Peugeot 207
Owners Workshop Manual

Peter T Gill

Models covered

(4787 - 2AY2 - 400)

Hatchback & Estate (SW)
Petrol: 1.4 litre (1360cc & 1397cc) & 1.6 litre (1587cc & 1598cc)
Turbo-Diesel: 1.4 litre (1398cc) & 1.6 litre (1560cc)

Also covers major mechanical features of CC (Coupe Cabriolet) and Van
Does NOT cover models with 1.6 litre turbo petrol engine

© J H Haynes & Co. Ltd. 2019

ABCDE
FG

A book in the **Haynes Owners Workshop Manual Series**

ISBN **978 1 78521 438 7**

British Library Cataloguing in Publication Data
A catalogue record for this book is available from the British Library.

Printed in India

J H Haynes & Co. Ltd.
Sparkford, Yeovil, Somerset BA22 7JJ, England

Haynes North America, Inc
859 Lawrence Drive, Newbury Park, California 91320, USA

Contents

LIVING WITH YOUR PEUGEOT 207

MAINTENANCE

Routine Maintenance and Servicing

Contents

REPAIRS & OVERHAUL

Engine and Associated Systems

Transmission

Brakes, Suspension and Steering

Body Equipment

Wiring Diagrams

REFERENCE

Index

The Peugeot 207 range was introduced in the UK in May 2006 in the form of the Hatchback model. Originally, the 207 was available with a choice of 1.4 litre (1360cc) and 1.6 litre (1587cc) petrol engines, and 1.4 litre (1398cc) and 1.6 litre (1560 cc) DOHC diesel engines. All models were available in both three- and five-door Hatchback form.

All these early petrol engines are derived from the well-proven TU series engines, which have appeared in many Peugeot and Citroën vehicles. The engine is of four-cylinder, overhead camshaft design, mounted transversely, with the transmission mounted on the left-hand side.

In 2007 the 1.4 litre and 1.6 litre VTi petrol engine was introduced, this being a newly-developed engine in conjunction with BMW. This engine is of four-cylinder double overhead camshaft design with variable valve timing.

In 2010 the 1.6 litre SOHC diesel engine was introduced in the Peugeot 207, this being used previously in the Ford Focus. This engine is a single overhead camshaft design of the earlier 1.6 litre DOHC engine.

Other additions to the 207 range include the Estate (SW), the Cabriolet Coupe (CC) and Van models.

Most models have a five-speed manual transmission, with the option of a new six-speed transmission on later models. A four-speed automatic transmission being offered on some early models.

All models have fully independent front suspension, incorporating shock absorbers, coil springs and an anti-roll bar. The rear suspension is semi-independent, with torsion bars and trailing arms.

A wide range of standard and optional equipment is available within the 207 range to suit most tastes, including central locking, electric windows and front, side and curtain airbags. An air conditioning system is available on all models.

Provided that regular servicing is carried out in accordance with the manufacturer's recommendations, the Peugeot 207 should prove reliable and very economical. The engine compartment is well-designed, and most of the items requiring frequent attention are easily accessible.

Your Peugeot manual

The aim of this manual is to help you get the best value from your vehicle. It can do so in several ways. It can help you decide what work must be done (even should you choose to get it done by a garage), provide information on routine maintenance and servicing, and give a logical course of action and diagnosis when random faults occur. However, it is hoped that you will use the manual by tackling the work yourself. On simpler jobs it may even be quicker than booking the car into a garage and going there twice, to leave and collect it. Perhaps most important, a lot of money can be saved by avoiding the costs a garage must charge to cover its labour and overheads.

The manual has drawings and descriptions to show the function of the various components so that their layout can be understood. Tasks are described and photographed in a clear step-by-step sequence.

References to the left-hand and right-hand sides of the vehicle are always in the sense of when viewed by a person sat in the driver's seat, facing forwards.

Acknowledgements

Thanks are due to Bakers of Gillingham who provided several of the project vehicles used in the origination of this manual. Thanks are also due to Draper Tools Limited and Auto Service Tools Limited (www.asttools.co.uk), who provided some of the workshop tools, and to all those people at Sparkford who helped in the production of this manual.

We take great pride in the accuracy of information given in this manual, but vehicle manufacturers make alterations and design changes during the production run of a particular vehicle of which they do not inform us. No liability can be accepted by the authors or publishers for loss, damage or injury caused by errors in, or omissions from, the information given.

Working on your car can be dangerous. This page shows just some of the potential risks and hazards, with the aim of creating a safety-conscious attitude.

General hazards

Scalding

• Don't remove the radiator or expansion tank cap while the engine is hot.
• Engine oil, transmission fluid or power steering fluid may also be dangerously hot if the engine has recently been running.

Burning

• Beware of burns from the exhaust system and from any part of the engine. Brake discs and drums can also be extremely hot immediately after use.

Crushing

• When working under or near a raised vehicle, always supplement the jack with axle stands, or use drive-on ramps.
Never venture under a car which is only supported by a jack.
• Take care if loosening or tightening high-torque nuts when the vehicle is on stands. Initial loosening and final tightening should be done with the wheels on the ground.

Fire

• Fuel is highly flammable; fuel vapour is explosive.
• Don't let fuel spill onto a hot engine.
• Do not smoke or allow naked lights (including pilot lights) anywhere near a vehicle being worked on. Also beware of creating sparks (electrically or by use of tools).
• Fuel vapour is heavier than air, so don't work on the fuel system with the vehicle over an inspection pit.
• Another cause of fire is an electrical overload or short-circuit. Take care when repairing or modifying the vehicle wiring.
• Keep a fire extinguisher handy, of a type suitable for use on fuel and electrical fires.

Electric shock

• Ignition HT and Xenon headlight voltages can be dangerous, especially to people with heart problems or a pacemaker. Don't work on or near these systems with the engine running or the ignition switched on.

• Mains voltage is also dangerous. Make sure that any mains-operated equipment is correctly earthed. Mains power points should be protected by a residual current device (RCD) circuit breaker.

Fume or gas intoxication

• Exhaust fumes are poisonous; they can contain carbon monoxide, which is rapidly fatal if inhaled. Never run the engine in a confined space such as a garage with the doors shut.
• Fuel vapour is also poisonous, as are the vapours from some cleaning solvents and paint thinners.

Poisonous or irritant substances

• Avoid skin contact with battery acid and with any fuel, fluid or lubricant, especially antifreeze, brake hydraulic fluid and Diesel fuel. Don't syphon them by mouth. If such a substance is swallowed or gets into the eyes, seek medical advice.
• Prolonged contact with used engine oil can cause skin cancer. Wear gloves or use a barrier cream if necessary. Change out of oil-soaked clothes and do not keep oily rags in your pocket.
• Air conditioning refrigerant forms a poisonous gas if exposed to a naked flame (including a cigarette). It can also cause skin burns on contact.

Asbestos

• Asbestos dust can cause cancer if inhaled or swallowed. Asbestos may be found in gaskets and in brake and clutch linings. When dealing with such components it is safest to assume that they contain asbestos.

Special hazards

Hydrofluoric acid

• This extremely corrosive acid is formed when certain types of synthetic rubber, found in some O-rings, oil seals, fuel hoses etc, are exposed to temperatures above 4000C. The rubber changes into a charred or sticky substance containing the acid. *Once formed, the acid remains dangerous for years. If it gets onto the skin, it may be necessary to amputate the limb concerned.*
• When dealing with a vehicle which has suffered a fire, or with components salvaged from such a vehicle, wear protective gloves and discard them after use.

The battery

• Batteries contain sulphuric acid, which attacks clothing, eyes and skin. Take care when topping-up or carrying the battery.
• The hydrogen gas given off by the battery is highly explosive. Never cause a spark or allow a naked light nearby. Be careful when connecting and disconnecting battery chargers or jump leads.

Air bags

• Air bags can cause injury if they go off accidentally. Take care when removing the steering wheel and trim panels. Special storage instructions may apply.

Diesel injection equipment

• Diesel injection pumps supply fuel at very high pressure. Take care when working on the fuel injectors and fuel pipes.

⚠ *Warning: Never expose the hands, face or any other part of the body to injector spray; the fuel can penetrate the skin with potentially fatal results.*

Remember...

DO

• Do use eye protection when using power tools, and when working under the vehicle.

• Do wear gloves or use barrier cream to protect your hands when necessary.

• Do get someone to check periodically that all is well when working alone on the vehicle.

• Do keep loose clothing and long hair well out of the way of moving mechanical parts.

• Do remove rings, wristwatch etc, before working on the vehicle – especially the electrical system.

• Do ensure that any lifting or jacking equipment has a safe working load rating adequate for the job.

DON'T

• Don't attempt to lift a heavy component which may be beyond your capability – get assistance.

• Don't rush to finish a job, or take unverified short cuts.

• Don't use ill-fitting tools which may slip and cause injury.

• Don't leave tools or parts lying around where someone can trip over them. Mop up oil and fuel spills at once.

• Don't allow children or pets to play in or near a vehicle being worked on.

The following pages are intended to help in dealing with common roadside emergencies and breakdowns. You will find more detailed fault finding information at the back of the manual, and repair information in the main chapters.

If your car won't start and the starter motor doesn't turn

☐ If it's a model with automatic transmission, make sure the selector is in P or N.
☐ Open the bonnet and make sure that the battery terminals are clean and tight.
☐ Switch on the headlights and try to start the engine. If the headlights go very dim when you're trying to start, the battery is probably flat. Get out of trouble by jump starting (see next page) using a friend's car.

If your car won't start even though the starter motor turns as normal

☐ Is there fuel in the tank?
☐ Is there moisture on electrical components under the bonnet? Switch off the ignition, then wipe off any obvious dampness with a dry cloth. Spray a water-repellent aerosol product (WD-40 or equivalent) on ignition and fuel system electrical connectors like those shown in the photos.
☐ Pay special attention to the ignition coil wiring connector and HT leads. (Note that diesel engines don't normally suffer from damp.)

A Check the security and condition of the battery connections.

B On petrol models, check that the ignition HT coil(s) are securely connected by checking their locking clip (remove the engine cover for access).

C Check that all the fuses and connections in the engine fusebox.

Check that electrical connections are secure (with the ignition switched off) and spray them with a water-dispersant spray like WD-40 if you suspect a problem due to damp.

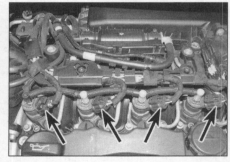

D On diesel engines, check the injector wiring connectors (arrowed) are securely connected (remove the engine cover for access).

Jump starting

When jump-starting a car using a booster battery, observe the following precautions:

✔ Before connecting the booster battery, make sure that the ignition is switched off.
✔ Ensure that all electrical equipment (lights, heater, wipers, etc) is switched off.
✔ Take note of any special precautions printed on the battery case.

✔ Make sure that the booster battery is the same voltage as the discharged one in the vehicle.
✔ If the battery is being jump-started from the battery in another vehicle, the two vehicles MUST NOT TOUCH each other.
✔ Make sure that the transmission is in neutral (or PARK, in the case of automatic transmission).

> **HAYNES HiNT**
>
> *Jump starting will get you out of trouble, but you must correct whatever made the battery go flat in the first place. There are three possibilities:*
>
> **1** *The battery has been drained by repeated attempts to start, or by leaving the lights on.*
>
> **2** *The charging system is not working properly (alternator drivebelt slack or broken, alternator wiring fault or alternator itself faulty).*
>
> **3** *The battery itself is at fault (electrolyte low, or battery worn out).*

1 Connect one end of the red jump lead to the positive (+) terminal of the flat battery

2 Connect the other end of the red lead to the positive (+) terminal of the booster battery.

3 Connect one end of the black jump lead to the negative (-) terminal of the booster battery

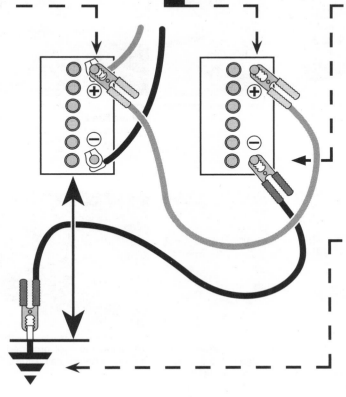

4 Connect the other end of the black jump lead to a bolt or bracket on the engine block, well away from the battery, on the vehicle to be started.

5 Make sure that the jump leads will not come into contact with the fan, drive-belts or other moving parts of the engine.

6 Start the engine using the booster battery and run it at idle speed. Switch on the lights, rear window demister and heater blower motor, then disconnect the jump leads in the reverse order of connection. Turn off the lights etc.

Wheel changing

Some of the details shown here will vary according to model. However, the basic principles apply to all vehicles.

 Warning: Do not change a wheel in a situation where you risk being hit by other traffic. On busy roads, try to stop in a lay-by or a gateway. Be wary of passing traffic while changing the wheel – it is easy to become distracted by the job in hand.

Preparation

- ☐ When a puncture occurs, stop as soon as it is safe to do so.
- ☐ Park on firm level ground, if possible, and well out of the way of other traffic.
- ☐ Use hazard warning lights if necessary.

- ☐ If you have one, use a warning triangle to alert other drivers of your presence.
- ☐ Apply the handbrake and engage first or reverse gear.

- ☐ Chock the wheel diagonally opposite the one being removed – a couple of large stones will do for this.
- ☐ If the ground is soft, use a flat piece of wood to spread the load under the jack.

Changing the wheel

1 The spare wheel and tools are stored in the luggage compartment. Lift up the luggage compartment carpet and remove the tool kit from the centre of the spare wheel.

2 Where applicable (steel wheels), remove the wheel trim cover.

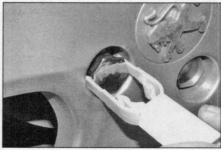

3 On models where anti-theft wheel bolts are fitted (alloy wheels), pull off the plastic cover using the yellow plastic tool in the tool kit...

4 ... then unscrew the anti-theft bolt (one on each wheel) using the special tool provided – normally stored in thepassenger glovebox or tool kit.

5 Place the chock (arrowed) provided in the vehicle tool kit against the wheel diagonally opposite the wheel to be removed, or use a stone/rock to stop the car rolling.

6 Using the tool provided, slacken each wheel bolt by half-a-turn.

7 Engage the jack head with the reinforced jacking point nearest the wheel to be changed; the jacking point is the area by the cut-out on the sill. Ensure the head of the jack is positioned securely then raise the jack until its base is in contact with the ground. Ensure the jack base is located directly below the sill then raise the vehicle until the wheel is clear of the ground. If the tyre is flat, remember to raise the vehicle sufficiently to allow the spare wheel to befitted.

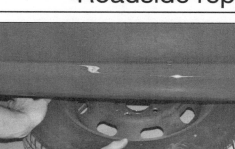

8 Remove the bolts and lift off the wheel. Place the wheel beneath the sill as a precaution against the jack failing then fit the spare wheel. Fit the wheel bolts and moderately tighten them with the wheel brace. Remove the punctured wheel fromunder the sill then lower the vehicle to the ground.

9 Tighten the wheel bolts in a diagonal sequence then refit the wheel trim (where applicable). Note that the wheelbolts should be slackened and retightened to the specified torque at the earliest possible opportunity. Store the puncturedwheel/tyre and tools back in the luggage compartment, and secure them in position.

Finally . . .

- ☐ Remove any remaining wheel chocks.
- ☐ Have the damaged tyre or wheel repaired as soon as possible.
- ☐ Check the tyre pressure on the wheel just fitted. If it is low, or if you don't have a pressure gauge with you, drive slowly to the nearest garage and inflate the tyre to the right pressure.
- ☐ Note that the space-saver wheel is only designed for emergency use; never exceed 50 mph whilst the wheel is fitted to the vehicle.

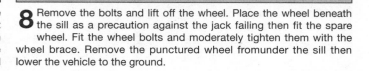

Towing

When all else fails, you may find yourself having to get a tow home – or of course you may be helping somebody else. Long-distance recovery should only be done by a garage or breakdown service. For shorter distances, DIY towing using another car is easy enough, but observe the following points:

☐ Use a proper tow-rope – they are not expensive. The vehicle being towed must display an ON TOW sign in its rear window.

☐ Only attach the tow-rope to the towing eyes provided in the tool kit (see Wheel changing).

☐ The driver of the car being towed must keep the tow-rope taut at all times to avoid snatching.

☐ Before being towed, release the handbrake and select neutral on the transmission.

☐ On models with an automatic transmission unit, the vehicle must only be towed forwards with the selector lever in the N position. Never tow the vehicle at speeds in excess of 30 mph or over a distance in excess of 30 miles. Failure to observe these warning will lead to serious transmission damage.

☐ Always turn the ignition key to the 'On' position when the vehicle is being towed, so that the steering lock is released, and the direction indicator and brake lights work.

☐ Note that greater-than-usual pedal pressure will be required to operate the brakes, since the vacuum servo unit is only operational with the engine running.

☐ On models with power steering, greater-than-usual steering effort will also be required.

☐ Make sure that both drivers know the route before setting off.

☐ Only drive at moderate speeds and keep the distance towed to a minimum. Drive smoothly and allow plenty of time for slowing down at junctions.

Identifying leaks

Puddles on the garage floor or drive, or obvious wetness under the bonnet or underneath the car, suggest a leak that needs investigating. It can sometimes be difficult to decide where the leak is coming from, especially if an engine undershield is fitted. Leaking oil or fluid can also be blown rearwards by the passage of air under the car, giving a false impression of where the problem lies.

 Warning: Most automotive oils and fluids are poisonous. Wash them off skin, and change out of contaminated clothing, without delay.

 The smell of a fluid leaking from the car may provide a clue to what's leaking. Some fluids are distinctively coloured. It may help to remove the engine undershield, clean the car carefully and to park it over some clean paper overnight as an aid to locating the source of the leak. Remember that some leaks may only occur while the engine is running.

Sump oil

Engine oil may leak from the drain plug...

Oil from filter

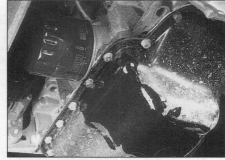

...or from the base of the oil filter.

Gearbox oil

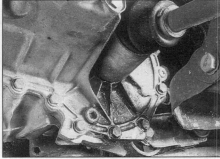

Gearbox oil can leak from the seals at the inboard ends of the driveshafts.

Antifreeze

Leaking antifreeze often leaves a crystalline deposit like this.

Brake fluid

A leak occurring at a wheel is almost certainly brake fluid.

Introduction

There are some very simple checks which need only take a few minutes to carry out, but which could save you a lot of inconvenience and expense.

These checks require no great skill or special tools, and the small amount of time they take to perform could prove to be very well spent, for example:

☐ Keeping an eye on tyre condition and pressures, will not only help to stop them wearing out prematurely, but could also save your life.

☐ Many breakdowns are caused by electrical problems. Battery-related faults are particularly common, and a quick check on a regular basis will often prevent the majority of these.

☐ If your car develops a brake fluid leak, the first time you might know about it is when your brakes don't work properly. Checking the level regularly will give advance warning of this kind of problem.

☐ If the oil or coolant levels run low, the cost of repairing any engine damage will be far greater than fixing the leak, for example.

Underbonnet check points

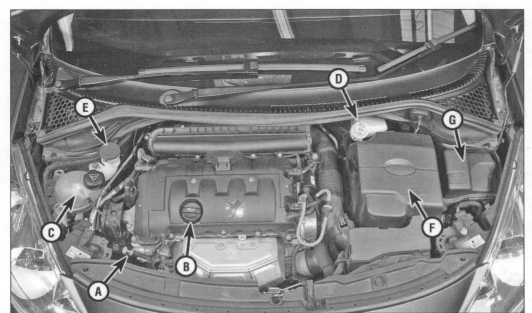

◄ **1.6 litre VTi petrol engine (others similar)**

A *Engine oil level dipstick*

B *Engine oil filler cap*

C *Coolant expansion tank*

D *Brake (and clutch) fluid reservoir*

E *Screen washer fluid reservoir*

F *Battery*

G *Engine compartment fuse/ relay box*

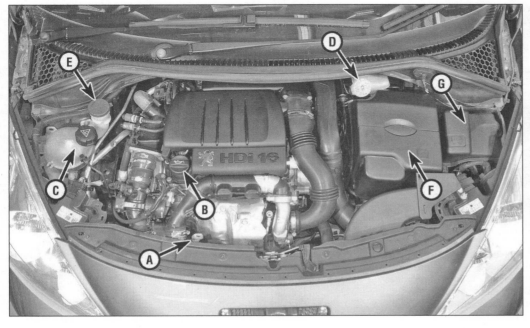

◄ **1.6 litre DOHC diesel engine (others similar)**

A *Engine oil level dipstick*

B *Engine oil filler cap*

C *Coolant expansion tank*

D *Brake (and clutch) fluid reservoir*

E *Screen washer fluid reservoir*

F *Battery*

G *Engine compartment fuse/ relay box*

Engine oil level

Before you start

✔ Make sure that the car is on level ground.
✔ Check the oil level before the car is driven, or at least 5 minutes after the engine has been switched off.

HAYNES HiNT *If the oil is checked immediately after driving the vehicle, some of the oil will remain in the upper engine components, resulting in an inaccurate reading on the dipstick.*

The correct oil

Modern engines place great demands on their oil. It is very important that the correct oil for your car is used (see *Lubricants and fluids*).

Car care

● On models equipped with an oil level gauge, don't be tempted to rely on the gauge alone – verify the level using the dipstick on a regular basis. Equally, don't ignore the gauge if it warns of low oil level.
● If you have to add oil frequently, you should check whether you have any oil leaks. Remove the engine undershield, place some clean paper under the car overnight, and check for stains in the morning. If there are no leaks, then the engine may be burning oil.
● Always maintain the level between the upper and lower dipstick marks (see photo 3). If the level is too low, severe engine damage may occur. Oil seal failure may result if the engine is overfilled by adding too much oil.

1 The engine oil level is checked with a dipstick that extends through the dipstick tube and into the sump at the bottom of the engine. The dipstick is located at the front of the engine (see Underbonnet check points for exact location). Withdraw the dipstick.

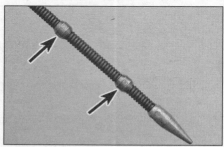
3 Note the oil level on the end of the dipstick (VTi-petrol model shown, others similar). Add oil as necessary until the level is between the upper (MAX) mark and lower (MIN) mark on the dipstick. Note that approximately 1.0 litre of oil will be required to raise the level from the lower mark to the upper mark.

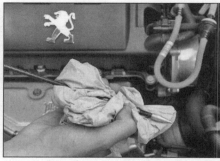
2 Wipe all the oil from the end with a clean rag or paper towel. Insert the clean dipstick back into the tube as far as it will go, then withdraw it once more.

4 Oil is added to the engine via the filler cap on the cylinder head cover. Unscrew the cap and top-up the level. A funnel may help to reduce spillage. Add the oil slowly, checking the level on the dipstick frequently. Do not overfill.

Coolant level

Warning: Do not attempt to remove the expansion tank pressure cap when the engine is hot, as there is a very great risk of scalding. Do not leave open containers of coolant about, as it is poisonous.

Car care

● With a sealed-type cooling system, adding coolant should not be necessary on a regular basis. If frequent topping-up is required, it is likely there is a leak. Check the radiator, all hoses and joint faces for signs of staining or wetness, and rectify as necessary.

● It is important that antifreeze is used in the cooling system all year round, not just during the winter months. Don't top up with water alone, as the antifreeze will become diluted.

1 The coolant level varies with the temperature of the engine. The level is checked in the expansion tank located in the right-hand, rear corner of the engine compartment. When the engine is cold, the coolant level should be between the MAX and MIN level marks on the tank.

2 If topping up is necessary, wait until the engine is cold. Slowly unscrew the expansion tank cap, to release any pressure present in the cooling system, and remove it.

3 Add the specified coolant to the expansion tank until the coolant level is correct. Refit the cap and tighten it securely.

Brake (and clutch*) fluid level

On manual transmission models, the brake fluid reservoir also supplies the clutch master cylinder with fluid,

Warning:
• **Brake fluid can harm your eyes and damage painted surfaces, so use extreme caution when handling and pouring it.**
• **Do not use fluid that has been standing open for some time, as it absorbs moisture from the air, which can cause a dangerous loss of braking effectiveness.**

Safety first!

● If the reservoir requires repeated topping-up this is an indication of a fluid leak somewhere in the system, which should be investigated immediately.

● If a leak is suspected, the car should not be driven until the braking system has been checked. Never take any risks where brakes are concerned

HAYNES HINT
• **Make sure that your car is on level ground.**
• **The fluid level in the reservoir will drop slightly as the brake pads wear down, but the fluid level must never be allowed to drop below the DANGER mark.**

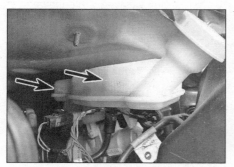

1 The brake fluid reservoir is located on the left-hand side of the engine compartment. The MAX and MIN marks are indicated on the side of the reservoir. The fluid level must be kept between the marks at all times.

2 If topping-up is necessary, first wipe clean the area around the filler cap to prevent dirt entering the hydraulic system.

3 Carefully add fluid, taking care not to spill it onto the surrounding components. Use only the specified fluid;mixing different types can cause damage to the system. After topping-up to the correct level, securely refit the cap and wipe off any spilt fluid.

Washer fluid level

● Screenwash additives not only keep the windscreen clean during bad weather, they also prevent the washer system freezing in cold weather – which is when you are likely to need it most. Don't top-up using plain water, as the screenwash will become diluted, and will freeze in cold weather.

Warning: On no account use engine coolant antifreeze in the screenwasher system – this may damage the paintwork.

1 The screenwasher fluid reservoir filler neck is located in the right-hand side of the engine compartment, behind the coolant reservoir. The screenwasher level cannot easily be seen. Remove the filler cap, and look down the filler neck – if fluid is not visible, topping-up may be required.

2 When topping-up the reservoir, add a screenwash additive in the quantities recommended on the additive bottle. The exact level is not critical – add fluid slowly until the level reaches the base of the filler neck

Tyre condition and pressure

It is very important that tyres are in good condition, and at the correct pressure - having a tyre failure at any speed is highly dangerous. Tyre wear is influenced by driving style - harsh braking and acceleration, or fast cornering, will all produce more rapid tyre wear. As a general rule, the front tyres wear out faster than the rears. Interchanging the tyres from front to rear ("rotating" the tyres) may result in more even wear. However, if this is completely effective, you may have the expense of replacing all four tyres at once!

Remove any nails or stones embedded in the tread before they penetrate the tyre to cause deflation. If removal of a nail does reveal that the tyre has been punctured, refit the nail so that its point of penetration is marked. Then immediately change the wheel, and have the tyre repaired by a tyre dealer.

Regularly check the tyres for damage in the form of cuts or bulges, especially in the sidewalls. Periodically remove the wheels, and clean any dirt or mud from the inside and outside surfaces. Examine the wheel rims for signs of rusting, corrosion or other damage. Light alloy wheels are easily damaged by "kerbing" whilst parking; steel wheels may also become dented or buckled. A new wheel is very often the only way to overcome severe damage.

New tyres should be balanced when they are fitted, but it may become necessary to re-balance them as they wear, or if the balance weights fitted to the wheel rim should fall off. Unbalanced tyres will wear more quickly, as will the steering and suspension components. Wheel imbalance is normally signified by vibration, particularly at a certain speed (typically around 50 mph). If this vibration is felt only through the steering, then it is likely that just the front wheels need balancing. If, however, the vibration is felt through the whole car, the rear wheels could be out of balance. Wheel balancing should be carried out by a tyre dealer or garage.

1 Tread Depth - visual check
The original tyres have tread wear safety bands (B), which will appear when the tread depth reaches approximately 1.6 mm. The band positions are indicated by a triangular mark on the tyre sidewall (A).

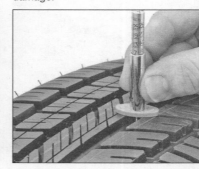

2 Tread Depth - manual check
Alternatively, tread wear can be monitored with a simple, inexpensive device known as a tread depth indicator gauge.

3 Tyre Pressure Check
Check the tyre pressures regularly with the tyres cold. Do not adjust the tyre pressures immediately after the vehicle has been used, or an inaccurate setting will result.

Tyre tread wear patterns

Shoulder Wear

Underinflation (wear on both sides)
Under-inflation will cause overheating of the tyre, because the tyre will flex too much, and the tread will not sit correctly on the road surface. This will cause a loss of grip and excessive wear, not to mention the danger of sudden tyre failure due to heat build-up.
Check and adjust pressures
Incorrect wheel camber (wear on one side)
Repair or renew suspension parts
Hard cornering
Reduce speed!

Centre Wear

Overinflation
Over-inflation will cause rapid wear of the centre part of the tyre tread, coupled with reduced grip, harsher ride, and the danger of shock damage occurring in the tyre casing.
Check and adjust pressures

If you sometimes have to inflate your car's tyres to the higher pressures specified for maximum load or sustained high speed, don't forget to reduce the pressures to normal afterwards.

Uneven Wear

Front tyres may wear unevenly as a result of wheel misalignment. Most tyre dealers and garages can check and adjust the wheel alignment (or "tracking") for a modest charge.
Incorrect camber or castor
Repair or renew suspension parts
Malfunctioning suspension
Repair or renew suspension parts
Unbalanced wheel
Balance tyres
Incorrect toe setting
Adjust front wheel alignment
Note: *The feathered edge of the tread which typifies toe wear is best checked by feel.*

Wiper blades

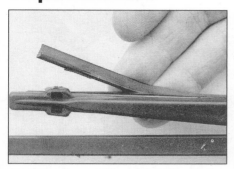

1 Check the condition of the wiper blades; if they are cracked or show any signs of deterioration, or if the glass swept area is smeared, renew them. For maximum clarity of vision, wiper blades should be renewed annually, as a matter of course.

EARLY MODELS

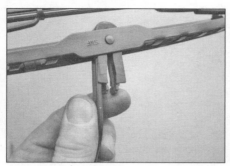

2 To remove a windscreen wiper blade, pull the arm fully away from the glass until it locks. Swivel the blade through 90°, then squeeze the locking clip

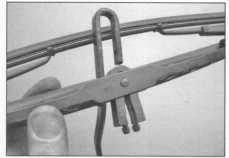

3 Slide the blade out of the arm's hooked end, disengaging it from the wiper arm, taking care not to allow the wiper arm to spring back and damage the windscreen.

LATER MODELS

4 To remove a windscreen wiper blade, pull the arm fully away from the glass until it locks. Swivel the blade through 90°, then pull the blade from the peg on the end of the wiper arm. Take care not to allow the wiper arm to spring back and damage the windscreen.

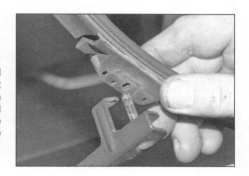

Electrical systems

✔ Check all external lights and the horn. Refer to the appropriate Sections of Chapter 12 for details if any of the circuits are found to be inoperative.

✔ Visually check all accessible wiring connectors, harnesses and retaining clips for security, and for signs of chafing or damage.

 HAYNES HINT *If you need to check your brake lights and indicators unaided, back up to a wall or garage door and operate the lights. The reflected light should show if they are working properly.*

1 If a single indicator light, stoplight or headlight bulb has failed, it is likely that a bulb has blown and will need renewing. Refer to Chapter 12 for details. If both stop-lights have failed, it is possible that the stop-light switch has failed (see Chapter 9).

2 If more than one indicator light or headlight has failed, it is likely that either a fuse has blown or there is a fault in the circuit (see Chapter 12). The main fuses are located behind a small cover inside the glovebox on the passenger side of the facia. Unclip the cover to gain access. Additional fuses and relays are located in the fuse/relay box located on the left-hand side of the engine compartment.

3 To renew a blown fuse, remove it using the plastic tool supplied (where applicable). Fit a new fuse of the correct rating, available from car accessory shops. If the new fuse blows immediately, there is a fault, which must be traced and rectified (see *Electrical fault finding* in Chapter 12)

Battery

Caution: Before carrying out any work on the vehicle battery, read the precautions given in 'Safety first!' at the start of this manual.

✔ The battery is located on the left-hand side of the engine compartment, make sure that the battery tray is in good condition, and that the clamp is tight. Depending on model/year the cover may be either a one or two piece cover. Corrosion on the metal lower tray, retaining clamp and the battery itself can be removed with a solution of water and baking soda. Thoroughly rinse all cleaned areas with water. Any metal parts damaged by corrosion should be covered with a zinc-based primer, and then painted.

✔ Periodically (approximately every three months), check the charge condition of the battery as described in Chapter 5A.

✔ If the battery is flat, and you need to jump start your vehicle, see *Roadside Repairs*.

 HAYNES HiNT *Battery corrosion can be kept to a minimum by applying a layer of petroleum jelly to the clamps and terminals after they are reconnected.*

1 Unclip the cover from the battery tray to gain access (early type, two-piece cover shown). The exterior of the battery should be inspected periodically for damage such as a cracked case or cover.

2 Check the tightness of the battery cable clamps to ensure good electrical connections, and check the entire length of each cable for cracks and frayed conductors.

3 If corrosion (visible as white, fluffy deposits) is evident, remove the cables from the battery terminals, clean them with a small wire brush, then refit them. Automotive stores sell tools for cleaning the battery terminals...

4 ... and the battery lead clamps

Lubricants and fluids

Petrol engine oil

TU and ET engines .... SAE 10W40, 5W40, 5W30 or 0W30 multigrade engine oil to ACEA A3 and API SJ/SL specification*

EP VTi engines .... SAE 5W30 or 0W30 multigrade engine oil to ACEA A3 and API SJ/SL specification*

Diesel engine oil

All diesels without particulate filter .... SAE 10W40, 5W40, 5W30 or 0W30 multigrade engine oil to ACEA B3 and API CD/CF specification*

All diesels with particulate filter....................... SAE 10W40, 5W40 or 5W30 multigrade engine oil to ACEA B3 and API CD/CF specification*

Cooling system................................... BASF Glysantin G33-23F or Gurit Essex Revkogel 2000 antifreeze

Manual transmission .... Esso Gear Oil BV 75W80 or Total Transmission BV 75W80

Automatic transmission........................... Special oil, Part number 9736 22

Brake (and clutch) hydraulic system .... BP BF PSA DOT4, Shell BF 40 or Gurit Essex Betabrake 303 DOT4 – hydraulic fluid to DOT 4

Particulate filter additives .... Eolys DPX42 or Eolys 176

* Due to the extended service intervals Peugeot specify, it is essential that semi-synthetic or fully-synthetic engine oil be used.

Tyre pressures

Note: *Always refer to the tyre pressure data sticker on the rear edge of the driver's door (visible when the door is open) for the correct tyre pressures for your particular vehicle. Pressures apply only to original-equipment tyres, and may vary if any other make or type is fitted; check with the tyre manufacturer or supplier for correct pressures if necessary.*

Chapter 1A
Routine maintenance and servicing – petrol models

Contents

Degrees of difficulty

Easy, suitable for novice with little experience 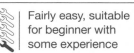	Fairly easy, suitable for beginner with some experience	Fairly difficult, suitable for competent DIY mechanic 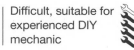	Difficult, suitable for experienced DIY mechanic	Very difficult, suitable for expert DIY or professional

1 Servicing specifications

Lubricants and fluids...................................... Refer to *Lubricants, fluids and tyre pressures*

Capacities

Engine oil
Including filter.. 4.25 litres
Difference between MAX and MIN dipstick marks................ 1.5 litres
Cooling system... 6.0 litres

Transmission
Manual .... 2.0 litres
Automatic:
  Refilling after draining.................................. 4.5 litres
  From dry.. 6.0 litres
Fuel tank .... 50 litres

Engine

Auxiliary drivebelt tension with belt tensioning tool (non-VTi engines) – see text:
  Without air conditioning:
    New belt .... 87 SEEM units
    Used belt .... 61 SEEM units
  With air conditioning:
    New belt .... 120 SEEM units
    Used belt .... 58 SEEM units

Cooling system

Frost and corrosion protection............................. Refer to antifreeze manufacturer's concentration recommendations

Ignition system

Spark plugs:
  1.4 litre EP3 engine..................................... Beru 12ZR 6SP03
  1.6 litre EP6 engine..................................... Beru 12ZR 6SP03
Electrode gap.. 0.9 mm

Brakes

Brake pad friction material minimum thickness.............. 2.0 mm

Tyres

Tyre pressures .... See *Lubricants, fluids and tyre pressures*

Torque wrench settings	Nm	lbf ft
Alternator mounting bolts.	37	27
Automatic transmission:		
Filler plug	24	18
Level plug	35	26
Auxiliary drivebelt tensioner pulley nut.	45	33
Manual transmission drain plug	35	26
Manual transmission filler/level plug (where fitted).	25	18
Oil filter cover	25	18
Roadwheel bolts.	90	66
Spark plugs	25	18
Sump drain plug.	30	22

2   Maintenance schedule

Note: *This maintenance schedule is a guide recommended by Haynes for servicing your own vehicle. Check with your local dealer for the manufacturer's maintenance schedule.*

The maintenance intervals in this manual are provided with the assumption that you, not the dealer, will be carrying out the work. These are the minimum maintenance intervals recommended by us for vehicles driven daily. If you wish to keep your vehicle in peak condition at all times, you may wish to perform some of these procedures more often. We encourage frequent maintenance, because it enhances the efficiency, performance and resale value of your vehicle.

If the vehicle is driven in dusty areas, used to tow a trailer, or driven frequently at slow speeds (idling in traffic) or on short journeys, more frequent maintenance intervals are recommended.

When the vehicle is new, it should be serviced by a dealer service department (or other workshop recognised by the vehicle manufacturer as providing the same standard of service) in order to preserve the warranty. The vehicle manufacturer may reject warranty claims if you are unable to prove that servicing has been carried out as and when specified, using only original equipment parts or parts certified to be of equivalent quality.

Valve clearance checking on 1.4 litre SOHC engines (Chapter 2A Section 9) is no longer specified as part of the routine maintenance schedule (DOHC engines have hydraulic adjusters). Check the valve clearances if there is any tapping or rattling from the top of the engine, or in the event of an unexplained lack of performance. The prudent owner may wish to check the clearances, perhaps at 40 000 mile or four-yearly intervals.

Every 250 miles or weekly

- ☐ Refer to *Weekly checks*

Every 10 000 miles or 12 months – whichever comes sooner

- ☐ Renew the engine oil and filter (Section 6).

Note: *Peugeot recommend the engine oil and filter are changed every 20 000 miles or two years. However, oil and filter changes are good for the engine and we recommend changing the oil more frequently, especially if the vehicle is used on a lot of short journeys.*

- ☐ Check all underbonnet components for fluid leaks (Section 7).
- ☐ Check the condition of the driveshaft rubber gaiters and CV joints (Section 8).
- ☐ Lubricate all hinges and locks (Section 9).
- ☐ Carry out a road test (Section 10).

Every 20 000 miles or 2 years – whichever comes sooner

- ☐ Reset the service interval indicator (Section 11).
- ☐ Check the pollen filter (Section 12).
- ☐ Check the condition of the auxiliary drivebelt (Section 13).
- ☐ Check the condition of the brake pads and shoes (Section 14).
- ☐ Check the operation of the handbrake (Section 15).
- ☐ Check the steering and suspension components (Section 16).

Every 40 000 miles or 3 years – whichever comes sooner

- ☐ Renew the timing belt – non-VTi engines (Section 17).

Note: *Although the normal interval for timing belt renewal is 80 000 miles, it is strongly recommended that the interval is reduced to 40 000 miles, especially on vehicles which are subjected to intensive use, ie, mainly short journeys or a lot of stop-start driving. The actual belt renewal interval is therefore very much up to the individual owner, but bear in mind that severe engine damage will result if the belt breaks.*

- ☐ Renew the brake fluid (Section 18).

Note: *The hydraulic clutch shares its fluid reservoir with the braking system, and will also need to be bled.*

Every 40 000 miles or 4 years – whichever comes sooner

- ☐ Renew the spark plugs (Section 19).
- ☐ Renew the fuel filter (Section 20).

Note: *Only* fitted to markets where inferior quality fuel is sold.

- ☐ Renew the air cleaner filter element (Section 21).
- ☐ Check the manual transmission oil level (Section 22).
- ☐ Check the automatic transmission fluid level (Section 23).
- ☐ Check the exhaust emissions (Section 24).
- ☐ Renew the coolant (Section 25).

Every 10 years

- ☐ Renew the airbags and seat belt pretensioners (Section 26).

3 Component location

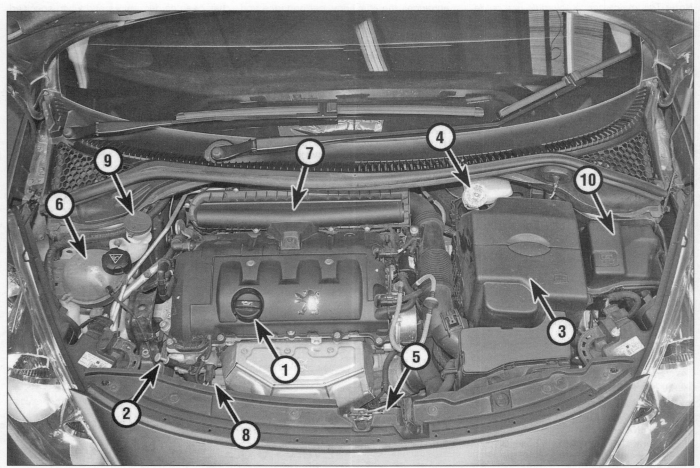

Underbonnet view of a 1.6 litre VTi model

1 Engine oil filler cap
2 Engine oil level dipstick
3 Battery
4 Brake/clutch fluid reservoir

5 Radiator
6 Coolant expansion tank
7 Air filter housing

8 Alternator
9 Washer fluid reservoir
10 Fuse/electrical box

Front underbody view

1 Engine oil drain plug
2 Air conditioning compressor
3 Right-hand driveshaft
4 Brake calipers
5 Suspension lower arms
6 Track rod arms
7 Catalytic converter
8 Automatic transmission
9 Rear lower mounting link
10 Lower radiator hose

Rear underbody view

1 Fuel tank
2 Beam axle
3 Handbrake cables
4 Brake calipers
5 Coil springs
6 Rear exhaust silencer
7 Spare wheel well
8 Fuel tank filler neck
9 Exhaust heat shield

4 General Information

1 This Chapter is designed to help the home mechanic maintain his/her vehicle for safety, economy, long life and peak performance.

2 The Chapter contains a master maintenance schedule, followed by Sections dealing specifically with each task in the schedule. Visual checks, adjustments, component renewal and other helpful items are included. Refer to the accompanying illustrations of the engine compartment and the underside of the vehicle for the locations of the various components.

3 Servicing your vehicle in accordance with the mileage/time maintenance schedule and the following Sections will provide a planned maintenance programme, which should result in a long and reliable service life. This is a comprehensive plan, so maintaining some items but not others at the specified service intervals will not produce the same results.

4 As you service your vehicle, you will discover that many of the procedures can – and should – be grouped together, because of the particular procedure being performed, or because of the close proximity of two otherwise-unrelated components to one another. For example, if the vehicle is raised for any reason, the exhaust can be inspected at the same time as the suspension and steering components.

5 The first step in this maintenance programme is to prepare you before the actual work begins. Read through all the Sections relevant to the work to be carried out, then make a list and gather together all the parts and tools required. If a problem is encountered, seek advice from a parts specialist, or a dealer service department.

5 Routine Maintenance

1 If, from the time the vehicle is new, the routine maintenance schedule is followed closely, and frequent checks are made of fluid levels and high-wear items, as suggested

throughout this manual, the engine will be kept in relatively good running condition, and the need for additional work will be minimised.

2 It is possible that there will be times when the engine is running poorly due to the lack of regular maintenance. This is even more likely if a used vehicle, which has not received regular and frequent maintenance checks, is purchased. In such cases, additional work may need to be carried out, outside of the regular maintenance intervals.

3 If engine wear is suspected, a compression test (refer to Chapter 2A Section 2 or Chapter 2B Section 2) will provide valuable information regarding the overall performance of the main internal components. Such a test can be used as a basis to decide on the extent of the work to be carried out. If, for example, a compression test indicates serious internal engine wear, conventional maintenance as described in this Chapter will not greatly improve the performance of the engine, and may prove a waste of time and money, unless extensive overhaul work (Chapter 2F) is carried out first.

4 The following series of operations are those often required to improve the performance of a generally poor-running engine:

Primary operations

- Clean, inspect and test the battery (See *Weekly checks*).
- Check all the engine-related fluids (See *Weekly checks*).
- Check the condition and tension of the auxiliary drivebelt (Section 13).
- Renew the spark plugs (Section 19).
- Check the condition of the air cleaner filter element, and renew if necessary (Section 21).
- Renew the fuel filter – where fitted (Section 20).
- Check the condition of all hoses, and check for fluid leaks (Section 7).

5 If the above operations do not prove fully effective, carry out the following operations:

Secondary operations

6 All items listed under Primary operations, plus the following:
- Check the charging system (Chapter 5A).
- Check the ignition system (Chapter 5B).
- Check the fuel system (Chapter 4A).

6 Engine oil and filter renewal

Note: *A suitable square-section wrench may be required to undo the sump drain plug on certain models. These wrenches can be obtained from most motor factors or your Peugeot dealer.*

1 Frequent oil and filter changes are the most important preventative maintenance procedures, which can be undertaken by the DIY owner. As engine oil ages, it becomes diluted and contaminated, which leads to premature engine wear.

2 Before starting this procedure, gather together all the necessary tools and materials. Also make sure that you have plenty of clean rags and newspapers handy, to mop-up any spills. Ideally, the engine oil should be warm, as it will drain better, and more built-up sludge will be removed with it. Take care, however, not to touch the exhaust or any other hot parts of the engine when working under the vehicle. To avoid any possibility of scalding, and to protect yourself from possible skin irritants and other harmful contaminants in used engine oils, it is advisable to wear gloves when carrying out this work. Access to the underside of the vehicle will be greatly improved if it can be raised on a lift, driven onto ramps, or jacked up and supported on axle stands (see *Jacking and vehicle support*). Whichever method is chosen, make sure that the vehicle remains level, or if it is at an angle, that the drain plug is at the lowest point.

3 Undo the screws and remove the engine undershield – where fitted **(see illustration)**.

4 Slacken the drain plug about half a turn **(see illustration)**. Position the draining container under the drain plug, and then remove the plug completely. If possible, try to keep the plug pressed into the sump while unscrewing it by hand the last couple of turns (see **Haynes Hint**). Recover the sealing ring from the drain plug.

6.3 Remove the screws securing the engine undershield

6.4 Slacken the sump drain plug

HAYNES HINT

As the drain plug releases from the sump threads, move it away sharply, so the stream of oil issuing from the sump runs into the container, not up your sleeve.

6.8a Slacken the filter cover...

6.8b... and remove the filter

6.11a Fit the new oil seal to the cover...

5 Allow some time for the old oil to drain, noting that it may be necessary to reposition the container as the oil flow slows to a trickle.
6 After all the oil has drained, wipe off the drain plug with a clean rag, and fit a new sealing washer. Clean the area around the drain plug opening, and refit the plug, tightening it to the specified torque.
7 Move the container into position under the oil filter, which is located on the front of the cylinder block.
8 The filter element is contained within a filter cover. Using a socket or spanner, slacken and remove the filter cover from above **(see illustrations)**. Be prepared for fluid spillage, and recover the O-ring seal from the cover.
9 Pull the filter element from the filter cover.
10 Use a clean rag to remove all oil, dirt and sludge from the inside and outside of the filter cover.
11 Fit the new O-ring seal to the filter cover, insert the new filter element, then apply a little clean engine oil to the seal, and fit it to the filter cover **(see illustrations)**.
12 Refit the filter/cover to the housing and tighten the cover to the specified torque.
13 Remove the old oil and all tools from under the car, then lower the car to the ground (if applicable).
14 Remove the dipstick, and then unscrew the oil filler cap from the cylinder head cover. Fill the engine, using the correct grade and type of oil (see Lubricants and fluids0,6). An oil can spout or funnel may help to reduce spillage. Pour in half the specified quantity of oil first, and then wait a few minutes for the oil to run to the sump. Continue adding oil a small quantity at a time until the level is up to the lower mark on the dipstick. Refit the filler cap.
15 Start the engine and run it for a few minutes; check for leaks around the oil filter seal and the sump drain plug. Note that there may be a delay of a few seconds before the oil pressure warning light goes out when the engine is first started, as the oil circulates through the engine oil galleries and the new oil filter before the pressure builds-up.
16 Refit the engine undershield (where applicable), and secure it in place with the screw fasteners.
17 Switch off the engine, and wait a few minutes for the oil to settle in the sump once

6.11b... and the filter element...

more. With the new oil circulated and the filter completely full, recheck the level on the dipstick, and add more oil as necessary.
18 Dispose of the used engine oil safely, with reference to *General Repair Procedures*.

7 Hose and fluid leak check

Cooling system

 Warning: Refer to the safety information given in 'Safety first!' and Chapter 3 before disturbing any of the cooling system components.

HAYNES HINT

A leak in the cooling system will usually show up as white- or antifreezecoloured deposits on the area adjoining the leak.

6.11c... then refit the oil filter

1 Carefully check the radiator and heater coolant hoses along their entire length. Renew any hose which is cracked, swollen or which shows signs of deterioration. Cracks will show up better if the hose is squeezed. Pay close attention to the clips that secure the hoses to the cooling system components. Hose clips that have been overtightened can pinch and puncture hoses, resulting in cooling system leaks.
2 Inspect all the cooling system components (hoses, joint faces, etc) for leaks **(see Haynes Hint)**.
3 Where any problems of this nature are found on system components, renew the component or gasket with reference to Chapter 3.

Fuel

 Warning: Refer to the safety information given in 'Safety first!' and Chapter 4A before disturbing any of the fuel system components.

4 Check all fuel lines at their connections to the injection pump, injectors and fuel filter housing.
5 Examine each fuel hose/pipe along its length for splits or cracks. Check for leakage from the union nuts and examine the unions between the metal fuel lines and the fuel filter housing. Also check the area around the fuel injectors for signs of leakage.
6 To identify fuel leaks between the fuel tank and the engine bay, the vehicle should raised and securely supported on axle stands. Inspect the fuel tank and filler neck for

punctures, cracks and other damage. The connection between the filler neck and tank is especially critical. Sometimes a rubber filler neck or connecting hose will leak due to loose retaining clamps or deteriorated rubber.

7 Carefully check all rubber hoses and metal fuel lines leading awaty from the fuel tank. Check for loose connections, deteriorated hoses, kinked lines, and other damage. Pay particular attention to the vent pipes and hoses, which often loop up around the filler neck and can become blocked or kinked, making tank filling difficult. Follow the fuel supply and return lines to the front of the vehicle, carefully inspecting them all the way for signs of damage or corrosion. Renew damaged sections as necessary.

Engine oil

8 Inspect the area around the camshaft cover, cylinder head, oil filter and sump joint faces. Bear in mind that, over a period of time, some very slight seepage from these areas is to be expected – what you are really looking for is any indication of a serious leak caused by gasket failure. Engine oil seeping from the base of the timing belt/chain cover or the transmission bellhousing may be an indication of crankshaft or input shaft oil seal failure. Should a leak be found, renew the failed gasket or oil seal by referring to the appropriate Chapters in this manual.

Air conditioning refrigerant

 Warning: Refer to the safety information given in 'Safety first!' and Chapter 3, regarding the dangers of disturbing any of the air conditioning system components.

9 The air conditioning system is filled with a liquid refrigerant, which is retained under high pressure. If the air conditioning system is opened and depressurised without the aid of specialised equipment, the refrigerant will immediately turn into gas and escape into the atmosphere. If the liquid comes into contact with your skin, it can cause severe frostbite. In addition, the refrigerant contains substances, which are environmentally damaging; for this reason, it should not be allowed to escape into the atmosphere.

10 Any suspected air conditioning system leaks should be immediately referred to a Peugeot dealer or air conditioning specialist. Leakage will be shown up as a steady drop in the level of refrigerant in the system.

11 Note that water may drip from the condenser drain pipe, underneath the car, immediately after the air conditioning system has been in use. This is normal, and should not be cause for concern.

Brake (and clutch) fluid

 Warning: Refer to the safety information given in 'Safety first!' and Chapter 9, regarding the dangers of handling brake fluid.

12 With reference to Chapter 9, examine the area surrounding the brake pipe unions at the master cylinder for signs of leakage. Check the area around the base of fluid reservoir, for signs of leakage caused by seal failure. Also examine the brake pipe unions at the ABS hydraulic unit.

13 If fluid loss is evident, but the leak cannot be pinpointed in the engine bay, the brake calipers and underbody brake lines and should be carefully checked with the vehicle raised and supported on axle stands. Leakage of fluid from the braking system is serious fault that must be rectified immediately.

14 Refer to Chapter 6 Section 2 and check for leakage around the hydraulic fluid line connections to the clutch master cylinder at the bulkhead, and to the clutch slave cylinder, bolted to the side of the transmission bellhousing.

15 Brake/clutch hydraulic fluid is a toxic substance with a watery consistency. New fluid is almost colourless, but it becomes darker with age and use.

Unidentified fluid leaks

16 If there are signs that a fluid of some description is leaking from the vehicle, but you cannot identify the type of fluid or its exact origin, remove the engine undershield, park the vehicle overnight and slide a large piece of card underneath it. Providing that the card is positioned in roughly in the right location, even the smallest leak will show up on the card. Not only will this help you to pinpoint the exact location of the leak, it should be easier to identify the fluid from its colour. Bear in mind, though, that the leak may only be occurring when the engine is running!

Vacuum hoses

17 Although the braking system is hydraulically operated, the brake servo unit amplifies the effort you apply at the brake pedal, by making use of the vacuum created by the engine or vacuum pump (see Chapter 9). Vacuum is ported to the servo by means of a large-bore hose. Any leaks that develop in this hose will reduce the effectiveness of the braking system.

18 In addition, many of the underbonnet components, particularly the emission control components, are driven by vacuum supplied from the vacuum pump via narrow-bore hoses. A leak in a vacuum hose means that air is being drawn into the hose (rather than escaping from it) and this makes leakage very difficult to detect. One method is to use an old length of vacuum hose as a kind of stethoscope – hold one end close to (but not in) your ear and use the other end to probe the area around the suspected leak. When the end of the hose is directly over a vacuum leak, a hissing sound will be heard clearly through the hose. Care must be taken to avoid contacting hot or moving components, as the engine must be running when testing in this manner. Renew any vacuum hoses that are found to be defective.

8.1 Check the driveshaft gaiters for signs of damage or deterioration

8 Driveshaft gaiter and CV joints check

1 With the vehicle raised and securely supported on stands (see *Jacking and vehicle support*), turn the steering onto full lock, then slowly rotate the roadwheel. Inspect the condition of the outer constant velocity (CV) joint gaiters, squeezing the gaiters to open out the folds **(see illustration)**. Check for signs of cracking, splits or deterioration of the gaiter, which may allow the grease to escape, and lead to water and grit entry into the joint. Also check the security and condition of the retaining clips. Repeat these checks on the inner CV joints. If any damage or deterioration is found, the gaiters should be renewed (see Chapter 8).

2 At the same time, check the general condition of the CV joints themselves by first holding the driveshaft and attempting to rotate the wheel. Repeat this check by holding the inner joint and attempting to rotate the driveshaft. Any appreciable movement indicates wear in the joints; wear in the driveshaft splines, or a loose driveshaft retaining nut.

9 Hinge and lock lubrication

1 Work around the vehicle, and lubricate the hinges of the bonnet, doors and tailgate with a small amount of general-purpose oil.

2 Lightly lubricate the bonnet release mechanism and exposed section of inner cable with a smear of grease.

3 Check carefully the security and operation of all hinges, latches and locks, adjusting them where required. Check the operation of the central locking system.

4 Check the condition and operation of the tailgate struts, renewing them if either is leaking or no longer able to support the tailgate securely when raised.

10 Road test

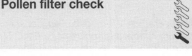

Instruments and electrical equipment

1 Check the operation of all instruments and electrical equipment.
2 Make sure that all instruments read correctly, and switch on all electrical equipment in turn to check it functions properly.

Steering and suspension

3 Check for any abnormalities in the steering, suspension, handling or road 'feel'.
4 Drive the vehicle, and check that there are no unusual vibrations or noises.
5 Check that the steering feels positive, with no excessive 'sloppiness', or roughness, and check for any suspension noises when cornering, or when driving over bumps.

Drivetrain

6 Check the performance of the engine, clutch, transmission and driveshafts.
7 Listen for any unusual noises from the engine, clutch and transmission.
8 Make sure the engine idles smoothly, and that there is no hesitation when accelerating.
9 Check that the clutch action is smooth and progressive, that the drive is taken up smoothly, and that the pedal travel is not excessive. Also listen for any noises when the clutch pedal is depressed.
10 Check that all gears can be engaged smoothly, without noise, and that the gear lever action is smooth and not vague or 'notchy'.
11 On automatic transmission models, make sure that all gearchanges occur smoothly, without snatching, and without an increase in engine speed between changes. Check that all the gear positions can be selected with the vehicle at rest. If any problems are found, they should be referred to a Peugeot dealer.
12 Listen for a metallic clicking sound from the front of the vehicle, as the vehicle is driven slowly in a circle with the steering on full lock. Carry out this check in both directions. If a clicking noise is heard, this indicates wear in a driveshaft joint; in which case, the complete driveshaft must be renewed (see Chapter 8 Section 2).

Braking system

13 Make sure that the vehicle does not pull to one side when braking, and that the wheels do not lock when braking hard.
14 Check that there is no vibration through the steering when braking.
15 Check that the handbrake operates correctly, without excessive movement of the lever, and that it holds the vehicle on a slope.
16 Test the operation of the brake servo unit as follows. With the engine off, depress the footbrake four or five times to exhaust the vacuum. Start the engine, holding the brake pedal depressed. As the engine starts, there should be a noticeable 'give' in the brake pedal as vacuum builds-up. Allow the engine to run for at least two minutes, and then switch it off. If the brake pedal is depressed now, it should be possible to detect a hiss from the servo as the pedal is depressed. After about four or five applications, no further hissing should be heard, and the pedal should feel considerably firmer.

11 Resetting the service indicator

Note: *If you need to disconnect the battery after carrying out this procedure, lock the vehicle and wait at least 5 minutes. Otherwise the display reset may not register.*
1 On completion of the service, reset the service interval indicator as follows.

12.0 There are two parts (arrowed) to the pollen filter

2 With the ignition switched off, press and hold trip meter button.
3 Turn on the ignition switch, and the display begins a countdown. When the countdown reaches 0, release the trip meter button, and the spanner service symbol in the display will disappear.
4 Turn off the ignition switch.
5 Turn on the ignition switch and check the correct mileage to the next service interval is displayed on the indicator.

12 Pollen filter check

Note: *There are two parts to the pollen filter (see illustration).*
1 Open the bonnet and the pollen filter is positioned in the right-hand rear of the engine compartment.
2 Unclip the plastic access cover from the rear of the bulkhead (see illustration).
3 Reaching in through the bulkhead, release the securing clips at each end of the pollen filter cover and hinge the flap downwards (see illustration).
4 Slide the first part of the filter out from the housing (see illustration). Note any markings or arrows to aid refitting.
5 Reaching in through the bulkhead once again, slide the second part of the pollen filter sideways and then out from the housing (see illustration).
6 Check the condition of the filter, and renew it if dirty.

12.2 Unclip the cover from the scuttle panel...

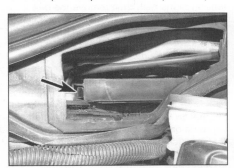

12.3... then release the securing clips (one side arrowed) and open the flap

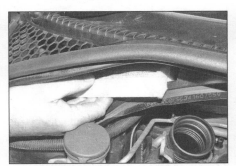

12.4 Slide the first part of the pollen filter out...

12.5... then reach in and slide the second part of the filter out

7 Wipe clean the inside of the housing and fit both of the pollen filter elements, making sure they are correctly fitted.
8 Close the flap on the pollen filter housing, making sure the clips are located securely.
9 Refit the pollen filter access cover to the rear of the bulkhead.
10 Close the bonnet.

13 Auxiliary drivebelt check and renewal

Note: *For non-VTi models, Peugeot specify the use of a special electronic tool (SEEM C.TRONIC type 105.5 belt tension measuring tool) to correctly set the auxiliary drivebelt tension. If access to this equipment cannot be obtained, an approximate setting can be achieved using the method described below. If this method is used, the tension should be checked using the special electronic tool at the earliest opportunity.*

Check

1 Apply the handbrake, slacken the front right-hand roadwheel bolts, then jack up the front of the car and support it on axle stands (see *Jacking and vehicle support*). Remove the right-hand front roadwheel.
2 Remove the fixings securing the wheel arch liner to the body, and then manoeuvre the liner out from underneath the wing.
3 Using a suitable socket and extension bar fitted to the crankshaft sprocket bolt, rotate the crankshaft so that the entire length of the drivebelt can be examined. Examine the drivebelt for cracks, splitting, fraying or damage. Check also for signs of glazing (shiny patches) and for separation of the belt plies. Renew the belt if worn or damaged.
4 If the condition of the belt is satisfactory, on non-VTi models, check the drivebelt tension as described below. **Note:** *On VTi models, there is no need to check the drivebelt tension (an automatic tensioner is fitted).*
5 Refit the wheel arch liner and the roadwheel, then lower the vehicle to the ground; tighten the wheel bolts to the specified torque.
6 Some models may use 'elastic/stretch' belts, these are belts which do not have any form of adjustment. Replacement of these belts requires the use of special tools.
7 If renewing the auxiliary belt idler pulley (depending on model), place a jack under the right-hand end of the engine and remove the right-hand engine mounting. This will enable the engine to be moved up or down slightly to access the bolt/nut and remove the idler pulley. Take care not to damage any components (hoses, cables, wiring and exhaust front pipe), as the engine is moved up or down.

Non-VTi engines without air conditioning

Renewal

8 If not already done, proceed as described in paragraphs 1 and 2. On 1.4 litre models,

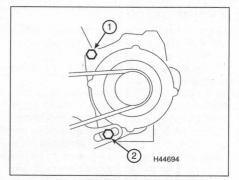

13.11a Auxiliary belt routing and adjustment (1.4 litre models without air conditioning)

1 Alternator pivot bolt   2 Adjuster bolt

slacken both the alternator upper and lower mounting bolts, whilst on 1.6 litre models it is only necessary to slacken the lower mounting bolt.
9 Back off the adjuster bolt to relieve the tension in the drivebelt, then slip the drivebelt from the pulleys. **Note:** *If the belt is going to be re-used, mark the direction of rotation on the belt prior to removal. This will ensure it is refitted the correct way around.*
10 If the belt is being renewed, ensure that the correct type is used. If the original belt is being refitted, use the mark made on removal to ensure it is fitted the correct way around.
11 Fit the belt around the pulleys, and take up the slack in the belt by tightening the adjuster bolt **(see illustrations)**. Tension the drivebelt as described in the following paragraphs.

Tensioning

12 If not already done, proceed as described in paragraphs 1 and 2.
13 If the special measuring tool is available, fit the measuring equipment to the 'lower run' of the belt, approximately midway between the crankshaft and alternator pulleys. The belt

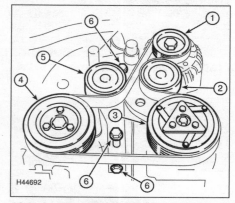

13.21 Auxiliary belt routing and adjustment (1.4 and 1.6 litre models with air conditioning)

1 Alternator pulley   4 Crankshaft pulley
2 Idler pulley   5 Tensioner pulley
3 Compressor pulley   6 Tensioner bolts

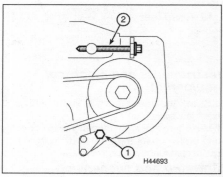

13.11b Auxiliary belt routing and adjustment (1.6 litre models without air conditioning)

1 Alternator pivot bolt   2 Adjuster bolt

tension should be set to the figure given in the Specifications at the start of this Chapter.
14 If the measuring tool is not available, the belt should be tensioned so that, under firm thumb pressure, there is about 5.0 mm of free movement at the mid-point between the pulleys on the lower belt run.
Caution: Correct tensioning of the drivebelt will ensure it has a long life. A belt that is too slack will slip and squeal. Beware of overtightening, as this can cause wear in the alternator bearings.
15 To adjust the belt tension, with the mounting bolt(s) just slackened, turn the adjuster bolt until the correct tension is achieved.
16 Rotate the crankshaft a couple of times, recheck the tension, and then tighten the alternator mounting bolt(s) to the specified torque.
17 Refit the wheel arch liner, securing it in position with the plastic expanding rivets.
18 Refit the roadwheel then lower the vehicle to the ground and tighten the wheel bolts to the specified torque. Reconnect the battery.

Non-VTi engines with air conditioning

Renewal

19 If not already done, proceed as described in paragraphs 1 and 2.
20 Slacken the tensioner pulley bracket bolts and rotate the adjuster bolt to release the tension in the belt, then remove the belt from the pulleys. **Note:** *If the belt is to be re-used, mark the direction of rotation on the belt prior to removal. This will ensure it is refitted the correct way around.*
21 If the belt is being renewed, ensure that the correct type is used. If the original belt is being refitted, use the mark made on removal to ensure it is fitted the correct way around. Fit the drivebelt around the pulleys in the following order **(see illustration)**:
- Air conditioning compressor.
- Crankshaft.
- Alternator.
- Idler roller
- Tensioner pulley.

13.30a Turn the tensioner arm clockwise...

13.30b... and then push the locking pin (arrowed) into position

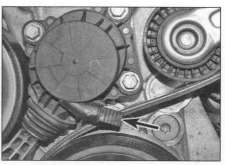

13.31a Pull out the spring (arrowed)...

22 Ensure that the ribs on the belt are correctly engaged with the grooves in the pulleys, and that the drivebelt is correctly routed. Tension the belt as follows.

Tensioning

23 If not already done, proceed as described in paragraphs 1 and 2.
24 If the special measuring tool is available, fit the measuring equipment to the belt, approximately midway between the crankshaft and air conditioning compressor pulleys. Check the belt tension is as given in the Specifications at the start of this Chapter.
25 If the measuring tool is not available, the belt should be tensioned so that, under firm thumb pressure, there is about 5.0 mm of free movement at the mid-point between the crankshaft and air conditioning compressor pulleys.
Caution: Correct tensioning of the drivebelt will ensure it has a long life. A belt that is too slack will slip and squeal. Beware of overtightening, as this can cause wear in the alternator bearings.
26 To adjust the tension, rotate the adjuster bolt until the correct tension is achieved. Once the belt is correctly tensioned, tighten the tensioner pulley bracket bolts to the specified torque. Rotate the crankshaft a couple of times and recheck the tension.
27 When the belt is correctly tensioned, refit the wheel arch liner.
28 Refit the roadwheel, and then lower the vehicle to the ground; tighten the wheel bolts to the specified torque. Reconnect the battery.

VTi engines

Removal

29 If not already done, proceed as described in paragraphs 1 and 2.
30 Move the tensioner pulley away from the drivebelt, using a spanner on the tensioner arm. Rotate the tensioner arm clockwise away from the belt. When the notch at the top of the arm is aligned with the spring-loaded pin, push the pin in to the stop and release the tension on the spanner **(see illustrations)**.
31 Once the tension arm is secured in the released position, reach under the wheel arch and pull out the spring locking tab from the friction wheel drive and secure it on the

13.31b... and lock it onto the locating peg (arrowed)

13.32 Remove the belt from the pulleys

locating peg on the friction wheel housing **(see illustrations)**. Note: *This needs to be released to allow removal of the belt from the crankshaft pulley.*
32 Working under the wheel arch, disengage the belt from all the pulleys, noting its correct routing. Remove the drivebelt from the engine **(see illustration)**. Note: *If the belt is going to be re-used, mark the direction of rotation on the belt prior to removal. This will ensure it is refitted the correct way around.*

Refitting and tensioning

33 If the belt is being renewed, ensure that the correct type is used. If the original belt is being refitted, use the mark made on removal to ensure it is fitted the correct way around. Fit the drivebelt around the pulleys in the following order **(see illustration)**:
● Alternator.
● Air conditioning compressor (where applicable).
● Crankshaft.
● Automatic tensioner pulley.

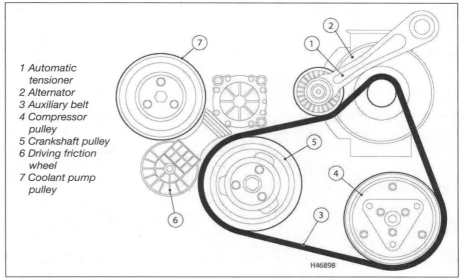

1 Automatic tensioner
2 Alternator
3 Auxiliary belt
4 Compressor pulley
5 Crankshaft pulley
6 Driving friction wheel
7 Coolant pump pulley

H46898

13.33 Auxiliary belt routing and adjustment (VTi-models with air conditioning)

13.39 Cut through the drivebelt

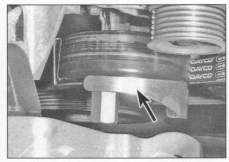

13.42a Fit the installation tool (arrowed) to the coolant pump pulley

13.42b Fit the tool to the crankshaft pulley in the 12 o'clock position...

13.42c ...with the curved side (arrowed) of the tool towards the engine

13.43a Rotate the coolant pump pulley/tool by hand until it catches the belt...

13.43b ...then use a spanner to fully rotate the pulley/tool

34 Ensure that the ribs on the belt are correctly engaged with the grooves in the pulleys
Caution: Do not allow the tensioner pulley to spring forcefully onto the belt as this could result in damage.
35 Refit the wheel arch liner.
36 Refit the roadwheel, and then lower the vehicle to the ground; tighten the wheel bolts to the specified torque.

Elastic/Stretch belts

37 If not already done so, jack up and support the front of the vehicle (see Jacking and vehicle support 13 Section 5 in the reference section). Remove the right-hand wing liner and the engine undershield.
38 Note the routing of the belt(s) before removing them.
39 Where two belts are fitted (models with

hydraulic power steering) cut off the outer belt first with a sharp knife **(see illustration)** and then cut off and remove the inner belt.
40 Genuine Peugeot replacement belts may be supplied with a fitting kit. Aftermarket replacement belts may not be supplied with a fitting kit. Where no fitting kit is supplied it will be necessary to purchase a 'universal' stretch belt fitting kit (such as Draper tools part No EABT-1).
41 To replace the outer belt on models with two belt, a special tool will be required.
42 To replace the main belt, locate the special tool on the waterpump pulley and then fit the second part of the special tool over the crankshaft pulley. Route the belt over the pulleys and then onto the special tool **(see illustrations)**.
43 Using a suitable spanner on the special

tool rotate the waterpump pulley and stretch the belt over the tool and onto the pulley **(see illustrations)**. Check that the belt is correctly located on all the pulleys. Remove the tools.
44 Using a suitable spanner or socket on the crankshaft pulley, rotate the engine twice in the normal (clockwise) direction, checking that the belt is correctly located on all the pulleys as the engine is rotated.
45 Where a second belt is fitted, fit the special tool to the crankshaft pulley. Locate the drivebelt over the AC compressor and then over the special tool. Use a suitable spanner or socket on the crankshaft pulley and rotate the engine approximately 180 degrees, allowing the special tool to lift the belt up and over the crankshaft pulley as the engine is rotated **(see illustrations)**.
46 Check that the belt is correctly located

13.45a Fit the compressor drivebelt installation tool in the 7 o'clock position

13.45b Fit the belt around the tool...

13.45c ...then rotate the crankshaft pulley clockwise

Routine maintenance and servicing – petrol models 1A•13

and then rotate the engine twice in the normal direction of rotation, checking that the new belt is correctly located as the engine is rotated.
47 Refit the remaining components in reverse order.

14 Brake pad and shoe check

1 Slacken the front roadwheel bolts. Firmly apply the handbrake, and then jack up the front of the car and support it securely on axle stands (see *Jacking and vehicle support*). Remove the front roadwheels.
2 For a quick check, the pad thickness can be carried out via the inspection hole on the front caliper **(see Haynes Hint)**. Using a steel rule, measure the thickness of the pad friction material. This must not be less than the specified minimum given in the Specifications.
3 For a comprehensive check, the brake pads should be removed and cleaned. The operation of the caliper can then be checked, and the brake disc itself can be fully examined on both sides. Refer to Chapter 9 for details.
4 If any pad's friction material is worn to the specified minimum thickness or less; all four pads must be renewed as a set. Refer to Chapter 9 for details.
5 On completion, refit the roadwheels then lower the vehicle to the ground and tighten the wheel bolts to the specified torque.
6 On models with rear brake discs, slacken the rear roadwheel bolts. Jack up the rear of the car and support it securely on axle stands. Remove the rear roadwheels. Repeat the procedure described in Paragraphs 2 to 5 on the rear brake pads.
7 On models with rear brake drums, check the brake shoes as described in Chapter 9.

15 Handbrake check

1 The handbrake should be fully applied before 5 clicks can be heard from the lever ratchet mechanism. Check and, if necessary, adjust the handbrake as described in Chapter 9 Section 17.

16 Steering and suspension check

Front suspension and steering

1 Raise the front of the vehicle, and securely support it on axle stands (see *Jacking and vehicle support*).
2 Visually inspect the balljoint dust covers and the steering gear gaiters for splits, chafing or deterioration. Any wear of these components will cause loss of lubricant, together with dirt

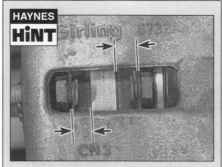
For a quick check, the thickness of the arrowed friction material on each brake pad can be measured through the aperture in the caliper body.

and water entry, resulting in rapid deterioration of the balljoints or steering gear.
3 Grasp the roadwheel at the 12 o'clock and 6 o'clock positions, and try to rock it **(see illustration)**. Very slight free play may be felt, but if the movement is appreciable, further investigation is necessary to determine the source. Continue rocking the wheel while an assistant depresses the footbrake. If the movement is now eliminated or significantly reduced, it is likely that the hub bearings are at fault. If the free play is still evident with the footbrake depressed, then there is wear in the suspension joints or mountings.
4 Now grasp the wheel at the 9 o'clock and 3 o'clock positions, and try to rock it as before. Any movement felt now may again be caused by wear in the hub bearings or the steering track rod balljoints. If the inner or outer balljoint is worn, the visual movement will be obvious.
5 Using a large screwdriver or flat bar, check for wear in the suspension mounting bushes by levering between the relevant suspension component and its attachment point. Some movement is to be expected as the mountings are made of rubber, but excessive wear should be obvious. Also check the condition of any visible rubber bushes, looking for splits, cracks or contamination of the rubber.
6 With the car standing on its wheels, have an assistant turn the steering wheel back-and-

16.3 Check for wear in the hub bearings by grasping the wheel and trying to rock it

forth about an eighth of a turn each way. There should be very little, if any, lost movement between the steering wheel and roadwheels. If this is not the case, closely observe the joints and mountings previously described, but in addition, check the steering column universal joints for wear, and the steering gear itself.

Suspension strut/ shock absorber

7 Check for any signs of fluid leakage around the suspension strut/shock absorber body, or from the rubber gaiter around the piston rod. Should any fluid be noticed, the suspension strut/shock absorber is defective internally, and should be renewed. **Note:** *Suspension struts/shock absorbers should always be renewed in pairs on the same axle, or the handling of the vehicle will be adversely affected.*
8 The efficiency of the suspension strut/shock absorber may be checked by bouncing the vehicle at each corner. Generally speaking, the body will return to its normal position and stop after being depressed. If it rises and returns on a rebound, the suspension strut/shock absorber is probably suspect. Examine also the suspension strut/shock absorber upper and lower mountings for any signs of wear.

17 Timing belt renewal – non-VTi engines

1 Refer to Chapter 2A Section 7.

18 Brake fluid renewal

⚠️ *Warning: Brake hydraulic fluid can harm your eyes and damage painted surfaces, so use extreme caution when handling and pouring it. Do not use fluid that has been standing open for some time, as it absorbs moisture from the air. Excess moisture can cause a dangerous loss of braking effectiveness.*
Note: *A hydraulic clutch shares its fluid reservoir with the braking system, and will also need to be bled (see Chapter 6 Section 2).*
1 The procedure is similar to that for the bleeding of the hydraulic system as described in Chapter 9 Section 2, except that the brake fluid reservoir should be emptied by siphoning, using a clean shringe or similar before starting, and allowance should be made for the old fluid to be expelled when bleeding a section of the circuit.
2 Working as described in Chapter 9, open the first bleed screw in the sequence, and pump the brake pedal gently until nearly all the old fluid has been emptied from the master cylinder reservoir.

3 Top-up to the MAX level with new fluid **(see illustration)**, and continue pumping until only the new fluid remains in the reservoir, and new fluid can be seen emerging from the bleed screw. Tighten the screw, and top the reservoir level up to the MAX level line.

4 Work through all the remaining bleed screws in the sequence until new fluid can be seen at all of them. Be careful to keep the master cylinder reservoir topped-up to above the DANGER level at all times, or air may enter the system and increase the length of the task.

5 When the operation is complete, check that all bleed screws are securely tightened, and that their dust caps are refitted. Wash off all traces of spilt fluid, and recheck the master cylinder reservoir fluid level.

6 Check the operation of the brakes before taking the car on the road.

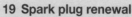

19 Spark plug renewal

1 The correct functioning of the spark plugs is vital for the correct running and efficiency of the engine. It is essential that the plugs fitted are appropriate for the engine (see Specifications1). If this type is used and the engine is in good condition, the spark plugs should not need attention between scheduled renewal intervals. Spark plug cleaning is rarely necessary, and should not be attempted unless specialised equipment is available, as damage can easily be caused to the firing ends.

2 To gain access to the spark plugs, remove the ignition HT coils as described in Chapter 5B Section 3.

3 Unscrew the plugs using a spark plug spanner, suitable box spanner or a deep socket and extension bar **(see illustration)**. Keep the socket aligned with the spark plug – if it is forcibly moved to one side, the ceramic insulator may be broken off. As each plug is removed, examine it as follows.

4 Examination of the spark plugs will give a good indication of the condition of the engine **(see illustration)**. If the insulator nose of the spark plug is clean and white, with no deposits, this is indicative of a weak mixture or too hot a plug (a hot plug transfers heat

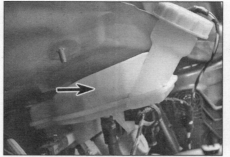
18.3 Brake/clutch fluid MAX level – arrowed

away from the electrode slowly, a cold plug transfers heat away quickly).

5 If the tip and insulator nose are covered with hard black-looking deposits, then this is indicative that the mixture is too rich. Should the plug be black and oily, and then it is likely that the engine is fairly worn, as well as the mixture being too rich.

6 If the insulator nose is covered with light tan to greyish-brown deposits, then the mixture is correct and it is likely that the engine is in good condition.

7 The spark plug electrode gap is of considerable importance as, if it is too large or too small, the size of the spark and its efficiency will be seriously impaired. The gap should be set to the value given in the Specifications at the beginning of this Chapter. **Note:** *The electrode gap on multi-electrode spark plugs cannot be adjusted.*

8 To set the gap on single-electrode plugs, measure the gap with a feeler blade, and then bend open, or closed, the outer plug electrode until the correct gap is achieved **(see illustration)**. The centre electrode should never be bent, as this may crack the insulator and cause plug failure, if nothing worse. If using feeler blades, the gap is correct when the appropriate-size blade is a firm sliding fit.

9 Special spark plug electrode gap adjusting tools are available from most motor accessory shops, or from spark plug manufacturers.

10 Before fitting the spark plugs, check that the threaded connector sleeves are tight, and that the plug exterior and threads are clean **(see Haynes Hint)**.

19.3 Unscrew the spark plugs

11 Remove the rubber hose (if used), and tighten the plug to the specified torque using the spark plug socket and a torque wrench. Refit the remaining spark plugs in the same manner.

12 Refit the ignition HT coil as described in Chapter 5B Section 3.

20 Fuel filter renewal

⚠️ *Warning: Before carrying out the following operation, refer to the precautions given in 'Safety first!' at the beginning of this manual, and follow them implicitly. Petrol is a highly dangerous and volatile liquid, and the precautions necessary when handling it cannot be overstressed.*

Note: *Only fitted to vehicles available in countries where inferior quality fuel is sold.*

Note: *Before disconnecting any fuel lines, depressurise the fuel system,* as described in Chapter 4A.

HAYNES HINT

It is very often difficult to insert spark plugs into their holes without crossthreading them. To avoid this possibility, fit a short length of 8 mm internal diameter rubber hose over the end of the spark plug. The flexible hose acts as a universal joint to help align the plug with the plug hole. Should the plug begin to cross-thread, the hose will slip on the spark plug, preventing thread damage to the cylinder head.

19.4 Examine the spark plugs to check the condition of the engine – see text

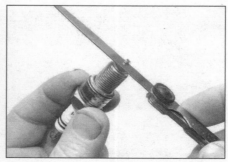
19.8 Measure the spark plug electrode gap with a feeler gauge

1 The fuel filter is situated underneath the rear of the vehicle, on the right-hand side of the front of the fuel tank. To improve access to the filter, chock the front wheels, and then jack up the rear of the vehicle and support it on axle stands (see *Jacking and vehicle support*).

2 Undo the nuts, release the retaining clips and remove the plastic tray from the underside of the fuel tank. Place a container beneath the fuel filter to catch all spilt fuel.

3 Position a large rag around the fuel pipe union, to catch any fuel spray which may be expelled as the fuel pressure is released, then depress the retaining clips and slowly disconnect the fuel pipe. Disconnect the other pipe from the opposite end of the filter and allow the filter contents to drain into the container.

4 Release the retaining clips and slide the fuel filter out of its holder, noting which way around it is fitted. Dispose of the old filter safely; it will be highly inflammable, and may explode if thrown on a fire.

5 Slide the new filter into position, ensuring it is fitted the correct way around; the filter will either have an arrow on its body (indicating the correct direction of fuel flow) or be stamped OUT on one end (indicating the fuel outlet end of the filter).

6 Ensure the filter is clipped securely in its holder then reconnect both fuel pipes. Ensure the pipes 'click' into position on the filter and are securely retained by their quick-release fittings.

7 Start the engine and check the fuel filter for signs leaks.

21 Air cleaner filter element renewal

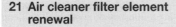

1 Undo the retaining screws securing the lid to the air cleaner housing **(see illustration)**.

2 Lift the lid and remove the air filter element from the housing, noting which way up it is fitted **(see illustration)**. If necessary, slacken the retaining clip securing the intake duct to the air cleaner housing lid then remove the lid to improve access.

3 Wipe clean the inside of the housing then

21.1 Remove the air cleaner housing (VTi model shown)…

fit the new element, ensuring it is correctly located.

4 Locate the lid correctly on the housing and securely tighten the retaining screws. Where necessary, reconnect the intake duct and securely tighten the retaining clip.

22 Manual transmission oil level check (early models)

Note: *On later models, the oil level cannot be checked, as there is no filler/level plug fitted. These transmissions do not require regular maintenance and are filled for life. If the transmission develops a leak or is removed for other work, the oil needs to be completely drained and refilled with the correct amount of oil. The transmission will then be refilled through the vent on the top of the transmission (see illustration).*

Note: *A suitable square-section wrench may be required to undo the transmission filler/ level plug on some models. These wrenches can be obtained from most motor factors or your Peugeot dealer. A new sealing washer will be required for the transmission filler/level plug when refitting.*

1 Park the car on a level surface. The oil level must be checked before the car is driven, or at least 5 minutes after the engine has been switched off. If the oil is checked immediately after driving the car, some of the oil will remain distributed around the transmission, resulting in an inaccurate level reading.

21.2… and remove the filter element

2 If required, to gain better access, remove the left-hand front wheel and then release the securing clips, and remove the wheel arch liner.

3 Wipe clean the area around the filler/level plug, which is on the left-hand end of the transmission. Unscrew the plug and clean it; discard the sealing washer **(see illustrations)**.

4 The oil level should reach the lower edge of the filler/level hole. A certain amount of oil will have gathered behind the filler/level plug, and will trickle out when it is removed; this does not necessarily indicate that the level is correct. To ensure that a true level is established, wait until the initial trickle has stopped, then add oil as necessary until a trickle of new oil can be seen emerging. The level will be correct when the flow ceases; use only good-quality oil of the specified type (see Lubricants and fluids0,6).

5 Filling the transmission with oil is an extremely awkward operation; above all, allow plenty of time for the oil level to settle properly before checking it. If a large amount is added to the transmission, and a large amount flows out on checking the level, refit the filler/level plug and take the vehicle on a short journey so that the new oil is distributed fully around the transmission components, then recheck the level when it has settled again.

6 If the transmission has been overfilled so that oil flows out as soon as the filler/level plug is removed, Check that the car is completely level (front-to-rear and side-to-side), allow the surplus to drain off into a container.

7 When the level is correct, fit a new sealing

22.0 Removing the cap from the transmission vent

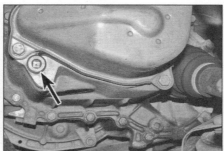

22.3a Oil level/filler plug – MA5 transmission

22.3b Oil level/filler plug – BE4 transmission

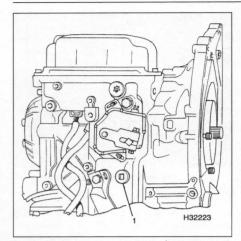

23.2 Unscrew the automatic transmission filler plug (1)

washer to the filler/level plug. Refit the plug, tightening it to the specified torque setting. Wash off any spilt oil then refit the wheel arch liner, securing it in position with the screws and fasteners.

8 Frequent need for topping-up indicates a leak, which should be found and corrected before it becomes serious.

23 Automatic transmission fluid level check

Note: The transmission unit is equipped with a fluid wear sensor to inform the driver when the fluid needs renewing (the ECU flashes the Sport and Snow mode indicator lights when fluid renewal is necessary). Every time the transmission unit is topped-up, this sensor should be adjusted to compensate for the new fluid being added, however this can only be done using the Peugeot diagnostic test box. Adding fluid without adjusting the sensor will not cause any problems but will mean the sensor is giving an inaccurate reading, resulting in fluid renewal being recommended earlier than is actually necessary.

1 Take the vehicle on a short journey, to warm the transmission up to normal operating temperature, and then park the vehicle on

23.5 The level plug is the smaller plug (arrowed)

level ground. Firmly apply the handbrake and place the selector lever in the P position.

2 Wipe clean the area around the filler plug, which is situated on the top of the transmission, directly beneath the battery. Remove the battery and battery tray/box as described in Chapter 5A Section 4, then unscrew the filler plug from the transmission and recover the sealing washer **(see illustration)**.

3 Carefully add 0.5 litre of the specified type of fluid to the transmission via the filler plug aperture. Fit a new sealing washer to the filler plug then refit the plug, tightening it to the specified torque.

4 Undo the screws and remove the engine undershield – where fitted **(see illustration 3.3)**.

5 Position a suitable container under the drain/filler plug arrangement, situated on the base of the transmission. The level plug is the smaller plug fitted to the centre of the larger drain plug **(see illustration)**.

Caution: Do not remove the drain plug by mistake.

6 Start the engine and allow it to idle. With the engine running, retain the drain plug then slacken and remove the level plug and sealing washer.

 Warning: The fluid will be hot, take precautions against scalding.

7 If there is sufficient fluid in the transmission unit, fluid should trickle out the centre of the drain plug before slowing to a drip. **Note:** *If no fluid trickles out, or just a few drips appear when the plug is removed, the fluid level is too low. Refit the level plug then switch off the engine. Add a further 0.5 litre of fluid to the transmission then refit the filler plug and repeat the check.*

8 Once the flow of fluid stops, the level is correct. Fit a new sealing washer to the level plug then refit the plug and tighten it to the specified torque. Switch off the engine.

24 Emissions control systems check

1 This check specified by Peugeot involves checking the engine management system by plugging an electronic tester into the system

25.4 Squeeze together the tabs to release the hose clamp

diagnostic socket to check the electronic control unit (ECU) memory for faults (see Chapter 4A).

2 In reality, if the vehicle is running correctly and the engine management warning light on the instrument panel is functioning normally, then this check need not be carried out.

25 Coolant renewal

 Warning: Wait until the engine is cold before starting this procedure. Do not allow antifreeze to come in contact with your skin, or with the painted surfaces of the vehicle. Rinse off spills immediately with plenty of water. Never leave antifreeze lying around in an open container, or in a puddle on the driveway or on the garage floor. Children and pets are attracted by its sweet smell, but antifreeze can be fatal if ingested.

Cooling system draining

1 With the engine completely cold, unscrew the expansion tank filler cap.

2 Remove the engine undershield (where fitted). The undershield is secured by several screw type fasteners.

3 Position a suitable container beneath the coolant hoses at the lower part of the radiator.

4 Release the retaining clips and disconnect the lower hoses, allowing the coolant to drain into the container **(see illustration)**.

5 To assist draining, remove the cooling system bleed cap/screw (as applicable) from the heater matrix outlet hose union on the engine compartment bulkhead and, on some models, the bleed screw and sealing washer from the top of the coolant housing on the left-hand end of the cylinder head **(see illustration)**. In order to improve access to the bleed screw on the heater union, remove the air filter housing and air ducts, as described in Chapter 4A Section 2.

6 If the coolant has been drained for a reason other than renewal, then provided it is clean and less than four years old, it can be re-used, though new fresh coolant would be recommended.

25.5 Undo the bleed screw from the heater outlet hose union (arrowed)

7 Refit the radiator hose and secure it with the hose clamp.

Cooling system flushing

8 If coolant renewal has been neglected, or if the antifreeze mixture has become diluted, then in time, the cooling system may gradually lose efficiency, as the coolant passages become restricted due to rust, scale deposits, and other sediment. The cooling system efficiency can be restored by flushing the system clean.

9 The radiator should be flushed separately from the engine, to avoid excess contamination.

Radiator flushing

10 Disconnect the top and bottom hoses and any other relevant hoses from the radiator (see Chapter 3 Section 2).

11 Insert a garden hose into the radiator top inlet. Direct a flow of clean water through the radiator, and continue flushing until clean water emerges from the radiator bottom outlet.

12 If after a reasonable period, the water still does not run clear, the radiator can be flushed with a good proprietary cleaning agent. It is important that their manufacturer's instructions are followed carefully. If the contamination is particularly bad, insert the hose in the radiator bottom outlet, and reverse-flush the radiator.

Engine flushing

13 To flush the engine, remove the thermostat (see Chapter 3 Section 5).

14 With the bottom hose disconnected from the radiator, insert a garden hose into the coolant housing. Direct a clean flow of water through the engine, and continue flushing until clean water emerges from the radiator bottom hose.

15 When flushing is complete, refit the thermostat and reconnect the hoses (see Chapter 3 Section 5).

Cooling system filling

16 Before attempting to fill the cooling system, make sure that all hoses and clips are in good condition, and that the clips are tight. Note that an antifreeze mixture must be used all year round, to prevent corrosion of the engine components (see following sub-Section).

17 Remove the expansion tank filler cap.

18 Remove the cooling system bleed screws (see paragraph 5).

19 Peugeot recommend the use of a 'header tank' when refilling the cooling system, to reduce the possibility of air being trapped in the system. Although Peugeot dealers use a special header tank which screws onto the expansion tank, the same effect can be achieved by using a suitable 1.0 litre bottle, with a seal between the bottle and the expansion tank **(see illustration)**.

20 Fit the header tank to the expansion tank and slowly fill the system whilst observing the bleed holes. Coolant will emerge from each of the bleed holes in turn, starting with the heater matrix hose. As soon as coolant free from air bubbles emerges from the heater matrix hose outlet, securely refit the cap/screw (as applicable) then watch the bleed hole on the coolant housing. Once coolant free from air bubbles emerges from the housing hole, refit the bleed screw and sealing washer and tighten securely.

21 Continue to fill the cooling system until bubbles stop appearing in the expansion tank. Help to bleed the air from the system by repeatedly squeezing the radiator bottom hose.

22 When no more bubbles appear, ensure the header tank is full (at least 1.0 litre of coolant) then start the engine. Run the engine at a fast idle speed (do not exceed 2000 rpm) until the cooling fan cuts in and out TWICE, then when the fan has stopped for the second time, switch the engine off.

23 The coolant will be hot. Take great care not to scald yourself.

Caution: Allow the engine to cool, and then remove the header tank. Wash off any spilt coolant with cold water.

24 When the engine has cooled, check the coolant level with reference to *Weekly checks*. Top-up the level if necessary, and refit the expansion tank cap.

Antifreeze mixture

25 The antifreeze should always be renewed at the specified intervals. This is necessary

25.19 Use a 1.0 litre plastic bottle as a header tank

not only to maintain the antifreeze properties, but also to prevent corrosion, which would otherwise occur as the corrosion inhibitors become progressively less effective.

26 Always use an ethylene glycol based antifreeze, which is suitable for use in mixed-metal cooling systems.

27 Before adding antifreeze, the cooling system should be completely drained, preferably flushed, and all hoses checked for condition and security.

28 After filling with antifreeze, a label should be attached to the expansion tank, stating the type and concentration of antifreeze used, and the date installed. Any subsequent topping-up should be made with the same type and concentration of antifreeze.

Caution: Do not use engine antifreeze in the windscreen/tailgate washer system, as it will damage the vehicle paintwork. A screen wash additive should be added to the washer system in the quantities stated on the bottle.

26 Airbags and seat belt pretensioners renewal

1 Peugeot recommend that the airbags and seat belt pretensioners are renewed regardless of their condition every ten years. Refer to Chapter 12 Section 22 for airbag renewal, and Chapter 11 Section 24 for seat belt pretensioner renewal.

Chapter 1B
Routine maintenance and servicing – diesel models

Contents

Degrees of difficulty

Easy, suitable for novice with little experience	Fairly easy, suitable for beginner with some experience 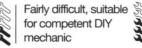	Fairly difficult, suitable for competent DIY mechanic	Difficult, suitable for experienced DIY mechanic	Very difficult, suitable for expert DIY or professional

1 Servicing specifications

Lubricants and fluids . . . .   Refer to *Lubricants, fluids and tyre pressures*

Capacities

Engine oil (including oil filter)
1.4 litre engines . . . .   3.75 litres
1.6 litre engines . . . .   3.75 litres
Cooling system . . . .   6.0 litres

Transmission
Manual transmission (approximate):
   MA5   . . . .   2.0 litres
   BE4/5 . . . .   1.9 litres
Fuel tank . . . .   50 litres

Cooling system
Frost and corrosion protection . . . .   Refer to antifreeze manufacturer's concentration recommendations

Brakes
Brake pad friction material minimum thickness . . . .   2.0 mm

Tyres
Tyre pressures . . . .   See Lubricants, fluids and tyre pressures

Torque wrench settings

	Nm	lbf ft
Automatic transmission:		
Filler plug	24	18
Level plug	35	26
Engine oil filter cover	25	18
Engine sump drain plug	16	12
Manual transmission drain plug	35	26
Manual transmission filler/level plug (where fitted)	25	18
Roadwheel bolts	90	66

2 Maintenance schedule

Note: *This maintenance schedule is a guide recommended by Haynes for servicing your own vehicle. Check with your local dealer for the manufacturer's maintenance schedule.*

The maintenance intervals in this manual are provided with the assumption that you, not the dealer, will be carrying out the work. These are the minimum maintenance intervals recommended by us for vehicles driven daily. If you wish to keep your vehicle in peak condition at all times, you may wish to perform some of these procedures more often. We encourage frequent maintenance, because it enhances the efficiency, performance and resale value of your vehicle.

If the vehicle is driven in dusty areas, used to tow a trailer, or driven frequently at slow speeds (idling in traffic) or on short journeys, more frequent maintenance intervals are recommended.

When the vehicle is new, it should be serviced by a dealer service department (or other workshop recognised by the vehicle manufacturer as providing the same standard of service) in order to preserve the warranty. The vehicle manufacturer may reject warranty claims if you are unable to prove that servicing has been carried out as and when specified, using only original equipment parts or parts certified to be of equivalent quality.

Every 250 miles or weekly
☐ Refer to *Weekly checks*

Every 6000 miles or 12 months – whichever comes sooner
☐ Renew the engine oil and filter (Section 6)

Note: *Peugeot recommend that the engine oil and filter are changed every 12 000 miles or 2 years. However, oil and filter changes are good for the engine and we recommend that the oil and filter are renewed more frequently, especially if the vehicle is used on a lot of short journeys.*

☐ Drain any water from the fuel filter (Section 7)
☐ Check all underbonnet components and hoses for fluid leaks (Section 8)
☐ Check the steering, suspension, driveshaft rubber gaiters and CV joints (Section 9)
☐ Lubricate all hinges and locks (Section 10)

Every 12 000 miles
☐ Reset the service interval indicator (Section 11)
☐ Check the pollen filter (Section 12)
☐ Check the condition of the brake pads and shoes (Section 13)
☐ Check the operation of the handbrake (Section 14)
☐ Carry out a road test (Section 15)
☐ Check the condition of the auxiliary drivebelt, and renew if necessary (Section 16)

Every 24 000 miles
☐ Renew the air filter (Section 17)
☐ Renew the fuel filter (Section 18)
☐ Check the manual transmission oil level, and top-up if necessary (Section 19)

Every 36 000 miles or 3 years – whichever comes sooner
☐ Renew the timing belt (Section 20)

Note: *Although the Peugeot interval for timing belt renewal is 96 000 miles for normal use, and 80 000 miles for use in adverse conditions, it is strongly recommended that the timing belt renewal interval is reduced to 36 000 miles on vehicles which are subjected to intensive use, ie, mainly short journeys or a lot of stop-start driving. The actual belt renewal interval is therefore very much up to the individual owner, but bear in mind that severe engine damage will result if the belt breaks.*

☐ Renew the brake fluid (Section 21)

Note: *A hydraulic clutch shares its fluid reservoir with the braking system, and will also need to be bled.*

Every 48 000 miles
☐ Renew the coolant (Section 22)

Every 72 000 miles or 5 years – whichever comes sooner
☐ Check the particulate emission system – where fitted (Section 23)

Every 10 years
☐ Renew the airbags and seat belt pretensioners (Section 24)

3 Component location

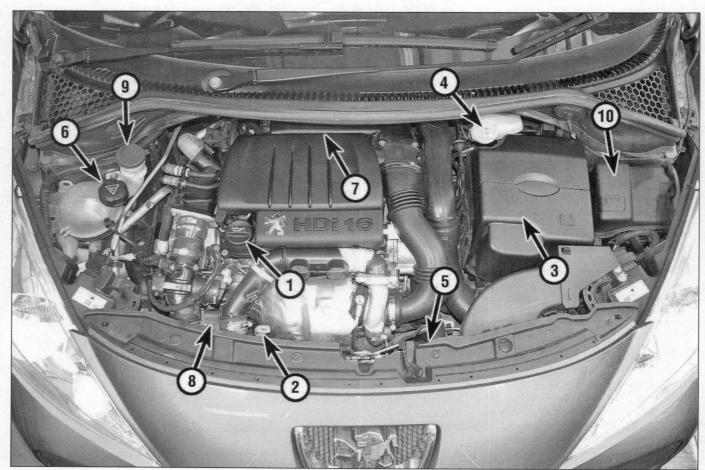

Underbonnet view of a 1.6 litre DOHC model

1 Engine oil filler cap
2 Engine oil level dipstick
3 Battery
4 Brake/clutch fluid reservoir

5 Radiator
6 Coolant expansion tank
7 Air filter housing

8 Alternator
9 Washer fluid reservoir
10 Fuse/electrical box

Front underbody view

1 Engine oil drain plug
2 Air conditioning compressor
3 Right-hand driveshaft
4 Brake calipers
5 Suspension lower arms
6 Track rod arms
7 Catalytic converter
8 Rear lower mounting link
9 Manual transmission
10 Lower radiator hose

Rear underbody view

1 Fuel tank
2 Beam axle
3 Handbrake cables
4 Brake calipers
5 Coil springs
6 Rear exhaust silencer
7 Spare wheel well
8 Fuel tank filler neck
9 Exhaust heat shield

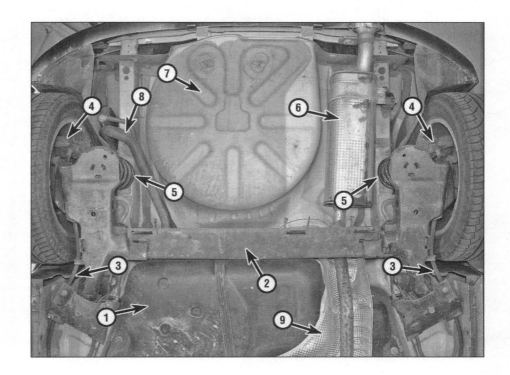

4 General Information

1 This Chapter is designed to help the home mechanic maintain his/her vehicle for safety, economy, long life and peak performance.

2 The Chapter contains a master maintenance schedule, followed by Sections dealing specifically with each task in the schedule. Visual checks, adjustments, component renewal and other helpful items are included. Refer to the accompanying illustrations of the engine compartment and the underside of the vehicle for the locations of the various components.

3 Servicing your vehicle in accordance with the mileage/time maintenance schedule and the following Sections will provide a planned maintenance programme, which should result in a long and reliable service life. This is a comprehensive plan, so maintaining some items but not others at the specified service intervals will not produce the same results.

4 As you service your vehicle, you will discover that many of the procedures can – and should – be grouped together, because of the particular procedure being performed, or because of the proximity of two otherwise-unrelated components to one another. For example, if the vehicle is raised for any reason, the exhaust can be inspected at the same time as the suspension and steering components.

5 The first step in this maintenance programme is to prepare yourself before the actual work begins. Read through all the Sections relevant to the work to be carried out, then make a list and gather all the parts and tools required. If a problem is encountered, seek advice from a parts specialist, or a dealer service department.

5 Routine Maintenance

1 If, from the time the vehicle is new, the routine maintenance schedule is followed closely, and frequent checks are made of fluid levels and high-wear items, as suggested throughout this manual, the engine will be kept in relatively good running condition, and the need for additional work will be minimised.

2 It is possible that there will be times when the engine is running poorly due to the lack of regular maintenance. This is even more likely if a used vehicle, which has not received regular and frequent maintenance checks, is purchased. In such cases, additional work may need to be carried out, outside of the regular maintenance intervals.

3 If engine wear is suspected, a compression test (refer to Chapter 2C Section 2 for 1.4 litre engine, Chapter 2D Section 2 for 1.6 litre DOHC engine and Chapter 2E Section 2 for 1.6 litre SOHC engine) will provide valuable information regarding the overall performance of the main internal components. Such a test can be used as a basis to decide on the extent of the work to be carried out. If, for example, a compression test indicates serious internal engine wear, conventional maintenance as described in this Chapter will not greatly improve the performance of the engine, and may prove a waste of time and money, unless extensive overhaul work is carried out first.

4 The following series of operations are those most often required to improve the performance of a generally poor-running engine:

Primary operations

● Clean, inspect and test the battery (refer to *Weekly checks*).
● Check all the engine-related fluids (refer to *Weekly checks*).
● Check the condition and tension of the auxiliary drivebelt (Section 16).
● Check the condition of the air filter, and renew if necessary (Section 17).
● Check the condition of all hoses, and check for fluid leaks (Section 8).
● Renew the fuel filter (Section 18).

5 If the above operations do not prove fully effective, carry out the following secondary operations:

Secondary operations

6 All items listed under Primary operations, plus the following:

● Check the charging system (refer to Chapter 5A).
● Check the preheating system (refer to Chapter 5C).
● Check the fuel system (refer to Chapter 4B).

6 Engine oil and filter renewal

1 Frequent oil and filter changes are the most important preventative maintenance procedures, which can be undertaken by the DIY owner. As engine oil ages, it becomes diluted and contaminated, which leads to premature engine wear.

2 Before starting this procedure, gather together all the necessary tools and materials. Also make sure that you have plenty of clean rags and newspapers handy, to mop-up any spills. Ideally, the engine oil should be warm, as it will drain better, and more built-up sludge will be removed with it. Take care, however, not to touch the exhaust or any other hot parts of the engine when working under the vehicle. To avoid any possibility of scalding, and to protect yourself from possible skin irritants and other harmful contaminants in used engine oils, it is advisable to wear gloves when carrying out this work. Access to the underside of the vehicle will be greatly improved if it can be raised on a lift, driven onto ramps, or jacked up and supported on axle stands. Whichever method is chosen, make sure that the vehicle remains level, or if it is at an angle, that the drain plug is at the lowest point. Release the screws and remove the engine undershield **(see illustration)**.

3 Slacken the drain plug about half a turn, position the draining container under the drain plug, then remove the plug completely **(see illustrations)**. If possible, try to keep the plug pressed into the sump while unscrewing it by hand the last couple of turns. Recover the sealing ring from the drain plug.

> **HAYNES HINT**
> *As the drain plug releases from the threads, move it away sharply so the stream of oil issuing from the sump runs into the container, not up your sleeve.*

6.2 Undo the engine undershield screws

6.3a Slacken the drain plug...

6.3b ... and unscrew it from the sump

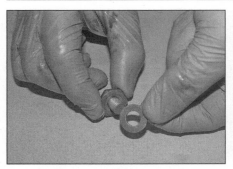

6.5a Fit a new sealing washer...

6.5b ... and tighten to the correct torque

6.6 Engine oil filter cover (arrowed)

4 Allow some time for the old oil to drain, noting that it may be necessary to reposition the container as the oil flow slows to a trickle.

5 After all the oil has drained, wipe off the drain plug with a clean rag, and fit a new sealing washer **(see illustrations)**. Clean the area around the drain plug opening, and refit the plug. Tighten the plug securely.

6 If the filter is also to be renewed, move the container into position under the oil filter, which is located on the front side of the cylinder block **(see illustration)**.

7 The filter element is contained within a filter cover. Using a socket or spanner, slacken and remove the filter cover, complete with filter element from above **(see illustration)**. Be prepared for fluid spillage, and recover the O-ring seal from the cover.

8 Pull the filter element from the filter housing and remove the old O-ring seals from the filter cover **(see illustrations)**.

9 Use a clean rag to remove all oil, dirt and sludge from the inside and outside of the filter cover.

10 Fit the new O-ring to the filter cover, then insert the new filter element into the housing, ensuring that the element locating peg engages correctly with the corresponding hole in the housing **(see illustrations)**.

6.7 Withdraw the filter cover and element

6.8a Pull the filter from the cover...

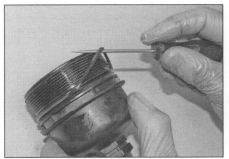

6.8b ... and remove the O-ring seal

6.10a Fit the new O-ring to the cover

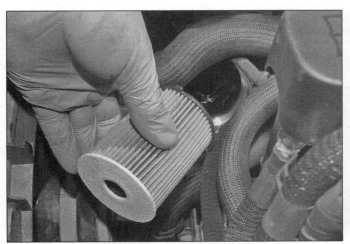

6.10b Fit the new filter element...

6.10c ... making sure the filter locating peg (arrowed) locates into the corresponding hole in the housing (arrowed)

6.11a Apply oil to the O-ring seal

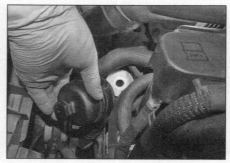

6.11b Fit cover to filter housing...

6.11c ... and tighten to the correct torque

11 Apply a little clean engine oil to the O-ring seal, then refit the filter/cover to the housing and tighten the cover to the specified torque **(see illustrations)**.

12 Remove the old oil and all tools from under the car, then lower the car to the ground (if applicable).

13 Remove the dipstick, and then unscrew the oil filler cap from the top of the filler tube on the front side of the cylinder block. Fill the engine, using the correct grade and type of oil (see Lubricants and fluids0,6). An oil can spout or funnel may help to reduce spillage **(see illustration)**. Pour in half the specified quantity of oil first, and then wait a few minutes for the oil to run to the sump. Continue adding oil a small quantity at a time until the level is up to the lower mark on the dipstick. Adding approximately 1.0 litre will bring the level up to the upper mark on the dipstick. Refit the filler cap.

14 Start the engine and run it for a few minutes; check for leaks around the oil filter seal and the sump drain plug. Note that there may be a delay of a few seconds before the oil pressure warning light goes out when the engine is first started, as the oil circulates through the engine oil galleries and the new oil filter (where fitted) before the pressure builds-up.

15 Switch off the engine, and wait a few minutes for the oil to settle in the sump once more. With the new oil circulated and the filter completely full, recheck the level on the dipstick, and add more oil as necessary.

16 Dispose of the used engine oil safely, with reference to *General Repair Procedures*.

7 Fuel filter water draining

1 To make access easier, remove the battery as described in Chapter 5A. Unclip the plastic cover from the top of the engine.

2 Where fitted, a water drain plug and tube are provided at the base of the fuel filter housing **(see illustration)**. **Note:** *A water drain facility is not provided on later models – if an air purge screw/pump is located on top of the fuel filter, there is no water drain facility.*

3 Place a suitable container beneath the drain tube, and cover the surrounding area with rags.

4 Open the drain plug, and allow fuel and water to drain until fuel which is free from water emerges from the end of the tube. Close the drain plug.

5 Dispose of the drained fuel safely.

6 Start the engine. If difficulty is experienced, bleed the fuel system (Chapter 4B Section 3).

8 Hose and fluid leak check

Cooling system

⚠ *Warning: Refer to the safety information given in 'Safety first!' and Chapter 3 before disturbing any of the cooling system components.*

1 Carefully check the radiator and heater coolant hoses along their entire length. Renew any hose which is cracked, swollen or which shows signs of deterioration. Cracks will show up better if the hose is squeezed. Pay close attention to the clips that secure the hoses to the cooling system components. Hose clips that have been overtightened can pinch and puncture hoses, resulting in cooling system leaks.

2 Inspect all the cooling system components (hoses, joint faces, etc) for leaks.

3 Where any problems of this nature are found on system components, renew the component or gasket with reference to Chapter 3 **(see Haynes Hint)**.

Fuel

⚠ *Warning: Refer to the safety information given in 'Safety first!' and Chapter 4B before disturbing any of the fuel system components.*

4 Check all fuel lines at their connections to the injection pump, injectors and fuel filter housing.

5 Examine each fuel hose/pipe along its length for splits or cracks. Check for leakage from the union nuts and examine the unions between the metal fuel lines and the fuel filter housing. Also check the area around the fuel injectors for signs of leakage.

6 To identify fuel leaks between the fuel tank and the engine bay, the vehicle should raised and securely supported on axle stands.

6.13 Using a funnel, to prevent spillage

7.2 Fuel filter water drain plug (arrowed) – 1.4 litre engine

HAYNES HiNT

A leak in the cooling system will usually show up as white- or antifreezecoloured deposits on the area adjoining the leak.

Inspect the fuel tank and filler neck for punctures, cracks and other damage. The connection between the filler neck and tank is especially critical. Sometimes a rubber filler neck or connecting hose will leak due to loose retaining clamps or deteriorated rubber.

7 Carefully check all rubber hoses and metal fuel lines leading away from the fuel tank. Check for loose connections, deteriorated hoses, kinked lines, and other damage. Pay particular attention to the vent pipes and hoses, which often loop up around the filler neck and can become blocked or kinked, making tank filling difficult. Follow the fuel supply and return lines to the front of the vehicle, carefully inspecting them all the way for signs of damage or corrosion. Renew damaged sections as necessary.

Engine oil

8 Inspect the area around the camshaft cover, cylinder head, oil filter and sump joint faces. Bear in mind that, over a period of time, some very slight seepage from these areas is to be expected – what you are really looking for is any indication of a serious leak caused by gasket failure. Engine oil seeping from the base of the timing belt cover or the transmission bellhousing may be an indication of crankshaft or input shaft oil seal failure. Should a leak be found, renew the failed gasket or oil seal by referring to the appropriate Chapters in this manual.

Air conditioning refrigerant

 Warning: Refer to the safety information given in 'Safety first!' and Chapter 3, regarding the dangers of disturbing any of the air conditioning system components.

9 The air conditioning system is filled with a liquid refrigerant, which is retained under high pressure. If the air conditioning system is opened and depressurised without the aid of specialised equipment, the refrigerant will immediately turn into gas and escape into the atmosphere. If the liquid comes into contact with your skin, it can cause severe frostbite. In addition, the refrigerant contains substances, which are environmentally damaging; for this reason, it should not be allowed to escape into the atmosphere.

10 Any suspected air conditioning system leaks should be immediately referred to a Peugeot dealer or air conditioning specialist. Leakage will be shown up as a steady drop in the level of refrigerant in the system.

11 Note that water may drip from the condenser drain pipe, underneath the car, immediately after the air conditioning system has been in use. This is normal, and should not be cause for concern.

Brake (and clutch) fluid

Warning: Refer to the safety information given in 'Safety first!' and Chapter 9, regarding the dangers of handling brake fluid.

12 With reference to Chapter 9 Section 13, examine the area surrounding the brake pipe unions at the master cylinder for signs of leakage. Check the area around the base of fluid reservoir, for signs of leakage caused by seal failure. Also examine the brake pipe unions at the ABS hydraulic unit.

13 If fluid loss is evident, but the leak cannot be pinpointed in the engine bay, the brake calipers and underbody brake lines and should be carefully checked with the vehicle raised and supported on axle stands. Leakage of fluid from the braking system is serious fault that must be rectified immediately.

14 Refer to Chapter 6 and check for leakage around the hydraulic fluid line connections to the clutch master cylinder at the bulkhead, and to the clutch slave cylinder, bolted to the side of the transmission bellhousing.

15 Brake/clutch hydraulic fluid is a toxic substance with a watery consistency. New fluid is almost colourless, but it becomes darker with age and use.

Unidentified fluid leaks

16 If there are signs that a fluid of some description is leaking from the vehicle, but you cannot identify the type of fluid or its exact origin, remove the engine undershield, park the vehicle overnight and slide a large piece of card underneath it. Providing that the card is positioned in roughly in the right location, even the smallest leak will show up on the card. Not only will this help you to pinpoint the exact location of the leak, it should be easier to identify the fluid from its colour. Bear in mind, though, that the leak may only be occurring when the engine is running!

Vacuum hoses

17 Although the braking system is hydraulically operated, the brake servo unit amplifies the effort you apply at the brake pedal, by making use of the vacuum created by the vacuum pump (see Chapter 9 Section 24). Vacuum is ported to the servo by means of a large-bore hose. Any leaks that develop in this hose will reduce the effectiveness of the braking system.

18 In addition, many of the underbonnet components, particularly the emission control components, are driven by vacuum supplied

from the vacuum pump via narrow-bore hoses. A leak in a vacuum hose means that air is being drawn into the hose (rather than escaping from it) and this makes leakage very difficult to detect. One method is to use an old length of vacuum hose as a kind of stethoscope – hold one end close to (but not in) your ear and use the other end to probe the area around the suspected leak. When the end of the hose is directly over a vacuum leak, a hissing sound will be heard clearly through the hose. Care must be taken to avoid contacting hot or moving components, as the engine must be running when testing in this manner. Renew any vacuum hoses that are found to be defective.

9   Steering, suspension, driveshaft gaiter and CV joint check

Front suspension and steering

1 Raise the front of the vehicle, and securely support it on axle stands.

2 Visually inspect the balljoint dust covers and the steering rack-and-pinion gaiters for splits, chafing or deterioration **(see illustration)**. Any wear of these components will cause loss of lubricant, together with dirt and water entry, resulting in rapid deterioration of the balljoints or steering gear.

3 Grasp the roadwheel at the 12 o'clock and 6 o'clock positions, and try to rock it **(see illustration)**. Very slight free play may be felt, but if the movement is appreciable, further investigation is necessary to determine the source. Continue rocking the wheel while an assistant depresses the footbrake. If the movement is now eliminated or significantly reduced, it is likely that the hub bearings are at fault. If the free play is still evident with the footbrake depressed, then there is wear in the suspension joints or mountings.

4 Now grasp the wheel at the 9 o'clock and 3 o'clock positions, and try to rock it as before. Any movement felt now may again be caused by wear in the hub bearings or the steering track rod balljoints. If the inner or outer balljoint is worn, the visual movement will be obvious.

9.2 Check the steering rack gaiters for damage

9.3 Check for wear in the hub bearings by grasping the wheel and trying to rock it

9.9 Check the driveshaft gaiter for damage

12.0 There are two parts (arrowed) to the pollen filter

5 Using a large screwdriver or flat bar, check for wear in the suspension mounting bushes by levering between the relevant suspension component and its attachment point. Some movement is to be expected as the mountings are made of rubber, but excessive wear should be obvious. Also check the condition of any visible rubber bushes, looking for splits, cracks or contamination of the rubber.

6 With the car standing on its wheels, have an assistant turn the steering wheel back-and-forth about an eighth of a turn each way. There should be very little, if any, lost movement between the steering wheel and roadwheels. If this is not the case, closely observe the joints and mountings previously described, but in addition, check the steering column universal joints for wear, and the rack-and-pinion steering gear itself.

Suspension strut/shock absorber

7 Check for any signs of fluid leakage around the suspension strut/shock absorber body, or from the rubber gaiter around the piston rod. Should any fluid be noticed, the suspension strut/shock absorber is defective internally, and should be renewed. **Note:** *Suspension struts/shock absorbers should always be renewed in pairs on the same axle, or the handling of the vehicle will be adversely affected.*

8 The efficiency of the suspension strut/shock absorber may be checked by bouncing the vehicle at each corner. Generally speaking, the body will return to its normal position and stop after being depressed. If it rises and returns on a rebound, the suspension strut/shock

absorber is probably suspect. Examine also the suspension strut/shock absorber upper and lower mountings for any signs of wear.

Driveshaft gaiter and CV joints

9 With the vehicle raised and securely supported on axle stands, turn the steering to full left or right lock, and then slowly rotate the roadwheel. Inspect the outer constant velocity (CV) joint rubber gaiters, squeezing the gaiters to open out the folds **(see illustration)**. Check for signs of cracking, splits or deterioration of the rubber, which may allow the grease to escape, or water and grit to enter. Also check the security and condition of the retaining clips. Repeat these checks on the inner CV joints. If any damage or deterioration is found, the gaiters should be renewed (see Chapter 8 Section 3).

10 At the same time, check the general condition of the CV joints themselves by first holding the driveshaft and attempting to rotate the wheel. Repeat this check whilst holding the inner joint and attempting to rotate the driveshaft. Any appreciable movement indicates wear in the CV joints; wear in the driveshaft splines, or a loose driveshaft retaining nut.

10 Hinge and lock lubrication

1 Work around the vehicle, and lubricate the hinges of the bonnet, doors and tailgate with a small amount of general-purpose oil.

2 Lightly lubricate the bonnet release

mechanism and exposed section of inner cable with a smear of grease.

3 Check carefully the security and operation of all hinges, latches and locks, adjusting them where required. Check the operation of the central locking system.

4 Check the condition and operation of the tailgate struts, renewing them if either is leaking or no longer able to support the tailgate securely when raised.

11 Resetting the service indicator

Note: *If you need to disconnect the battery after carrying out this procedure, lock the vehicle and wait at least 5 minutes. Otherwise the display reset may not register.*

1 On completion of the service, reset the service interval indicator as follows.

2 With the ignition switched off, press and hold trip meter button.

3 Turn on the ignition switch, and the display begins a countdown. When the countdown reaches 0, release the trip meter button, and the spanner service symbol in the display will disappear.

4 Turn off the ignition switch.

5 Turn on the ignition switch and check the correct mileage to the next service interval is displayed on the indicator.

12 Pollen filter check

Note: *There are two parts to the pollen filter* **(see illustration)**.

1 Open the bonnet and the pollen filter is positioned in the right-hand rear of the engine compartment.

2 Unclip the plastic access cover from the rear of the bulkhead **(see illustration)**.

3 Reaching in through the bulkhead, release the securing clips at each end of the pollen filter cover and hinge the flap downwards **(see illustration)**.

4 Slide the first part of the filter out from the housing **(see illustration)**. Note any markings or arrows to aid refitting.

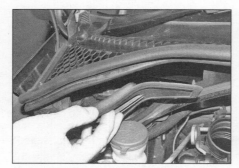

12.2 Unclip the cover from the scuttle panel...

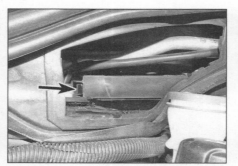

12.3... then release the securing clips (one side arrowed) and open the flap

12.4 Slide the first part of the pollen filter out...

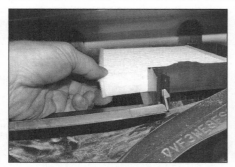

12.5... then reach in and slide the second part of the filter out

5 Reaching in through the bulkhead once again, slide the second part of the pollen filter sideways and then out from the housing **(see illustration)**.

6 Check the condition of the filter, and renew it if dirty.

7 Wipe clean the inside of the housing and fit both of the pollen filter elements, making sure they are correctly fitted.

8 Close the flap on the pollen filter housing, making sure the clips are located securely.

9 Refit the pollen filter access cover to the rear of the bulkhead.

10 Close the bonnet.

13 Brake pad and shoe check

1 Slacken the front roadwheel bolts. Firmly apply the handbrake, and then jack up the front of the car and support it securely on axle stands (see *Jacking and vehicle support*). Remove the front roadwheels.

2 For a quick check, the pad thickness can be carried out via the inspection hole on the front caliper **(see Haynes Hint)**. Using a steel rule, measure the thickness of the pad friction material. This must not be less than the minimum given in the Specifications.

3 For a comprehensive check, the brake pads should be removed and cleaned. The operation of the caliper can then be checked, and the brake disc itself can be fully examined on both sides. Refer to Chapter 9 for details.

4 If any pad's friction material is worn to the specified minimum thickness or less; all four pads must be renewed as a set (see Chapter 9).

5 On completion, refit the roadwheels then lower the vehicle to the ground and tighten the wheel bolts to the specified torque.

6 On models with rear brake discs, slacken the rear roadwheel bolts. Jack up the rear of the car and support it securely on axle stands. Remove the rear roadwheels. Repeat the procedure described in Paragraphs 2 to 5 on the rear brake pads.

7 On models with rear brake drums, check the brake shoes as described in Chapter 9 Section 6.

For a quick check, the thickness of the friction material remaining on each brake pad can be measured through the aperture in the caliper body.

14 Handbrake check

1 The handbrake should be fully applied before 5 clicks can be heard from the lever ratchet mechanism. Check and, if necessary, adjust the handbrake as described in Chapter 9 Section 17.

15 Road test

Instruments and electrical equipment

1 Check the operation of all instruments and electrical equipment.

2 Make sure that all instruments read correctly, and switch on all electrical equipment in turn to check it functions properly.

Steering and suspension

3 Check for any abnormalities in the steering, suspension, handling or road 'feel'.

4 Drive the vehicle, and check that there are no unusual vibrations or noises.

5 Check that the steering feels positive, with no excessive 'sloppiness', or roughness, and check for any suspension noises when cornering, or when driving over bumps.

Drivetrain

6 Check the performance of the engine, clutch, transmission and driveshafts.

7 Listen for any unusual noises from the engine, clutch and transmission.

8 Make sure the engine idles smoothly, and that there is no hesitation when accelerating.

9 Check that the clutch action is smooth and progressive, that the drive is taken up smoothly, and that the pedal travel is not excessive. Also listen for any noises when the clutch pedal is depressed.

10 Check that all gears can be engaged smoothly, without noise, and that the gear lever action is smooth and not vague or 'notchy'.

11 Listen for a metallic clicking sound from the front of the vehicle, as the vehicle is driven slowly in a circle with the steering on full lock. Carry out this check in both directions.

12 If a clicking noise is heard, this indicates wear in a driveshaft joint; in which case, the complete driveshaft must be renewed (see Chapter 8 Section 2).

Braking system

13 Make sure that the vehicle does not pull to one side when braking, and that the wheels do not lock when braking hard.

14 Check that there is no vibration through the steering when braking.

15 Check that the handbrake operates correctly, without excessive movement of the lever, and that it holds the vehicle on a slope.

16 Test the operation of the brake servo unit as follows. With the engine off, depress the footbrake four or five times to exhaust the vacuum. Start the engine, holding the brake pedal depressed. As the engine starts, there should be a noticeable 'give' in the brake pedal as vacuum builds-up. Allow the engine to run for at least two minutes, and then switch it off. If the brake pedal is depressed now, it should be possible to detect a hiss from the servo as the pedal is depressed. After about four or five applications, no further hissing should be heard, and the pedal should feel considerably firmer.

16 Auxiliary drivebelt check and renewal

1 Most models are equipped with a single poly-V type, multi-ribbed auxiliary drivebelt. The belt tension is adjusted automatically by means of a spring-loaded tensioner.

2 Some models may use 'elastic/stretch' belts, these are belts which do not have any form of adjustment. Replacement of these belts requires the use of special tools.

3 If renewing the auxiliary belt idler pulley (depending on model), place a jack under the right-hand end of the engine and remove the right-hand engine mounting. This will enable the engine to be moved up or down slightly to access the bolt/nut and remove the idler pulley. Take care not to damage any components (hoses, cables, wiring and exhaust front pipe), as the engine is moved up or down.

Checking condition

4 Apply the handbrake and slacken the right-hand front roadwheel bolts, then jack up the front of the car and support it securely on axle stands (see Chapter 13 Section 5). Remove the right-hand front roadwheel. Remove the plastic expanding rivets (push in the centre pin a little, then prise out the rivet)

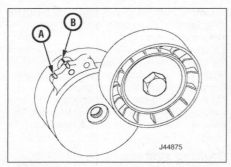

16.6 When the groove (A) lines up with the mark (B) on the mounting bracket, the belt requires renewal

16.8 Use an open-ended spanner to rotate the tensioner arm clockwise, then lock it in place by inserting a 4 mm drill into the hole in the tensioner body (arrowed)

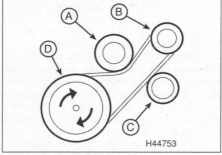

16.10a Auxiliary drivebelt routing (models without air conditioning)

A Tensioner   *C Idler pulley*
B Alternator   *D Crankshaft*

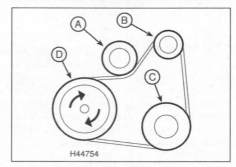

16.10b Auxiliary drivebelt routing (models with air conditioning)

A Tensioner   *C Compressor*
B Alternator   *D Crankshaft*

enable the alignment of the locking holes to be more easily seen in the limited space available.

9 Note how the belt is routed, then remove the belt from around the pulleys. If the belt is to be re-used, mark the direction of rotation, as the belt must be refitted the same way around.

Refitting and tensioning

10 Fit the belt around the pulleys, ensuring that the ribs on the belt are correctly engaged with the grooves in the pulleys, and the drivebelt is correctly routed (see illustrations). If refitting a used belt, use the mark made on removal to ensure it's fitted the correct way around.

11 Using an open-ended spanner, hold the tensioner arm so that the locking drill bit/rod can be removed, then release the pressure on the spanner so that the automatic tensioner takes up the slack in the drivebelt.

12 Refit the wheel arch liner.

Elastic/Stretch belts

13 If not already done so, jack up and support the front of the vehicle (see Jacking and vehicle support 13 Section 5 in the reference section). Remove the right-hand wing liner and the engine undershield.

14 Note the routing of the belt(s) before removing them.

15 Where two belts are fitted (models with hydraulic power steering) cut off the outer belt first with a sharp knife (see illustration) and then cut off and remove the inner belt.

16 Genuine Peugeot replacement belts may be supplied with a fitting kit. Aftermarket replacement belts may not be supplied with a fitting kit. Where no fitting kit is supplied it will be necessary to purchase a 'universal' stretch belt fitting kit (such as Draper tools part No EABT-1).

17 To replace the outer belt on models with two belt, a special tool will be required.

18 To replace the main belt, locate the special tool on the waterpump pulley and then fit the second part of the special tool over the crankshaft pulley. Route the belt over the pulleys and then onto the special tool (see illustrations).

and remove the wheel arch liner from under the right-hand front wing for access to the crankshaft pulley bolt.

5 Using a suitable socket and bar fitted to the crankshaft pulley bolt, rotate the crankshaft so that the entire length of the drivebelt can be examined. Examine the drivebelt for cracks, splitting, fraying or damage. Check also for signs of glazing (shiny patches) and for separation of the belt plies. Renew the belt if worn or damaged.

6 On 1.6 litre DOHC models, the automatic tensioner has markings, which align with each other when the belt is in need of renewal.

The small square lug aligns with the large square on the front of the tensioner body (see illustration).

Removal

7 If not already done, proceed as described in paragraphs 2 and 3.

8 Using an open-ended spanner, reach down and rotate the tensioner arm clockwise to release the belt tension. Insert a 4 mm drill bit or rod into the hole in the tensioner body, so that the tensioner arm rests against it, and locks it in this position (see illustration). It is useful to have a small mirror available to

16.15 Cut through the drivebelt

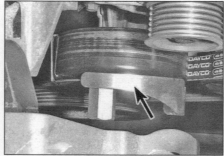

16.18a Fit the installation tool (arrowed) to the coolant pump pulley

16.18b Fit the tool to the crankshaft pulley in the 12 o'clock position...

16.18c ...with the curved side (arrowed) of the tool towards the engine

16.19a Rotate the coolant pump pulley/tool by hand until it catches the belt...

16.19b ...then use a spanner to fully rotate the pulley/tool

16.21a Fit the compressor drivebelt installation tool in the 7 o'clock position

16.21b Fit the belt around the tool...

16.21c ...then rotate the crankshaft pulley clockwise

19 Using a suitable spanner on the special tool rotate the waterpump pulley and stretch the belt over the tool and onto the pulley **(see illustrations).** Check that the belt is correctly located on all the pulleys. Remove the tools.
20 Using a suitable spanner or socket on the crankshaft pulley, rotate the engine twice in the normal (clockwise) direction, checking that the belt is correctly located on all the pulleys as the engine is rotated.
21 Where a second belt is fitted, fit the special tool to the crankshaft pulley. Locate the drivebelt over the AC compressor and

then over the special tool. Use a suitable spanner or socket on the crankshaft pulley and rotate the engine approximately 180 degrees, allowing the special tool to lift the belt up and over the crankshaft pulley as the engine is rotated **(see illustrations).**
22 Check that the belt is correctly located and then rotate the engine twice in the normal direction of rotation, checking that the new belt is correctly located as the engine is rotated.
23 Refit the remaining components in reverse order.

17 Air filter element renewal

1.4 litre engines

1 Remove the plastic cover from the top of the engine. The cover is retained by rubber grommets, and pulls upwards to release.
2 Undo the screws at the front of the filter cover, then lift the cover and withdrawn the filter element. Note which way up the element was fitted **(see illustrations).**

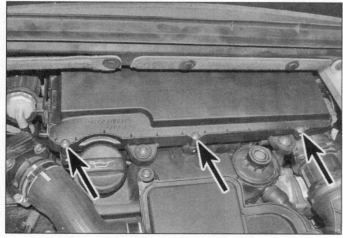

17.2a Undo the three air filter cover screws (arrowed), lift off the cover...

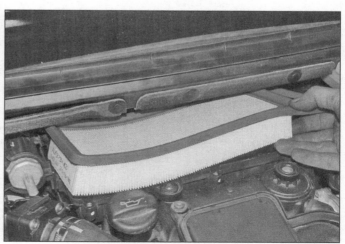

17.2b... and remove the filter element

17.7a Slacken the air cleaner retaining clip (arrowed)...

17.7b ... and the retaining clip (arrowed) on the turbo...

17.7c ... release the securing clip...

17.7d ... and remove the air intake hose

17.8 Disconnect the wiring connector

3 Using a rag, or air-line if available (wear safety glasses), clean out the filter housing.

4 Position the new element in the filter housing and refit the filter cover. Note the three lugs at the rear of the cover, which engage with the housing. Tighten the retaining screws securely.

5 Refit the plastic cover to the top of the engine.

1.6 litre DOHC engines

6 Remove the plastic cover from the top of the engine. The cover is retained by rubber grommets, and pulls upwards to release.

7 Remove the primary air inlet duct from the front of the engine compartment, and then remove the turbocharger inlet duct (see illustrations), and the air cleaner inlet duct.

8 Disconnect the wiring connector from the air mass meter (see illustration).

9 Release the fuel priming pump and support from the top of the air cleaner, then place it to one side (see illustrations).

10 Undo the retaining screws at the front of the air cleaner, then unhook and remove the cover (see illustrations).

11 Withdraw the filter element; noting which way up it is fitted.

12 Using a rag, or air-line if available (wear safety glasses), clean out the filter housing.

13 Position the new element in the air cleaner housing and refit the cover, making sure

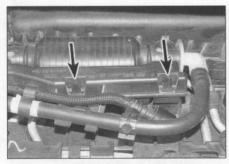

17.9a Release the two locking clips (arrowed)...

17.9b ... and move the priming pump to one side

17.10a Undo the retaining screws (arrowed)...

17.10b ... and remove the upper housing

17.11 Remove the air filter element

the rear lugs engage properly. Tighten the retaining screws securely.

14 Refit the remaining parts using a reversal of the removal procedure.

1.6 litre SOHC engines

15 Remove the cover from the top of the engine **(see illustration)**. The cover is retained by rubber grommets, and pulls upwards to release.

16 Undo the retaining screws at the front of the air cleaner, then release the securing clip on the side of the housing and remove the cover **(see illustrations)**.

17 Withdraw the filter element**(see illustration)**; noting which way up it is fitted.

18 Using a rag **(see illustration)**, or air-line if available (wear safety glasses), clean out the filter housing.

19 Position the new filter element in the air cleaner lower housing and refit the cover, making sure the rear lugs engage properly **(see illustration)**. Tighten the retaining screws securely.

20 Refit the remaining parts using a reversal of the removal procedure.

---

18 Fuel filter renewal

Note: *Check with your dealer for the availability of fuel filter/housing before removal. On some models the fuel filter/housing may come as a complete assembly.*

Removal

1 Remove the battery as described in Chapter 5A.

2 Remove the engine upper plastic cover and air inlet ducting from across the top of the fuel filter housing **(see illustrations)**.

1.4 litre engines

3 Place a suitable container beneath the drain screw, and cover the surrounding area with rags. Take care not to allow fuel to enter the transmission bellhousing, which is just below. If available, fit a length of hose over the drain screw **(see illustration 4.2a)**.

4 Open the drain plug by turning it anti-clockwise. Allow fuel and water to drain. Close the drain plug.

5 Release the retaining clips and disconnect

the fuel feed and return pipes from the filter **(see illustration)**. Plug the pipes to prevent dirt ingress and fuel loss.

6 Undo the filter retaining screw, and

17.15 Unclip the engine cover

17.16a Undo the screws...

17.16b ... and release the securing clip

17.17 Withdraw the filter element

17.18 Clean out the filter housing

17.19 Locate the rear lugs of the cover correctly

18.2a Release the securing clips...

18.2b... and remove the air ducting

18.5 Depress the button (arrowed) and disconnect the fuel feed and return pipes

18.6a Undo the filter retaining screw (arrowed)...

18.6b... then disengage the filter lug from the bracket

18.9 Disconnect the fuel lines

18.10a Release the securing clip...

18.10b... and withdraw the fuel filter

manoeuvre the filter from the bracket. Disconnect the fuel heater and water detector wiring plugs (where fitted) as the filter is withdrawn (see illustrations).

7 Unscrew the fuel heater and water detector (where fitted) from the filter. Discard the O-ring seals, new ones must be fitted.

1.6 litre DOHC engines

8 Disconnect the wiring from the fuel heater.

9 Place cloth rags beneath the filter, then disconnect the fuel inlet and outlet pipes (see illustration).

10 Release the clip and remove the fuel filter housing from the engine compartment (see illustrations).

11 The new filter is supplied as one complete housing. As applicable, remove the water detector and fuel heater from the old filter housing and transfer them to the new unit.

1.6 litre SOHC engines

12 Remove the cover from the top of the engine. The cover is retained by rubber grommets, pull upwards to release (see illustration 14.15).

13 Place cloth rags beneath the fuel line connections, then release the securing clips and disconnect the fuel inlet and outlet pipes from the top of the filter (see illustrations).

14 Disconnect the wiring connector from the fuel heater on top of the filter housing (see illustration).

18.13a Lift up to release the securing clip...

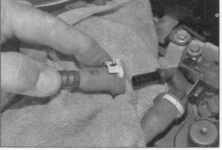

18.13b ... and withdraw the fuel line

18.13c Push down on the coloured clip...

18.13d ... to release the other fuel lines

18.14 Disconnect the wiring connector

18.15 Withdraw the fuel filter

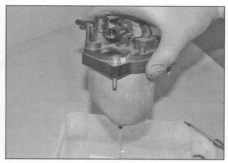

18.16a Lift the sensor up slightly...

18.16b ... and drain the fuel from the filter

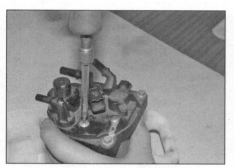

18.17a Undo the retaining screws...

18.17b ... to release the upper housing from the filter

18.18 Fit seal to new filter

15 Pull the filter housing upwards to release it from the mounting bracket at the rear of the engine compartment **(see illustration)**.

16 Turn the sensor at the centre of the upper housing clockwise and lift it upwards slightly, to drain the fuel from inside the filter into a container **(see illustrations)**.

17 Undo the three retaining screws and remove the upper housing from the filter **(see illustrations)**.

18 Fit the new seal to the top of the new filter and refit the upper housing **(see illustration)**, making sure the screws are tightened securely to prevent any leakage.

19 Turn the sensor anti-clockwise to secure it back in position **(see illustration)**.

Refitting

1.4 litre engines

20 Renew the water detector and fuel heater O-ring seals, and refit them to the new filter, tightening them securely.

21 Manoeuvre the filter into position and secure it in place with the fixing screw.

22 Reconnect the fuel feed/return pipes and the wiring plugs.

23 Refit the retaining bracket – tighten the screw securely.

24 Close the fuel drain plug and prime the fuel system as described in Chapter 4B Section 3. The remainder of refitting is a reversal of removal.

1.6 litre engines

25 Fit the new filter using a reversal of the removal procedure, then prime the fuel system as described in Chapter 4B Section 3.

19 Manual transmission oil level check (early models)

Note: *On later models, the oil level cannot be checked, as there is no filler/level plug fitted. These transmissions do not require maintenance and are filled for life. If the transmission develops a leak or is removed for other work, the oil needs to be completely drained and refilled with the correct amount of oil. The transmission will then be refilled through the vent on the top of the transmission* **(see illustration)**.

Note: *A suitable square-section wrench may be required to undo the transmission filler/level plug on some models. These wrenches can be obtained from most motor factors or your Peugeot dealer. A new sealing washer will be required for the transmission filler/level plug when refitting.*

1 Park the car on a level surface. The oil level must be checked before the car is driven, or at least 5 minutes after the engine has been switched off. If the oil is checked immediately after driving the car, some of the oil will remain distributed around the transmission, resulting in an inaccurate level reading.

18.19 Make sure the sensor is back in position

19.0a Remove the vent cap from the top of the transmission

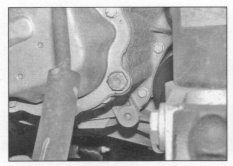

19.3 Manual transmission oil filler/level plug (where fitted)

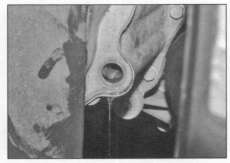

19.4 Add oil until a trickle emerges

2 If required, to gain better access, remove the left-hand front wheel and then release the securing clips, and remove the wheel arch liner.

3 Wipe clean the area around the filler/level plug, which is on the left-hand end of the transmission. Unscrew the plug and clean it; discard the sealing washer **(see illustration)**.

4 The oil level should reach the lower edge of the filler/level hole. A certain amount of oil will have gathered behind the filler/level plug, and will trickle out when it is removed; this does not necessarily indicate that the level is correct. To ensure that a true level is established, wait until the initial trickle has stopped, then add oil as necessary until a trickle of new oil can be seen emerging **(see illustration)**. The level will be correct when the flow ceases; use only good-quality oil of the specified type (see Lubricants and fluids0,6).

5 Filling the transmission with oil is an extremely awkward operation; above all, allow plenty of time for the oil level to settle properly before checking it. If a large amount is added to the transmission, and a large amount flows out on checking the level, refit the filler/level plug and take the vehicle on a short journey so that the new oil is distributed fully around the transmission components, then recheck the level when it has settled again.

6 If the transmission has been overfilled so that oil flows out as soon as the filler/level plug is removed, Check that the car is completely level (front-to-rear and side-to-side), allow the surplus to drain off into a container.

7 When the level is correct, fit a new sealing washer to the filler/level plug. Refit the plug, tightening it to the specified torque setting. Wash off any spilt oil then refit the wheel arch liner, securing it in position with the screws and fasteners.

8 Frequent need for topping-up indicates a leak, which should be found and corrected before it becomes serious.

20 Timing belt renewal

1 Refer to Chapter 2C Section 7 for 1.4 litre engines, Chapter 2D Section 7 for 1.6 litre DOHC engine and Chapter 2E Section 7 for 1.6 litre SOHC engines.

21 Brake fluid renewal

⚠️ *Warning: Brake hydraulic fluid can harm your eyes and damage painted surfaces, so use extreme caution when handling and pouring it. Do not use fluid that has been standing open for some time, as it absorbs moisture from the air. Excess moisture can cause a dangerous loss of braking effectiveness.*
Note: *A hydraulic clutch shares its fluid*

reservoir with the braking system, and will also need to be bled (see Chapter 6).

1 The procedure is similar to that for the bleeding of the hydraulic system as described in Chapter 9 Section 2, except that the brake fluid reservoir should be emptied by siphoning, using a clean ladle or similar before starting, and allowance should be made for the old fluid to be expelled when bleeding a section of the circuit.

2 Working as described in Chapter 9 Section 2, open the first bleed screw in the sequence, and pump the brake pedal gently until nearly all the old fluid has been emptied from the master cylinder reservoir.

3 Top-up to the MAX level with new fluid **(see illustration)**, and continue pumping until only the new fluid remains in the reservoir, and new fluid can be seen emerging from the bleed screw. Tighten the screw, and top the reservoir level up to the MAX level line.

4 Work through all the remaining bleed screws in the sequence until new fluid can be seen at all of them. Be careful to keep the master cylinder reservoir topped-up to above the MIN level at all times, or air may enter the system and increase the length of the task.

5 When the operation is complete, check that all bleed screws are securely tightened, and that their dust caps are refitted. Wash off all traces of spilt fluid, and recheck the master cylinder reservoir fluid level.

6 Check the operation of the brakes before taking the car on the road.

22 Coolant renewal

⚠️ *Warning: Wait until the engine is cold before starting this procedure. Do not allow antifreeze to come in contact with your skin, or with the painted surfaces of the vehicle. Rinse off spills immediately with plenty of water. Never leave antifreeze lying around in an open container, or in a puddle in the driveway or on the garage floor. Children and pets are attracted by its sweet smell, but antifreeze can be fatal if ingested.*

Cooling system draining

1 With the engine completely cold, unscrew the expansion tank filler cap.

2 Remove the engine undershield (where fitted). The undershield is secured by several screw type fasteners.

3 Position a suitable container beneath the coolant hoses at the lower part of the radiator.

4 Release the retaining clips and disconnect the lower hoses, allowing the coolant to drain into the container **(see illustration)**.

5 To assist draining, remove the cooling system bleed cap/screw (as applicable) from the heater matrix outlet hose union on the engine compartment bulkhead and the bleed screw and sealing washer from the top of the

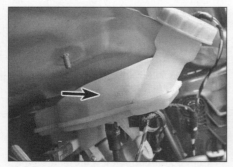

21.3 Brake/clutch fluid MAX level (arrowed)

22.4 Squeeze together the tabs to release the hose retaining clip

22.5a Heater matrix outlet hose bleed screw

22.5b Coolant housing bleed screw (arrowed) – 1.6 litre DOHC engine

22.5c Coolant housing bleed screw (1.6 litre SOHC engine)

coolant housing on the left-hand end of the cylinder head **(see illustrations)**. In order to improve access to the bleed screw on the heater union, remove the air filter housing and air ducts, as described in Chapter 4B Section 4.

6 If the coolant has been drained for a reason other than renewal, then provided it is clean and less than four years old, it can be re-used, though new fresh coolant would be recommended.

7 Refit the radiator hose and secure it with the hose clamp.

Cooling system flushing

8 If coolant renewal has been neglected, or if the antifreeze mixture has become diluted, then in time, the cooling system may gradually lose efficiency, as the coolant passages become restricted due to rust, scale deposits, and other sediment. The cooling system efficiency can be restored by flushing the system clean.

9 The radiator should be flushed independently of the engine, to avoid unnecessary contamination.

Radiator flushing

10 Disconnect the top hose and any other relevant hoses from the radiator, with reference to Chapter 3 Section 4.

11 Insert a garden hose into the radiator top inlet. Direct a flow of clean water through the radiator, and continue flushing until clean water emerges from the radiator bottom outlet.

12 If after a reasonable period, the water still does not run clear, the radiator can be flushed with a good proprietary cleaning agent. it is important that the manufacturer's instructions are followed carefully. If the contamination is particularly bad, insert the hose in the radiator bottom outlet, and reverse-flush the radiator.

Engine flushing

13 To flush the engine, first refit the cylinder block drain plug, and tighten the cooling system bleed screws.

14 Remove the thermostat as described in Chapter 3 Section 5, then temporarily refit the thermostat cover.

15 With the top and bottom hoses disconnected from the radiator, insert a garden hose into the radiator top hose. Direct a clean flow of water through the engine, and continue flushing until clean water emerges from the radiator bottom hose.

16 On completion of flushing, refit the thermostat and reconnect the hoses with reference to Chapter 3.

Cooling system filling

17 Before attempting to fill the cooling system, make sure that all hoses and clips are in good condition, and that the clips are tight. Note that an antifreeze mixture must be used all year round, to prevent corrosion of the engine components (see following sub-Section). Also check that the radiator and cylinder block drain plugs are in place and tight.

18 Remove the expansion tank filler cap.

19 Open all the cooling system bleed screws (see paragraph 5).

20 Some of the cooling system hoses are positioned at a higher level than the top of the radiator expansion tank. It is therefore necessary to use a 'header tank' when refilling the cooling system, to reduce the possibility of air being trapped in the system. Although Peugeot dealers use a special header tank, the same effect can be achieved by using a suitable 1.0 litre bottle, with a seal between the bottle and the expansion tank **(see Haynes Hint)**.

21 Fit the header tank to the expansion tank and slowly fill the system. Coolant will emerge from the bleed screw. As soon as coolant free from air bubbles emerges from the screw, tighten the screw.

22 Ensure that the header tank is full (at least 1.0 litre of coolant). Refit the battery (where removed), start the engine. Run the engine at a fast idle speed (do not exceed 2000 rpm) until the cooling fan cuts in, and then cuts out TWICE, then switch the engine off.

Caution: The coolant will be hot. Take great care not to scald yourself.

23 Allow the engine to cool, and then remove the header tank. Wash off any spilt coolant with cold water.

24 When the engine has cooled, check the coolant level as described in *Weekly checks*.

Top-up the level if necessary, and refit the expansion tank cap.

Antifreeze mixture

25 The antifreeze should always be renewed at the specified intervals. This is necessary not only to maintain the antifreeze properties, but also to prevent corrosion, which would otherwise occur as the corrosion inhibitors become progressively less effective.

26 Always use an ethylene glycol based antifreeze, which is suitable for use in mixed-metal cooling systems.

27 Before adding antifreeze, the cooling system should be completely drained, preferably flushed, and all hoses checked for condition and security.

28 After filling with antifreeze, a label should be attached to the expansion tank, stating the type and concentration of antifreeze used, and the date installed. Any subsequent topping-up should be made with the same type and concentration of antifreeze.

Caution: Do not use engine antifreeze in the washer system, as it will cause damage to the vehicle paintwork. A screen wash additive should be added to the washer system in the quantities stated on the bottle.

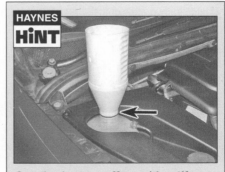

HAYNES HiNT

Cut the bottom off an old antifreeze container to make a 'header tank' for use when refilling the cooling system. The seal at the point arrowed should be as tight as possible – use an O-ring if available, or seal the joint by some other means.

23 Particulate emission system check

1 A particulate filter is fitted to some 1.6 litre models. This filter is combined with the catalytic converter in the exhaust front pipe. An additive is used to help clean the filter element. This additive is stored in a separate reservoir adjacent to the fuel tank on the right-hand side. However, checking the filter and refilling the reservoir should be entrusted to a Peugeot dealer or specialist, as parameters of the engine management ECU must be re-initialised, and special equipment/tools must be used due to the hazardous nature of the additive.

2 Peugeot recommends that the additive is topped-up at this interval (see Lubricants and fluids0,6).

24 Airbags and seat belt pretensioners renewal

1 Peugeot recommend that the airbags and seat belt pretensioners are renewed regardless of their condition every ten years. Refer to Chapter 12 Section 22 for airbag renewal, and Chapter 11 Section 24 for seat belt pretensioner renewal.

Chapter 2 Part A:
Non-VTi petrol engines in-car repair procedures

Contents

Degrees of difficulty

Easy, suitable for novice with little experience	**Fairly easy,** suitable for beginner with some experience	**Fairly difficult,** suitable for competent DIY mechanic	**Difficult,** suitable for experienced DIY mechanic	**Very difficult,** suitable for expert DIY or professional

Specifications

Engine (general)

Capacity:	
1.4 litre engine	1360cc
1.6 litre engine	1587cc
Designation:	
1.4 litre engine:	
SOHC	TU3A
DOHC	ET3J4
1.6 litre engine	TU5JP4
Engine codes:*	
1.4 litre engine:	
SOHC	KFV
DOHC	KFU
1.6 litre engine	NFU
Bore:	
1.4 litre engine	75.00 mm
1.6 litre engine	78.50 mm
Stroke:	
1.4 litre engine	77.00 mm
1.6 litre engine	82.00 mm
Direction of crankshaft rotation	Clockwise (viewed from right-hand side of vehicle)
No 1 cylinder location	At transmission end of the block
Compression ratio:	
1.4 litre engine:	
SOHC	10.2 : 1
DOHC	11.1 : 1
1.6 litre engine	10.8 : 1
Maximum power output:	
1.4 litre engine:	
SOHC	55 kW @ 5500 rpm
DOHC	65 kW @ 5250 rpm
1.6 litre engine	80 kW @ 5500 rpm
Maximum torque output:	
1.4 litre engine:	
SOHC	120 Nm @ 3000 rpm
DOHC	135 Nm @ 3250 rpm
1.6 litre engine	150 Nm @ 4500 rpm

* The engine code is situated on front, left-hand end of the cylinder block.

Camshaft(s)

Drive. . . . . Toothed belt

Valve clearances (engine cold)

1.4 litre SOHC engine:
  Inlet. . . . . 0.20 mm
  Exhaust. . . . . 0.40 mm
1.4 and 1.6 litre DOHC engines . . . . Hydraulic adjusters

Lubrication system

Oil pump type. . . . . Gear type, chain-driven off the crankshaft
Minimum oil pressure at 80°C:
  1000 rpm . . . . 1.5 bars
  2000 rpm . . . . 3.0 bars
  4000 rpm . . . . 4.0 bars
Oil pressure warning switch operating pressure . . . . 0.8 bars

Torque wrench settings

	Nm	lbf ft
Big-end bearing cap nuts:*		
1.4 litre SOHC and 1.6 litre engines	40	30
1.4 litre DOHC engine:		
Stage 1	30	22
Stage 2	Angle-tighten a further 45°	
Camshaft bearing housing to cylinder head (DOHC engines)	10	7
Camshaft sprocket retaining bolt(s):		
1.4 litre SOHC and 1.6 litre engines	45	33
1.4 litre DOHC engine:		
Exhaust sprocket retaining bolt	45	33
Inlet sprocket retaining bolt:		
Stage 1	20	15
Stage 1	60	44
Inlet sprocket retaining bolt cover	40	30
Camshaft thrust fork retaining bolt (SOHC engine)	16	12
Crankshaft oil seal housing bolts	8	6
Crankshaft pulley retaining bolts	25	18
Crankshaft sprocket retaining bolt:*		
Stage 1	40	30
Stage 2	Angle-tighten a further 45°	
Cylinder head bolts:		
1.4 litre SOHC engine:		
Stage 1	20	15
Stage 2	Angle-tighten a further 240°	
1.4 litre DOHC engine:		
Stage 1	15	11
Stage 2	25	18
Stage 3	Angle-tighten a further 200°	
1.6 litre engine:		
Stage 1	20	15
Stage 2	Angle-tighten a further 260°	
Cylinder head cover screws/nuts (SOHC engine)	8	6
Cylinder head cover bolts (DOHC engines)	10	7
Driveplate bolts	67	49
Engine-to-transmission bolts:		
Manual transmission models	40	30
Automatic transmission models	35	26
Engine/transmission left-hand mounting:		
Mounting centre nut	65	48
Mounting-to-bracket bolts	30	22
Mounting bracket-to-body bolts	19	14
Mounting bracket-to-manual transmission nuts	25	18
Mounting bracket-to-automatic transmission bolts	45	33
Mounting stud/nut (automatic transmission)	40	30
Engine/transmission rear mounting:		
Mounting-to-cylinder block bolts	40	30
Mounting link-to-mounting bolt	55	41
Mounting link-to-subframe bolt	39	29

Torque wrench settings (continued)

	Nm	lbf ft
Engine/transmission right-hand mounting:		
Mounting bracket nuts	45	33
Support bracket:		
Bracket to cylinder head	45	33
Bracket to mounting bracket	60	44
Bracket to engine	26	19
Mounting bolts to body	60	44
Mounting vibration damper	32	24
Flywheel bolts*	70	52
Inlet sprocket retaining bolt:		
Stage 1	20	15
Stage 2	60	44
Main bearing cap bolts (1.6 litre engine):		
Stage 1	20	15
Stage 2	Angle-tighten a further 49°	
Main bearing ladder casting (1.4 litre engine):		
M11 bolts:		
Stage 1	20	15
Stage 2	Angle-tighten a further 44°	
M6 bolts	8	6
Oil filter	25	18
Oil filter housing to engine block (1.6 litre engine)	10	7
Oil pressure switch:		
SOHC engine	30	22
DOHC engines	20	15
Oil pump retaining bolts	9	7
Piston oil jet spray tube bolts	10	7
Roadwheel bolts	90	66
Sump drain plug	30	22
Sump retaining nuts and bolts	8	6
Timing belt cover bolts	8	6
Timing belt tensioner pulley nut:		
1.4 litre engine	20	15
1.6 litre engine	22	16

Do not re-use

1 General information

How to use this Chapter

1 This Part of Chapter 2 describes those repair procedures that can reasonably be carried out on the petrol engine while it remains in the car. If the engine has been removed from the car and is being dismantled, as described in Part E, any preliminary dismantling procedures can be ignored.

2 Note that, while it may be possible physically to overhaul items such as the piston/connecting rod assemblies while the engine is in the car, such tasks are not normally carried out as separate operations. Usually, several additional procedures (not to mention the cleaning of components and of oilways) have to be carried out. For this reason, all such tasks are classed as major overhaul procedures, and are described in Part E of this Chapter.

3 Part E describes the removal of the engine/transmission from the vehicle, and the full overhaul procedures that can then be carried out.

Petrol engine description

4 The petrol engines in this Part of Chapter 2 are from the TU and ET series, and are well-proven engines, which have been fitted to many previous Peugeot and Citroën vehicles. 1.4 litre single overhead camshaft (SOHC) 8-valve or 1.4 and 1.6 litre double overhead camshaft (DOHC) 16-valve, in-line four cylinder engines are fitted, being mounted transversely at the front of the car with the transmission attached to the left-hand end. The 1.4 litre SOHC and DOHC engines share the same block incorporating wet liners. Both 1.4 and 1.6 litre DOHC engines have similar cylinder heads and repair procedures are identical, except in the area of the hydraulic followers. On the 1.6 litre, the camshaft operates directly on the hydraulic followers which are located in the cylinder head beneath the camshaft. On the 1.4 litre, the valves are operated by roller rocker arms between the camshaft and the tops of the valves – one end of the rocker arm is clipped to the hydraulic follower and the other end rests on top of the valve stem.

5 The crankshaft runs in five main bearings. Thrustwashers are fitted to No 2 main bearing (upper half) to control crankshaft endfloat.

6 The connecting rods rotate on horizontally split bearing shells at their big ends. The pistons are attached to the connecting rods by gudgeon pins, which are an interference fit in the connecting rod small-end eyes. The aluminium-alloy pistons are fitted with three piston rings – two compression rings and an oil control ring.

7 On 1.4 litre engines, the cylinder block is made of aluminium, and wet liners are fitted to the cylinder bores. Sealing O-rings are fitted at the base of each liner, to prevent the escape of coolant into the sump.

8 On 1.6 litre engines, the cylinder block is made from cast-iron, and the cylinder bores are an integral part of the cylinder block. On this type of engine, the cylinder bores are sometimes referred to as having dry liners.

9 The inlet and exhaust valves are each closed by coil springs, and operate in guides pressed into the cylinder head; the valve seat inserts are also pressed into the cylinder head, and can be renewed separately if worn.

10 On SOHC engines, the camshaft is driven by a toothed timing belt, and operates the eight valves via rocker arms. Valve clearances are adjusted by a screw-and-locknut arrangement. The camshaft rotates directly in the cylinder head. The timing belt also drives the coolant pump.

11 On DOHC engines, the camshafts are driven by a timing belt, and operate the 16 valves. The camshafts rotate directly in the cylinder head and are retained by a one-piece bearing housing. The belt also drives the coolant pump.

12 Lubrication is by means of an oil pump, which is driven (via a chain and sprocket) off the right-hand end of the crankshaft. It draws oil through a strainer located in the sump, and then forces it through an externally mounted filter into galleries in the cylinder block/crankcase. From there, the oil is distributed to the crankshaft (main bearings) and camshaft. The big-end bearings are supplied with oil via internal drillings in the crankshaft, while the camshaft bearings also receive a pressurised supply. On 1.6 litre engines, piston cooling oil spray jets are fitted to spray oil on the underside of each piston. The camshaft lobes and valves are lubricated by splash, as are all other engine components.

Operations with engine in car

13 The following work can be carried out with the engine in the car:

a) *Compression pressure – testing.*
b) *Cylinder head cover – removal and refitting.*
c) *Timing belt covers – removal and refitting.*
d) *Timing belt – removal, refitting and adjustment.*
e) *Timing belt tensioner and sprockets – removal and refitting.*
f) *Camshaft oil seal(s) – renewal.*
g) *Camshaft(s) and rocker arms/followers – removal, inspection and refitting.*
h) *Cylinder head – removal and refitting.*
i) *Cylinder head and pistons – decarbonising.*
j) *Sump – removal and refitting.*
k) *Oil pump – removal, overhaul and refitting.*
l) *Crankshaft oil seals – renewal.*
m) *Engine/transmission mountings – inspection and renewal.*
n) *Flywheel/driveplate – removal, inspection and refitting.*

2 Compression test – description and interpretation

1 When engine performance is down, or if misfiring occurs which cannot be attributed to the ignition or fuel systems, a compression test can provide diagnostic clues as to the engine's condition. If the test is performed regularly, it can give warning of trouble before any other symptoms become apparent.

2 The engine must be fully warmed-up to normal operating temperature, the battery must be fully-charged. The aid of an assistant will also be required.

3 Remove the ignition HT coil assembly (see Chapter 5B) then remove the spark plugs (see Chapter 1A).

4 Fit a compression tester to the No 1 cylinder spark plug hole – the type of tester which screws into the plug thread is to be preferred.

5 Have the assistant hold the throttle wide open, and crank the engine on the starter motor; after one or two revolutions, the compression pressure should build-up to a maximum figure, and then stabilise. Record the highest reading obtained.

6 Repeat the test on the remaining cylinders, recording the pressure in each.

7 All cylinders should produce very similar pressures; a difference of more than 2 bars between any two cylinders indicates a fault. Note that the compression should build-up quickly in a healthy engine; low compression on the first stroke, followed by gradually increasing pressure on successive strokes, indicates worn piston rings. A low compression reading on the first stroke, which does not build-up during successive strokes, indicates leaking valves or a blown head gasket (a cracked head could also be the cause). Deposits on the undersides of the valve heads can also cause low compression.

8 Although Peugeot do not specify exact compression pressures, as a guide, any cylinder

pressure of below 10 bars can be considered as less than healthy. Refer to a Peugeot dealer or other specialist if in doubt as to whether a particular pressure reading is acceptable.

9 If the pressure in any cylinder is low, carry out the following test to isolate the cause. Introduce a teaspoonful of clean oil into that cylinder through its spark plug hole, and repeat the test.

10 If the addition of oil temporarily improves the compression pressure, this indicates that bore or piston wear is responsible for the pressure loss. No improvement suggests that leaking or burnt valves, or a blown head gasket, may be to blame.

11 A low reading from two adjacent cylinders is almost certainly due to the head gasket having blown between them; the presence of coolant in the engine oil will confirm this.

12 If one cylinder is about 20 percent lower than the others and the engine has a slightly rough idle; a worn camshaft lobe could be the cause.

13 If the compression reading is unusually high, the combustion chambers are probably coated with carbon deposits. If this is the case, the cylinder head should be removed and decarbonised.

14 On completion of the test, refit the spark plugs and ignition HT coil (see Chapters 1A and 5B).

3 Engine assembly/ valve timing holes – general information and usage

Note: *Do not attempt to rotate the engine whilst the crankshaft/camshaft are locked in position. If the engine is to be left in this state for a long period of time, it is a good idea to place warning notices inside the vehicle, and in the engine compartment. This will reduce the possibility of the engine being accidentally cranked on the starter motor, which is likely to cause damage with the locking pins in place.*

3.4 Insert a 6 mm diameter bolt/pin (arrowed) into the hole in the cylinder block flange and into the flywheel hole

3.5 Lock the camshaft sprocket in position with a 10 mm diameter bolt/pin (arrowed) (SOHC engine)

1 On all models, timing holes are drilled in the camshaft sprocket(s) and in the rear of the flywheel/driveplate. The holes are used to ensure that the crankshaft and camshaft(s) are correctly positioned when assembling the engine (to prevent the possibility of the valves contacting the pistons when refitting the cylinder head), or refitting the timing belt. When the timing holes are aligned with access holes in the cylinder head and the front of the cylinder block, suitable diameter bolts/pins can be inserted to lock both the camshaft and crankshaft in position, preventing them from rotating. Proceed as follows.
2 Remove the timing belt upper cover as described in Section 5.

SOHC engines

3 The crankshaft must now be turned until the timing hole in the camshaft sprocket is aligned with the corresponding hole in the cylinder head. The holes are aligned when the camshaft sprocket hole is in the 2 o'clock position, when viewed from the right-hand end of the engine. The crankshaft can be turned by using a spanner on the crankshaft sprocket bolt, noting that it should always be rotated in a clockwise direction (viewed from the right-hand end of the engine).
4 With the camshaft sprocket hole correctly positioned, insert a 6 mm diameter stud or pin, 90 mm long, welded to a length of weld rod bent to the appropriate shape, through the hole in the front left-hand flange of the cylinder block, and locate it in the timing hole in the rear of the flywheel (see illustration). A purpose-made Peugeot tool No 0132-QY is available from dealers. Note that it may be necessary to rotate the crankshaft slightly to get the holes to align.
5 With the flywheel correctly positioned, insert a 10 mm diameter bolt or a pin through the timing hole in the camshaft sprocket, and locate it in the hole in the cylinder head (see illustration).

DOHC engines

6 Turn the crankshaft until the holes in the camshaft sprockets align with the corresponding holes in the cylinder head. The crankshaft can be turned by using a spanner on the crankshaft sprocket bolt, noting that it should always be rotated in a clockwise direction (viewed from the right-hand end of the engine).
7 With the camshaft sprocket holes correctly positioned, insert a 6 mm diameter stud or pin, 90 mm long, welded to a length of weld rod bent to the appropriate shape, through the hole in the front left-hand flange of the cylinder block, and locate it in the timing hole in the rear of the flywheel/driveplate (see illustrations). A purpose-made Peugeot tool No 0132-QY is available from dealers. Note that it may be necessary to rotate the crankshaft slightly to get the holes to align.
8 With the crankshaft correctly positioned, insert suitable bolts or pins through the timing holes in the camshaft sprockets, and locate them in the

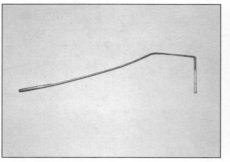

3.7a Weld a 90 mm length of 6 mm rod/ stud to a length of weld rod . . .

3.8a Use suitable bolts/pins (arrowed) to lock the camshaft sprockets in position (1.6 litre DOHC engine)

holes in the cylinder head (see illustrations).
Note: The holes on all engines is 8 mm diameter except for the inlet camshaft sprocket hole on 1.4 litre engines which is 5 mm.

All models

9 The crankshaft and camshaft are now locked in position, preventing unnecessary rotation.

4 Cylinder head cover – removal and refitting

SOHC engine

Removal

1 Disconnect the battery (see Chapter 5A).

4.2 Disconnect the breather hose from the cylinder head cover

3.7b . . . and insert it into the hole in the cylinder block flange (arrowed)

3.8b Lock the camshaft sprockets in position using 5 mm and 8 mm diameter drill bits/bolts (1.4 litre DOHC engine)

2 Depress the clip and disconnect the breather hose from the cylinder head cover (see illustration).
3 Remove the ignition HT coil as described in Chapter 5B.
4 Undo the two retaining nuts and sealing washers (where fitted) then lift off the cylinder head cover, complete with its rubber seal. Examine the seal for signs of damage and deterioration, and if necessary, renew it.
5 Remove the spacer from each cover stud then lift off the oil baffle plate (see illustrations).

Refitting

6 Carefully clean the cylinder head and cover mating surfaces, and remove all traces of oil.
7 Fit the rubber seal over the edge of the cylinder head cover, ensuring that it is correctly located along its entire length (see illustration).

4.5a Remove the spacers (arrowed) from the studs . . .

4.5b . . . then lift off the baffle plate

4.7 Ensure the rubber seal is correctly located on the cylinder head cover

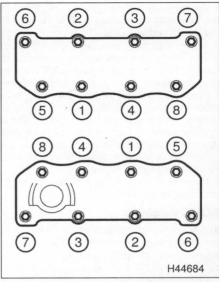

4.16 Cylinder head cover bolts tightening sequence

8 Refit the oil baffle plate then fit the spacers to the cover studs.

9 Carefully refit the cylinder head cover to the engine, taking great care not to displace the rubber seal.

10 Fit the sealing washers (where fitted) and cover retaining nuts, tightening them to the specified torque.

11 Refit the ignition HT coil (see Chapter 5B) then reconnect the breather hose securely to the cylinder head cover. On completion reconnect the battery.

DOHC engines

Removal

12 Disconnect the battery (see Chapter 5A), and remove the ignition coil as described in Chapter 5B.

13 Working in a spiral pattern, progressively and evenly slack the cylinder head cover bolts, and remove the covers. Recover the gaskets.

Refitting

14 Carefully clean the cylinder head and cover mating surfaces, and remove all traces of oil.

15 Check the condition of the cover's composite gasket, and re-use it if undamaged. If it is damaged, a repair may be effected using silicone sealing compound.

16 Refit the cover(s) and tighten the bolts in sequence (see illustration).

17 Refit the ignition coils (Chapter 5B).

18 Reconnect the battery.

5 Timing belt covers – removal and refitting

Upper cover removal

1.4 litre engines

1 Slacken and remove the two retaining

bolts (one at the front and one at the rear), and remove the upper timing cover from the cylinder head (see illustrations).

1.6 litre engines

2 Position a trolley jack under the engine, with a block of wood between the jack head and the sump to prevent damage. Raise the jack to take the weight of the engine.

3 Slacken the right-hand engine mounting bolts, and then remove the mounting and brackets from the end of the engine (see illustrations).

4 Slacken the two lower bolts, then undo the five upper bolts and remove the upper timing belt cover (see illustration).

Lower cover removal

5 Remove the upper cover as described previously.

6 Remove the auxiliary drivebelt as described in Chapter 1A.

7 Undo the three crankshaft pulley retaining bolts and remove the pulley, noting which way round it is fitted (see illustrations).

8 Slacken and remove the retaining bolts then remove the lower cover from the engine (see illustration).

5.1a Unscrew the retaining bolts (arrowed) . . .

5.1b . . . and remove the timing belt upper cover (SOHC engine)

5.3a Undo the bolts (arrowed) securing the mounting and bracket . . .

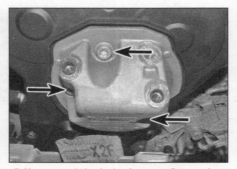

5.3b . . . and the bolts (arrowed) securing the bracket to the engine

5.4 Undo the screws (arrowed) and remove the upper timing belt cover

Inner cover removal

9 Remove the camshaft sprocket(s) and tensioner pulley as described in Section 7.
10 Undo the bolts and remove the inner cover **(see illustration)**.

Refitting

Upper cover

11 Refitting is the reverse of removal.

Lower cover

12 Locate the lower cover over the timing belt sprocket, and tighten its retaining bolts.
13 Fit the pulley to the end of the crankshaft, ensuring it is fitted the correct way round, and tighten its bolts to the specified torque.
14 Refit the upper cover as described above.
15 Refit and tension the auxiliary drivebelt as described in Chapter 1A.

Inner cover

16 Refitting is a reversal of removal.

---

6 Timing belt –
general information, removal and refitting

Note: *With early 1.4 litre engines (up to engine number 3666765) Peugeot specify the use of a special electronic tool (SEEM C.TRONIC type 105.5 belt tensioning measuring tool) and the rocker arm contact plate (0132-AE) to correctly set the timing belt tension. If access to this equipment cannot be obtained, an approximate setting can be achieved using the method described below. If this method is used, the tension must be checked using the special electronic tool at the earliest possible opportunity. Do not drive the vehicle over large distances, or use high engine speeds, until the belt tension is known to be correct. Refer to a Peugeot dealer for advice.*
Note: *Timing belts, tensioners and sprockets are not interchangeable between early (up to engine number 3666765) and late 1.4 litre engines.*

General information

1 The timing belt drives the camshaft(s) and coolant pump from a toothed sprocket on the front of the crankshaft. If the belt breaks or slips in service, the pistons are likely to hit the valve heads, resulting in extensive (and expensive) damage.
2 The timing belt should be renewed at the specified intervals (see Chapter 1A), or earlier if it is contaminated with oil or if it is at all noisy in operation (a 'scraping' noise due to uneven wear).
3 If the timing belt is being removed, it is a wise precaution to check the condition of the coolant pump at the same time (check for signs of coolant leakage). This may avoid the need to remove the timing belt again at a later stage, should the coolant pump fail.

5.7a Undo the retaining bolts (arrowed) . . .

5.7b . . . and remove the crankshaft pulley

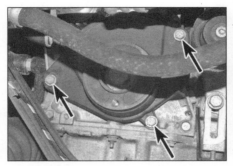
5.8 Unscrew the bolts (arrowed) and remove the timing belt lower cover

Removal

4 Disconnect the battery (see Chapter 5A).
5 Align the engine assembly/valve timing holes as described in Section 3, and lock both the camshaft sprocket(s) and the flywheel/driveplate in position.
Caution: Do not attempt to rotate the engine whilst the locking tools are in position.
6 Remove the timing belt lower cover as described in Section 5.

SOHC engines

7 Loosen the timing belt tensioner pulley retaining nut **(see illustration)**. Pivot the pulley approximately 60° in a clockwise direction, using a key fitted to the hole in the pulley hub, then retighten the retaining nut. On early engines (up to engine number 3666765), an 8 mm square section key will be required, and a hexagonal key on later engines.

6.7 Slacken the nut then pivot the tensioner pulley clockwise to relieve the timing belt tension

5.10 Undo the bolts (arrowed) and remove the inner cover (1.6 litre DOHC engine)

DOHC engines

8 Slacken the timing belt tensioner pulley retaining nut and, using a hexagonal key, rotate the pulley clockwise until the index arm is in the minimum tension position **(see illustration)**. Temporarily tighten the tensioner pulley nut in this position.

All models

9 If the timing belt is to be re-used, use white

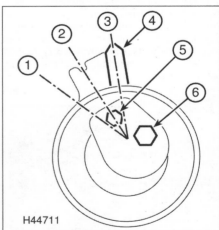
6.8 Timing belt tensioner (DOHC engines)

1 Minimum tension position
2 Normal tension position
3 Maximum tension position
4 Index arm
5 Hole for hexagonal key
6 Tensioner pulley bolt

paint or similar to mark the direction of rotation on the belt (if markings do not already exist). Slip the belt off the sprockets.

10 Check the timing belt carefully for any signs of uneven wear, splitting, or oil contamination. Pay particular attention to the roots of the teeth. Renew the belt if there is the slightest doubt about its condition. If the engine is undergoing an overhaul, and has covered more than 40 000 miles with the existing belt fitted, renew the belt as a matter of course, regardless of its apparent condition. The cost of a new belt is nothing when compared to the cost of repairs, should the belt break in service. If signs of oil contamination are found, trace the source of the oil leak, and rectify it. Wash down the engine timing belt area and all related components, to remove all traces of oil.

11 Prior to refitting, thoroughly clean the timing belt sprockets. Check that the tensioner pulley rotates freely, without any sign of roughness. If necessary, renew the tensioner pulley as described in Section 7. Make sure that the locking tools are still in place, as described in Section 3.

Refitting – early SOHC engine (up to engine number 3666765)

12 Manoeuvre the timing belt into position, ensuring that the arrows on the belt are pointing in the direction of rotation (clockwise, when viewed from the right-hand end of the engine).

13 Do not twist the timing belt sharply while refitting it. Fit the belt over the crankshaft and camshaft sprockets. Make sure that the 'front run' of the belt is taut – ie, ensure that any slack is on the tensioner pulley side of the belt. Fit the belt over the coolant pump sprocket and tensioner pulley. Ensure that the belt teeth are seated centrally in the sprockets.

14 Loosen the tensioner pulley retaining nut. Pivot the pulley anti-clockwise to remove all freeplay from the timing belt, and then retighten the nut **(see illustration 6.7)**. Tension the timing belt as described under the relevant sub-heading.

To hold their arms clear of the camshaft, fix a stout metal bar to the cylinder head cover studs with the nuts, and lift the arms using shorter lengths of metal bar pivoted on large sockets.

Tensioning without the electronic tool

Note: *If this method is used, ensure that the belt tension is checked by a Peugeot dealer at the earliest possible opportunity.*

15 If the special tool is not available, an approximate setting may be achieved by pivoting the tensioner pulley anti-clockwise until it is just possible to twist the timing belt through 90° by finger and thumb (without using excessive force), midway between the crankshaft and camshaft sprockets. The deflection of the belt at the mid-point between the sprockets should be approximately 6.0 mm.

16 Remove the locking tools from the camshaft sprocket and flywheel.

17 Using a suitable socket and extension bar on the crankshaft sprocket bolt, rotate the crankshaft through four complete rotations in a clockwise direction (viewed from the right-hand end of the engine). Refit the flywheel locking tool and check that the camshaft timing hole is correctly aligned with the cylinder head hole.

Caution: Do not at any time rotate the crankshaft anti-clockwise.

18 Slacken the tensioner pulley nut, retension the belt as described in paragraph 15, then tighten the tensioner pulley nut to the specified torque.

19 Remove the flywheel locking tool then rotate the crankshaft through a further two turns clockwise.

20 Check that both the camshaft sprocket and flywheel timing holes are still correctly aligned.

21 If all is well, refit the timing belt covers as described in Section 5.

22 Clip the wiring harness back into position then reconnect the battery.

Tensioning with the electronic tool

23 Fit the special belt tensioning measuring equipment to the 'front run' of the timing belt, approximately midway between the camshaft and crankshaft sprockets. Position the tensioner pulley so that the belt is tensioned to a setting of 44 SEEM units, then retighten its retaining nut.

24 Remove the locking tools from the camshaft sprocket and flywheel, and remove the measuring tool from the belt.

25 Using a suitable socket and extension bar on the crankshaft sprocket bolt, rotate the crankshaft through four complete rotations in a clockwise direction (viewed from the right-hand end of the engine). Refit the flywheel locking tool and check that the camshaft timing hole is correctly aligned with the cylinder head hole.

Caution: Do not at any time rotate the crankshaft anti-clockwise.

26 To ensure an accurate reading, it is necessary to remove the valve spring load from the camshaft by fitting the rocker arm plate (0132-AE). Remove the cylinder head cover (see Section 4) then back off all the rocker arm contact bolts on the plate (0132-AE). Fit the plate to the cylinder head

cover studs, ensuring it is fitted the correct way around then secure it in position with the cylinder head cover nuts. Tighten each rocker arm contact bolt until all rockers are lifted clear of the camshaft lobes. If the rocker arm plate is not available, obtain clearance between the rocker arms and camshaft by slackening the locknut and backing off the adjusting screws on all the necessary rocker arms. It will be found that two of the rocker arms remain in contact with the camshaft, even with the adjusting screws backed fully off. To hold these arms clear of the camshaft, use an arrangement similar to that shown **(see Tool Tip)**.

Caution: Do not overtighten the contact bolts any more than is necessary to obtain a small amount of clearance between the rocker arm roller and cam lobe. If the bolts are overtightened, there is a risk of the valves being forced into contact with the pistons, resulting in serious engine damage.

27 Refit the tensioning measuring equipment to the front run of the belt.

28 Slacken the tensioner pulley retaining nut whilst holding the pulley stationary. Gradually release the tensioner pulley until a tension setting of between 29 and 33 SEEM units is indicated on the measuring equipment. With the belt correctly tensioned, hold the pulley stationary and tighten its retaining nut to the specified torque.

29 Remove the measuring tool from the belt then unscrew the nuts and remove the rocker arm contact plate (or home-made alternative) from the cylinder head.

30 Remove the flywheel locking tool, then rotate the crankshaft through another four complete rotations in a clockwise direction. Refit the flywheel locking tool and check that the camshaft timing hole is correctly aligned with the cylinder head hole.

31 If all is well, refit the timing belt covers and cylinder head cover as described in Sections 4 and 5. **Note:** *If the rocker arm adjusting screws were moved, adjust the valve clearances before refitting the cylinder head cover.*

Refitting – later SOHC engine (from engine number 3666766)

32 These engines are equipped with a spring-loaded tensioner, so access to the belt tensioning gauge is unnecessary.

33 Manoeuvre the timing belt into position, ensuring that the arrows on the belt are pointing in the direction of rotation (clockwise, when viewed from the right-hand end of the engine).

34 Do not twist the timing belt sharply while refitting it. Fit the belt over the crankshaft and camshaft sprockets. Make sure that the 'front run' of the belt is taut – ie, ensure that any slack is on the tensioner pulley side of the belt. Fit the belt over the coolant pump sprocket and tensioner pulley. Ensure that the belt teeth are seated centrally in the sprockets.

35 Remove the crankshaft and camshaft locking tools, then slacken the tensioner pulley nut and, using a hexagonal key, rotate the pulley anti-clockwise until the index arm is in the maximum tension position **(see illustration)**. Tighten the pulley retaining nut.

36 Using a socket on the crankshaft pulley bolt, rotate the crankshaft clockwise 10 complete revolutions, and refit the crankshaft locking tool as described in Section 3.

37 Check the timing is correct by inserting the camshaft sprocket locking tool (Section 3). If the tool cannot be inserted, slacken the tensioner, remove the belt, refit the locking tools, and start again from Paragraph 33.

38 Remove the crankshaft and camshaft locking tools.

39 Hold the hexagonal key in the tensioner pulley to maintain the tension, then slacken the pulley nut, and rotate the tensioner to bring the index arm to the normal tension position **(see illustration 6.35)**. Tighten the pulley nut to the specified torque.

40 Rotate the crankshaft two complete revolutions, and check that the crankshaft and camshaft locking tools can still be inserted.

41 The remainder of refitting is a reversal of removal.

Refitting – DOHC engines

42 Manoeuvre the timing belt into position, ensuring that the arrows on the belt are pointing in the direction of rotation (clockwise, when viewed from the right-hand end of the engine). Note that there are three marks on a new belt, which correspond to marks on the crankshaft and camshaft sprockets **(see illustration)**.

43 Do not twist the timing belt sharply while refitting it. Fit the belt over the crankshaft and camshaft sprockets aligning the marks on the belt with those on the crankshaft and camshaft sprockets. Make sure that the 'front run' of the belt is taut – ie, ensure that any slack is on the tensioner pulley side of the belt. Fit the belt over the coolant pump sprocket and tensioner pulley. Ensure that the belt teeth are seated centrally in the sprockets.

44 Insert the hexagonal key on the tensioner pulley, slacken the pulley nut and rotate the key to bring the index arm to the maximum tension position **(see illustration 6.8)**. Tighten the tensioner roller nut securely.

45 Remove the camshaft and crankshaft locking tools, and rotate the crankshaft 4 complete revolutions clockwise, and refit the crankshaft locking tool.

46 Insert the hexagon key in the tensioner, slacken the nut and rotate the tensioner using the key, until the index arm is in the normal tension position **(see illustration 6.8)**. Tighten the tensioner nut to the specified torque.

47 Remove the crankshaft locking tool, and rotate the crankshaft two complete revolutions clockwise. Check the position of the tensioner index arm – it should be no more than 2.0 mm away from the normal tension position. If it is not, repeat the belt fitting procedure from Paragraph 42.

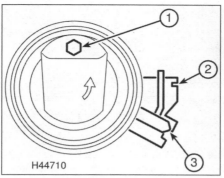

6.35 Timing belt tensioner (later 1.4 litre engine)

1 Hole for hexagonal key
2 Normal tension position
3 Maximum tension position

48 The remainder of refitting is a reversal of removal.

---

7 Timing belt tensioner and sprockets – removal, inspection and refitting

Removal

Camshaft sprocket – SOHC engine

1 Remove the timing belt as described in Section 6.

2 Withdraw the crankshaft and camshaft locking tools, and using a spanner or socket on the crankshaft pulley bolt, rotate the crankshaft backwards (anti-clockwise) 90°. This is to prevent any accidental contact between the pistons and valves.

3 Slacken the camshaft sprocket retaining bolt and remove it, along with its washer. To prevent the camshaft rotating as the bolt is slackened, a sprocket-holding tool will be required. In the absence of the special Peugeot tool, an acceptable substitute can be fabricated as follows. Use two lengths of steel strip (one long, the other short), and three nuts and bolts; one nut and bolt forms the pivot of a forked tool, with the remaining two nuts and

TOOL TIP

Using a home-made tool to hold the camshaft sprocket stationary whilst the bolt is tightened (shown with the cylinder head removed).

6.42 Note the timing belt marks which correspond to the camshaft sprockets and crankshaft sprocket

bolts at the tips of the 'forks' to engage with the sprocket spokes **(see Tool Tip)**.

Caution: Do not attempt to use the sprocket locking pin to prevent the sprocket from rotating whilst the bolt is slackened.

4 With the retaining bolt removed, slide the sprocket off the end of the camshaft. If the sprocket locating pin is a loose fit, remove it for safekeeping. Examine the camshaft oil seal for signs of oil leakage and, if necessary, renew it as described in Section 8.

Camshaft sprockets – DOHC engines

5 Remove the cylinder head covers as described in Section 4.

6 Remove the timing belt as described in Section 6.

7 Withdraw the crankshaft and camshaft locking tools, and using a spanner or socket on the crankshaft pulley bolt, rotate the crankshaft backwards (anti-clockwise) 90°. This is to prevent any accidental contact between the pistons and valves.

8 Using an open-ended spanner on the square section to counterhold the camshaft, undo the sprocket retaining-bolt **(see illustration)**.

Caution: Do not attempt to use the sprocket locking pin to prevent the sprocket from rotating whilst the bolt is slackened.

9 With the retaining bolt removed, slide the sprocket off the end of the camshaft. Note that the key is integral with the sprocket. Examine the camshaft oil seals for signs of oil leakage and, if necessary, renew it as described in Section 8.

7.8 Use an open-ended spanner to counterhold the camshaft whilst slackening the bolt

7.12a Remove the retaining bolt and washer . . .

7.12b . . . then slide off the crankshaft sprocket

7.13 Remove the Woodruff key and flanged spacer (where fitted) from the crankshaft

Crankshaft sprocket

10 Remove the timing belt as described in Section 6.

11 Slacken the crankshaft sprocket bolt. To prevent crankshaft rotation on manual transmission models, select top gear, and have an assistant apply the brakes firmly. If the engine has been removed from the vehicle or the vehicle is equipped with an automatic transmission unit, It will be necessary to lock the flywheel/driveplate (see Section 15).

Caution: Do not be tempted to use the flywheel/driveplate locking pin to prevent the crankshaft from rotating; temporarily remove the locking pin prior to slackening the pulley bolt, then refit it once the bolt has been slackened.

12 Unscrew the retaining bolt and washer, then slide the sprocket off the end of the crankshaft **(see illustrations)**.

13 If the Woodruff key is a loose fit in the crankshaft, remove it and store it with the sprocket for safe-keeping. If necessary, also slide the flanged spacer (where fitted) off the end of the crankshaft **(see illustration)**. Examine the crankshaft oil seal for signs oil leakage and, if necessary, renew as described in Section 14.

Tensioner pulley

14 Remove the lower timing belt cover (see Section 5).

15 Lock the camshaft and crankshaft at TDC on No 1 cylinder as described in Section 3.

16 Slacken and remove the timing belt tensioner pulley retaining nut, and slide the pulley off its mounting stud. Examine the

mounting stud for signs of damage and, if necessary, renew it.

Inspection

17 Clean the sprockets thoroughly, and renew any that show signs of wear, damage or cracks.

18 Clean the tensioner assembly, but do not use any strong solvent, which may enter the pulley bearing. Check that the pulley rotates freely about its hub, with no sign of stiffness or of free play. Renew the tensioner pulley if there is any doubt about its condition, or if there are any obvious signs of wear or damage.

19 Inspect the timing belt (see Section 6). Renew the belt is there is any doubt about its condition.

Refitting

Camshaft sprocket

20 Refit the locating pin (where removed) then locate the sprocket on the end of the camshaft. Ensure that the locating pin is correctly engaged with the sprocket and the cut-out in the camshaft end. Note that on 1.6 litre engines, the exhaust sprocket is marked E and the inlet sprocket marked A **(see illustrations)**.

21 Refit the sprocket retaining bolt and washer. Tighten the bolt to the specified torque, whilst retaining the sprocket/camshaft with the method used on removal.

22 Realign the timing hole in the camshaft sprocket (see Section 3) with the corresponding hole in the cylinder head, and refit the locking pin.

23 Rotate the crankshaft 90° in the normal direction of rotation (clockwise), until the crankshaft locking pin can be inserted.

24 Refit the timing belt as described in Section 6. Refit the cylinder head covers as described in Section 4.

Crankshaft sprocket

25 Locate the Woodruff key in the crankshaft end, then slide on the flanged spacer (where fitted) aligning its slot with the Woodruff key.

26 Align the crankshaft sprocket slot with the Woodruff key, and slide it onto the end of the crankshaft.

27 Temporarily remove the locking pin from the rear of the flywheel/driveplate, and then refit the crankshaft sprocket retaining bolt and washer. Tighten the bolt to the specified torque, whilst preventing crankshaft rotation using the method employed on removal. Refit the locking pin to the rear of the flywheel/driveplate.

28 Refit the timing belt as described in Section 6.

Tensioner pulley

29 Refit the tensioner pulley to its mounting stud, ensuring the cut-out aligns with the pin **(see illustration)**, and fit the retaining nut.

30 Ensure that the 'front run' of the belt is taut – ie, ensure that any slack is on the pulley side of the belt. Check that the belt is centrally located on all its sprockets. Rotate the pulley anti-clockwise to remove all free play from the timing belt, and then tighten the pulley retaining nut securely.

31 Tension the timing belt as described in Section 6.

32 Once the belt is correctly tensioned, refit the timing belt covers as described in Section 5.

7.20a The locating pin must engage with the slot (arrowed)

7.20b On 1.6 litre engines, the inlet sprocket is marked A (arrowed) and the exhaust E

7.29 The cut-out aligns the locating pin (arrowed)

8 Camshaft oil seal(s) – renewal

Note: *If the camshaft oil seal has been leaking, check the timing belt for signs of oil contamination; the belt must be renewed if signs of oil contamination are found. Ensure that all traces of oil are removed from the sprockets and surrounding area before the new belt is fitted.*

1 Remove the camshaft sprocket as described in Section 7.

2 Punch or drill two small holes opposite each other in the oil seal. Screw a self-tapping screw into each, and pull on the screws with pliers to extract the seal. Alternatively, carefully prise the seal out using a flat-bladed screwdriver **(see illustration)**.

3 Clean the seal housing, and polish off any burrs or raised edges, which may have caused the seal to fail in the first place.

4 Lubricate the lips of the new seal with clean engine oil, and drive it into position until it seats on its locating shoulder. Use a suitable tubular drift, such as a socket, which bears only on the hard outer edge of the seal. Take care not to damage the seal lips during fitting. Note that the seal lips should face inwards.

5 Refit the camshaft sprocket as described in Section 7.

9 Valve clearances – checking and adjustment

Note: *The valve clearances must be checked and adjusted only when the engine is cold.*

Note: *This procedure applies only to the 1.4 litre SOHC 8V engine – the valve clearances on DOHC engines are maintained by hydraulic compensator units built into the cam followers.*

1 The importance of having the valve clearances correctly adjusted cannot be overstressed, as they vitally affect the performance of the engine. If the clearances are too big, the engine will be noisy (characteristic rattling or tapping noises) and engine efficiency will be reduced, as the valves open too late and close too early. A more serious problem arises if the clearances are too small, however. If this is the case, the valves may not close fully when the engine is hot, resulting in serious damage to the engine (eg, burnt valve seats and/or cylinder head warping/cracking). The clearances are checked and adjusted as follows.

2 Remove the cylinder head cover as described in Section 4.

3 The engine can now be turned using a suitable socket and extension bar fitted to the crankshaft sprocket bolt.

4 It is important that the clearance of each valve is checked and adjusted only when the valve is fully closed, with the rocker

8.2 Carefully prise the camshaft oil seal out with a flat-bladed screwdriver

arm resting on the heel of the cam (directly opposite the peak). This can be ensured by carrying out the adjustments in the following sequence, noting that No 1 cylinder is at the transmission end of the engine. The correct valve clearances are given in the Specifications at the start of this Chapter. The valve locations can be determined from the position of the manifolds.

Valve fully open	Adjust valves
No 1 exhaust	No 3 inlet, No 4 exhaust
No 3 exhaust	No 4 inlet, No 2 exhaust
No 4 exhaust	No 2 inlet, No 1 exhaust
No 2 exhaust	No 1 inlet, No 3 exhaust

5 With the relevant valve fully open, check the clearances of the two valves specified. The clearances are checked by inserting a feeler blade of the correct thickness between the valve stem and the rocker arm adjusting screw. The feeler blade should be a light, sliding fit. If adjustment is necessary, slacken the adjusting screw locknut, and turn the screw as necessary **(see illustration)**. Once the correct clearance is obtained, hold the adjusting screw and tighten the locknut securely. Once the locknut has been tightened, recheck the valve clearance, and adjust again if necessary.

6 Rotate the crankshaft until the next valve in the sequence is fully open, and check the clearances of the next two specified valves.

7 Repeat the procedure until all the eight valve clearances have been checked (and if necessary, adjusted). Refit the cylinder head cover as described in Section 4.

10.4 Remove the circlip and slide the components from the rocker shaft

9.5 Check the valve clearances using feeler gauges

10 Camshaft(s) and rocker arms/followers – removal, inspection and refitting

General information

1 On SOHC engines, the valves are operated by rockers arms between the camshaft and the top of the valves. The rocker arm assembly is secured to the top of the cylinder head by the cylinder head bolts. Although in theory it is possible to undo the head bolts and remove the rocker arm assembly without removing the head, in practice, this is not recommended. Once the bolts have been removed, the head gasket will be disturbed, and the gasket will almost certainly leak or blow after refitting. For this reason, removal of the rocker arm assembly cannot be done without removing the cylinder head and renewing the head gasket.

2 On DOHC engines, the camshafts and followers can be removed upwards from the cylinder head. On SOHC engines, the camshaft is slid out of the right-hand end of the cylinder head, and it therefore cannot be removed without first removing the cylinder head, due to a lack of clearance.

Removal

Rocker arms – SOHC engine

3 Remove the cylinder head as described in Section 11.

4 To dismantle the rocker arm assembly, carefully prise off the circlip from the right-hand end of the rocker shaft; retain the rocker pedestal, to prevent it being sprung off the end of the shaft. Slide the various components off the end of the shaft, keeping all components in their correct fitted order **(see illustration)**. Make a note of each component's correct fitted position and orientation as it is removed, to ensure it is fitted correctly on reassembly. **Note:** *Avoid touching the rocker arm roller bearing surfaces with your fingers.*

5 To separate the left-hand pedestal and shaft, first unscrew the cylinder head cover retaining stud from the top of the pedestal; this can be achieved using a stud extractor, or two nuts locked together **(see illustration)**. With

10.5 Lock two nuts together to enable the stud to be unscrewed from the left-hand end pedestal

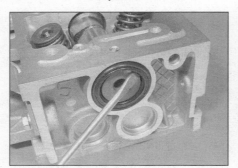

10.10a Prise out the oil seal . . .

10.9 Undo the bolt and slide out the camshaft thrust fork (arrowed)

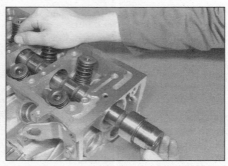

10.10b . . . then slide out the camshaft from the cylinder head

the stud removed, unscrew the grub screw from the top of the pedestal, and withdraw the rocker shaft.

Camshaft – SOHC engine

6 Remove the cylinder head as described in Section 11.

7 With the head on a bench, remove the locking pin, then remove the camshaft sprocket as described in Section 7.

8 Unbolt the coolant housing from the left-hand end of the cylinder head.

9 Undo the retaining bolt and slide out the camshaft thrust fork **(see illustration)**.

10 Using a large flat-bladed screwdriver, carefully prise the oil seal out of the right-hand end of the cylinder head, and then slide out the camshaft **(see illustrations)**.

Camshafts/followers – DOHC engine

11 Remove the camshaft sprockets as described in Section 7. Undo the screws and

securing the inner timing cover to the cylinder head.

12 Starting from the outside, working in a spiral pattern, progressively and evenly slacken the camshaft bearing housing retaining bolts, and lift the housing from the cylinder head **(see illustration)**.

13 Identify each camshaft for position – the inlet camshaft is at the rear and the exhaust camshaft is at the front of the cylinder head. Also note the TDC position of each camshaft for correct refitting.

14 Remove the camshafts by pressing on the transmission ends to release the opposite ends from their bearings. Withdrawn the camshafts from the cylinder head and slide the oil seals from the ends.

15 Obtain 16 small, clean plastic containers, and number them inlet 1 to 8 and exhaust 1 to 8; alternatively divide a large container into 16 compartments and number each

compartment accordingly. On 1.6 litre engines, use a rubber sucker to withdraw each follower in turn, and place it in its respective container. On 1.4 litre engines, withdraw each rocker arm complete with hydraulic follower, and place it in its respective container **(see illustrations)**. Don't interchange the followers since the wear rate will be much increased.

Inspection

Rocker arm assembly

16 Examine the rocker arm surfaces, which contact the camshaft lobes for wear ridges and scoring. Renew any rocker arms on which the rollers show signs of damage. If a rocker arm roller surface is badly scored, also examine the corresponding lobe on the camshaft for wear, as both will likely be worn. Renew worn components as necessary. The rocker arm assembly can be dismantled as described in paragraphs 4 and 5.

17 Inspect the ends of the (valve clearance) adjusting screws for signs of wear or damage, and renew as required.

18 If the rocker arm assembly has been dismantled, examine the rocker arm and shaft bearing surfaces for wear ridges and scoring. If there are obvious signs of wear, the relevant rocker arm(s) and/or the shaft must be renewed.

Camshaft(s)

19 Examine the camshaft bearing surfaces and cam lobes for signs of wear ridges and scoring. Renew the camshaft if any of these conditions are apparent. Examine the condition of the bearing surfaces, both on the camshaft journals and in the cylinder head/bearing housing. If the head bearing surfaces are worn excessively, the cylinder head will need to be renewed. If the necessary measuring equipment is available, camshaft bearing journal wear can be checked by direct measurement, noting that No 1 journal is at the transmission end of the head.

20 On SOHC engines, examine the thrust fork for signs of wear or scoring, and renew as necessary.

21 On DOHC engines, examine the hydraulic follower surfaces, which contact the camshaft lobes for wear ridges and scoring. Renew any follower where these conditions are apparent.

10.12 Evenly and progressively slacken the camshaft housing retaining bolts

10.15a Remove the rocker arms complete with hydraulic lifter . . .

10.15b . . . and keep them in a clean container

If a follower bearing surface is badly scored, also examine the corresponding lobe on the camshaft for wear, as it is likely that both will be worn (see illustration). Renew any components as necessary.

Refitting

Rocker arms – SOHC engine

22 If the rocker arm assembly was dismantled, refit the rocker shaft to the left-hand pedestal, aligning its locating hole with the pedestal threaded hole. Refit the grub screw, and tighten it securely. With the grub screw in position, refit the cylinder head cover mounting stud to the pedestal, and tighten it securely. Apply a smear of clean engine oil to the shaft, and then slide on all removed components, ensuring each is correctly fitted in its original position. **Note:** *Avoid touching the rocker arm roller bearing surfaces with your fingers.* Once all components are in position on the shaft, compress the right-hand pedestal and refit the circlip. Ensure that the circlip is correctly located in its groove on the shaft.

23 Refit the cylinder head and rocker arm assembly as described in Section 11.

Camshaft – SOHC engine

24 Ensure that the cylinder head and camshaft bearing surfaces are clean, and then liberally oil the camshaft bearings and lobes. Slide the camshaft back into position in the cylinder head.

25 Locate the thrust fork with the left-hand end of the camshaft. Refit the fork retaining bolt, tightening it to the specified torque setting.

26 Ensure that the coolant housing and cylinder head mating surfaces are clean and dry, then apply a smear of sealant to the housing mating surface. Refit the housing to the left-hand end of the head, and securely tighten its retaining bolts.

27 Lubricate the lips of the new seal with clean engine oil, then drive it into position until it seats on its locating shoulder. Use a suitable tubular drift, such as a socket, which bears only on the hard outer edge of the seal. Take care not to damage the seal lips during fitting. Note that the seal lips should face inwards.

28 Refit the camshaft sprocket as described in Section 7.

29 Refit the cylinder head as described in Section 11.

Camshafts/followers – DOHC engines

30 Before commencing refitting, remove all traces of oil from the bearing housing retaining bolts holes in the cylinder head, using a clean rag. Also ensure that both the cylinder head and bearing housing mating faces are clean and free from oil.

31 Liberally oil the cylinder head hydraulic follower bores and the followers. Carefully refit the followers to the cylinder head; ensuring that each follower is refitted to its original bore. Some care will be required to enter the followers

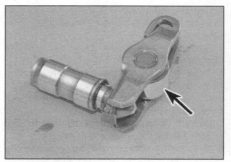

10.21 Check the roller surface (arrowed) on the rocker arm

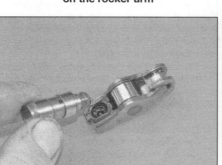

10.31b . . . making sure the hydraulic lifter is clipped into the rocker arm securely

squarely into their bores. Check that each follower rotates freely. On the 1.4 litre engine, make sure the rocker arms are clipped to the hydraulic follower securely (see illustrations).

32 Liberally oil the camshaft bearings in the cylinder head and the camshaft lobes, and then refit the camshafts to the cylinder head in the previously-noted positions. The locating notch in the right-hand end of the camshafts should be positioned at the 7 o'clock position

10.31a Refit the rocker arm and hydraulic lifter . . .

10.32 Position the inlet camshaft locking notch at the 7 o'clock position and the exhaust camshaft at 8 o'clock (arrowed)

on the inlet camshaft, and the 8 o'clock position on the exhaust camshaft (see illustration).

33 Apply a bead of silicone-based jointing compound around the perimeter of the mating faces and around the retaining bolt hole locations (see illustration).

34 Refit the bearing housing, and tighten the bolts progressively, in sequence, to the specified torque (see illustration).

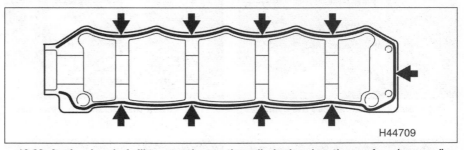

10.33 Apply a bead of silicone sealant to the cylinder head mating surface (arrowed)

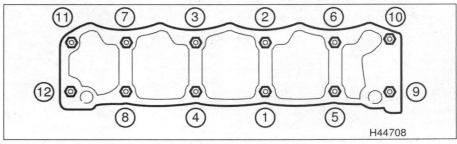

10.34 Camshaft bearing housing bolts tightening sequence

10.36 Ensure the lower edge of the inner timing belt cover engages correctly (arrowed)

35 Fit new oil seals with reference to Section 8.

36 Ensure that the lower edge of the inner timing belt cover engages correctly with the upper edge of the crankshaft oil seal housing (see illustration).

37 Refit the camshaft sprockets as described in Section 7.

11 Cylinder head – removal and refitting

Note: *Ensure the engine is cold before removing the cylinder head.*

Removal

1 Disconnect the battery (see Chapter 5A).

2 Drain the cooling system as described in Chapter 1A.

11.11 Slacken and remove the cylinder head bolts

11.14 Use two stout screwdrivers to rock the cylinder head free from the block

3 Remove the ignition HT coil assembly (see Chapter 5B) then remove the spark plugs (see Chapter 1A).

4 Remove the cylinder head cover(s) as described in Section 4.

5 Align the engine assembly/valve timing holes as described in Section 3, and lock both the camshaft sprocket(s) and flywheel/driveplate in position.

Caution: Do not attempt to rotate the engine whilst the tools are in position.

6 Note that the following text assumes that the cylinder head will be removed with both inlet and exhaust manifolds attached; this is easier, but makes it a bulky and heavy assembly to handle. If it is wished to remove the manifolds first, proceed as described in Chapter 4A.

7 Carry out the following operations as described in Chapter 4A:

a) *Disconnect the exhaust system front pipe from the manifold. Disconnect or release the oxygen sensor wiring.*

b) *Remove the air cleaner housing and inlet duct assembly.*

c) *Disconnect the fuel feed and return hoses from the fuel rail (plug all openings, to prevent loss of fuel and entry of dirt into the fuel system).*

d) *Note their fitted positions, then disconnect the relevant electrical connectors and vacuum/breather hoses from the inlet manifold.*

e) *Where necessary unbolt the support bracket from the inlet manifold.*

f) *Disconnect the accelerator cable (where fitted).*

11.13 Lift off the rocker arm assembly

11.15 On 1.4 litre engines, clamp the cylinder liners in position before rotating the crankshaft (clamps arrowed)

8 Remove the timing belt inner cover as described in Section 5.

9 Undo the mounting bolt and remove the upper section of the oil dipstick guide tube. Note their fitted positions, then slacken the retaining clips, and disconnect the coolant hoses from the cylinder head. Likewise, note the routing, and then disconnect all electrical connectors from the cylinder head.

10 On DOHC engines, remove the camshafts as described in Section 10.

11 Working in the *reverse* of the tightening sequence **(see illustration 11.30a or 11.30b)**, progressively slacken the cylinder head bolts by half a turn at a time, until all bolts can be unscrewed by hand **(see illustration)**.

12 On DOHC engines, lift the cylinder head away; seek assistance if possible, as it is a heavy assembly, especially if it is being removed complete with the manifolds.

13 On SOHC engines, with all the cylinder head bolts removed, lift the rocker arm assembly off the cylinder head **(see illustration)**. **Note:** *Avoid touching the rocker arm roller bearing surfaces with your fingers. Note the locating pins, which are fitted to the base of each rocker arm pedestal. If any pin is a loose fit in the head or pedestal, remove it for safekeeping.*

14 On 1.4 litre engines, the joint between the cylinder head and gasket, and the cylinder block/crankcase must now be broken without disturbing the wet liners. To break the joint, obtain two stout screwdrivers, which fit into the cylinder head bolt holes. Gently 'rock' the cylinder head free towards the front of the car **(see illustration)**. Do not try to swivel the head on the cylinder block/crankcase; it is located by dowels, as well as by the tops of the liners. **Note:** *If care is not taken and the liners are moved, there is also a possibility of the bottom seals being disturbed, causing leakage after refitting the head.* When the joint is broken, lift the cylinder head away; seek assistance if possible, as it is a heavy assembly, especially if it is being removed complete with the manifolds.

15 On all models, remove the gasket from the top of the block, noting the two locating dowels. If the locating dowels are a loose fit, remove them and store them with the head for safekeeping. Do not discard the gasket – on some models it will be needed for identification purposes (see paragraphs 20 and 21). Operations that require the rotation of the crankshaft (eg, cleaning the piston crowns) should only be carried out on 1.4 litre engines once the cylinder liners are firmly clamped in position **(see illustration)**. In the absence of the special Peugeot liner clamps, the liners can be clamped in position using large flat washers positioned underneath suitable-length bolts. Alternatively, the original head bolts could be temporarily refitted, with suitable spacers fitted to their shanks.

Caution: On 1.4 litre engines, do not attempt to rotate the crankshaft with the cylinder head removed, otherwise the wet liners may be displaced.

16 If the cylinder head is to be dismantled for overhaul, refer to Part E of this Chapter.

Preparation for refitting

17 The mating faces of the cylinder head and cylinder block/crankcase must be perfectly clean before refitting the head. Use a hard plastic or wood scraper to remove all traces of gasket and carbon; also clean the piston crowns. **Note:** *On 1.4 litre engines, clamp the liners in position before turning the crankshaft (see paragraph 15).* Take particular care during the cleaning operations, as aluminium alloy is easily damaged. Also, make sure that the carbon is not allowed to enter the oil and water passages – this is particularly important for the lubrication system, as carbon could block the oil supply to the engine's components. Using adhesive tape and paper, seal the water, oil and bolt holes in the cylinder block/crankcase. To prevent carbon entering the gap between the pistons and bores, smear a little grease in the gap. After cleaning each piston, use a small brush to remove all traces of grease and carbon from the gap, and then wipe away the remainder with a clean rag. Clean all the pistons in the same way.

18 Check the mating surfaces of the cylinder block/crankcase and the cylinder head for nicks, deep scratches and other damage. If slight, they may be removed carefully with a file, but if excessive, machining may be the only alternative to renewal.

19 If warpage of the cylinder head gasket surface is suspected, use a straight-edge to check it for distortion. Refer to Part E of this Chapter if necessary.

20 When purchasing a new cylinder head gasket, it is essential that a gasket of the correct thickness is obtained. On some models only one thickness of gasket is available, so this is not a problem. On other models, there are two different thicknesses available – the standard gasket, and a slightly thicker 'repair' gasket (+ 0.2 mm). The gaskets can be identified as described in the following paragraph, using the cut-outs on the left-hand end of the gasket.

21 With the gasket fitted the correct way up on the cylinder block, there will be a single or double cut-out at the rear of the left-hand side of the gasket identifying the engine type (eg, TU3A engine). In the centre of the gasket there will likely be another series of between 0 and 4 cut-outs, identifying the manufacturer of the gasket and whether or not it contains asbestos (these cut-outs are of little importance). The important cut-out location is at the front of the gasket; on the standard gasket there will be no cut-out in this position, whereas on the thicker 'repair' gasket there will be a single cut-out **(see illustration)**. Identify the gasket type, and ensure that the new gasket obtained is of the correct thickness. If there is any doubt as to which gasket is fitted, take the old gasket along to your Peugeot dealer, and have him confirm the gasket type.

22 Check the condition of the cylinder head bolts, and particularly their threads, whenever they are removed. Wash the bolts in suitable solvent, and wipe them dry. Check each for any sign of visible wear or damage, renewing any bolt if necessary. Measure the length of each bolt, from the underside of its head to the bolt end, to check for stretching **(see illustration)**. The bolts for the SOHC engine are 175.5 mm in length when new, if any bolt has stretched to more than 176.5mm; renew all the cylinder head bolts as a set. On the 1.4 litre DOHC engine, the maximum length for the bolts is 118.6 mm and they can only be re-used 2 times. On 1.6 litre engines, the maximum length for the bolts is 122.6 mm. Although Peugeot do not actually specify that the bolts must be renewed, it is strongly recommended that the bolts should be renewed as a complete set, regardless of their apparent condition, whenever they are disturbed.

23 On 1.4 litre engines, prior to refitting the cylinder head, check the cylinder liner protrusion as described Chapter 2E, Section 11.

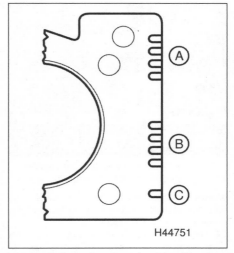

11.21 Cylinder head gasket identification markings

A *Engine type identification cut-out locations*
B *Gasket manufacturer identification cut-out locations*
C *Gasket thickness identification cut-out locations*

Refitting

24 Wipe clean the mating surfaces of the cylinder head and cylinder block/crankcase. Check that the two locating dowels are in position at each end of the cylinder block/crankcase surface and, if necessary, remove the cylinder liner clamps **(see illustration)**.

25 Position a new gasket on the cylinder block/crankcase surface, ensuring that its identification cut-outs are at the left-hand end of the gasket, and the side marked TOP is uppermost.

26 Check that the flywheel/driveplate and camshaft sprocket(s) are still correctly locked in position with their respective tools then, with the aid of an assistant, carefully refit the cylinder head assembly to the block, aligning it with the locating dowels. On DOHC engines,

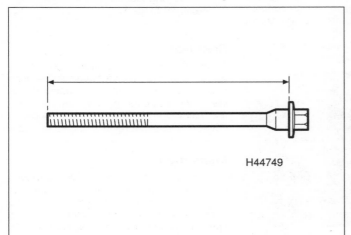

11.22 Measure the bolt length from the underside of the bolt head to the end of the bolt

11.24 Ensure the locating dowels (arrowed) are in position then fit the new head gasket

11.30a Cylinder head bolt tightening sequence (SOHC engine)

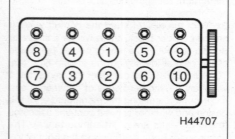

11.30b Cylinder head bolt tightening sequence (DOHC engine)

ensure that the inner timing cover lower edge engages correctly with the upper edge of the crankshaft oil seal housing.

27 On SOHC engines, ensure that the locating pins are in position in the base of each rocker pedestal, and then refit the rocker arm assembly to the cylinder head.

28 On all engines, lubricate the threads and underside of the heads of the cylinder head bolts lightly with clean engine oil.

29 Carefully enter each bolt into its relevant hole (do not drop them in) and screw in, by hand only, until finger-tight.

30 Working progressively and in the sequence shown, tighten the cylinder head bolts to their Stage 1 torque setting, using a torque wrench and suitable socket **(see illustrations)**.

31 Once all the bolts have been tightened to their Stage 1 setting, working again in the given sequence, angle-tighten the bolts through the specified Stage 2 angle, using a socket and extension bar. It is recommended that an angle-measuring gauge be used during this stage of the tightening, to ensure accuracy. If a gauge is not available, use white paint to make alignment marks between the bolt head and cylinder head prior to tightening; the marks can then be used to check that the bolt has been rotated through the correct angle during tightening.

32 Refit the timing belt inner cover as described in Section 5. Reconnect the all wiring plugs to the cylinder head and manifold.

33 On DOHC engines, refit the camshafts with reference to Section 10.

34 Working as described in the Chapter 4A, carry out the following tasks:

a) Refit all disturbed wiring, hoses and control cable(s) to the inlet manifold and fuel system components.

b) Reconnect and adjust the accelerator cable (where fitted).

c) Reconnect the exhaust system front pipe to the manifold and reconnect the oxygen sensor wiring connector.

d) Refit the air cleaner and inlet duct.

35 On SOHC engines, check and, if necessary, adjust the valve clearances as described in Section 9.

36 Refit the cylinder head cover(s) as described in Section 4.

37 Refit the spark plugs and install the ignition HT coil (see Chapters 1A and 5B).

38 On completion, reconnect the battery (Chapter 5A), and refill the cooling system as described in Chapter 1A.

12 Sump – removal and refitting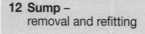

Removal

1 Firmly apply the handbrake, and then jack up the front of the vehicle and support it on axle stands (see Jacking and vehicle support). Undo the screws and remove the engine undershield.

2 Drain the engine oil, then clean and refit the engine oil drain plug, tightening it to the

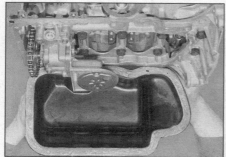

12.4a Undo the nuts and bolts, then remove the sump from the engine (1.4 litre engine)

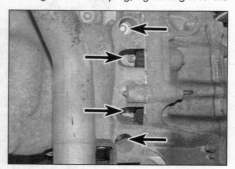

12.4b Access to the sump end bolts/nuts is through holes in the casing (arrowed) (1.6 litre engine)

specified torque. If the engine is nearing its service interval when the oil and filter are due for renewal, it is recommended that the filter is also removed, and a new one fitted. After reassembly, the engine can then be refilled with fresh oil. Refer to Chapter 1A for further information.

3 Remove the exhaust system front pipe as described in Chapter 4A.

4 Progressively slacken and remove all the sump nuts and bolts/nuts and position the wiring harness guide clear of the sump **(see illustrations)**.

5 Break the joint by striking the sump with the palm of your hand, then lower and withdraw the sump from under the car. On 1.6 litre engines, recover the gasket.

6 While the sump is removed, take the opportunity to check the oil pump pick-up/strainer for signs of clogging or splitting. If necessary, remove the pump as described in Section 13, and clean or renew the strainer.

Refitting

7 Clean all traces of sealant from the mating surfaces of the cylinder block/crankcase and sump, and then use a clean rag to wipe out the sump and the engine's interior.

8 Ensure that the sump and cylinder block/crankcase mating surfaces are clean and dry, then on 1.4 litre engines, apply a coating of suitable sealant to the sump mating surface. On 1.6 litre engines, if the gasket is undamaged, refit it to the sump. If required, fit a new sump gasket.

9 Offer up the sump and locate it on its studs. Locate the wiring harness guide back in position then refit the sump retaining nuts and bolts. Tighten the nuts and bolts evenly and progressively to the specified torque.

10 Refit the exhaust front pipe as described in Chapter 4A, and refit the engine undershield.

11 Replenish the engine oil (see Chapter 1A).

13 Oil pump – removal, inspection and refitting

Removal

1 Remove the sump (see Section 12).

2 Slacken and remove the three bolts securing the oil pump in position **(see illustration)**. Disengage the pump sprocket from the chain, and remove the oil pump. If the pump locating dowel is a loose fit, remove and store it with the bolts for safe-keeping.

Inspection

3 Examine the oil pump sprocket for signs of damage and wear, such as chipped or missing teeth. If the sprocket is worn, the pump assembly must be renewed, as the sprocket is not available separately. It is also recommended that the chain and drive sprocket, fitted to the crankshaft, are renewed at the same time. On 1.4 litre engines, renewal

of the chain and drive sprocket is an involved operation requiring the removal of the main bearing ladder, and therefore cannot be carried out with the engine still fitted to the vehicle. On 1.6 litre engines, the oil pump drive sprocket and chain can be removed with the engine still in the vehicle, once the crankshaft sprocket has been removed and the crankshaft oil seal housing has been unbolted.

4 Slacken and remove the bolts securing the strainer cover to the pump body, and then lift off the strainer cover. Remove the relief valve piston and spring (and guide pin – 1.6 litre engines only), noting which way round they are fitted.

5 Examine the pump rotors and body for signs of wear ridges and scoring. If worn, the complete pump assembly must be renewed.

6 Examine the relief valve piston for signs of wear or damage, and renew if necessary. The condition of the relief valve spring can only be measured by comparing it with a new one; if there is any doubt about its condition, it should also be renewed. Both the piston and spring are available individually.

7 Thoroughly clean the oil pump strainer with a suitable solvent, and check it for signs of clogging or splitting. If the strainer is damaged, the strainer and cover assembly must be renewed.

8 Locate the relief valve spring, piston and (where fitted) the guide pin in the strainer cover, then refit the cover to the pump body. Align the relief valve piston with its bore in the pump. Refit the cover retaining bolts, tightening them securely.

Refitting

9 Ensure that the locating dowel is in position, and then engage the pump sprocket with its drive chain. Locate the pump on its dowel, and refit the pump retaining bolts, tightening them to the specified torque setting.

10 Refit the sump as described in Section 12.

14 Crankshaft oil seals – renewal

Right-hand oil seal

1 Remove the crankshaft sprocket and flanged spacer (where fitted) as described in Section 7.

2 Make a note of the correct fitted depth of the seal in its housing then carefully punch or drill two small holes opposite each other in the seal. Screw a self-tapping screw into each, and pull on the screws with pliers to extract the seal. Alternatively, the seal can be levered out of position using a suitable flat-bladed screwdriver, taking great care not to damage the crankshaft/oil pump drivegear shoulder or seal housing **(see illustration)**.

3 Clean the seal housing, and polish off any burrs or raised edges, which may have caused the seal to fail in the first place.

13.2 Unscrew the three bolts securing the oil pump in position

4 Lubricate the lips of the new seal with clean engine oil, and carefully locate the seal on the end of crankshaft. Note that its sealing lip must face inwards. Take care not to damage the seal lips during fitting.

5 Using a suitable tubular drift (such as a socket), which bears only on the hard outer edge of the seal, tap the seal into position, to the same depth in the housing as the original was prior to removal. The inner face of the seal must be flush with the inner wall of the crankcase.

6 Wash off any traces of oil, and then refit the crankshaft sprocket as described in Section 7.

Left-hand oil seal

7 Remove the flywheel/driveplate (see Section 15).

8 Make a note of the correct fitted depth of the seal in its housing. Punch or drill two small holes opposite each other in the seal. Screw a self-tapping screw into each, and pull on the screws with pliers to extract the seal.

9 Clean the seal housing, and polish off any burrs or raised edges, which may have caused the seal to fail in the first place.

10 Lubricate the lips of the new seal with clean engine oil, and carefully locate the seal on the end of the crankshaft.

11 Using a suitable tubular drift, which bears only on the hard outer edge of the seal, drive the seal into position, to the same depth in the housing as the original was prior to removal.

12 Wash off any traces of oil, and then refit the flywheel/driveplate as described in Section 15.

14.2 Use a screwdriver to lever out the crankshaft right-hand oil seal

15 Flywheel/driveplate – removal, inspection and refitting

Flywheel

Removal

1 Remove the transmission as described in Chapter 7A, then remove the clutch assembly as described in Chapter 6.

2 Prevent the flywheel from turning by locking the ring gear teeth **(see illustration)**. Alternatively, bolt a strap between the flywheel and the cylinder block/crankcase.

Caution: Do not attempt to lock the flywheel in position using the locking pin described in Section 3.

3 Slacken and remove the flywheel retaining bolts.

4 Remove the flywheel. Do not drop it, as it is very heavy. If the locating dowel is a loose fit in the crankshaft end, remove and store it with the flywheel for safe-keeping.

Inspection

5 If the flywheel's clutch mating surface is deeply scored, cracked or otherwise damaged, the flywheel must be renewed. However, it may be possible to have it surface-ground; seek the advice of a Peugeot dealer or engine reconditioning specialist.

6 If the ring gear is badly worn or has missing teeth, it must be renewed. This job is best left to a Peugeot dealer or engine reconditioning specialist. The temperature to which the new ring gear must be heated for installation is critical and, if not done accurately, the hardness of the teeth will be destroyed.

Refitting

7 Clean the mating surfaces of the flywheel and crankshaft.

8 If the new flywheel retaining bolts are not supplied with their threads already pre-coated, apply a suitable thread-locking compound to the threads of each bolt.

9 Ensure that the locating dowel is in position. Offer up the flywheel, locating it on the dowel, and fit the retaining bolts.

10 Lock the flywheel using the method employed on dismantling, and tighten the

15.2 Use a tool to lock the flywheel ring gear and prevent rotation

retaining bolts evenly and progressively to the specified torque.

11 Refit the clutch as described in Chapter 6. Remove the locking tool, and refit the transmission as described in Chapter 7A.

Driveplate

Removal

12 Remove the transmission as described in Chapter 7B.

13 Prevent the driveplate from turning by locking the ring gear teeth with a similar arrangement to that for the flywheel **(see illustration 15.2)**. Alternatively, bolt a strap between the driveplate and the cylinder block/crankcase. *Caution: Do not attempt to lock the driveplate in position using the locking pin described in Section 3.*

14 Slacken and remove the driveplate retaining bolts and remove the outer spacer plate and torque converter mounting plate.

15 Remove the driveplate and inner spacer plate from the end of the crankshaft. If the locating dowel is a loose fit in the crankshaft end, remove and store it with the driveplate for safe-keeping. **Note:** *The inner and outer spacer plates are different and are not interchangeable.*

Inspection

16 Inspect the driveplate and torque converter mounting plate for signs of wear or damage. If damage is found, the worn component must be renewed (it is not possible to renew the driveplate ring gear separately).

Refitting

17 Ensure all mating surfaces are clean and dry.

18 Remove any traces of locking compound from the threads of the driveplate bolts and apply a small amount of fresh locking compound (Peugeot recommend Loctite Frenbloc) to the bolt threads.

19 Ensure that the locating dowel is in position then refit the inner spacer plate, driveplate, torque converter mounting plate and outer spacer plate. Ensure all components are correctly located on the dowel then fit the retaining bolts.

20 Lock the driveplate using the method employed on dismantling, and tighten the retaining bolts evenly and progressively to the specified torque.

21 Refit the transmission as described in Chapter 7B.

16 Engine/transmission mountings – inspection and renewal

Inspection

1 If improved access is required, raise the front of the car and support it on axle stands (see *Jacking and vehicle support*).

2 Check the mounting rubber to see if it is cracked, hardened or separated from the metal at any point; renew the mounting if any such damage or deterioration is evident.

3 Check that all the mounting's fasteners are securely tightened; use a torque wrench to check if possible.

4 Using a large screwdriver or a crowbar, check for wear in the mounting by carefully levering against it to check for free play. Where this is not possible, enlist the aid of an assistant to move the engine/transmission back-and-forth, or from side-to-side, while you watch the mounting. While some free play is to be expected even from new components, excessive wear should be obvious. If excessive free play is found, check first that the fasteners are secure, and then renew any worn components as described below.

Renewal

Right-hand mounting

5 Place a jack beneath the engine, with a block of wood on the jack head. Raise the jack until it is supporting the weight of the engine.

6 Slacken and remove the bolts securing the mounting to the body, and the mounting bracket to the bracket bolted to the cylinder head.

7 If required, undo the bolts and remove the bracket from the cylinder head. Release the wiring loom and fuel lines from the retaining clips as it is removed.

8 Check for signs of wear or damage on all components, and renew as necessary.

9 On reassembly, refit the bracket to the cylinder head, tightening the bolts to the specified torque.

10 Install the mounting and mounting bracket and tighten its retaining bolts to the specified torque setting.

11 Remove the jack from under the engine.

Left-hand mounting

12 Remove the battery, and battery tray/box as described in Chapter 5A.

13 Place a jack beneath the transmission, with a block of wood on the jack head. Raise the jack until it is supporting the weight of the transmission.

14 Slacken and remove the mounting's two upper retaining bolts **(see illustration)**.

15 Undo the four retaining bolts from the mounting bracket on the body and remove the mounting from the engine compartment **(see illustration)**.

16 Check carefully for signs of wear or damage on all components, and renew them where necessary.

17 Refit the mounting bracket to the vehicle body and tighten its bolts to the specified torque.

18 Fit the mounting bolts to the bracket on the transmission and tighten the retaining bolts to the specified torque.

19 Remove the jack from underneath the transmission, then refit the battery as described in Chapter 5A.

16.14 Left-hand transmission mounting upper bolts (arrowed)

16.15 Left-hand transmission mounting bracket bolts (arrowed)

16.21 Undo the mounting bolts (arrowed) . . .

16.22 . . . and remove the lower link

Rear lower mounting

20 If not already done, firmly apply the handbrake, then jack up the front of the vehicle and support it securely on axle stands (see *Jacking and vehicle support*).

21 Unscrew and remove the bolt securing the rear mounting link to the bracket on the transmission **(see illustration)**.

22 Remove the bolt securing the rear mounting link to the subframe and remove the mounting torque reaction link **(see illustration)**.

23 To remove the mounting bracket undo the retaining bolts and remove the mounting bracket from the rear of the transmission **(see illustration)**.

24 Check carefully for signs of wear or damage on all components, and renew them where necessary.

25 On reassembly, fit the rear mounting bracket to the transmission, and tighten its retaining bolts to the specified torque.

26 Refit the rear mounting torque reaction link, and tighten both its bolts to their specified torque settings.

27 Lower the vehicle to the ground.

16.23 Undo the nut/bolts and remove the mounting bracket

Chapter 2 Part B
VTi petrol engines in-car repair procedures

Contents

Degrees of difficulty

Easy, suitable for novice with little experience	Fairly easy, suitable for beginner with some experience	Fairly difficult, suitable for competent DIY mechanic	Difficult, suitable for experienced DIY mechanic	Very difficult, suitable for expert DIY or professional

Specifications

Engine (general)

Capacity:
  1.4 litre engine 1397cc
  1.6 litre engine 1598cc
Designation:
  1.4 litre engine EP3
  1.6 litre engine EP6
Engine codes: *
  1.4 litre engine .... 8FP & 8FR
  1.6 litre engine 5FS
Bore:
  1.4 litre engine .... 77.00 mm
  1.6 litre engine .... 77.00 mm
Stroke:
  1.4 litre engine .... 75.00 mm
  1.6 litre engine .... 85.80 mm
Direction of crankshaft rotation .... Clockwise (viewed from the right-hand side of vehicle)
No 1 cylinder location.. At the transmission end of the block
Compression ratio:
  1.4 litre engine .... 10.8 : 1
  1.6 litre engine .... 11.0 : 1
Maximum power output:
  1.4 litre engine:
    8FP .... 70 kW @ 5250 rpm
    8FR .... 72 kW @ 5250 rpm
  1.6 litre engine .... 88 kW @ 6000 rpm
Maximum torque output:
  1.4 litre engine
    8FP .... 140 Nm @ 4100 rpm
    8FR
  1.6 litre engine .... 160 Nm @ 4250 rpm

*The engine code is stamped on a plate attached to the front right-hand end of the cylinder block, below the right-hand branch of the exhaust manifold. The code is the first 3-digits on the first line, and this is the code most often used by Peugeot.

Camshafts
Drive . . . .   Chain

Lubrication system
Oil pump type. . . . .   Gear type, chain-driven off the crankshaft
Minimum oil pressure at 80°C (with correct oil level):
   1000 rpm . . . .   2.0 bars
   2000 rpm . . . .   2.9 bars
   4000 rpm . . . .   3.3 bars
Oil pressure warning switch operating pressure . . . .   0.5 bars

Torque wrench settings

	Nm	lbf ft
Big-end bearing bolts: *		
Stage 1	5	4
Stage 2	10	7
Stage 3	Angle-tighten a further 130°	
Camshaft sprocket centre bolts (inlet and exhaust):		
Stage 1	20	15
Stage 2	Angle-tighten a further 180°	
Crankshaft pulley centre hub bolt:		
Stage 1	50	37
Stage 2	Angle-tighten a further 180°	
Crankshaft pulley-to-centre hub bolts (3)	28	21
Cylinder head bolts:		
Main bolts (10):		
Stage 1	30	22
Stage 2	Angle-tighten a further 90°	
Stage 3	Angle-tighten a further 90°	
Timing chain end bolts (2):		
Stage 1	15	11
Stage 2	Angle-tighten a further 90°	
Stage 3	Angle-tighten a further 90°	
Small bolt at rear of head (1)		
Stage 1	25	18
Stage 2	Angle-tighten a further 30°	
Cylinder head cover bolts	9	7
Engine-to-transmission fixing bolts	55	41
Flywheel/driveplate retaining bolts: *		
Stage 1	8	6
Stage 2	30	22
Stage 3	Angle-tighten a further 90°	
Left-hand engine/transmission mounting:		
Mounting bracket-to-body bolts	55	41
Mounting bolts to transmission bracket	60	44
Mounting bracket to transmission casing	30	22
Main bearing outer housing/ladder bolts	9	7
Main bearing bolts:		
Stage 1	30	22
Stage 2	Angle-tighten a further 150°	
Oil filter cap	25	18
Oil filter housing to cylinder block	10	7
Oil pump-to-engine bolts	25	18
Rear engine/transmission mounting:		
Connecting link-to-mounting bracket bolt	60	44
Connecting link-to-subframe bolt	60	44
Mounting bracket-to-transmission bolts	85	62
Right-hand engine/transmission mounting:		
Mounting bracket to support bracket	60	44
Rubber mounting to body	45	33
Support bracket to engine	45	33
Roadwheels	90	66
Sump retaining bolts	12	9
Sump baffle plate bolts	10	7
Sump drain plug	30	22
Timing chain guide securing bolts	25	18
Timing chain tensioner	65	48
Timing control solenoid valves (2) securing bolts	9	7
Variable timing actuator	8	6

Do not re-use

1 General Information

How to use this Chapter

1 This Part of Chapter 2 describes those repair procedures that can reasonably be carried out on the engine while it remains in the car. If the engine has been removed from the car and is being dismantled as described in Part F, any preliminary dismantling procedures can be ignored.

2 Note that, while it may be possible physically to overhaul items such as the piston/connecting rod assemblies while the engine is in the car, such tasks are not usually carried out as separate operations. Usually, several additional procedures (not to mention the cleaning of components and oilways) have to be carried out. For this reason, all such tasks are classed as major overhaul procedures, and are described in Part F of this Chapter.

3 Part F describes the removal of the engine/transmission unit from the vehicle, and the full overhaul procedures that can then be carried out.

EP series engine

4 The engine is of in-line four-cylinder, double-overhead camshaft, 16-valve type, mounted transversely at the front of the car. The clutch and transmission are attached to its left-hand end.

5 The engine is of conventional 'dry-liner' type, and the cylinder block is cast in aluminium.

6 The crankshaft runs in five main bearings. Thrustwashers are fitted to No 2 main bearing cap, to control crankshaft endfloat.

7 The connecting rods rotate on horizontally-split bearing shells at their big-ends. The pistons are attached to the connecting rods by gudgeon pins. The gudgeon pins are an interference fit in the connecting rod small-end eyes. The aluminium alloy pistons are fitted with three piston rings – two compression rings and an oil control ring.

8 The camshafts are driven by a chain, and operate sixteen valves by rocker arms located beneath each cam lobe. The valve clearances are self-adjusting by means of hydraulic followers in the cylinder head. The camshafts run in bearing cap housings, which are bolted to the top of the cylinder head. The inlet and exhaust valves are each closed by coil springs, and operate in guides pressed into the cylinder head. The engine has a variable valve timing arrangement, which has two electrovalves one for the exhaust camshaft and one for the inlet camshaft; these are positioned at the timing chain end at the front and rear of the cylinder head. Also an eccentric shaft actuator is fitted to the left-hand rear of the cylinder head and this alters the inlet valve opening and closing.

9 At the time of writing, there was no procedure available for the removal of the camshafts and valve assembly. The timing components: camshafts, bearings, rockers, followers, springs, valves and valve seals cannot be renewed individually. Peugeot recommend that if there is any damage to any of these components that the complete cylinder head assembly be renewed.

Caution: Work on the inlet valve spring mechanism is prohibited as a considerable risk of injury may occur.

10 The coolant pump is driven by the auxiliary belt and located in the right-hand end, at the rear of the cylinder block.

11 Lubrication is by means of an oil pump, which is chain driven off the crankshaft right-hand end. It draws oil through a strainer located in the sump, and then forces it through an externally-mounted filter into galleries in the cylinder block/crankcase. From there, the oil is distributed to the crankshaft (main bearings) and camshaft. The big-end bearings are supplied with oil via internal drillings in the crankshaft; the camshaft bearings also receive a pressurised supply. The camshaft lobes and valves are lubricated by splash, as are all other engine components.

12 Throughout the manual, it is often necessary to identify the engines not only by their cubic capacity, but also by their engine code. The engine code consists of three digits (eg, 8FP). The code is stamped on a plate attached to the front, left-hand end of the cylinder block, or stamped directly onto the front face of the cylinder block, on the machined surface located just to the left of the oil filter (next to the crankcase vent hose union).

Operations with engine in the car

13 The following work can be carried out with the engine in the car:
- Compression pressure – testing.
- Cylinder head covers – removal and refitting.
- Crankshaft pulley – removal and refitting.
- Timing chain – removal, refitting and adjustment.
- Timing chain tensioner and sprockets – removal and refitting.
- Cylinder head – removal and refitting.
- Cylinder head and pistons – decarbonising.
- Sump – removal and refitting.
- Oil pump – removal, overhaul and refitting.
- Crankshaft oil seals – renewal.
- Engine/transmission mountings – inspection and renewal.
- Flywheel/driveplate – removal, inspection and refitting.

2 Compression test – description and interpretation

1 Refer to.

3 Engine assembly/valve timing holes – general information and usage

1 Special tools are required to lock the camshafts in position (see illustrations).

2 Each camshaft has flats on the transmission end to accommodate the locking tools. The special tools are bolted down to the top of the cylinder head, locking the camshafts in position.

3 A timing hole is drilled in the lower cylinder block; when the timing hole is aligned with the corresponding hole in the flywheel, the pin can be inserted to lock the crankshaft in position, preventing it from rotating (see illustration).

3.1a Special tools...

3.1b... to lock the camshafts in position

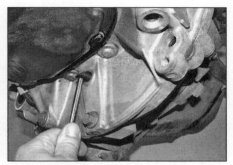

3.3 When the timing hole is aligned with the hole in the flywheel, the pin can be inserted to lock the crankshaft in position

3.7 Bolt the special tool over the camshafts to lock them in position

4.3 Remove the cylinder head cover

4.5 Disconnect the earth cable

4 This ensures that the camshafts and crankshaft are correctly positioned when assembling the engine (to prevent the possibility of the valves contacting the pistons

4.6 Disconnect the camshaft sensors

when refitting the cylinder head), or refitting the timing chain. To set the engine in the timing position, proceed as follows.

5 Undo the retaining bolts and remove the cylinder head cover (see Section 4).

6 Using a socket and extension bar fitted to the crankshaft pulley centre hub bolt, turn the crankshaft in the normal direction of rotation until the hole in the flywheel aligns with the hole in the lower part of the cylinder block. When the timing hole is aligned correctly the pistons should be halfway down the cylinders. **Note:** *Do not attempt to rotate the engine whilst the crankshaft/camshafts are locked in position. If the engine is to be left in this state for a long period of time, it is a good idea to place suitable warning notices inside the vehicle, and in the engine compartment. This will reduce the possibility of the engine*

being accidentally cranked on the starter motor, which is likely to cause damage with the locking rods/tool in place.

7 With the flats on the camshafts correctly positioned, fit the special tools over the camshafts to lock them in position on the cylinder head **(see illustration)** and insert the flywheel positioning tool **(see illustration 3.2)**.

8 The crankshaft and camshafts are now locked in position, preventing rotation.

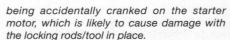

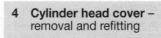

4 Cylinder head cover –
  removal and refitting

Removal

1 Remove the battery cover and disconnect the battery. **Note:** *Wait 15 minutes after switching off the ignition before* Disconnecting the battery, *to ensure that the ECU's memory is stored.*

2 Remove the air filter housing and air inlet hoses as described in Chapter 4A Section 2.

3 Undo the two retaining screws and unclip the plastic cover from the front of the cylinder head cover **(see illustration)**.

4 Remove the ignition coils as described in Chapter 5B Section 3.

5 Release the wiring loom from across the front of the cylinder head cover including the earth connection **(see illustration)**.

6 Disconnect the wiring connectors from the camshaft position sensors in the transmission end of the cylinder head cover **(see illustration)**.

7 Slide the wiring loom bracket from the end of the cylinder head cover upwards and move it to one side **(see illustration)**.

8 Disconnect the breather pipe from the right-hand rear of the cylinder head cover **(see illustration)**.

9 Unclip the fuel pipes from the right-hand rear of the cylinder head cover and move them to one side **(see illustration)**.

10 Progressively unscrew the bolts securing the cylinder head cover to the cylinder head. Noting the two bolts in the centre of the cylinder head cover **(see illustration)**.

4.7 Unclip the wiring harness bracket

4.8 Unclip the breather pipe

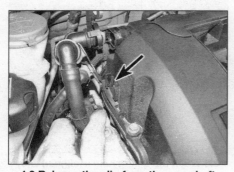

4.9 Release the clip from the camshaft cover

4.10 Two inner camshaft cover retaining bolts – arrowed

4.11 Remove the camshaft cover

4.13 Clip the rubber gasket into the cover

5.3a Undo the retaining bolts...

11 Remove the cylinder head cover and gaskets **(see illustration)**.

Refitting

12 Thoroughly clean the surfaces of the covers and cylinder head.
13 Fit new gaskets and locate the cover on the head **(see illustration)**. Insert all the retaining bolts and finger-tighten them.
14 Progressively tighten the bolts to the correct torque setting.
15 The remainder of refitting is a reversal of removal.

5	Crankshaft pulley – removal and refitting

Removal

1 Remove the auxiliary drivebelt (Chapter 1A Section 13)
2 If required, to prevent the crankshaft turning whilst the pulley retaining bolts are being slackened on manual transmission models, select 5th gear and have an assistant apply the brakes firmly. On automatic transmission models it will be necessary to remove the starter motor (Chapter 5A Section 10) and lock the driveplate with a suitable tool. If the engine has been removed from the vehicle, lock the flywheel ring gear as described in Section 8. Do not attempt to lock the pulley by inserting a bolt/drill through the timing hole.

If the locking pin is in position, temporarily remove it prior to slackening the pulley bolt, then refit it once the bolt has been slackened.
3 Undo the three crankshaft pulley retaining bolts and remove the pulley from the centre hub on the end of the crankshaft **(see illustrations)**.

Refitting

4 Locate the pulley on the hub on the end of the crankshaft, refit the three retaining bolts and tighten them to the specified torque.
5 Refit and tension the auxiliary drivebelt as described in Chapter 1A Section 13.

6	Timing chain assembly – general information, removal and refitting

General information

1 The timing chain drives the camshafts from a toothed sprocket on the end of the crankshaft.
2 The chain should be renewed if the sprocket or chain is worn, indicated by excessive lateral play between the links, and excessive noise in operation. It is wise to renew the chain in any case if the engine is to be dismantled for overhaul. Note that the rollers on a very badly worn chain may be slightly grooved. To avoid future problems, if there is any doubt at all about the condition of the chain, renew it.
3 The timing chain and guides are removed as

5.3b... and remove the crankshaft pulley

a complete assembly and are withdrawn out through the top of the cylinder head.
4 To check the wear of the timing chain a special tool is required **(see illustration 3.0)**. Insert the tool into the cylinder head where the tensioner fits, and tighten the outer part (see paragraph 11). Run the threaded centre part of the tool in until it contacts the timing chain guide and tighten to 0.6 Nm/0.4 lbf ft (hand-tight). Lock the nut on the centre thread and remove the special tool. Check the length of the tool to make sure that it does not exceed 68 mm **(see illustrations)**.

Removal

5 Remove the cylinder head cover, as described in Section 4.
6 Set the engine valve timing and lock in position, as described in Section 3.

6.4a Insert the tool into the cylinder head where the chain tensioner fits

6.4b Screw the threaded centre part of the tool in until it contacts the timing chain guide and hand-tighten

6.4c Make sure the length does not exceed 68 mm

6.8 Hold the camshafts in position and slacken the camshaft sprocket/dephaser unit retaining bolts

6.11 Remove the timing chain tensioner

6.12 Remove the guide/anti-knock pad from the cylinder head

6.13 Remove the engine mounting bracket

6.14a Remove the upper guide securing bolts...

6.14b... and the two lower securing bolts – arrowed

7 Slacken the crankshaft pulley centre hub retaining bolt. To prevent the crankshaft turning whilst the bolt is being slackened on manual transmission models, select 5th gear and have an assistant apply the brakes firmly. On automatic transmission models it will be necessary to remove the starter motor (Chapter 5A Section 10) and lock the driveplate with a suitable tool. If the engine has been removed from the vehicle, lock the flywheel ring gear as described in Section 8. Do not attempt to lock the pulley by inserting a bolt/drill through the timing hole. If the locking pin is in position, temporarily remove it prior to slackening

the bolt, then refit it once the bolt has been slackened.

8 Holding the camshafts in position with an open-ended spanner on the flats on the camshaft, slacken the camshaft sprocket/ dephaser unit retaining bolts (see illustration).

9 Remove the crankshaft pulley, as described in Section 5.

10 Remove the throttle housing unit from the inlet manifold, as described in Chapter 4A Section 11.

11 Slacken and remove the timing chain tensioner from the rear of the cylinder head (see illustration). Before the tensioner is removed, make sure the camshafts and

crankshaft are locked in position as described in Section 3.

12 Undo the two retaining bolts and remove the chain guide/anti-knock pad from the top of the cylinder head (see illustration).

13 Position a trolley jack under the engine, placing a block of wood between the jack head and the sump. Take the weight of the engine, undo the bolts/nuts and remove the right-hand engine mounting and bracket (see illustration).

14 Slacken and remove the timing chain guide retaining bolts (see illustrations).

15 Remove the crankshaft pulley centre bolt and hub (see illustrations).

6.15a Remove the crankshaft hub retaining bolt...

6.15b... and then withdraw the hub

6.17a Undo the retaining bolts...

6.17b... then remove the inlet...

6.17c... and exhaust camshaft sprockets

16 Withdraw the dipstick and remove it from the dipstick tube. The dipstick goes down through the chain guide; if this is not removed it will prevent the timing chain assembly from being withdrawn out through the cylinder head.

17 Undo the retaining bolts and remove the camshaft sprocket/dephaser units from the ends of the camshafts, keeping the timing chain held in position **(see illustrations)**. **Note:** *The camshafts are marked IN for inlet and EX for exhaust.*

18 Withdraw the timing chain and guide assembly out through the top of the cylinder head, complete with crankshaft sprocket **(see illustrations)**.

19 Check the timing chain assembly carefully for any signs of wear. Renew it if there is the slightest doubt about its condition. If the engine is undergoing an overhaul, it is

advisable to renew the chain as a matter of course, regardless of its apparent condition.

Refitting

20 Before refitting, thoroughly clean the crankshaft sprockets. The sprockets are a compression fit between the pulley centre hub and the crankshaft. The mating faces need to be clean and free from any oil when assembling, use a dry product like brake cleaner or similar.

21 Check the camshaft sprocket/dephaser units are in the rest position **(see illustration)**. If these are not aligned the sprocket/dephaser unit will need to be renewed.

22 Lower the timing chain assembly down through the top of the cylinder head, complete with crankshaft sprocket **(see illustration)**.

23 Refit the crankshaft pulley hub; making sure it locates correctly with the crankshaft

sprockets. Tighten the bolt to the torque setting specified, preventing the crankshaft from turning as carried out for removal.

24 Refit the timing chain guide retaining bolts and renew the seals/washer.

25 Check that the camshafts and crankshaft are still locked in correct position as described in Section 3.

26 Refit the camshaft sprocket/dephaser units to the ends of the camshafts and tighten to the correct torque setting. Make sure the timing chain is located correctly around the sprockets **(see illustration)**. **Note:** *The camshaft sprockets are marked IN for inlet and EX for exhaust.*

27 Refit the chain guide/anti-knock pad to the top of the cylinder head **(see illustration)**.

28 Refit the timing chain tensioner and tighten to the specified torque setting.

29 Remove the camshaft and crankshaft

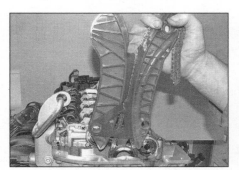

6.18a Withdraw the timing chain guide assembly...

6.18b... complete with crankshaft sprocket

6.21 Check the alignment marks are in position – arrowed

6.22 Lower the sprocket into position

6.26 Refit the camshaft sprockets

6.27 Refit the guide/anti-knock pad securing bolts – arrowed

locking tools, and rotate the crankshaft four complete revolutions clockwise (viewed from the right-hand end of the engine). Realign the engine valve timing holes and refit the locking tools, to check the timing is still aligned. If required, refer to Section 3 ; to check timing mark alignment is correct. When correct remove the timing locking tools from the engine.

Caution: Do not attempt to rotate the engine whilst the locking tools are in position.

30 Refit the right-hand engine mounting with reference to Section 13.

31 Refit the throttle housing unit, as described in Chapter 4A Section 11.

32 Refit the crankshaft pulley, as described in Section 5.

8.4 Disconnect the vacuum pipe

33 Refit the camshaft cover with reference to Section 4.

34 Refit the engine oil dipstick and reconnect the battery lead.

7 Camshafts and valve assembly – general information

1 At the time of writing, there was no procedure available for the removal of the camshafts and valve assembly. The timing components: camshafts, bearings, rockers, followers, springs, valves and valve seals cannot be renewed individually. Peugeot recommend that if there is any damage to any of these components that the complete cylinder head assembly be renewed.

Caution: Work on the inlet valve spring mechanism is prohibited as a considerable risk of injury may occur.

8 Cylinder head – removal and refitting

Note: *The cylinder head cannot be stripped (see Section 7); this procedure is for just the removal and refitting of the cylinder head.*

Removal

1 Disconnect the battery (see Chapter 5A,4).

Note: *Wait 15 minutes after switching off the ignition before disconnecting the battery, to ensure that the ECU's memory is stored.*

2 Apply the handbrake, then jack up the front of the vehicle and support it on axle stands (see *Jacking and vehicle support*). Undo the screws and remove the engine undershield. For improved access, remove the bonnet.

3 Drain the cooling system as described in Chapter 1A Section 25.

4 Disconnect the pipe from the vacuum pump, release the securing clip and move the pipe to one side **(see illustration)**.

5 Disconnect the wiring connectors from the thermostat, temperature sensor and oil pressure sensor on the end of the cylinder head **(see illustrations)**.

6 Disconnect the wiring connectors from the camshaft position sensors in the transmission end of the cylinder head cover **(see illustration)**.

7 Slide the wiring loom bracket upwards from the end of the cylinder head cover and move it to one side **(see illustration)**.

8 Disconnect the four coolant hoses from the thermostat housing **(see illustration)**.

9 Release the retaining clip at the rear of the cylinder head, where the thermostat housing joins the pipe to the coolant pump **(see illustration)**.

10 Undo the retaining bolts and remove the thermostat housing from the cylinder head

8.5a Disconnect the thermostat wiring connector

8.5b Disconnect the oil pressure sensor and temperature sensor wiring connector

8.6 Disconnect the camshaft sensor wiring connectors

8.7 Unclip the wiring harness mounting bracket

8.8 Disconnect the coolant hoses

8.9 release the securing clip at the rear of the housing

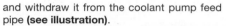

8.10 Withdraw the housing from the cylinder head

8.11a Undo the retaining bolts – arrowed...

8.11b... and using an Allen key withdraw the actuator from the cylinder head

and withdraw it from the coolant pump feed pipe **(see illustration)**.

11 Disconnect the wiring connector from the eccentric shaft actuator at the left-hand rear of the cylinder head. Undo the actuator retaining bolts and then remove it from the cylinder head by using a 4 mm Allen key, and turning the centre shaft anti-clockwise, while withdrawing the actuator from the cylinder head **(see illustrations)**.

12 Remove the exhaust front pipe/catalytic converter and inlet manifold, with reference to Chapter 4A.

13 Remove the timing chain assembly, as described in Section 6.

14 If not already done, undo the retaining bolts and remove the mounting bracket from the right-hand end of the cylinder head. Release the wiring loom and fuel pipes from the securing clips where required **(see illustration)**.

15 Disconnect the wiring connectors from the inlet and exhaust variable timing electrovalves at the front and rear of the cylinder head at the timing chain end **(see illustrations)**.

16 Slacken and remove the cylinder head bolt at the right-hand rear of the cylinder head **(see illustration)**.

17 Slacken and remove the two cylinder head bolts at the timing chain end of the cylinder head **(see illustration)**.

18 Progressively slacken and remove the remaining ten cylinder head bolts starting from the middle and spiralling outwards.

19 With all the cylinder head bolts removed,

the joint between the cylinder head and gasket, and the cylinder block/crankcase must now be broken. Carefully 'rock' the cylinder head free towards the front of the car. Do not try to swivel the head on the cylinder block/crankcase; it is located by dowels. When the joint is broken, lift the cylinder head away. Use a hoist or seek assistance if possible, as it is a heavy assembly. Remove the gasket from the top of the block, noting the two locating dowels. If the locating dowels are a loose fit, remove them and store them with the head for safe-keeping. Do not discard the gasket; it will be needed for identification purposes.

Preparation for refitting

20 The mating faces of the cylinder head and cylinder block/crankcase must be perfectly clean before refitting the head. Use a hard

8.14 Remove the engine mounting bracket

8.15a Disconnect the exhaust electrovalve connector...

plastic or wooden scraper to remove all traces of gasket and carbon and also clean the piston crowns. Make sure that the carbon is not allowed to enter the oil and water passages – this is particularly important for the lubrication system, as carbon could block the oil supply to the engine's components. Using adhesive tape and paper, seal the water, oil and bolt holes in the cylinder block/crankcase. To prevent carbon entering the gap between the pistons and bores, smear a little grease in the gap. After cleaning each piston, use a small brush to remove all traces of grease and carbon from the gap, and then wipe away the remainder with a clean rag. Clean all the pistons in the same way.

21 Check the mating surfaces of the cylinder block/crankcase and the cylinder head for

8.15b... and the inlet electrovalve connector

8.16 Cylinder head securing bolt – arrowed

8.17 Cylinder head securing bolts – arrowed

8.22 Cylinder head thickness markings – arrowed

nicks, deep scratches and other damage. If slight, they may be removed carefully with a file, but if excessive, machining may be the only alternative to renewal. If warpage of the cylinder head gasket surface is suspected, use a straight-edge to check it for distortion. Refer to Part F of this Chapter if necessary.

22 Obtain a new cylinder head gasket before starting the refitting procedure. There are different thicknesses available – check the old head gasket for markings on the rear right-hand side of the gasket **(see illustration)**. Note that modifications to the cylinder head gasket material, type, and manufacturer are constantly taking place; seek the advice of a Peugeot dealer as to the latest recommendations.

23 Due to the stress that the cylinder head bolts are under, it is highly recommended that they be renewed along with the washers, regardless of their apparent condition.

Refitting

24 Wipe clean the mating surfaces of the cylinder head and cylinder block/crankcase. Check that the two locating dowels are in position at each end of the cylinder block/crankcase surface.

25 Position a new gasket on the cylinder block/crankcase surface.

26 Check that the crankshaft pulley and camshaft sprockets are still at their locked positions (see Section 3).

27 With the aid of an assistant, carefully lower the cylinder head assembly onto the block,

aligning it with the locating dowels.

28 Apply a smear of grease to the threads, and to the underside of the heads, of the cylinder head bolts. Peugeot recommend the use of Molykote G Rapid Plus (available from your Peugeot dealer); in the absence of the specified grease, any good-quality high melting-point grease may be used.

29 Carefully enter each of the new bolts and washers into there relevant hole (do not drop them in) and then screw them in finger-tight.

30 Working progressively tighten the main ten cylinder head bolts starting from the middle and spiraling outwards. Then tighten the two bolts at the timing chain end of the cylinder head and the one at the rear of the head. Tighten all the cylinder head bolts to their Stage 1 torque setting.

31 Once all the bolts have been tightened to their Stage 1 torque setting, proceed to tighten them through the remaining stages as given in the Specifications. It is recommended that an angle-measuring gauge be used for the angle-tightening stages, however, if a gauge is not available, use white paint to make alignment marks between the bolt head and cylinder head prior to tightening; the marks can then be used to check that the bolt has rotated sufficiently. Each step must be completed in one movement without stopping.

32 The remainder of the refitting procedure is a reversal of removal, referring to the relevant Chapters or Sections as required. On completion, refill the cooling system as described in Chapter 1A Section 25. Initialise the engine management ECU as follows. Start the engine and run to normal temperature. Carry out a road test during which the following procedure should be made. Engage third gear and stabilise the engine at 1000 rpm. Now accelerate fully to 3500 rpm.

---

9 **Sump** – removal and refitting

Removal

1 Apply the handbrake, then jack up the front

of the vehicle and support it on axle stands (see *Jacking and vehicle support*). Undo the screws and remove the engine undershield (if fitted).

2 Drain the engine oil then clean and refit the engine oil drain plug, tightening it securely. If the engine is nearing its service interval when the oil and filter are due for renewal, it is recommended that the filter is also removed, and a new one fitted. After reassembly, the engine can then be refilled with fresh oil. Refer to Chapter 1A Section 6 for further information.

3 Withdraw the engine oil dipstick from the guide tube.

4 Undo the two retaining bolts and remove the mounting plate from the rear of the sump **(see illustration)**.

5 Progressively slacken and remove all of the sump retaining bolts. Make a note of the fitting position of the bolts, as they may be different lengths. This will avoid the possibility of installing the bolts in the wrong locations on refitting.

6 Break the joint by striking the sump with the palm of your hand. Lower the sump, and withdraw it from underneath the vehicle **(see illustration)**. While the sump is removed, take the opportunity to check the oil pump pick-up/strainer for signs of clogging or splitting. If necessary, remove the pump as described in Section 10, and clean or renew the strainer. If required, unbolt the oil baffle plate from the bottom of the main bearing ladder, noting which way round it is fitted.

Refitting

7 Where removed, refit the baffle plate to the main bearing ladder and tighten the bolts securely.

8 Where removed, refit the oil pump and pick-up/strainer with reference to Section 10.

9 Clean all traces of sealant/gasket from the mating surfaces of the main bearing ladder and sump, and then use a clean rag to wipe out the sump and the engine's interior.

10 Ensure that the sump mating surfaces are clean and dry, and then apply a thin coating of suitable sealant to the sump mating surface **(see illustration)**.

9.4 Undo the two bolts – arrowed

9.6 Remove the sump

9.10 Apply a thin bead of RTV sealant to the sump mating surface

11 Refit the sump onto the main bearing ladder and insert the bolts and finger-tighten them at this stage, so that it is still possible to move the sump. Make sure the bolts are refitted in their correct locations.

12 Refit the mounting plate to the rear of the sump and tighten all the retaining bolts.

13 Check that the oil drain plug is tightened securely, then refit the engine undershield (where applicable) and lower the vehicle to the ground.

14 Refit the dipstick and refill the engine with oil as described in Chapter 1A Section 6.

10.2 Unclip the cover...

10.3... and undo the sprocket retaining bolt

---

10 Oil pump – removal, inspection and refitting

Removal

1 Remove the sump as described in Section 9.

2 Unclip the cover from the oil pump drive sprocket **(see illustration)**.

3 Slacken and remove the drive sprocket retaining bolt, withdraw the sprocket from the drive chain **(see illustration)**.

4 Undo the oil pump retaining bolts and withdraw the pump from the bottom of main bearing ladder **(see illustration)**.

Inspection

5 At the time of writing, checking specifications for the oil pump were not available, however, clean the pump and inspect it for damage and excessive wear.

6 Thoroughly clean the oil pump strainer with a suitable solvent, and check it for signs of clogging or splitting. If the strainer is damaged, the strainer and cover assembly must be renewed.

7 If the oil pump drive chain needs renewing, the timing chain assembly will need to be removed first as described in Section 6. The chain is around a sprocket on the end of the crankshaft, at the rear of the crankshaft sprocket for the timing chain **(see illustration)**.

Refitting

8 Clean the mating surfaces of the oil pump and main bearing ladder/cylinder block and fit the retaining bolts. Tighten to the specified torque setting.

9 Locate the sprocket onto the pump making sure it is located correctly in the drive chain. Tighten the sprocket retaining bolt securely.

10 Refit the sprocket cover to the end of the oil pump.

11 Refit the sump as described in Section 9.

12 Before starting the engine, prime the oil pump as follows. Disconnect the fuel injector wiring connectors, and then turn the engine over on the starter motor until the oil pressure warning light goes out. Reconnect the injector wiring on completion.

10.4 Undo the oil pump housing retaining bolts

10.7 Oil pump drive chain sprocket – arrowed

---

11 Crankshaft oil seals – renewal

Right-hand oil seal

1 Remove the crankshaft pulley, with reference to Section 5.

2 Check the depth of the seal in the engine casing before removing **(see illustration)**.

3 Punch or drill two small holes opposite each other in the seal. Screw a self-tapping screw into each, and pull on the screws with pliers to extract the seal **(see illustrations 11.10a and 11.10b)**. Alternatively, the seal can be levered out of position. Use

a flat-bladed screwdriver, and take great care not to damage the crankshaft shoulder or seal housing.

4 Clean the seal housing, and polish off any burrs or raised edges which may have caused the seal to fail in the first place.

5 Lubricate the lips of the new seal with clean engine oil, and carefully locate the seal on the end of the crankshaft. The new seal will normally be supplied with a plastic fitting sleeve to protect the seal lips as the seal is fitted. If so, lubricate the fitting sleeve and locate it over the end of the crankshaft **(see illustration)**.

6 Fit the new seal using a suitable tubular drift, which bears only on the hard outer edge of the seal. Tap the seal into position, to the

11.2 Check the depth of the fitted oil seal

11.5 Locate the oil seal and fitting sleeve over the end of the crankshaft

11.6 Tap the seal squarely into position

11.10a Drill a hole...

11.10b... then use a self-tapping screw and pliers to extract the oil seal

11.11 Clean out the recess

11.12a The new oil seal comes with a protective sleeve...

11.12b... which fits over the end of the crankshaft

same depth in the housing as the original was prior to removal **(see illustration)**.

7 Wash off any traces of oil, then refit the crankshaft pulley as described in Section 5.

Left-hand oil seal

8 Remove the flywheel/driveplate and crank- shaft timing plate, as described in Section 12.

9 Make a note of the correct fitted depth of the seal in its housing **(see illustration 11.2)**.

10 Punch or drill two small holes opposite each other in the seal. Screw a self-tapping screw into each, and pull on the screws with pliers to extract the seal **(see illustrations)**.

11 Clean the seal housing, and polish off

any burrs or raised edges which may have caused the seal to fail in the first place **(see illustration)**.

12 Lubricate the lips of the new seal with clean engine oil, and carefully locate the seal on the end of the crankshaft. The new seal will normally be supplied with a plastic fitting sleeve to protect the seal lips as the seal is fitted. If so, lubricate the fitting sleeve and locate it over the end of the crankshaft **(see illustrations)**.

13 Before driving the seal fully into position, put a small amount of sealer at each side of the seal, where the upper and lower crankcases meet **(see illustration)**. Drive the seal into position, to the same depth in the housing as the original was prior to removal.

14 Clean off any excess sealer or oil and then refit the crankshaft timing plate and flywheel/driveplate as described in Section 12.

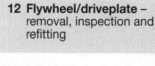

12 Flywheel/driveplate – removal, inspection and refitting

Removal

Flywheel

1 Remove the transmission as described in Chapter 7A Section 7, then remove the clutch assembly as described in Chapter 6 Section 6.

2 Prevent the crankshaft from turning by locking the flywheel with a wide-bladed screwdriver between the ring gear teeth and the transmission casing. Alternatively, bolt a strap between the flywheel and the cylinder block/crankcase **(see illustration)**. Do not attempt to lock the flywheel in position using the crankshaft pulley locking pin described in Section 3.

3 Slacken and remove the flywheel retaining bolts, and remove the flywheel from the end of the crankshaft **(see illustrations)**. Be careful not to drop it; it is heavy. If the flywheel locating dowel is a loose fit in the crankshaft end, remove it and store it with the flywheel for safe-keeping. Discard the flywheel bolts; new ones must be used on refitting.

11.13 Apply a small amount of sealer at the casing joints

12.2 Use a tool to lock the flywheel ring gear and prevent rotation

12.3a Slacken the securing bolts...

12.3b... and remove the flywheel

12.4 Remove the TDC timing plate from the crankshaft

4 If required, remove the crankshaft TDC timing plate from the end of the crankshaft (see illustration).

Driveplate

5 Remove the transmission as described in Chapter 7A Section 7. Lock the driveplate as described in paragraph 2. Mark the relationship between the torque converter plate and the driveplate, and slacken all the driveplate retaining bolts.

6 Remove the retaining bolts, along with the torque converter plate and (where fitted) the two shims (one fitted on each side of the torque converter plate). Note that the shims are of different thickness, the thicker one being on the outside of the torque converter plate. Discard the driveplate retaining bolts; new ones must be used on refitting.

7 Remove the driveplate from the end of the crankshaft. If the locating dowel is a loose fit in the crankshaft end, remove it and store it with the driveplate for safe-keeping.

8 If required remove the crankshaft TDC timing plate from the end of the crankshaft.

Inspection

9 On models with manual transmission, examine the flywheel for scoring of the clutch face, and for wear or chipping of the ring gear teeth. If the clutch face is scored, the flywheel may be surface-ground, but renewal is preferable. Seek the advice of a Peugeot dealer or engine reconditioning specialist to see if machining is possible. If the ring gear is worn or damaged, the flywheel must be renewed, as it is not possible to renew the ring gear separately.

10 On models with automatic transmission, check the torque converter driveplate carefully for signs of distortion. Look for any hairline cracks around the bolt holes or radiating outwards from the centre, and inspect the ring gear teeth for signs of wear or chipping. If any sign of wear or damage is found, the driveplate must be renewed.

11 Check the crankshaft TDC timing plate for any damage; make sure that none of the teeth around the circumference of the disc are bent.

Refitting

Flywheel

12 Clean the mating surfaces of the flywheel and crankshaft. Remove any remaining locking compound from the threads of the crankshaft holes, using the correct-size tap, if available.

13 If the new flywheel retaining bolts are not supplied with their threads already pre-coated, apply a suitable thread-locking compound to the threads of each bolt.

14 If removed, refit the crankshaft TDC timing plate to the end of the crankshaft.

15 Ensure the locating dowel is in position. Offer up the flywheel, locating it on the dowel, and fit the new retaining bolts.

16 Lock the flywheel using the method employed on dismantling, and tighten the retaining bolts to the specified torque and angle.

17 Refit the clutch and remove the flywheel locking tool, then refit the transmission.

Driveplate

18 Carry out the operations described above in paragraphs 12 and 13, substituting 'driveplate' for all references to the flywheel.

19 If removed, refit the crankshaft TDC timing plate to the end of the crankshaft.

20 Locate the driveplate on its locating dowel.

21 Offer up the torque converter plate, with the thinner shim positioned behind the plate and the thicker shim on the outside, and align the marks made prior to removal.

22 Fit the new retaining bolts, then lock the driveplate using the method employed on dismantling. Tighten the retaining bolts to the specified torque wrench setting and angle.

23 Remove the driveplate locking tool, and refit the transmission.

13 Engine/transmission mountings – inspection and renewal

Inspection

1 If improved access is required, raise the front of the car and support it on axle stands (see *Jacking and vehicle support*).

2 Check the mounting rubber to see if it is cracked, hardened or separated from the metal at any point; renew the mounting if any such damage or deterioration is evident.

3 Check that all the mounting's fasteners are securely tightened; use a torque wrench to check if possible.

4 Using a large screwdriver or a crowbar, check for wear in the mounting by carefully levering against it to check for free play. Where this is not possible, enlist the aid of an assistant to move the engine/transmission back-and-forth, or from side-to-side, while you watch the mounting. While some free play is to be expected even from new components, excessive wear should be obvious. If excessive free play is found, check first that the fasteners are secure, and then renew any worn components as described below.

Renewal

Right-hand mounting

5 Place a jack beneath the engine, with a block of wood on the jack head. Raise the jack until it is supporting the weight of the engine.

6 Slacken and remove the bolts securing the mounting to the body, and the mounting bracket bolted to the cylinder head (see illustration).

7 If required, undo the bolts and remove the bracket from the cylinder head (see

13.6 Slacken the engine mounting bolts – arrowed

13.7 Remove the engine mounting bracket

13.14 Left-hand transmission mounting upper bolts – arrowed

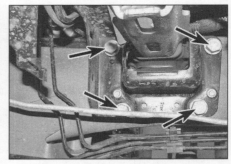

13.15 Left-hand transmission mounting bracket bolts – arrowed

illustration). Release the wiring loom and fuel lines from the retaining clips as it is removed.
8 Check for signs of wear or damage on all components, and renew as necessary.
9 On reassembly, refit the bracket to the cylinder head, tightening the bolts to the specified torque.
10 Install the mounting and mounting bracket and tighten its retaining bolts to the specified torque setting.
11 Remove the jack from under the engine.

Left-hand mounting

12 Remove the battery, and battery tray/box as described in Chapter 5A Section 4.
13 Place a jack beneath the transmission, with a block of wood on the jack head. Raise the jack until it is supporting the weight of the transmission.
14 Slacken and remove the mounting's two upper retaining bolts **(see illustration).**

15 Undo the four retaining bolts from the mounting bracket on the body and remove the mounting from the engine compartment **(see illustration).**
16 Check carefully for signs of wear or damage on all components, and renew them where necessary.
17 Refit the mounting bracket to the vehicle body and tighten its bolts to the specified torque.
18 Fit the mounting bolts to the bracket on the transmission and tighten the retaining bolts to the specified torque.
19 Remove the jack from underneath the transmission, then refit the battery and tray.

Rear lower mounting

20 If not already done, firmly apply the handbrake, then jack up the front of the vehicle and support it securely on axle stands (see *Jacking and vehicle support*).

21 Unscrew and remove the bolt securing the rear mounting link to the bracket on the transmission **(see illustration).**
22 Remove the bolt securing the rear mounting link to the subframe and remove the mounting torque reaction link **(see illustration).**
23 To remove the mounting bracket undo the retaining bolts and remove the mounting bracket from the rear of the transmission **(see illustration).**
24 Check carefully for signs of wear or damage on all components, and renew them where necessary.
25 On reassembly, fit the rear mounting bracket to the transmission, and tighten its retaining bolts to the specified torque.
26 Refit the rear mounting torque reaction link, and tighten both its bolts to their specified torque settings.
27 Lower the vehicle to the ground.

13.21 Undo the mounting bolts – arrowed...

13.22... and remove the lower link

13.23 Undo the nut/bolts and remove the mounting bracket

Chapter 2 Part C
1.4 litre diesel engine in-car repair procedures

Contents

Degrees of difficulty

| Easy, suitable for novice with little experience | | Fairly easy, suitable for beginner with some experience | | Fairly difficult, suitable for competent DIY mechanic | | Difficult, suitable for experienced DIY mechanic | | Very difficult, suitable for expert DIY or professional | |

Specifications

General

Designation	DV4C
Engine codes*	8HR
Bore	73.70 mm
Stroke	82.00 mm
Direction of crankshaft rotation	Clockwise (viewed from the right-hand side of vehicle)
No 1 cylinder location	At the transmission end of the block
Maximum power output	50 kW @ 4000 rpm
Maximum torque output	160 Nm @ 2000 rpm
Compression ratio	18.0 : 1

* The engine code is stamped on a plate attached to the front of the cylinder block, next to the oil filter

Compression pressures (engine hot, at cranking speed)

Normal	25 to 30 bars
Minimum	18 bars
Maximum difference between any two cylinders	5 bars

Camshaft

Drive . . . . Toothed belt

Lubrication system

Oil pump type. . . . . Gear type, driven directly by the right-hand end of the crankshaft, by two flats machined along the crankshaft journal

Minimum oil pressure. . . . . 3.5 bars @ 4000 rpm, 2.3 bars @ 2000 rpm (110°C)

Oil pressure warning switch operating pressure . . . . 0.8 bars

Torque wrench settings

	Nm	lbf ft
Auxiliary drivebelt tensioner roller	20	15
Big-end bolts: *		
Stage 1.	10	7
Stage 2.	Slacken 180°	
Stage 3.	10	7
Stage 4.	Angle-tighten a further 100°	
Camshaft bearing housing	10	7
Camshaft position sensor bolt.	5	4
Camshaft sprocket.	45	33
Coolant outlet housing bolts	10	7
Crankshaft position/speed sensor bolt	5	4
Crankshaft pulley/sprocket bolt:		
Stage 1.	30	22
Stage 2.	Angle-tighten a further 180°	
Cylinder head bolts:		
Stage 1.	20	15
Stage 2.	40	30
Stage 3.	Angle-tighten a further 260°	
Cylinder head cover bolts	10	7
Engine-to-transmission fixing bolts	45	33
Flywheel/driveplate bolts: *		
Stage 1.	15	11
Stage 2.	Angle-tighten a further 75°	
Fuel pump sprocket nut	50	37
Left-hand engine/transmission mounting:		
Mounting bracket-to-body bolts	20	15
Mounting stud-to-transmission bolts.	20	15
Mounting to bracket	30	22
Rubber mounting centre nut	60	44
Main bearing ladder seam bolts:		
Stage 1.	5	4
Stage 2.	10	7
Main bearing ladder to cylinder block: *		
Stage 1.	10	7
Stage 2.	Slacken 180°	
Stage 3.	30	22
Stage 4.	Angle-tighten a further 140°	
Piston oil jet spray tube bolt.	20	15
Oil pump to cylinder block	10	7
Rear engine/transmission mounting:		
Connecting link to mounting assembly	55	41
Connecting link-to-subframe nut/bolt	40	30
Mounting to engine	45	33
Right-hand engine mounting:		
Mounting to body	60	44
Mounting to support bracket	60	44
Support bracket to engine	55	41
Sump bolts/nuts.	10	7
Sump plug	16	12
Timing belt idler pulley	35	26
Timing belt tensioner pulley.	25	18

*Do not re-use

1 General Information

How to use this Chapter

1 This Part of Chapter 2 describes the repair procedures that can reasonably be carried out on the engine while it remains in the vehicle. If the engine has been removed from the vehicle and is being dismantled as described in Part F, any preliminary dismantling procedures can be ignored.

2 Note that, while it may be possible physically to overhaul items such as the piston/connecting rod assemblies while the engine is in the car, such tasks are not usually carried out as separate operations. Usually, several additional procedures are required (not to mention the cleaning of components and oilways); for this reason, all such tasks are classed as major overhaul procedures, and are described in Part F of this Chapter.

3 Part F describes the removal of the engine/transmission from the car, and the full overhaul procedures that can be carried out.

DV series engines

4 The DV series engine is the result of development collaboration between Peugeot/Citroën and Ford. It is a single overhead camshaft 8-valve design. The turbocharged, four-cylinder engine is mounted transversely, with the transmission mounted on the left-hand side.

5 A toothed timing belt drives the camshaft, high-pressure fuel pump and coolant pump. The camshaft operates the inlet and exhaust valves via rocker arms, which are supported at their pivot ends by hydraulic self-adjusting followers. The camshaft is supported by bearings machined directly in the cylinder head and camshaft bearing housing.

6 The high-pressure fuel pump supplies fuel to the fuel rail, and subsequently to the electronically-controlled injectors, which inject the fuel directly into the combustion chambers. This design differs from the previous type where an injection pump supplies the fuel at high pressure to each injector. The earlier, conventional type injection pump required fine calibration and timing, and these functions are now completed by the high-pressure pump, electronic injectors and engine management ECU.

7 The crankshaft runs in five main bearings of the usual shell type. Endfloat is controlled by thrustwashers either side of No 2 main bearing.

8 The pistons are selected to be of matching weight, and incorporate fully-floating gudgeon pins retained by circlips.

9 The oil pump is a gear type pump, which is fitted over the end of the crankshaft, and is driven by interlocking machined flats on the crankshaft and pump gear.

10 Throughout the manual, it is often necessary to identify the engines not only by their cubic capacity, but also by their engine code. The engine code consists of three letters (8HR). The code is stamped on a plate attached to the front of the cylinder block.

Precautions

11 The engine is a complex unit with numerous accessories and ancillary components. The design of the engine compartment is such that every conceivable space has been utilised, and access to virtually all of the engine components is extremely limited. In many cases, ancillary components will have to be removed, or moved to one side, and wiring, pipes and hoses will have to be disconnected or removed from various cable clips and support brackets.

12 When working on this engine, read through the entire procedure first, look at the car and engine at the same time, and establish whether you have the necessary tools, equipment, skill and patience to proceed. Allow considerable time for any operation, and be prepared for the unexpected. Any major work on these engines is not for the faint hearted!

13 Because of the limited access, many of the engine photographs appearing in this Chapter were, by necessity, taken with the engine removed from the vehicle.

⚠ **Warning: It is essential to observe strict precautions when working on the fuel system components of the engine, particularly the high-pressure side of the system. Before carrying out any engine operations that entail working on, or near, any part of the fuel system, refer to the special information given in Chapter 4A Section 1.**

Operations with engine in car

● Compression pressure – testing.
● Cylinder head cover – removal and refitting.
● Crankshaft pulley – removal and refitting.
● Timing belt covers – removal and refitting.
● Timing belt – removal, refitting and adjustment.
● Timing belt tensioner and sprockets – removal and refitting.
● Camshaft oil seal – renewal.
● Camshaft, rocker arms and hydraulic followers – removal, inspection and refitting.
● Sump – removal and refitting.
● Oil pump – removal and refitting.
● Crankshaft oil seals – renewal.
● Engine/transmission mountings – inspection and renewal.
● Flywheel/driveplate – removal, inspection and refitting.

2 Compression and leakdown tests – description and interpretation

Compression test

Note: *A compression tester specifically designed for diesel engines must be used for this test.*

1 When engine performance is down, or if misfiring occurs which cannot be attributed to the fuel system, a compression test can provide diagnostic clues as to the engine's condition. If the test is performed regularly, it can give warning of trouble before any other symptoms become apparent.

2 A compression tester specifically intended for diesel engines must be used, because of the higher pressures involved. The tester is connected to an adapter which screws into the glow plug or injector hole. On these engines, an adapter suitable for use in the glow plug holes will be required, so as not to disturb the fuel system components. It is unlikely to be worthwhile buying such a tester for occasional use, but it may be possible to borrow or hire one – if not, have the test performed by a garage.

3 Unless specific instructions to the contrary are supplied with the tester, observe the following points:

● The battery must be in a good state of charge, the air filter must be clean, and the engine should be at normal operating temperature.

● All the glow plugs should be removed as described in Chapter 5C Section 2 before starting the test.

● The wiring connector on the engine management system ECU (located in the plastic box behind the battery) must be disconnected.

4 The compression pressures measured are not so important as the balance between cylinders. Values are given in the Specifications.

5 The cause of poor compression is less easy to establish on a diesel engine than on a petrol engine. The effect of introducing oil into the cylinders ('wet' testing) is not conclusive, because there is a risk that the oil will sit in the swirl chamber or in the recess on the piston crown instead of passing to the rings. However, the following can be used as a rough guide to diagnosis.

6 All cylinders should produce very similar pressures; any difference greater than that specified indicates the existence of a fault. Note that the compression should build-up quickly in a healthy engine; low compression on the first stroke, followed by gradually increasing pressure on successive strokes, indicates worn piston rings. A low compression reading on the first stroke, which does not build-up during successive strokes, indicates leaking valves or a blown head gasket (a cracked head could also be

the cause). Deposits on the undersides of the valve heads can also cause low compression.

7 A low reading from two adjacent cylinders is almost certainly due to the head gasket having blown between them; the presence of coolant in the engine oil will confirm this.

8 If the compression reading is unusually high, the cylinder head surfaces, valves and pistons are probably coated with carbon deposits. If this is the case, the cylinder head should be removed and decarbonised (see Part F).

Leakdown test

9 A leakdown test measures the rate at which compressed air fed into the cylinder is lost. It is an alternative to a compression test, and in many ways it is better, since the escaping air provides easy identification of where pressure loss is occurring (piston rings, valves or head gasket).

10 The equipment needed for leakdown testing is unlikely to be available to the home mechanic. If poor compression is suspected, have the test performed by a suitably-equipped garage.

3 Engine assembly/valve timing holes – general information and usage

Note: *Do not attempt to rotate the engine whilst the crankshaft and camshaft are locked in position. If the engine is to be left in this state for a long period of time, it is a good idea to place suitable warning notices inside the vehicle, and in the engine compartment. This will reduce the possibility of the engine being accidentally cranked on the starter motor, which is likely to cause damage with the locking pins in place.*

1 Timing holes or slots are located in the crankshaft pulley flange and camshaft sprocket hub. The holes/slots are used to align the crankshaft and camshaft at the position when the pistons are halfway up the cylinder bores. This will ensure that the valve timing is maintained during operations that require removal and refitting of the timing belt. When the holes/slots are aligned with their corresponding holes in the cylinder block and cylinder head, suitable diameter bolts/pins can be inserted to lock the crankshaft and camshaft in position, preventing rotation.

2 Note that the HDi type fuel system used on these engines does not have a conventional diesel injection pump, but instead uses a high-pressure fuel pump. The alignment of the fuel pump sprocket (and hence the fuel pump itself) with respect to crankshaft and camshaft position is irrelevant, however Peugeot include this procedure for engines fitted with a Bosch high-pressure fuel pump. **Note:** *On the Bosch pump, the drive sprocket is keyed to the shaft. In addition, note that on these engines, the hole in the fuel pump sprocket only aligns correctly with the hole in the mounting bracket*

3.9 Insert a 5 mm drill through the hole in the crankshaft sprocket flange, and into the corresponding hole in the oil pump

every 12 revolutions of the crankshaft (or every 6 revolutions of the camshaft sprocket).

3 To align the engine assembly/valve timing holes, proceed as follows.

4 Apply the handbrake, then jack up the front of the vehicle and support it on axle stands (see *Jacking and vehicle support*). Remove the right-hand front roadwheel.

5 To gain access to the crankshaft pulley, to enable the engine to be turned, the wheel arch plastic liner must be removed. The liner is secured by several plastic expanding rivets. To remove the rivets, push in the centre pins a little, and then prise the clips from place. Remove the liner from under the front wing. The crankshaft can then be turned using a suitable socket and extension bar fitted to the pulley bolt.

6 Remove the upper and lower timing belt covers as described in Section 6.

7 Turn the crankshaft until the timing hole in the camshaft sprocket hub is aligned with the corresponding hole in the cylinder head. Note that the crankshaft must always be turned in a clockwise direction (viewed from the right-hand side of vehicle). Use a small mirror so that the position of the sprocket hub timing slot can be observed. When the slot is aligned with the corresponding hole in the cylinder head, the camshaft is positioned correctly.

8 Remove the crankshaft drivebelt pulley as described in Section 5.

9 Insert a 5 mm diameter bolt, rod or drill through the hole in crankshaft sprocket flange and into the corresponding hole in the oil pump **(see illustration)**, if necessary, carefully

4.3 Disconnect the mass airflow meter wiring plug

3.10 Insert an 8 mm drill through the hole in the camshaft sprocket, and into the corresponding hole in the cylinder head

turn the crankshaft either way until the rod enters the timing hole in the block.

10 Insert an 8 mm bolt, rod or drill through the hole in the camshaft sprocket hub and into engagement with the cylinder head **(see illustration)**.

11 If using this procedure during refitting of the timing belt on engines fitted with a Bosch high-pressure fuel pump, insert a 5 mm diameter bolt, rod or drill through the hole in the fuel pump sprocket and into the corresponding hole in the cylinder head. Note the comment in paragraph 2 – if the fuel pump sprocket holes are not aligned during removal of the timing belt, it is of no consequence, however it is important to align the holes during the refitting procedure. If timing alignment alone is being checked there is no need to check alignment of the pump sprocket.

4 Cylinder head cover – removal and refitting

Removal

1 Remove the plastic cover from the top of the engine, this simply pulls up from its place.

2 Remove the timing belt upper cover, as described in Section 6.

3 The cylinder head cover is integral with the inlet manifold and oil separator. Disconnect the mass airflow meter wiring plug **(see illustration)**.

4 Slacken the retaining clip, and remove the turbocharger outlet elbow **(see illustration)**.

4.4 Slacken the retaining clamps and disconnect the turbo outlet hose

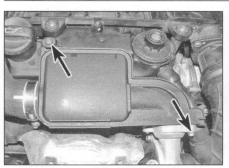

4.5a Undo the bolts (arrowed) and lift up
the right-hand end...

4.5b... to disengage the resonator box
from the turbocharger

4.7 Undo the two bolts (arrowed) and pull
the air filter housing up from its place

5 Undo the retaining bolts, lift up the right-hand end and remove the resonator **(see illustrations)**. Recover the O-ring seal.
6 Slacken the retaining clips and remove the air inlet ducting and turbocharger inlet hose. Slide up the plastic trim in the left-hand front corner of the engine compartment, push in the centre pin a little, prise out the rivet and remove the inlet ducting from the bonnet slam panel.
7 Unscrew the air filter housing bolts, and the filter cover bolts, then remove the cover and filter element – refer to Chapter 4B Section 4 **(see illustration)**. Release the diesel priming pump bulb from its retaining brackets at the right-hand end of the cylinder head, and remove the air filter housing. Disconnect any wiring plugs as necessary as the housing is withdrawn, having first noted their fitted positions.
8 Remove the diesel fuel filter as described in Chapter 1B Section 18, then undo the 3 bolts securing the diesel filter support bracket.
9 Disconnect the wiring plugs from the top of each injector, then make sure all wiring harnesses are freed from any retaining brackets on the cylinder head cover/inlet manifold. Disconnect any vacuum pipes as necessary, having first noted their fitted positions.
10 Prise out the retaining clips and disconnect the fuel return pipes from the injectors. Plug the openings to prevent dirt ingress.
11 Disconnect the fuel feed and return pipes

4.11 Depress the locking buttons (arrowed)
and disconnect the fuel feed and return
hoses

at the right-hand end of the cylinder head cover. Undo the Torx screw securing the fuel pipes bracket **(see illustration)**.
12 Unclip the fuel temperature sensor from the retaining bracket and move the pipe/priming bulb assembly to the rear.
13 Undo the two screws securing the EGR pipe to the cylinder head cover, and the bolt securing the pipe to the rear of the cylinder head **(see illustration)**.
14 Undo the two bolts securing the EGR valve to the left-hand end of the cylinder head, disconnect the vacuum hose, and then remove the valve along with the EGR pipe. Recover the O-ring seal from the pipe.
15 Undo the eight bolts securing the cylinder

4.13 Undo the bolt securing the EGR pipe
to the rear of the block (arrowed)

head cover and inlet manifold at the front, and the two retaining bolts along the rear edge of the cover. Lift the assembly away **(see illustrations)**. Recover the manifold rubber seals.

Refitting

16 Refitting is a reversal of removal, bearing in mind the following points:
● Examine the cover seal(s) for signs of damage and deterioration, and renew if necessary. Smear a little clean engine oil on the manifold seals.
● Tighten the cylinder head cover bolts to the specified torque, in the order shown **(see illustration)**.

4.15a Undo the 8 bolts (arrowed) at the
front...

4.15b... and the two bolts (arrowed) at the
rear

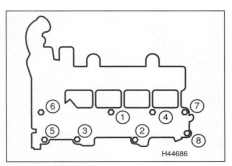

4.16 Cylinder head cover tightening
sequence

5.1 Insert a drill or pin to lock the auxiliary drivebelt tensioner in position

5.2 The locking pin/bolt (arrowed) must locate in the hole in the flywheel (arrowed) to prevent rotation

5.3 Undo the crankshaft pulley retaining bolt

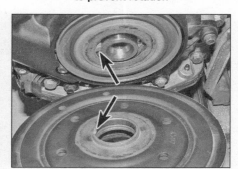

5.4 The notch in the pulley (arrowed) must align with the key in the sprocket (arrowed)

5 Crankshaft pulley – removal and refitting

Removal

1 Remove the auxiliary drivebelt as described in Chapter 1B Section 16. Turn the tensioner anti-clockwise and insert a pin or drill to hold it away from the drivebelt **(see illustration)**.

2 To lock the crankshaft, working underneath the engine, insert Peugeot tool No 0194-C into the hole in the right-hand face of the engine block casting over the lower section of the flywheel. Rotate the crankshaft until the tool engages in the corresponding hole in the flywheel. In the absence of the Peugeot tool,

insert a 12 mm rod or drill into the hole **(see illustration)**. Note: *The hole in the casting and the hole in the flywheel are provided purely to lock the crankshaft whilst the pulley bolt is undone, it does not position the crankshaft at TDC.*

3 Using a suitable socket and extension bar, unscrew the retaining bolt, remove the washer, then slide the pulley off the end of the crankshaft **(see illustration)**. If the pulley is a tight fit, it can be drawn off the crankshaft using a suitable puller. If a puller is being used, refit the pulley retaining bolt without the washer to avoid damaging the crankshaft as the puller is tightened.

Caution: Do not touch the outer magnetic sensor ring of the sprocket with your fingers, or allow metallic particles to come into contact with it.

Refitting

4 Refit the pulley to the end of the crankshaft **(see illustration)**.
5 Thoroughly clean the threads of the pulley retaining bolt, and then apply a coat of locking compound to the bolt threads. Peugeot recommend the use of Loctite (available from your Peugeot dealer); in the absence of this, any good-quality locking compound may be used.
6 Refit the crankshaft pulley retaining bolt and washer. Tighten the bolt to the specified torque, then through the specified angle, preventing the crankshaft from turning using the method employed on removal.
7 Refit and tension the auxiliary drivebelt.

6 Timing belt covers – removal and refitting

> **Warning: Refer to the precautionary information contained in Section 1 before proceeding.**

Upper cover removal

1 Remove the plastic covers from the top of the engine; this simply pulls up from its place.
2 Release the wiring harness and fuel pipes from the upper cover **(see illustration)**.
3 Undo the five screws and remove the timing belt upper cover **(see illustration)**.

Lower cover removal

4 Remove the upper cover as described previously.
5 Remove the crankshaft pulley as described in Section 5.
6 Undo the five bolts and withdraw the lower cover **(see illustration)**.

Refitting

7 Refitting of the covers is a reversal of the relevant removal procedure, ensuring that each cover section is correctly located, and that the cover retaining bolts are securely tightened. Ensure that any disturbed hoses or wiring are reconnected and retained by their relevant clips.

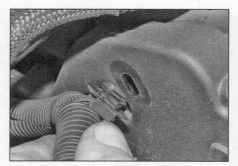

6.2 Release the wiring harness from the timing belt upper cover

6.3 Undo the 5 screws (arrowed) and remove the upper timing belt cover

6.6 Lower cover retaining bolts (arrowed)

7.8 Undo the bolt securing the crankshaft position sensor (arrowed)

7.9 Timing belt protection bracket retaining bolt (arrowed)

7.13 Insert an Allen key into the hole (arrowed), slacken the pulley bolt and allow the tensioner to rotate

7 Timing belt – removal, inspection, refitting and tensioning

Note: *Early models are identified by three bolts securing the camshaft sprocket to the hub. Later engines are identified by the camshaft sprocket being retained by one central bolt.*

General

1 The timing belt drives the camshaft(s), high-pressure fuel pump and coolant pump from a toothed sprocket on the end of the crankshaft. If the belt breaks or slips in service, the pistons are likely to hit the valve heads, resulting in expensive damage.

2 The timing belt should be renewed at the specified intervals, or earlier if it is contaminated with oil or at all noisy in operation (a 'scraping' noise due to uneven wear).

3 If the timing belt is being removed, it is a wise precaution to check the condition of the coolant pump at the same time (check for signs of coolant leakage). This may avoid the need to remove the timing belt again at a later stage, should the coolant pump fail.

Removal

4 Apply the handbrake, then jack up the front of the vehicle and support it on axle stands (see *Jacking and vehicle support*). Remove the front right-hand roadwheel, and remove the wheel arch liner and the engine undershield.

5 Refer to Chapter 4B Section 18 and remove the complete exhaust system.

Caution: If the exhaust system is not removed, the front pipe flexible section will be damaged when the right-hand engine mounting is detached.

6 Remove the auxiliary drivebelt as described in Chapter 1B Section 16.

7 Remove the upper and lower timing belt covers, as described in Section 6.

8 Undo the screw and remove the crankshaft position sensor adjacent to the crankshaft sprocket flange, and move it to one side **(see illustration)**.

9 Undo the retaining screw and remove the

timing belt protection bracket, again adjacent to the crankshaft sprocket flange **(see illustration)**.

10 Lock the crankshaft and camshaft in the correct position as described in Section 3. If necessary, temporarily refit the crankshaft pulley bolt to enable the crankshaft to be rotated.

11 Position a trolley jack under the engine, and using a block of wood on the jack head, take the weight of the engine.

12 Undo the bolts and remove the right hand engine mounting and support bracket – see Section 17.

13 Insert a hexagon key into belt tensioner pulley centre, slacken the pulley bolt, and allow the tensioner to rotate, relieving the belt tension **(see illustration)**. With the belt slack, temporarily tighten the pulley bolt.

7.17 Timing belt routing

1 Camshaft sprocket
2 Idler pulley
3 Crankshaft sprocket
4 Coolant pump sprocket
5 Tensioner pulley
6 High-pressure fuel pump pulley

14 Note its routing, then remove the timing belt from the sprockets.

Inspection

15 Renew the belt as a matter of course, regardless of its apparent condition. The cost of a new belt is nothing compared with the cost of repairs, should the belt break in service. If signs of oil contamination are found, trace the source of the oil leak and rectify it. Wash down the engine timing belt area and all related components, to remove all traces of oil. Check that the tensioner and idler pulleys rotate freely without any sign of roughness, and also check that the coolant pump pulley rotates freely. If necessary, renew these items. **Note:** *Peugeot recommend that the tensioner and idler pulleys should not be re-used, regardless of apparent condition.*

Refitting and tensioning

16 Commence refitting by ensuring that the crankshaft and camshaft timing pins are still in position correctly.

17 Locate the timing belt on the crankshaft sprocket then, keeping it taut, locate it around the idler pulley, camshaft sprocket, high-pressure pump sprocket, coolant pump sprocket, and the tensioner roller **(see illustration)**.

18 Refit the timing belt protection bracket and tighten the retaining bolt securely.

19 Slacken the tensioner pulley bolt and, using a hexagonal key, rotate the tensioner anti-clockwise, which moves the index arm clockwise, until the index arm is aligned **(see illustration)**.

7.19 Align the index arm (A) with the locating stud (B)

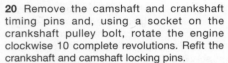

A sprocket holding tool can be made from two lengths of steel strip bolted together to form a forked end. Bend the end of the strip through 90° to form the fork 'prongs'.

20 Remove the camshaft and crankshaft timing pins and, using a socket on the crankshaft pulley bolt, rotate the engine clockwise 10 complete revolutions. Refit the crankshaft and camshaft locking pins.

21 Check that the tensioner index arm is still aligned between the edges of the area **(see illustration 7.19)**. If it is not, remove and belt and begin the refitting process again, starting at Paragraph 17.

22 The remainder of refitting is a reversal of removal. Tighten all fasteners to the specified torque where given.

8 Timing belt sprockets and tensioner – removal and refitting

Camshaft sprocket

Removal

1 Remove the timing belt as described in Section 7.

2 Remove the locking tool from the camshaft sprocket/hub. Slacken the sprocket hub retaining bolt, and the three sprocket-to-hub retaining bolts (where applicable). To prevent the camshaft rotating as the bolts are slackened, a sprocket holding tool will be required. In the absence of the special Peugeot tool, an acceptable substitute can

8.11 Slide the crankshaft sprocket off the end of the crankshaft

8.3 Undo the retaining bolt and remove the camshaft sprocket

be fabricated at home **(see Tool Tip 1)**. Do not attempt to use the engine assembly/valve timing locking tool to prevent the sprocket from rotating whilst the bolt is slackened.

3 Remove the sprocket hub retaining bolt and washer (where fitted), and slide the sprocket and hub off the end of the camshaft **(see illustration)**. Examine the camshaft oil seal for signs of oil leakage and, if necessary, renew it as described in Section 14.

4 Clean the camshaft sprocket thoroughly, and renew it if there are any signs of wear, damage or cracks.

Refitting

5 Refit the camshaft sprocket and hub onto the end of the camshaft **(see illustration)**.

6 Refit the sprocket hub retaining bolt and washer. Tighten the bolt to the specified torque, preventing the camshaft from turning as during removal.

7 Align the engine assembly/valve timing slot in the camshaft sprocket hub with the hole in the cylinder head and refit the timing pin to lock the camshaft in position.

8 Fit the timing belt around the pump sprocket and camshaft sprocket, and tension the timing belt as described in Section 7.

Crankshaft sprocket

Removal

9 Remove the timing belt as described in Section 7.

10 Check that the engine assembly/valve timing holes are still aligned as described in Section 3, and the camshaft sprocket/hub and flywheel/driveplate are locked in position.

8.17 Insert a suitable drill bit through the sprocket into the hole in the backplate

8.5 Align the sprocket lug with the notch in the end of the camshaft (arrowed)

11 Slide the sprocket off the end of the crankshaft **(see illustration)**.

12 Examine the crankshaft oil seal for signs of oil leakage and, if necessary, renew it as described in Section 14.

13 Clean the crankshaft sprocket thoroughly, and renew it if there are any signs of wear, damage or cracks.

Refitting

14 Refit the crankshaft sprocket (with the flange facing the crankshaft pulley).

15 Fit the timing belt around the crankshaft sprocket, and tension the timing belt as described in Section 7.

Fuel pump sprocket

Removal

16 Remove the timing belt as described in Section 7.

17 Using a suitable socket, undo the pump sprocket retaining nut. The sprocket can be held stationary by inserting a suitably-sized locking pin, drill or rod through the hole in the sprocket, and into the corresponding hole in the backplate **(see illustration)**, or by using a suitable forked tool engaged with the holes in the sprocket **(see Tool Tip 1)**.

18 The pump sprocket is a taper fit on the pump shaft and it will be necessary to make up another tool to release it from the taper **(see Tool Tip 2)**.

Make a sprocket releasing tool from a short strip of steel. Drill two holes in the strip to correspond with the two holes in the sprocket. Drill a third hole just large enough to accept the flats of the sprocket retaining nut.

9.4 Undo the vacuum pump bolts (arrowed)

9.6 Upper camshaft bearing housing bolts (arrowed)

19 Partially unscrew the sprocket retaining nut, fit the homemade tool, and secure it to the sprocket with two suitable bolts. Prevent the sprocket from rotating as before, and unscrew the sprocket retaining nut. The nut will bear against the tool, as it is undone, forcing the sprocket off the shaft taper. Once the taper is released, remove the tool, unscrew the nut fully, and remove the sprocket from the pump shaft.
20 Clean the sprocket thoroughly, and renew it if there are any signs of wear, damage or cracks.

Refitting

21 Refit the pump sprocket and retaining nut, and tighten the nut to the specified torque. Prevent the sprocket rotating as the nut is tightened using the sprocket holding tool.
22 Fit the timing belt around the pump sprocket, and tension the timing belt as described in Section 7.

Coolant pump sprocket

23 The coolant pump sprocket is integral with the pump, and cannot be removed. Coolant pump removal is described in Chapter 3 Section 8.

Tensioner pulley

Removal

24 Remove the timing belt as described in Section 7.
25 Remove the tensioner pulley retaining bolt, and slide the pulley off its mounting stud.
26 Clean the tensioner pulley, but do not use any strong solvent, which may enter the bearings. Check that the pulley rotates freely, with no sign of stiffness or free play. Renew the pulley if there is any doubt about its condition, or if there are any obvious signs of wear or damage.
27 Examine the pulley mounting stud for signs of damage and if necessary, renew it.

Refitting

28 Refit the tensioner pulley to its mounting stud, and fit the retaining bolt.

29 Refit the timing belt as described in Section 7.

Idler pulley

Removal

30 Remove the timing belt as described in Section 7.
31 Undo the retaining bolt/nut and withdraw the idler pulley from the engine.
32 Clean the idler pulley, but do not use any strong solvent, which may enter the bearings. Check that the pulley rotates freely, with no sign of stiffness or free play. Renew the idler pulley if there is any doubt about its condition, or if there are any obvious signs of wear or damage.

Refitting

33 Locate the idler pulley on the engine, and fit the retaining bolt/nut. Tighten the bolt/nut to the specified torque.
34 Refit the timing belt as described in Section 7.

9 Camshaft, rocker arms and hydraulic followers – removal, inspection and refitting

Removal

1 Remove the cylinder head cover as described in Section 4.
2 Remove the camshaft sprocket as described in Section 8.
3 Refit the right-hand engine mounting, but only tighten the bolts moderately; this will keep the engine supported during the camshaft removal.
4 Undo the bolts and remove the vacuum pump. Recover the pump O-ring seals (see illustration).
5 Disconnect the wiring plug, unscrew the retaining bolt, and remove the camshaft position sensor from the cylinder head.
6 Working in a spiral pattern, progressively

and evenly unscrew the camshaft upper bearing housing bolts (see illustration). Carefully lift the housing away.
7 Note the orientation of the camshaft, then lift it upwards from the housing and slide off and discard the oil seal.
8 To remove the rocker arms and hydraulic followers, undo the 13 bolts and remove the lower half of the camshaft bearing housing.
9 Obtain eight small, clean plastic containers, and number them 1 to 8; alternatively, divide a larger container into eight compartments.
10 Lift out each rocker arm. Place the rocker arms in their respective positions in the box or containers (see illustration).
11 A compartmentalised container filled with engine oil is now required to retain the hydraulic followers while they are removed from the cylinder head. Withdraw each hydraulic follower and place it in the container, keeping them each identified for correct refitting. The followers must be totally submerged in the oil to prevent air entering them.
12 Recover the 5 O-ring seals between the housing and the cylinder head.

Inspection

13 Inspect the cam lobes and the camshaft bearing journals for scoring or other visible evidence of wear. Once the surface hardening

9.10 Remove the rocker arms

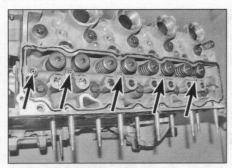

9.22 Apply a bead of sealant, and fit the new O-rings (arrowed)

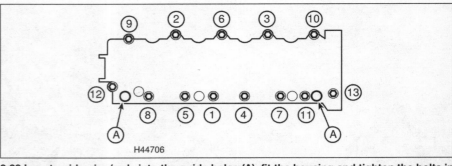

9.23 Insert guide pins/rods into the guide holes (A), fit the housing and tighten the bolts in sequence

9.25 Lay the camshaft in position, and apply a bead of sealant to the housing mating face

of the cam lobes has been eroded, wear will occur at an accelerated rate. **Note:** *If these symptoms are visible on the tips of the camshaft lobes, check the corresponding rocker arm, as it will probably be worn as well.*
14 Examine the condition of the bearing surfaces in the cylinder head and camshaft bearing housing. If wear is evident, the cylinder head and bearing housing will both have to be renewed, as they are a matched assembly.
15 Inspect the rocker arms and followers for scuffing, cracking or other damage and renew any components as necessary. Also check the condition of the tappet bores in the cylinder head. As with the camshafts, any wear in this area will necessitate cylinder head renewal.

Refitting

16 Thoroughly clean the sealant from the mating surfaces of the cylinder head and camshaft bearing housing. Use a suitable liquid gasket-dissolving agent (available from Peugeot dealers) together with a soft putty knife; do not use a metal scraper or the faces will be damaged. As there is no conventional gasket used, the cleanliness of the mating faces is of the utmost importance.
17 Clean off any oil, dirt or grease from both components and dry with a clean lint-free cloth. Ensure that all the oilways are completely clean.
18 With the timing marks aligned as described in Section 3, the pistons should be positioned halfway down the cylinder bores.
19 Liberally lubricate the hydraulic tappet bores in the cylinder head with clean engine oil.
20 Insert the hydraulic followers into their original bores in the cylinder head unless they have been renewed.
21 Lubricate the rocker arms and place them over their respective followers and valve stems.
22 Sparingly apply a bead of silicone sealant to the mating face of the cylinder head-to-camshaft lower bearing housing, and position the 5 new O-ring seals **(see illustration)**.
23 Insert two 12 mm rods or drill bits into the locating holes in the cylinder head to guide the bearing housing into position. Suitable guide rods, No 194-N, are available from Peugeot dealers. Refit the lower bearing housing over the tools, insert the bolts and finger-tighten them in order **(see illustration)**.
24 Remove the guide pins/rods and tighten the housing bolts in the sequence shown previously to the specified torque.

25 Lubricate the camshaft bearing journals with clean engine oil, and lay the camshaft in position. Sparingly apply a bead of silicone sealant to the mating face of the camshaft lower bearing housing **(see illustration)**.
26 Insert two 12 mm rods or drill bits into the locating holes in the lower camshaft bearing housing to guide the upper housing into position. Suitable guide rods, No 194-N, are available from Peugeot dealers.
27 Lower the upper housing over the guide pins/rods, and finger-tighten the bolts gradually and evenly, in sequence until the housing makes firm contact with the lower housing **(see illustration)**.
28 Remove the guide pins/rods and tighten the housing to the specified torque in the same sequence.
29 Fit a new camshaft oil seal as described in Section 14.
30 Ensure the key is fitted to the camshaft, then refit the camshaft sprocket to the camshaft and tighten the bolt to the specified torque.
31 Refit the camshaft position sensor to the camshaft housing, and position the sensor so that the gap between the sprocket and the sensor end is 1.2 mm for a used sensor. If fitting a new sensor, the small tip of the sensor must be just touching one of the three webs of the signal ring **(see illustration)**. Tighten the bolt to the specified torque.
32 Turn the camshaft sprocket the position where the timing tool can be inserted, then refit the timing belt as described in Section 7.
33 The remainder of refitting is a reversal of removal.

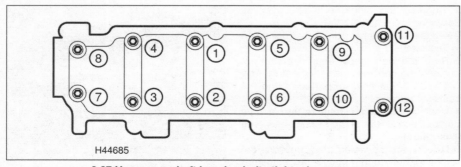

9.27 Upper camshaft housing bolts tightening sequence

9.31 When fitting a used sensor, the gap between the sensor end and the sensor ring web should be 1.2 mm

10.8 Auxiliary drivebelt tensioner bolts (arrowed)

10.13a Fuel pump rear support bracket bolts (arrowed)...

10.13b... and front support bracket upper bolt

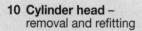

10 Cylinder head – removal and refitting

Note: *This is an involved procedure, and it is suggested that the Section is read thoroughly before starting work. To aid refitting, make notes on the locations of all relevant brackets and the routing of hoses and cables before removal.*

Removal

1 Apply the handbrake, then jack up the front of the vehicle and support it on axle stands (see *Jacking and vehicle support*). Remove the front right-hand roadwheel, the engine undershield, and the front wheel arch liner.
2 Remove the battery (see Chapter 5A Section 4).
3 Drain the cooling system as described in Chapter 1B Section 22. For improved general access, remove the bonnet.
4 Remove the cylinder head cover as described in Section 4.
5 Remove the timing belt as described in Section 7.
6 Disconnect the exhaust front pipe from the manifold, as described in Chapter 4B Section 18. **Note:** *Do not allow any strain to be placed on the flexible section of the exhaust pipe, as damage will result.*
7 Remove the glow plugs as described in Chapter 5C Section 2.
8 Undo the three bolts and remove the auxiliary drivebelt tensioner from the front of the engine **(see illustration)**.
9 Remove the catalytic converter as described in Section of Chapter 4B.
10 Remove the alternator (see Chapter 5A Section 7) and mounting bracket.
11 Undo the union bolts and remove the oil feed pipe from the engine block and the turbocharger. Recover the unions sealing washers.
12 Slacken the retaining clamp and disconnect the turbocharger oil return hose from the engine block.
13 Slacken and remove the high-pressure fuel pump rear support bracket bolts and front support bracket upper bolt **(see illustrations)**.
14 Remove the injectors as described in Chapter 4B Section 11.

15 Undo the coolant outlet housing (left-hand end of the cylinder head) retaining bolts, slacken the two bolts securing the housing support bracket to the top of the transmission bellhousing, and move the outlet housing away from the cylinder head a little **(see illustration)**. There is no need to disconnect the hoses.
16 Disconnect the wiring plug, then undo the bolt and remove the camshaft position sensor from the cylinder head.
17 Undo the 13 bolts and remove the camshaft bearing housing from the cylinder head, complete with camshaft. Recover the 5 small O-ring seals between the housing and the cylinder head.
18 Obtain eight small, clean plastic containers, and number them 1 to 8; alternatively, divide a larger container into eight compartments.
19 Lift out each rocker arm. Place the rocker arms in their respective positions in the box or containers **(see illustration 9.10)**.
20 A compartmentalised container filled with engine oil is now required to retain the hydraulic followers while they are removed from the cylinder head. Withdraw each hydraulic follower and place it in the container, keeping them each identified for correct refitting. The followers must be totally submerged in the oil to prevent air entering them.
21 Working in the reverse of the tightening sequence **(see illustration 10.42)** undo the cylinder head bolts.
22 Release the cylinder head from the cylinder block and location dowels by rocking it. The Peugeot tool for doing this consists

10.15 Coolant housing bolts (arrowed)

simply of two metal rods with 90-degree angled ends **(see illustration)**. Do not prise between the mating faces of the cylinder head and block, as this may damage the gasket faces.
23 Lift the cylinder head from the block, and recover the gasket.
24 If necessary, remove the manifolds (if not already done) with reference to Chapter 4B.

Preparation for refitting

25 The mating faces of the cylinder head and cylinder block must be perfectly clean before refitting the head. Peugeot recommend the use of a scouring agent for this purpose, but acceptable results can be achieved by using a hard plastic or wood scraper to remove all traces of gasket and carbon. The same method can be used to clean the piston crowns. Take particular care to avoid scoring or gouging the cylinder head/cylinder block mating surfaces during the cleaning operations, as aluminium alloy is easily damaged. Make sure that the carbon is not allowed to enter the oil and water passages – this is particularly important for the lubrication system, as carbon could block the oil supply to the engine's components. Using adhesive tape and paper, seal the water, oil and bolt holes in the cylinder block. To prevent carbon entering the gap between the pistons and bores, smear a little grease in the gap. After

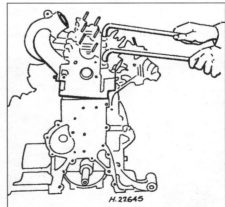

10.22 Free the cylinder head using angled rods

10.31 Measure the piston protrusion using a DTI gauge

10.33 Cylinder head gasket thickness identification notches (arrowed)

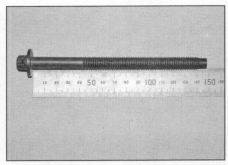

10.34 Measure the length of from under the bolt head to its end

cleaning each piston, use a small brush to remove all traces of grease and carbon from the gap, then wipe away the remainder with a clean rag.

26 Check the mating surfaces of the cylinder block and the cylinder head for nicks, deep scratches and other damage. If slight, they may be removed carefully with a file, but if excessive, machining may be the only alternative to renewal. If warpage of the cylinder head gasket surface is suspected, use a straight-edge to check it for distortion. Refer to Part F of this Chapter if necessary.

27 Thoroughly clean the threads of the cylinder head bolt holes in the cylinder block. Ensure that the bolts run freely in their threads, and that all traces of oil and water are removed from each bolt hole.

Gasket selection

28 Remove the crankshaft timing pin, then turn the crankshaft until pistons 1 and 4 are at TDC (Top Dead Centre). Position a dial test indicator (dial gauge) on the cylinder block adjacent to the rear of No 1 piston, and zero it on the block face. Transfer the probe to the crown of No 1 piston (10.0 mm in from the rear edge), and then slowly turn the crankshaft back-and-forth past TDC, noting the highest reading on the indicator. Record this reading as protrusion A.

29 Repeat the check described in para- graph 28, this time 10.0 mm in from the front edge of the No 1 piston crown. Record this reading as protrusion B.

30 Add protrusion A to protrusion B, then

divide the result by 2 to obtain an average reading for piston No 1.

31 Repeat the procedure described in para- graphs 28 to 30 on piston No 4, then turn the crankshaft through 180°, and carry out the procedure on the piston Nos 2 and 3 **(see illustration)**. Check that there is a maximum difference of 0.07 mm protrusion between any two pistons.

32 If a dial test indicator is not available, piston protrusion may be measured using a straight-edge and feeler blades or Vernier calipers. However, this is much less accurate, and cannot therefore be recommended.

33 Note the greatest piston protrusion measurement, and use this to determine the correct cylinder head gasket from the following table. The series of notches/holes on the side of the gasket are used for thickness identification **(see illustration)**.

Piston protrusion	Gasket identification
0.618 to 0.725 mm	2 notches
0.726 to 0.775 mm	3 notches
0.776 to 0.825 mm	1 notch
0.826 to 0.875 mm	4 notches
0.876 to 0.983 mm	5 notches

Head bolt examination

34 Carefully examine the cylinder head bolts for signs of damage to the threads or head, and for any sign of corrosion. If the bolts are in a satisfactory condition, measure the length of each bolt from the underside of the head,

to the end of the shank. The bolts may be re-used providing that the measured length does not exceed 149.0 mm **(see illustration)**. **Note:** *Considering the stress to which the cylinder head bolts are subjected, it is highly recommended that they are all renewed, regardless of their apparent condition.*

Refitting

35 Turn the crankshaft and position Nos 1 and 4 pistons at TDC, then turn the crankshaft a quarter turn (90°) anti-clockwise.

36 Thoroughly clean the surfaces of the cylinder head and block.

37 Make sure that the locating dowels are in place, then fit the correct gasket the right way round on the cylinder block **(see illustration)**.

38 If necessary refit the exhaust manifold to the cylinder head as described in Chapter 4B Section 14.

39 Carefully lower the cylinder head onto the gasket and block, making sure that it locates correctly onto the dowels.

40 Apply a smear of grease to the threads, and to the underside of the heads, of the cylinder head bolts. Peugeot recommend the use of Molykote G Rapid Plus (available from your Peugeot dealer); in the absence of the specified grease, any good-quality high melting-point grease may be used.

41 Carefully insert the cylinder head bolts into their holes (do not drop them in) and initially finger-tighten them.

42 Working progressively and in sequence, tighten the cylinder head bolts to their Stage 1 torque setting, using a torque wrench and suitable socket **(see illustration)**.

43 Once all the bolts have been tightened to their Stage 1 torque setting, working again in the specified sequence, tighten each bolt to the specified Stage 2 setting. Finally, angle-tighten the bolts through the specified Stage 3 angle. It is recommended that an angle-measuring gauge is used during this stage of tightening, to ensure accuracy. **Note:** *Retightening of the cylinder head bolts after running the engine is not required.*

44 Refit the hydraulic followers, rocker arms, and camshaft housing (complete with camshaft) as described in Section 9.

45 Refit the timing belt as described in Section 7.

10.37 Ensure the gasket fits correctly over the locating dowels

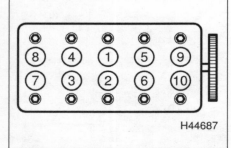

10.42 Cylinder head bolt tightening sequence

H44687

46 The remainder of refitting is a reversal of removal, noting the following points.

● Use a new seal when refitting the coolant outlet housing.

● When refitting a cylinder head, it is good practice to renew the thermostat.

● Refit the camshaft position sensor and set the air gap with reference to Chapter 4B Section 12.

● Tighten all fasteners to the specified torque where given.

● Refill the cooling system as described in Chapter 1B Section 22.

● The engine may run erratically for the first few miles, until the engine management ECM relearns its stored values.

11 Sump – removal and refitting

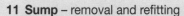

Removal

1 Drain the engine oil, then clean and refit the engine oil drain plug, tightening it securely. If the engine is nearing its service interval when the oil and filter are due for renewal, it is recommended that the filter is also removed, and a new one fitted. After reassembly, the engine can then be refilled with fresh oil. Refer to Chapter 1B Section 6 for further information.

2 Apply the handbrake, then jack up the front of the vehicle and support it on axle stands (see *Jacking and vehicle support*). Undo the screws and remove the engine undershield.

3 To improve access, remove the exhaust front pipe as described in Chapter 4B Section 18.

4 Where necessary, disconnect the wiring connector from the oil temperature sender unit, which is screwed into the sump.

5 Progressively slacken and remove all of the sump retaining bolts/nuts. Since the sump bolts vary in length, remove each bolt in turn, and store it in its correct fitted order by pushing it through a clearly marked cardboard template. This will avoid the possibility of installing the bolts in the wrong locations on refitting.

6 Try to break the joint by striking the sump with the palm of your hand, then lower and

11.9 Apply a bead of sealant to the sump of crankcase mating surface

withdraw the sump from under the car. If the sump is stuck, use a putty knife or similar carefully inserted between the sump and block. Ease the knife along the joint until the sump is released.

7 While the sump is removed, take the opportunity to check the oil pump pick-up/strainer for signs of clogging or splitting. If necessary, remove the pump as described in Section 12, and clean or renew the strainer.

Refitting

8 Clean all traces of sealant/gasket from the mating surfaces of the cylinder block/crankcase and sump, and then use a clean rag to wipe out the sump and the engine's interior.

9 On engines where the sump was fitted without a gasket, ensure that the sump mating surfaces are clean and dry, then apply a thin coating of suitable sealant to the sump or crankcase mating surface **(see illustration)**.

10 Offer up the sump to the cylinder block/crankcase. Refit its retaining bolts/nuts, ensuring that each bolt is screwed into its original location. Tighten the bolts evenly and progressively to the specified torque setting **(see illustration)**.

11 Where necessary, align the air conditioning compressor with its mountings on the sump, and insert the retaining bolts. Securely tighten the compressor retaining bolts, and then refit the drivebelt as described in chapter 1B Section 16.

12 Reconnect the wiring connector to the oil temperature sensor (where fitted).

11.10 Refit the sump and tighten the bolts

13 Lower the vehicle to the ground, and then refill the engine with oil as described in Chapter 1B Section 6.

12 Oil pump – removal, inspection and refitting

Removal

1 Remove the sump as described in Section 11.

2 Remove the crankshaft sprocket as described in Section 8. Recover the locating key from the crankshaft.

3 Disconnect the wiring plug, undo the bolts and remove the crankshaft position sensor, located on the right-hand end of the cylinder block.

4 Undo the three Allen bolts and remove the oil pump pick-up tube from the pump/block, complete with the dipstick guide tube **(see illustration)**. Discard the oil seal; a new one must be fitted.

5 Undo the 8 bolts, and remove the oil pump **(see illustration)**.

Inspection

6 Undo and remove the Torx screws securing the cover to the oil pump **(see illustration)**. Examine the pump rotors and body for signs of wear and damage. If worn, the complete pump must be renewed.

7 Remove the circlip, and extract the cap, valve piston and spring, noting which way

12.4 Undo the three Allen bolts (arrowed) and remove the oil pick-up tube

12.5 Undo the 8 bolts (arrowed) and remove the oil pump

12.6 Undo the Torx screws and remove the pump cover

12.7a Remove the circlip...

12.7b... cap...

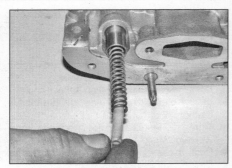

12.7c... spring...

12.7d... and piston

12.11 Apply a bead of sealant to the cylinder block mating surface

around they are fitted **(see illustrations)**. The condition of the relief valve spring can only be measured by comparing it with a new one; if there is any doubt about its condition, it should also be renewed.

8 Refit the relief valve piston and spring, then secure them in place with the circlip.

9 Refit the cover to the oil pump, and tighten the Torx screws securely.

Refitting

10 Remove all traces of sealant, and thoroughly clean the mating surfaces of the oil pump and cylinder block.

11 Apply a 4 mm wide bead of silicone sealant to the mating face of the cylinder block **(see illustration)**. Ensure that no sealant enters any of the holes in the block.

12 With a new oil seal fitted, refit the oil pump over the end of the crankshaft, aligning the flats in the pump drivegear with the flats machined in the crankshaft **(see illustrations)**. Note that new oil pumps are supplied with the oil seal already fitted, and a seal protector

sleeve. The sleeve fits over the end of the crankshaft to protect the seal as the pump is fitted.

13 Install the oil pump bolts and tighten them to the specified torque.

14 Refit the oil pick-up tube to the pump/cylinder block using a new O-ring seal. Ensure the oil dipstick guide tube is correctly refitted.

15 Refit the Woodruff key to the crankshaft, and slide the crankshaft sprocket into place.

16 The remainder of refitting is a reversal of removal.

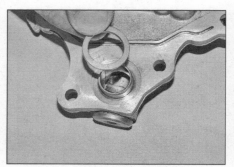

12.12a Fit a new oil seal...

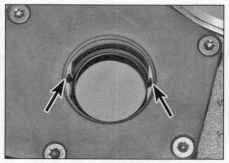

12.12b... align the pump gear flats (arrowed)...

12.12c... with those of the crankshaft (arrowed)

13 Oil cooler –
removal and refitting

Removal

1 Apply the handbrake, then jack up the front of the vehicle and support it on axle stands (see *Jacking and vehicle support*). Undo the screws and remove the engine undershield.
2 The oil cooler is fitted to the front of the oil filter housing. Drain the coolant as described in Chapter 1B Section 22.
3 Drain the engine oil as described in Chapter 1B Section 6, or be prepared for fluid spillage.
4 Undo the bolts and remove the oil cooler. Recover the O-ring seals **(see illustrations)**. **Note:** *depending on model there may either 4 or 5 mounting bolts on the oil cooler.*

Refitting

5 Fit new O-ring seals into the recesses in the oil filter housing, and refit the cooler. Tighten the bolts securely.
6 Refill or top-up the cooling system and engine oil level as described in Chapter 1B or *Weekly checks* (as applicable). Start the engine, and check the oil cooler for signs of leakage.

14 Oil seals – renewal

Crankshaft right-hand oil seal

1 Remove the crankshaft sprocket as described in Section 8.
2 Measure and note the fitted depth of the oil seal.
3 Pull the oil seal from the housing using a hooked instrument. Alternatively, drill a small hole in the oil seal, and use a self-tapping screw and a pair of pliers to remove it **(see illustration)**.
4 Clean the oil seal housing and the crankshaft sealing surface.

13.4a Undo the bolts (arrowed), remove the oil cooler...

5 The seal has a Teflon lip and must not be oiled or marked. The new seal should be supplied with a protector sleeve, which fits over the end of the crankshaft to prevent any damage to the seal lip. With the sleeve in place, press the seal (open end first) into the pump to the previously-noted depth, using a suitable tube or socket.
6 Where applicable, remove the plastic or tape from the end of the crankshaft.
7 Refit the timing belt crankshaft sprocket as described in Section 8.

Crankshaft left-hand oil seal

8 Remove the flywheel/driveplate, as described in Section 16.
9 Measure and note the fitted depth of the oil seal.
10 Pull the oil seal from the housing using a hooked instrument. Alternatively, drill a small hole in the oil seal, and use a self-tapping screw and a pair of pliers to remove it **(see illustration 14.3)**.
11 Clean the oil seal housing and the crankshaft sealing surface.
12 The seal has a Teflon lip and must not be oiled or marked. The new seal should be supplied with a protector sleeve, which fits over the end of the crankshaft to prevent any damage to the seal lip **(see illustration)**. With the sleeve in place, press the seal (open end first) into the housing to the previously-noted depth, using a suitable tube or socket.

13.4b... and recover the O-ring seals

13 Where applicable, remove the plastic or tape from the end of the crankshaft.
14 Refit the flywheel/driveplate, as described in Section 16.

Camshaft right-hand oil seal

15 Remove the camshaft sprocket (and hub where applicable) as described in Section 8. In principle there is no need to remove the timing belt completely, but remember that if the belt has been contaminated with oil, it must be renewed.
16 Pull the oil seal from the housing using a hooked instrument. Alternatively, drill a small hole in the oil seal and use a self-tapping screw and a pair of pliers to remove it **(see illustration 14.3)**.
17 Clean the oil seal housing and the camshaft sealing surface.
18 The seal has a Teflon lip and must not be oiled or marked. The new seal should be supplied with a protector sleeve, which fits over the end of the camshaft to prevent any damage to the seal lip **(see illustration)**. With the sleeve in place, press the seal (open end first) into the housing, using a suitable tube or socket that bears only of the outer edge of the seal.
19 Refit the camshaft sprocket (and hub where applicable) as described in Section 8.
20 Where necessary, fit a new timing belt with reference to Section 7.

14.3 Drill a hole then use a self-tapping screw and pliers to extract the oil seal

14.12 The new oil seal comes with a protective sleeve (arrowed) which fits over the end of the crankshaft

14.18 The new oil seal comes with a protective sleeve (arrowed) which fits over the end of the camshaft

15.3 The oil pressure switch is on the front face of the cylinder block

15.8 Oil level sensor (arrowed)

16.10 If the new bolts are not supplied with their threads pre-coated, apply thread-locking compound to them...

15 Oil pressure switch and level sensor – removal and refitting

Oil pressure switch

Removal

1 The oil pressure switch is located at the front of the cylinder block, adjacent to the oil dipstick guide tube. Note that on some models, access to the switch may be improved if the vehicle is jacked up and supported on axle stands, then undo the screws and remove the engine undershield so that the switch can be reached from underneath (see *Jacking and vehicle support*).
2 Remove the protective sleeve from the wiring plug (where applicable), and then disconnect the wiring from the switch.
3 Unscrew the switch from the cylinder block, and recover the sealing washer **(see illustration)**. Be prepared for oil spillage, and if the switch is to be left removed from the engine for any length of time, plug the hole in the cylinder block.

Refitting

4 Examine the sealing washer for any signs of damage or deterioration, and if necessary renew.
5 Refit the switch, complete with washer, and tighten it securely.
6 Refit the engine undershield, and lower the vehicle to the ground.

Oil level sensor

Removal

7 The oil level sensor is located at the rear of the cylinder block. Jack up the front of the vehicle and support it securely on axle stands (see *Jacking and vehicle support*). Undo the screws and remove the engine undershield.
8 Reach up between the driveshaft and the cylinder block and disconnect the wiring plug from the sensor **(see illustration)**.
9 Using an open-ended spanner, unscrew the sensor and withdraw it from position.

Refitting

10 Smear a little silicone sealant on the threads and refit the sensor to the cylinder block, tightening it securely.
11 Reconnect the wiring plug to the oil level sensor.
12 Refit the engine under shield, and lower the vehicle to the ground.

16 Flywheel/driveplate – removal, inspection and refitting

Removal

Flywheel

1 Remove the transmission as described in Chapter 7A Section 7, then remove the clutch assembly as described in Chapter 6 Section 6.
2 Prevent the flywheel from turning by locking the ring gear teeth. Alternatively, bolt a strap between the flywheel and the cylinder block/crankcase. Do not attempt to lock the flywheel in position using the crankshaft pulley locking tool described in Section 3. Insert a 12 mm diameter rod or drill bit through the hole in the flywheel cover casting, and into a slot in the flywheel **(see illustration 5.2)**.
3 Make alignment marks between the flywheel and crankshaft to aid refitment. Slacken and remove the flywheel retaining bolts, and remove the flywheel from the end of the crankshaft. Be careful not to drop it; it is heavy. If the flywheel locating dowel (where fitted) is a loose fit in the crankshaft end, remove it and store it with the flywheel for safe-keeping. Discard the flywheel bolts; new ones must be used on refitting.

Driveplate

4 Remove the transmission as described in Chapter 7B Section 9. Lock the driveplate as described in paragraph 2 of this Section. Mark the relationship between the torque converter plate and the driveplate, and slacken all the driveplate retaining bolts.

5 Remove the retaining bolts, along with the torque converter plate and the two shims (one fitted on each side of the torque converter plate). Note that the shims are of different thickness, the thicker one being on the outside of the torque converter plate. Discard the driveplate retaining bolts; new ones must be used on refitting.
6 Remove the driveplate from the end of the crankshaft. If the locating dowel is a loose fit in the crankshaft end, remove it and store it with the driveplate for safe-keeping.

Inspection

7 On models with manual transmission, examine the flywheel for scoring of the clutch face, and for wear or chipping of the ring gear teeth. If the clutch face is scored, the flywheel may be surface-ground, but renewal is preferable. Seek the advice of a Peugeot dealer or engine reconditioning specialist to see if machining is possible. If the ring gear is worn or damaged, the flywheel must be renewed, as it is not possible to renew the ring gear separately.
8 On models with automatic transmission, check the torque converter driveplate carefully for signs of distortion. Look for any hairline cracks around the bolt holes or radiating outwards from the centre, and inspect the ring gear teeth for signs of wear or chipping. If any sign of wear or damage is found, the driveplate must be renewed.

Refitting

Flywheel

9 Clean the mating surfaces of the flywheel and crankshaft. Remove any remaining locking compound from the threads of the crankshaft holes, using the correct size of tap, if available.
10 If the new flywheel retaining bolts are not supplied with their threads already pre-coated, apply a suitable thread-locking compound to the threads of each bolt **(see illustration)**.
11 Ensure that the locating dowel is in position. Offer up the flywheel, locating it

16.12... then refit the flywheel and tighten the bolts to the specified torque

on the dowel (where fitted) and fit the new retaining bolts. Where no locating dowel is fitted, align the previously-made marks to ensure the flywheel is refitted in its original position.

12 Lock the flywheel using the method employed on dismantling, and tighten the retaining bolts to the specified torque **(see illustration)**.

13 Refit the clutch and remove the flywheel locking tool, then refit the transmission.

Driveplate

14 Carry out the operations described above in paragraphs 9 and 10, substituting 'driveplate' for all references to the flywheel.

15 Locate the driveplate on its locating dowel.

16 Offer up the torque converter plate, with the thinner shim positioned behind the plate and the thicker shim on the outside, and align the marks made prior to removal.

17 Fit the new retaining bolts, then lock the driveplate using the method employed on dismantling. Tighten the retaining bolts to the specified torque wrench setting.

18 Remove the driveplate locking tool, and refit the transmission.

17 Engine/transmission mountings – inspection and renewal

Inspection

1 If improved access is required, firmly apply the handbrake, then jack up the front of the car and support it on axle stands (see *Jacking and vehicle support*). Undo the screws and remove the engine undershield.

2 Check the mounting rubbers to see if they are cracked, hardened or separated from the metal at any point; renew the mounting if any such damage or deterioration is evident.

3 Check that all the mountings' fasteners are securely tightened; use a torque wrench to check if possible.

4 Using a large screwdriver or a crowbar, check for wear in each mounting by carefully levering against it to check for free play. Where this is not possible, enlist the aid of an assistant to move the engine/transmission back-and-forth, or from side-to-side, while you watch the mounting. While some free play is to be expected even from new components, excessive wear should be obvious. If excessive free play is found, check first that the fasteners are correctly secured, and then renew any worn components as described below.

Renewal

Right-hand mounting

5 Release all the relevant hoses and wiring from their retaining clips. Place the hoses/wiring clear of the mounting so that the removal procedure is not hindered. Undo screws and remove the engine undershield.

6 Place a jack beneath the engine, with a block of wood on the jack head. Raise the jack until it is supporting the weight of the engine.

7 Undo the bolts securing the engine mounting to the body and the support bracket.

8 If required. undo the bolts/nuts securing the support bracket to the cylinder head/cylinder block and remove the mounting.

9 Check all components carefully for signs of wear or damage, and renew as necessary.

10 Where removed, refit the support bracket to the cylinder head, and tighten the bolts securely.

11 Refit the mount to the body and support bracket, and then tighten the bolts to the specified torque.

12 Remove the jack from underneath the engine.

Left-hand mounting

13 Remove the battery, and battery tray/box as described in Chapter 5A Section 4.

14 Place a jack beneath the transmission, with a block of wood on the jack head. Raise the jack until it is supporting the weight of the transmission.

15 Slacken and remove the mounting's two upper retaining bolts **(see illustration)**.

16 Undo the four retaining bolts from the mounting bracket on the body and remove the mounting from the engine compartment **(see illustration)**.

17 Check carefully for signs of wear or damage on all components, and renew them where necessary.

18 Refit the mounting bracket to the vehicle body and tighten its bolts to the specified torque.

19 Fit the mounting bolts to the bracket on the transmission and tighten the retaining bolts to the specified torque.

20 Remove the jack from underneath the transmission, then refit the battery.

Rear lower mounting

21 If not already done, firmly apply the handbrake, then jack up the front of the vehicle and support it securely on axle stands (see *Jacking and vehicle support*).

17.15 Left-hand transmission mounting upper bolts – arrowed

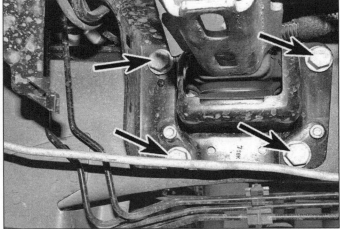

17.16 Left-hand transmission mounting bracket bolts – arrowed

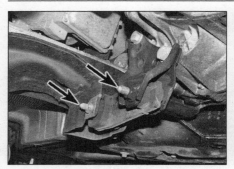

17.22 Undo the mounting bolts – arrowed...

17.23... and remove the lower link

17.24 Undo the nut/bolts and remove the mounting bracket

22 Unscrew and remove the bolt securing the rear mounting link to the bracket on the transmission **(see illustration)**.
23 Remove the bolt securing the rear mounting link to the subframe and remove the mounting torque reaction link **(see illustration)**.

24 To remove the mounting bracket undo the retaining bolts and remove the mounting bracket from the rear of the transmission **(see illustration)**.
25 Check carefully for signs of wear or damage on all components, and renew them where necessary.

26 On reassembly, fit the rear mounting bracket to the transmission, and tighten its retaining bolts to the specified torque.
27 Refit the rear mounting torque reaction link, and tighten both its bolts to their specified torque settings.
28 Lower the vehicle to the ground.

Chapter 2 Part D
1.6 litre DOHC diesel engine in-car repair procedures

Contents

Degrees of difficulty

Easy, suitable for novice with little experience	Fairly easy, suitable for beginner with some experience	Fairly difficult, suitable for competent DIY mechanic	Difficult, suitable for experienced DIY mechanic	Very difficult, suitable for expert DIY or professional

Specifications

General

Designation:
Without intercooler	DV6TED4
With intercooler	DV6ATED4

Engine codes: *
DV6ATED4	9HX
DV6DTED	9HP
DV6TED4	9HV, 9HY & 9HZ
Capacity	1560 cc
Bore	75.0 mm
Stroke	88.3 mm
Direction of crankshaft rotation	Clockwise (viewed from the right-hand side of vehicle)
No 1 cylinder location.....................................	At the transmission end of block
Maximum power output.....................................	80 kW @ 4000 rpm
Maximum torque output.....................................	245 Nm @ 2000 rpm
Compression ratio	18.0 : 1

* The engine code is stamped on a plate attached to the front of the cylinder block, next to the oil filter

Compression pressures (engine hot, at cranking speed)

Normal	20 ± 5 bar
Minimum	15 bar
Maximum difference between any two cylinders................	5 bar

Camshaft

Drive:
Inlet camshaft..	Toothed belt from crankshaft
Exhaust camshaft..	Chain-drive from inlet camshaft
Number of teeth	19

Length:
Inlet camshaft..	401.0 ± 0.15 mm
Exhaust camshaft..	389.0 ± 0.5 mm
Endfloat	0.195 to 0.300 mm

Lubrication system

Oil pump type	Gear-type, driven directly by the right-hand end of the crankshaft, by two flats machined along the crankshaft journal

Minimum oil pressure at 80°C:
    1000 rpm . . . . 1.3 bar
    4000 rpm . . . . 3.5 bar

Torque wrench settings

	Nm	lbf ft
Ancillary drivebelt tensioner roller	20	15
Big-end bolts: *		
Stage 1	10	7
Stage 2	Slacken 180°	
Stage 3	30	22
Stage 4	Angle-tighten a further 140°	
Camshaft bearing caps	10	7
Camshaft cover/bearing ladder:		
Studs	10	7
Bolts	10	7
Camshaft position sensor bolt	5	4
Camshaft sprocket:		
Stage 1	20	15
Stage 2	Angle-tighten a further 50°	
Coolant outlet housing bolts	7	5
Crankshaft position/speed sensor bolt	5	4
Crankshaft pulley/sprocket bolt: *		
Stage 1	35	26
Stage 2	Angle-tighten a further 190 °	
Cylinder head bolts:		
Stage 1	20	15
Stage 2	40	30
Stage 3	Angle-tighten a further 230°	
Cylinder head cover/manifold	10	7
EGR valve.	10	7
Engine-to-transmission fixing bolts	60	44
Flywheel bolt: *		
Dual mass flywheel:		
Stage 1	25	18
Stage 2	Fully slacken	
Stage 3	8	6
Stage 4	30	22
Stage 5	Angle-tighten a further 90°	
Normal flywheel:		
Stage 1	25	18
Stage 2	Fully slacken	
Stage 3	8	6
Stage 4	17	13
Stage 5	Angle-tighten a further 75°	
Fuel pump sprocket	50	37
Left-hand engine/transmission mounting:		
Mounting bracket to transmission	55	41
Mounting to bracket	60	44
Main bearing ladder outer seam bolts:		
Stage 1	5	4
Stage 2	10	7
Main bearing ladder to cylinder block:		
Stage 1	10	7
Stage 2	Slacken 180°	
Stage 3	30	22
Stage 4	Angle-tighten a further 140°	
Piston oil jet spray tube bolt.	20	15
Oil filter cover	25	18
Oil pick-up pipe	10	7
Oil pressure switch	32	24
Oil pump to cylinder block	10	7
Rear engine/transmission mounting:		
Connecting link to mounting assembly	60	44
Connecting link-to-subframe nut/bolt	60	44
Mounting to engine.	60	44

Torque wrench settings (continued)

	Nm	lbf ft
Right-hand engine mounting:		
Mounting to body	60	44
Mounting to support bracket	60	44
Support bracket to engine	55	41
Sump drain plug	25	18
Sump bolts/nuts	12	9
Timing belt idler pulley	35	26
Timing belt tensioner pulley	25	18
Timing chain tensioner	10	7
Vacuum pump:		
Stage 1	18	13
Stage 2	Angle-tighten a further 5°	

*Do not re-use

1 General Information

How to use this Chapter

1 This Part of Chapter 2 describes the repair procedures that can reasonably be carried out on the engine whilst it remains in the vehicle. If the engine has been removed from the vehicle and is being dismantled as described in Part F, any preliminary dismantling procedures can be ignored.

2 Note that, while it may be possible physically to overhaul items such as the piston/connecting rod assemblies while the engine is in the car, such tasks are not usually carried out as separate operations. Usually, several additional procedures are required (not to mention the cleaning of components and oilways); for this reason, all such tasks are classed as major overhaul procedures, and are described in Part F of this Chapter.

3 Part F describes the removal of the engine/transmission from the car, and the full overhaul procedures that can then be carried out.

DV series engines

4 The DV series engine is the result of development collaboration between Peugeot/Citroën and Ford. The engine is of double overhead camshaft (DOHC) 16-valve design. The direct injection, turbocharged, four-cylinder engine is mounted transversely, with the transmission mounted on the left-hand side.

5 A toothed timing belt drives the inlet camshaft, high-pressure fuel pump and coolant pump. The inlet camshaft drives the exhaust camshaft via a chain. The camshafts operate the inlet and exhaust valves via rocker arms, which are supported at their pivot ends by hydraulic self-adjusting followers. The camshafts are supported by bearings machined directly in the cylinder head and camshaft bearing housing.

6 The high-pressure fuel pump supplies fuel to the fuel rail, and subsequently to the electronically-controlled injectors that inject the fuel direct into the combustion chambers. This design differs from the previous type where an injection pump supplies the fuel at high pressure to each injector. The earlier, conventional type injection pump required fine calibration and timing, and these functions are now completed by the high-pressure pump, electronic injectors and engine management ECM.

7 The crankshaft runs in five main bearings of the usual shell type. Endfloat is controlled by thrustwashers either side of No 2 main bearing.

8 The pistons are selected to be of matching weight, and incorporate fully floating gudgeon pins retained by circlips.

Repair operations precaution

9 The engine is a complex unit with numerous accessories and ancillary components. The design of the engine compartment is such that every conceivable space has been utilised, and access to virtually all of the engine components is extremely limited. In many cases, ancillary components will have to be removed, or moved to one side, and wiring, pipes and hoses will have to be disconnected or removed from various cable clips and support brackets.

10 When working on this engine, read through the entire procedure first, look at the car and engine at the same time, and establish whether you have the necessary tools, equipment, skill and patience to proceed. Allow considerable time for any operation, and be prepared for the unexpected.

11 Because of the limited access, many of the engine photographs appearing in this Chapter were, by necessity, taken with the engine removed from the vehicle.

Warning: It is essential to observe strict precautions when working on the fuel system components of the engine, particularly the high-pressure side of the system. Before carrying out any engine operations that entail working on, or near, any part of the fuel system, refer to the special information given in Chapter 4B.

Operations with engine in vehicle

● Compression pressure – testing.
● Cylinder head cover – removal and refitting.

● Crankshaft pulley – removal and refitting.
● Timing belt covers – removal and refitting.
● Timing belt – removal, refitting and adjustment.
● Timing belt tensioner and sprockets – removal and refitting.
● Camshaft oil seal – renewal.
● Camshaft, rocker arms and hydraulic followers – removal, inspection and refitting.
● Sump – removal and refitting.
● Oil pump – removal and refitting.
● Crankshaft oil seals – renewal.
● Engine/transmission mountings – inspection and renewal.
● Flywheel – removal, inspection and refitting.

2 Compression and leakdown tests – description and interpretation

Compression test

Note: *A compression tester specifically designed for diesel engines must be used for this test.*

1 When engine performance is down, or if misfiring occurs which cannot be attributed to the fuel system, a compression test can provide diagnostic clues as to the engine's condition. If the test is performed regularly, it can give warning of trouble before any other symptoms become apparent.

2 A compression tester specifically intended for diesel engines must be used, because of the higher pressures involved. The tester is connected to an adapter, which screws into the glow plug or injector hole. On this engine, an adapter suitable for use in the glow plug holes will be required, so as not to disturb the fuel system components. It is unlikely to be worthwhile buying such a tester for occasional use, but it may be possible to borrow or hire one – if not, have the test performed by a garage.

3 Unless specific instructions to the contrary are supplied with the tester, observe the following points:

● The battery must be in a good state of charge, the air filter must be clean, and the engine should be at normal operating temperature.

● All the glow plugs should be removed as described in Chapter 5C Section 2 before starting the test.

● The wiring connectors on the engine management system ECM (located in the plastic box behind the battery) must be disconnected.

4 The compression pressures measured are not so important as the balance between cylinders. Values are given in the Specifications.

5 The cause of poor compression is less easy to establish on a diesel engine than on a petrol engine. The effect of introducing oil into the cylinders ('wet' testing) is not conclusive, because there is a risk that the oil will sit in the swirl chamber or in the recess on the piston crown instead of passing to the rings. However, the following can be used as a rough guide to diagnosis.

6 All cylinders should produce very similar pressures; any difference greater than that specified indicates the existence of a fault. Note that the compression should build-up quickly in a healthy engine; low compression on the first stroke, followed by gradually increasing pressure on successive strokes, indicates worn piston rings. A low compression reading on the first stroke, which does not build-up during successive strokes, indicates leaking valves or a blown head gasket (a cracked head could also be the cause). Deposits on the undersides of the valve heads can also cause low compression.

7 A low reading from two adjacent cylinders is almost certainly due to the head gasket having blown between them; the presence of coolant in the engine oil will confirm this.

8 If the compression reading is unusually high, the cylinder head surfaces, valves and pistons are probably coated with carbon deposits. If this is the case, the cylinder head should be removed and decarbonised (see Part F of this Chapter).

Leakdown test

9 A leakdown test measures the rate at which compressed air fed into the cylinder is lost. It is an alternative to a compression test, and in many ways it is better, since the escaping air provides easy identification of where pressure loss is occurring (piston rings, valves or head gasket).

10 The equipment needed for leakdown testing is unlikely to be available to the home mechanic. If poor compression is suspected, have the test performed by a suitably-equipped garage.

---

3 Engine assembly/valve timing holes – general information and usage

Note: *Do not attempt to rotate the engine whilst the crankshaft and camshaft are locked in position. If the engine is to be left in this state for a long period of time, it is a good idea to place suitable warning notices inside the vehicle, and in the engine compartment. This will reduce the possibility of the engine being accidentally cranked on the starter motor, which is likely to cause damage with the locking pins in place.*

1 Timing holes or slots are located only in the crankshaft pulley flange and camshaft sprocket hub. The holes/slots are used to position the pistons halfway up the cylinder bores. This will ensure that the valve timing is maintained during operations that require removal and refitting of the timing belt. When the holes/slots are aligned with their corresponding holes in the cylinder block and cylinder head, suitable diameter bolts/pins can be inserted to lock the crankshaft in position, preventing rotation.

2 Note that the HDi type fuel system used on these engines does not have a conventional diesel injection pump, but instead uses a high-pressure fuel pump. Although it may be argued that timing of the fuel pump is irrelevant because it merely pressurises the fuel in the fuel rail, Peugeot include this procedure for engines fitted with a Bosch high-pressure fuel pump, using the same timing rod/pin used for crankshaft sprocket timing. **Note:** *On the Bosch pump, the drive sprocket is keyed to the shaft. In addition, note that the hole in the fuel pump sprocket only aligns correctly with the hole in the mounting bracket every 12 revolutions of the crankshaft (or every 6 revolutions of the camshaft sprocket).*

3 To align the engine assembly/valve timing holes, proceed as follows.

4 Chock the rear wheels then jack up the front of the vehicle and support it on axle stands (see *Jacking and vehicle support*). Remove the right-hand front roadwheel.

5 To gain access to the crankshaft pulley, to enable the engine to be turned, the wheel arch plastic liner must be removed. The liner is secured by several plastic expanding rivets/nut/screws. To remove the rivets, push in the centre pins a little, and then prise the clips from place. Remove the liner from under the front wing. The crankshaft can then be turned using a suitable socket and extension bar fitted to the pulley bolt.

6 Remove the upper and lower timing belt covers as described in Section 6.

7 Temporarily refit the crankshaft pulley bolt, remove the crankshaft locking tool, and then turn the crankshaft until the timing hole in the camshaft sprocket hub is aligned with the corresponding hole in the cylinder head. Note that the crankshaft must always be turned in a clockwise direction (viewed from the right-hand side of vehicle). Use a small mirror so that the position of the sprocket hub timing slot can be observed. When the slot is aligned with the corresponding hole in the cylinder head, the camshaft is positioned correctly.

8 Remove the crankshaft drivebelt pulley as described in Section 5.

9 Insert a 5 mm diameter bolt, rod or drill through the hole in the crankshaft sprocket flange and into the corresponding hole in the oil pump **(see illustration)**, if necessary, carefully turn the crankshaft either way until the rod enters the timing hole in the block.

10 Insert an 8 mm bolt, rod or drill through the hole in the camshaft sprocket hub and into engagement with the cylinder head. Note that a modified 3-segment camshaft sprocket is fitted to later models **(see illustration)**.

11 If using this procedure during refitting of the timing belt, insert a 5 mm diameter bolt, rod or drill through the hole in the fuel pump sprocket and into the corresponding hole in the cylinder head **(see illustration)**. **Note:** *On some engines, a hole is provided at the 5 o'clock position for locking purposes only, however, the timing hole*

3.9 Insert a 5.0 mm drill bit/bolt through the round hole in the sprocket flange into the hole in the oil pump housing (lower timing belt cover removed for clarity)

3.10 Insert an 8.0 mm drill bit/bolt through the hole in the camshaft sprocket into the corresponding hole in the cylinder head

3.11 Insert a 5.0 mm drill bit/bolt through the round hole in the fuel pump sprocket into the cylinder head

4.2 Release the clip (arrowed) and disconnect the mass airflow meter wiring plug

4.3a Undo the screw (arrowed) and remove the inlet ducting

4.3b Disconnect the hose to the turbocharger…

is at the 12 o'clock position. Note the comment in paragraph 2 – if the fuel pump sprocket holes are not aligned during removal of the timing belt, it is of no consequence, however it is important to align the holes during the refitting procedure. If timing alignment alone is being checked there is no need to check alignment of the pump sprocket.

12 The crankshaft and camshaft are now locked in position, preventing unnecessary rotation.

4 Cylinder head cover/ manifold – removal and refitting

Removal

1 Pull the plastic cover upwards from the top of the engine. Remove the scuttle trim panel and crossmember.

2 Disconnect the wiring plug from the mass airflow meter **(see illustration)**.

3 Remove the inlet and outlet air ducting from the air filter housing **(see illustrations)**.

4 Unscrew the air filter housing cover bolts, then remove the cover and filter element – refer to Chapter 4B Section 4 **(see illustrations)**. Pull the air filter housing from its mountings.

5 Disconnect the wiring plugs from the top of each injector, undo the guide bolts, then make sure all wiring harnesses are freed from any retaining brackets on the cylinder head cover/ inlet manifold **(see illustration)**. Disconnect

4.3c… release the clips (arrowed) and disconnect the breather hose…

4.4a… then undo the cover screws (arrowed)…

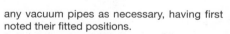

4.4b… and remove the ducting/cover assembly

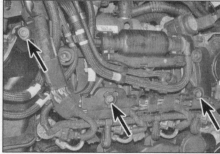

4.5 Undo the bolts (arrowed) and position the wiring harness/guide to one side

any vacuum pipes as necessary, having first noted their fitted positions.

6 Remove the EGR heat exchanger as described in Chapter 4C Section 2.

7 Depress the release buttons and

disconnect the fuel feed and return hoses at the right-hand end of the cylinder head, then disconnect the fuel temperature sensor wiring plug, and move the pipe/priming bulb assembly to the rear **(see illustrations)**.

4.7a Depress the release buttons (arrowed) and disconnect the fuel feed and return hoses

4.7b Disconnect the fuel temperature sensor wiring plug (arrowed)…

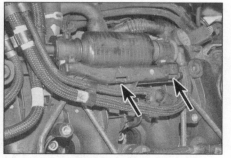

4.7c… then unclip the fuel priming bulb/ pipes (arrowed)

4.8a Slacken the left-hand turbocharger outlet hose bolt, undo the right-hand bolt (arrowed)…

4.8c… undo the bolt on the end (arrowed)…

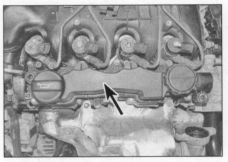

4.9 Undo the bolts and remove the oil separator (arrowed)

4.10b Use a second spanner to hold the injector port whilst slackening the fuel pipe unions

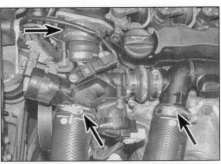

4.8b… then slacken the hose clamps (arrowed), disconnect the wiring plugs…

4.8d… and the 2 at the front (arrowed), then remove the assembly

4.10a Prise out the clip and pull the return hose from the top of each injector

4.11 Undo the 2 remaining bolts (arrowed) and pull the cover/manifold upwards

8 Release the clamps, undo the bolts and remove the inlet ducting between the turbocharger and the inlet manifold. Make a note of their fitted positions, and then disconnect the various wiring plugs as the assembly is withdrawn **(see illustrations)**.

9 Undo the retaining bolts and remove the oil separator from the top of the cylinder head **(see illustration)**. Recover the rubber seal.

10 Prise out the retaining clips and disconnect the fuel return pipes from the injectors, then undo the unions and remove the high-pressure fuel pipes from the injectors and the common fuel rail at the rear of the cylinder head – counterhold the unions with a second spanner **(see illustrations)**. Plug the openings to prevent dirt ingress.

11 Undo the 2 bolts securing the cylinder head cover/inlet manifold. Lift the assembly away **(see illustration)**. Recover the manifold rubber seals.

Refitting

12 Refitting is a reversal of removal, bearing in mind the following points:
- Examine the seals for signs of damage and deterioration, and renew if necessary. Smear a little clean engine oil on the manifold seals.
- Renew the fuel injector high-pressure pipes – see Chapter 4B Section 11.

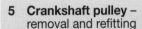

5 Crankshaft pulley – removal and refitting

Removal

1 Remove the auxiliary drivebelt as described in Chapter 1B Section 16.

2 To lock the crankshaft, working underneath the engine, insert Peugeot tool No 0194-C into the hole in the face of the engine block casting over the lower section of the flywheel. Rotate the crankshaft until the tool engages in the corresponding hole in the flywheel. In the absence of the Peugeot tool, insert a 12 mm rod or drill into the hole **(see illustration)**.

5.2 The locking pin/bolt (arrowed) must locate in the hole in the flywheel (arrowed) to prevent rotation

5.3 Undo the crankshaft pulley retaining bolt (arrowed)

6.2a Unclip the fuel pipes (arrowed)...

6.2b ... and the wiring harness (arrowed) from the timing belt upper cover

Note: *The hole in the casting and the hole in the flywheel are provided purely to lock the crankshaft whilst the pulley bolt is undone, it does not position the crankshaft at TDC.*

3 Using a suitable socket and extension bar, unscrew the retaining bolt, remove the washer, then slide the pulley off the end of the crankshaft **(see illustration)**. If the pulley is tight fit, it can be drawn off the crankshaft using a suitable puller. If a puller is being used, refit the pulley retaining bolt without the washer to avoid damaging the crankshaft as the puller is tightened.

Caution: Do not touch the outer magnetic sensor ring of the sprocket with your fingers, or allow metallic particles to come into contact with it.

Refitting

4 Refit the pulley to the end of the crankshaft.
5 Thoroughly clean the threads of the pulley retaining bolt, and then apply a coat of locking compound to the bolt threads. Peugeot recommend the use of Loctite (available from your Peugeot dealer); in the absence of this, any good-quality locking compound may be used.
6 Refit the crankshaft pulley retaining bolt and washer. Tighten the bolt to the specified torque, then through the specified angle, preventing the crankshaft from turning using the method employed on removal.
7 Refit and tension the auxiliary drivebelt as described in Chapter 1B Section 16.

6 Timing belt covers – removal and refitting

Removal

Upper cover

1 Remove the plastic cover from the top of the engine. Remove the scuttle trim panel and crossmember.
2 Release the wiring harness and fuel pipes from the upper cover **(see illustrations)**.
3 Undo the five screws and remove the timing belt upper cover **(see illustration)**.

Lower cover

4 Remove the upper cover as described previously.
5 Remove the crankshaft pulley as described in Section 5.
6 Remove the auxiliary drivebelt tensioner locking tool (where applicable), then undo the five bolts and remove the lower cover **(see illustration)**.

Refitting

7 Refitting of all the covers is a reversal of the relevant removal procedure, ensuring that each cover section is correctly located, and that the cover retaining bolts are securely tightened. Ensure that all disturbed hoses are reconnected and retained by their relevant clips.

7 Timing belt – removal, inspection, refitting and tensioning

General

1 The timing belt drives the inlet camshaft, high-pressure fuel pump, and coolant pump from a toothed sprocket on the end of the crankshaft. If the belt breaks or slips in service, the pistons are likely to hit the valve heads, resulting in expensive damage.
2 The timing belt should be renewed at the specified intervals, or earlier if it is contaminated with oil or at all noisy in operation (a 'scraping' noise due to uneven wear).
3 If the timing belt is being removed, it is a wise precaution to check the condition of the coolant pump at the same time (check for signs of coolant leakage). This may avoid the need to remove the timing belt again at a later stage should the coolant pump fail.

Removal

4 Chock the rear wheels then jack up the front of the vehicle and support it on axle stands (see *Jacking and vehicle support*). Remove the front right-hand roadwheel, wheel arch liner (to expose the crankshaft pulley), and the engine undershield.
5 Remove the auxiliary drivebelt as described in Chapter 1B Section 16.
6 Remove the upper and lower timing belt covers, as described in Section 6.
7 Refer to Chapter 4B Section 18 and disconnect the front exhaust pipe at the flexible section.
8 Position a trolley jack under the engine, and using a block of wood on the jack head, take the weight of the engine.
9 Undo the bolts/nut and remove the right-hand engine mounting and support bracket – see Section 17.
10 Undo the screw and remove the crankshaft position sensor adjacent to the

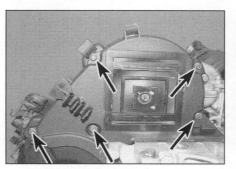

6.3 Upper timing belt cover screws (arrowed)

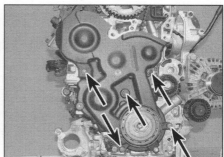

6.6 Lower timing belt cover bolts (arrowed)

7.10 Undo the bolt (arrowed) and remove the crankshaft position sensor

7.13 Slacken the bolt and allow the tensioner to rotate, relieving the tension on the belt

20 Remove the camshaft and crankshaft and fuel pump timing pins and, using a socket on the crankshaft pulley bolt, crankshaft clockwise 10 complete revolutions. Align the camshaft and crankshaft timing holes and check that the timing pins can be inserted, then remove them. There is no requirement to check the fuel pump sprocket alignment, as it will only be aligned after 12 complete revolutions.

21 Check that the tensioner index arm is still aligned between the edges of the area shown **(see illustration 7.19)**. If it is not, remove and belt and begin the refitting process again, starting at Paragraph 19.

22 The remainder of refitting is a reversal of removal. Tighten all fasteners to the specified torque where given.

crankshaft sprocket flange, and move it to one side **(see illustration)**.

11 Undo the retaining screw and remove the timing belt protection bracket, again adjacent to the crankshaft sprocket flange.

12 Lock the crankshaft and camshaft in the correct position as described in Section 3. If necessary, temporarily refit the crankshaft pulley bolt to enable the crankshaft to be rotated. At this stage, it is of no consequence that the fuel pump sprocket aligns correctly with the hole in the pump mounting bracket.

13 Insert a hexagon key into the belt tensioner pulley centre, slacken the pulley bolt, and allow the tensioner to rotate, relieving the belt tension **(see illustration)**. With the belt slack, temporarily tighten the pulley bolt.

14 Note its routing, and then remove the timing belt from the sprockets.

Inspection

15 Renew the belt as a matter of course, regardless of its apparent condition. The cost of a new belt is nothing compared with the cost of repairs should the belt break in service. If signs of oil contamination are found, trace the source of the oil leak and rectify it. Wash down the engine timing belt area and all

related components, to remove all traces of oil. Check that the tensioner and idler pulleys rotate freely without any sign of roughness, and also check that the coolant pump pulley rotates freely. If necessary, renew these items.

Refitting and tensioning

16 Commence refitting by ensuring that the crankshaft and camshaft timing pins are still in position correctly. Also, where a Bosch high-pressure fuel pump is fitted, locate and lock the fuel pump sprocket in its correct position as described in Section 3.

17 Locate the timing belt on the crankshaft sprocket, then keeping it taut, locate it around the idler pulley, camshaft sprocket, high-pressure pump sprocket, coolant pump sprocket, and the tensioner pulley **(see illustration)**. If the timing belt has directional arrows on it, make sure that they point in the direction of normal engine rotation.

18 Refit the timing belt protection bracket and tighten the retaining bolt securely.

19 Slacken the tensioner pulley bolt, and using a hexagonal key, rotate the tensioner anti-clockwise, which moves the index arm clockwise, until the index arm is aligned as shown **(see illustration)**.

8 Timing belt sprockets and tensioner – removal and refitting

Camshaft sprocket

Removal

1 Remove the timing belt as described in Section 7.

2 Remove the locking tool from the camshaft sprocket/hub. Slacken the sprocket hub retaining bolt. To prevent the camshaft rotating as the bolt is slackened, a sprocket holding tool will be required. In the absence of the special Peugeot tool, an acceptable substitute can be fabricated at home **(see Tool Tip 1)**. Do not attempt to use the engine assembly/valve timing locking tool to prevent the sprocket from rotating whilst the bolt is slackened.

3 Remove the sprocket hub retaining bolt, and slide the sprocket and hub off the end of the camshaft.

4 Clean the camshaft sprocket thoroughly, and renew it if there are any signs of wear, damage or cracks.

7.17 Timing belt routing

7.19 The index arm must align with the lug (arrowed)

TOOL TiP 1

A sprocket holding tool can be made from two lengths of steel strip bolted together to form a forked end. Drill holes and insert bolts in the ends of the fork to engage with the sprocket spokes.

8.5 Ensure the lug on the sprocket hub engages with the slot on the end of the camshaft (arrowed)

8.11a Slide the sprocket from the crankshaft...

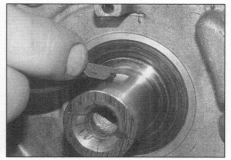

8.11b... and recover the Woodruff key

Refitting

5 Refit the camshaft sprocket to the camshaft **(see illustration)**.

6 Refit the sprocket hub retaining bolt. Tighten the bolt to the specified torque, preventing the camshaft from turning as during removal.

7 Align the engine assembly/valve timing slot in the camshaft sprocket hub with the hole in the cylinder head and refit the timing pin to lock the camshaft in position.

8 Fit the timing belt around the pump sprocket and camshaft sprocket, and tension the timing belt as described in Section 7.

Crankshaft sprocket

Removal

9 Remove the timing belt as described in Section 7.

10 Check that the engine assembly/valve timing holes are still aligned as described in Section 3, and the camshaft sprocket and flywheel are locked in position.

11 Slide the sprocket off the end of the crankshaft and collect the Woodruff key **(see illustrations)**.

12 Examine the crankshaft oil seal for signs of oil leakage and, if necessary, renew it as described in Section 14.

13 Clean the crankshaft sprocket thoroughly, and renew it if there are any signs of wear, damage or cracks. Recover the crankshaft locating key.

Refitting

14 Refit the key to the end of the crankshaft, then refit the crankshaft sprocket (with the flange facing the crankshaft pulley).

15 Fit the timing belt around the crankshaft sprocket, and tension the timing belt as described in Section 7.

Fuel pump sprocket

Removal

16 Remove the timing belt as described in Section 7.

17 Using a suitable socket, undo the pump sprocket retaining nut. The sprocket can be held stationary by inserting a suitably-sized locking pin, drill or rod through the hole in the sprocket, and into the corresponding hole in the

backplate **(see illustration)**, or by using a suitable forked tool engaged with the holes in the sprocket **(see Tool Tip 1)**. **Note:** *On some engines, a hole is provided at the 5 o'clock position for locking purposes only, and the timing position hole is at the 12 o'clock position.*

18 The pump sprocket is a taper fit on the pump shaft and it will be necessary to make up another tool to release it from the taper **(see Tool Tip 2)**.

19 On late models where the sprocket is keyed to the shaft, unscrew the retaining nut and remove the sprocket, then recover the Woodruff key. On early models where the sprocket is not keyed to the shaft, partially unscrew the sprocket retaining nut, then fit the home-made tool, and secure it to the sprocket with two suitable bolts. Prevent the sprocket from rotating as before, and unscrew the sprocket retaining nut. The nut will bear against the tool as it is undone, forcing the sprocket off the shaft taper. Once the taper is released, remove the tool, unscrew the nut fully, and remove the sprocket from the pump shaft.

20 Clean the sprocket thoroughly, and renew it if there are any signs of wear, damage or cracks.

Refitting

21 Refit the Woodruff key (late models only) then refit the pump sprocket and retaining nut, and tighten the nut to the specified torque. Prevent the sprocket rotating as the nut is tightened using the sprocket holding tool.

22 Fit the timing belt around the pump

8.17 Insert a suitable drill bit through the sprocket into the hole in the backplate

sprocket, and tension the timing belt as described in Section 7.

Coolant pump sprocket

23 The coolant pump sprocket is integral with the pump, and cannot be removed. Coolant pump removal is described in Chapter 3 Section 8.

Tensioner pulley

Removal

24 Remove the timing belt as described in Section 7.

25 Remove the tensioner pulley retaining bolt, and slide the pulley off its mounting stud.

26 Clean the tensioner pulley, but do not use any strong solvent, which may enter the pulley bearings. Check that the pulley rotates freely, with no sign of stiffness or free play. Renew the pulley if there is any doubt about its condition, or if there are any obvious signs of wear or damage.

27 Examine the pulley mounting stud for signs of damage and if necessary, renew it.

Refitting

28 Refit the tensioner pulley to its mounting stud, and fit the retaining bolt.

29 Refit the timing belt as described in Section 7.

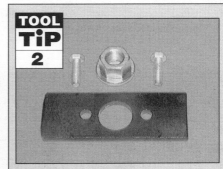

TOOL TiP 2

Make a sprocket releasing tool from a short strip of steel. Drill two holes in the strip to correspond with the two holes in the sprocket. Drill a third hole just large enough to accept the flats of the sprocket retaining nut.

8.31 Timing belt idler pulley retaining nut (arrowed)

9.5 Vacuum pump bolts (arrowed)

9.7 Timing belt inner, upper cover bolts (arrowed)

Idler pulley

Removal

30 Remove the timing belt as described in Section 7.

31 Undo the retaining bolt/nut and withdraw the idler pulley from the engine **(see illustration)**.

32 Clean the idler pulley, but do not use any strong solvent, which may enter the bearings. Check that the pulley rotates freely, with no sign of stiffness or free play. Renew the idler pulley if there is any doubt about its condition, or if there are any obvious signs of wear or damage.

Refitting

33 Locate the idler pulley on the engine, and fit the retaining bolt/nut. Tighten the bolt/nut to the specified torque.

34 Refit the timing belt (see Section 7).

9 Camshafts, rocker arms and hydraulic followers – removal, inspection and refitting

Removal

1 Remove the cylinder head cover/manifold as described in Section 4.

2 Remove the injectors as described in Chapter 4B Section 11.

3 Remove the camshaft sprocket as described in Section 8.

4 Refit the right-hand engine mounting, but only tighten the bolts moderately; this will keep the engine supported during the camshaft removal.

5 Undo the bolts and remove the vacuum pump. Recover the pump O-ring seals **(see illustration)**.

6 Remove the fuel filter (see Chapter 1B Section 18), then undo the bolts and remove the fuel filter mounting bracket.

7 Release the wiring harness clips, then undo the 3 bolts and remove the timing belt inner, upper cover **(see illustration)**.

8 Disconnect the wiring plug, unscrew the retaining bolt, and remove the camshaft position sensor from the camshaft cover/bearing ladder.

9 Undo the 5 bolts and remove the upper rear section of the turbocharger heat shield, then working gradually and evenly, slacken and remove the bolts securing the camshaft cover/bearing ladder to the cylinder head in sequence **(see illustration)**. Lift the cover/ladder from position complete with the camshafts.

10 Undo the retaining bolts and remove the bearing caps. Note their fitted positions, as they must be refitted into their original positions **(see illustration)**. Note that the bearing caps are marked A for inlet, and E for exhaust, and 1 to 4 from the flywheel end of the cylinder head.

11 Undo the bolts securing the chain tensioner assembly to the camshaft cover/bearing ladder, and then lift the camshafts, chain and tensioner from place **(see illustrations)**. Discard the camshaft oil seal.

12 Obtain 16 small, clean plastic containers, and number them 1 to 8 inlet and 1 to 8 exhaust; alternatively, divide a larger container into 16 compartments.

13 Lift out each rocker arm. Place the rocker arms in their respective positions in the box or containers.

14 A compartmentalised container filled with engine oil is now required to retain the hydraulic followers while they are removed from the cylinder head. Withdraw each hydraulic follower and place it in the container, keeping them each identified for correct refitting. The followers must be totally submerged in the oil to prevent air entering them.

Inspection

15 Inspect the cam lobes and the camshaft bearing journals for scoring or other visible evidence of wear. Once the surface hardening of the cam lobes has been eroded, wear will occur at an accelerated rate. **Note:** *If these symptoms are visible on the tips of the*

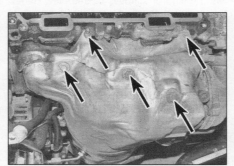

9.9 Undo the bolts (arrowed) and remove the heat shield

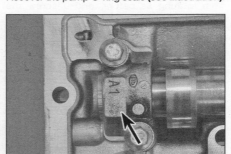

9.10 The camshaft bearing caps are numbered 1 to 4 from the flywheel end – A for inlet, and E for exhaust (arrowed)

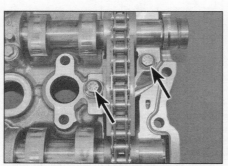

9.11a Undo the tensioner bolts (arrowed)...

9.11b... then lift the camshafts, chain and tensioner from place

9.21 Refit the hydraulic tappets...

9.22... and rocker arms to their original locations

9.23 Align the marks on the sprockets with the centre of the black-coloured chain links (arrowed). There must be 12 link pins between the sprocket marks

camshaft lobes, check the corresponding rocker arm, as it will probably be worn as well.
16 Examine the condition of the bearing surfaces in the cylinder head and camshaft bearing housing. If wear is evident, the cylinder head and bearing housing will both have to be renewed, as they are a matched assembly.
17 Inspect the rocker arms and followers for scuffing, cracking or other damage and renew any components as necessary. Also check the condition of the follower bores in the cylinder head. As with the camshafts, any wear in this area will necessitate cylinder head renewal.

Refitting

18 Thoroughly clean the sealant from the mating surfaces of the cylinder head and camshaft bearing housing. Use a suitable liquid gasket-dissolving agent (available from Peugeot dealers) together with a soft putty knife; do not use a metal scraper or the faces will be damaged. As there is no conventional gasket used, the cleanliness of the mating faces is of the utmost importance. Prise out the oil injector oil seals from the camshaft bearing housing.
19 Clean off any oil, dirt or grease from both components and dry with a clean lint-free cloth. Ensure that all the oilways are completely clean.
20 Liberally lubricate the hydraulic follower bores in the cylinder head with clean engine oil.
21 Insert the hydraulic followers into their original bores in the cylinder head unless they have been renewed **(see illustration)**.
22 Lubricate the rocker arms and place them over their respective followers and valve stems **(see illustration)**.

9.24a Assemble the chain tensioner between the upper and lower runs of the chain...

9.24b... and lower the camshafts, chain and tensioner into position

23 Engage the timing chain around the camshaft sprockets, aligning the black-coloured links with the marked teeth on the camshaft sprockets **(see illustration)**. If the black colouring has been lost, there must be 12 chain link pins between the marks on the sprockets.
24 Fit the chain tensioner between the upper and lower runs of the chain, then lubricate the bearing surfaces with clean engine oil, and fit the camshafts into position on the underside of the camshaft cover/bearing ladder. Refit the bearing caps to their original positions and tighten the retaining bolts to the specified torque **(see illustrations)**. Tighten the tensioner retaining bolts to the specified torque.
25 Apply a thin bead of sealant to the mating surface of the camshaft cover/bearing ladder as shown. Peugeot recommend the use of Autojoint Noir. Do not allow the sealant to

obstruct the oil channels for the hydraulic chain tensioner.
26 Check that the black-coloured links on the chain are still aligned with the marks on the camshaft sprockets, then refit the camshaft cover/bearing ladder, and gradually and evenly tighten the retaining bolts until the cover/ladder is in contact with the cylinder head, then tighten the bolts to the specified torque in sequence. **Note:** *Ensure the cover/ladder is correctly located by checking the bores of the vacuum pump and camshaft oil seal at each end of the cover/ladder.*
27 Fit a new camshaft oil seal as described in Section 14.
28 Refit the camshaft sprocket, and tighten the retaining bolt finger-tight.
29 Using a spanner on the camshaft sprocket bolt, rotate the camshafts approxi- mately 40 complete revolutions clockwise. Check the black-coloured links on the chain still align with the marks on the camshaft sprockets.
30 If the marks still align, refit the camshaft sprocket as described in Section 8.
31 Refit and adjust the camshaft position sensor as described in Chapter 4B Section 12.
32 Press the new oil seals into the bearing housing, using a tube/socket of approximately 20 mm outside diameter, ensuring the inner lip of the seal fits around the injector guide tube **(see illustrations)**. Refit the injectors as described in Chapter 4B Section 11.
33 Refit the cylinder head cover/manifold as described in Section 4.

9.32a Fit the new seal around a 20 mm outside diameter socket...

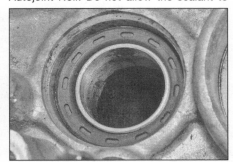

9.32b... and push it into place

10 Cylinder head – removal and refitting

Removal

1 Chock the rear wheels then jack up the front of the vehicle and support it on axle stands (see *Jacking and vehicle support*). Remove the front right-hand roadwheel, the engine undershield, and the front wheel arch liner.
2 Disconnect the battery as described in Chapter 5A Section 4.
3 Drain the cooling system as described in Chapter 1B Section 22.
4 Remove the camshafts, rocker arms and hydraulic followers as described in Section 9.
5 Remove the turbocharger as described in Chapter 4B Section 16.
6 Remove the glow plugs as described in Chapter 5C Section 2.
7 Where applicable, undo the 3 mounting bolts and move the power steering pump to one side (there's no need to disconnect the hoses).
8 Undo the upper mounting bolts, and pivot the alternator away from the engine, undo the oil dipstick guide tube bolt, then undo the bolts securing the alternator mounting bracket to the cylinder head/block **(see illustration)**.
9 Undo the coolant outlet housing (left-hand end of the cylinder head) retaining bolts, slacken the two bolts securing the housing

support bracket to the top of the transmission bellhousing, and move the outlet housing away from the cylinder head a little **(see illustration)**. There is no need to disconnect the hoses.
10 Disconnect the high-pressure fuel pipe from the common rail to the pump, and disconnect the fuel supply and return hoses. Remove the bracket at the rear of the pump, then undo the bolt/nut and remove the pump and mounting bracket as an assembly **(see illustrations)**. Note that a new high-pressure pipe must be fitted – see Chapter 4B Section 9.
11 Working in the reverse of the sequence shown **(see illustration 10.32)** undo the cylinder head bolts.
12 Release the cylinder head from the cylinder block and location dowels by rocking it. The Peugeot tool for doing this consists simply of two metal rods with 90-degree angled ends **(see illustration)**. Do not prise between the mating faces of the cylinder head and block, as this may damage the gasket faces.
13 Lift the cylinder head from the block, and recover the gasket.
14 If necessary, remove the exhaust manifold with reference to Chapter 4B Section 14.

Preparation for refitting

15 The mating faces of the cylinder head and cylinder block must be perfectly clean before refitting the head. Peugeot recommend the use of a scouring agent for this purpose, but acceptable results can be achieved by using

a hard plastic or wood scraper to remove all traces of gasket and carbon. The same method can be used to clean the piston crowns. Take particular care to avoid scoring or gouging the cylinder head/cylinder block mating surfaces during the cleaning operations, as aluminium alloy is easily damaged. Make sure that the carbon is not allowed to enter the oil and water passages – this is particularly important for the lubrication system, as carbon could block the oil supply to the engine's components. Using adhesive tape and paper, seal the water, oil and bolt holes in the cylinder block. To prevent carbon entering the gap between the pistons and bores, smear a little grease in the gap. After cleaning each piston, use a small brush to remove all traces of grease and carbon from the gap, then wipe away the remainder with a clean rag.
16 Check the mating surfaces of the cylinder block and the cylinder head for nicks, deep scratches and other damage. If slight, they may be removed carefully with a file, but if excessive, machining may be the only alternative to renewal. If warpage of the cylinder head gasket surface is suspected, use a straight-edge to check it for distortion. Refer to Part F of this Chapter if necessary.
17 Thoroughly clean the threads of the cylinder head bolt holes in the cylinder block. Ensure that the bolts run freely in their threads, and that all traces of oil and water are removed from each bolt hole. If required, pull the oil feed non-return valve from the cylinder head, and

10.8 The engine oil level dipstick is secured to the alternator bracket by a Torx bolt (arrowed)

10.9 Undo the bolts (arrowed) and pull the coolant outlet housing from the left-hand end of the cylinderhead

10.10a Remove the high-pressure pipe (arrowed)...

10.10b... and the bracket (arrowed)

10.10c Pump mounting bracket upper nut and lower mounting bolt (arrowed)

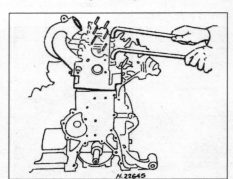

10.12 Free the cylinder head using angled rods

10.17a Pull the non-return valve from the cylinder head...

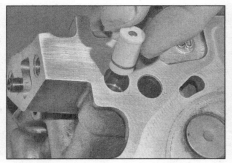

10.17b... and push a new one into place

10.21 Measure the piston protrusion using a DTI gauge

check the ball moves freely. Push a new valve into place if necessary **(see illustrations)**.

Gasket selection

18 Remove the crankshaft timing pin, then turn the crankshaft until pistons 1 and 4 are at TDC (Top Dead Centre). Position a dial test indicator (dial gauge) on the cylinder block adjacent to the rear of No 1 piston, and zero it on the block face. Transfer the probe to the crown of No 1 piston (10.0 mm in from the rear edge), and then slowly turn the crankshaft back-and-forth past TDC, noting the highest reading on the indicator. Record this reading as protrusion A.

19 Repeat the check described in para- graph 18, this time 10.0 mm in from the front edge of the No 1 piston crown. Record this reading as protrusion B.

20 Add protrusion A to protrusion B, then divide the result by 2 to obtain an average reading for piston No 1.

21 Repeat the procedure described in paragraphs 18 to 20 on piston 4, then turn the crankshaft through 180° and carry out the procedure on the piston Nos 2 and 3 **(see illustration)**. Check that there is a maximum difference of 0.07 mm protrusion between any two pistons.

22 If a dial test indicator is not available, piston protrusion may be measured using a straight-edge and feeler blades or Vernier calipers. However, this is much less accurate, and cannot therefore be recommended.

23 Note the greatest piston protrusion measurement, and use this to determine

the correct cylinder head gasket from the following table. The series of notches/holes on the side of the gasket are used for thickness identification **(see illustration)**.

Piston protrusion	Gasket identification
0.6115 to 0.720 mm	2 notches
0.721 to 0.770 mm	3 notches
0.771 to 0.820 mm	1 notches
0.821 to 0.870 mm	4 notches
0.871 to 0.977 mm	5 notches

Head bolt examination

24 Carefully examine the cylinder head bolts for signs of damage to the threads or head, and for any sign of corrosion. If the bolts are in a satisfactory condition, measure the length of each bolt from the underside of the head to the end of the shank. The bolts may be re-used providing that the measured length does not exceed 149.0 mm **(see illustration)**. **Note:** *Considering the stress to which the cylinder head bolts are subjected, it is highly recommended that they are all renewed, regardless of their apparent condition.*

Refitting

25 Turn the crankshaft and position Nos 1 and 4 pistons at TDC, then turn the crankshaft a quarter turn (90°) anti-clockwise.

26 Thoroughly clean the surfaces of the cylinder head and block.

27 Make sure that the locating dowels are in place, then fit the correct gasket the right way round on the cylinder block **(see illustration)**.

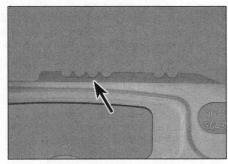

10.23 Cylinder head gasket thickness identification notches (arrowed)

28 If necessary, refit the exhaust manifold to the cylinder head as described in Chapter 4B Section 14.

29 Carefully lower the cylinder head onto the gasket and block, making sure that it locates correctly onto the dowels.

30 Apply a smear of grease to the threads, and to the underside of the heads, of the cylinder head bolts. Peugeot recommend the use of Molykote G Rapid Plus (available from your Peugeot dealer); in the absence of the specified grease, any good-quality high melting-point grease may be used.

31 Carefully insert the cylinder head bolts into their holes (do not drop them in) and initially finger-tighten them.

32 Working progressively and in sequence, tighten the cylinder head bolts to their Stage 1 torque setting, using a torque wrench and suitable socket **(see illustration)**.

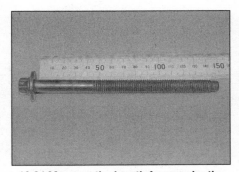

10.24 Measure the length from under the bolt head to its end

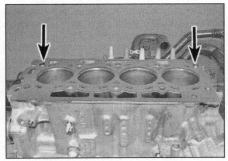

10.27 Ensure the gasket locates over the dowels (arrowed)

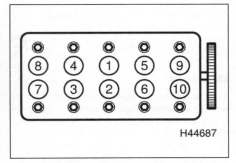

10.32 Cylinder head bolt tightening sequence

11.8 Apply a bead of sealant to the sump or crankcase mating surface. Ensure the sealant is applied on the inside of the retaining bolt holes

11.9 Refit the sump and tighten the bolts

33 Once all the bolts have been tightened to their Stage 1 torque setting, working again in the specified sequence, tighten each bolt to the specified Stage 2 setting. Finally, angle-tighten the bolts through the specified Stage 3 angle. It is recommended that an angle-measuring gauge is used during this stage of tightening, to ensure accuracy. **Note:** *Retightening of the cylinder head bolts after running the engine is not required.*

34 Refit the hydraulic followers, rocker arms, and camshaft housing (complete with camshafts) as described in Section 9.

35 Refit the timing belt as described in Section 7.

36 The remainder of refitting is a reversal of removal, noting the following points.
● Use a new seal when refitting the coolant outlet housing.
● When refitting a cylinder head, it is good practice to renew the thermostat.
● Refit the camshaft position sensor and set the air gap with reference to Chapter 4B Section 12.
● Tighten all fasteners to the specified torque where given.
● Refill the cooling system as described in Chapter 1B Section 22.
● The engine may run erratically for the first few miles, until the engine management ECM relearns its stored values.

11 Sump – removal and refitting

Removal

1 Drain the engine oil, then clean and refit the engine oil drain plug, tightening it securely. If the engine is nearing the service interval when the oil and filter are due for renewal, it is recommended that the filter is also removed, and a new one fitted. After reassembly, the engine can then be refilled with fresh oil. Refer to Chapter 1B Section 6 for further information.

2 Chock the rear wheels then jack up the front of the vehicle and support it on axle stands (see *Jacking and vehicle support*). Undo the screws and remove the engine undershield.

3 Remove the exhaust front pipe as described in Chapter 4B Section 18.

4 Where necessary, disconnect the wiring connector from the oil temperature sender unit, which is screwed into the sump.

5 Progressively slacken and remove all the sump retaining bolts/nuts. Since the sump bolts vary in length, remove each bolt in turn, and store it in its correct fitted order by pushing it through a clearly marked cardboard template. This will avoid the possibility of installing the bolts in the wrong locations on refitting.

6 Try to break the joint by striking the sump with the palm of your hand, then lower and withdraw the sump from under the car. If the sump is stuck (which is quite likely) use a putty knife or similar, carefully inserted between the sump and block. Ease the knife along the joint until the sump is released. While the sump is removed, take the opportunity to check the oil pump pick-up/strainer for signs of clogging or splitting. If necessary, remove the pump as described in Section 12, and clean or renew the strainer.

Refitting

7 Clean all traces of sealant from the mating surfaces of the cylinder block/crankcase and sump, and then use a clean rag to wipe out the sump and the engine's interior.

8 On engines where the sump was fitted without a gasket, ensure that the sump mating surfaces are clean and dry, then apply a thin coating of suitable sealant to the sump or crankcase mating surface **(see illustration)**.

9 Offer up the sump to the cylinder block/crankcase. Refit its retaining bolts/nuts, ensuring that each bolt is screwed into its original location. Tighten the bolts evenly and progressively to the specified torque setting **(see illustration)**.

10 Where necessary, align the air conditioning

compressor with its mountings on the sump, and insert the retaining bolts. Securely tighten the compressor retaining bolts, then refit the drivebelt as described in Chapter 1B Section 16.

11 Reconnect the wiring connector to the oil temperature sensor (where fitted).

12 Lower the vehicle to the ground, then refill the engine with oil as described in Chapter 1B Section 6.

12 Oil pump – removal, inspection and refitting

Removal

1 Remove the sump as described in Section 11.

2 Remove the crankshaft sprocket as described in Section 8. Recover the locating key from the crankshaft.

3 Disconnect the wiring plug, undo the bolts and remove the crankshaft position sensor, located on the right-hand end of the cylinder block.

4 Undo the three Allen screws and remove the oil pump pick-up tube from the pump/block **(see illustration)**. Discard the oil seal; a new one must be fitted.

12.4 Oil pick-up tube Allen screws (arrowed)

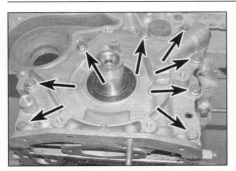

12.5 Oil pump retaining bolts (arrowed)

12.6 Undo the Torx bolts and remove the pump cover

12.7a Remove the circlip...

5 Undo the 8 bolts, and remove the oil pump **(see illustration)**.

Inspection

6 Undo and remove the Torx bolts securing the cover to the oil pump **(see illustration)**. Examine the pump rotors and body for signs of wear and damage. If worn, the complete pump must be renewed.
7 Remove the circlip, and extract the cap, valve piston and spring, noting which way around they are fitted **(see illustrations)**. The condition of the relief valve spring can only be measured by comparing it with a new one; if there is any doubt about its condition, it should also be renewed.
8 Refit the relief valve piston and spring, and then secure them in place with the circlip.
9 Refit the cover to the oil pump, and tighten the Torx bolts securely.

Refitting

10 Remove all traces of sealant, and thoroughly clean the mating surfaces of the oil pump and cylinder block.
11 Apply a 4 mm wide bead of silicone sealant to the mating face of the cylinder block **(see illustration)**. Ensure that no sealant enters any of the holes in the block.
12 With a new oil seal fitted, refit the oil pump over the end of the crankshaft, aligning the flats in the pump drivegear with the flats machined in the crankshaft **(see illustrations)**. Note that new oil pumps are supplied with the

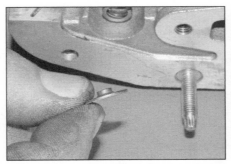

12.7b... cap...

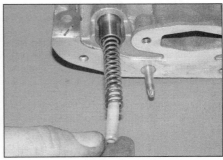

12.7c... spring...

12.7d... and piston

12.11 Apply a bead of sealant to the cylinder block mating surface

12.12a Fit a new seal...

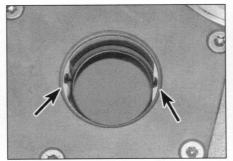

12.12b... align the pump gear flats (arrowed)...

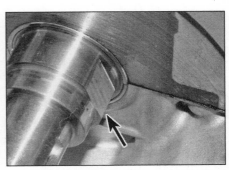

12.12c... with those of the crankshaft (arrowed)

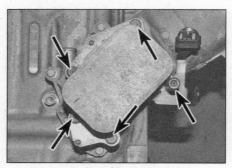

13.4a Undo the oil cooler bolts/stud (arrowed)

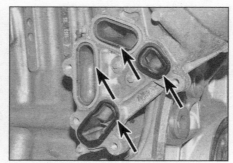

13.4b Renew the O-ring seals (arrowed)

14.3 Take great care not to mark the crankshaft whilst levering out the oil seal

oil seal already fitted, and a seal protector sleeve. The sleeve fits over the end of the crankshaft to protect the seal as the pump is fitted.

13 Install the oil pump bolts and tighten them to the specified torque.

14 Refit the oil pick-up tube to the pump/ cylinder block using a new O-ring seal. Ensure the oil dipstick guide tube is correctly refitted.

15 Refit the Woodruff key to the crankshaft, and slide the crankshaft sprocket into place.

16 The remainder of refitting is a reversal of removal.

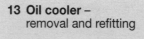

13 Oil cooler –
removal and refitting

Removal

1 Chock the rear wheels then jack up the front of the vehicle and support it on axle stands (see *Jacking and vehicle support*). Undo the screws and remove the engine undershield.

2 The oil cooler is fitted to the front of the oil filter housing. Drain the coolant as described in Chapter 1B Section 22.

3 Drain the engine oil as described in Chapter 1B Section 6, or be prepared for fluid spillage.

4 Undo the 5 bolts/stud and remove the oil cooler. Recover the O-ring seals **(see illustrations)**.

Refitting

5 Fit new O-ring seals into the recesses in the

oil filter housing, and refit the cooler. Tighten the bolts securely.

6 Refill or top-up the cooling system and engine oil level, then start the engine, and check the oil cooler for signs of leakage.

14 Oil seals – renewal

Crankshaft

Right-hand oil seal

1 Remove the crankshaft sprocket and Woodruff key as described in Section 8.

2 Measure and note the fitted depth of the oil seal.

3 Pull the oil seal from the housing using a screwdriver. Alternatively, drill a small hole in the oil seal, and use a self-tapping screw and a pair of pliers to remove it **(see illustration)**.

4 Clean the oil seal housing and the crankshaft sealing surface.

5 The seal has a Teflon lip and must not be oiled or marked. The new seal should be supplied with a protector sleeve, which fits over the end of the crankshaft to prevent any damage to the seal lip. With the sleeve in place, press the seal (open end first) into the pump to the previously-noted depth, using a suitable tube or socket **(see illustrations)**.

6 Where applicable, remove the plastic sleeve from the end of the crankshaft.

7 Refit the timing belt crankshaft sprocket as described in Section 8.

Left-hand oil seal

8 Remove the flywheel, as described in Section 16.

9 Measure and note the fitted depth of the oil seal.

10 Pull the oil seal from the housing using a screwdriver. Alternatively, drill a small hole in the oil seal, and use a self-tapping screw and a pair of pliers to remove it **(see illustration 14.3)**.

11 Clean the oil seal housing and the crankshaft sealing surface.

12 The seal has a Teflon lip and must not be oiled or marked. The new seal should be supplied with a protector sleeve, which fits over the end of the crankshaft to prevent any damage to the seal lip **(see illustration)**. With the sleeve in place, press the seal (open end first) into the housing to the previously-noted depth, using a suitable tube or socket.

13 Where applicable, remove the plastic sleeve from the end of the crankshaft.

14 Refit the flywheel, as described in Section 16.

Camshaft

15 Remove the camshaft sprocket as described in Section 8. In principle there is no need to remove the timing belt completely, but remember that if the belt has been contaminated with oil, it must be renewed.

16 Pull the oil seal from the housing using a hooked instrument. Alternatively, drill a small

14.5a Slide the seal and protective sleeve over the end of the crankshaft...

14.5b... and press the seal into place

14.12 Slide the seal and protective sleeve over the left-hand end of the crankshaft

hole in the oil seal and use a self-tapping screw and a pair of pliers to remove it **(see illustration)**.

17 Clean the oil seal housing and the camshaft sealing surface.

18 The seal has a Teflon lip and must not be oiled or marked. The new seal should be supplied with a protector sleeve, which fits over the end of the camshaft to prevent any damage to the seal lip **(see illustration)**. With the sleeve in place, press the seal (open end first) into the housing, using a suitable tube or socket that bears only of the outer edge of the seal.

19 Refit the camshaft sprocket as described in Section 8.

20 Where necessary, fit a new timing belt with reference to Section 7.

15 Oil pressure switch and level sensor – removal and refitting

Oil pressure switch

Removal

1 The oil pressure switch is located at the front of the cylinder block, adjacent to the oil dipstick guide tube. Note that on some models, access to the switch may be improved if the vehicle is jacked up and supported on axle stands, then undo the screws and remove the engine undershield so that the switch can be reached from underneath (see *Jacking and vehicle support*).

2 Remove the protective sleeve from the wiring plug (where applicable), and then disconnect the wiring from the switch.

3 Unscrew the switch from the cylinder block, and recover the sealing washer **(see illustration)**. Be prepared for oil spillage, and if the switch is to be left removed from the engine for any length of time, plug the hole in the cylinder block.

Refitting

4 Examine the sealing washer for any signs of damage or deterioration, and if necessary renew.

5 Refit the switch, complete with washer, and tighten it to the specified torque.

15.3 The oil pressure switch is located on the front face of the cylinder block (arrowed)

14.16 Drill a hole, insert a self-tapping screw, and pull the seal from place using pliers

6 Refit the engine undershield, and lower the vehicle to the ground.

Oil level sensor

Removal

7 The oil level sensor is located at the rear of the cylinder block **(see illustration)**. Jack up the front of the vehicle and support it securely on axle stands (see *Jacking and vehicle support*). Undo the screws and remove the engine undershield.

8 Reach up between the driveshaft and the cylinder block and disconnect the wiring plug from the sensor.

9 Using an open-ended spanner, unscrew the sensor and withdraw it from position.

Refitting

10 Smear a little silicone sealant on the threads and refit the sensor to the cylinder block, tightening it securely.

11 Reconnect the wiring plug to the sensor.

12 Refit the engine undershield, and lower the vehicle to the ground.

16 Flywheel – removal, inspection and refitting

Removal

1 Remove the transmission as described in Chapter 7A Section 7, then remove the clutch assembly as described in Chapter 6 Section 6.

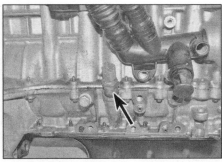

15.7 The oil level sensor is located on the rear face of the cylinder block (arrowed)

14.18 Fit the protective sleeve and seal over the end of the camshaft

2 Prevent the flywheel from turning by locking the ring gear teeth **(see illustration 5.2)**. Alternatively, bolt a strap between the flywheel and the cylinder block/crankcase. Do not attempt to lock the flywheel in position using the crankshaft pulley locking tool described in Section 3. Insert a 12 mm diameter rod or drill bit through the hole in the flywheel cover casting, and into a slot in the flywheel.

3 Make alignment marks between the flywheel and crankshaft to aid refitting. Slacken and remove the flywheel retaining bolts, and remove the flywheel from the end of the crankshaft. Be careful not to drop it; it is heavy. If the flywheel locating dowel (where fitted) is a loose fit in the crankshaft end, remove it and store it with the flywheel for safe-keeping. Discard the flywheel bolts; new ones must be used on refitting.

Inspection

4 Examine the flywheel for scoring of the clutch face, and for wear or chipping of the ring gear teeth. If the clutch face is scored, the flywheel may be surface-ground, but renewal is preferable. Seek the advice of a Peugeot dealer or engine-reconditioning specialist to see if machining is possible. If the ring gear is worn or damaged, the flywheel must be renewed, as it is not possible to renew the ring gear separately.

Refitting

5 Clean the mating surfaces of the flywheel and crankshaft. Remove any remaining locking compound from the threads of the crankshaft holes, using the correct size of tap, if available.

6 If the new flywheel retaining bolts are not supplied with their threads already pre-coated, apply a suitable thread-locking compound to the threads of each bolt.

Engines with normal flywheel

7 Ensure that the locating dowel is in position. Offer up the flywheel, locating it on the dowel (where fitted), and fit the new retaining bolts. Where no locating dowel is fitted, align the previously-made marks to ensure the flywheel is refitted in its original position.

8 Lock the flywheel using the method employed on dismantling, and tighten the

16.8 Flywheel retaining Torx bolts

retaining bolts to the specified torque **(see illustration)**.

Engines with dual mass flywheel

9 The dual mass flywheel is designed to reduce harshness and vibration in the action of the engine, clutch and transmission. With this type of flywheel, two flywheel centralising tools are needed (available from Peugeot dealers). These are screwed into two opposite flywheel bolt holes in the crankshaft. As the tools are screwed down, their conical shape centralises the flywheel with regard to the crankshaft.

10 With the flywheel centralised, fit the new bolts into the remaining flywheel holes, then lock the flywheel using the same method employed on dismantling, and tighten the bolts to the specified torque.

11 Remove the two centralising tools, fit the new bolts and tighten them to the specified torque.

All models

12 Refit the clutch, remove the flywheel locking tool, and then refit the transmission.

---

17 Engine/transmission mountings – inspection and renewal

Inspection

1 If improved access is required, chock the rear wheels then jack up the front of the car and support it on axle stands (see *Jacking and vehicle support*). Undo the screws and remove the engine undershield.

2 Check the mounting rubbers to see if they are cracked, hardened or separated from the metal at any point; renew the mounting if any such damage or deterioration is evident.

3 Check that all the mountings' fasteners are securely tightened; use a torque wrench to check if possible.

4 Using a large screwdriver or a crowbar, check for wear in each mounting by carefully levering against it to check for free play. Where this is not possible, enlist the aid of an assistant to move the engine/transmission back-and-forth, or from side-to-side, while you watch the mounting. While some free play is to be expected even from new components, excessive wear should be obvious. If excessive free play is found, check first that the fasteners are correctly secured, and then renew any worn components as described below.

Renewal

Right-hand mounting

5 Release all the relevant hoses and wiring from their retaining clips. Place the hoses/wiring clear of the mounting so that the removal procedure is not hindered. Undo the screws and remove the engine undershield.

6 Place a jack beneath the engine, with a block of wood on the jack head. Raise the jack until it is supporting the weight of the engine.

7 Undo the bolts/nut securing the engine mounting to the body and the support bracket.

8 If required, undo the bolts/nuts securing the support bracket to the cylinder head/cylinder block.

9 Check all components carefully for signs of wear or damage, and renew as necessary.

10 Where removed, refit the support bracket to the cylinder head, and tighten the bolts securely.

11 Refit the mount to the body and support bracket, and then tighten the bolts to the specified torque.

12 Remove the jack from underneath the engine.

Left-hand mounting

13 Remove the battery, and battery tray/box as described in Chapter 5A Section 4.

14 Place a jack beneath the transmission, with a block of wood on the jack head. Raise the jack until it is supporting the weight of the transmission.

15 Slacken and remove the mounting's upper retaining bolts.

16 Undo the retaining bolts from the mounting bracket on the body and remove the mounting from the engine compartment.

17 Check carefully for signs of wear or damage on all components, and renew them where necessary.

18 Refit the mounting bracket to the vehicle body and tighten its bolts to the specified torque.

19 Fit the mounting bolts to the bracket on the transmission and tighten the retaining bolts to the specified torque.

20 Remove the jack from underneath the transmission, then refit the battery and tray.

Rear lower mounting

21 If not already done, firmly apply the handbrake, then jack up the front of the vehicle and support it securely on axle stands (see *Jacking and vehicle support*).

22 Unscrew and remove the bolt securing the rear mounting link to the bracket on the transmission **(see illustration)**.

23 Remove the bolt securing the rear mounting link to the subframe and remove the mounting torque reaction link **(see illustration)**.

24 To remove the mounting bracket undo the retaining bolts and remove the mounting bracket from the rear of the transmission **(see illustration)**.

25 Check carefully for signs of wear or damage on all components, and renew them where necessary.

26 On reassembly, fit the rear mounting bracket to the transmission, and tighten its retaining bolts to the specified torque.

27 Refit the rear mounting torque reaction link, and tighten both its bolts to their specified torque settings.

28 Lower the vehicle to the ground.

17.22 Undo the mounting bolts – arrowed...

17.24 Undo the nut/bolts and remove the mounting bracket

17.23... and remove the lower link

Chapter 2 Part E
1.6 litre SOHC diesel engine in-car repair procedures

Contents

Degrees of difficulty

Easy, suitable for novice with little experience | Fairly easy, suitable for beginner with some experience 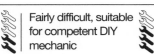 | Fairly difficult, suitable for competent DIY mechanic | Difficult, suitable for experienced DIY mechanic | Very difficult, suitable for expert DIY or professional

Specifications

General

Designation	DV6C
Engine codes	9HR
Capacity	1560 cc
Bore	75.0 mm
Stroke	88.3 mm
Direction of crankshaft rotation	Clockwise (viewed from the right-hand side of vehicle)
No 1 cylinder location	At the transmission end of block
Maximum power output	82 kW (110 PS) @ 4000 rpm
Maximum torque output	270 Nm @ 1750 rpm
Compression ratio	16 : 1

*The engine code is stamped onto a plate attached to the front of the cylinder block, next to the oil filter.

Valves

Valve clearances (cold)
Inlet	0.103 to 0.118 mm
Exhaust	0.113 to 0.128 mm

Compression pressures (engine hot, at cranking speed)

Normal	20 ± 5 bar
Minimum	15 bar
Maximum difference between any two cylinders	5 bar

Camshaft

Camshaft end float	0.195 – 0.3 mm

Lubrication system

Oil pump type...	Gear-type, driven directly by the right-hand end of the crankshaft, by two flats machined along the crankshaft journal.

Minimum oil pressure at 80°C:
 Idle speed.. 1.0 to 2.0 bar
 2000 rpm .... 2.3 to 3.7 bar

Torque wrench settings

	Nm	lbf ft
Ancillary drivebelt tensioner roller	20	15
Big-end bolts: *		
Stage 1...	10	7
Stage 2...	Slacken 180°	
Stage 3...	10	7
Stage 4...	Angle-tighten a further 130°	
Camshaft bearing caps	10	7
Camshaft cover/bearing ladder:		
Studs	10	7
Bolts	10	7
Camshaft position sensor bolt.............................	5	4
Camshaft sprocket bolt:		
Stage 1...	20	15
Stage 2...	Angle-tighten a further 50°	
Coolant outlet housing bolts	8	6
Crankshaft position/speed sensor bolt	10	7
Crankshaft pulley/sprocket bolt: *		
Stage 1...	35	26
Stage 2...	Angle-tighten a further 190°	
Cylinder head bolts: *		
Stage 1...	20	15
Stage 2...	40	30
Stage 3...	Angle-tighten a further 260°	
Cylinder head cover/manifold	13	10
EGR valve..	10	7
Engine-to-transmission fixing bolts	47	35
Flywheel bolts: *		
Stage 1...	30	22
Stage 2...	Angle-tighten a further 90°	
Fuel pump sprocket	50	37
Left-hand engine/transmission mounting:		
Mounting-to-bracket centre nut..........................	148	109
Mounting-to-bracket outer nuts..........................	48	35
Mounting bracket to transmission	80	59
Main bearing ladder outer seam bolts:		
Stage 1...	5	4
Stage 2...	10	7
Main bearing ladder to cylinder block:		
Stage 1...	10	7
Stage 2...	Slacken 180°	
Stage 3...	30	22
Stage 4...	Angle-tighten a further 140°	
Piston oil jet spray tube bolt...............................	20	15
Oil cooler retaining bolts...................................	10	7
Oil filter cover	25	18
Oil pick-up pipe	10	7
Oil pressure switch.......................................	30	22
Oil pump to cylinder block:		
Stage 1...	5	4
Stage 2...	9	7
Rear engine/transmission mounting.........................	25	18
Right-hand engine mounting:		
Mounting to Inner wing (nuts/bolts)	48	35
Mounting bracket to engine block	55	41
Sump drain plug...	35	26
Sump bolts/nuts...	10	7
Timing belt idler pulley	37	27
Timing belt tensioner pulley	30	22
Vacuum pump bolts	20	15

*Do not re-use

1 General Information

How to use this Chapter

1 This Part of Chapter 2 describes the repair procedures that can reasonably be carried out on the engine while it remains in the vehicle. If the engine has been removed from the vehicle and is being dismantled as described in Part F, any preliminary dismantling procedures can be ignored.

2 Note that, while it may be possible physically to overhaul items such as the piston/connecting rod assemblies while the engine is in the car, such tasks are not usually carried out as separate operations. Usually, several additional procedures are required (not to mention the cleaning of components and oilways); for this reason, all such tasks are classed as major overhaul procedures, and are described in Part F of this Chapter.

3 Part F describes the removal of the engine/transmission from the car, and the full overhaul procedures that can then be carried out.

DV series engines

4 The 1.6 litre DV series of engines are the result of development collaboration between Citroën/Peugeot and Ford. Originally specified as a double overhead camshaft (DOHC) 16-valve design, the latest version fitted to the Peugeot 207 is a single overhead cam (SOHC), 8 valve variant. The direct injection, turbocharged, four-cylinder engine is mounted transversely, with the transmission mounted on the left-hand side.

5 A toothed timing belt drives the camshaft, high-pressure fuel pump and coolant pump. The camshaft operates the inlet and exhaust valves via rocker arms which are supported at their pivot ends by hydraulic self-adjusting tappets. The camshaft Is supported by bearings machined directly in the cylinder head and camshaft bearing housing.

6 The high-pressure fuel pump supplies fuel to the fuel rail, and subsequently to the electronically-controlled injectors which inject the fuel direct into the combustion chambers. This design differs from the previous type where an injection pump supplies the fuel at high pressure to each injector. The earlier, conventional type injection pump required fine calibration and timing, and these functions are now completed by the high-pressure pump, electronic injectors and engine management ECM.

7 The crankshaft runs in five main bearings of the usual shell type. Endfloat is controlled by thrustwashers either side of No 2 main bearing.

8 The pistons are selected to be of matching weight, and incorporate fully-floating gudgeon pins retained by circlips.

Repair operations precaution

9 The engine is a complex unit with numerous accessories and ancillary components. The design of the engine compartment is such that every conceivable space has been utilised, and access to virtually all of the engine components is extremely limited. In many cases, ancillary components will have to be removed, or moved to one side, and wiring, pipes and hoses will have to be disconnected or removed from various cable clips and support brackets.

10 When working on this engine, read through the entire procedure first, look at the car and engine at the same time, and establish whether you have the necessary tools, equipment, skill and patience to proceed. Allow considerable time for any operation, and be prepared for the unexpected.

11 Because of the limited access, many of the engine photographs appearing in this Chapter were, by necessity, taken with the engine removed from the vehicle.

⚠ **Warning: It is essential to observe strict precautions when working on the fuel system components of the engine, particularly the high-pressure side of the system. Before carrying out any engine operations that entail working on, or near, any part of the fuel system, refer to the special information given in Chapter. 4B**

Operations with engine in vehicle

● Compression pressure – testing.
● Cylinder head cover – removal and refitting.
● Crankshaft pulley – removal and refitting.
● Timing belt covers – removal and refitting.
● Timing belt – removal, refitting and adjustment.
● Timing belt tensioner and sprockets – removal and refitting.
● Camshaft oil seal – renewal.
● Camshaft, rocker arms and hydraulic tappets – removal, inspection and refitting.
● Sump – removal and refitting.
● Oil pump – removal and refitting.
● Crankshaft oil seals – renewal.
● Engine/transmission mountings – inspection and renewal.
● Flywheel – removal, inspection and refitting.

2 Compression and leakdown tests – description and interpretation

Compression test

Note: *A compression tester specifically designed for diesel engines must be used for this test.*

1 When engine performance is down, or if misfiring occurs which cannot be attributed to the fuel system, a compression test can provide diagnostic clues as to the engine's condition. If the test is performed regularly, it can give warning of trouble before any other symptoms become apparent.

2 A compression tester specifically intended for diesel engines must be used, because of the higher pressures involved. The tester is connected to an adapter which screws into the glow plug or injector hole. On this engine, an adapter suitable for use in the glow plug holes will be required, so as not to disturb the fuel system components. It is unlikely to be worthwhile buying such a tester for occasional use, but it may be possible to borrow or hire one – if not, have the test performed by a garage.

3 Unless specific instructions to the contrary are supplied with the tester, observe the following points:
The battery must be in a good state of charge, the air filter must be clean, and the engine should be at normal operating temperature.
All the glow plugs should be removed as described in Chapter 5C Section 2 before starting the test.
Disconnect the fuel injector wiring plugs.

4 The compression pressures measured are not so important as the balance between cylinders. Values are given in the Specifications.

5 The cause of poor compression is less easy to establish on a diesel engine than on a petrol one. The effect of introducing oil into the cylinders ('wet' testing) is not conclusive, because there is a risk that the oil will sit in the swirl chamber or in the recess on the piston crown instead of passing to the rings. However, the following can be used as a rough guide to diagnosis.

6 All cylinders should produce very similar pressures; any difference greater than that specified indicates the existence of a fault. Note that the compression should build-up quickly in a healthy engine; low compression on the first stroke, followed by gradually-increasing pressure on successive strokes, indicates worn piston rings. A low compression reading on the first stroke, which does not build-up during successive strokes, indicates leaking valves or a blown head gasket (a cracked head could also be the cause). Deposits on the undersides of the valve heads can also cause low compression.

7 A low reading from two adjacent cylinders is almost certainly due to the head gasket having blown between them; the presence of coolant in the engine oil will confirm this.

8 If the compression reading is unusually high, the cylinder head surfaces, valves and pistons are probably coated with carbon deposits. If this is the case, the cylinder head should be removed and decarbonised.

Note: *After performing this test, a fault code may be generated and stored in the PCM memory. Have the PCM self-diagnosis facility interrogated by a Ford dealer or suitably-equipped specialist, and the fault code erased. Inexpensive fault code readers/scanners are readily available.*

Leakdown test

9 A leakdown test measures the rate at which compressed air fed into the cylinder is lost. It is an alternative to a compression test, and in many ways it is better, since the escaping air provides easy identification of where pressure loss is occurring (piston rings, valves or head gasket).

10 The equipment needed for leakdown testing is unlikely to be available to the home mechanic. If poor compression is suspected, have the test performed by a suitably-equipped garage.

3 Engine assembly/valve timing holes – general information and usage

Note: *Do not attempt to rotate the engine whilst the crankshaft and camshaft are locked in position. If the engine is to be left in this state for a long period of time, it is a good idea to place suitable warning notices inside the vehicle, and in the engine compartment. This will reduce the possibility of the engine being accidentally cranked on the starter motor, which is likely to cause damage with the locking pins in place.*

1 Timing holes or slots are located only in the crankshaft pulley flange and camshaft sprocket hub. The holes/slots are used to position the pistons halfway up the cylinder bores. This will ensure that the valve timing is maintained during operations that require removal and refitting of the timing belt. When the holes/slots are aligned with their corresponding holes in the cylinder block and cylinder head, suitable diameter bolts/pins can be inserted to lock the crankshaft and camshaft in position, preventing rotation.

2 Note that the fuel system used on these engines does not have a conventional diesel injection pump, but instead uses a high-pressure fuel pump. However, the fuel pump sprocket must be pegged in position in a similar fashion to the camshaft sprocket.

3 To align the engine assembly/valve timing holes, proceed as follows.

4 Apply the handbrake, then jack up the front of the vehicle and support it on axle stands

3.9 Insert a 5.0 mm drill bit/bolt through the round hole in the sprocket flange into the hole in the oil pump housing (lower timing belt removed for clarity)

(see Chapter 13 Section 5). Remove the right-hand front roadwheel.

5 To gain access to the crankshaft pulley, to enable the engine to be turned, the wheel arch plastic liner must be removed. The liner is secured by several plastic expanding rivets/nut/bolts. To remove the rivets, push in the centre pins a little, then prise the clips from place. Remove the liner from under the front wing.

6 Remove the starter motor and remove the crankshaft pulley as described in Section 5.

7 Remove the upper and lower timing belt covers as described in Section 6.

8 Temporarily refit the crankshaft pulley bolt (without the crankshaft pulley) and then remove the crankshaft locking tool.

9 Turn the crankshaft until the timing hole in the crankshaft sprocket aligns with the hole in the oil pump casing (this is at the 12 o'clock position). Fit the special tool 303-732, or a suitable alternative and lock the crankshaft in position **(see illustration)**.

10 With the crankshaft locked in position fit the camshaft locking tool (303-735 or similar). The hole in the camshaft sprocket should be at approximately the 1 o'clock position **(see illustration)**. If this is not the case remove the crankshaft locking pin and rotate the engine one revolution. Note that the crankshaft must always be turned in a clockwise direction (viewed from the right-hand side of vehicle).

3.10 Insert an 8.0 mm bolt through the hole in the camshaft sprocket into the corresponding hole in the cylinder head

11 When refitting the timing belt, insert tool No 303-732 through the slot in the fuel pump sprocket and into the corresponding hole in the fuel pump mounting bracket. In the absence of this tool use a 5 mm bolt or drill bit.

12 The crankshaft and camshaft are now locked in position, preventing unnecessary rotation.

4 Cylinder head cover – removal and refitting

Removal

1 Disconnect the battery negative lead as described in Chapter 13 Section 6.

2 Release the securing lugs **(see illustrations 10.2a and 10.2b)** and lift the cover upwards from the top of the engine.

3 Remove the air cleaner assembly Chapter 4B Section 4.

4 Remove the sound insulation from the top of the engine **(see illustration)**.

5 Unclip the wiring loom from the rear of the cover and move it to one side, then remove the breather hose from the front corner of the valve cover.

6 Unbolt and then remove the timing belt upper cover Section 6.

7 Remove the bolts and remove the cover from the top of the cylinder head, then recover the rubber seal.

Refitting

8 Refitting is a reversal of removal, but ensure that the valve cover seal is correctly located in the valve cover **(see illustration)**.

5 Crankshaft pulley – removal and refitting

Removal

1 Jack up and support the front of the vehicle (see *Jacking and vehicle support*).

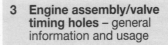

4.4 Remove the insulation

4.8 Fit the seal correctly

2 Disconnect the battery (Chapter 13 Section 6) and remove the engine undershield.

3 Remove the starter motor as described in Chapter 5A Section 10.

4 Remove wing liner and then remove the auxiliary drivebelt as described in Chapter 1B Section 16.

5 To lock the crankshaft, fit the special tool 303-393 (or suitable equivalent) to the flywheel ring gear **(see illustration)**.

6 Using a suitable socket and extension bar, unscrew the retaining bolt, remove the washer, then slide the pulley off the end of the crankshaft **(see illustrations)**. If the pulley is tight fit, it can be drawn off the crankshaft using a suitable puller. If a puller is being used, refit the pulley retaining bolt without the washer, to avoid damaging the crankshaft as the puller is tightened.

Caution: Do not touch the outer magnetic sensor ring of the sprocket with your fingers, or allow metallic particles to come into contact with it.

Refitting

7 Refit the pulley to the end of the crankshaft.

8 Refit the crankshaft pulley. Fit a new bolt and retaining washer. Tighten the bolt to the specified torque, then through the specified angle.

9 Remove the locking tool and refit the starter motor

10 Refit and tension the auxiliary drivebelt as described in Chapter 1B Section 16

11 Refit the remaining components in reverse order of removal.

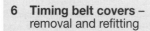

6   Timing belt covers –
    removal and refitting

⚠️ *Warning: Refer to the precautionary information contained in Section 1 before proceeding.*

Removal

Upper cover

1 Remove the engine cover from the top of the engine.

2 Remove the fuel lines and wiring loom from the support bracket next to the cover and then work the bracket free **(see illustrations)**.

3 Undo the 4 bolts and remove the timing belt upper cover **(see illustration)**.

Lower cover

4 Remove the crankshaft pulley as described in Section 5.

5 Position a trolley/workshop jack under the engine. Place a block of wood on the jack head (to help spread the load on the sump), then take the weight of the engine.

6 Prise up the coolant expansion tank and move it to one side – there is no need to drain the coolant.

7 Undo the nuts/bolts, and remove the right-hand engine mounting **(see illustration)**.

5.5 Install the flywheel locking tool (arrowed)

5.6a Where fitted remove the cover

5.6b Remove the bolt and...

5.6c ...then the pulley

6.2a Release the fuel lines and...

6.2b ...remove the bracket

6.3 Remove the upper cover

6.7 Remove the engine mounting

6.9 Remove the lower timing belt cover from below

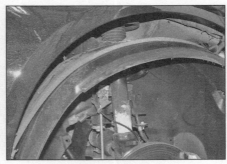

7.4 Remove the wing liner

7.6 Undo the bolt (arrowed) and remove the crankshaft position sensor

8 Whilst not strictly necessary access is greatly improved if the mounting bracket is removed from the engine.

9 Undo the 4 bolts and remove the lower cover **(see illustration)**.

Refitting

10 Refitting of all the covers is a reversal of the relevant removal procedure, ensuring that each cover section is correctly located, and that the cover retaining bolts are securely tightened. Ensure that all disturbed hoses are reconnected and retained by their relevant clips.

7 Timing belt – removal, inspection, refitting and tensioning

General

1 The timing belt drives the camshaft, high-pressure fuel pump, and coolant pump from a toothed sprocket on the end of the crankshaft. If the belt breaks or slips in service, the pistons are likely to hit the valve heads, resulting in expensive damage.

2 The timing belt should be renewed at the specified intervals, or earlier if it is contaminated with oil, or at all noisy in operation (a 'scraping' noise due to uneven wear).

3 If the timing belt is being removed, it is a wise precaution to renew the coolant pump at the same time. This may avoid the need to remove the timing belt again at a later stage, should the coolant pump fail. The timing belt tensioner should always be replaced when a new timing belt is fitted.

Removal

4 Apply the handbrake, then jack up the front of the vehicle and support it on axle stands (see *Jacking and vehicle support*). Remove the front right-hand roadwheel, wing liner **(see illustration)** and the engine undershield.

5 Remove the upper and lower timing belt covers, as described in Section 6.

6 Undo the bolt and remove the crankshaft position sensor adjacent to the crankshaft sprocket flange, and move it to one side **(see illustration)**.

7 Undo the retaining bolt and remove the timing belt protection bracket, again, adjacent to the crankshaft sprocket flange **(see illustration)**.

8 Lock the crankshaft and camshaft in the correct position as described in Section 3. If necessary, temporarily refit the crankshaft pulley bolt to enable the crankshaft to be rotated.

9 Insert a hexagon key into the belt tensioner pulley centre, slacken the pulley bolt, and allow the tensioner to rotate, relieving the belt

tension **(see illustration)**. With the belt slack, temporarily tighten the pulley bolt.

10 Note its routing, then remove the timing belt from the sprockets **(see illustration)**.

Inspection

11 Renew the belt as a matter of course, regardless of its apparent condition. The cost of a new belt is nothing compared with the cost of repairs should the belt break in service. If signs of oil contamination are found, trace the source of the oil leak and rectify it. Wash down the engine timing belt area and all related components, to remove all traces of oil. The tensioner must always be replaced. Check that the idler pulleys rotate freely without any sign of roughness, and also check that the coolant pump pulley rotates freely. It is highly recommended that both the coolant pump and the idler pulley are replaced at the same time as the timing belt and tensioner.

Refitting and tensioning

12 Commence refitting by ensuring that the crankshaft, camshaft and fuel pump sprocket timing pins are in position as described in Section 3.

13 Locate the timing belt on the crankshaft sprocket, then keeping it taut, locate it around the idler pulley, camshaft sprocket, high-pressure pump sprocket, coolant

7.7 Remove the timing belt protection bracket

7.9 Slacken the bolt and allow the tensioner to rotate, relieving the tension on the belt

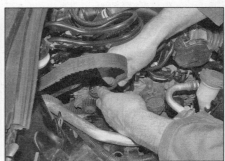

7.10 Remove the timing belt

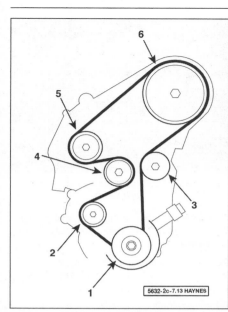

7.13 Timing belt routing

1 Crankshaft   4 Tensioner
2 Waterpump   5 Fuel pump
3 Idler   6 Camshaft

pump sprocket, and the tensioner roller **(see illustration)**.

14 Refit the timing belt protection bracket and tighten the retaining bolt securely.

15 Slacken the tensioner pulley bolt, and using a hexagonal key, rotate the tensioner anti-clockwise, which moves the index arm clockwise, until the index arm is aligned as shown **(see illustration)**.

16 Remove the camshaft, crankshaft and fuel pump sprocket (where applicable) timing pins and, using a socket on the crankshaft pulley bolt, rotate the crankshaft clockwise 10 complete revolutions. Refit the crankshaft and camshaft locking pins.

17 Check that the tensioner index arm is still aligned between the edges of the area shown **(see illustration 7.15)**. If it is not, remove and belt and begin the refitting process again, starting at Paragraph 12.

7.15 The index arm must align with the lug (arrowed)

18 The remainder of refitting is a reversal of removal. Tighten all fasteners to the specified torque where given.

8 Timing belt sprockets and tensioner – removal and refitting

Camshaft sprocket

Removal

1 Remove the timing belt as described in Section 7.

2 Remove the locking tool from the camshaft sprocket/hub. Slacken the sprocket hub retaining bolt. To prevent the camshaft rotating as the bolt is slackened, a sprocket holding tool will be required. In the absence of the special Peugeot tool, an acceptable substitute can be fabricated at home **(see Tool Tip 1)**. **Do not** attempt to use the engine assembly/valve timing locking tool to prevent the sprocket from rotating whilst the bolt is slackened.

3 Remove the sprocket hub retaining bolt, and slide the sprocket and hub off the end of the camshaft.

4 Clean the camshaft sprocket thoroughly, and renew it if there are any signs of wear, damage or cracks.

A sprocket holding tool can be made from two lengths of steel strip bolted together to form a forked end. Drill holes and insert bolts in the ends of the fork to engage with the sprocket spokes.

Refitting

5 Refit the camshaft sprocket to the camshaft **(see illustration)**.

6 Refit the sprocket hub retaining bolt. Tighten the bolt to the specified torque, preventing the camshaft from turning as during removal.

7 Align the engine assembly/valve timing slot in the camshaft sprocket hub with the hole in the cylinder head and refit the timing pin to lock the camshaft in position.

8 Fit the timing belt around the pump sprocket and camshaft sprocket, and tension the timing belt as described in Section 7.

Crankshaft sprocket

Removal

9 Remove the timing belt as described in Section 7.

10 Check that the engine assembly/valve timing holes are still aligned as described in Section 3, and the camshaft sprocket and flywheel are locked in position.

11 Slide the sprocket off the end of the crankshaft and collect the Woodruff key **(see illustrations)**.

12 Examine the crankshaft oil seal for signs of oil leakage and, if necessary, renew it as described in Section 14.

13 Clean the crankshaft sprocket thoroughly,

8.5 Ensure the lug on the sprocket hub engages with the slot on the end of the camshaft (arrowed)

8.11a Slide the sprocket from the crankshaft...

8.11b ...and recover the Woodruff key

TOOL TiP 2

Make a sprocket releasing tool from a short strip of steel. Drill two holes in the strip to correspond with the two holes in the sprocket. Drill a third hole just large enough to accept the flats of the sprocket retaining nut.

and renew it if there are any signs of wear, damage or cracks. Recover the crankshaft locating key.

Refitting

14 Refit the key to the end of the crankshaft, then refit the crankshaft sprocket (with the flange facing the crankshaft pulley).
15 Fit the timing belt around the crankshaft sprocket, and tension the timing belt as described in Section 7.

Fuel pump sprocket

Removal

16 Remove the timing belt as described in Section 7.
17 Using a suitable socket, undo the pump sprocket retaining nut. The sprocket can be held stationary by inserting a suitably-sized locking pin, drill or rod through the slot in the sprocket, and into the corresponding hole in the backplate, or by using a suitable forked tool engaged with the holes in the sprocket **(see Tool Tip 1)**.
18 The pump sprocket is a taper fit on the pump shaft and it will be necessary to make up another tool to release it from the taper **(see Tool Tip 2)**.
19 Partially unscrew the sprocket retaining nut, fit the home-made tool, and secure it to the sprocket with two suitable bolts. Prevent the

9.4 Remove the vacuum pump

8.25 Remove the tensioner

sprocket from rotating as before, and unscrew the sprocket retaining nut. The nut will bear against the tool as it is undone, forcing the sprocket off the shaft taper. Once the taper is released, remove the tool, unscrew the nut fully, and remove the sprocket from the pump shaft.
20 Clean the sprocket thoroughly, and renew it if there are any signs of wear, damage or cracks.

Refitting

21 Refit the pump sprocket and retaining nut, and tighten the nut to the specified torque. Prevent the sprocket rotating as the nut is tightened using the sprocket holding tool.
22 Refit the timing belt as described in Section 7.

Coolant pump sprocket

23 The coolant pump sprocket is integral with the pump, and cannot be removed. Coolant pump removal is described in Chapter 3 Section 8.

Tensioner pulley

Removal

24 Remove the timing belt as described in Section 7.
25 Remove the tensioner pulley retaining bolt, and then remove the tensioner **(see illustration)**.
26 Clean the tensioner pulley, but do not use any strong solvent which may enter the pulley bearings. Check that the pulley rotates freely, with no sign of stiffness or free play. The pulley should always be replaced when the timing belt is replaced.

9.6 Remove the camshaft position sensor (arrowed)

8.31 Timing belt idler pulley retaining nut (arrowed)

27 Examine the pulley mounting stud for signs of damage and if necessary, renew it.

Refitting

28 Refitting is a reversal of removal.
29 Refit the timing belt as described in Section 7.

Idler pulley

Removal

30 Remove the timing belt as described in Section 7.
31 Undo the retaining bolt/nut and withdraw the idler pulley from the engine **(see illustration)**.
32 Clean the idler pulley, but do not use any strong solvent which may enter the bearings. Check that the pulley rotates freely, with no sign of stiffness or free play. Renew the idler pulley if there is any doubt about its condition, or if there are any obvious signs of wear or damage.

Refitting

33 Locate the idler pulley on the engine, and fit the retaining bolt/nut. Tighten the bolt/nut to the specified torque.
34 Refit the timing belt as described in Section 7.

---

9 Camshaft, rocker arms and hydraulic tappets – removal, inspection and refitting

Removal

1 Remove the cylinder head cover/manifold as described in Section 4.
2 Remove the timing belt (Section 7) and the camshaft sprocket as described in Section 8.
3 Refit the right-hand engine mounting, but only tighten the bolts moderately; this will keep the engine supported during the camshaft removal.
4 Undo the bolts and remove the vacuum pump (see Chapter 9 Section 23). Recover the pump O-ring seals **(see illustration)**.
5 Unbolt the fuel filter (see Chapter 1B Section 18) and move it to one side.
6 Disconnect the wiring plug from the camshaft position sensor **(see illustration)**. Unbolt and remove the sensor from the bearing ladder.

9.7 Remove the bearing ladder

9.8 Remove the camshaft

9.10 Remove the rocker arms (cam followers)

7 Working in reverse order to that shown **(see illustration 9.22)** remove the retaining bolts and then remove camshaft bearing cap ladder **(see illustration)**.
8 Lift out the camshaft **(see illustration)** and dispose of the oil seal. A new one will be required.
9 Obtain 8 small, clean plastic containers, and number them 1 to 4 inlet and 1 to 4 exhaust; alternatively, divide a larger container into 8 compartments.
10 Lift out each rocker arm. Place the rocker arms in their respective positions in the box or containers **(see illustration)**.
11 A compartmentalised container filled with engine oil is now required to retain the hydraulic tappets while they are removed from the cylinder head. Withdraw each hydraulic follower **(see illustration)** and place it in the container, keeping them each identified for correct refitting. The tappets must be totally submerged in the oil to prevent air entering them.

Inspection

12 Inspect the cam lobes and the camshaft bearing journals for scoring or other visible evidence of wear. Once the surface hardening of the cam lobes has been eroded, wear will occur at an accelerated rate. **Note:** *If these symptoms are visible on the tips of the camshaft lobes, check the corresponding rocker arm, as it will probably be worn as well.*
13 Examine the condition of the bearing surfaces in the cylinder head and camshaft bearing housing. If wear is evident, the cylinder head and bearing housing will both have to be renewed, as they are a matched assembly.

14 Inspect the rocker arms and tappets for scuffing, cracking or other damage and renew any components as necessary. Also check the condition of the tappet bores in the cylinder head. As with the camshafts, any wear in this area will necessitate cylinder head renewal.

Refitting

15 Thoroughly clean the sealant from the mating surfaces of the cylinder head and camshaft bearing housing. Use a suitable liquid gasket dissolving agent (available from Ford dealers) together with a soft putty knife; do not use a metal scraper or the faces will be damaged. As there is no conventional gasket used, the cleanliness of the mating faces is of the utmost importance.
16 Clean off any oil, dirt or grease from both components and dry with a clean lint-free cloth. Ensure that all the oilways are completely clean.

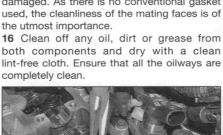

9.11 Use long nose pliers to remove the hydraulic tappets

17 Liberally lubricate the hydraulic tappet bores in the cylinder head with clean engine oil.
18 Insert the hydraulic tappets into their original bores in the cylinder head unless they have been renewed.
19 Lubricate the rocker arms and place them over their respective tappets and valve stems. Lubricate the bearing surfaces **(see illustration)** and then refit the camshaft.
20 Apply a thin bead of silicone sealant to the mating surface of the camshaft cover/bearing ladder as shown **(see illustration)**.
21 Assembly the bearing ladder within 10 minutes of applying the sealant **(see illustration)**. Technicians use a special tool (303-245) to align the bearing ladder, however 2 suitable bolts (with their heads and threads cut off) can be used if the tool is not available.
22 Tighten the bolts to the specified torque in sequence **(see illustration)**.

9.19 Lubricate the bearing surfaces

9.20 Apply sealant to the camshaft housing

9.21 Refit the bearing ladder

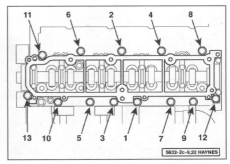

9.22 Tighten the bolts to the specified torque in the order shown

23 Fit a new camshaft oil seal as described in Section 14.

24 Refit the camshaft sprocket, and tighten the retaining bolt.

25 Refit the timing belt and temporarily refit the crankshaft pulley bolt – use the old bolt. Rotate the engine at least 20 revolutions to allow the oil pump to deliver oil to the camshaft and associated components. Refit the timing belt cover.

26 Refit the remainder of the components in the reverse order of removal.

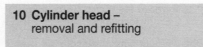

10 Cylinder head – removal and refitting

Removal

1 Apply the handbrake, then jack up the front of the vehicle and support it on axle stands (see *Jacking and vehicle support*). Remove the front right-hand roadwheel, the engine undershield, and the right-hand front wheel arch liner.

2 Remove the engine cover **(see illustrations)** and then disconnect the battery negative lead as described in Chapter 5A Section 4. With reference to Chapter 12 Section 13 remove the wiper arms and screen cowl panel.

3 Drain the cooling system as described in Chapter 1B Section 22.

4 Remove the timing belt, camshaft, rocker arms and hydraulic tappets as described in Section 9.

10.2a Pull up on the retaining lugs…

10.2b … and remove the engine cover

5 Remove the turbocharger and exhaust manifold as described in Chapter 4B Section 16.

6 Unbolt the fuel filter assembly (and move it to one side) and the remove the glow plugs as described in Chapter 5C Section 2.

7 Undo the upper mounting bolts, and pivot the alternator away from the engine, undo the oil dipstick guide tube bolt, then undo the bolts securing the alternator mounting bracket to the cylinder head/block **(see illustration)**.

8 Undo the coolant outlet housing (left-hand end of the cylinder head) retaining bolts, slacken the two bolts securing the housing support bracket to the top of the transmission bellhousing, and move the outlet housing away from the cylinder head a little **(see illustration)**. There is no need to disconnect the hoses.

9 Remove the brake vacuum pump as described in Chapter 9 Section 23.

10 Disconnect the high-pressure fuel pipe from the common rail to the pump, and disconnect the fuel supply and return hoses. Where fitted, remove the bracket at the rear of the pump, then undo the bolt/nut and remove the pump and mounting bracket as an assembly **(see illustrations)**. Immediately seal all the openings in the fuel system. Note that a new high-pressure pipe must be fitted – see Chapter 4B Section 9.

11 Unbolt the EGR pipe and inlet duct from the rear of the cylinder head.

12 Check that no components or electrical connectors are still fitted to the cylinder head.

13 Working in the **reverse** of the sequence shown **(see illustration 10.32)** undo the cylinder head bolts. Discard the bolts – new ones must be fitted.

14 Release the cylinder head from the cylinder block and location dowels by rocking it. The special tool for doing this consists simply of two metal rods with 90-degree angled ends **(see illustration)**. Do not prise

10.7 The engine oil level dipstick guide tube is secured to the alternator bracket by a Torx bolt (arrowed)

10.8 Access to the coolant outlet housing will be improved if the vacuum pump is removed first

10.10a Remove the high-pressure pipe (arrowed)

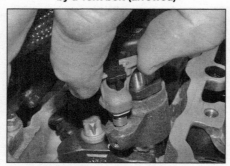

10.10b Compress the collars and…

10.10c …remove the fuel bleed hoses from the injectors

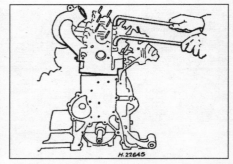

10.14 Free the cylinder head using angled rods

10.18a Pull the non-return valve from the cylinder head…

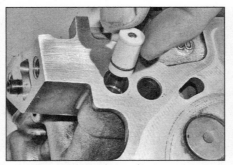

10.18b …and push a new one into place

10.23 Measure the piston protrusion using a DTI gauge

between the mating faces of the cylinder head and block, as this may damage the gasket faces.

15 Lift the cylinder head from the block, and recover the gasket.

Preparation for refitting

16 The mating faces of the cylinder head and cylinder block must be perfectly clean before refitting the head. Peugeot recommend the use of a scouring agent for this purpose, but acceptable results can be achieved by using a hard plastic or wood scraper to remove all traces of gasket and carbon. The same method can be used to clean the piston crowns. Take particular care to avoid scoring or gouging the cylinder head/cylinder block mating surfaces during the cleaning operations, as aluminium alloy is easily damaged. Make sure that the carbon is not allowed to enter the oil and water passages – this is particularly important for the lubrication system, as carbon could block the oil supply to the engine's components. Using adhesive tape and paper, seal the water, oil and bolt holes in the cylinder block. To prevent carbon entering the gap between the pistons and bores, smear a little grease in the gap. After cleaning each piston, use a small brush to remove all traces of grease and carbon from the gap, then wipe away the remainder with a clean rag.

17 Check the mating surfaces of the cylinder block and the cylinder head for nicks, deep scratches and other damage. If slight, they may be removed carefully with a file, but if excessive, machining may be the only alternative to renewal. If warpage of the cylinder head gasket surface is suspected, use a straight-edge to check it for distortion. Refer to Part F of this Chapter if necessary.

18 Thoroughly clean the threads of the cylinder head bolt holes in the cylinder block. Ensure that the bolts run freely in their threads, and that all traces of oil and water are removed from each bolt hole. If required, pull the oil feed non-return valve from the cylinder head, and check the ball moves freely. Push a new valve into place if necessary **(see illustrations)**.

Gasket selection

19 The gasket thickness is indicated by notches/holes on the front edge of the gasket. If the crankshaft or pistons/connecting rods have not been disturbed, fit a new gasket with the same number of notches/holes as the previous one. If the crankshaft/piston or connecting rods have been disturbed, it's necessary to work out the piston protrusion as follows:

20 Remove the crankshaft timing pin, then turn the crankshaft until pistons 1 and 4 are at TDC (Top Dead Centre). Position a dial test indicator (dial gauge) on the cylinder block adjacent to the rear of No 1 piston, and zero it on the block face. Transfer the probe to the crown of No 1 piston (10.0 mm in from the rear edge), then slowly turn the crankshaft back-and-forth past TDC, noting the highest reading on the indicator. Record this reading as protrusion A.

21 Repeat the check described in paragraph 18, this time 10.0 mm in from the front edge of the No 1 piston crown. Record this reading as protrusion B.

22 Add protrusion A to protrusion B, then divide the result by 2 to obtain an average reading for piston No 1.

23 Repeat the procedure described in paragraphs 20 to 22 on piston 4, then turn the crankshaft through 180° and carry out the procedure on the piston Nos 2 and 3 **(see illustration)**. Check that there is a maximum difference of 0.07 mm protrusion between any two pistons.

24 If a dial test indicator is not available, piston protrusion may be measured using a straight-edge and feeler blades or Vernier calipers. However, this is much less accurate, and cannot therefore be recommended.

25 Note the greatest piston protrusion measurement, and use this to determine the correct cylinder head gasket from the table below. The series of notches/holes on the side of the gasket are used for thickness identification **(see illustration)**.

Refitting

26 Turn the crankshaft and position Nos 1 and 4 pistons at TDC, then turn the crankshaft a quarter turn (90°) anti-clockwise.

27 Thoroughly clean the surfaces of the cylinder head and block.

28 Make sure that the locating dowels are in place, then fit the correct gasket the right way round on the cylinder block **(see illustration)**.

29 Carefully lower the cylinder head onto the gasket and block, making sure that it locates correctly onto the dowels.

30 Apply a smear of grease to the threads, and to the underside of the heads of the new cylinder head bolts.

31 Carefully insert the cylinder head bolts into their holes (do not drop them in) and initially finger-tighten them.

32 Working progressively and in sequence, tighten the cylinder head bolts to their

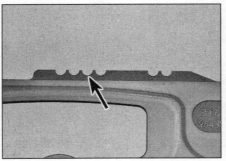

10.25 Cylinder head gasket thickness identification notches (arrowed)

10.28 Ensure the gasket locates over the dowels (arrowed)

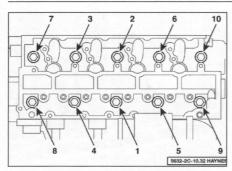

10.32 Cylinder head bolt tightening sequence

Stage 1 torque setting, using a torque wrench and suitable socket **(see illustration).**

33 Once all the bolts have been tightened to their Stage 1 torque setting, working again in the specified sequence, tighten each bolt to the specified Stage 2 setting. Finally, angle-tighten the bolts through the specified Stage 3 angle. It is recommended that an angle-measuring gauge is used during this stage of tightening, to ensure accuracy. **Note:** *Retightening of the cylinder head bolts after running the engine is not required.*

34 Refit the hydraulic tappets, rocker arms, and camshaft housing (complete with camshafts) as described in Section 9.

35 Refit the timing belt as described in Section 7.

36 The remainder of refitting is a reversal of removal, noting the following points.
● Use a new seal when refitting the coolant outlet housing.
● When refitting a cylinder head, it is good practice to renew the thermostat.
● Refit the camshaft position sensor and set the air gap with reference to Chapter 4B Section 12.
● Tighten all fasteners to the specified torque where given.

● Refill the cooling system as described in Chapter 1B Section 22.
● The engine may run erratically for the first few miles, until the engine management ECM relearns its stored values.

11 Sump – removal and refitting

Removal

1 Drain the engine oil, then clean and refit the engine oil drain plug, tightening it securely. If the engine is nearing its service interval when the oil and filter are due for renewal, it is recommended that the filter is also removed, and a new one fitted. After reassembly, the engine can then be refilled with fresh oil. Refer to Chapter 1B Section 6 for further information.

2 Apply the handbrake, then jack up the front of the vehicle and support it on axle stands (see *Jacking and vehicle support*). Undo the bolts and remove the engine undershield.

3 Remove the exhaust front pipe as described in Chapter 4B Section 18.

4 Where necessary, disconnect the wiring connector from the oil temperature sender unit, which is screwed into the sump.

5 Progressively slacken and remove all the sump retaining bolts/nuts. Since the sump bolts vary in length, remove each bolt in turn, and store it in its correct fitted order by pushing it through a clearly-marked cardboard template. This will avoid the possibility of installing the bolts in the wrong locations on refitting.

6 Try to break the joint by striking the sump with the palm of your hand, then lower and withdraw the sump from under the car. If the sump is stuck (which is quite likely) use a putty knife or similar, carefully inserted between the

sump and block. Ease the knife along the joint until the sump is released. While the sump is removed, take the opportunity to check the oil pump pick-up/strainer for signs of clogging or splitting. If necessary, remove the pump as described in Section 12, and clean or renew the strainer.

Refitting

7 Clean all traces of sealant from the mating surfaces of the cylinder block/crankcase and sump, then use a clean rag to wipe out the sump and the engine's interior.

8 Ensure that the sump mating surfaces are clean and dry, then apply a 3mm diameter bead of sealant to the sump mating surface **(see illustration).** The sealant must be applied to the inside of the bolt holes. Note that the sump must be installed within 10 minutes of applying the sealant, and the bolts tightened within a further 5 minutes.

9 Offer up the sump to the cylinder block/crankcase. Refit its retaining bolts/nuts, ensuring that each bolt is screwed into its original location. Tighten the bolts evenly and progressively to the specified torque setting **(see illustration).**

10 Reconnect the wiring connector to the oil temperature sensor (where fitted).

11 Lower the vehicle to the ground, wait at least 30 minutes (to allow the sealant to set) and then refill the engine with oil as described in Chapter 1B Section 6.

12 Oil pump – removal, inspection and refitting

Removal

1 Remove the sump as described in Section 11.
2 Remove the crankshaft sprocket as described in Section 8. Recover the locating key from the crankshaft.

11.8 Apply a bead of sealant to the sump or crankcase mating surface. Ensure the sealant is applied to the inside of the retaining bolt holes

11.9 Refit the sump and tighten the bolts

12.4 Oil pick-up tube bolts (arrowed)

12.5 Oil pump retaining bolts (arrowed)

12.6 Undo the Torx bolts and remove the pump cover

12.7a Remove the circlip...

12.7b ...cap...

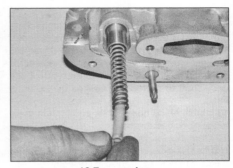

12.7c ...spring...

3 Disconnect the wiring plug, undo the bolts and remove the crankshaft position sensor, located on the right-hand end of the cylinder block.

4 Undo the three bolts and remove the oil pump pick-up tube from the pump/block **(see illustration)**. Discard the oil seal, a new one must be fitted.

5 Undo the 8 bolts, and remove the oil pump **(see illustration)**.

Inspection

6 Undo and remove the Torx bolts securing the cover to the oil pump **(see illustration)**. Examine the pump rotors and body for signs of wear and damage. If worn, the complete pump must be renewed.

7 Remove the circlip, and extract the cap, valve piston and spring, noting which way around they are fitted **(see illustrations)**. The condition of the relief valve spring can only be measured by comparing it with a new one; if there is any doubt about its condition, it should also be renewed.

8 Refit the relief valve piston and spring, then secure them in place with the circlip.

9 Refit the cover to the oil pump, and tighten the Torx bolts securely.

Refitting

10 Remove all traces of sealant, and thoroughly clean the mating surfaces of the oil pump and cylinder block.

11 Apply a 4 mm diameter bead of silicone sealant to the mating face of the cylinder block **(see illustration)**. Ensure that no sealant enters any of the holes in the block.

12 With a new oil seal fitted, refit the oil pump over the end of the crankshaft, aligning the

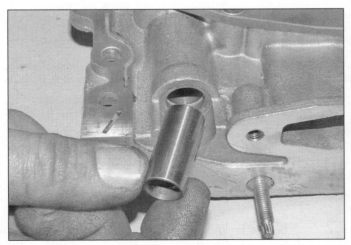

12.7d ...and piston

12.11 Apply a bead of sealant to the cylinder block mating surface

12.12a Fit a new seal...

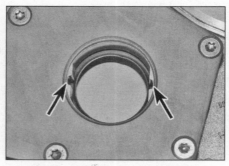

12.12b ...align the pump gear flats (arrowed)...

12.12c ...with those of the crankshaft (arrowed)

flats in the pump drive gear with the flats machined in the crankshaft **(see illustrations)**. Note that new oil pumps are supplied with the oil seal already fitted, and a seal protector sleeve. The sleeve fits over the end of the crankshaft to protect the seal as the pump is fitted.

13 Install the oil pump bolts and tighten them to the specified torque.

14 Refit the oil pick-up tube to the pump/cylinder block using a new O-ring seal. Ensure the oil dipstick guide tube is correctly refitted.

15 Refit the woodruff key to the crankshaft, and slide the crankshaft sprocket into place.

16 The remainder of refitting is a reversal of removal.

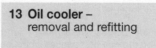

13 Oil cooler –
removal and refitting

Removal

1 Apply the handbrake, then jack up the front of the vehicle and support it on axle stands (see *Jacking and vehicle support*). Undo the fasteners and remove the engine undershield.

2 The oil cooler is fitted to the front of the oil filter housing. Drain the coolant as described in Section 13.

3 Drain the engine oil as described in Chapter 1B Section 6, or be prepared for fluid spillage.

4 Undo the bolts/stud and remove the oil cooler **(see illustration)**. Recover the gasket.

Refitting

5 Fit a new gasket into the recesses in the oil filter housing, and refit the cooler. Tighten the bolts securely.

6 Refill or top-up the cooling system and engine oil level, then start the engine, and check the oil cooler for signs of leakage.

14 Oil seals – renewal

Crankshaft

Right-hand oil seal

1 Remove the crankshaft sprocket and Woodruff key as described in Section 8.

2 Measure and note the fitted depth of the oil seal.

3 Pull the oil seal from the housing using a screwdriver. Alternatively, drill a small hole in the oil seal, and use a self-tapping screw and a pair of pliers to remove it **(see illustration)**.

4 Clean the oil seal housing and the crankshaft sealing surface.

5 The new seal should be supplied with a protective sleeve, which fits over the end of the crankshaft to prevent any damage to the seal lip. With the sleeve in place, press the seal (open end first) into the pump to the previously-noted depth, using a suitable tube or socket **(see illustrations)**.

13.4 Undo the oil cooler bolts/stud (arrowed)

6 Where applicable, remove the plastic sleeve from the end of the crankshaft.

7 Refit the crankshaft sprocket as described in Section 8.

Left-hand oil seal

8 Remove the flywheel, as described in Section 16.

9 Measure and note the fitted depth of the oil seal.

10 Pull the oil seal from the housing using a screwdriver. Alternatively, drill a small hole in the oil seal, and use a self-tapping screw and a pair of pliers to remove it **(see illustration 14.3)**.

11 Clean the oil seal housing and the crankshaft sealing surface.

12 The new seal should be supplied with a protective sleeve, which fits over the end of

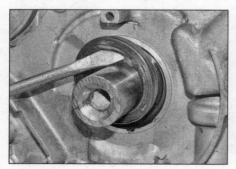

14.3 Take great care not to mark the crankshaft whilst levering out the oil seal

14.5a Slide the seal and protective sleeve over the end of the crankshaft...

14.5b ...and press the seal into place

the crankshaft to prevent any damage to the seal lip **(see illustration)**. With the sleeve in place, press the seal (open end first) into the housing to the previously-noted depth, using a suitable tube or socket.

13 Where applicable, remove the plastic sleeve from the end of the crankshaft.

14 Refit the flywheel, as described in Section 16.

Camshaft

15 Remove the camshaft sprocket as described in Section 8. In principle there is no need to remove the timing belt completely, but remember that if the belt has been contaminated with oil, it must be renewed.

16 Pull the oil seal from the housing using a hooked instrument. Alternatively, drill a small hole in the oil seal and use a self-tapping screw and a pair of pliers to remove it **(see illustration)**.

17 Clean the oil seal housing and the camshaft sealing surface.

18 Press the seal (open end first) into the housing to the previously-noted depth, using either the correct tool (303-684), a suitable tube or a socket which bears only of the outer edge of the seal **(see illustrations)**. If the seal was supplied with a protective sleeve, remove it.

19 Refit the camshaft sprocket as described in Section 8.

20 Where necessary, fit a new timing belt with reference to Section 7.

15 Oil pressure switch and level sensor – removal and refitting

Removal

Oil pressure switch

1 The oil pressure switch is located at the front of the cylinder block, adjacent to the oil dipstick guide tube. Note that on some models, access to the switch may be improved if the vehicle is jacked up and supported on axle stands, then undo the bolts and remove the engine undershield so that the switch can be reached from underneath (see *Jacking and vehicle support*).

2 Remove the protective sleeve from the wiring plug (where applicable), then disconnect the wiring from the switch.

3 Unscrew the switch from the cylinder block, and recover the sealing washer **(see illustration)**. Be prepared for oil spillage, and if the switch is to be left removed from the engine for any length of time, plug the hole in the cylinder block.

Oil level sensor

4 The oil level sensor is located at the rear of the cylinder block. Jack up the front of the vehicle and support it securely on axle stands (see *Jacking and vehicle support*). Undo the bolts and remove the engine undershield.

14.12 Slide the seal and protective sleeve over the left-hand end of the crankshaft

14.18a Use the correct tool to fit the seal...

5 Reach up between the driveshaft and the cylinder block, and disconnect the sensor wiring plug **(see illustration)**.

6 Using an open-ended spanner, unscrew the sensor and withdraw it from position.

Refitting

Oil pressure switch

7 Examine the sealing washer for any signs of damage or deterioration, and if necessary renew.

8 Refit the switch, complete with washer, and tighten it to the specified torque where given.

9 Refit the engine undershield, and lower the vehicle to the ground.

Oil level sensor

10 Smear a little silicone sealant on the

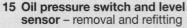
15.3 The oil pressure switch is located on the front face of the cylinder block (arrowed)

14.16 Drill a hole, insert a self-tapping screw, and pull the seal from place using pliers

14.18b ...or a suitable socket

threads and refit the sensor to the cylinder block, tightening it securely.

11 Reconnect the sensor wiring plug.

12 Refit the engine undershield, and lower the vehicle to the ground.

16 Flywheel – removal, inspection and refitting

Removal

1 Remove the transmission as described in Chapter 7A Section 7, then remove the clutch assembly as described in Chapter 6 Section 6.

2 Prevent the flywheel from turning. *Do not attempt to lock the flywheel in position using*

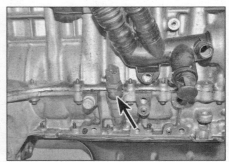
15.5 The oil level sensor is located on the rear face of the cylinder block (arrowed)

16.2 Lock the flywheel with a 12mm diameter rod or bolt (arrowed)

16.9 Flywheel retaining Torx bolts

the crankshaft pulley locking tool described in Section 3. Insert a 12 mm diameter rod or drill bit through the hole in the flywheel cover casting, and into a slot in the flywheel **(see illustration)**.

3 Make alignment marks between the flywheel and crankshaft to aid refitment. Slacken and remove the flywheel retaining bolts, and remove the flywheel from the end of the crankshaft. Be careful not to drop it; it is heavy. If the flywheel locating dowel (where fitted) is a loose fit in the crankshaft end, remove it and store it with the flywheel for safe-keeping. Discard the flywheel bolts; new ones must be used on refitting.

Inspection

4 Examine the flywheel for scoring of the clutch face, and for wear or chipping of the ring gear teeth. If the clutch face is scored, the flywheel may be surface-ground, but renewal is preferable. Seek the advice of a Ford dealer or engine reconditioning specialist to see if machining is possible. If the ring gear is worn or damaged, the flywheel must be renewed, as it is not possible to renew the ring gear separately.

5 All engines are fitted with a dual-mass flywheel. The maximum travel of the primary mass in relation to the secondary must not exceed 15 teeth (or 20 degrees). If in doubt remove the flywheel and have a suitably equipped specialist check the flywheel. Inspect the flywheel for any grease or debris from the interface between the fixed part and the movable part of the flywheel. If any doubt to the condition of the flywheel exists, despite the expense we recommend replacing it.

Refitting

6 Clean the mating surfaces of the flywheel and crankshaft. Remove any remaining locking compound from the threads of the crankshaft holes, using the correct size of tap, if available.
7 If the new flywheel retaining bolts are not supplied with their threads already pre-coated, apply a suitable thread-locking compound to the threads of each bolt.
8 Ensure that the locating dowel is in position.

Offer up the flywheel, locating it on the dowel (where fitted), and fit the new retaining bolts. Where no locating dowel is fitted, align the previously-made marks to ensure the flywheel is refitted in its original position.
9 Lock the flywheel using the method employed on dismantling, and tighten the retaining bolts to the specified torque **(see illustration)**.
10 Refit the clutch, remove the flywheel locking tool, and then refit the transmission.

17 Engine/transmission mountings – inspection and renewal

General

1 The engine/transmission mountings seldom require attention, but broken or deteriorated mountings should be renewed immediately, or the added strain placed on the driveline components may cause damage or wear.
2 While separate mountings may be removed and refitted individually, if more than one is disturbed at a time – such as if the engine/transmission unit is removed from its mountings – they must be reassembled and their fasteners tightened in the position marked on removal.
3 On reassembly, the complete weight of the engine/transmission unit must not be taken by the mountings until all are correctly aligned with the marks made on removal. Tighten the engine/transmission mounting fasteners to their specified torque wrench settings.

Inspection

4 During the check, the engine/transmission unit must be raised slightly, to remove its weight from the mountings.
5 Raise the front of the vehicle, and support it securely on axle stands. Position a jack under the sump, with a large block of wood between the jack head and the sump, then carefully raise the engine/transmission just enough to take the weight off the mountings.

Warning: DO NOT place any part of your body under the engine when it is supported only by a jack.

6 Check the mountings to see if the rubber is cracked, hardened or separated from the metal components. Sometimes the rubber will split right down the centre.
7 Check for relative movement between each mounting's brackets and the engine/transmission or body (use a large screwdriver or lever to attempt to move the mountings). If movement is noted, lower the engine and check-tighten the mounting fasteners.

Renewal

Note: *The following paragraphs assume the engine is supported beneath the sump as described earlier.*

Right-hand mounting

8 If required, to make access easier, undo the bolts and lift up the coolant expansion tank, then position it to one side. Note there is no need to disconnect the coolant pipes.
9 Mark the position of the mounting on the vehicle on the right-hand inner wing panel, and then undo the 2 bolts securing the mounting.
10 Undo the 3 retaining bolts from the engine side of the mounting and then remove the mounting from the engine compartment **(see illustration)**.

17.10 Undo the bolts and remove the mounting

17.14 Remove the battery support panel

17.15 Remove the centre bolt (arrowed)

11 Re-align the marks made on removal. Tighten all fasteners to the torque wrench settings specified.

Left-hand mounting

12 Remove the air filter housing as described in Chapter 4B Section 4.
13 Remove the battery as described in Chapter 5A Section 4. Undo the bolts and withdraw the battery tray, disconnecting any wiring securing clips, as the tray is withdrawn.
14 Unclip the wiring loom from the battery tray support panel, remove the bolts and withdraw the support panel **(see illustration)**.
15 With the transmission supported, note the position of the mounting bracket on the top of the transmission, then unscrew the retaining bolts to release the mounting from the transmission **(see illustration)**.
16 On six speed transmissions (depending on model), lower the transmission slightly to access the 3 mounting bolts on the transmission **(see illustration)**. On five speed transmission access the bolts from the engine bay. Remove the bolts and recover the mounting.

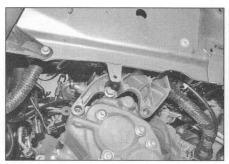

17.16 Lower the transmission and remove the bolts

17 Refitting is a reversal of removal. Re-align the mounting in the position noted on removal, then tighten all fasteners to the specified torque wrench settings.

Rear mounting (roll restrictor)

18 Remove the mounting bolts from the transmission mounting bracket and the subframe **(see illustration)**. If required, undo the bolts and remove the mounting bracket

17.18 Remove the bolts (arrowed)

from the rear of the transmission. Note, that the bolts may be different lengths.
19 With the aid of an assistant pivot the engine (assuming the two main engine mountings are in position) and work the mounting free.
20 On refitting, ensure that the bolts are securely tightened to the specified torque wrench setting.

Chapter 2 Part F
Engine removal and overhaul procedures

Contents

Degrees of difficulty

Easy, suitable for novice with little experience	Fairly easy, suitable for beginner with some experience	Fairly difficult, suitable for competent DIY mechanic	Difficult, suitable for experienced DIY mechanic	Very difficult, suitable for expert DIY or professional

Specifications

Engine identification

Petrol engines	Designation	Engine code
1.4 litre:		
Non-VTi engine:		
SOHC	TU3A	KFV
DOHC	ET3JP4	KFU
VTi engine	EP3	8FP, 8FR & 8FS
1.6 litre:		
Non-VTi engine	TU5JP4	NFU
VTi engine	EP6	5FS & 5FW
Diesel engines		
1.4 litre	DV4TD & DV4C	8HZ & 8HR
1.6 litre DOHC	DV6ATED4 & DV6TED4	9HX, 9HY & 9HZ
1.6 litre SOHC	DV6C	9HR

Cylinder head

Maximum gasket face distortion . . . . 0.05 mm
New cylinder head height:
Petrol engines:
1.4 litre . . . . 111.20 mm
1.6 litre . . . . N/A
Diesel engines:
1.4 litre . . . . 88.0 mm
1.6 litre . . . . 124.0 ± 0.05 mm
Minimum cylinder head height after machining:
Petrol engines:
1.4 litre . . . . 111.0 mm
1.6 litre . . . . N/A
Diesel engines:
1.4 litre . . . . 87.60 mm
1.6 litre . . . . N/A
Valve head-to-cylinder head measurement – diesel engines:
1.4 litre . . . . 1.25 mm maximum
1.6 litre . . . . N/A

Cylinder block

Cylinder bore diameter:
Petrol engines:
  1.4 litre . . . .   75.00 mm (nominal)
  1.6 litre . . . .   78.50 mm (nominal)
Diesel engines:
  1.4 litre . . . .   73.70 mm (nominal)
  1.6 litre (reboring not possible) . . . .   75.00 mm (nominal)
Liner protrusion – 1.4 litre non-VTi petrol engine:
  Standard . . . .   0.03 to 0.10 mm
  Maximum difference between any two liners . . . .   0.05 mm

Valves

	Inlet	Exhaust
Valve head diameter:		
Petrol engines:		
1.4 litre	36.7 mm	29.4 mm
1.6 litre	N/A	N/A
Diesel engines:		
1.4 litre	32.8 mm	30.3 mm
1.6 litre	N/A	N/A
Valve stem diameter:		
Petrol engines:		
1.4 litre	6.965 to 6.980 mm	6.945 to 6.960 mm
1.6 litre	N/A	N/A
Diesel engines:		
1.4 litre	N/A	N/A
1.6 litre	5.485 +0.0, -0.015 mm	5.475 +0.0, -0.015 mm

Pistons

Piston diameter:
Petrol engines:
  1.4 litre . . . .   74.950 mm (nominal)
  1.6 litre . . . .   78.455 mm (nominal)
Diesel engines:
  1.4 litre . . . .   73.520 mm (nominal)
  1.6 litre . . . .   N/A
Check with your Peugeot dealer or engine specialist regarding piston oversizes

Piston ring end gaps

Petrol engines:
  Top compression ring . . . .   0.20 to 0.45 mm
  Second compression ring . . . .   0.30 to 0.50 mm
  Oil control ring . . . .   0.30 to 0.50 mm
Diesel engines:
  1.4 litre:
    Top compression ring . . . .   0.20 to 0.35 mm
    Second compression ring . . . .   0.20 to 0.40 mm
    Oil control ring . . . .   0.80 to 1.00mm
  1.6 litre:
    Top compression ring . . . .   0.15 to 0.25 mm
    Second compression ring . . . .   0.30 to 0.50 mm
    Oil control ring . . . .   0.35 to 0.55 mm

Crankshaft

Endfloat:
  Petrol engines . . . .   0.07 to 0.27 mm
  Diesel engines:
    1.4 litre . . . .   0.10 to 0.30 mm
    1.6 litre . . . .   0.10 to 0.30 mm (thrustwasher thickness 2.40 ± 0.05 mm)
Main bearing journal diameter:
  Petrol engines . . . .   49.965 to 49.981 mm
  Diesel engines . . . .   49.962 to 49.981 mm
Big-end bearing journal diameter:
  Petrol engines . . . .   44.975 to 44.991 mm
  Diesel engines:
    1.4 litre . . . .   44.975 to 44.991 mm
    1.6 litre . . . .   46.975 to 46.991 mm
Maximum bearing journal out-of-round (all models) . . . .   0.007 mm

Torque wrench settings

Non-VTi petrol engines. . . . .   Refer to Chapter 2A Specifications
VTi petrol engines. . . . .   Refer to Chapter 2B Specifications
1.4 litre diesel engines . . . .   Refer to Chapter 2C Specifications
1.6 litre DOHC diesel engines . . . .   Refer to Chapter 2D Specifications
1.6 litre SOHC diesel engines. . . . .   Refer to Chapter 2E Specifications.

1 General Information

1 Included in this Part of Chapter 2 are details of removing the engine/transmission from the car and general overhaul procedures for the cylinder head, cylinder block/crankcase and all other engine internal components.
2 The information given ranges from advice concerning preparation for an overhaul and the purchase of parts, to detailed step-by-step procedures covering removal, inspection, renovation and refitting of engine internal components.
3 After Section 5, all instructions are based on the assumption that the engine has been removed from the car. For information concerning in-car engine repair, as well as the removal and refitting of those external components necessary for full overhaul, refer to Part A, B, C, D or E of this Chapter, as applicable and to Section 5. Ignore any preliminary dismantling operations that are no longer relevant once the engine has been removed from the car.
4 Apart from torque wrench settings, which are given at the beginning of Parts A, B, C, D and E, all specifications relating to engine overhaul are at the beginning of this Part of Chapter 2F.

2 Engine overhaul – general information

1 It is not always easy to determine when, or if, an engine should be completely overhauled, as a number of factors must be considered.
2 High mileage is not necessarily an indication that an overhaul is needed, while low mileage does not preclude the need for an overhaul. Frequency of servicing is probably the most important consideration. An engine, which has had regular and frequent oil and filter changes, as well as other required maintenance, should give many thousands of miles of reliable service. Conversely, a neglected engine may require an overhaul very early in its life.
3 Excessive oil consumption is an indication that piston rings, valve seals and/or valve guides are in need of attention. Make sure that oil leaks are not responsible before deciding that the rings and/or guides are worn. Perform a compression test, as described in Part A, B, C, D or E of this Chapter (as applicable), to determine the likely cause of the problem.
4 Check the oil pressure with a gauge fitted in place of the oil pressure switch, and compare it with that specified. If it is extremely low, the main and big-end bearings, and/or the oil pump, are probably worn out.
5 Loss of power, rough running, knocking or metallic engine noises, excessive valve gear noise, and high fuel consumption may also point to the need for an overhaul, especially if they are all present at the same time. If a complete service does not remedy the situation, major mechanical work is the only solution.
6 A full engine overhaul involves restoring all internal parts to the specification of a new engine. During a complete overhaul, the pistons and the piston rings are renewed. New main and big-end bearings are generally fitted; if necessary, the crankshaft may be reground, to compensate for wear in the journals. The valves are also serviced as well, since they are usually in less-than-perfect condition at this point. While the engine is being overhauled, other components, such as the starter and alternator, can be overhauled as well. Always pay careful attention to the condition of the oil pump when overhauling the engine, and renew it if there is any doubt as to its serviceability. The end result should be an as-new engine that will give many trouble-free miles.
7 Critical cooling system components such as the hoses, thermostat and water pump should be renewed when an engine is overhauled. The radiator should be checked carefully, to ensure that it is not clogged or leaking. Also, it is a good idea to renew the oil pump whenever the engine is overhauled.
8 Before beginning the engine overhaul, read through the entire procedure, to familiarise yourself with the scope and requirements of the job. Overhauling an engine is not difficult if you follow carefully all of the instructions, have the necessary tools and equipment, and pay close attention to all specifications. It can, however, be time-consuming. Plan on the car being off the road for a minimum of two weeks, especially if parts must be taken to an engineering works for repair or reconditioning. Check on the availability of parts and make sure that any necessary special tools and equipment are obtained in advance. Most work can be done with typical hand tools, although a number of precision measuring tools are required for inspecting parts to determine if they must be renewed. Often the engineering works will handle the inspection of parts and offer advice concerning reconditioning and renewal.
9 Always wait until the engine has been completely dismantled, and until all components (especially the cylinder block/crankcase and the crankshaft) have been inspected, before deciding what service and repair operations must be performed by an engineering works. The condition of these components will be the major factor to consider when determining whether to overhaul the original engine, or to buy a reconditioned unit. Do not, therefore, purchase parts or have overhaul work done on other components until they have been thoroughly inspected. As a general rule, time is the primary cost of an overhaul, so it does not pay to fit worn or sub-standard parts.
10 As a final note, to ensure maximum life and minimum trouble from a reconditioned engine, everything must be assembled with care, in a spotlessly clean environment.

3 Engine removal – methods and precautions

1 If you have decided that the engine must be removed for overhaul or major repair work, several preliminary steps should be taken.
2 Locating a suitable place to work is extremely important. Adequate workspace, along with storage space for the car, will be needed. Engine/transmission removal is extremely complicated and involved on these vehicles. It must be stated, that unless the vehicle can be positioned on a ramp, or raised and supported on axle stands over an inspection pit, it will be more difficult to carry out the work involved.
3 Cleaning the engine compartment and engine/transmission before beginning the removal procedure will help keep tools clean and organised.
4 An engine hoist or A-frame will also be necessary. Make sure the equipment is rated in excess of the weight of the engine. Safety is of primary importance, considering the potential hazards involved in lifting the engine/transmission out of the car.
5 The help of an assistant is essential. Apart from the safety aspects involved, there are many instances when one person cannot simultaneously perform all of the operations required during engine/transmission removal.
6 Plan the operation ahead of time. Before starting work, arrange for the hire of or obtain all of the tools and equipment you will need. Some of the equipment necessary to perform engine/transmission removal and installation safely and with relative ease (in addition to an engine hoist) is as follows: a heavy duty trolley

jack, complete sets of spanners and sockets (see Tools and working facilities), wooden blocks, and plenty of rags and cleaning solvent for mopping-up spilled oil, coolant and fuel. If the hoist must be hired, make sure that you arrange for it in advance, and perform all of the operations possible without it beforehand. This will save you money and time.

7 Plan for the car to be out of use for quite a while. An engineering machine shop or engine reconditioning specialist will be required to perform some of the work, which cannot be accomplished without special equipment. These places often have a busy schedule, so it would be a good idea to consult them before removing the engine, in order to accurately estimate the amount of time required to rebuild or repair components that may need work.

8 During the engine/transmission removal procedure, it is advisable to make notes of the locations of all brackets, cable ties, earthing points, etc, as well as how the wiring harnesses, hoses and electrical connections are attached and routed around the engine and engine compartment. An effective way of doing this is to take a series of photographs of the various components before they are disconnected or removed; the resulting photographs will prove invaluable when the engine/transmission is refitted.

9 The engine can be removed complete with the transmission as an assembly. Remove the front bumper, crossmember, radiator panel, and then the assembly is removed from the front of the vehicle.

10 Always be extremely careful when removing and refitting the engine/transmission. Serious injury can result from careless actions. Plan ahead and take your time, and a job of this nature, although major, can be accomplished successfully.

Note: *Such is the complexity of the power unit arrangement on these vehicles, and the variations that may be encountered according to model and optional equipment fitted, that the following should be regarded as a guide to the work involved, rather than a step-by-step procedure. Where differences are encountered, or additional component disconnection or removal is necessary, make notes of the work involved as an aid to refitting.*

4 Engine – removal and refitting

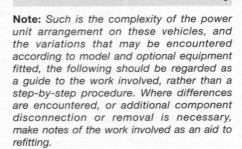

Note: *Such is the complexity of the power unit arrangement on these vehicles, and the variations that may be encountered according to model and optional equipment fitted, the following should be regarded as a guide to the work involved, rather than a step-by-step procedure. Where differences are encountered, or additional component disconnection or removal is necessary, make notes of the work involved as an aid to refitting.*

Removal

1 Remove the battery and battery support tray (see Chapter 5A Section 4). Wait five minutes, and then disconnect the engine wiring harness plugs at the fusebox or ECM depending on model **(see illustration)**. Release the wiring harness from the retaining clips on the timing cover at the right-hand end of the engine (where applicable).

2 Apply the handbrake, then jack up the front of the vehicle and support it on axle stands (see *Jacking and vehicle support*). Remove both front roadwheels. Undo the screws/fasteners and remove the engine undershield and front wheel arch liners.

3 Where fitted, remove the plastic covers from the top of the engine. On diesel engines, the engine cover simply pulls up from place. Other covers are retained by either plastic nut type fasteners or plastic expanding rivets. Rotate the nuts 90° anti-clockwise, or push in the centre pins a little and prise up the complete rivets

4 Drain the cooling system.

5 Drain the transmission oil/fluid, refit the drain plug (with a new sealing washer), and then tighten to the specified torque settings.

6 If the engine is to be dismantled, drain the engine oil and remove the oil filter. Clean and refit the drain plug (with a new sealing washer), tightening it securely.

7 Refer to Chapter 8 Section 2 and remove both front driveshafts.

8 Remove the front bumper and bumper bar as described in Chapter 11 Section 6.

Also, remove the headlamps (see Chapter 12 Section 7).

9 Remove the auxiliary drivebelt.

10 Remove the radiator/cooling fan and front panel assembly as described in Chapter 3 Section 4. On air conditioned models, tie the condenser to one side. Do not disconnect the refrigerant pipes.

11 Undo the securing bolts and remove the front panel lower crossmember and side rails **(see illustrations)**.

12 On 1.6 litre diesel engines, remove the air hoses leading from the intercooler to the turbocharger located on the right-hand side of the radiator, and to the inlet manifold.

13 Remove the air cleaner housing and ducting, then remove the exhaust system.

14 Note their fitted positions and harness routing, then disconnect all wiring plugs from the transmission. If necessary label the connectors as they are unplugged. On diesel models, undo the nut and remove the heater control box (still connected) from the front left-hand corner of the engine compartment.

15 Disconnect the hose from the vacuum pump on the left-hand end of the cylinder head (diesel models) or the brake servo unit vacuum pipe (petrol models).

16 Disconnect the fuel feed and return hoses. Plug the end of the hoses to prevent dirt ingress.

17 Disconnect the selector cable(s) from the transmission.

18 On manual transmission models, unbolt the clutch slave cylinder, then tie it to one side, without disconnecting the fluid pipe (see Chapter 6 Section 4). Use an elastic band around the cylinder to prevent the piston from coming out.

19 From underneath the vehicle, slacken and remove the nuts and bolts securing the rear engine mounting connecting link to the mounting assembly and subframe, and remove the connecting link.

20 On models with air conditioning, refer to Chapter 3 Section 12 and unbolt the compressor from the engine. Do not disconnect the refrigerant lines. Support or tie the compressor to one side.

21 Using a hoist attached to the lifting eyes on the cylinder head, take the weight of the engine and transmission.

4.1 Disconnect the ECM wiring plugs

4.11a Remove the front panel lower crossmember…

4.11b… and the side rails

22 Remove the right-hand and left-hand engine mountings and support brackets.

23 Completely pull out the wire retaining clips and disconnect the heater hoses at the engine compartment bulkhead.

24 Make a final check to ensure all wiring, hoses and brackets that would prevent the removal of the assembly have been disconnected.

25 Move the engine/transmission forwards and out from the front of the vehicle. Enlist the help of an assistant during this procedure, as it may be necessary to tilt and twist the assembly slightly to clear the body panels and adjacent components. Move the unit clear of the car and lower it to the ground

Separation

26 With the engine/transmission assembly removed, support the assembly on suitable blocks of wood on a workbench (or failing that, on a clean area of the workshop floor).

27 Undo the retaining bolts, and remove the flywheel lower cover plate (where fitted) from the transmission.

28 Slacken and remove the retaining bolts, and remove the starter motor from the transmission.

29 Disconnect any remaining wiring connectors at the transmission, then move the main engine wiring harness to one side.

30 On automatic transmission models, locate the access hole at the lower rear of the cylinder block, then turn the crankshaft by means of a socket on the crankshaft pulley bolt, until one of the three torque converter retaining nuts is accessible through the access hole. Undo the accessible torque converter bolt, then turn the crankshaft as necessary and undo the remaining two bolts.

31 Ensure that both engine and transmission are adequately supported, then slacken and remove the remaining bolts securing the transmission housing to the engine. Note the correct fitted positions of each bolt (and the relevant brackets) as they are removed, to use as a reference on refitting. On diesel models, the left-hand catalytic converter mounting stud must be removed to access the front transmission-to-engine bolt **(see illustration)**.

32 Carefully withdraw the transmission from the engine, ensuring that the weight of the transmission is not allowed to hang on the

4.31 The stud must be removed to access the front transmission-to-engine bolt

input shaft while it is engaged with the clutch friction disc (manual transmission models) or that the torque converter does not slip from the input shaft (automatic transmission models).

33 If they are loose, remove the locating dowels from the engine or transmission, and keep them in a safe place.

Refitting

34 If the engine and transmission have not been separated, perform the operations described below from paragraph 41 onwards.

35 Apply a smear of high melting-point grease (Peugeot recommend the use of Molykote BR2 plus – available from your Peugeot dealer) to the splines of the transmission input shaft. Do not apply too much; otherwise there is a possibility of the grease contaminating the clutch friction disc. **Note:** *On late models, Peugeot recommend no grease be applied.*

36 On automatic transmission models, prior to reconnection it is necessary to make a simple tool to align the torque converter with the driveplate as the transmission is refitted. To make the tool, carry out the following:

● Obtain a bolt of the same size as the torque converter retaining bolts, but long enough to extend through the access hole in the cylinder block when the transmission is refitted.

● Cut the head off the bolt and cut a slot (to enable it to be unscrewed) in the plain end. Check that the tool will slide easily through the torque converter retaining bolt hole in the driveplate.

● Turn the engine crankshaft so that one of the torque converter retaining bolt holes in the driveplate is aligned with the access hole in the cylinder block. Screw the alignment tool (finger-tight only) into one of the retaining bolt holes in the torque converter. Turn the torque converter so that the alignment tool is in approximately the correct position, relative to the cylinder block access hole. As the transmission is refitted, the alignment tool will pass through the retaining bolt hole in the driveplate and through the access hole. It can then be unscrewed with a screwdriver and the first torque converter retaining bolt fitted in its place.

● Check that the torque converter support bush fitted to the centre of the crankshaft is in good condition, and in place.

37 Ensure that the locating dowels are correctly positioned in the engine or transmission, and then carefully offer the transmission to the engine until the locating dowels are engaged. On manual transmission models, ensure that the weight of the transmission is not allowed to hang on the input shaft as it is engaged with the clutch friction disc. On automatic transmission models, ensure the torque converter studs engage correctly with the corresponding holes in the driveplate.

38 Refit the transmission housing-to-engine bolts, ensuring that all the necessary brackets

are correctly positioned, and tighten them securely.

39 Refit the starter motor, and securely tighten its retaining bolts.

40 Refit the lower flywheel cover plate (where fitted) to the transmission, and securely tighten the bolts.

41 Reconnect the hoist and lifting tackle to the engine lifting brackets. With the aid of an assistant, lift the assembly into the engine compartment, taking care not to damage surrounding components.

42 Refit the right-hand engine mounting and support bracket, but leave the bolts finger-tight at this stage.

43 Working on the left-hand mounting, refit the mounting to the transmission and finger-tighten.

44 Remove the hoist.

45 From underneath the vehicle, refit the rear mounting connecting link and finger-tighten the bolts.

46 Rock the engine to settle it on its mountings, then go around and tighten all the mounting nuts and bolts to their specified torque settings.

47 The remainder of the refitting procedure is a direct reversal of the removal sequence, with reference to the relevant chapters and noting the following points:

● Ensure that the wiring loom is correctly routed and retained by all the relevant retaining clips; all connectors should be correctly and securely reconnected.

● Prior to refitting the driveshafts to the transmission, renew the driveshaft oil seals as described in Chapter 7A Section 4.

● Ensure that all coolant hoses are correctly reconnected, and securely retained by their retaining clips.

● Refill the engine and transmission with the correct quantity and type of lubricant.

● Refill the cooling system and check for cooling fan operation.

● Initialise the engine management ECU as follows. Start the engine and run to normal temperature. Carry out a road test during which the following procedure should be made. Engage third gear and stabilise the engine at 1000 rpm. Now accelerate fully to 3500 rpm.

5 Engine overhaul – dismantling sequence

1 It is much easier to dismantle and work on the engine if it is mounted on a portable engine stand. These stands can often be hired from a tool hire shop. Before the engine is mounted on a stand, the flywheel/driveplate should be removed, so that the stand bolts can be tightened into the end of the cylinder block/crankcase.

2 If a stand is not available, it is possible to dismantle the engine with it blocked up on a sturdy workbench, or on the floor. Be extra careful not to tip or drop the engine when working without a stand.

3 If you are going to obtain a reconditioned engine, all the external components must be removed first, to be transferred to the new engine (just as they will if you are doing a complete engine overhaul yourself). These components include the following:

● Ancillary unit mounting brackets (oil filter, starter, alternator, power steering pump, etc)
● Thermostat and housing (Chapter 3 Section 5).
● Dipstick tube/sensor.
● All electrical switches and sensors.
● Inlet and exhaust manifolds.
● Ignition coils and spark plugs (petrol engines).
● Flywheel/driveplate (Part A, B, C, D or E of this Chapter).

Note: *When removing the external components from the engine, pay close attention to details that may be helpful or important during refitting. Note the fitted position of gaskets, seals, spacers, pins, washers, bolts, and other small items.*

4 If you are obtaining a 'short' engine (which consists of the engine cylinder block/crankcase, crankshaft, pistons and connecting rods all assembled), then the cylinder head, sump, oil pump, and timing belt will have to be removed also.

5 If you are planning a complete overhaul, the engine can be dismantled, and the internal components removed, in the order given below, referring to Part A, B, C, D or E of this Chapter unless otherwise stated.

● Inlet and exhaust manifolds.
● Timing belts, sprockets and tensioner(s).
● Cylinder head.
● Flywheel/driveplate.
● Sump.
● Oil pump.
● Piston/connecting rod assemblies (Section 9). **Note:** *On diesel engines, remove the crankshaft before the pistons.*
● Crankshaft (Section 10).

6 Before beginning the dismantling and overhaul procedures, make sure that you have all of the correct tools necessary. Refer to Tools and working facilities for further information.

6 Cylinder head – dismantling

Note: *New and reconditioned cylinder heads are available from the manufacturer, and from engine overhaul specialists. Be aware that some specialist tools are required for the dismantling and inspection procedures, and new components may not be readily available. It may therefore be more practical and economical for the home mechanic to purchase a reconditioned head, rather than dismantle, inspect and recondition the original head.*

1 Remove the cylinder head as described in Part A, B, C, D or E of this Chapter (as applicable).

2 If not already done, remove the Inlet and the exhaust manifolds. Remove any remaining brackets or housings as required.

3 Remove the camshaft(s), hydraulic followers and rockers (as applicable) as described in Part A, B, C, D or E of this Chapter.

4 If not already done on petrol models, remove the spark plugs as described in Chapter 1A Section 19.

5 If not already done on diesel models, remove the glow plugs as described in Chapter 5C Section 2.

6 On all models, using a valve spring compressor, compress each valve spring in turn until the split collets can be removed. Release the compressor, and lift off the spring retainer, spring and, where fitted, the spring seat. Using a pair of pliers, carefully extract the valve stem oil seal from the top of the guide. On 16-valve engines, the valve stem oil seal also forms the spring seat and is deeply recessed in the cylinder head. It is also a tight fit on the valve guide making it difficult to remove with pliers or a conventional valve stem oil seal removal tool. It can be easily removed, however, using a self-locking nut of suitable diameter screwed onto the end of a bolt and locked with a second nut. Push the nut down onto the top of the seal; the locking portion of the nut will grip the seal allowing it to be withdrawn from the top of the valve guide. Access to the valves is limited, and it may be necessary to make up an adapter out of metal tube – cut out a 'window' so that the valve collets can be removed **(see illustrations)**.

7 If, when the valve spring compressor is screwed down, the spring retainer refuses to free and expose the split collets, gently tap the top of the tool, directly over the retainer,

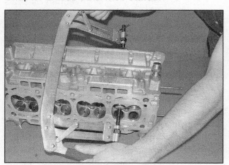

6.6a Compress the valve spring using a spring compressor...

6.6b... then extract the collets and release the spring compressor

6.6c Remove the spring retainer...

6.6d... followed by the valve spring...

6.6e... and the spring seat (not all models)

6.6f Use a pair of pliers to remove the valve stem oil seal. On some models the spring seat is integral with the seal

with a light hammer. This will free the retainer.

8 Withdraw the valve from the combustion chamber. Remove the valve stem oil seal from the top of the guide, then lift out the spring seat where fitted.

9 It is essential that each valve is stored together with its collets, retainer, spring, and spring seat. The valves should also be kept in their correct sequence, unless they are so badly worn that they are to be renewed. If they are going to be kept and used again, place each valve assembly in a labelled polythene bag or similar small container **(see illustration)**. Note that No 1 valve is nearest to the transmission (flywheel/driveplate) end of the engine.

---

7 Cylinder head and valves – cleaning and inspection

1 Thorough cleaning of the cylinder head and valve components, followed by a detailed inspection, will enable you to decide how much valve service work must be carried out during the engine overhaul. **Note:** *If the engine has been severely overheated, it is best to assume that the cylinder head is warped – check carefully for signs of this.*

Cleaning

2 Scrape away all traces of old gasket material from the cylinder head.

3 Scrape away the carbon from the combustion chambers and ports, then wash the cylinder head thoroughly with paraffin or a suitable solvent.

4 Scrape off any heavy carbon deposits that may have formed on the valves, then use a power-operated wire brush to remove deposits from the valve heads and stems.

Inspection

Note: *Be sure to perform all the following inspection procedures before concluding that the services of a machine shop or engine overhaul specialist are required. Make a list of all items that require attention.*

Cylinder head

5 Inspect the head very carefully for cracks,

6.9 Place each valve and its associated components in a labelled bag

evidence of coolant leakage, and other damage. If cracks are found, a new cylinder head should be obtained. Use a straight-edge and feeler blade to check that the cylinder head gasket surface is not distorted **(see illustration)**. If it is, it may be possible to have it machined, provided that the cylinder head height is not significantly reduced.

6 Examine the valve seats in each of the combustion chambers. If they are severely pitted, cracked, or burned, they will need to be renewed or recut by an engine overhaul specialist. If they are only slightly pitted, this can be removed by grinding-in the valve heads and seats with fine valve grinding compound, as described below. If in any doubt, have the cylinder head inspected by an engine overhaul specialist.

7 Check the valve guides for wear by inserting the relevant valve, and checking for side-to-side motion of the valve. A very small amount of movement is acceptable. If the movement seems excessive, remove the valve. Measure the valve stem diameter (see below), and renew the valve if it is worn. If the valve stem is not worn, the wear must be in the valve guide, and the guide must be renewed. The renewal of valve guides is best carried out by a Peugeot dealer or engine overhaul specialist, who will have the necessary tools available. Where no valve stem diameter is specified, seek the advice of a Peugeot dealer on the best course of action.

8 If renewing the valve guides, the valve seats should be recut or reground only after the guides have been fitted.

9 Where applicable, examine the camshaft oil

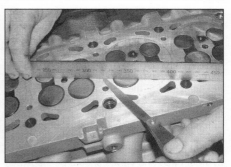

7.5 Check the cylinder head gasket surface for distortion

supply non-return valve in the oil feed bore at the timing belt end of the cylinder head. Check that the valve is not loose in the cylinder head and that the ball is free to move within the valve body. If the valve is a loose fit in its bore, or if there is any doubt about its condition, it should be renewed. The non-return valve can be removed (assuming it is not loose), using compressed air, such as that generated by a tyre foot pump. Place the pump nozzle over the oil feed bore of the camshaft bearing journal and seal the corresponding oil feed bore with a rag. Apply the compressed air and the valve will be forced out of its location in the underside of the cylinder head **(see illustrations)**. Fit the new non-return valve to its bore on the underside of the head ensuring it is fitted the correct way. Oil should be able to pass upwards through the valve to the camshafts, but the ball in the valve should prevent the oil from returning back to the cylinder block. Use a thin socket or similar to push the valve fully into position.

Valves

10 Examine the head of each valve for pitting, burning, cracks, and general wear. Check the valve stem for scoring and wear ridges. Rotate the valve, and check for any obvious indication that it is bent. Look for pits or excessive wear on the tip of each valve stem. Renew any valve that shows any such signs of wear or damage.

11 If the valve appears satisfactory at this stage, measure the valve stem diameter at several points using a micrometer **(see illustration)**. Any significant difference in the

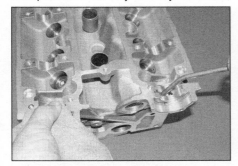

7.9a Apply compressed air to the oil feed bore of the inlet camshaft, seal the bore in the exhaust camshaft bore with a rag...

7.9b... and the camshaft oil supply non-return valve will be ejected from the underside of the cylinder head

7.11 Measure the valve stem diameter with a micrometer

readings obtained indicates wear of the valve stem. Should any of these conditions be apparent, the valve must be renewed.

12 If the valves are in satisfactory condition, they should be ground (lapped) into their respective seats, to ensure a smooth, gas-tight seal. If the seat is only lightly pitted, or if it has been recut, fine grinding compound only should be used to produce the required finish. Coarse valve-grinding compound should not be used, unless a seat is badly burned or deeply pitted. If this is the case, the cylinder head and valves should be inspected by an expert, to decide whether seat recutting, or even the renewal of the valve or seat insert (where possible) is required.

13 Valve grinding is carried out as follows. Place the cylinder head upside-down on a bench.

14 Smear a trace of (the appropriate grade of) valve-grinding compound on the seat face, and press a suction grinding tool onto the valve head **(see illustration)**. With a semi-rotary action, grind the valve head to its seat, lifting the valve occasionally to redistribute the grinding compound. A light spring placed under the valve head will greatly ease this operation.

15 If coarse grinding compound is being used, work only until a dull, matt even surface is produced on both the valve seat and the valve, then wipe off the used compound, and repeat the process with fine compound. When a smooth unbroken ring of light grey matt

finish is produced on both the valve and seat, the grinding operation is complete. Do not grind-in the valves any further than absolutely necessary, or the seat will be prematurely sunk into the cylinder head.

16 When all the valves have been ground-in, carefully wash off all traces of grinding compound using paraffin or a suitable solvent, before reassembling the cylinder head.

Valve components

17 Examine the valve springs for signs of damage and discoloration. No minimum free length is specified by Peugeot, so the only way of judging valve spring wear is by comparison with a new component.

18 Stand each spring on a flat surface, and check it for squareness. If any of the springs are damaged, distorted or have lost their tension, obtain a complete new set of springs. It is normal to renew the valve springs as a matter of course if a major overhaul is being carried out.

19 Renew the valve stem oil seals regardless of their apparent condition.

8 Cylinder head – reassembly

1 Working on the first valve assembly, refit the spring seat then dip the new valve stem oil seal in fresh engine oil. Locate the seal

on the valve guide and press the seal firmly onto the guide using a suitable socket **(see illustrations)**. Note that on diesel engines, the seal is integral with the lower spring seat.

2 Lubricate the stem of the first valve, and insert it in the guide **(see illustration)**.

3 Locate the valve spring on top of its seat, and then refit the spring retainer.

4 Compress the valve spring, and locate the split collets in the recess in the valve stem. Release the compressor, then repeat the procedure on the remaining valves. Ensure that each valve is inserted into its original location. If new valves are being fitted, insert them into the locations to which they have been ground.

5 With all the valves installed, support the cylinder head and, using a hammer and interposed block of wood, tap the end of each valve stem to settle the components.

6 Refit the camshafts, hydraulic followers and rocker arms (as applicable) as described in Part A, B, C, D or E of this Chapter.

7 Refit any remaining components using the reverse of the removal sequence and with new seals or gaskets as necessary.

8 The cylinder head can then be refitted as described in Part A, B, C, D or E of this Chapter.

9 Piston/connecting rod assembly – removal

1 Remove the cylinder head, sump and oil pump as described in Part A, B, C, D or E of this Chapter.

2 If there is a pronounced wear ridge at the top of any bore, it may be necessary to remove it with a scraper or ridge reamer, to avoid piston damage during removal. Such a ridge indicates excessive wear of the cylinder bore.

3 Using quick-drying paint, mark each connecting rod and big-end bearing cap with its respective cylinder number on the flat machined surface provided; if the engine has been dismantled before, note carefully any identifying marks made previously **(see**

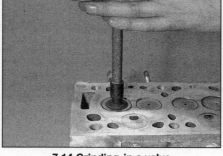

7.14 Grinding-in a valve

8.1a Locate the valve stem oil seal on the valve guide...

8.1b... and press the seal firmly onto the guide using a suitable socket

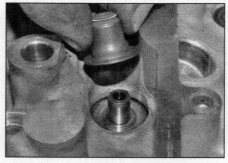

8.1c On some models, the valve stem oil seal is integral with the spring seat

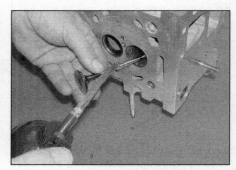

8.2 Lubricate the stem of the valve and insert it into the guide

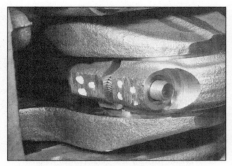

9.3 Connecting rod and big-end bearing cap identification marks (No 3 shown)

9.5 Remove the big-end bearing shell and cap

9.6 To protect the crankshaft journals, tape over the connecting rod stud threads

illustration). Note that No 1 cylinder is at the transmission (flywheel) end of the engine.

4 Turn the crankshaft to bring pistons 1 and 4 to BDC (Bottom Dead Centre). On diesel engines and VTi petrol engines, remove the main bearing ladder as described in Section 10 of this Chapter.

5 Unscrew the nuts or bolts, as applicable, from No 1 piston big-end bearing cap. Take off the cap, and recover the bottom half bearing shell **(see illustration)**. If the bearing shells are to be re-used, tape the cap and the shell together.

6 Where applicable, to prevent the possibility of damage to the crankshaft bearing journals, tape over the connecting rod stud threads **(see illustration)**.

7 Using a hammer handle, push the piston up through the bore, and remove it from the top of the cylinder block. Recover the bearing shell, and tape it to the connecting rod for safe-keeping.

8 Loosely refit the big-end cap to the connecting rod, and secure with the nuts/bolts – this will help to keep the components in their correct order.

9 Remove number 4 piston assembly in the same way.

10 Turn the crankshaft through 180° to bring pistons 2 and 3 to BDC (Bottom Dead Centre), and remove them in the same way.

10 Crankshaft – removal

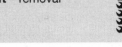

1 Remove the crankshaft sprocket and the oil pump as described in Part A, B, C, D or E of this Chapter (as applicable).

2 Remove the pistons and connecting rods, as described in Section 9. If no work is to be done on the pistons and connecting rods, there is no need to remove the cylinder head, or to push the pistons out of the cylinder bores. The pistons should just be pushed far enough up the bores so that they are positioned clear of the crankshaft journals.

Note: *On diesel engines and VTi petrol engines, the main bearing ladder must be removed before the piston/connecting rods.*

3 Check the crankshaft endfloat as described in Section 13, then proceed as follows.

Non-VTi petrol engine

1.4 litre

4 Work around the outside of the cylinder block, and unscrew all the small (M6) bolts securing the main bearing ladder to the base of the cylinder block. Note the correct fitted depth of both the left- and right-hand crankshaft oil seals in the cylinder block/main bearing ladder.

5 Working in a diagonal sequence, evenly and progressively slacken the ten large (M11) main bearing ladder retaining bolts by a turn at a time. Once all the bolts are loose, remove them from the ladder.

6 With all the retaining bolts removed, carefully lift the main bearing ladder casting away from the base of the cylinder block. Recover the lower main bearing shells, and tape them to their respective locations in the casting. If the two locating dowels are a loose fit, remove them and store them with the casting for safe-keeping.

7 Lift out the crankshaft, and discard both the oil seals. Remove the oil pump drive chain from the end of the crankshaft. Where necessary, slide off the drive sprocket, and recover the Woodruff key.

8 Recover the upper main bearing shells, and store them along with the relevant lower bearing shell. Also recover the two thrustwashers (one fitted either side of No 2 main bearing) from the cylinder block.

1.6 litre

9 Unbolt and remove the crankshaft left- and right-hand oil seal housings from each end of the cylinder block, noting the correct fitted locations of the locating dowels. If the locating dowels are a loose fit, remove them and store them with the housings for safe-keeping.

10 Remove the oil pump drive chain, and slide the drive sprocket off the end of the crankshaft. Remove the Woodruff key, and store it with the sprocket for safe-keeping.

11 The main bearing caps should be numbered 1 to 5 from the transmission (flywheel/driveplate) end of the engine. If not, mark them accordingly using a centre-punch or paint.

12 Unscrew and remove the main bearing cap retaining bolts, and withdraw the caps. Recover the lower main bearing shells, and tape them to their respective caps for safe-keeping.

13 Carefully lift out the crankshaft, taking care not to displace the upper main bearing shell.

14 Recover the upper bearing shells from the cylinder block, and tape them to their respective caps for safe-keeping. Remove the thrustwasher halves from the side of No 2 main bearing, and store them with the bearing cap.

VTi petrol engine

15 Work around the outside of the cylinder block, and unscrew all the small bolts securing the main bearing ladder to the base of the cylinder block. Note the correct fitted depth of the left-hand crankshaft oil seal in the cylinder block/main bearing ladder.

16 Working in a diagonal sequence, evenly and progressively slacken the large main bearing ladder retaining bolts by a turn at a time. Once all the bolts are loose, remove them from the ladder.

17 With all the retaining bolts removed, carefully lift the main bearing ladder casting away from the base of the cylinder block. Recover the lower main bearing shells, and tape them to their respective locations in the casting. If the two locating dowels are a loose fit, remove them and store them with the casting for safe-keeping.

18 Lift out the crankshaft, and discard both the oil seals.

19 Recover the upper main bearing shells, and store them along with the relevant lower bearing shell. Also recover the two thrustwashers (one fitted either side of No 2 main bearing) from the cylinder block.

Diesel engine

20 Work around the outside of the cylinder block, and unscrew all the small bolts securing the main bearing ladder to the base of the cylinder block. Note the correct fitted depth of the left-hand crankshaft oil seal in the cylinder block/main bearing ladder.

21 Working in a diagonal sequence, evenly and progressively slacken the large main bearing ladder retaining bolts by a turn at a

10.21 On diesel engines, prise up the two caps to expose the main bearing bolts at the flywheel end

time. Once all the bolts are loose, remove them from the ladder. **Note:** *Prise up the two caps at the flywheel end of the ladder to expose the two end main bearing bolts* **(see illustration)**.

22 With all the retaining bolts removed, carefully lift the main bearing ladder casting away from the base of the cylinder block. Recover the lower main bearing shells, and tape them to their respective locations in the casting. If the two locating dowels are a loose fit, remove them and store them with the casting for safe-keeping. Undo the big-end bolts and remove the pistons/connecting rods as described in Section 9.

23 Lift out the crankshaft, and discard both the oil seals.

24 Recover the upper main bearing shells, and store them along with the relevant lower bearing shell. Also recover the two thrustwashers (one fitted either side of No 2 main bearing) from the cylinder block.

11 Cylinder block/crankcase – cleaning and inspection

Cleaning

1 Remove all external components and electrical switches/sensors from the block. For complete cleaning, the core plugs should ideally be removed **(see illustration)**. Drill a small hole in the plugs, and then insert a self-tapping screw into the hole. Pull out the plugs by pulling on the screw with a pair of grips, or by using a slide hammer.

2 On 1.4 litre non-VTi petrol engines, remove the cylinder liners – see paragraph 18.

3 Where applicable, undo the retaining bolts and remove the piston oil jet spray tubes (there is one for each piston) from inside the cylinder block **(see illustration)**.

4 Scrape all traces of gasket from the cylinder block/crankcase, and from the main bearing ladder/caps (as applicable), taking care not to damage the gasket/sealing surfaces.

5 Remove all oil gallery plugs (where fitted). The plugs are usually very tight – they may have to be drilled out, and the holes re-tapped. Use new plugs when the engine is reassembled.

6 If any of the castings are extremely dirty, all should be steam-cleaned.

7 After the castings are returned, clean all oil holes and oil galleries one more time. Flush all internal passages with warm water until the water runs clear. Dry thoroughly, and apply a light film of oil to all mating surfaces, to prevent rusting. On cast-iron block engines, also oil the cylinder bores. If you have access to compressed air, use it to speed up the drying process, and to blow out all the oil holes and galleries.

Warning: Wear eye protection when using compressed air.

8 If the castings are not very dirty, you can do an adequate cleaning job with hot (as hot as you can stand), soapy water and a stiff brush. Take plenty of time, and do a thorough job. Regardless of the cleaning method used, be sure to clean all oil holes and galleries very thoroughly, and to dry all components well. On cast-iron block engines, protect the cylinder bores as described above, to prevent rusting.

9 All threaded holes must be clean, to ensure accurate torque readings during reassembly. To clean the threads, run the correct-size tap into each of the holes to remove rust, corrosion, thread sealant or sludge, and to restore damaged threads **(see illustration)**. If possible, use compressed air to clear the holes of debris produced by this operation.

10 Apply suitable sealant to the new oil gallery plugs, and insert them into the holes in the block. Tighten them securely. Also apply suitable sealant to new core plugs, and drive them into the block using a tube or socket.

11 Where applicable, clean the threads of the piston oil jet retaining bolts, and apply a drop of thread-locking compound (Peugeot recommend Loctite Frenetanch) to each bolt threads. Refit the piston oil jet spray tubes to the cylinder block, and tighten the retaining bolts to the specified torque setting.

12 If the engine is not going to be reassembled right away, cover it with a large plastic bag to keep it clean; protect all mating surfaces and the cylinder bores as described above, to prevent rusting.

Inspection

Cast-iron cylinder block

13 Visually check the castings for cracks and corrosion. Look for stripped threads in the threaded holes. If there has been any history of internal water leakage, it may be worthwhile having an engine overhaul specialist check the cylinder block/crankcase with special equipment. If defects are found, have them repaired if possible, or renew the assembly.

14 Check each cylinder bore for scuffing and scoring. Check for signs of a wear ridge at the top of the cylinder, indicating that the bore is excessively worn.

15 If the necessary measuring equipment is available, measure the bore diameter of each cylinder at the top (just under the wear ridge), centre, and bottom of the cylinder bore, parallel to the crankshaft axis.

16 Next, measure the bore diameter at the same three locations, at right angles to the crankshaft axis. Compare the results with the figures given in the Specifications. If there is any doubt about the condition of the cylinder bores, seek the advice of a Peugeot dealer or suitable engine reconditioning specialist.

17 At the time of writing, it was not clear whether oversize pistons were available for all models. Consult your Peugeot dealer or engine specialist for the latest information on piston availability. If oversize pistons are available, then it may be possible to have the cylinder bores rebored and fit the oversize pistons. If oversize pistons are not available, and the bores are worn, renewal of the block seems to be the only option.

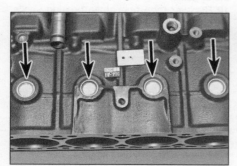

11.1 Cylinder block core plugs (arrowed)

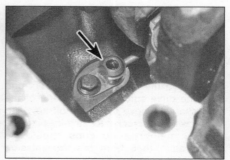

11.3 Piston oil jet spray tube (arrowed) in the cylinder block

11.9 Use a suitable tap to clean the cylinder block threaded holes

Aluminium cylinder block

18 Remove the liner clamps (where used), and then use a hardwood drift to tap out each liner from the inside of the cylinder block. When all the liners are released, tip the cylinder block/crankcase on its side and remove each liner from the top of the block. As each liner is removed, stick masking tape on its left-hand (transmission side) face, and write the cylinder number on the tape. No 1 cylinder is at the transmission (flywheel/driveplate) end of the engine. Remove the sealing ring from the base of each liner, and discard **(see illustrations)**.

19 Check each cylinder liner for scuffing and scoring. Check for signs of a wear ridge at the top of the liner, indicating that the bore is excessively worn.

20 Take the liners to a Peugeot dealer or engine reconditioning specialist and have their bores measured to determine if renewal is necessary. If it is, the dealer or specialist will be able to advise you regarding piston/liner availability.

21 Prior to installing the liners, check the liner protrusion as follows. Thoroughly clean the mating surfaces of the liner and cylinder block. Insert the liners into the block, without a sealing ring, ensuring each one is correctly seated; if the original liners are being refitted, ensure the liners are fitted in their original locations. With all four liners correctly installed, use a dial gauge (or a straight-edge and feeler blade) to check that the protrusion of each liner above the upper surface of the cylinder block is within the limits given in the Specifications. The maximum difference between any two liners must not be exceeded. **Note:** *If new liners are being fitted, it is permissible to interchange them to bring the difference in protrusion within limits. Remember to keep each piston with its respective liner. If liner protrusion is not within the specified limits, seek the advice of a Peugeot dealer or engine reconditioning specialist before proceeding with the engine rebuild.*

22 Once the protrusions have been checked, remove the liners from the block and fit a new sealing ring carefully to the base of each liner. Lubricate the base of each liner with a smear of oil to aid installation.

23 Insert each liner into the cylinder block, taking care not to damage the O-ring, and press it home as far as possible by hand. Using a hammer and a block of wood, tap each liner lightly but fully onto its locating shoulder. If the original liners are being refitted, use the marks made on removal to ensure that each is refitted the correct way round, and is inserted into its original bore.

24 Wipe clean, then lightly oil all exposed liner surfaces, to prevent rusting. Where necessary, clamp the liners back in position.

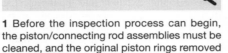

12 Piston/connecting rod assembly – inspection

1 Before the inspection process can begin, the piston/connecting rod assemblies must be cleaned, and the original piston rings removed from the pistons.

2 Carefully expand the old rings over the top of the pistons. The use of two or three old feeler blades will be helpful in preventing the rings dropping into empty grooves **(see illustration)**. Be careful not to scratch the piston with the ends of the ring. The rings are brittle, and will snap if they are spread too far. They are also very sharp – protect your hands and fingers. Note that the third ring incorporates an expander. Always remove the rings from the top of the piston. Keep each set of rings with its piston if the old rings are to be re-used.

3 Scrape away all traces of carbon from the top of the piston. A hand-held wire brush (or a piece of fine emery cloth) can be used, once the majority of the deposits have been scraped away.

4 Remove the carbon from the ring grooves in the piston, using an old ring. Break the ring in half to do this (be careful not to cut your fingers – piston rings are sharp). Be careful to remove only the carbon deposits – do not remove any metal, and do not nick or scratch the sides of the ring grooves.

5 Once the deposits have been removed, clean the piston/connecting rod assembly with paraffin or a suitable solvent, and dry thoroughly. Make sure that the oil return holes in the ring grooves are clear.

6 If the pistons and cylinder bores are not damaged or worn excessively, and if the cylinder block does not need to be re-bored (where possible), the original pistons can be refitted. Normal piston wear shows up as even vertical wear on the piston thrust surfaces, and slight looseness of the top ring in its groove. New piston rings should always be used when the engine is reassembled.

7 Carefully inspect each piston for cracks around the skirt, around the gudgeon pin holes, and at the piston ring 'lands' (between the ring grooves).

8 Look for scoring and scuffing on the piston skirt, holes in the piston crown, and burned areas at the edge of the crown. If the skirt is scored or scuffed, the engine may have been suffering from overheating, and/or abnormal combustion, which caused excessively high operating temperatures. The cooling and lubrication systems should be checked thoroughly. Scorch marks on the sides of the pistons show that blow-by has occurred. A hole in the piston crown, or burned areas at the edge of the piston crown, indicates that abnormal combustion (pre-ignition, knocking, or detonation) has been occurring. If any of the above problems exist, the causes must be investigated and corrected, or the damage will occur again. The causes may include incorrect ignition/injection pump timing, or a faulty injector (as applicable).

9 Corrosion of the piston, in the form of pitting, indicates that coolant has been leaking into the combustion chamber and/or the crankcase. Again, the cause must be corrected, or the problem may persist in the rebuilt engine.

10 On engines with wet liners, it is not possible to renew the pistons separately; pistons are only supplied with piston rings and a liner, as a part of a matched assembly (see Section 11). On iron-block engines, pistons can be purchased from a Peugeot dealer or engine reconditioning specialist.

11 Examine each connecting rod carefully for signs of damage, such as cracks around the big-end and small-end bearings. Check that the rod is not bent or distorted. Damage is highly unlikely, unless the engine has been seized or badly overheated. Detailed checking of the connecting rod assembly can only be

11.18a On aluminium block engines, remove each liner...

11.18b... and recover the bottom O-ring seal (arrowed)

12.2 Remove the piston rings with the aid of a feeler gauge

12.15a Prise out the circlip...

12.15b... and withdraw the gudgeon pin

carried out by a Peugeot dealer or engine specialist with the necessary equipment.

12 The connecting rod big-end cap bolts/nuts must be renewed whenever they are disturbed. Although Peugeot do not specify that the bolts must also renewed, it is recommended that the nuts and bolts are renewed as a complete set.

Petrol engines

13 On petrol engines, the gudgeon pins are an interference fit in the connecting rod small-end bearing. Therefore, piston and/or connecting rod renewal should be entrusted to a Peugeot dealer or engine repair specialist, who will have the necessary tooling to remove and install the gudgeon pins.

Diesel engines

14 On diesel engines, the gudgeon pins are of the floating type, secured in position by two circlips. On these engines, the pistons and connecting rods can be separated as described in the following paragraphs.

15 Using a small flat-bladed screwdriver, prise out the circlips, and push out the gudgeon pin **(see illustrations)**. Hand pressure should be sufficient to remove the pin. Identify the piston and rod to ensure correct reassembly. Discard the circlips – new ones must be used on refitting.

16 Examine the gudgeon pin and connecting rod small-end bearing for signs of wear or damage. Wear can be cured by renewing both the pin and bush (where possible) or connecting rod. Bush renewal, however, is a specialist job – press facilities are required, and the new bush must be reamed accurately.

17 The connecting rods themselves should not be in need of renewal, unless seizure or some other major mechanical failure has occurred. Check the alignment of the connecting rods visually, and if the rods are not straight, take them to an engine overhaul specialist for a more detailed check.

18 Examine all components, and obtain any new parts from your Peugeot dealer. If new pistons are purchased, they will be supplied complete with gudgeon pins and circlips. Circlips can also be purchased individually.

19 Position the piston as shown **(see illustration)**.

20 Ensure the piston and connecting rod are correctly positioned then apply a smear of clean engine oil to the gudgeon pin. Slide it into the piston and through the connecting rod small-end. Check that the piston pivots freely on the rod, then secure the gudgeon pin in position with two new circlips. Ensure that each circlip is correctly located in its groove in the piston.

Checking endfloat

1 If the crankshaft endfloat is to be checked, this must be done when the crankshaft is still installed in the cylinder block/crankcase, but is free to move (see Section 10).

2 Check the endfloat using a dial gauge in contact with the end of the crankshaft. Push the crankshaft fully one way, and then zero the gauge. Push the crankshaft fully the other way, and check the endfloat. The result can be compared with the specified amount, and will give an indication as to whether new thrustwashers are required **(see illustration)**.

3 If a dial gauge is not available, feeler blades can be used. First push the crankshaft fully towards the flywheel end of the engine, and then use feeler blades to measure the gap between the web of No 2 crankpin and the thrustwasher**(see illustration)**.

Inspection

4 Clean the crankshaft using paraffin or a suitable solvent, and dry it, preferably with compressed air if available. Be sure to clean the oil holes with a pipe cleaner or similar probe, to ensure that they are not obstructed.
Warning: Wear eye protection when using compressed air.

5 Check the main and big-end bearing journals for uneven wear, scoring, pitting and cracking.

6 Big-end bearing wear is accompanied by distinct metallic knocking when the engine is running (particularly noticeable when the engine is pulling from low speed) and some loss of oil pressure.

7 Main bearing wear is accompanied by severe engine vibration and rumble – getting progressively worse as engine speed increases – and again by loss of oil pressure.

8 Check the bearing journal for roughness by running a finger lightly over the bearing surface. Any roughness (which will be accompanied by obvious bearing wear) indicates that the crankshaft requires regrinding (where possible) or renewal.

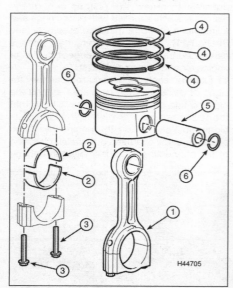

12.19 Piston and connecting rod assembly (diesel engine)

1 Connecting rod	4 Piston rings
2 Big-end shells	5 Gudgeon pin
3 Big-end bolt	6 Circlips

13.2 The crankshaft endfloat can be checked with a dial gauge...

13.3... or with feeler gauges

9 Check the oil seal contact surfaces at each end of the crankshaft for wear and damage. If the seal has worn a deep groove in the surface of the crankshaft, consult an engine overhaul specialist; repair may be possible, but otherwise a new crankshaft will be required.

10 Take the crankshaft to a Peugeot dealer or engine reconditioning specialist to have it measured for journal wear. If excessive wear is evident, they will be able to advise you with regard to regrinding the crankshaft and supplying new bearing shells.

11 If the crankshaft has been reground, check for burrs around the crankshaft oil holes (the holes are usually chamfered, so burrs should not be a problem unless regrinding has been carried out carelessly). Remove any burrs with a fine file or scraper, and thoroughly clean the oil holes as described previously.

12 At the time of writing, it was not clear whether Peugeot produce undersize bearing shells for all of these engines. On some engines, if the crankshaft journals have not already been reground, it may be possible to have the crankshaft reconditioned, and to fit undersize shells. If no undersize shells are available and the crankshaft has worn beyond the specified limits, it will have to be renewed. Consult your Peugeot dealer or engine specialist for further information on parts availability.

14 Main and big-end bearings – inspection

1 Even though the main and big-end bearings should be renewed during the engine overhaul, the old bearings should be retained for close examination, as they may reveal valuable information about the condition of the engine. The bearing shells are graded by thickness, the grade of each shell being indicated by the colour code marked on it.

2 Bearing failure can occur due to lack of lubrication, the presence of dirt or other foreign particles, overloading the engine, or corrosion **(see illustration)**. Regardless of the cause of bearing failure, the cause must be corrected (where applicable) before the engine is reassembled, to prevent it from happening again.

3 When examining the bearing shells, remove them from the cylinder block/crankcase, the main bearing ladder/caps (as appropriate), the connecting rods and the connecting rod big-end bearing caps. Lay them out on a clean surface in the same general position as their location in the engine. This will enable you to match any bearing problems with the corresponding crankshaft journal. Do not touch any shell's bearing surface with your fingers while checking it, or the delicate surface may be scratched.

4 Dirt and other foreign matter gets into the engine in a variety of ways. It may be left in

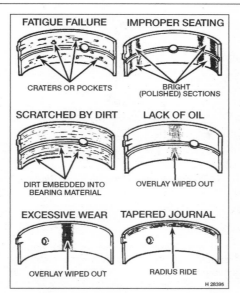

FATIGUE FAILURE	IMPROPER SEATING
CRATERS OR POCKETS	BRIGHT (POLISHED) SECTIONS
SCRATCHED BY DIRT	LACK OF OIL
DIRT EMBEDDED INTO BEARING MATERIAL	OVERLAY WIPED OUT
EXCESSIVE WEAR	TAPERED JOURNAL
OVERLAY WIPED OUT	RADIUS RIDE

H 28395

14.2 Typical bearing failures

the engine during assembly, or it may pass through filters or the crankcase ventilation system. It may get into the oil, and from there into the bearings. Metal chips from machining operations and normal engine wear are often present. Abrasives are sometimes left in engine components after reconditioning, especially when parts are not thoroughly cleaned using the proper cleaning methods. Whatever the source, these foreign objects often end up embedded in the soft bearing material, and are easily recognised. Large particles will not embed in the bearing, and will score or gouge the bearing and journal. The best prevention for this cause of bearing failure is to clean all parts thoroughly, and keep everything spotlessly clean during engine assembly. Frequent and regular engine oil and filter changes are also recommended.

5 Lack of lubrication (or lubrication breakdown) has a number of interrelated causes. Excessive heat (which thins the oil), overloading (which squeezes the oil from the bearing face) and oil leakage (from excessive bearing clearances, worn oil pump or high engine speeds) all contribute to lubrication breakdown. Blocked oil passages, which usually are the result of misaligned oil holes in a bearing shell, will also oil-starve a bearing, and destroy it. When lack of lubrication is the cause of bearing failure, the bearing material is wiped or extruded from the steel backing of the bearing. Temperatures may increase to the point where the steel backing turns blue from overheating.

6 Driving habits can have a definite effect on bearing life. Full-throttle, low-speed operation (labouring the engine) puts very high loads on bearings, tending to squeeze out the oil film. These loads cause the bearings to flex, which produces fine cracks in the bearing face (fatigue failure). Eventually, the bearing

material will loosen in pieces, and tear away from the steel backing.

7 Short-distance driving leads to corrosion of bearings, because insufficient engine heat is produced to drive off the condensed water and corrosive gases. These products collect in the engine oil, forming acid and sludge. As the oil is carried to the engine bearings, the acid attacks and corrodes the bearing material.

8 Incorrect bearing installation during engine assembly will lead to bearing failure as well. Tight-fitting bearings leave insufficient bearing running clearance, and will result in oil starvation. Dirt or foreign particles trapped behind a bearing shell result in high spots on the bearing, which lead to failure.

9 Do not touch any shell's bearing surface with your fingers during reassembly; there is a risk of scratching the delicate surface, or of depositing particles of dirt on it.

10 As mentioned at the beginning of this Section, the bearing shells should be renewed as a matter of course during engine overhaul; to do otherwise is false economy.

15 Engine overhaul – reassembly sequence

1 Before reassembly begins, ensure that all new parts have been obtained, and that all necessary tools are available. Read through the entire procedure to familiarise yourself with the work involved, and to ensure that all items necessary for reassembly of the engine are at hand. In addition to all normal tools and materials, thread-locking compound will be needed. A tube of suitable liquid sealant will also be required for the joint faces that are fitted without gaskets. It is recommended that Peugeot's own product(s) be used, which are specially formulated for this purpose; the relevant product names are quoted in the text of each Section where they are required.

2 In order to save time and avoid problems, engine reassembly can be carried out in the following order, referring to Part A, B, C, D or E of this Chapter unless otherwise stated:
● Crankshaft (See Section 17). **Note:** *On 1.4 litre diesel engines, the piston/connecting rods must be fitted before the crankshaft.*
● Piston/connecting rod assemblies (See Section 18).
● Oil pump.
● Sump.
● Flywheel/driveplate.
● Cylinder head.
● Injection pump and mounting bracket – diesel engine (Chapter 4B Section 9).
● Timing belt tensioner pulley(s) and sprockets, and timing belt.
● Engine external components.

3 At this stage, all engine components should be absolutely clean and dry, with all faults repaired. The components should be laid out (or in individual containers) on a completely clean work surface.

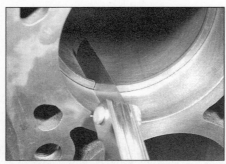

16.5 Measure the piston rings end gaps with a feeler gauge

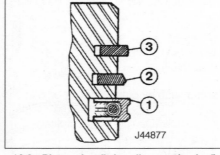

16.9a Piston ring fitting diagram (typical)

1 Oil control ring
2 Second compression ring
3 Top compression ring

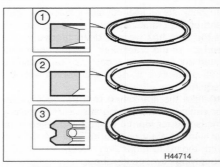

16.9b Piston rings (diesel engine)

1 Top compression ring
2 Second compression ring
3 Oil control ring

16 Piston rings – refitting

1 Before fitting new piston rings, the ring end gaps must be checked as follows.

2 Lay out the piston/connecting rod assemblies and the new piston ring sets, so that the ring sets will be matched with the same piston and cylinder during the end gap measurement and subsequent engine reassembly.

3 Insert the top ring into the first cylinder, and push it down the bore using the top of the piston. This will ensure that the ring remains square with the cylinder walls. Position the ring near the bottom of the cylinder bore, at the lower limit of ring travel. Note that the top and second compression rings are different. The second ring can be identified by its taper; on petrol engines it also has a step on its lower surface. On diesel engines, the top ring has a chamfer on its upper/outer edge.

4 Measure the end gap using feeler blades.

5 Repeat the procedure with the ring at the top of the cylinder bore, at the upper limit of its travel **(see illustration)**, and compare the measurements with the figures given in the Specifications. If the end gaps are incorrect, check that you have the correct rings for your engine and for the cylinder bore size.

6 Repeat the checking procedure for each ring in the first cylinder, and then for the rings in the remaining cylinders. Remember to keep rings, pistons and cylinders matched up.

7 Once the ring end gaps have been checked and if necessary corrected, the rings can be fitted to the pistons.

8 Fit the oil control ring expander (where fitted) then install the ring. The ring gap should be positioned 180° from the expander gap.

9 The second and top rings are different and can be identified from their cross-sections; the top ring is symmetrical whilst the second ring is tapered. Fit the second ring, ensuring its identification (TOP) marking is facing upwards, and then install the top ring **(see illustrations)**. Arrange the second

and top ring end gap so they are equally spaced 120° apart. **Note:** *Always follow any instructions supplied with the new piston ring sets – different manufacturers may specify different procedures. Do not mix up the top and second compression rings, as they have different cross-sections.*

17 Crankshaft – refitting

Selection of bearing shells

1 Have the crankshaft inspected and measured by a Peugeot dealer or engine reconditioning specialist. They will be able to carry out any regrinding/repairs, and supply suitable main and big-end bearing shells.

Crankshaft refitting

Note: *New main bearing cap/lower crankcase bolts must be used when refitting the crankshaft.*

2 Where applicable, ensure that the oil spray jets are fitted to the bearing locations in the cylinder block.

1.4 litre non-VTi petrol engine

3 Using a little grease, stick the upper thrustwashers to each side of the No 2 main

bearing upper location; ensure that the oilway grooves on each thrustwasher face outwards (away from the block).

4 Clean the backs of the bearing shells, and the bearing locations in both the cylinder block/crankcase and the main bearing ladder/bearing caps.

5 Press the bearing shells into their locations, ensuring that the tab on each shell engages in the notch in the cylinder block/crankcase or main bearing ladder/bearing cap. Take care not to touch any shell's bearing surface with your fingers. Note that the grooved bearing shells, both upper and lower, are fitted to numbers 2 and 4 main bearings **(see illustration)**.

6 Liberally lubricate each bearing shell in the cylinder block/crankcase with clean engine oil.

7 Refit the Woodruff key, then slide on the oil pump drive sprocket, and locate the drive chain on the sprocket **(see illustration)**. Lower the crankshaft into position so that numbers 2 and 3 cylinder crankpins are at TDC; numbers 1 and 4 cylinder crankpins will be at BDC, ready for fitting No 1 piston. Check the crankshaft endfloat as described in Section 13.

8 Thoroughly de-grease the mating surfaces of the cylinder block/crankcase and the main bearing ladder. Apply a thin bead of suitable sealant to the cylinder block, mating surface

17.5 Fit the grooved bearing shells to No 2 and 4 main bearings (non-VTi petrol engine)

17.7 Fit the oil pump drive chain and sprocket

of the main bearing ladder casting, then spread to an even film **(see illustration)**.

9 Ensure that the locating dowels are in position then lubricate the lower bearing shells with clean engine oil. Refit the main bearing ladder to the cylinder block, ensuring that the lower bearings remain correctly fitted.

10 Install the main bearing ladder retaining bolts, and tighten them all by hand only. Working in a spiral pattern from the centre bolts outwards, evenly and progressively tighten the bolts to the specified Stage 1 torque wrench setting. Once all the bolts have been tightened to the Stage 1 setting, working in the same sequence, angle-tighten the bolts through the specified Stage 2 angle using a socket and extension bar. It is recommended that an angle-measuring gauge is used during this stage of the tightening, to ensure accuracy **(see illustration)**. If a gauge is not available, use a dab of white paint to make alignment marks between the bolt head and casting prior to tightening; the marks can then be used to check that the bolt has been rotated sufficiently during tightening.

11 Refit all the smaller bolts securing the main bearing ladder to the base of the cylinder block, and tighten them to the specified torque. Check that the crankshaft rotates freely.

12 Refit the piston/connecting rod assemblies to the crankshaft as described in Section 18.

13 Ensuring that the drive chain is correctly located on the sprocket, refit the oil pump and sump as described in Part A of this Chapter.

14 Fit two new crankshaft oil seals as described in Part A.

15 Refit the flywheel/driveplate as described in Part A of this Chapter.

16 Refit the cylinder head (where removed) as described in Part A. Also refit the crankshaft sprocket and timing belt (see Part A).

1.6 litre non-VTi petrol engine

17 Using a little grease, stick the upper thrustwashers to each side of the No 2 main bearing upper location. Ensure that the oilway grooves on each thrustwasher face outwards (away from the cylinder block) **(see illustration)**.

18 Place the bearing shells in their locations as described in paragraphs 4 and 5 **(see illustration)**. If new shells are being fitted, ensure that all traces of protective grease are cleaned off using paraffin. Wipe dry the shells and connecting rods with a lint-free cloth. Liberally lubricate each bearing shell in the cylinder block/crankcase and cap with clean engine oil.

19 Lower the crankshaft into position so that numbers 2 and 3 cylinder crankpins are at TDC; numbers 1 and 4 cylinder crankpins will be at BDC, ready for fitting No 1 piston. Check the crankshaft endfloat as described in Section 13.

20 Lubricate the lower bearing shells in the main bearing caps with clean engine oil. Make sure that the locating lugs on the shells

17.8 Apply a thin film of sealant to the cylinder block mating surface

17.10 Tighten the ten main bearing bolts to the specified torque

engage with the corresponding recesses in the caps.

21 Fit the main bearing caps to their correct locations, ensuring that they are fitted the correct way round (the bearing shell lug recesses in the block and caps must be on the same side).

22 Lightly lubricate the threads and the underside of the heads of the main bearing cap bolts with engine oil then refit the bolts. Working in a spiral sequence from the centre bolts outwards, tighten the main bearing cap bolts evenly and progressively to the specified Stage 1 torque wrench setting. Once all the bolts have been tightened to the Stage 1 setting, working in the same sequence, angle-tighten the bolts through the specified Stage 2 angle, using a socket and extension bar. It is recommended that an angle-measuring gauge be used during this stage of the tightening, to ensure accuracy. If a gauge is not available, use a dab of white paint to make alignment marks between the bolt head and casting prior to tightening; the marks can then be used to check that the bolt has been rotated sufficiently during tightening.

23 Check that the crankshaft rotates freely.

24 Refit the piston/connecting rod assemblies to the crankshaft as described in Section 18.

25 Refit the Woodruff key to the crankshaft groove, and slide on the oil pump drive sprocket. Locate the drive chain on the sprocket.

26 Ensure that the mating surfaces of right-hand (timing belt end) oil seal housing and

cylinder block are clean and dry. Note the correct fitted depth of the oil seal then, using a large flat-bladed screwdriver, lever the seal out of the housing.

27 Apply a smear of suitable sealant to the oil seal housing mating surface, and make sure that the locating dowels are in position. Slide the housing over the end of the crankshaft, and into position on the cylinder block. Tighten the housing retaining bolts securely.

28 Repeat the operations in paragraphs 26 and 27, and fit the left-hand (flywheel/drive-plate end) oil seal housing.

29 Fit new crankshaft oil seals as described in Part A of this Chapter.

30 Ensuring that the chain is correctly located on the drive sprocket, refit the oil pump and sump as described in Part A of this Chapter.

31 Refit the flywheel/driveplate as described in Part A of this Chapter.

32 Refit the cylinder head (where removed) and install the crankshaft sprocket and timing belt as described in the relevant Sections of Part A.

VTi petrol engines

33 Clean the backs of the bearing shells in both the cylinder block/crankcase and the main bearing ladder. If new shells are being fitted, ensure that all traces of protective grease are cleaned off using paraffin. Wipe dry the shells with a lint-free cloth.

34 Press the bearing shells into their locations, ensuring that the tab on each shell engages in the notch in the cylinder block/crankcase

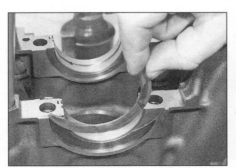

17.17 Fit the thrustwashers to either side of the No 2 main bearing, with the oilway grooves facing outwards

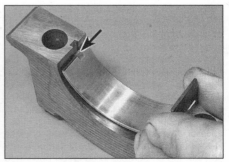

17.18 Ensure the tab (arrowed) is located in the cut-out when fitting the bearing shells

17.41a Cylinder head timing chain end bolts – arrowed

17.41b Cylinder head rear bolt – arrowed

and bearing ladder. Take care not to touch any shell's bearing surface with your fingers. Note that the upper bearing shells all have a grooved surface, whereas the lower shells have a plain bearing surface.

35 Liberally lubricate each bearing shell in the cylinder block with clean engine oil then lower the crankshaft into position.

36 Insert the thrustwashers to either side of No 2 main bearing upper location and push them around the bearing journal until their edges are horizontal. Ensure that the oilway grooves on each thrustwasher face outwards (away from the cylinder block).

37 Thoroughly degrease the mating surfaces of the cylinder block and the crankshaft bearing cap housing/main bearing ladder. Apply a thin bead of RTV sealant to the bearing cap housing mating surface. Peugeot recommend the use of Loctite Autojoint Noir for this purpose.

38 Lubricate the lower bearing shells with clean engine oil, then refit the bearing cap housing, ensuring that the shells are not displaced, and that the locating dowels engage correctly.

39 Install the large and small crankshaft bearing cap housing/ladder retaining bolts, and screw them in until they are just making contact with the housing.

40 Working in sequence, tighten all the main bearing ladder bolts to the torque setting given in the Specifications.

41 Tighten the two timing chain end bolts and the single bolt at the rear of the cylinder head to the Stage 1 torque setting, given in the Specifications **(see illustrations)**.

42 Using an angle tightening gauge, tighten all bolts to their stage 2 setting, working in the correct sequence.

43 Finally tighten all the bolts (except for the single bolt at the rear of the cylinder head), in the correct sequence, through the specified Stage 3 angle, using an angle tightening gauge.

44 With the bearing cap housing in place, check that the crankshaft rotates freely.

45 Refit the piston/connecting rod assemblies to the crankshaft as described in Section 18.

46 Refit the oil pump and sump as described in Part B.

47 Fit a new crankshaft left-hand oil seal, then refit the flywheel as described in Part B.

48 Where removed, refit the crankshaft sprocket and timing belt also as described in Part B.

1.4 litre diesel engine

49 Clean the backs of the bearing shells in both the cylinder block/crankcase and the main bearing ladder. If new shells are being fitted, ensure that all traces of protective grease are cleaned off using paraffin. Wipe dry the shells with a lint-free cloth.

50 Press the bearing shells into their locations, ensuring that the tab on each shell engages in the notch in the cylinder block/crankcase and bearing ladder. Take care not to touch any shell's bearing surface with your fingers. Note that the upper bearing shells all have a grooved surface, whereas the lower shells have a plain bearing surface. It is essential that the lower bearing shell halves are centrally located in the ladder. To ensure this use Peugeot tool No 0194-Q positioned over the ladder, and insert the bearing shells through the slots in the tool **(see illustration)**.

51 Liberally lubricate each bearing shell in the cylinder block with clean engine oil then lower the crankshaft into position.

52 Insert the thrustwashers to either side of No 2 main bearing upper location and push them around the bearing journal until their edges are horizontal. Ensure that the oilway grooves on each thrustwasher face outwards

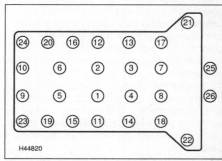

17.50 Main bearing shell refitment (diesel engine)

1 Bearing shell   *3 Peugeot tool*
2 Main bearing ladder   *4 Aligning pins*

(away from the cylinder block). Now refit the piston and connecting rod assemblies as described in Section 18.

53 Thoroughly degrease the mating surfaces of the cylinder block and the crankshaft bearing cap housing/main bearing ladder. Apply a thin bead of RTV sealant to the bearing cap housing mating surface. Peugeot recommend the use of Loctite Autojoint Noir for this purpose. Use two aligning pins (available from Peugeot) inserted into the main bearing ladder, to ensure the correct positioning of the assembly.

54 Lubricate the lower bearing shells with clean engine oil, then refit the bearing cap housing, ensuring that the shells are not displaced, and that the locating dowels engage correctly. Remove the aligning pins from the bearing ladder.

55 Install the large and small crankshaft bearing cap housing/ladder retaining bolts, and screw them in until they are just making contact with the housing. Note that new large (M11) bolts must be used.

56 Tighten all the main bearing ladder bolts to their Stage 1 setting in the sequence shown **(see illustration)**.

57 Slacken (Stage 2) the large diameter bearing ladder bolts half a turn (180°), then tighten them in sequence to the Stage 3 torque setting, followed by the Stage 4 angle-tightening setting. Apply sealant to the two new bearing ladder bolt caps, and tap them into place over the two flywheel bolts.

58 Finally, tighten the small diameter bearing ladder bolts to their Stage 2 setting.

59 With the bearing cap housing in place, check that the crankshaft rotates freely.

60 Refit the oil pump and sump as described in Part C.

61 Fit a new crankshaft left-hand oil seal, then refit the flywheel as described in Part C.

62 Where removed, refit the cylinder head, crankshaft sprocket and timing belt also as described in Part C.

1.6 litre diesel engine

63 Place the bearing shells in their locations. If new shells are being fitted, ensure that all traces of protective grease are cleaned off using paraffin. Wipe dry the shells with a lint-free cloth. The upper bearing shells all

17.56 Main bearing ladder bolts tightening sequence (diesel engine)

17.65 Place the thrustwashers each side of the No 2 bearing upper location

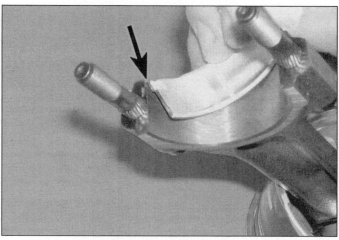
18.4 Ensure the bearing shell tab (arrowed) locates correctly in the cut-out

have a grooved surface, whereas the lower shells have a plain surface. On these engines, it's essential that the lower bearing shells are centrally located in the bearing cap housing/ladder. To ensure this use Peugeot tool No 0194-QZ positioned over the housing/ladder, and insert the bearing shells through the slots in the tool **(see illustration 17.50)**.
64 Liberally lubricate each bearing shell in the cylinder block with clean engine oil then lower the crankshaft into position.
65 Insert the thrustwashers to either side of No 2 main bearing upper location and push them around the bearing journal until their edges are horizontal **(see illustration)**. Ensure that the oilway grooves on each thrustwasher face outwards (away from the bearing journal).
66 Thoroughly degrease the mating surfaces of the cylinder block and the crankshaft bearing cap housing. Apply a thin bead of RTV sealant to the bearing cap housing mating surface. Peugeot recommend the use of Loctite Autojoint Noir for this purpose.
67 Lubricate the lower bearing shells with clean engine oil, then refit the bearing cap housing, ensuring that the shells are not displaced, and that the locating dowels engage correctly.
68 Install the ten large diameter and sixteen smaller diameter crankshaft bearing cap

housing retaining bolts, and screw them in until they are just making contact with the housing.
69 Working in sequence, tighten the bolts to the torque settings given in the Specifications **(see illustration 17.56)**.
70 With the bearing cap housing in place, check that the crankshaft rotates freely.
71 Refit the piston/connecting rod assemblies to the crankshaft as described in Section 18.
72 Refit the oil pump and sump.
73 Fit a new crankshaft left-hand oil seal, then refit the flywheel.
74 Where removed, refit the cylinder head, crankshaft sprocket and timing belt.

18 Piston/connecting rod assembly – refitting

1 New big-end cap nuts/bolts must be used on refitting.
2 Note that the following procedure assumes that, where applicable, the cylinder liners are in position in the cylinder block/crankcase as described in Section 11, and that the crankshaft and main bearing ladder/caps are in place – except on the 1.4 litre diesel engine where the crankshaft is fitted after the pistons (see Section 17).

3 Clean the backs of the bearing shells, and the bearing locations in both the connecting rod and bearing cap.

Petrol engines
4 Press the bearing shells into their locations, ensuring that the tab on each shell engages in the notch in the connecting rod and cap. Take care not to touch any shell's bearing surface with your fingers **(see illustration)**.

All engines
5 Lubricate the cylinder bores, the pistons, and piston rings, then lay out each piston/connecting rod assembly in its respective position.
6 Start with assembly No 1. Make sure that the piston rings are still spaced as described in Section 16, and then clamp them in position with a piston ring compressor.
7 Insert the piston/connecting rod assembly into the top of cylinder/liner number 1; ensuring the piston is correctly positioned as follows.
● On petrol engines, ensure that the arrow on the piston crown is pointing towards the timing belt/chain end of the engine.
● On diesel engines, ensure that the DIST mark or arrow on the piston crown is towards the timing belt end of the engine.
8 Once the piston is correctly positioned, using a block of wood or hammer handle against the piston crown, tap the assembly into the cylinder/liner until the piston crown is flush with the top of the cylinder/liner **(see illustration)**.

Petrol engines
9 Ensure that the bearing shell is still correctly installed. Liberally lubricate the crankpin and both bearing shells. Taking care not to mark the cylinder/liner bores, pull the piston/connecting rod assembly down the bore and onto the crankpin. Refit the big-end bearing cap and fit the new nuts, tightening them finger-tight at first **(see illustration)**. Note that

18.8 Tap the piston into the bore using a hammer handle

18.9 Fit the big-end bearing cap, ensuring it is fitted the right way around, and screw on the new nuts

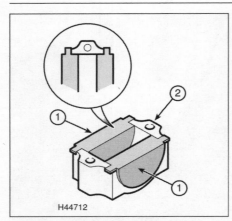

18.12 Big-end bearing shell positioning (diesel engine)

1 Peugeot tool No 0194-P   2 Bearing shell

the faces with the identification marks must match (which means that the bearing shell locating tabs abut each other).

10 Tighten the bearing cap retaining nuts evenly and progressively to the specified torque setting.

Diesel engine

11 On these engines, the connecting rod is made in one piece, and the big-end bearing cap is 'cracked' off. This ensures that the cap fits onto the connecting rod only in one position, and with maximum rigidity. Consequently, there are no locating notches for the bearing shells to fit into.

12 To ensure that the big-end bearing shells are centrally located in the connecting rod and cap, two special tools are available from Peugeot. These half-moon shaped tools are pressed in from either side of the rod/cap and locate the shell exactly in the centre **(see illustration)**. Fit the shells into the connecting rods and big-end caps and lubricate them with plenty of clean engine oil.

13 Pull the connecting rods and pistons down the bores and onto the crankshaft journals. Fit the big-end caps – they will only fit properly one way round (see paragraph 10), and insert the new bolts.

14 Tighten the bolts to the Stage 1 torque setting, then slacken them 180° (Stage 2). Tighten the bolts to the Stage 3 setting, followed by the Stage 4 angle-tightening setting.

15 Continue refitting the main bearing shells and ladder as described in Section 17.

All engines

16 Once the bearing cap retaining nuts have been correctly tightened, rotate the crankshaft. Check that it turns freely; some stiffness is to be expected if new components have been fitted, but there should be no signs of binding or tight spots.

17 Refit the cylinder head and oil pump as described in Part A, B, C, D or E, of this Chapter (as applicable).

19 Engine – initial start-up after overhaul

1 With the engine refitted in the vehicle, double-check the engine oil and coolant levels. Make a final check that everything has been reconnected, and that there are no tools or rags left in the engine compartment.

Petrol engine models

2 Remove the spark plugs and disable the fuel system by disconnecting the wiring connectors from the fuel injectors, referring to Chapter 4A for further information.

3 Turn the engine on the starter until the oil pressure warning light goes out. Refit the spark plugs, and reconnect the wiring.

Diesel engine models

4 On the models covered in this Manual, the oil pressure warning light is linked to the STOP warning light, and is not illuminated when the ignition is initially switched on. Therefore it is not possible to check the oil pressure warning light when turning the engine on the starter motor.

5 Prime the fuel system (refer to Chapter 4B Section 3).

6 Fully depress the accelerator pedal, turn the ignition key to position M, and wait for the preheating warning light to go out.

All models

7 Start the engine, noting that this may take a little longer than usual, due to the fuel system components having been disturbed.

8 While the engine is idling, check for fuel, water and oil leaks. Don't be alarmed if there are some odd smells and smoke from parts getting hot and burning off oil deposits.

9 Assuming all is well; keep the engine idling until hot water is felt circulating through the top hose, then switch off the engine.

10 After a few minutes, recheck the oil and coolant levels as described in *Weekly checks*, and top-up as necessary.

11 Note that there is no need to retighten the cylinder head bolts once the engine has first run after reassembly.

12 If new pistons, rings or crankshaft bearings have been fitted, the engine must be treated as new, and run-in for the first 500 miles. Do not operate the engine at full-throttle, or allow it to labour at low engine speeds in any gear. It is recommended that the oil and filter be changed at the end of this period.

Chapter 3
Cooling, heating and ventilation systems

Contents

Degrees of difficulty

Easy, suitable for novice with little experience	Fairly easy, suitable for beginner with some experience	Fairly difficult, suitable for competent DIY mechanic	Difficult, suitable for experienced DIY mechanic	Very difficult, suitable for expert DIY or professional

Specifications

General

Maximum system pressure	1.4 bars
Engine coolant temperature sensor resistance (approximately):	
Petrol engines:	
20°C	6100 ohms
80°C	620 ohms
Diesel engines:	
60°C	1266 ohms
80°C	642 ohms

Thermostat

Start of opening temperature:	
Petrol engine models:	
Non-VTi engines.	89°C
VTi engines	82°C
Diesel engine models	83°C

Air conditioning compressor

Make	Sanden or Denso
Model	SD6V12 (Sanden) or ND8 (Denso)
Compressor oil:	
Quantity	135 cc
Type	SP10

Refrigerant

Quantity	450 ± 25 g
Type	R134a

Torque wrench settings

	Nm	lbf ft
Air conditioning compressor mounting bolts.	25	18
Coolant outlet housing.	10	7
Coolant pump:		
Non-VTi petrol engines:		
Upper bolt.	16	12
Lower bolt.	8	6
VTi petrol engines.	10	7
Diesel engines	10	7

1 General information and precautions

1 The cooling system is of pressurised type, comprising a coolant pump driven by the timing belt or auxiliary belt on VTi petrol engines, an aluminium radiator, an expansion tank, an electric cooling fan, a thermostat, a heater matrix, and all associated hoses and switches.

2 The system functions as follows. Cold coolant in the bottom of the radiator passes through the bottom hose to the coolant pump, where it is pumped around the cylinder block and head passages. After cooling the cylinder bores, combustion surfaces and valve seats, the coolant reaches the underside of the thermostat, which is initially closed. The coolant passes through the heater, and is returned via the cylinder block to the coolant pump.

3 When the engine is cold, the coolant circulates only through the cylinder block, cylinder head, and heater. When the coolant reaches a predetermined temperature, the thermostat opens, and the coolant passes through the top hose to the radiator. As the coolant passes down through the radiator, it is cooled by the inrush of air when the car is in forward motion. The airflow is supplemented by the action of the electric cooling fan when necessary. Upon reaching the bottom of the radiator, the coolant has now cooled, and the cycle is repeated.

4 On models with automatic transmission, a proportion of the coolant is recirculated through the transmission fluid cooler mounted on the transmission. On models fitted with an engine oil cooler, the coolant is also passed through the oil cooler.

5 The operation of the electric cooling fan(s) is controlled by the engine management control unit.

⚠️ *Warning: Do not attempt to remove the expansion tank filler cap, or to disturb any part of the cooling system, while the engine is hot, as there is a high risk of scalding.*

2.5 Release the retaining clip and move it along the hose

If the expansion tank filler cap must be removed before the engine and radiator have fully cooled (even though this is not recommended), the pressure in the cooling system must first be relieved. Cover the cap with a thick layer of cloth to avoid scalding, and slowly unscrew the filler cap until a hissing sound is heard. When the hissing has stopped, indicating that the pressure has reduced, slowly unscrew the filler cap until it can be removed; if more hissing sounds are heard, wait until they have stopped before unscrewing the cap. At all times keep well away from the filler cap opening, and protect your hands.

● Do not allow antifreeze to come into contact with your skin, or with the painted surfaces of the vehicle. Rinse off spills immediately, with plenty of water. Never leave antifreeze lying around in an open container, or in a puddle in the driveway or on the garage floor. Children and pets are attracted by its sweet smell, but antifreeze can be fatal if ingested.

● If the engine is hot, the electric cooling fan(s) may start rotating even if the engine is not running. Be careful to keep your hands, hair, and any loose clothing well clear when working in the engine compartment.

● Refer to Section 11 for precautions to be observed when working on models equipped with air conditioning.

2 Cooling system hoses – disconnection and renewal

Note: *Refer to the warnings given in Section 1 of this Chapter before proceeding. Hoses should only be disconnected once the engine has cooled sufficiently to avoid scalding.*

1 If the checks described in the Hose and fluid leak check Section in Chapter 1A Section 7 (petrol engines) or Chapter 1B Section 8 (diesel engines) reveal a faulty hose, it must be renewed as follows.

2 First drain the cooling system. If the coolant

2.13 Where click-fit connectors are used, prise out the circlip then disconnect the hose

is not due for renewal, it may be re-used, providing it is collected in a clean container.

3 To disconnect a hose, proceed as follows, according to the type of hose connection.

Conventional connections

4 On conventional connections, the clips used to secure the hoses in position may be standard worm-drive (Jubilee) clips, spring clips or disposable crimped types. The crimped type of clip is not designed to be re-used and should be renewed with a worm-drive type on reassembly.

5 To disconnect a hose, release the retaining clips and move them along the hose, clear of the relevant inlet/outlet. Carefully work the hose free. The hoses can be removed with relative ease when new – on an older car; they may have stuck **(see illustration)**.

6 If a hose proves to be difficult to remove, try to release it by rotating its ends before attempting to free it. Gently prise the end of the hose with a blunt instrument (such as a flat-bladed screwdriver), but do not apply too much force, and take care not to damage the pipe stubs or hoses. Note in particular that the radiator inlet stub is fragile; do not use excessive force when attempting to remove the hose. If all else fails, cut the hose with a sharp knife, then slit it so that it can be peeled off in two pieces. Although this may prove expensive if the hose is otherwise undamaged, it is preferable to buying a new radiator. Check first, however, that a new hose is readily available.

7 When fitting a hose, first slide the clips onto the hose, then work the hose into position. If crimped-type clips were originally fitted, use standard worm-drive clips when refitting the hose.

8 Work the hose into position, checking that it is correctly routed, and then slide each clip back along the hose until it passes over the flared end of the relevant inlet/outlet, before tightening the clip securely.

9 Refill the cooling system.

10 Check thoroughly for leaks as soon as possible after disturbing any part of the cooling system.

Click-fit connections

11 New sealing ring should be used when reconnecting the hose.

12 On certain models, some cooling system hoses are secured in position with click-fit connectors where the hose is retained by a large circlip.

13 To disconnect this type of hose fitting, carefully prise the wire clip out of position then disconnect the hose connection **(see illustration)**. Once the hose has been disconnected, refit the wire clip to the hose union. Inspect the hose unit sealing ring for signs of damage or deterioration and renew if necessary.

14 On refitting, ensure that the sealing ring is in position and the wire clip is correctly located in the groove in the union **(see illustration)**. Lubricate the sealing ring with

2.14 Ensure the sealing ring and circlip (arrowed) are correctly fitted to the hose union before reconnecting

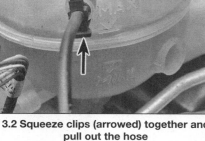

3.2 Squeeze clips (arrowed) together and pull out the hose

3.3 Slide out the retaining clip (arrowed) and pull out the hose

a smear of soapy water, to ease installation, and then push the hose into its union until it is heard to click into position.

15 Ensure the hose is securely retained by the wire clip then refill the cooling system.

16 Check thoroughly for leaks as soon as possible after disturbing any part of the cooling system.

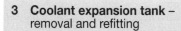

3   Coolant expansion tank –
removal and refitting

Removal

1 Referring to Chapter 1A Section 25, drain the cooling system sufficiently to empty the contents of the expansion tank. Do not drain any more coolant than is necessary.

2 Squeeze the clips on the collar of the pipe together, then pull the plastic hose from the top of the expansion tank **(see illustration)**.

3 Slide out the retaining clip, then pull the hose from the lower part of the expansion tank **(see illustration)**. Note: *On some models, the hoses may be secured by expanding clamps.*

4 Where fitted, disconnect the level sensor wiring plug.

5 Unscrew the mounting bolts and free the tank from its mount.

Refitting

6 Refitting is the reverse of removal, ensuring the hoses are securely reconnected. On completion, top-up the coolant level as described in *Weekly checks*.

4   Radiator – removal,
inspection and refitting

Note: *If leakage is the reason for removing the radiator, bear in mind that minor leaks can often be cured using a radiator sealant with the radiator still in position.*

Removal

1 Drain the cooling system (see Chapter 1A Section 25).

2 Remove the air inlet resonator and inlet hoses from side of the battery tray, with reference to Chapter 4A or 4B

3 Squeeze the clips on the collar of the pipe together, then pull the plastic hose from the top of the radiator **(see illustration)**.

4 Unclip the battery ventilation pipe from the front crossmember above the radiator top hose **(see illustration)**.

5 Release the retaining clips and disconnect

the upper and lower coolant hoses from the radiator **(see illustrations)**.

6 Release the securing clips and disconnect the wiring connectors from the radiator fan assembly **(see illustrations)**.

7 Using a small screwdriver release the two upper radiator mountings from the

4.3 Squeeze clips together and disconnect the hose

4.4 Disconnect the air vent pipe

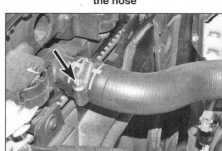

4.5a Undo the hose clip (arrowed)

4.5b Squeeze clips (arrowed) together and disconnect the hose

4.6a Release the securing clips...

4.6b... and disconnect the wiring connectors

4.7 Release the radiator upper mountings…

4.9 … and remove the radiator

crossmember and tilt the radiator towards the engine **(see illustration).**

8 On some models, it may be necessary to remove the front bumper as described in Chapter 11 Section 6. Then slacken the upper crossmember retaining bolts and carefully pull the radiator/condenser plastic housing forwards to allow room for the radiator to be withdrawn.

9 Carefully lift the radiator out of position, taking care not to damage the radiator fins **(see illustration).** If required, recover the radiator lower mounting rubbers.

Inspection

10 If the radiator has been removed due to suspected blockage, reverse-flush it as described in Chapter 1A or 1B. Clean dirt and debris from the radiator fins, using an airline (in which case, wear eye protection) or a soft brush. Be careful, as the fins are sharp, and easily damaged.

11 If necessary, a radiator specialist can perform a 'flow test' on the radiator, to establish whether an internal blockage exists.

12 A leaking radiator must be referred to a specialist for permanent repair. Do not attempt to weld or solder a leaking radiator,

as damage to the plastic components may result.

13 Inspect the condition of the radiator mounting rubbers, and renew them if necessary.

Refitting

14 Refitting is a reversal of removal, bearing in mind the following points:

● Ensure that the lower lugs on the radiator are correctly engaged with the mounting rubbers in the body panel.

● Reconnect the hoses with reference to Section 2, using new sealing rings where applicable.

● On completion, refill the cooling system as described in Chapter 1A or 1B.

5 Thermostat – removal, testing and refitting

Removal

1 Drain the cooling system (see Chapter 1A or 1B).

2 The thermostat is located in the coolant outlet housing on the left-hand end of the cylinder head. It is integral with the housing, requiring removal of the complete housing.

3 Where applicable, remove the engine upper cover. Remove the battery and battery tray as described in Chapter 5A Section 4, then remove the air cleaner and air ducting as described in Chapter 4A or 4B. In the following paragraphs, note that some of the hoses are disconnected after pressing down on the white-coloured release button **(see illustration).**

4 Disconnect the wiring connectors from the sensors on the thermostat housing.

5 On VTi petrol models, disconnect the wiring connectors from the camshaft position sensors and oil pressure sensor on the end of the cylinder head. Slide the wiring loom bracket upwards from the end of the cylinder head cover and move it to one side **(see illustration).** Release the retaining clip at the rear of the cylinder head, where the thermostat housing joins the pipe to the coolant pump **(see illustration).**

6 Disconnect all the hoses from the coolant

5.3 Press down the release button and disconnect the hose

5.5a Disconnect the wiring loom bracket from the cylinder head

5.5b Release the securing clip from the rear of the coolant housing

5.6 Note the fitted position of the hoses on the housing – VTi petrol engine

5.7a Undo the coolant outlet housing retaining bolts (arrowed) – 1.4 litre diesel engine

5.7b Remove the coolant housing – VTi petrol engine

5.11a Renew the gasket/seal

5.11b Renew the sealing rings

6.3 Disconnect the air vent pipe

housing, having noted their fitted locations (see illustration).

7 Unscrew the retaining bolts and remove the housing (see illustrations). Recover the gasket/seals.

Testing

8 A rough test of the thermostat may be made by suspending it with a piece of string in a container full of water. Heat the water to bring it to the boil – the thermostat must open by the time the water boils. If not, renew it.

9 If a thermometer is available, the precise opening temperature of the thermostat may be determined; compare with the figures given in the Specifications.

10 A thermostat which fails to close as the water cools, must also be renewed.

Refitting

11 Refitting is a reversal of removal, bearing in mind the following points.

● Renew the coolant housing gasket/seal (see illustration).

● Examine the sealing ring for damage or deterioration, and if necessary, renew (see illustration).

● On completion, refill the cooling system as described in Chapter 1A or 1B.

6 Electric cooling fan – removal and refitting

Note: The cooling fan can be removed on its own as below or complete with the radiator assembly as described in Section 4 of this Chapter.

Removal

1 Drain the cooling system (see Chapter 1A or 1B). This only needs to be drained until the level of coolant is below the top hose outlet on the radiator.

2 Remove the air inlet resonator and inlet hoses from side of the battery tray.

3 Unclip the battery ventilation pipe from the front crossmember above the radiator top hose (see illustration).

4 Release the retaining clip and disconnect the upper coolant hose from the radiator (see illustration).

5 Release the securing clips and disconnect the wiring connectors from the radiator fan assembly (see illustration).

6 Undo the retaining screws from the cooling fan cowling (see illustration). Carefully lift the

6.4 Undo the hose clip (arrowed)

6.5 Disconnect the wiring connectors from the relay

6.6 Undo the two upper retaining screws – arrowed

6.9 Relay retaining screw – arrowed

7.1a Coolant temperature sensor – VTi petrol engine...

7.1b... and 1.4 litre diesel engine

fan assembly out of position, taking care not to damage the radiator fins.

7 On some models, it may be necessary to remove the front bumper as described in Chapter 11 Section 6. Then slacken the upper crossmember retaining bolts and carefully pull the radiator/condenser plastic housing forwards to allow room for the fan and cowling to be withdrawn.

Refitting

8 Refitting is a reversal of removal.

Cooling fan resistor/relay

9 The relays are fitted to the fan cowling. Disconnect the wiring connectors and undo the retaining screw to release the relay from the cowling (see illustration).

7.2 Coolant temperature sensors (arrowed) – 1.6 litre non-VTi petrol engine

7 Cooling system electrical sensors – general information, removal and refitting

General information

1 There is only one coolant temperature sensor on most models, which is fitted to the coolant outlet housing on the left-hand end of the cylinder head (see illustrations). The coolant temperature gauge and the cooling fan are all operated by the engine management ECU using the signal supplied by this sensor.

2 On some non-VTi petrol models, two sensors are fitted (see illustration). The one fitted to the outlet housing is for the

7.3 Disconnect the thermostat – VTi petrol engines

temperature gauge, and the one screwed into the left-hand end of the cylinder head is for the engine management ECU.

3 On VTi petrol models, there is a second wiring connector on the coolant housing, which is for the electrically-controlled thermostat (see illustration).

Removal

Note: Ensure the engine is cold before removing a temperature sensor.

4 Partially drain the cooling system to just below the level of the sensor (as described in Chapter 1A or 1B). Alternatively, have ready a suitable bung to plug the sensor aperture whilst the sensor is removed. If this method is used, take great care not to damage the switch aperture or use anything which will allow foreign matter to enter the cooling system. On diesel models, to improve access, remove the battery as described in Chapter 5A Section 4.

5 Disconnect the wiring connector from the sensor (see illustration).

6 On some engines, the sensor is clipped in place. Prise out the sensor retaining circlip, and then remove the sensor and sealing ring from the housing (see illustrations). If the system has not been drained, plug the sensor aperture to prevent further coolant loss.

7 On all other engines, unscrew the sensor and recover the sealing washer (where applicable). If the system has not been drained, plug the sensor aperture to prevent further coolant loss.

7.5 Disconnect the wiring connector from the sensor

7.6a Prise out the clip...

7.6b... and pull out the sensor and sealing ring

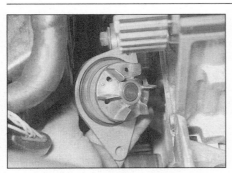

8.3a Remove the coolant pump...

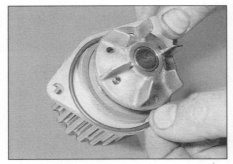

8.3b... and recover the sealing ring –
1.4 litre non-VTi petrol engine

8.3c Undo the coolant pump bolts
(arrowed) – 1.4 litre diesel engine

Refitting

8 Where the sensor was clipped in place, fit a new sealing ring to the sensor. Push the sensor firmly into the housing and secure it in position with the circlip, ensuring it is correctly located in the housing groove.

9 On all other engines, if the sensor was originally fitted using sealing compound, clean the sensor threads thoroughly, and coat them with fresh sealing compound. If the sensor was originally fitted using a sealing washer, use a new sealing washer. Fit the sensor and tighten securely.

10 Reconnect the wiring connector then refit any components removed from access. If removed, refit the battery.

11 Top-up the cooling system as described in *Weekly checks*.

8   Coolant pump –
     removal and refitting

Removal

1 Drain the cooling system (see Chapter 1A or 1B).

All except VTi petrol engines

2 Remove the timing belt as described in Chapter 2A, 2C, 2D or 2E, as applicable.

3 Slacken and remove the retaining bolts and withdraw the pump assembly from the engine. Recover the pump sealing ring/gasket (as applicable) and discard it; a new one must be used on refitting **(see illustrations)**. Note

that on some engines, the sealing ring is not available separately from the pump – check with your Peugeot dealer.

VTi petrol engines

4 Slacken the coolant pump pulley retaining bolts **(see illustration)**; do not remove completely at this point.

5 Remove the auxiliary drivebelt as described in Chapter 1A Section 13.

6 Undo the retaining bolts and remove the friction wheel drive from the cylinder block **(see illustrations)**.

7 Remove the retaining bolts and withdraw the pulley from the coolant pump **(see illustration)**.

8 Undo the bolts securing the pump to the cylinder block, and then withdraw the pump from the cylinder block **(see illustrations)**.

8.4 Slacken the coolant pump pulley
securing bolts – arrowed

8.6a Undo the retaining bolts (arrowed)...

8.6b... and remove the friction wheel drive
unit

8.7 Remove the coolant pump pulley

8.8a Undo the coolant pump bolts
(arrowed)...

8.8b... and remove the coolant pump

8.10 Renew the gasket/seal

9.9 Diagnostic plug connector (arrowed)

Refitting

9 Ensure that the pump and cylinder block/ housing mating surfaces are clean and dry.

10 Fit the new sealing ring/gasket (as applicable) to the pump (see illustrations), and then refit the pump assembly, tightening its retaining bolts securely.

11 On all models, except VTi petrol engines, refit the timing belt.

12 On VTi petrol models, refit the friction wheel drive to the cylinder block.

13 Refit the auxiliary drivebelt, as described in Chapter 1A or 1B.

14 Refill the cooling system as described in Chapter 1A Section 25.

9 Heating and ventilation system – general information

Note: Refer to Section 11 for information on the air conditioning side of the system.

Manually-controlled system

1 The heating/ventilation system consists of a four-speed blower motor (housed behind the facia), face level vents in the centre and at each end of the facia, and air ducts to the front footwells.

2 The control unit is located in the facia, and the controls operate flap valves to deflect and mix the air flowing through the various parts of the heating/ventilation system. The flap valves

are contained in the air distribution housing, which acts as a central distribution unit, passing air to the various ducts and vents.

3 Cold air enters the system through the grille in the scuttle. If required, the airflow is boosted by the blower, and then flows through the various ducts, according to the settings of the controls. Stale air is expelled through ducts at the rear of the vehicle. If warm air is required, the cold air is passed over the heater matrix, which is heated by the engine coolant.

4 A recirculation lever enables the outside air supply to be closed off, while the air inside the vehicle is recirculated. This can be useful to prevent unpleasant odours entering from outside the vehicle, but should only be used briefly, as the recirculated air inside the vehicle will soon become stale.

5 On some engine models an electric heater is fitted into the heater housing. When the coolant temperature is cold, the heater warms the air before it enters the heater matrix. This quickly increases the temperature of the heater matrix on cold starts, resulting in warm air being available to heat the vehicle interior soon after start-up.

Automatic climate control

6 A fully-automatic electronic climate control system was offered as an option on some models. The main components of the system are exactly the same as those described for the manual system, the only major difference being that the temperature and distribution

flaps in the heating/ventilation housing are operated by electric motors rather than cables.

7 The operation of the system is controlled by the electronic control module (which is incorporated in the blower motor assembly) along with the following sensors.

● The passenger compartment sensor – informs the control module of the temperature of the air inside the passenger compartment.

● Evaporator temperature sensor – informs the control module of the evaporator temperature.

● Heater matrix temperature sensor – informs the control module of the heater matrix temperature.

8 Using the information from the above sensors, the control module determines the appropriate settings for the heating/ ventilation system housing flaps to maintain the passenger compartment at the desired setting on the control panel.

9 If the system develops a fault, the vehicle should be taken to a Peugeot dealer. A complete test of the system can then be carried out, using a special electronic diagnostic test unit, which is simply plugged into the system's diagnostic connector, located inside the glovebox, behind a plastic panel (see illustration).

10 Heater/ventilation components – removal and refitting

Control panel

1 Remove the audio unit (see Chapter 12 Section 17).

2 Unclip the trim panels from each side of the control panel (see illustration).

3 Undo the two retaining screws and remove the switch panel from below the heater control panel (see illustration).

4 Unclip the storage compartment from above the heater control panel (see illustration).

5 Undo the two retaining screws, release the retaining clips and tilt the control

10.2 Unclip the side trims

10.3 Remove the switch panel

10.4 Unclip the storage compartment

10.5a Undo the two screws (arrowed)...

10.5b... and unclip the control panel

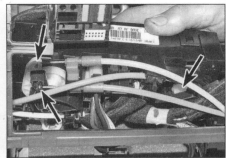

10.6 Note the position of the cables (arrowed)

10.10a Three cables (arrowed) are on the right of the unit...

10.10b... and one (arrowed) is on the left

10.13 Clamp the heater hoses

panel forward, then manoeuvre it from the console **(see illustrations)**.

6 On models with a manual control panel, disconnect the wiring connectors from the rear of the control panel. Note the correct fitted location of each control cables (the end fittings are colour-coded) then unhook the cable retaining clips **(see illustration)**. Detach the cables and remove the control panel from the vehicle.

7 On models with an automatic climate control system, disconnect the wiring connectors and remove the control panel from the vehicle.

8 Refitting is the reverse of removal. On models with a manual control panel, ensure the control cables are correctly reconnected and securely held by the retaining clips; check

the operation of the control knobs before securing the control panel to the facia.

Control cables

9 Remove the centre console and front lower panels (see Chapter 11).

10 Release the retaining clip and detach the relevant cable from the rear of the control panel as described in paragraph 6. Then release the retaining clip and disconnect the cable from the heating/ventilation housing control flaps. Remove the cable, noting its correct routing and colour **(see illustrations)**.

11 Refitting is the reverse of removal, ensuring that the cables are secured by their retaining clips. Check the operation of the

control panel and cables before refitting the centre console (see Chapter 11 Section 26).

Heater matrix

12 To improve access to the matrix unions on the bulkhead, remove the air cleaner housing and air inlet ducting as described in Chapter 4A Section 2 for petrol engines and Chapter 4B Section 4 for diesel engines.

13 Drain the cooling system (see Chapter 1A Section 25). Alternatively, clamp the heater matrix coolant hoses to minimise coolant loss **(see illustration)**.

14 Release the retaining clips and disconnect the coolant hoses from the heater matrix pipe unions on the engine compartment bulkhead **(see illustrations)**.

10.14a Prise out the wire retaining clip...

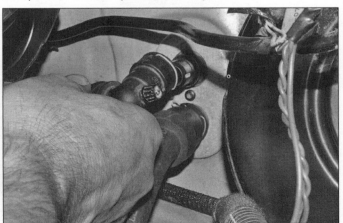

10.14b... and disconnect the heater hose

10.15a Remove the retaining plate...

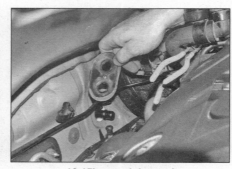

10.15b... and the seal

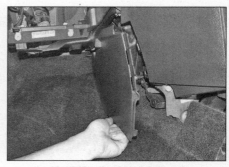

10.17 Unclip the trim panel

15 Slacken and remove the screw securing the heater matrix pipes to the bulkhead and remove the retaining plate and seal **(see illustrations)**.

16 Position a container (or rags) beneath the heater matrix pipe union on the left-hand side of the heating/ventilation housing to catch any spilt coolant.

17 Release the securing clips and unclip the trim panel from the front left-hand side of the facia centre panel **(see illustration)**. To make access easier, it may be necessary to remove the glovebox assembly and centre console as described in Chapter 11.

18 Release the retaining clips and remove the air ducting from below the glovebox housing **(see illustration)**. **Note:** *Make sure the heater control switch is positioned in the hot position, to allow for the easier removal of the ducting*

and heater matrix pipes. If this is not in the hot position, the control arm will prevent them from being removed and damage may occur.

19 Slacken and remove the screw securing the pipes to the heater matrix and remove the two screws securing the matrix to the heater housing **(see illustration)**.

20 As the heater matrix is withdrawn from the housing, release the coolant pipes from the matrix **(see illustration)**. Recover the sealing rings fitted to each end of the pipe unions and discard them; new ones will be required for refitting.

21 Carefully withdraw the matrix out from the housing. Keep the matrix unions uppermost as the matrix is removed to prevent coolant spillage **(see illustration)**.

22 If required, free the pipes from the bulkhead and remove them from the vehicle

(see illustration). If not already done, recover the sealing rings and discard them; new ones will be required for refitting.

23 If removed, refit the coolant pipes, making sure they are located in the bulkhead correctly. Fit new seals to the end of the coolant pipes.

24 Ease the matrix into the housing, whilst aligning the coolant pipes into position, then tighten the retaining screws.

25 Working in the engine compartment, refit the seal and retaining plate to the heater matrix pipes and securely tighten the retaining screw. Remove the clamps from the hoses (where fitted) then reconnect the coolant hoses, securing them in position with the retaining clips.

26 Refit the air ducting back into place below the glovebox housing.

27 Refit the trim panel, centre console and glovebox assembly (where applicable).

28 Refit the air cleaner housing and air ducting.

29 Refill the cooling system as required.

Heater blower motor

30 The blower motor is fitted to the top of the heating/ventilation housing, on the left-hand side.

31 On right-hand drive models, remove the glovebox (see Chapter 11, Section 27). Access to the motor can then be gained through the glovebox aperture.

32 On left-hand drive models, remove the steering column as described in Chapter 10 Section 18 to gain access to the motor.

10.18 Remove the air ducting

10.19 Undo the retaining screws (arrowed)...

10.20... disengage the coolant pipes...

10.21... and withdraw the heater matrix

10.22 Withdraw the coolant pipes from the bulkhead

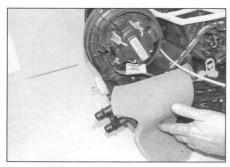

10.33 Pull back the foam soundproofing

10.34 Disconnect the wiring connector

10.35a Release the securing clips...

10.35b... and withdraw the blower motor/ fan

10.37 Blower motor resistor (arrowed)

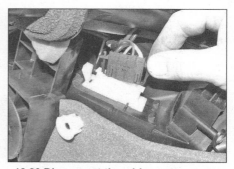

10.39 Disconnect the wiring connector...

33 Reaching up to the motor, unclip and pull back the foam insulation from over the motor housing **(see illustration)**.
34 Disconnect the wiring connector from the blower motor **(see illustration)**.
35 Release the securing clip and rotate the motor anti-clockwise to free it from the housing and then manoeuvre it out of position **(see illustrations)**.
36 Refitting is the reverse of removal. Make sure the motor is a secure fit in the housing, by turning it clockwise until the securing clip is located. Refit the foam insulation when motor is in place.

Heater blower motor resistor

37 The blower motor resistor is fitted to the lower part of the heating/ventilation housing, at the front left-hand side, below the blower motor **(see illustration)**.

38 Remove the glovebox and facia lower trim panel, with reference to Chapter 11 Section 27.
39 Disconnect the wiring connector from the blower motor resistor **(see illustration)**.
40 Release the retaining clip and withdraw the resistor from the heater housing **(see illustration)**.
41 Manoeuvre the resistor into position in the housing and connect the wiring connector. **Note:** *If the securing clip on the resistor has broken, fit a small securing screw to the small hole provided in the housing* **(see illustration)**.
42 Refit any components removed for access.

Housing assembly

Models without air conditioning

43 To improve access to the matrix unions on the bulkhead, remove the air cleaner housing and air inlet ducting as described in Chapters 4A or 4B.

44 Drain the cooling system (see Chapter 1A Section 25). Alternatively, working in the engine compartment, clamp the heater matrix coolant hoses to minimise coolant loss.
45 Release the retaining clips and disconnect the coolant hoses from the heater matrix pipe unions on the engine compartment bulkhead **(see illustration 10.14b)**.
46 Slacken and remove the screw securing the heater matrix pipes to the bulkhead and remove the retaining plate and seal **(see illustrations 10.15a and 10.15b)**.
47 Slacken and remove the bolt securing the heating/ventilation housing to the bulkhead **(see illustration)**.
48 Remove the facia assembly as described in Chapter 11 Section 27.
49 Disconnect the wiring connectors from the heating/ventilation housing components then remove the housing and control panel

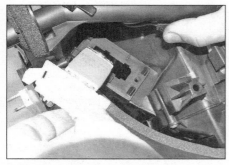

10.40.. and unclip the resistor from the housing

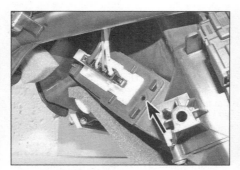

10.41 If required fit a screw (arrowed) to secure

10.47 Heater/ventilation housing retaining bolt (arrowed)

10.54 Undo the two nuts (arrowed) securing the air conditioning pipes

assembly from the vehicle. Keep the heater matrix pipe unions uppermost as the assembly is removed to prevent coolant spillage.

50 Recover the seal and retaining plate from the heater matrix pipes, and the seal from the housing mounting. Renew the seals if they show signs of damage or deterioration.

51 Refitting is the reverse of removal ensuring the seals are in position on the pipes and housing mounting. On completion, refill the cooling system (see Chapter 1A or 1B).

Models with air conditioning

 Warning: Refer to Section 11 for precautions to be observed when working on models equipped with air conditioning. Do not attempt the following procedure unless the system has been professionally discharged.

52 Have the air conditioning system discharged by an air conditioning specialist and obtain some plugs to seal the air conditioning pipe unions whilst the system is disconnected.

53 Carry out the operations described in paragraphs 43 to 46.

54 Unscrew the two nuts securing the air conditioning pipe union to the bulkhead **(see illustration)**. Separate the pipes from the evaporator and quickly seal the pipe and evaporator unions to prevent the entry of moisture into the refrigerant circuit. Discard the sealing rings, new ones must be used on refitting.

 Warning: Failure to seal the refrigerant pipe unions will result in the dehydrator reservoir become saturated, necessitating its renewal.

55 Remove the heating/ventilation housing assembly as described in paragraphs 47 to 50 and recover the seal from the evaporator.

56 Ensure the bulkhead seals are correctly fitted to the evaporator, matrix pipes and housing mounting. Manoeuvre the housing assembly into position, locating the housing drain hose correctly in its hole in the floor.

57 Loosely refit the housing mounting bolt then refit the retaining plate to the heater matrix pipe and loosely install the retaining screw.

58 Lubricate the new evaporator union sealing

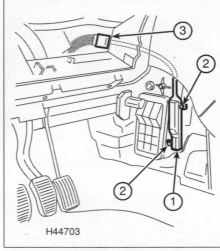

10.64 Additional heater on some diesel models

1 Heater   2 Screw and clip   3 Wiring plug

rings with compressor oil. Remove the plugs and install the sealing rings then quickly fit the refrigerant pipe union to the evaporator. Ensure the refrigerant pipes and evaporator are correctly joined then refit the retaining nuts, tighten them securely.

59 Tighten the matrix pipe retaining screw securely and securely tighten the housing mounting bolt.

60 The remainder of refitting is the reverse of removal. On completion, refill the cooling system.

Additional heater/resistor – diesel models

61 On right-hand drive models, remove the glovebox and passenger side central kick panel as described in Chapter 11 Section 27.

62 On left-hand drive models, remove the trim panel above the pedals, undo the two fasteners and remove the trim panel at the front of the centre console, adjacent to the pedals.

63 Undo the bolt securing the heater earth connection.

64 Disconnect the heater wiring plug, then undo the screw(s), release the retaining clip, and slide the heater from the housing **(see illustration)**.

65 Refitting is the reverse of removal.

Air recirculation motor

66 On right-hand drive models, remove the lower facia trim panel, then undo the fasteners and remove the centre console side panel at the front (adjacent to the pedals).

67 Disconnect the motor wiring plug, undo the bolts, and remove the motor **(see illustration)**.

68 Refitting is a reversal of removal. **Note:** *The drivegear on the rear of the motor can only be fitted in one position on the shaft, make sure it located correctly.*

10.67 Air recirculation motor

Ambient temperature sensor

69 The ambient temperature sensor is located on the underside of the driver's side exterior mirror. To remove the sensor, remove the mirror cover as described in Chapter 11 Section 18.

70 Unclip the sensor from the mirror housing. To disconnect the wiring plug, it is necessary to remove the door trim panel as described in Chapter 11 Section 12.

11 Air conditioning system – general information and precautions

General information

1 An air conditioning system is available on certain models. It enables the temperature of incoming air to be lowered, and also dehumidifies the air, which makes for rapid demisting and increased comfort.

2 The cooling side of the system works in the same way as a domestic refrigerator. Refrigerant gas is drawn into a belt-driven compressor, and passes into a condenser mounted on the front of the radiator, where it loses heat and becomes liquid. The liquid passes through an expansion valve to an evaporator, where it changes from liquid under high pressure to gas under low pressure. This change is accompanied by a drop in temperature, which then cools the evaporator. The refrigerant returns to the compressor, and the cycle begins again.

3 Air blown through the evaporator passes to the heating/ventilation housing, where it is mixed with hot air blown through the heater matrix to achieve the desired temperature in the passenger compartment.

4 The heating side of the system works in the same way as on models without air conditioning (see Section 9).

5 The operation of the system is controlled electronically by the ECU integral with the control panel. Any problems with the system should be referred to a Peugeot dealer, or suitably-equipped specialist.

Precautions

6 When an air conditioning system is fitted, it is necessary to observe special precautions whenever dealing with any part of the system, or its associated components. The refrigerant

is potentially dangerous, and should only be handled by qualified persons. Uncontrolled discharging of the refrigerant is dangerous and damaging to the environment for the following reasons.

● If it is splashed onto the skin, it can cause frostbite.

● The refrigerant is heavier then air and so displaces oxygen. In a confined space, which is not adequately ventilated, this could lead to a risk of suffocation. The gas is odourless and colourless so there is no warning of its presence in the atmosphere.

● Although not poisonous, in the presence of a naked flame (including a cigarette) it forms a noxious gas that causes headaches, nausea, etc.

⚠ *Warning: Never attempt to open any air conditioning system refrigerant pipe/hose union without first having the system fully discharged by an air conditioning specialist. On completion of work, have the system recharged with the correct type and amount of fresh refrigerant.*

⚠ *Warning: Always seal disconnected refrigerant pipe/ hose unions as soon as they are disconnected. Failure to form an airtight seal on any union will result in the dehydrator reservoir become saturated, necessitating its renewal. Also renew all sealing rings disturbed.*

Caution: Do not operate the air conditioning system if it is known to be short of refrigerant as this could damage the compressor.

12 Air conditioning system components – removal and refitting

⚠ *Warning: Refer to the precautions given in Section 11 and have the system discharged by an air conditioning specialist before carrying out any work on the air conditioning system.*

Compressor

Removal

1 Have the air conditioning system fully

12.4 Undo the two nuts (arrowed) securing the air conditioning pipes

discharged and evacuated by an air conditioning specialist.

2 Remove the auxiliary drivebelt as described in Chapter 1A Section 13 for petrol engines and Chapter 1B Section 16 for diesel engines.

3 Disconnect the compressor wiring connector from the engine harness.

4 Unscrew the nuts securing the refrigerant pipes retaining plates to the compressor **(see illustration)**. Separate the pipes from the compressor and quickly seal the pipe and compressor unions to prevent the entry of moisture into the refrigerant circuit. Discard the sealing rings, new ones must be used on refitting.

⚠ *Warning: Failure to seal the refrigerant pipe unions will result in the dehydrator reservoir become saturated, necessitating its renewal.*

5 Unscrew the compressor mounting bolts and nuts then free the compressor from its mounting bracket and remove it from the engine **(see illustration)**. Take care not to lose the spacers from the compressor rear mountings (where fitted).

6 If the compressor is to be renewed, drain the refrigerant oil from the old compressor. The specialist who recharges the refrigerant system will need to add this amount of oil to the system.

Refitting

7 If a new compressor is being fitted, drain the refrigerant oil.

8 Manoeuvre the compressor into position and fit the mounting bolts. Tighten the compressor

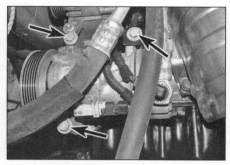

12.5 Remove the compressor mounting bolts (arrowed) – VTi petrol engine

front (drivebelt pulley) end mounting bolts to the specified torque first then tighten the rear bolt.

9 Lubricate the new refrigerant pipe sealing rings with compressor oil. Remove the plugs and install the sealing rings then quickly fit the refrigerant pipes to the compressor. Ensure the refrigerant pipes are correctly joined then refit the retaining bolt, tighten it securely.

10 Reconnect the wiring connector then refit the auxiliary drivebelt.

11 Have the air conditioning system recharged with the correct type and amount of refrigerant by a specialist before using the system. Remember to inform the specialist which components have been renewed, so they can add the correct amount of oil.

Condenser

Removal

12 Have the air conditioning system fully discharged by an air conditioning specialist.

13 Remove the front bumper as described in Chapter 11 Section 6.

14 Undo the retaining nuts and disconnect the refrigerant pipes from the right-hand side of the condenser. Recover the O-ring seals **(see illustrations)**.

⚠ *Warning: Failure to seal the refrigerant pipe unions will result in the dehydrator reservoir become saturated, necessitating its renewal.*

15 Release the retaining clips at the top of the condenser and remove it from the front panel **(see illustration)**.

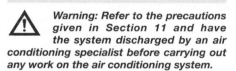

12.14a Undo the nuts (arrowed) securing the refrigerant pipes...

12.14b... and plug the ends of the pipes

12.15 Release the condenser upper mountings

12.23a Remove the cover…

12.23b… to access the evaporator (arrowed)

Refitting

16 Refitting is a reversal of removal. Noting the following points:
● Ensure the upper mountings are secure when the condenser is in position in the front panel.
● Lubricate the sealing rings with compressor oil. Remove the plugs and install the sealing rings then quickly fit the refrigerant pipes to the condenser. Securely tighten the dehydrator pipe union nut and ensure the compressor pipe is correctly joined.
● Have the air conditioning system recharged with the correct type and amount of refrigerant by a specialist before using the system.

Receiver/drier

17 The receiver/drier is located on the left-hand side of the condenser and is part of the condenser, which cannot be renewed separately.
18 Remove the condenser (receiver/drier) as described in paragraphs 12 to 15 of this Section.

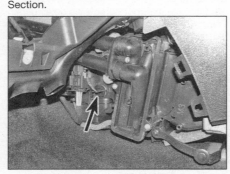

12.25 Evaporator sensor (arrowed)

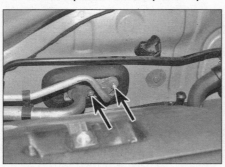

12.33 Undo the two nuts (arrowed) securing the air conditioning pipes

⚠ **Warning: Prior to slackening the clamp, clean the dehydrator and wipe it dry, to avoid moisture/debris entering the air conditioning circuit**

Evaporator

Note: *At the time of writing the evaporator was not available as a separate item and had to be supplied complete in heater housing unit. See your local dealer for availability of parts.*

Removal

19 Have the air conditioning system fully discharged and evacuated by an air conditioning specialist.
20 Remove the heating/ventilation housing as described in Section 10.
21 Note their fitted positions, and then disconnect the wiring plugs and harness from the housing.
22 Remove any heater/ventilation components from the heater housing as described in Section 10.

12.28 Turn the sensor to remove from housing

12.35 Expansion valve retaining bolts (arrowed)

23 Undo the retaining screws and remove the plastic cover to access the evaporator **(see illustrations)**.

Refitting

24 Refitting is a reversal of removal but have the air conditioning system recharged with the correct type and amount of refrigerant by a specialist prior to using the system.

Evaporator sensor
Removal

25 The evaporator sensor is fitted to the lower part of the heating/ventilation housing, at the left-hand side, below the heater matrix coolant pipes **(see illustration)**.
26 Remove the lower trim panel from the front of the centre console.
27 Trace the wiring back from the sensor and disconnect the wiring connector. If a wiring connector is not available, it may be part of the wiring loom. In this case, the wiring will need to be cut approximately 50mm from the sensor.
28 Rotate the sensor anti-clockwise and withdraw it from the heater housing **(see illustration)**.

Refitting

29 Refit the sensor into position in the housing and connect the wiring connector. If required, join the wiring where it has been cut.
30 Refit any components removed for access.

Expansion valve
Removal

31 Have the air conditioning system fully discharged and evacuated by an air conditioning specialist.
32 Remove the sound insulation material/heat shield from the engine compartment bulkhead (where fitted).
33 Undo the nuts securing the refrigerant pipes to the connection at the engine compartment bulkhead **(see illustration)**. Plug/cover the openings to prevent contamination/saturation. Recover and discard the O-ring seals – new ones must be fitted.

⚠ **Warning: Failure to seal the refrigerant pipe unions will result in the receiver/drier becoming saturated, necessitating its renewal**

34 Pull the seal from around the pipes connection at the bulkhead.
35 Undo the upper bolt and insert a piece of threaded rod (or stud), then undo the lower bolt and insert another piece of threaded rod (or stud). The expansion/relief valve can then be withdrawn out from the bulkhead along the length of the threaded rods. **Note:** *If the threaded rods (studs) are not used the spacer at the rear of the expansion/relief valve may drop down behind the heater unit housing* **(see illustration)**. *Recover and discard the O-ring seals – new ones must be fitted.*

Refitting

36 Refitting is a reversal of removal but have the air conditioning system recharged with the correct type and amount of refrigerant by a specialist prior to using the system.

Chapter 4 Part A
Fuel and exhaust systems – petrol models

Contents

Degrees of difficulty

Easy, suitable for novice with little experience	Fairly easy, suitable for beginner with some experience	Fairly difficult, suitable for competent DIY mechanic	Difficult, suitable for experienced DIY mechanic	Very difficult, suitable for expert DIY or professional

Specifications

Engine identification

	Designation	Engine code
1.4 litre:		
Non-VTi engine:		
SOHC	TU3A	KFV & KFT
DOHC	ET3JP4	KFU
VTi engine.	EP3	8FS, 8FR & 8 FP
1.6 litre:		
Non-VTi engine.	TU5JP4	NFU
VTi engine.	EP6	5FW & 5FS

System type

1.4 litre models:	
TU3	Johnson Controls J34P
ET3	Marelli 6LP
EP3	Bosch MEV 17.4
1.6 litre models:	
TU5JP4.	Bosch ME7.4
EP6	Bosch MEV 17.4

Fuel system data

Fuel pump type	Electric, immersed in tank
Fuel pump regulated constant pressure.	3.5 ± 0.2 bars
Specified idle speed.	850 ± 100 rpm (not adjustable – controlled by ECU)
Idle mixture CO content	Less than 1.0% (not adjustable – controlled by ECU)

Recommended fuel

Minimum octane rating.	95 RON unleaded (UK unleaded premium). Leaded/lead replacement fuel (LRP) must not be used

Torque wrench settings

	Nm	lbf ft
Catalytic converter-to-cylinder block bolts (VTi engine).	25	18
Exhaust manifold to catalytic converter (non-VTi engine)	40	30
Exhaust manifold-to-cylinder head nuts	25	18
Inlet manifold nuts:		
M6	10	7
M8	20	15
Oxygen sensor	45	33
Roadwheel bolts.	90	66

1 General information and precautions

1 The fuel supply system consists of a fuel tank, which is mounted under the rear of the car, with an electric fuel pump immersed in it, a fuel filter (depending on model), fuel feed and return lines. The fuel pump supplies fuel to the fuel rail, which acts as a reservoir for the four fuel injectors, which inject fuel into the inlet tracts. The fuel filter incorporated in the feed line from the pump to the fuel rail ensures that the fuel supplied to the injectors is clean.

2 Refer to Section 5 for further information on the operation of the engine management system, and to Section 15 for information on the exhaust system.

 Warning: Many of the procedures in this Chapter require the removal of fuel lines and connections, which may result in some fuel spillage. Before carrying out any operation on the fuel system, refer to the precautions given in 'Safety first!' at the beginning of this manual, and follow them implicitly. Petrol is a highly dangerous and volatile liquid, and the precautions necessary when handling it cannot be overstressed.

Note: *Residual pressure will remain in the fuel lines long after the vehicle was last used. When disconnecting any fuel line, first depressurise the fuel system as described in Section 6.*

2 Air cleaner assembly and inlet ducts – removal and refitting

Removal

VTi engines

1 Undo the retaining bolt from the top of the cam cover (see illustration).

2 Slacken the retaining screws and remove the upper cover from the top of the air cleaner housing (see illustration).

2.5b.. and remove the air ducting

2.1 Undo the retaining bolt (arrowed)

2.3... and remove the air filter element

3 Lift out the air filter from the lower housing (see illustration).

4 Undo the two retaining screws, and remove the middle section of the air cleaner housing, releasing the air inlet hose as it is removed (see illustrations).

5 Undo the retaining bolt and unclip any

2.4b... and remove the centre section

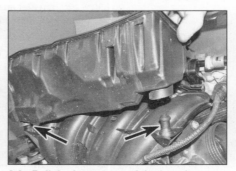
2.6a Pull the lower part of the housing up...

2.2 Unscrew the upper cover...

2.4a Undo the two retaining screws (arrowed)...

wiring from the air ducting, then remove it from the engine compartment (see illustrations).

6 Pull the lower part of the air cleaner housing upwards to release from its mountings on the manifold, and then turn the housing and withdraw it out from the rear of the engine compartment (see illustrations).

2.5a Undo the retaining bolt (arrowed)...

2.6b... and out from the engine compartment

2.7a Release the securing clip...

2.7b... unclip the vent pipe...

2.7c... and remove the resonator box

7 To remove the resonator box, remove the securing clips, unclip the hoses and withdraw the resonator housing out from the front of the engine compartment **(see illustrations)**.

Non-VTi engines

8 Slacken the retaining clips then free the duct from the manifold and air cleaner housing, and remove it from the engine compartment.
9 Depress the retaining clip at the side, then lift the air cleaner housing assembly off of its mounting bracket and remove it from the engine compartment. Recover the mounting rubber fitted to the housing lower locating peg and the sealing ring from the housing inlet duct.
10 To remove the inlet duct, firmly apply the handbrake then jack up the front of the car and support it on axle stands (see *Jacking and vehicle support*). Push in the centre pins a little, then prise out the complete expanding plastic rivets, and remove the left-hand wheel arch liner. Remove the retaining bolts and remove the duct assembly from the vehicle (a resonator chamber is incorporated into the duct to reduce inlet noise).

Refitting

11 Refitting is a reversal of the removal procedure, ensuring that all hoses and ducts are properly reconnected and correctly seated and, where necessary, securely held by their retaining clips.

3 Accelerator pedal –
removal and refitting

Removal

1 Release the fasteners and remove trim panel above the pedals **(see illustration)**.
2 Disconnect the accelerator pedal position sensor wiring plug from the top of the pedal **(see illustration)**.
3 Undo the three nuts and remove the pedal assembly **(see illustration)**.

Refitting

4 Refitting is a reversal of the removal procedure.

4 Unleaded petrol – general
information and usage

Note: *The information given in this Chapter is correct at the time of writing. If updated information is thought to be required, check with a Peugeot dealer. If traveling abroad, consult one of the motoring organisations (or a similar authority) for advice on the fuel available.*
1 The fuel recommended by Peugeot is given in the Specifications Section of this Chapter,

followed by the equivalent petrol currently on sale in the UK.
2 All models are designed to run on fuel with a minimum octane rating of 95 (RON). All models have a catalytic converter, and so must be run on unleaded fuel only. Under no circumstances should leaded/lead replacement fuel (UK 4-star/LRP) be used, as this may damage the converter.
3 Super unleaded petrol (97, 98 or 99 octane) can also be used in all models if wished, though there is no advantage in doing so.

5 Engine management system
– general information

Note: *The fuel injection ECU is of the 'self-learning' type, meaning that as it operates, it also monitors and stores the settings, which give optimum engine performance under all operating conditions. When the battery is disconnected, these settings are lost and the ECU reverts to the base settings programmed into its memory at the factory. On restarting, this may lead to the engine running/idling roughly for a short while, until the ECU has relearned the optimum settings. This process is best accomplished by taking the vehicle on a road test (for approximately 15 minutes), covering all engine speeds and loads, concentrating mainly in the 2500 to 3500 rpm region.*

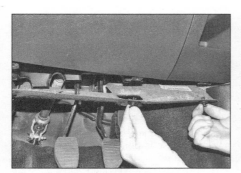

3.1 Unclip the lower trim panel

3.2 Disconnect the wiring connector

3.3 Undo the retaining bolts (arrowed)

1 On all engines, the fuel injection and ignition functions are combined into a single engine management system. The systems fitted are manufactured by Bosch, Magneti Marelli and Johnson Controls, and are very similar to each other in most respects, the only significant differences being in the software contained in the system ECU, and specific component location according to engine type. Each system incorporates a closed-loop catalytic converter and an evaporative emission control system, and complies with the latest emission control standards. Refer to Chapter 5B for information on the ignition side of each system; the fuel side of the system operates as follows.

2 The fuel pump, which is situated in the fuel tank, supplies fuel from the tank to the fuel rail. The pump motor is permanently immersed in fuel, to keep it cool. The fuel rail is mounted directly above the fuel injectors and acts as a fuel reservoir.

3 Fuel rail supply pressure is controlled by the pressure regulator, also located in the fuel tank. The regulator contains a spring-loaded valve, which lifts to allow excess fuel to recirculate within the tank when the optimum operating pressure of the fuel system is exceeded (eg, during low speed, light load cruising).

4 The fuel injectors are electromagnetic pintle valves, which spray atomised fuel into the inlet manifold tracts under the control of the engine management system ECU. There are four injectors, one per cylinder, mounted in the inlet manifold close to the cylinder head on non-VTi engines, and in the cylinder head close to the inlet manifold on VTi engines. Each injector is mounted at an angle that allows it to spray fuel directly onto the back of the inlet valves. The ECU controls the volume of fuel injected by varying the length of time for which each injector is held open. The fuel injection systems are of the sequential type, whereby each injector operates individually in cylinder sequence.

5 The electrical control system consists of the ECU, along with the following sensors:

● Throttle potentiometer – informs the ECU of the throttle valve position, and the rate of throttle opening/closing.
● Coolant temperature sensor – informs the ECU of engine temperature.
● Inlet air temperature sensor – informs the ECU of the temperature of the air passing through the throttle housing.
● Oxygen sensors – inform the ECU of the oxygen content of the exhaust gases (explained in greater detail in Part C of this Chapter).
● Manifold pressure sensor – informs the ECU of the load on the engine (expressed in terms of inlet manifold vacuum).
● Crankshaft position sensor – informs the ECU of engine speed and crankshaft angular position.
● Vehicle speed sensor – informs the ECU of the vehicle speed (not all models).
● Knock sensor – informs the ECU of pre-ignition (detonation) within the cylinders (not all models).
● Camshaft sensor – informs the ECU which cylinder is on the firing stroke on systems with sequential injection.
● Accelerator pedal position sensor – informs the ECU of the pedal position and rate of change.
● Throttle valve positioner motor – allows the ECU to control the throttle valve position.
● Engine oil temperature sensor – informs the ECU of the engine oil temperature (not all models).
● Clutch and brake pedal position sensor – informs the ECU of the pedal positions (not all models).

6 Signals from each of the sensors are compared by the ECU and, based on this information, the ECU selects the response appropriate to those values, and controls the fuel injectors (varying the pulse width – the length of time the injectors are held open – to provide a richer or weaker air/fuel mixture, as appropriate). The air/fuel mixture is constantly varied by the ECU, to provide the best settings for cranking, starting (with either a hot or cold engine) and engine warm-up, idle, cruising and acceleration.

7 The ECU also has full control over the engine idle speed, via a stepper motor (depending on model) fitted to the throttle housing. The stepper motor either controls the amount of air passing through a bypass drilling at the side of the throttle or controls the position of the throttle valve itself, depending on model. A sensor informs the ECU of the position, and rate of change, of the accelerator pedal. The ECU then controls the throttle valve by means of a throttle positioning motor integral with the throttle body – no accelerator cable is fitted. The ECU also carries out 'fine tuning' of the idle speed by varying the ignition timing to increase or reduce the torque of the engine as it is idling. This helps to stabilise the idle speed when electrical or mechanical loads (such as headlights, air conditioning, etc) are switched on and off.

8 The throttle housing is also fitted with an electric heating element. The heater is supplied with current by the ECU, warming the throttle housing on cold starts to help prevent icing of the throttle valve.

9 The exhaust and evaporative loss emission control systems are described in more detail in Chapter 4C.

10 If there is any abnormality in any of the readings obtained from the coolant temperature sensor, the inlet air temperature sensor or the oxygen sensor, the ECU enters its 'back-up' mode. If this happens, the erroneous sensor signal is overridden, and the ECU assumes a preprogrammed 'back-up' value, which will allow the engine to continue running, albeit at reduced efficiency. If the ECU enters this mode, the warning lamp on the instrument panel will be illuminated, and the relevant fault code will be stored in the ECU memory.

11 If the warning light illuminates, the vehicle should be taken to a Peugeot dealer or specialist at the earliest opportunity. Once there, a complete test of the engine management system can be carried out, using a special electronic diagnostic test unit, which is plugged into the system's diagnostic connector, located behind the trim panel to the left of the glove compartment (see illustration).

6 Fuel system – depressurisation and pressurising

Note: *Refer to the warning note in Section 1 before proceeding.*

Depressurisation

⚠️ *Warning: The following procedure will merely relieve the pressure in the fuel system – remember that fuel will still be present in the system components and take precautions accordingly before disconnecting any of them.*

1 The fuel system referred to in this Section is defined as the tank-mounted fuel pump, the fuel filter (where fitted), the fuel injectors, the fuel rail and the pipes of the fuel lines between these components. All these contain fuel, which will be under pressure while the engine is running, and/or while the ignition is switched on. The pressure will remain for some time after the ignition has been switched off, and must be relieved in a controlled fashion when any of these components are disturbed for servicing work.

2 Some models are equipped with a pressure relief valve on the end of the fuel rail (see illustration). On these models, unscrew the

5.11 Diagnostic plug connector (arrowed)

6.2 Pressure relief valve – VTi engine

cap from the valve and position a container beneath the valve. Hold a wad of rag over the valve and relieve the pressure in the system by depressing the valve core with a suitable screwdriver. Be prepared for the squirt of fuel as the valve core is depressed and catch it with the rag. Hold the valve core down until no more fuel is expelled from the valve. Once the pressure is relieved, securely refit the valve cap.

3 Where no valve is fitted to the fuel rail, it will be necessary to release the pressure as the fuel pipe is disconnected. Place a container beneath the union and position a large rag around the union to catch any fuel spray, which may be expelled. Slowly release and disconnect the fuel pipe and catch any spilt fuel in the container. Plug the pipe/union to minimise fuel loss and prevent the entry of dirt into the fuel system.

Pressurising

4 After any work is carried out on the fuel system, the system should be pressurised as follows.

5 Depress the accelerator pedal fully then switch on the ignition. Hold the pedal depressed for approximately 1 second then release it. The ECU should then operate the fuel pump for between 20 and 30 seconds to refill the fuel system. Once the fuel pump stops the ignition can be switched off.

---

7 Fuel pump – removal and refitting

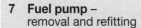

Note: *The fuel pump is only available as a complete assembly – no components are available separately.*

Removal

1 For access to the fuel pump, tilt or remove the rear seat cushion (see Chapter 11 Section 23).

2 Using a thin blade, carefully release the three plastic access cover retaining clips at the points indicated by the small arrows, and remove the cover from the floor to expose the fuel pump/sender unit **(see illustration)**.

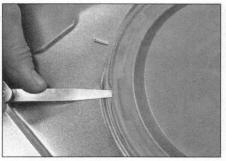

7.2 Release the fuel pump access cover retaining clips

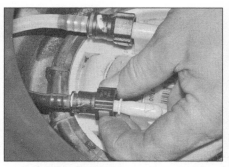

7.4a Depress the release button and disconnect the fuel pipe

3 Disconnect the wiring connector from the fuel pump, and tape the connector to the vehicle body, to prevent it from disappearing behind the tank**(see illustration)**.

4 Depress the retaining clip and detach the fuel pipe(s) from the top of the pump, bearing in mind the information given in Section 6 on depressurising the fuel system. Plug the pipe end(s) to minimise fuel loss and prevent the entry of dirt. On diesel models, note there are two pipes and they are identified with arrows indicating the fuel feed and return **(see illustrations)**.

5 Noting the alignment marks on the tank **(see illustration)**, pump cover and the locking ring, unscrew the ring and remove it from the tank. This is best accomplished by using a screwdriver on the raised ribs of the locking ring. Carefully tap the screwdriver to turn the ring anti-clockwise until it can be unscrewed

7.3 Disconnect the pump wiring plug

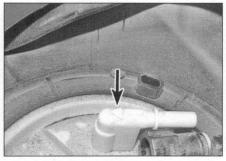

7.4b Note the fuel flow arrows on diesel models (arrowed)

by hand. Alternatively, a Peugeot special tool is available which fits over the collar and allows it to be released using a socket ratchet and extension.

6 Carefully lift the fuel pump assembly out of the fuel tank, taking great care not to damage the fuel gauge sender unit float arm, or to spill fuel onto the interior of the vehicle **(see illustration)**. Recover the rubber sealing ring and discard it – a new one must be used on refitting.

7 If the fuel pump is going to be left out of the fuel tank for a while, screw the ring back to the top of the fuel tank to prevent it from going out of shape. Cover the access hole in the tank to prevent dirt ingress.

Refitting

8 Fit the new sealing ring to the top of the fuel tank **(see illustration)**.

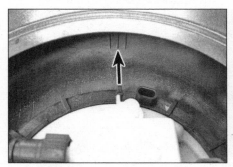

7.5 Fuel sender alignment marks (arrowed)

7.6 Lift the fuel pump assembly, taking care not to damage the float arm

7.8 Fit a new sealing ring to the top of the tank

9 Carefully manoeuvre the pump assembly into the fuel tank, taking care not to damage the float arm.

10 Align the arrow on the fuel pump cover with previously-noted mark on the fuel tank and clip the pump assembly into position.

11 Refit the locking ring and tighten it securely until its alignment mark aligns as noted on removal.

12 Securely reconnect the fuel pipe(s) to the pump cover then reconnect the pump wiring connector.

13 Pressurise the fuel system (see Section 6). Start the engine and check the fuel pump feed and return hoses unions for signs of leakage.

14 If all is well, refit the plastic access cover ensuring its tabs are located correctly.

15 Refit the rear seat cushion.

8 Fuel gauge sender unit – removal and refitting

1 The fuel gauge sender unit is an integral part of the fuel pump assembly and is not available separately. Refer to Section 7 for removal and refitting details.

9 Fuel tank – removal and refitting

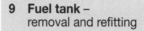

Note: *Refer to the warning note in Section 1 before proceeding.*

Removal

1 Before removing the fuel tank, all fuel must be drained from the tank. Since a fuel tank drain plug is not provided, it is therefore preferable to carry out the removal operation when the tank is nearly empty. Before proceeding, disconnect the battery (see Chapter 5A Section 4) and siphon or hand-pump the remaining fuel from the tank.

2 Remove the rear seat cushion and, using a

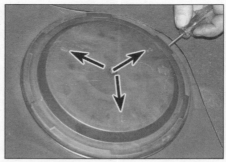

9.2 Fuel pump access cover retaining clips (arrowed)

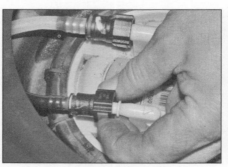

9.4 Depress the release button and disconnect the fuel pipes

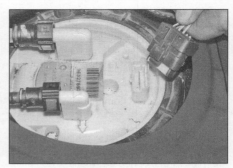

9.3 Disconnect the pump wiring plug

9.6 Remove the inner wheel arch liner

screwdriver, carefully release the three access cover retaining clips at the points indicated by the small arrows, and remove the cover from the floor to expose the fuel pump **(see illustration)**.

3 Disconnect the wiring connector from the fuel pump, and tape the connector to the vehicle body, to prevent it from disappearing behind the tank **(see illustration)**.

4 Depress the retaining clip and detach the fuel pipe(s) from the top of the pump, bearing in mind the information given in Section 6, on depressurising the fuel system **(see illustration)**. Plug the pipe end(s) to minimise fuel loss and prevent the entry of dirt.

5 Chock the front wheels then jack up the rear of the vehicle and support it on axle stands (see *Jacking and vehicle support*). Remove the right-hand rear roadwheel.

6 Remove the left-hand rear roadwheel and inner wheel arch liner **(see illustration)**.

7 Remove the left-hand rear suspension damper and spring (see Chapter 10 Section 13 & 14).

8 Remove the exhaust system as described in Section 15.

9 Undo the fasteners, and remove the heat shield from the tank underside.

10 Disconnect the hoses from the fuel vapour absorber **(see illustrations)**.

9.10a Disconnect the hose from the canister...

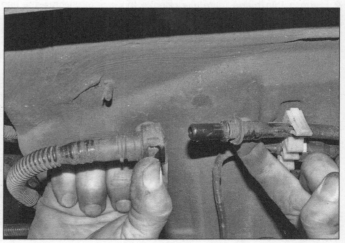

9.10b... and the return pipe

9.11a Unclip the vent pipe...

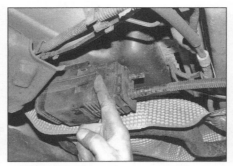

9.11b ... release the securing clip...

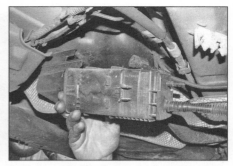

9.11c... and slide the canister out from the mounting bracket

9.12 Fuel filler neck securing bolt (arrowed)

9.14a Fuel tank strap retaining bolt (one arrowed)

9.14b Fuel tank front retaining nuts (one arrowed)

11 Unclip the vent pipe from the fuel tank, release the securing clip, and then slide the fuel vapour absorber out from the mounting bracket **(see illustrations)**.

12 Undo the retaining bolt from the fuel filler neck **(see illustration)**.

13 Place a trolley jack with an interposed block of wood beneath the tank, then raise the jack until it is supporting the weight of the tank.

14 Slacken and remove the four bolts securing the fuel tank to the body **(see illustrations)**. Release the filler neck seal from the body at the filler cap aperture.

15 Slowly lower the fuel tank; ensuring the filler neck assembly is guided out of position without placing any stress on it.

16 If the tank is contaminated with sediment or water, remove the fuel pump (Section 7), and swill the tank out with clean fuel. The tank is injection-moulded from a synthetic material – if seriously damaged, it should be renewed. However, in certain cases, it may be possible to have small leaks or minor damage repaired. Seek the advice of a specialist before attempting to repair the fuel tank.

17 It is not possible to separate the filler neck from the tank. If damaged, the complete assembly must be renewed.

Refitting

18 Refitting is the reverse of the removal procedure, noting the following points:
● Ensure the wiring connector and fuel pipes are securely reconnected and retained by all the relevant clips. When lifting the tank

back into position, take care to ensure that the pipes/wiring do not become trapped between the tank and vehicle body.
● Refit the rear suspension damper and spring.
● Refit the exhaust as described in Section 15.
● On completion, refill the tank with a small amount of fuel and pressurise the fuel system as described in Section 6. Check for signs of leakage prior to taking the vehicle out on the road.

10 Engine management system – testing and adjustment

Testing

1 If a fault appears in the engine management system, first ensure that all the system wiring connectors are securely connected and free of corrosion. Ensure that the fault is not due to poor maintenance; ie, check that the air cleaner filter element is clean, the spark plugs are in good condition and correctly gapped, the cylinder compression pressures are correct and that the engine breather hoses are clear and undamaged, referring to Chapters 1A, 2A, 2B, 2B and 5B for further information.

2 If these checks fail to reveal the cause of the problem, the vehicle should be taken to a suitably-equipped Peugeot dealer or specialist for testing using a diagnostic tester,

which is connected into the diagnostic socket located behind the trim panel to the left of the glove compartment **(see illustration)**. The tester will locate the fault quickly and simply, alleviating the need to test all the system components individually, which is a time-consuming operation that carries a risk of damaging the ECU.

Adjustment

3 Whilst it is possible to check the exhaust CO level and the idle speed, if these are found to be in need of adjustment, the car must be taken to a suitably-equipped Peugeot dealer or specialist or further testing. Neither the mixture adjustment (exhaust gas CO level) nor the idle speed is adjustable, and should either be incorrect, a fault must be present in the engine management system.

10.2 Diagnostic plug connector (arrowed)

11.3 Remove the inlet hose

11.4a Disconnect the wiring connectors – 1.4 litre non-VTi engine...

11.4b... from the throttle housing components – VTi engine

11 Throttle housing – removal and refitting

Removal

1 Where applicable, remove the plastic trim cover from the top of the engine.
2 Remove the air cleaner housing and air ducting as described in Section 2.

3 Slacken the securing clip and remove the inlet hose from the throttle housing **(see illustration)**.
4 Depress the retaining clip and disconnect the wiring connector(s) from the throttle body **(see illustrations)**. **Note:** *Depending on model there may be more than one connector.*
5 Undo the retaining screws and remove the throttle housing from the inlet manifold **(see illustrations)**. Recover the sealing ring from the manifold and discard it; a new one must be used on refitting.

Refitting

6 Refitting is a reversal of the removal procedure, noting the following points:
● Fit a new sealing ring to the manifold **(see illustration)**, then refit the throttle housing and securely tighten its retaining screws.
● Ensure all wiring is correctly routed, and that the connectors are securely reconnected.
● Refit the air cleaner housing and air ducts with reference to Section 2.

11.5a Undo the three retaining screws (arrowed) – 1.4 litre non-VTi engine...

11.5b... then remove the throttle housing from the manifold and recover the sealing ring

11.5c Undo the three retaining screws (arrowed) – VTi engine...

11.5d... then remove the throttle housing from the manifold and recover the sealing ring

11.6 Fit new sealing ring/gasket

12.5 Depress the retaining clip (arrowed) and disconnect the fuel hose from the fuel rail

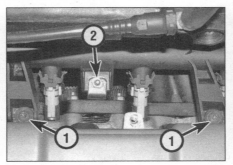

12.6 Unscrew the fuel rail mounting bolts (1) and the nut (2)...

12.7... then slacken the bolt (arrowed) and lift off the centre bracket

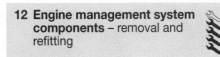

12 Engine management system components – removal and refitting

Note: *Refer to the warning note in Section 1 before proceeding.*

1 Before proceeding with removing any of the engine management system components, disconnect the battery (see Chapter 5A Section 4)

Fuel rail and injectors

Note: *If a faulty injector is suspected, before condemning the injector, it is worth trying the effect of one of the proprietary injector cleaning treatments, which are available from car accessory shops.*

2 Remove the air cleaner housing and air ducting as described in Section 2.

3 Before any work is carried out on the fuel system, depressurise the system as described in Section 6.

1.4 litre non-VTi models

4 Remove the ignition HT coil as described in Chapter 5B Section 3.

5 Depress the retaining clip and disconnect the fuel pipe from the right-hand end of the fuel rail **(see illustration)**.

6 Slacken and remove the two bolts securing the fuel rail to the cylinder head, and the nut securing the rail to the manifold **(see illustration)**.

7 Loosen the bolt securing the fuel rail

centre bracket to the inlet manifold, then lift off the bracket (the bracket is slotted to ease removal) **(see illustration)**.

8 Disconnect the injector wiring harness connector, and then unclip the connector from the rear of the inlet manifold. Also disconnect the wiring connectors from the throttle housing and position the wiring harness clear of the manifold so that it does not hinder fuel rail removal.

9 Carefully ease the fuel rail and injector assembly out from the cylinder head and manoeuvre it out of position. Remove the seals from the end of each injector and discard them; they must be renewed whenever they are disturbed **(see illustration)**.

10 Refitting is a reversal of the removal procedure, noting the following points.

● Fit new seals to all disturbed injector unions.

● Apply a smear of engine oil to the seals to aid installation, then ease the injectors and fuel rail into position ensuring that none of the seals are displaced.

● On completion, pressurise the fuel system as described in Section 6. Start the engine and check for fuel leaks.

1.6 litre non-VTi models

11 Remove the inlet manifold as described in Section 13.

12 Undo the two bolts and remove the fuel rail with injectors from the manifold **(see illustration)**.

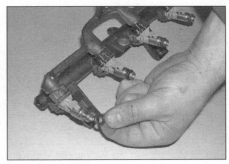

12.9 Remove the seal from the end of each injector

13 Disconnect the wiring connector(s) then slide out the retaining clip(s) and remove the relevant injector(s) from the fuel rail. Remove the seals from each disturbed injector and discard; all disturbed seals must be renewed **(see illustration)**.

14 Refitting is a reversal of the removal procedure, noting the following points.

● Fit new seals to all disturbed injector unions **(see illustration)**.

● Apply a smear of engine oil to the seals to aid installation, then ease the injectors and fuel rail into position ensuring that none of the seals are displaced.

● On completion, pressurise the fuel system as described in Section 6. Start the engine and check for fuel leaks.

12.12 Undo the two bolts (arrowed) and remove the injectors and fuel rail from the manifold

12.13 Slide off the retaining clip and remove the injector from the fuel rail

12.14 Renew all injector seals (arrowed) disturbed on removal

12.16a Unclip the wiring loom...

12.16b... undo the two retaining bolts...

12.17... and withdraw the fuel rail and injectors

12.18 Disconnect the wiring connectors

12.19 Remove the seal from the end of each injector

12.20 Remove the injector from the fuel rail

VTi models

15 Depress the release button and disconnect the fuel supply hose from the left-hand end of the fuel rail. **Note:** *Depressurise the system as described in Section 6, before disconnecting.*
16 Unclip the wiring loom from across the top of the cylinder head cover, and undo the two retaining bolts from the fuel rail **(see illustrations)**.
17 Carefully ease the fuel rail, complete with injectors, from the cylinder head **(see illustration)**.
18 Depress the retaining clip, and disconnect the wiring connectors from the four injectors **(see illustration)**.
19 Remove the O-rings from the end of each injector **(see illustration)**, and discard them; these must be renewed whenever they are disturbed.
20 Slide out the retaining clip and remove

the relevant injector from the fuel rail **(see illustration)**.
21 Remove the upper O-ring from each disturbed injector and discard; all disturbed O-rings must be renewed **(see illustration)**.
22 Refitting is a reversal of the removal procedure, noting the following points.
● Fit new O-rings to all disturbed injector unions.
● Apply a smear of clean engine oil to the O-rings to aid installation then ease the injectors and fuel rail into position ensuring that none of the O-rings are displaced.
● On completion start the engine and check for fuel leaks.

Fuel pressure regulator

23 The fuel pressure regulator is an integral part of the fuel pump assembly and is not available separately. Refer to Section 7 for removal and refitting details.

Throttle potentiometer

Note: *On VTi models, the potentiometer is an integral part of the throttle housing and is not available separately. Refer to Section 11 for removal and refitting details.*
24 Depress the retaining clip and disconnect the wiring connector from the throttle potentiometer **(see illustration)**.
25 Slacken and remove the two retaining screws, then disengage the potentiometer from the throttle valve spindle and remove it from the vehicle **(see illustration)**.
26 Refit in the reverse order of removal.
27 Ensure that the potentiometer is correctly engaged with the throttle valve spindle.

Electronic Control Unit (ECU)

Note: *If a new ECU is being fitted, the vehicle will not start until the immobiliser*

12.21 Remove the upper seal from the end of each injector

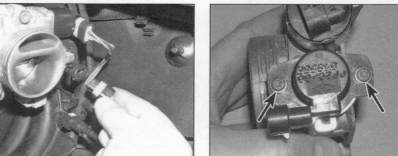

12.24 Disconnect the throttle potentiometer wiring plug...

12.25... then undo the retaining screws (arrowed) – 1.4 litre non-VTi engine

12.29 Remove the battery cover(s)

12.30 Release the lever catches and disconnect the ECU wiring plugs

12.31 Lift the ECU up from the battery box

ECU has been matched to the engine management ECU. This can only be performed using dedicated test equipment. Consequently, entrust the procedure to a Peugeot dealer or suitably-equipped specialist.

28 The ECU is located on the left-hand side of the engine compartment, next to the battery.

29 Remove the plastic cover from the top of the battery tray (see illustration).

30 Lift the ECU up from the battery box, and disconnect the wiring connectors (see illustrations). Release the wiring loom from its securing clips.

31 The ECU can be now be removed from the battery box, complete with plastic cover (see illustration).

32 Refitting is a reverse of the removal procedure ensuring the wiring connectors are securely reconnected.

Idle speed stepper motor
Non-VTi models

33 The idle speed stepper motor is fitted to the rear of the throttle housing.

34 Disconnect the wiring connector from the motor (see illustration).

35 Slacken and remove the retaining screws then remove the motor from the throttle housing (see illustration). If necessary, remove the throttle potentiometer to improve access to the motor lower screw.

36 Refitting is a reversal of the removal procedure ensuring the seal is in good condition.

Manifold pressure sensor

37 The MAP sensor is mounted on the inlet manifold.

38 Disconnect the wiring connector then undo the screw and remove the sensor from the manifold (see illustrations).

39 Refitting is a reversal of the removal procedure ensuring the sensor seal is in good condition.

Coolant temperature sensor

40 The coolant temperature sensor is either screwed, or secured by a retaining clip, in the coolant outlet housing on the left-hand end of the cylinder head. Refer to Chapter 3, Section 7, for removal and refitting information.

Inlet air temperature sensor

41 The inlet air temperature sensor is integral with the throttle housing and is not available separately.

Crankshaft position sensor
VTi engines

42 The crankshaft sensor is situated at the rear of the cylinder block, below the starter motor (see illustration).

12.34 Disconnect the idle speed stepper motor wiring plug (arrowed) – 1.4 litre non-VTi engine

12.35 Undo the retaining screw(s) and remove the motor from the housing

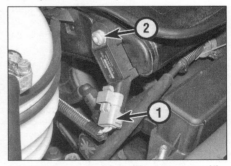

12.38a Disconnect the wiring connector (1) then undo the retaining screw (2) and remove the MAP sensor – 1.4 litre non-VTi engine...

12.38b... 1.6 litre non-VTi engine...

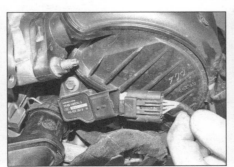

12.38c... and 1.6 litre VTi engine

12.42 Crankshaft position sensor (arrowed) – VTi engine

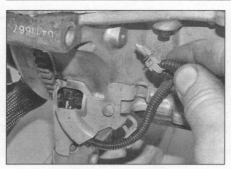

12.43a Remove the wiring clip…

12.43b… unclip the plastic cover…

12.43c… and disconnect the wiring connector

12.46a Disconnect the wiring plug then undo the retaining screw (arrowed)…

12.46b… and remove the crankshaft position sensor from the front of the transmission housing – non-VTi engines

12.49 Remove the throttle housing heating element – 1.4 litre non-VTi engine

43 Release the securing clips for the wiring loom, unclip the plastic cover and disconnect the sensor wiring connector. Undo the retaining bolt and remove the sensor from behind the flywheel **(see illustrations)**.
44 Refitting is reverse of the removal procedure.

Non-VTi engines

45 The crankshaft sensor is situated on the front face of the transmission clutch housing.
46 Disconnect the sensor wiring connector and unclip the wiring. Undo the retaining bolt and remove the sensor and bracket assembly from the transmission unit **(see illustrations)**.
47 Refitting is reverse of the removal procedure.

Throttle housing heating element

Note: *The heating element is only fitted to aluminium throttle housings. Plastic housings do not need a heater.*
48 The heating element is fitted to the top of the throttle housing.
49 Disconnect the wiring connector then unscrew the retaining screw and remove the heating element from the throttle housing **(see illustration)**.
50 Refitting is the reverse of removal.

Vehicle speed sensor

51 The vehicle speed sensor is an integral part of the speedometer drive on 1.4 litre TU engine models. Refer to Chapter 7A for removal and refitting details. On other models,

the ECU receives vehicle speed data from the wheel speed sensors, via the ABS ECU.

Knock sensor

52 Refer to Chapter 5B Section 5.

Air conditioning pressure switch

53 The air conditioning pressure switch is fitted to the refrigerant pipe located on the right-hand rear of the engine compartment **(see illustration)**. Switch renewal requires the air conditioning system to be discharged and drained (see Chapter 3 Section 11).

Camshaft position sensor

54 There are two camshaft position sensors located on the left-hand end of the cylinder head cover on VTi engines **(see illustration)**.
55 Disconnect the wiring plug, then undo the

12.53 Air conditioning pressure sensor (arrowed)

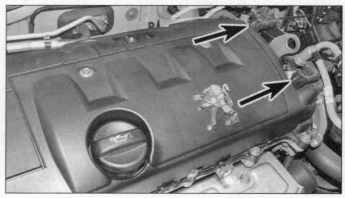

12.54 Camshaft position sensors (arrowed)

12.55a Disconnect the wiring connector...

12.55b... undo the bolt and withdraw the sensor

12.56 Renew the seals

bolt and remove the sensor from the cylinder head cover **(see illustrations)**.

56 Refitting is the reverse of removal ensuring the sensor seal is in good condition **(see illustration)**.

Throttle valve positioner motor

57 The throttle valve positioner motor (where fitted) is integral with the throttle body, and is not available separately.

Accelerator pedal position sensor

58 The sensor is integral with the accelerator pedal assembly – see Section 3.

13.3 Disconnect the pressure sensor wiring connector

13.4 Disconnect the breather pipe

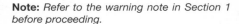

13 Inlet manifold –
removal and refitting

Note: *Refer to the warning note in Section 1 before proceeding.*

Removal

1 Remove the fuel rail and injectors as described in Section 12.

2 Remove the throttle housing as described in Section 11.

3 Disconnect the wiring connector from the manifold pressure sensor **(see illustration)**.

4 Disconnect the breather/vacuum pipe from the cylinder head cover **(see illustration)**.

5 Undo the retaining bolt and move the purge valve to one side, disconnect the vapour pipe(s) from the inlet manifold **(see illustration)**.

6 Working your way along the lower edge of the manifold, unclip the wiring loom and move it to one side, noting its fitted position **(see illustration)**.

7 On VTi models, disconnect the wiring connector from the eccentric shaft actuator at the left-hand rear of the cylinder head. Undo the actuator retaining bolts and then remove it from the cylinder head by using a 4 mm Allen key, and turning the centre shaft anti-clockwise, while withdrawing the actuator from the cylinder head **(see illustrations)**.

8 Undo the retaining bolts and remove

13.5 Undo the bracket mounting bolt (arrowed)

13.6 Unclip the wiring loom

13.7a Undo the retaining bolts (arrowed)...

13.7b... then using an Allen key withdraw the actuator from the cylinder head

13.8 Undo the bracket mounting bolts (arrowed)

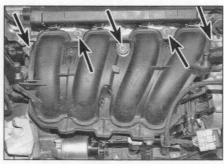

13.9a Inlet manifold nuts (arrowed) – VTi engine

13.9b Withdraw the manifold from the head

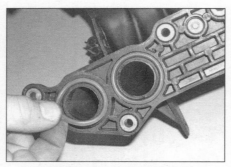

13.10a Ensure new manifold seals are fitted – 1.4 litre non-VTi engine…

13.10b… 1.6 litre non-VTi engine…

13.10c… and VTi engine

the lower mounting bracket from the inlet manifold **(see illustration)**.

9 Undo the manifold retaining nuts and withdraw the manifold from the engine compartment. Recover the four manifold seals and discard them; new ones must be used on refitting **(see illustrations)**.

Refitting

10 Refitting is a reverse of the removal procedure, noting the following points:
● Ensure that the manifold and cylinder head mating surfaces are clean and dry, then locate the new seals in their recesses in the manifold **(see illustrations)**. Refit the manifold and tighten its retaining nuts to the specified torque.
● Ensure that all relevant hoses are

reconnected to their original positions and are securely held (where necessary) by the retaining clips.
● Ensure the wiring is correctly routed and all connectors are securely reconnected.

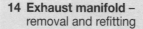

14 Exhaust manifold – removal and refitting

Removal

1 Disconnect the battery, as described in Chapter 5A Section 4.
2 Firmly apply the handbrake, and then jack up the front of the vehicle and support it on

axle stands (see *Jacking and vehicle support*). Release the screws and remove the engine undershield (where fitted).

Non-VTi models

3 Slacken and remove the retaining screws and remove the shroud from the top of the exhaust manifold. It may be necessary to remove the engine lifting eye bracket from the left-hand end of the cylinder head, and undo the bolt and remove the oil dipstick tube **(see illustrations)**.
4 On some models, a second heat shield is fitted on the underside of the manifold, above the oil filter. Undo the bolts and remove the heat shield.
5 Trace the oxygen sensors wiring back to the connectors and disconnect them.
6 Undo the nuts securing the exhaust front pipe to the manifold, and then remove the bolt securing the front pipe to its mounting bracket. Disconnect the front pipe from the manifold, and recover the gasket.
Caution: Do not place any strain on the flexible section of the exhaust front pipe (where fitted); it is easily damaged.
7 Undo the retaining nuts securing the manifold to the head. Manoeuvre the manifold out of the engine compartment, and discard the manifold gasket(s).

VTi models

Note: *The exhaust manifold and catalytic converter are a complete assembly, and cannot be renewed separately.*

14.3a Undo the heat shield bolts (arrowed)…

14.3b… and the dipstick guide tube bolt

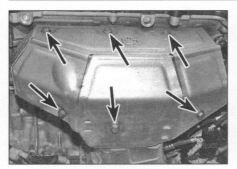

14.8a Undo the bolts (arrowed)…

14.8b… and remove the upper heat shield

14.9 Disconnect the sensor wiring connectors

8 Undo the bolts and remove the heat shield from the top of the exhaust manifold (see illustrations).
9 Disconnect the oxygen sensor wiring connectors and unclip them from the mounting bracket(see illustration).
10 Remove the upper oxygen sensor from the top of the catalytic converter (see illustration).
11 Undo the bolts and remove the heat shield from around the front of the catalytic converter (see illustration).
12 Working underneath the vehicle, undo the retaining clamp bolt and disconnect the front exhaust pipe from the bottom of the catalytic converter (see illustration).
13 Undo the two mounting bolts from each side of the catalytic converter (see illustration).
14 If necessary to gain better access, remove the radiator and fan assembly as described in Chapter 3 Section 4.
15 Undo the manifold-to-cylinder head nuts, and manoeuvre the manifold from the vehicle (see illustration). Note: *The lower oxygen sensor can remain fitted to the lower part of the catalytic converter; make sure the wiring is disconnected.*
16 Remove the manifold gasket/heat shield and discard, as a new one will be required for refitting.

Refitting

17 Refitting is the reverse of the removal procedure, noting the following points:
● Examine all the exhaust manifold studs for signs of damage and corrosion; remove all traces of corrosion, and repair or renew any damaged studs.
● Ensure that the manifold and cylinder head sealing faces are clean and flat, and fit the new manifold gasket/heat shield (see illustration). Tighten the manifold retaining nuts to the specified torque.
● Reconnect the front pipe to the catalytic converter.
● Where necessary (on non-VTi models), renew the oil dipstick tube O-ring.

14.10 Remove the oxygen sensor…

14.11… and then the lower heat shield

14.12 Undo the clamp from the front pipe

14.13 Undo the catalytic converter mounting bolts (arrowed)

14.15 Remove the exhaust manifold

14.17 Manifold gasket has built-in heat shield – VTi engines

15.3 Exhaust front rubber mountings

15.10 Front pipe/catalytic converter-to-flexible pipe retaining clamp

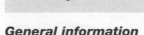

15 Exhaust system – general information, removal and refitting

General information

1 On non-VTi models, the exhaust system consists two sections; the front pipe with integral catalytic converter and the intermediate pipe/rear silencer with tailpipe; a flanged joint joins them.

2 On VTi models, the system is a one-piece section; as the catalytic converter is part of the exhaust manifold, see Section 14. A flanged joint joins the catalytic converter to the exhaust system.

3 The system is suspended throughout its entire length by rubber mountings **(see illustration)**.

4 To remove the system or part of the system, first jack up the front or rear of the car and support it on axle stands (see *Jacking and vehicle support*). Alternatively, position the car over an inspection pit or on car ramps. Undo the screws and remove the engine undershield.

5 If the intermediate pipe/rear silencer section of the exhaust needs renewing, it is available as a two-part system, check with your local exhaust dealer. The original exhaust will need to be cut, just in front of the rear axle. Before making any cuts, it is advisable to get the new part of the exhaust system; this can then be measured to fit the original.

Removal

Front pipe (non-VTi models)

Note: *The catalytic converter is integral with the front pipe.*

6 Trace the wiring back from the oxygen sensors to their wiring connectors. Disconnect the connectors and free the wiring from all its clips and ties so the sensors are free to be removed with the front pipe.

7 Undo the bolts securing the transmission support bracket to the underside of the transmission casing.

8 Undo the nuts securing the front pipe flange joint to the manifold, and the single bolt securing the front pipe to its mounting bracket. Separate the flange joint and collect the gasket.

9 Slacken and remove the two nut(s) securing the front pipe flange joint to the intermediate pipe/rear silencer. Withdraw the front pipe from underneath the vehicle. Recover the gasket.

Intermediate pipe/tailpipe/ rear silencer

10 Undo the retaining nut(s) and disconnect the exhaust system from the front pipe/catalytic converter **(see illustration)**.

11 Support the exhaust system and then undo the retaining nuts and free all the mounting rubbers from under the vehicle **(see illustrations)**.

12 If only part of the system needs to be renewed (see paragraph 5), the exhaust can be cut while it is still fitted to the vehicle; this will make it easier for removal.

13 If the system is being removed in one piece, it may be necessary to remove the rear shock absorbers and springs (see Chapter 10 Section 13 & 14), to allow enough room for the exhaust to be withdrawn from over the rear axle.

Heat shield(s)

14 The heat shields are secured to the underside of the body by various nuts and fasteners. If a shield is being removed to gain access to a component located behind it, remove the retaining nuts and/or fastener, exhaust mountings and manoeuvre the shield out of position **(see illustration)**. On some models it may be necessary to free the exhaust system from its mountings to gain the clearance necessary to remove the larger heat shield.

Refitting

15 Each section is refitted by reversing the removal sequence, noting the following points:
● Ensure that all traces of corrosion have been removed from the flanges and renew all necessary gaskets.
● Inspect the rubber mountings for signs of damage or deterioration, and renew as necessary.
● Where joints are secured together by a clamping ring, apply a smear of exhaust system jointing paste to the flange joint to ensure a gas-tight seal. Insert the bolt through the clamping ring and fit the washer.
● Prior to tightening the exhaust system fasteners, ensure that all rubber mountings are correctly located, and that there is adequate clearance between the exhaust system and vehicle underbody.

15.11a Undo the two upper retaining nuts (arrowed)

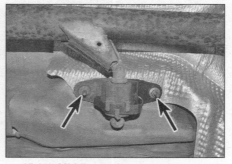

15.11b Middle section mounting nuts (arrowed)...

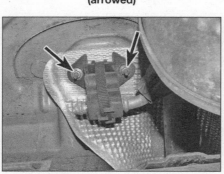

15.11c... and rear mounting retaining nuts (arrowed)

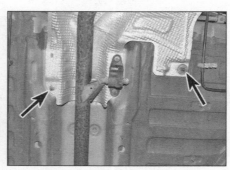

15.14 Heat shield has various fasteners (arrowed)

Chapter 4 Part B
Fuel and exhaust systems – diesel models

Contents

Degrees of difficulty

Easy, suitable for novice with little experience	Fairly easy, suitable for beginner with some experience	Fairly difficult, suitable for competent DIY mechanic	Difficult, suitable for experienced DIY mechanic	Very difficult, suitable for expert DIY or professional

Specifications

Engine identification

	Designation	Engine code
1.4 litre	DV4TD and DV4C	8HZ and 8HR
1.6 litre DOHC	DV6ATED4, DV6TED4 and DV6DTED	9HX, 9HY, 9HZ, 9HV and 9HP
1.6 litre SOHC	DV6C	9HR

General

System type . . . . HDi (High-pressure Diesel injection) with full electronic control, direct injection and turbocharger
Designation . . . . Bosch EDC 16
Firing order . . . . 1-3-4-2 (No 1 at flywheel end)
Fuel system operating pressure . . . . 200 to 1800 bars (according to engine speed)
Idle speed . . . . 800 ± 20 rpm (controlled by ECU)
Engine cut-off speed . . . . 5000 rpm (controlled by ECU)

Injectors

Type . . . . Electromagnetic or Piezo

Turbocharger

Type:
   1.4 litre . . . . KKK
   1.6 litre . . . . MHI – TD025S2 or Garrett GT1544V
Boost pressure (approximate) . . . . 0.9 bar @ 3500 rpm

Torque wrench settings

	Nm	lbf ft
Accumulator rail mounting bolts	23	17
Accumulator rail-to-fuel injector fuel pipe unions: *		
1.4 litre engine:		
Stage 1	17	13
Stage 2	22	16
1.6 litre engines:		
Injector end union:		
Stage 1	25	18
Stage 2	27	20
Rail end union:		
Stage 1	24	18
Stage 2	26	19
Camshaft position sensor bolt	5	4
Clamping ring nuts	20	15
Crankshaft speed/position sensor	5	4
Exhaust manifold nuts	20	15
Exhaust system fasteners:		
Catalytic converter-to-manifold nuts	40	30
Clamping ring nuts	20	15
Fuel injector clamp bolt:		
1.4 litre engine	20	15
1.6 litre engine:		
Stage 1	4	3
Stage 2	Angle-tighten a further 65°	
Fuel injector clamp stud	7	5
Fuel pressure sensor to accumulator rail	45	33
Fuel pump-to-accumulator rail fuel pipe unions: *		
1.4 litre engine:		
Stage 1	17	13
Stage 2	22	16
1.6 litre engine	25	18
High-pressure fuel pump mounting bolts:		
1.4 litre engine	25	18
1.6 litre engine	23	17
High-pressure fuel pump rear mounting bolts/nut (8 mm)	17	13
High-pressure fuel pump sprocket nut	50	37
Inlet manifold bolts	10	7
Turbocharger mounting bolts/nuts	25	18
Turbocharger oil feed pipe banjo bolts:		
1.4 litre engine	25	18
1.6 litre engine	30	20

Note: * *These torque settings are using Peugeot crow-foot adapters – see Section 2*

1 General information and system operation

1 The fuel system consists of a rear-mounted fuel tank and fuel lift pump, a fuel filter with integral water separator, on some models a fuel cooler mounted under the car, and an electronically-controlled High-pressure Diesel injection (HDi) system, together with a turbocharger.

2 The exhaust system is conventional, but to meet the latest emission levels an unregulated catalytic converter and an exhaust gas recirculation system are fitted to all models. On some 1.6 litre models, an exhaust emission particulate filter is fitted – refer to Chapter 4C for further details.

3 The HDi system (generally known as a 'common rail' system) derives its name from the fact that a common rail (referred to as an accumulator rail), or fuel reservoir, is used to supply fuel to all the fuel injectors. Instead of an in-line or distributor type injection pump, which distributes the fuel directly to each injector, a high-pressure pump is used, which generates a very high fuel pressure (1350 bars at high engine speed) in the accumulator rail. The accumulator rail stores fuel, and maintains a constant fuel pressure, with the aid of a pressure control valve. Each injector is supplied with high-pressure fuel from the accumulator rail, and the injectors are individually controlled via signals from the system electronic control unit (ECU). The injectors are electronically operated.

4 In addition to the various sensors used on models with a conventional fuel injection pump; common rail systems also have a fuel pressure sensor. The fuel pressure sensor allows the ECU to maintain the required fuel pressure, via the pressure control valve.

System operation

5 For the purposes of describing the operation of a common rail injection system, the components can be divided into three sub-systems; the low-pressure fuel system, the high-pressure fuel system and the electronic control system.

Low-pressure fuel system

6 The low-pressure fuel system consists of the following components:
- Fuel tank.
- Fuel lift pump.
- Fuel cooler (not all models).
- Fuel heater (not all models).
- Fuel filter/water trap.
- Low-pressure fuel lines.

7 The low-pressure system (fuel supply system) is responsible for supplying clean fuel to the high-pressure fuel system.

High-pressure fuel system

8 The high-pressure fuel system consists of the following components:
● High-pressure fuel pump with pressure control valve.
● High-pressure fuel accumulator rail.
● Fuel injectors.
● High-pressure fuel lines.

9 After passing through the fuel filter, the fuel reaches the high-pressure pump, which forces it into the accumulator rail. As diesel fuel has certain elasticity, the pressure in the accumulator rail remains constant, even though fuel leaves the rail each time one of the injectors operates. Additionally, a pressure control valve mounted on the high-pressure pump ensures that the fuel pressure is maintained within preset limits.

10 The pressure control valve is operated by the ECU. When the valve is opened, fuel is returned from the high-pressure pump to the tank, via the fuel return lines, and the pressure in the accumulator rail falls. To enable the ECU to trigger the pressure control valve correctly, a fuel pressure sensor measures the pressure in the accumulator rail.

11 The electronically-controlled fuel injectors are operated individually, via signals from the ECU, and each injector injects fuel directly into the relevant combustion chamber. The fact that high fuel pressure is always available allows very precise and highly flexible injection in comparison to a conventional injection pump: for example, combustion during the main injection process can be improved considerably by the pre-injection of a very small quantity of fuel.

Electronic control system

12 The electronic control system consists of the following components:
● Electronic control unit (ECU).
● Crankshaft speed/position sensor.
● Camshaft position sensor.
● Accelerator pedal position sensor.
● Coolant temperature sensor.
● Fuel temperature sensor.
● Air mass meter.
● Fuel pressure sensor.
● Fuel injectors.
● Fuel pressure control valve.
● Preheating control unit.
● EGR solenoid valve.
● Air temperature sensor
● Atmospheric pressure sensor – integral with the ECU (DV6TED4 engines only).
● Inlet manifold pressure sensor (DV6TED4 engines only).

13 The information from the various sensors is passed to the ECU, which evaluates the signals. The ECU contains electronic 'maps' which enable it to calculate the optimum quantity of fuel to inject, the appropriate start of injection, and even pre- and post-injection

fuel quantities, for each individual engine cylinder under any given condition of engine operation.

14 Additionally, the ECU carries out monitoring and self-diagnostic functions. Any faults in the system are stored in the ECU memory, which enables quick and accurate fault diagnosis using appropriate diagnostic equipment (such as a suitable fault code reader).

System components

Fuel lift pump

15 The fuel lift pump and integral fuel gauge sender unit is electrically operated, and is mounted in the fuel tank.

High-pressure pump

16 The high-pressure pump is mounted on the engine in the position normally occupied by the conventional distributor fuel injection pump. The pump is driven at half engine speed by the timing belt, and is lubricated by the fuel, which it pumps.

17 The fuel lift pump forces the fuel into the high-pressure pump chamber, via a safety valve.

18 The high-pressure pump consists of three radially-mounted pistons and cylinders. The pistons are operated by an eccentric cam mounted on the pump drive spindle. As a piston moves down, fuel enters the cylinder through an inlet valve. When the piston reaches bottom dead centre (BDC), the inlet valve closes, and as the piston moves back up the cylinder, the fuel is compressed. When the pressure in the cylinder reaches the pressure in the accumulator rail, an outlet valve opens, and fuel is forced into the accumulator rail. When the piston reaches top dead centre (TDC), the outlet valve closes, due to the pressure drop, and the pumping cycle is repeated. The use of multiple cylinders provides a steady flow of fuel, minimising pulses and pressure fluctuations.

19 As the pump needs to be able to supply sufficient fuel under full-load conditions, it will supply excess fuel during idle and part-load conditions. This excess fuel is returned from the high-pressure circuit to the low-pressure circuit (to the tank) via the pressure control valve.

20 The pump incorporates a facility to effectively switch off one of the cylinders to improve efficiency and reduce fuel consumption when maximum pumping capacity is not required. When this facility is operated, a solenoid-operated needle holds the inlet valve in the relevant cylinder open during the delivery stroke, preventing the fuel from being compressed.

Accumulator rail

21 As its name suggests, the accumulator rail (also known as common rail) acts as an accumulator, storing fuel and preventing pressure fluctuations. Fuel enters the rail from the high-pressure pump, and each injector

has its own connection to the rail. The fuel pressure sensor is mounted in the rail, and the rail also has a connection to the fuel pressure control valve on the pump.

Pressure control valve

22 The pressure control valve is operated by the ECU, and controls the system pressure. The valve is integral with the high-pressure pump and cannot be separated.

23 If the fuel pressure is excessive, the valve opens, and fuel flows back to the tank. If the pressure is too low, the valve closes, enabling the high-pressure pump to increase the pressure.

24 The valve is an electronically-operated ball valve. The ball is forced against its seat, against the fuel pressure, by a powerful spring, and also by the force provided by the electromagnet. The force generated by the electromagnet is directly proportional to the current applied to it by the ECU. The desired pressure can therefore be set by varying the current applied to the electromagnet. Any pressure fluctuations are damped by the spring.

Fuel pressure sensor

25 The fuel pressure sensor is mounted in the accumulator rail, and provides very precise information on the fuel pressure to the ECU.

Fuel injector

26 The injectors are mounted on the engine in a similar manner to conventional diesel fuel injectors. The injectors are electronically-operated via signals from the ECU, and fuel is injected at the pressure existing in the accumulator rail. The injectors are high-precision instruments and are manufactured to very high tolerances.

27 Fuel flows into the injector from the accumulator rail, via an inlet valve and an inlet throttle, and an electromagnet causes the injector nozzle to lift from its seat, allowing injection. Excess fuel is returned from the injectors to the tank via a return line. The injector operates on a hydraulic servo principle: the forces resulting inside the injector due to the fuel pressure effectively amplify the effects of the electromagnet, which does not provide sufficient force to open the injector nozzle directly. The injector functions as follows. Five separate forces are essential to the operation of the injector.
● A nozzle spring forces the nozzle needle against the nozzle seat at the bottom of the injector, preventing fuel from entering the combustion chamber.
● In the valve at the top of the injector, the valve spring forces the valve ball against the opening to the valve control chamber. The fuel in the chamber is unable to escape through the fuel return.
● When triggered, the electromagnet exerts a force, which overcomes the valve spring force, and moves the valve ball away from its seat. This is the triggering force for the start of injection. When the valve ball

moves off its seat, fuel enters the valve control chamber.

● The pressure of the fuel in the valve control chamber exerts a force on the valve control plunger, which is added to the nozzle spring force.

● A slight chamfer towards the lower end of the nozzle needle causes the fuel in the control chamber to exert a force on the nozzle needle.

28 When these forces are in equilibrium, the injector is in its rest (idle) state, but when a voltage is applied to the electromagnet, the forces work to lift the nozzle needle, injecting fuel into the combustion chamber. There are four phases of injector operation as follows:

● *Rest (idle) state* – all forces are in equilibrium. The nozzle needle closes off the nozzle opening, and the valve spring forces the valve ball against its seat.

● *Opening* – the electromagnet is triggered which opens the nozzle and triggers the injection process. The force from the electromagnet allows the valve ball to leave its seat. The fuel from the valve control chamber flows back to the tank via the fuel return line. When the valve opens, the pressure in the valve control chamber drops, and the force on the valve plunger is reduced. However, due to the effect of the input throttle, the pressure on the nozzle needle remains unchanged. The resulting force in the valve control chamber is sufficient to lift the nozzle from its seat, and the injection process begins.

● *Injection* – within a few milliseconds, the triggering current in the electromagnet is reduced to a lower holding current. The nozzle is now fully open, and fuel is injected into the combustion chamber at the pressure present in the accumulator rail.

● *Closing* – the electromagnet is switched off, at which point the valve spring forces the valve ball firmly against its seat, and in the valve control chamber, the pressure is the same as that at the nozzle needle. The force at the valve plunger increases, and the nozzle needle closes the nozzle opening. The forces are now in equilibrium once more, and the injector is once more in the idle state, awaiting the next injection sequence.

ECU and sensors

29 The ECU and sensors are described earlier in this Section – see Electronic control system.

Air inlet sensor and turbocharger

30 An airflow sensor is fitted downstream of the air filter to monitor the quantity of air supplied to the turbocharger. On 1.6 litre models, air from the high-pressure side of the turbocharger is either channeled through the intercooler, or into the manifold without being intercooled, depending on the air temperature. The flow and routing of inlet air is controlled by the engine management ECU. On these models, an engine coolant-heated matrix is fitted to the base of the air cleaner housing to warm the incoming air, which decreases harmful exhaust emissions. The turbochargers are of the variable nozzle geometry type.

2 High-pressure diesel injection system – special information

Warnings and precautions

1 It is essential to observe strict precautions when working on the fuel system components, particularly the high-pressure side of the system. Before carrying out any operations on the fuel system, refer to the precautions given in Safety first0,2 ! at the beginning of this manual, and to the following additional information.

● Do not carry out any repair work on the high-pressure fuel system unless you are competent to do so, have all the necessary tools and equipment required, and are aware of the safety implications involved.

● Before starting any repair work on the fuel system, wait at least 30 seconds after switching off the engine to allow the fuel circuit pressure to reduce.

● Never work on the high-pressure fuel system with the engine running.

● Keep well clear of any possible source of fuel leakage, particularly when starting the engine after carrying out repair work. A leak in the system could cause an extremely high pressure jet of fuel to escape, which could result in severe personal injury.

● Never place your hands or any part of your body near to a leak in the high-pressure fuel system.

● Do not use steam cleaning equipment or compressed air to clean the engine or any of the fuel system components.

Procedures and information

2 Strict cleanliness must be observed at all times when working on any part of the fuel system. This applies to the working area in general, the person doing the work, and the components being worked on.

3 Before working on the fuel system components, they must be thoroughly cleaned with a suitable degreasing fluid. Specific cleaning products may be obtained from Peugeot dealers. Alternatively, a suitable brake cleaning fluid may be used. Cleanliness is particularly important when working on the fuel system connections at the following components:

● Fuel filter.
● High-pressure fuel pump.
● Accumulator rail.
● Fuel injectors.
● High-pressure fuel pipes.

4 After disconnecting any fuel pipes or components, the open union or orifice must be immediately sealed to prevent the entry of dirt or foreign material. Plastic plugs and caps in various sizes are available in packs from motor factors and accessory outlets, and are particularly suitable for this application **(see illustration)**. Fingers cut from disposable rubber gloves should be used to protect components such as fuel pipes, fuel injectors and wiring connectors, and can be secured in place using elastic bands. Suitable gloves of this type are available at no cost from most petrol station forecourts.

5 Whenever any of the high-pressure fuel pipes are disconnected or removed, new pipes must be obtained for refitting.

6 On the completion of any repair on the high-pressure fuel system, Peugeot recommend the use of a leak-detecting compound. This is a powder which is applied to the fuel pipe unions and connections, and turns white when dry. Any leak in the system will cause the product to darken indicating the source of the leak.

7 The torque wrench settings given in the Specifications must be strictly observed when tightening component mountings and connections. This is particularly important when tightening the high-pressure fuel pipe unions. To enable a torque wrench to be used on the fuel pipe unions, two Peugeot crow-foot adapters are required. Suitable alternatives are available from motor factors and accessory outlets **(see illustration)**.

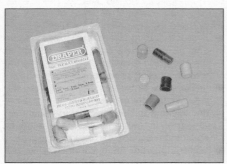

2.4 Typical plastic plug and cap set for sealing disconnected fuel pipes and components

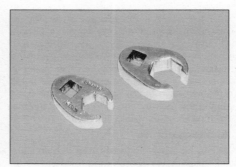

2.7 Two crow-foot adapters will be necessary for tightening the fuel pipe unions

3.1a Operate the hand priming pump 1.6 litre DOHC model...

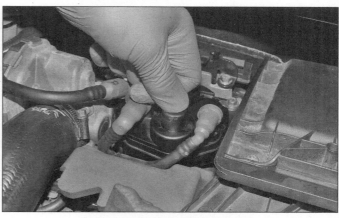

3.1b ... and 1.6 litre SOHC model

3 Fuel system –
priming and bleeding

1 Should the fuel supply system be disconnected between the fuel tank and high-pressure pump, it is necessary to prime the fuel system. This is achieved by operating the hand-priming pump (where fitted) until resistance is felt (1.6 litre models) or fuel

appears in the transparent fuel supply pipe in the engine compartment (1.4 litre models) **(see illustration)**. Remove the engine cover from the top of the engine to access the priming pump. Operate the hand-priming pump for approximately 2 minutes.

2 Where a hand-priming pump is not fitted, priming is achieved by connecting a suitable hose (if necessary, a special Peugeot hose No 444-T may be available) from the fuel filter outlet pipe to the fuel return pipe and forcing

fuel through the filter, into the return system. If the suitable hose is not available, it will suffice to connect a length of hose to the filter outlet, with the other end of the hose in a suitable container **(see illustration)**.

3 With the system primed, reconnect the hoses, and then operate the starter until the engine starts.

4 Air cleaner assembly
and inlet ducts –
removal and refitting

Air cleaner and inlet ducts removal

1.4 litre models

1 Pull the plastic engine cover up and remove it.

2 Slacken the turbocharger inlet hose clip, and release the diesel priming bulb from its brackets.

3 Slacken the clip securing the turbo outlet hose, undo the bolt securing the resonator box, and the bolt securing the resonator box to the turbocharger, swivel the box up and remove it **(see illustrations)**.

3.2 Attach a hose to the filter outlet and bleed the fuel into a container

4.3a Slacken the clip and disconnect the turbo outlet hose (arrowed)...

4.3b... then undo the retaining bolts (arrowed)...

4.3c... pivot the right-hand end of the box up and disengage it from the turbo outlet stud (arrowed)

4.4a Undo the two air cleaner housing screws (arrowed)

4.4b The rear of the air cleaner housing locates in two rubber mountings (arrowed)

4.5 Push in the centre pin, then prise the complete plastic rivet (arrowed) from place, and remove the air inlet ducting

4.9a Pull the housing upwards...

4.9b ... releasing it from the rubber grommets

4 Undo the two screws and remove the air cleaner housing, disconnecting any wiring plugs as necessary as the housing is withdrawn (see illustrations).

5 To remove the air inlet ducting, slacken the retaining clips and remove the relevant section of ducting. The air ducting in the left-hand front corner of the engine compartment is retained by a plastic expansion rivet. Push down the centre pin then pull the entire rivet from place (see illustration). The air deflector in the left-hand front corner of the engine compartment simply lifts from place and, upon refitting, locates over a clip on the front of the electrical box. The ducting at the rear of the engine is only accessible once the battery tray has been removed (see Chapter 5A Section 4).

1.6 litre DOHC models

6 Remove the air filter element as described in Chapter 1B Section 17.

7 Remove the screw/clip and withdraw the air inlet ducting, removing it from the front of the engine compartment to the air filter lower housing.

8 Check around the filter lower housing and unclip any wiring retaining clips.

9 Pull the air filter lower housing upwards from the rubber mounting grommets (see illustrations).

1.6 litre SOHC models

10 Remove the air filter element, as described in Chapter 1B Section 17.

11 Remove the inlet air resonator from the front of the engine compartment, as described later in this section. Releasing the air intake duct from the bottom of the air filter housing.

12 Slacken and remove the two retaining bolts (studs for locating engine cover), from the front of the lower housing (see illustration).

13 Disconnect the mass airflow sensor wiring plug, and unclip the wiring loom from the filter housing (see illustrations).

14 Release the retaining clips and remove the air inlet rubber hose/ducting from between the turbo and the airflow sensor (see illustration).

4.12 Remove the two retaining bolts/studs

4.13a Disconnect the wiring connector...

4.13b ... and unclip the wiring loom

4.14 Remove the air inlet rubber hose/ ducting

4.15a Pull the housing upwards…

4.15b … releasing it from the rubber grommets

15 Pull the air filter lower housing upwards from the rubber mounting grommets **(see illustrations)**.

Inlet air resonator removal

16 To remove the resonator, pull up and remove the plastic cover from the top of the engine, then make a note of its fitted position, and slacken the outlet ducting clamp. It must be refitted into its original position.
17 On 1.4 litre engines, undo the bolt securing the resonator box, and the bolt securing the turbocharger outlet pipe to the box **(see illustrations 4.3a, 4.3b and 4.3c)**.
18 On 1.6 litre engines (1.6 litre SOHC engine shown), remove the securing clip, release the retaining clip and withdraw the inlet air resonator upwards, releasing the

lower air ducting tube as it is removed **(see illustrations)**.
19 Lift up the right-hand end of the ducting, and remove the resonator box and ducting from position.

Refitting

20 Refitting is a reverse of the removal procedure, making sure the rubber grommets locate correctly. Examine the condition of the seals and retaining clips and renew if necessary.

5 Accelerator pedal –
removal and refitting

1 Refer to Chapter 4A Section 3.

6 Fuel lift pump –
removal and refitting

1 The diesel fuel lift pump is located in the same position as the conventional fuel pump on petrol models, and the removal and refitting procedures are virtually identical **(see illustration)**. Refer to Chapter 4A Section 7. **Note:** *No lift pump is fitted to the 1.4 litre engine, but the fuel gauge sender unit is located in the fuel tank – the same position as other models.*

7 Fuel gauge sender unit –
removal and refitting

1 The fuel gauge sender unit is integral with the fuel lift pump. Refer to Section 6.

8 Fuel tank and cooler –
removal and refitting

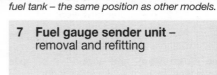

Fuel tank

1 Refer to Chapter 4A Section 9.

Fuel cooler
Removal

2 The fuel cooler is located under the right-hand side of the vehicle. Jack up the vehicle

4.18a Remove the securing clip…

4.18b …release the retaining clip…

4.18c …then disconnect the air ducting tube…

4.18d …as the resonator box is removed

4.18e Remove the air ducting tube from the filter housing

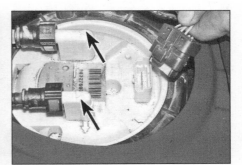

6.1 The arrows on the pump cover indicate supply and return (arrowed)

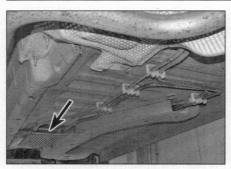

8.2 Fuel cooler (arrowed)

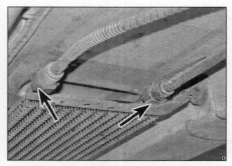

8.3 Depress the release buttons (arrowed) and disconnect the hoses

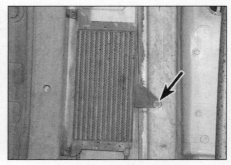

8.4 Undo the bolt (arrowed) securing the fuel cooler

(see illustration), and support it on axle stands (see *Jacking and vehicle support*).

3 Depress the release buttons and disconnect the fuel feed and return hoses from the cooler. Be prepared for fuel spillage, and plug the hose and cooler openings to prevent dirt ingress **(see illustration)**.

4 Working underneath the vehicle, undo the retaining bolt, and release the cooler from the locating holes **(see illustration)**.

Refitting

5 Refitting is a reversal of removal.

---

9 High-pressure fuel pump – removal and refitting

⚠️ **Warning: Refer to the information contained in Section 2 before proceeding.**

Note: *A new fuel pump-to-accumulator rail high-pressure fuel pipe will be required for refitting.*

Removal

1.4 litre engine

1 Disconnect the battery (see Chapter 5A

Section 4) and remove the timing belt as described in Chapter 2C Section 7. After removal of the timing belt, temporarily refit the right-hand engine mounting but do not fully tighten the bolts.

2 Remove the cylinder head cover/air filter housing as described in Chapter 2C Section 4.

3 Depress the clip buttons and disconnect the fuel supply and return hoses from the pump **(see illustration)**. Plug the end of the hoses to prevent dirt ingress.

4 Hold the pump sprocket stationary, and loosen the centre nut securing it to the pump shaft. The manufacturers recommend using an 8 mm pin inserted through the pulley and into the pump support **(see illustration)**.

5 The fuel pump sprocket is a taper fit on the pump shaft and it will be necessary to make up a tool to release it from the taper **(see Tool Tip 1)**. Partially unscrew the sprocket retaining nut, fit the home-made tool, and secure it to the sprocket with two 7.0 mm bolts and nuts. Prevent the sprocket from rotating as before, and screw down the nuts, forcing the sprocket off the shaft taper. Once the taper is released, remove the tool, unscrew

Make a sprocket releasing tool from a short strip of steel. Drill two holes in the strip to correspond with the two holes in the sprocket. Drill a third hole just large enough to accept the flats of the sprocket retaining nut.

the nut fully, and remove the sprocket from the pump shaft.

6 Undo the unions and remove the pump-to-accumulator rail metal pipe. Counterhold the pump union with a second spanner – the union screwed into the pump must not be

9.3 Depress the release buttons (arrowed) and disconnect the fuel supply and return hoses from the pump

9.4 Stop the fuel pump sprocket from rotating by inserting an 8 mm drill bit or pin through the sprocket into thebackplate

9.6 Counterhold the pump union with a second spanner whilst slackening the accumulator-to-pump pipe union

9.8a Undo the pump rear support bracket bolts/nut (arrowed)…

9.8b… and the bolts securing the bracket to the cylinder head

allowed to unscrew (see illustration). Discard the pipe; a new one must be fitted.

7 Disconnect the wiring plugs from the pump, noting their fitted positions.

8 Undo the nuts/bolts and remove the pump support bracket from the rear of the pump, and the bracket on the cylinder head (see illustrations).

9 Remove the EGR valve with reference to Chapter 4C Section 2.

10 Undo the three bolts, and remove the pump (see illustration).

Caution: The high-pressure fuel pump is manufactured to extremely close tolerances and must not be dismantled in any way. Do not unscrew the fuel pipe male union on the rear of the pump, or attempt to remove the sensor, piston de-activator switch, or the seal on the pump shaft. No parts for the pump are available separately and if the unit is in any way suspect, it must be renewed.

1.6 litre engine

11 Disconnect the battery (see Chapter 5A Section 4) and remove the timing belt as described in Chapter 2D Section 7 or Chapter 2E Section 7. After removal of the timing belt, temporarily refit the right-hand engine mounting but do not fully tighten the bolts.

12 Remove the air filter assembly as described in Section 4.

13 Remove the EGR cooler as described in Chapter 4C Section 2.

14 Undo the bolts/nuts and remove the 3

support brackets above the fuel accumulator rail and the high-pressure pump (see illustrations).

15 Undo the union nuts and remove the high-pressure fuel pipe between the fuel accumulator rail and the high-pressure pump. Plug the openings to prevent contamination.

16 Disconnect the wiring plug from the high-pressure fuel pump.

17 Depress the release buttons and disconnect the fuel supply and return hoses from the pump. Note that the hoses may have a release button on each side of the fitting. Plug the openings to prevent contamination.

18 Hold the pump sprocket stationary, and loosen the centre nut securing it to the pump shaft (see Tool Tip 2).

19 The fuel pump sprocket is a taper fit on the pump shaft and it will be necessary to make up a tool to release it from the taper (see Tool Tip 1). Partially unscrew the sprocket retaining nut, fit the home-made tool, and secure it to the sprocket with two 7.0 mm bolts and nuts. Prevent the sprocket from rotating as before, and screw down the nuts, forcing the sprocket off the shaft taper. Once the taper is released, remove the tool, unscrew the nut fully, and remove the sprocket from the pump shaft.

20 Undo the three bolts, and remove the pump from the mounting bracket.

Caution: The high-pressure fuel pump is manufactured to extremely close tolerances and must not be dismantled in

TOOL TiP 2

A sprocket holding tool can be made from two lengths of steel strip bolted together to form a forked end. Bend the end of the strip through 90° to form the fork 'prongs'.

any way. Do not unscrew the fuel pipe male union on the rear of the pump, or attempt to remove the sensor, piston de-activator switch, or the seal on the pump shaft. No parts for the pump are available separately and if the unit is in any way suspect, it must be renewed.

Refitting

21 Refitting is a reversal of removal, noting the following points:
● Always renew the pump-to-accumulator rail high-pressure pipe.
● With everything reassembled and

9.10 Unscrew the three bolts (arrowed) and remove the pump

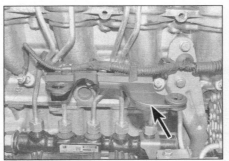

9.14a Remove the air filter support bracket (arrowed)…

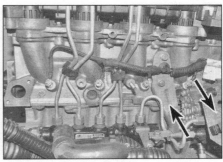

9.14b… and the brackets around the fuel pump (arrowed)

10.5 Use a second spanner to counterhold the fuel injector unions whilst slackening the pipe unions

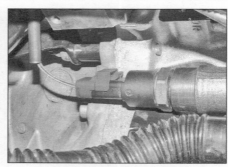

10.7 Disconnect the accumulator rail pressure sensor wiring plug

10.8 Depress the release button (arrowed) and disconnect the fuel return pipe

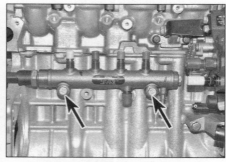

10.9 Remove the accumulator rail mounting bolts (arrowed)

reconnected, and observing the precautions listed in Section 2, start the engine and allow it to idle. Check for leaks at the high-pressure fuel pipe unions with the engine idling. If satisfactory, increase the engine speed to 3000 rpm and check again for leaks.

● Take the car for a short road test and check for leaks once again on return. If any leaks are detected, obtain and fit another new high-pressure fuel pipe. Do not attempt to cure even the slightest leak by further tightening of the pipe unions. During the road test, initialise the engine management ECU as follows – engage third gear and stabilise the engine at 1000 rpm, then accelerate fully up to 3500 rpm.

10 Accumulator rail – removal and refitting

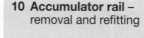

 Warning: Refer to the information contained in Section 2 before proceeding.

Note: *A complete new set of high-pressure fuel pipes will be required for refitting.*

Removal

1 Disconnect the battery (refer to Chapter 5A Section 4).

2 Remove the plastic cover from the top of the engine.

1.4 litre models

3 Remove the cylinder head cover/air filter housing as described in Chapter 2C Section 4.

4 Clean the area around the high-pressure fuel pipes to and from the accumulator rail, then unscrew the pump-to-accumulator rail pipe unions. Use a second spanner to counterhold the union screwed in to the pump body **(see illustration 9.6)**. The screwed-in union must not be allowed to move. Remove the pipe.

5 Repeat the procedure on the accumulator rail-to-injector fuel pipes. Use a second spanner to counterhold the unions screwed in to the injectors **(see illustration)**. These unions must not be allowed to move. Note their fitted locations and remove the pipes.

6 Plug the openings in the accumulator rail and fuel pump to prevent dirt ingress.

7 Disconnect the pressure sensor wiring plug from the accumulator rail **(see illustration)**.

8 Disconnect the fuel return pipe from the rail **(see illustration)**.

9 Unscrew the two rail mounting bolts and manoeuvre it from place **(see illustration)**. Peugeot insist that the fuel pressure sensor on the accumulator rail must not be removed.

1.6 litre engine

10 Remove the cylinder head cover/inlet manifold as described in Chapter 2D or 2E.

11 Drain the cooling system as described in Chapter 1B Section 22.

12 Remove the EGR cooler as described in Chapter 4C Section 2.

13 Undo the 2 mounting bolts, slacken the clamps, and move the coolant pump outlet assembly aside **(see illustration)**.

14 Clean around the pipe, then undo the unions and remove the high-pressure pipe from the accumulator rail to the high-pressure pump. Plug the openings to prevent contamination.

15 Disconnect the pressure sensor wiring plug from the accumulator rail **(see illustration)**.

16 Unscrew the two rail mounting bolts and manoeuvre it from place **(see illustration)**. Peugeot insist that the fuel pressure sensor on the accumulator rail must not be removed.

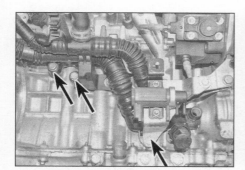

10.13 Undo the bolts (arrowed) and move the coolant pump outlet assembly aside

10.15 The pressure sensor is located at the end of the accumulator rail (arrowed)

10.16 Accumulator rail mounting bolt/stud (arrowed)

Note: *Do not attempt to remove the four high-pressure fuel pipe male unions from the accumulator rail. These parts are not available separately and if disturbed are likely to result in fuel leakage on reassembly.*

Refitting

17 Locate the accumulator rail in position, refit and finger-tighten the mounting bolts/nuts.
18 Reconnect the accumulator rail wiring plug(s).
19 Fit the new pump-to-rail high-pressure pipe, and only finger-tighten the unions at first, then tighten the unions to the specified torque setting. Use a second spanner to counterhold the union screwed into the pump body.
20 Fit the new set of rail-to-injector high-pressure pipes, and finger tighten the unions. If it's not possible to fit the new pipes to the injector unions, remove and refit the injectors as described in Section 11, and then try again.
21 Tighten the accumulator rail mounting bolts/nuts to the specified torque.
22 Tighten the rail-to-injector pipe unions to the specified torque setting. Use a second spanner to counterhold the injector unions.
23 The remainder of refitting is a reversal of removal, noting the following points:
● Ensure all wiring connectors and harnesses are correctly refitting and secured.
● Reconnect the battery.
● Observing the precautions listed in Section 2, start the engine and allow it to idle. Check for leaks at the high-pressure fuel pipe unions with the engine idling. If satisfactory, increase the engine speed to 3000 rpm and check again for leaks. Take the car for a short road test and check for leaks once again on return. If any leaks are detected, obtain and fit additional new high-pressure fuel pipes as required. Do not attempt to cure even the slightest leak by further tightening of the pipe unions.

11 Fuel injectors – removal and refitting

Warning: Refer to the information contained in Section 2 before proceeding.

Removal

1 Remove the plastic cover from the top of the engine.

1.4 litre models

Note: *The following procedure describes the removal and refitting of the injectors as a complete set, although each injector may be removed individually if required. New copper washers, upper seals, injector clamp retaining nuts and a high-pressure fuel pipe will be required for each disturbed injector when refitting.*

2 Remove the cylinder head cover/air filter housing as described in Chapter 2C Section 4.
3 Clean the area around the high-pressure fuel pipes between the injectors and the accumulator rail, then unscrew the pipe unions. Use a second spanner to counterhold the union screwed in to the injector body **(see illustration 10.5)**. The injectors' screwed-in unions must not be allowed to move. Remove the pipes. Plug the openings in the accumulator rail and injectors to prevent dirt ingress.
4 Extract the retaining circlip and disconnect the leak-off pipe from each fuel injector **(see illustration).**
5 Unscrew the injector retaining bolt, and remove the clamp. If loose, recover the clamp locating dowel from the cylinder head **(see illustrations).**
6 Carefully pull or lever the injector from place. Do not lever against or pull on the solenoid housing at the top of the injector.

11.4 Prise out the circlip and disconnect the fuel leak-off pipe

7 Remove the copper washer and the upper seal from each injector, or from the cylinder head if they remained in place during injector removal **(see illustration)**. New copper washers and upper seals will be required for refitting. Cover the injector hole in the cylinder head to prevent dirt ingress.
8 Examine each injector visually for any signs of obvious damage or deterioration. If any defects are apparent, renew the injector(s).
9 If the injectors are in a satisfactory condition, plug the fuel pipe union (if not already done) and suitably cover the electrical element and the injector nozzle.
Caution: The injectors are manufactured to extremely close tolerances and must not be dismantled in any way. Do not unscrew the fuel pipe union on the side of the injector, or separate any parts of the injector body. Do not attempt to clean carbon deposits from the injector nozzle or carry out any form of ultrasonic or pressure testing.

1.6 litre engine

Note: *The following procedure describes the removal and refitting of the injectors as a complete set, although each injector may be removed individually if required. New copper washers, upper seals, and a high-pressure fuel pipe will be required for each disturbed injector when refitting.*

10 Remove the EGR cooler as described in Chapter 4C Section 2.
11 Undo the bolts, slacken the clamps and remove the air inlet ducting assembly from between the turbocharger and the inlet

11.5a Undo the injector clamp bolt…

11.5b… and remove the clamp

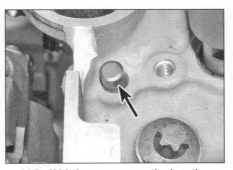

11.5c If it's loose, remove the locating dowel (arrowed)

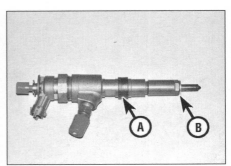

11.7 Fuel injector upper seal (A) and copper washer (B)

11.11a Inlet ducting clamps (arrowed)...

11.11b... and bolts (arrowed)

manifold. Note their fitted positions, and disconnect the various wiring plugs, as the assembly is withdrawn **(see illustrations)**.

12 Disconnect the injector wiring plugs.

13 Undo the bolts and move aside the wiring harness support bracket **(see illustration)**.

14 Release the manual fuel priming pump and its support.

15 Extract the retaining circlip and disconnect the leak-off pipe from each fuel injector **(see illustration)**.

16 Clean the area around the high-pressure fuel pipes between the injectors and the accumulator rail, then unscrew the pipe unions. Use a second spanner to counterhold the union screwed into the injector body **(see illustration)**. The injectors screwed-in unions must not be allowed to move. Remove the bracket above the accumulator rail unions, and then remove the pipes. Plug the openings in the accumulator rail and injectors to prevent dirt ingress.

17 Unscrew the injector retaining nuts, and carefully pull or lever the injector from place. If necessary, use an open-ended spanner and twist the injector to free it from position **(see illustrations)**. Do not lever against or pull on the solenoid housing at the top of the injector. Note down the injectors' position – if the injectors are to be refitted, they must be refitted to their original locations. If improved access is required, undo the bolts and remove the oil separator housing from the front of the cylinder head cover.

18 Remove the copper washer and the upper seal from each injector, or from the cylinder head if they remained in place during injector removal. New copper washers and upper seals will be required for refitting. Cover the injector hole in the cylinder head to prevent dirt ingress.

19 Examine each injector visually for any signs of obvious damage or deterioration. If any defects are apparent, renew the injector(s). Note down the 8-digit injector classification number – this may be needed during the refitting procedure if the ECU has been renewed **(see illustration)**.

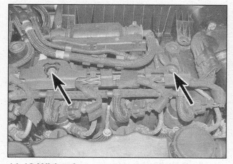

11.13 Wiring harness support bracket bolts (arrowed)

11.15 Prise out the clip and pull the return pipe from each injector

11.16 Use a second spanner to counterhold the high-pressure pipe union nuts

11.17a Injector retaining nuts (arrowed)

11.17b Use a spanner to twist the injector and free it from position

11.19 Note the injector classification number

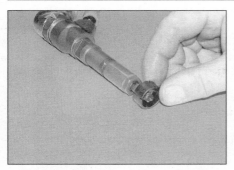

11.21a Locate a new upper seal on the body of the injector...

11.21b... and place a new copper washer on the injector nozzle

11.25 Fit the injectors into their original locations

20 If the injectors are in a satisfactory condition, plug the fuel pipe union (if not already done) and suitably cover the electrical element and the injector nozzle.

Caution: The injectors are manufactured to extremely close tolerances and must not be dismantled in any way. Do not unscrew the fuel pipe union on the side of the injector, or separate any parts of the injector body. Do not attempt to clean carbon deposits from the injector nozzle or carry out any form of ultrasonic or pressure testing.

Refitting

21 Locate a new upper seal on the body of each injector, and place a new copper washer on the injector nozzle **(see illustrations)**.
22 Refit the injector clamp locating dowels (where fitted) to the cylinder head.

1.4 litre engine

23 Place the injector clamp in the slot on each injector body and refit the injectors to the cylinder head. Guide the clamp over the mounting stud and onto the locating dowel as each injector is inserted. Ensure the upper injector seals are correctly located in the cylinder head.
24 Fit the washer and a new injector clamp retaining nut to each mounting stud. Tighten the nuts finger-tight only at this stage.

1.6 litre engine

25 Ensure the injector clamps are in place over their respective circlips on the injector bodies, and then fit the injectors into place in the cylinder head. If the original injectors are being refitted, ensure they are fitted into their original positions **(see illustration)**.
26 Fit the injector retaining bolts/nuts, but only finger-tighten them at this stage. When tightening the nuts/bolts, ensure the clamps stay horizontal.

All engines

27 Working on one fuel injector at a time, remove the blanking plugs from the fuel pipe unions on the accumulator rail and the relevant injector. Locate a new high-pressure fuel pipe over the unions and screw on the union nuts. Take care not to cross-thread the nuts or strain the fuel pipes as they are fitted. Once the union

nut threads have started, finger-tighten the nuts to the ends of the threads.
28 When all the fuel pipes are in place, tighten the injector clamp retaining nuts/bolts to the specified torque (and angle where applicable).
29 Using an open-ended spanner, hold each fuel pipe union in turn and tighten the union nut to the specified torque using a torque wrench and crow-foot adapter **(see illustration)**. Tighten all the disturbed union nuts in the same way.
30 On 1.6 litre engines, if new injectors have been fitted, their classification numbers must be programmed into the engine management ECU using dedicated diagnostic equipment/scanner. If this equipment is not available, entrust this task to a Peugeot dealer or suitably-equipped repairer. Note that it should be possible to drive the vehicle, albeit with reduced performance/increased emissions, to a repairer for the numbers to be programmed.
31 The remainder of refitting is a reversal of removal, noting the following points:
● Ensure all wiring connectors and harnesses are correctly refitting and secured.
● Reconnect the battery.
● Observing the precautions listed in Section 2, start the engine and allow it to idle. Check for leaks at the high-pressure fuel pipe unions with the engine idling. If satisfactory, increase the engine speed to 3000 rpm and check again for leaks. Take the car for a short road test and check for leaks once again on return. If any leaks are detected, obtain and fit additional new high-pressure fuel pipes as required. Do not attempt to cure even the slightest leak by further tightening of the pipe unions.

---

12 Electronic control system components – testing, removal and refitting

Testing

Note: *Before carrying out any of the following procedures, disconnect the battery (refer to Chapter 5A Section 4). Reconnect the battery on completion of work.*

11.29 Tighten the high-pressure pipe union nuts using a crow-foot adapter

1 If a fault is suspected in the electronic control side of the system, first ensure that all the wiring connectors are securely connected and free of corrosion. Ensure that the suspected problem is not of a mechanical nature, or due to poor maintenance; ie, check that the air cleaner filter element is clean, the engine breather hoses are clear and undamaged, and that the cylinder compression pressures are correct, referring to Chapters 1B and 2C or 2D for further information.
2 If these checks fail to reveal the cause of the problem, the vehicle should be taken to a Peugeot dealer or suitably-equipped garage for testing. A diagnostic socket is located behind the trim panel to the right of the steering column, to which a fault code reader or other suitable test equipment can be connected. By using the code reader or test equipment, the engine management ECU (and the various other vehicle system ECU's) can be interrogated, and any stored fault codes can be retrieved.
3 This will allow the fault to be quickly and simply traced, alleviating the need to test all the system components individually, which is a time-consuming operation that carries a risk of damaging the ECU.

Electronic control unit (ECU)

Note: *If a new ECU is to be fitted, this work must be entrusted to a Peugeot dealer or suitably-equipped specialist. It is necessary to initialise the new ECU after installation, which requires the use of dedicated Peugeot diagnostic equipment.*

12.5 Remove the battery cover(s)

12.6 Release the lever catches and disconnect the ECU wiring plugs

12.7a Lift the ECU up from the battery box – early models

12.7b ECU fitted between battery and inner wing panel – later models

4 The ECU is located on the left-hand side of the engine compartment, next to the battery.
5 Remove the plastic cover from the top of the battery tray (see illustration). The battery cover may vary depending on vehicle model and age.
6 Lift the ECU up from the battery box, and disconnect the wiring connectors (see illustration). Release the wiring loom from its securing clips.
7 The ECU can be now be removed from the battery box, complete with plastic cover (see illustrations).
8 Refitting is a reverse of the removal procedure ensuring the wiring connectors are securely reconnected.

Crankshaft speed/ position sensor

9 The crankshaft position sensor is located

12.11 Disconnect the crankshaft position sensor (arrowed) wiring plug

adjacent to the crankshaft pulley on the right-hand end of the engine.
10 Slacken the right-hand front road wheel bolts, and then jack the front of the vehicle up and support it on axle stands (see *Jacking and vehicle support*). Remove the right-hand front road wheel and inner wheel arch liner.
11 Disconnect the sensor wiring plug (see illustration).
12 Undo the bolt and remove the sensor.
13 Refitting is a reversal of removal, tightening the sensor retaining bolt securely.

Camshaft position sensor

Note: *Before carrying out the following procedure, disconnect the battery (refer to Chapter 5A Section 4). Reconnect the battery on completion of refitting.*

14 The camshaft position sensor is mounted on the right-hand end of the cylinder head cover, directly behind the camshaft sprocket.
15 Remove the upper timing belt cover.
16 Unplug the sensor wiring connector (see illustration).
17 Undo the bolt and pull the sensor from position (see illustration).
18 Upon refitting, position the sensor so that the air gap between the sensor end and the webs of the signal wheel is 1.2 mm, measured with feeler gauges, for a used sensor. If fitting a new sensor, the small tip of the sensor must be just touching one of the three webs of the signal wheel. Tighten the sensor retaining bolt to the specified torque (see illustration).
19 The remainder of refitting is a reversal of removal.

Accelerator pedal position sensor

20 On these models, the pedal sensor is integral with the accelerator pedal assembly. Refer to the relevant Section of Section 5 for the pedal removal procedure.

Coolant temperature sensor

21 Refer to Chapter 3, Section 7.

Fuel temperature sensor

Warning: Refer to the information contained in Section 2 before proceeding.
22 The sensor is clipped in to the plastic fuel manifold at the right-hand rear end of the cylinder head. To remove the sensor,

12.16 Disconnect the wiring connector

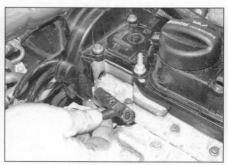

12.17 Remove the sensor

12.18 The gap between the end of the sensor and the webs of the signal wheel must be 1.2 mm (used sensor only)

12.22 Fuel temperature sensor (arrowed) – 1.4 litre engine

12.26a Air mass meter wiring plug (arrowed) – 1.4 litre engine...

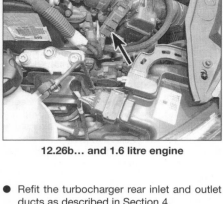

12.26b... and 1.6 litre engine

disconnect the wiring plug, and then unclip the sensor from the manifold. Be prepared for fuel spillage (see illustration).

23 Refitting is a reversal of removal.

24 Observing the precautions listed in Section 2, start the engine and allow it to idle. Check for leaks at the fuel temperature sensor with the engine idling. If satisfactory, increase the engine speed to 4000 rpm and check again for leaks. Take the car for a short road test and check for leaks once again on return. If any leaks are detected, obtain and fit a new sensor.

Air mass meter

25 Air mass meter is located in the inlet ducting from the air cleaner housing/intercooler. Remove the plastic cover from its mountings on top of the engine. Note: 1.6 litre DV6TED4 models fitted with particulate filter have a double air inlet mass meter, which is attached to four air pipes.

26 Disconnect the wiring plug connector(s) from the air mass meter (see illustrations).

27 Slacken the retaining clips and disconnect the air inlet ducting from either side of the air mass meter (two pipes each side on DV6TED4 engines). Plug or cover the turbocharger inlet duct, using clean rag to prevent any dirt or foreign material from entering. Where applicable, unbolt the air mass meter from the mounting bracket.

28 Refitting is reverse of the removal procedure.

Fuel pressure sensor

29 The fuel pressure sensor is integral with the accumulator rail, and is not available separately. Peugeot insist that the sensor is not removed from the rail.

Fuel pressure control valve

30 The fuel pressure control valve is integral with the high-pressure fuel pump and cannot be separated.

Preheating system control unit

31 Refer to Chapter 5C Section 3.

EGR solenoid valve

32 Refer to Chapter 4C, Section 2.

Vehicle speed sensor

33 The engine management ECU receives

the vehicle speed signal from the wheel speed sensors via the ABS ECU. Refer to Chapter 9 Section 22 for wheel speed sensor removal.

13 Inlet manifold – removal and refitting

1 The inlet manifold is an integral part of the cylinder head cover, see Chapters 2C, 2D or 2E or the removal of the cylinder head cover.

14 Exhaust manifold – removal and refitting

Removal

1 Remove the turbocharger as described in Section 16.

2 Undo the retaining nuts, recover the spacers, and remove the manifold. Recover the gasket (see illustrations).

Refitting

3 Refitting is a reverse of the removal procedure, bearing in mind the following points:

● Ensure that the manifold and cylinder head mating faces are clean, with all traces of old gasket removed.

● Use new gaskets when refitting the manifold to the cylinder head.

● Tighten the exhaust manifold retaining nuts to the specified torque.

● Refit the turbocharger rear inlet and outlet ducts as described in Section 4.

● Refit the exhaust front pipe as described in Section 18.

15 Turbocharger – description and precautions

Description

1 A turbocharger is fitted to increase engine efficiency by raising the pressure in the inlet manifold above atmospheric pressure. Instead of the air simply being sucked into the cylinders, it is forced in.

2 Energy for the operation of the turbocharger comes from the exhaust gas. The gas flows through a specially shaped housing (the turbine housing) and, in so doing, spins the turbine wheel. The turbine wheel is attached to a shaft, at the end of which is another vaned wheel known as the compressor wheel. The compressor wheel spins in its own housing, and compresses the inlet air on the way to the inlet manifold.

3 Boost pressure (the pressure in the inlet manifold) is limited by a wastegate, which diverts the exhaust gas away from the turbine wheel in response to a pressure-sensitive actuator. On later models, the turbocharger incorporates a variable inlet nozzle to improve boost pressure at low engine speeds.

4 The turbo shaft is pressure-lubricated by an oil feed pipe from the main oil gallery. The

14.2a Undo the exhaust manifold nuts, recover the spacers, and remove the manifold

14.2b Recover the manifold gasket

shaft 'floats' on a cushion of oil. A drain pipe returns the oil to the sump.

Precautions

5 The turbocharger operates at extremely high speeds and temperatures. Certain precautions must be observed, to avoid premature failure of the turbo, or injury to the operator.

● Do not operate the turbo with any of its parts exposed, or with any of its hoses removed. Foreign objects falling onto the rotating vanes could cause excessive damage, and (if ejected) personal injury.

● Do not race the engine immediately after start-up, especially if it is cold. Give the oil a few seconds to circulate.

● Always allow the engine to return to idle speed before switching it off – do not blip the throttle and switch off, as this will leave the turbo spinning without lubrication.

● Allow the engine to idle for several minutes before switching off after a high-speed run.

● Observe the recommended intervals for oil and filter changing, and use a reputable oil of the specified quality. Neglect of oil changing, or use of inferior oil, can cause carbon formation on the turbo shaft, leading to subsequent failure.

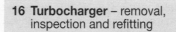

16 Turbocharger – removal, inspection and refitting

Removal

1 Apply the handbrake, then jack up the front of the vehicle and support it on axle stands (see *Jacking and vehicle support*). Undo the screws and remove the engine undershield. Disconnect the battery as described in Chapter 5A, Section 4.

2 Remove the radiator and fan assembly as described in Chapter 3 Section 4.

1.4 litre engine

3 Undo the heat shield mounting bolts **(see illustration)**, and remove the heat shield from above.

4 Release the clips and remove the turbocharger air inlet pipe and resonator box.

5 Undo the bolts and remove the upper heat shield from the manifold.

6 Slacken the clip securing the front pipe/catalytic converter to the turbocharger.

7 Undo the oil supply pipe banjo bolts and recover the sealing washers **(see illustrations)**.

8 Slacken the retaining clip and disconnect the oil return pipe from the turbocharger **(see illustration)**.

9 Unscrew the four nuts, and remove the turbocharger from the exhaust manifold **(see illustrations)**.

1.6 litre engine

10 Slacken the clamps, undo the bolts, and remove the air ducts to and from the

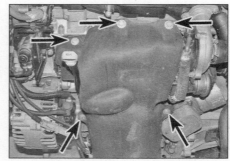

16.3 Undo the heat shield retaining bolts (arrowed)

16.7b... and the turbocharger

turbocharger and inlet manifold. Note their fitted positions and disconnect the various wiring plugs as the assembly is withdrawn.

16.8 Slacken the oil return hose clip (arrowed)

16.9b... and upper nuts securing the turbocharger

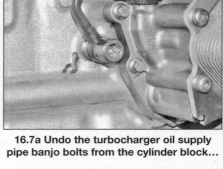

16.7a Undo the turbocharger oil supply pipe banjo bolts from the cylinder block...

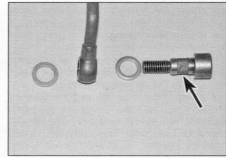

16.7c Note the filter incorporated into the banjo bolt (arrowed)

11 Disconnect the vacuum hose from the turbocharger wastegate control assembly **(see illustration)**.

12 Undo the mounting bolts **(see**

16.9a Undo the lower nuts (arrowed)...

16.11 Disconnect the vacuum pipe from the wastegate control assembly (arrowed)

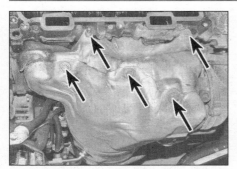

16.12 Undo the bolts and remove the turbocharger heat shield (arrowed)

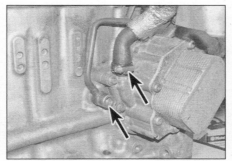

16.14 Turbocharger oil supply and return pipes (arrowed)

16.16 Undo the 3 nuts (arrowed – one hidden) and remove the support bracket (arrowed)

illustration), and remove the heat shield from above turbocharger.

13 Remove the catalytic converter/particulate filter (where applicable) as described in Section 18.

14 Undo the oil supply pipe banjo bolts and recover the sealing washers **(see illustration)**.

15 Slacken the retaining clip and disconnect the oil return pipe from the turbocharger and cylinder block.

16 Unscrew the four nuts, and the nut securing the support bracket, then remove the turbocharger from the exhaust manifold **(see illustration)**.

Inspection

17 With the turbocharger removed, inspect the housing for cracks or other visible damage.

18 Spin the turbine or the compressor wheel, to verify that the shaft is intact and to feel for excessive shake or roughness. Some play is normal, since in use, the shaft is 'floating' on a film of oil. Check that the wheel vanes are undamaged.

19 If oil contamination of the exhaust or induction passages is apparent, it is likely that turbo shaft oil seals have failed.

20 No DIY repair of the turbo is possible and none of the internal or external parts are available separately. If the turbocharger is suspect in any way a complete new unit must be obtained. Do not attempt to dismantle the turbocharger control assemblies.

Refitting

21 Refitting is a reverse of the removal procedure, bearing in mind the following points:
● Renew the turbocharger retaining nuts and gaskets.
● If a new turbocharger is being fitted, change the engine oil and filter. Also renew the filter in the oil feed pipe.
● Prime the turbocharger by injecting clean engine oil through the oil feed pipe union before reconnecting the union.

17 Intercooler –
removal and refitting

Note: *The following applies to the 1.6 litre models only.*

Removal

1 The intercooler is located at the front of the engine compartment, on the right-hand side of the radiator. First apply the handbrake, then jack up the front of the vehicle and support it on axle stands (see *Jacking and vehicle support*). Undo the screws and remove the engine undershield.

2 Where applicable, remove the engine top cover.

3 Remove the front bumper as described in Chapter 11 Section 6.

4 Remove the headlamps as described in Chapter 12 Section 7.

5 Remove the upper mounting bolts from each side of the radiator front panel **(see illustration)**.

6 Loosen the clips and disconnect the inlet and outlet ducts from the top of the intercooler **(see illustration)**.

7 Release the securing clip from the upper mounting on the intercooler, and then tilt it towards the engine **(see illustration)**.

8 Withdraw the intercooler upwards to release the lower locating pegs from the rubber grommets in the front panel, then remove it from the radiator front panel, making sure there are no hoses or wiring connected **(see illustration)**.

Refitting

9 Refitting is a reversal of removal.

17.5 Undo the front panel securing bolt (one side shown)

17.6 Disconnect the hose(s) from the intercooler

17.7 Unclip the intercooler – front panel removed for clarity

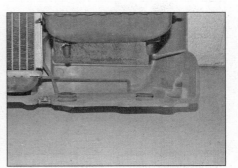

17.8 Check the lower rubber grommets are in position

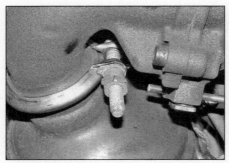

18.8 Catalytic converter-to-turbocharger clamp bolt

18.9 Catalytic converter mounting bolts (arrowed)

18.10a Unscrew the pressure take-off union from the side of the catalyst/filter...

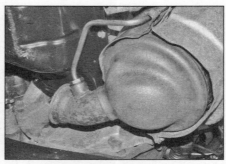

18.10b... and the one at the base

18 Exhaust system – general information and component renewal

General information

1 According to model, the exhaust system consists of either two or three sections. Three-section systems consist of a catalytic converter, an intermediate pipe, and a tailpipe. On two-section systems, the intermediate pipe and rear silencer are combined to form a single section.
2 The exhaust joints are of either the spring-loaded ball type (to allow for movement in the exhaust system) or clamp-ring type.

3 The system is suspended throughout its entire length by rubber mountings.
4 To remove the system or part of the system, first jack up the front or rear of the car and support it on axle stands (see *Jacking and vehicle support*). Alternatively, position the car over an inspection pit or on car ramps. Undo the screws and remove the engine undershield.
5 If the intermediate pipe/rear silencer section of the exhaust needs renewing, it is available as a two-part system, check with your local exhaust dealer. The original exhaust will need to be cut, just in front of the rear axle. Before making any cuts, it is advisable to get the new part of the exhaust system; this can then be measured to fit the original.

Catalytic converter removal

1.4 litre engine

6 To gain better access it may be necessary to remove the radiator and fan assembly as described in Chapter 3 Section 4.
7 Undo the bolts and remove the heat shield from the catalytic converter (see illustrations 16.3). Where applicable, disconnect the oxygen sensor wiring plug connectors.
8 Slacken the retaining clamps joining the catalytic converter to the turbocharger and exhaust pipe. Take care not to damage the flexible section of the front exhaust pipe (see illustration).
9 Undo the bolts securing the catalytic converter to the cylinder block and manoeuvre it down and out of the engine compartment (see illustration).

Catalytic converter/ particulate filter removal

1.6 litre engine

10 On models with a particulate filter fitted, unscrew the pressure take off unions from the side and base of the assembly (see illustrations).
11 On models without a particulate filter, disconnect the oxygen sensor wiring plug connectors.
12 Undo the bolts and remove the heat shield from the catalytic converter/particulate filter.
13 Slacken the retaining clamps joining the catalytic converter to the turbocharger, and exhaust pipe. Take care not to damage the flexible section of the front exhaust pipe (see illustration).
14 Slacken the clamp securing the catalytic converter to the turbocharger.
15 Undo the 2 nuts securing the catalytic converter to the cylinder block and manoeuvre it down and out of the engine compartment (see illustration).
16 If required, note its fitted position, then slacken the clamp and detach the particulate filter from the base of the catalytic converter (see illustration).

18.13 Exhaust pipe-to-catalyst/filter clamp (arrowed)

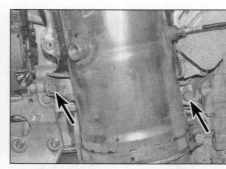

18.15 Catalytic converter/particulate filter retaining nuts (arrowed)

18.16 Undo the clamp (arrowed) and slide the particulate filter from the catalytic converter

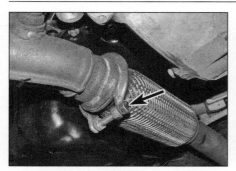

18.17 Front pipe/catalytic converter-to flexible-pipe retaining clamp

18.18a Undo the two upper retaining nuts (arrowed)

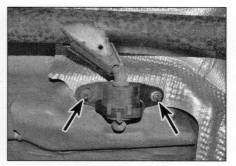

18.18b Middle section mounting nuts (arrowed)...

Intermediate pipe/ tailpipe/rear silencer removal

17 Undo the retaining nut(s) and disconnect the exhaust system from the front pipe/ catalytic converter **(see illustration)**.

18 Support the exhaust system and then undo the retaining nuts and free all the mounting rubbers from under the vehicle **(see illustrations)**.

19 If only part of the system needs to be renewed (see paragraph 5), the exhaust can be cut while it is still fitted to the vehicle; this will make it easier for removal.

20 If the system is being removed in one piece, it may be necessary to remove the rear shock absorbers and springs (see Chapter 10 Section 13 & 14), to allow enough room for the exhaust to be withdrawn from over the rear axle.

Heat shield(s) removal

21 The heat shields are secured to the underside of the body by various nuts and fasteners. If a shield is being removed to gain access to a component located behind it, remove the retaining nuts and/or fastener, and manoeuvre the shield out of position **(see illustration)**. On some models it may be necessary to free the exhaust system from its mountings to gain the clearance necessary to remove the larger heat shield.

18.18c... and rear mounting retaining nuts (arrowed)

18.21 Heat shield has various fasteners (arrowed)

Refitting

22 Each section is refitted by reversing the removal sequence, noting the following points:

● Ensure that all traces of corrosion have been removed from the flanges and renew all necessary gaskets.

● Inspect the rubber mountings for signs of damage or deterioration, and renew as necessary.

● Where joints are secured together by a clamping ring, apply a smear of exhaust system jointing paste to the flange joint

to ensure a gas-tight seal. Insert the bolt through the clamping ring and fit the washer.

● Prior to tightening the exhaust system fasteners, ensure that all rubber mountings are correctly located, and that there is adequate clearance between the exhaust system and vehicle underbody.

● On models fitted with a particulate filter, have the additive reservoir filled by your local dealer. If renewing the particulate filter, seal the old filter in the bag of the new filter and dispose of it correctly.

Chapter 4 Part C
Emission control systems

Contents

Degrees of difficulty

Easy, suitable for novice with little experience	Fairly easy, suitable for beginner with some experience	Fairly difficult, suitable for competent DIY mechanic	Difficult, suitable for experienced DIY mechanic	Very difficult, suitable for expert DIY or professional

1 General Information

1 All petrol engines use unleaded petrol and also have various other features built into the fuel system to help minimise harmful emissions. In addition, all engines are equipped with the crankcase emission control system described below. All engines are also equipped with a catalytic converter and an evaporative emission control system.

2 All diesel engines are also designed to meet the strict emission requirements and are equipped with a crankcase emission control system and a catalytic converter. To further reduce exhaust emissions, all diesel engines are also fitted with an exhaust gas recirculation (EGR) system. Additionally, some of the 1.6 litre diesel models may be equipped with a particulate emission filter, which uses porous silicon carbide substrate to trap particulates of carbon as the exhaust gases pass through.

3 The emission control systems function as follows.

Petrol engines

Crankcase emission control

4 To reduce the emission of unburned hydrocarbons from the crankcase into the atmosphere, the engine is sealed and the blow-by gases and oil vapour are drawn from inside the crankcase, through a wire mesh oil separator, into the inlet tract to be burned by the engine during normal combustion.

5 Under all conditions the gases are forced out of the crankcase by the (relatively) higher crankcase pressure; if the engine is worn, the raised crankcase pressure (due to increased blow-by) will cause some of the flow to return under all manifold conditions.

Exhaust emission control

6 To minimise the amount of pollutants which escape into the atmosphere, a catalytic converter is fitted in the exhaust system. On all models where a catalytic converter is fitted, the system is of the closed-loop type, in which oxygen (lambda) sensors in the exhaust system provides the fuel injection/ignition system ECU with constant feedback, enabling the ECU to adjust the mixture to provide the best possible conditions for the converter to operate.

7 The oxygen sensors have a heating element built-in that is controlled by the ECU through the oxygen sensor relay to quickly bring the sensor's tip to an efficient operating temperature. The sensor's tip is sensitive to oxygen and sends the ECU a varying voltage depending on the amount of oxygen in the exhaust gases; if the inlet air/fuel mixture is too rich, the exhaust gases are low in oxygen so the sensor sends a low-voltage signal, the voltage rising as the mixture weakens and the amount of oxygen rises in the exhaust gases. Peak conversion efficiency of all major pollutants occurs if the inlet air/fuel mixture is maintained at the chemically correct ratio for the complete combustion of petrol of 14.7 parts (by weight) of air to 1 part of fuel (the 'stoichiometric' ratio). The sensor output voltage alters in a large step at this point, the ECU using the signal change as a reference point and correcting the inlet air/fuel mixture accordingly by altering the fuel injector pulse width.

Evaporative emission control

8 To minimise the escape into the atmosphere of unburned hydrocarbons, an evaporative emission control system is fitted to models equipped with a catalytic converter. The fuel tank filler cap is sealed and a charcoal canister is mounted behind the wheel arch liner under the right-hand side front wing to collect the petrol vapours generated in the tank when the car is parked. It stores them until they can be cleared from the canister (under the control of the fuel injection/ignition system ECU) via the purge valve into the inlet tract to be burned by the engine during normal combustion.

9 To ensure that the engine runs correctly when it is cold and/or idling and to protect the catalytic converter from the effects of an over-rich mixture, the purge control valve is not opened by the ECU until the engine has warmed-up, and the engine is under load; the valve solenoid is then modulated on and off to allow the stored vapour to pass into the inlet tract.

Diesel models

Crankcase emission control

10 Refer to the description for petrol engines.

Exhaust emission control

11 To minimise the level of exhaust pollutants released into the atmosphere, a catalytic converter is fitted in the exhaust system of all models.

12 The catalytic converter consists of a canister containing a fine mesh impregnated with a catalyst material, over which the hot exhaust gases pass. The catalyst speeds up the oxidation of harmful carbon monoxide, un-burnt hydrocarbons and soot, effectively reducing the quantity of harmful products released into the atmosphere via the exhaust gases.

Exhaust gas recirculation system

13 This system is designed to recirculate small quantities of exhaust gas into the inlet tract, and therefore into the combustion process. This process reduces the level of oxides of nitrogen present in the final exhaust gas, which is released into the atmosphere.

14 The volume of exhaust gas recirculated is controlled by the system electronic control unit.

15 A vacuum-operated valve is fitted to the exhaust manifold, to regulate the quantity of exhaust gas recirculated. The valve is operated by the vacuum supplied by the solenoid valve.

Particulate filter system (where fitted)

16 The particulate filter is combined with the catalytic converter in the exhaust system, and its purpose it to trap particulates of carbon (soot) as the exhaust gases pass through, in order to comply with latest emission regulations.

17 The filter can be automatically regenerated (cleaned) by the system's ECU on-board the vehicle. The engine's high-pressure injection system is utilised to inject fuel into the exhaust gases during the post-injection period; this causes the filter temperature to increase sufficiently to oxidise the particulates, leaving an ash residue. The regeneration period is automatically controlled by the on-board ECU. Subsequently, at the correct service interval the filter must be removed from the exhaust system, and renewed.

18 To assist the combustion of the trapped carbon (soot) during the regeneration process, a fuel additive (cerium-based Eolys) is automatically mixed with the diesel fuel in the fuel tank. The additive is stored in a container attached to the right-hand side of the fuel tank, and the ECU regulates the amount of additive to send to the fuel tank by means of an additive injector located on the top of the fuel tank.

2 Emission control systems – testing and component renewal

Petrol models

Crankcase emission control

1 The components of this system require no attention other than to check that the hose(s) are clear and undamaged at regular intervals.

Evaporative emission control

2 If the system is thought to be faulty, disconnect the hoses from the charcoal canister and purge control valve and check that they are clear by blowing through them. If the purge control valve or charcoal canister is thought to be faulty, they must be renewed.

Charcoal canister renewal

3 On early models, the charcoal canister is located under the wheel arch on the right-hand side. To gain access, slacken the right-hand front roadwheel bolts, jack up the front of the car and support it on axle stands. Remove the roadwheel, push in the centre pins then prise out the plastic expanding rivets, and remove the wheel arch liner. Gently prise the canister from its three retaining clips and lower it from the top of the wheel arch.

4 On later models, it is located to the right-hand side of the fuel tank **(see**

2.4 Charcoal canister location (later models)

illustration), under the vehicle. To gain access, jack up the right-hand rear of the car and support it on axle stands. Gently prise the canister from its retaining clips and withdraw it from the side of the fuel tank.

5 Identify the location of the two hoses then depress the quick-release button and disconnect hoses from the purge valve and the canister. Disconnect the wiring plug connector from the purge valve **(see illustration)**.

6 Refitting is a reverse of the removal procedure ensuring that the hoses are correctly reconnected.

Purge valve renewal

7 The purge valve is integral with the canister, and cannot be renewed separately.

Exhaust emission control

8 The performance of the catalytic converter can be checked only by measuring the exhaust gases using a good-quality, carefully-calibrated exhaust gas analyser.

9 If the CO level at the tailpipe is too high, the vehicle should be taken to a Peugeot dealer or specialist so that the complete fuel injection and ignition systems, including the oxygen sensor, can be thoroughly checked using the special diagnostic equipment. Once these have been checked and are known to be free from faults, the fault must be in the catalytic converter, which must be renewed as described in Part A of this Chapter.

Catalytic converter renewal

10 Refer to Part A of this Chapter.

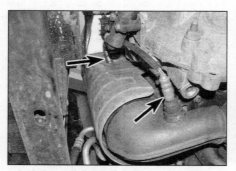

2.12 Oxygen (lambda) sensors – 1.6 litre VTi model

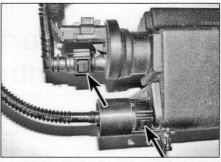

2.5 Depress the quick-release buttons, and disconnect the hoses (arrowed)

Oxygen sensor renewal

11 The oxygen sensor is delicate and will not work if it is dropped or knocked, if its power supply is disrupted, or if any cleaning materials are used on it.

12 Trace the wiring back from the oxygen sensor(s), which are located before and after the catalytic converters **(see illustration)**. Disconnect both wiring connectors and free the wiring from any relevant retaining clips or ties.

13 Unscrew the sensor from the exhaust system front pipe/manifold and remove it along with its sealing washer **(see illustration)**.

14 Refitting is a reverse of the removal procedure using a new sealing washer. Prior to installing the sensor apply a smear of high temperature grease to the sensor threads. Ensure that the sensor is securely tightened and that the wiring is correctly routed and in no danger of contacting either the exhaust system or engine.

Diesel models

Crankcase emission control

15 The components of this system require no attention other than to check that the hose(s) are clear and undamaged at regular intervals.

Exhaust emission control

16 The performance of the catalytic converter can be checked only by measuring the exhaust gases using a good-quality, carefully-calibrated exhaust gas analyser.

2.13 Removing the upper sensor

2.23a The EGR pipe is secured to the manifold by two screws (arrowed)…

2.23b… and to the cylinder block by one bolt (arrowed)

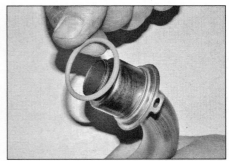

2.23c A new EGR pipe-to-manifold O-ring seal must be fitted

2.26a EGR solenoid valve retaining bolts (arrowed) – 1.4 litre

2.26b EGR valve mounting bolts (arrowed – one hidden) – 1.6 litre DOHC

2.26c EGR valve – 1.6 litre SOHC

17 If the catalytic converter is thought to be faulty, before assuming the catalytic converter is faulty, it is worth checking the problem is not due to a faulty injector. Refer to your Peugeot dealer for further information.

Catalytic converter renewal

18 Refer to Part B of this Chapter.

Exhaust gas recirculation system

19 Testing of the system should ideally be entrusted to a Peugeot dealer since a vacuum pump and vacuum gauge are required.

EGR valve renewal

20 The EGR valve is located on the left-hand rear of the cylinder head.
21 Carefully pull the plastic cover upwards from the top of the engine.
22 Remove the air cleaner housing and air ducting as described in Chapter 4B Sec-

tion 4. Disconnect the battery as described in Chapter 5A Section 4.
23 Undo the two retaining bolts and securing clamp, then disconnect the inlet supply pipe from the heat exchanger (where fitted) **(see illustrations)**.
24 On models with a heat exchanger fitted, slacken and remove the securing clamp from between the heat exchanger and EGR valve. Undo the heat exchanger mounting bolts and move it to one side.
25 Disconnect the wiring connector from the top of the EGR valve.
26 There are two bolts securing the EGR valve, undo the bolts and remove the valve. Discard the metal gasket from the valve, and the O-ring seal from the pipe – new ones must be fitted **(see illustrations)**.
27 Refitting is a reversal of removal.

EGR heat exchanger renewal

28 Drain the cooling system (see Chapter 1B Section 22). Alternatively, fit hose clamps to the hoses connected to the EGR heat exchanger.
29 Proceed as described in paragraphs 20 to 23.
30 Loosen the clips and disconnect the coolant hoses from the EGR heat exchanger **(see illustrations)**.
31 Refitting is a reversal of removal.

Particulate filter fuel additive system

32 It is possible to check the fuel additive pump delivery pressure, but this should be made by a Peugeot dealer or specialist.

Fuel additive reservoir renewal

Note: *Ideally, the additive reservoir should be empty before removing it, otherwise take precautions against spillage.*

 Warning: Wear protective gloves and eye protection when handling the reservoir.

33 To remove the fuel additive reservoir, chock the front wheels then jack up the rear of the vehicle and support on axle stands (see *Jacking and vehicle support*). The reservoir is attached to the left-hand side of the fuel tank.
34 Remove the undershield beneath the fuel tank/additive reservoir (where fitted).
35 Note the location of the additive pipes on the reservoir, then depress the release buttons and disconnect them. Tape over or plug the openings to prevent dirt ingress.
36 Disconnect the wiring from the level sensor on the reservoir.

2.30a EGR cooler-to-valve clamp (arrowed)…

2.30b… EGR cooler-to-pipe clamp (arrowed)

2.42 The pressure differential sensor is located at the top, right-hand corner of the radiator – 1.6 litre DOHC model show

37 Undo the securing nuts and remove the reservoir.

38 Have a suitable container available to catch spilled additive, undo the two retaining screws and detach the reservoir.

39 Refitting is a reversal of removal.

40 Have the reservoir refilled by a Peugeot dealer or specialist.

Particulate filter

41 Renewal of the particulate filter is described in part B of this Chapter.

Pressure differential sensor

42 This sensor measures the pressure at the entrance and exit of the particulate filter, and is located in the engine compartment **(see illustration)**.

43 Note their fitted positions, and then disconnect the rubber hoses and wiring plug from the sensor.

44 Undo the mounting bolts and remove the sensor.

---

3 Catalytic converter – general information and precautions

1 The catalytic converter is a reliable and simple device which needs no maintenance in itself, but there are some facts of which an owner should be aware if the converter is to function properly for its full service life.

Petrol models

- DO NOT use leaded petrol or LRP – the lead will coat the precious metals, and will eventually destroy the converter.
- Always keep the ignition and fuel systems well maintained to the service schedule.
- If the engine develops a misfire, do not drive the car at all (or at least as little as possible) until the fault is cured.
- DO NOT push- or tow-start the car – this will soak the catalytic converter in unburned fuel, causing it to overheat when the engine does start.
- DO NOT switch off the ignition at high engine speeds.
- DO NOT use fuel or engine oil additives – these may contain substances harmful to the catalytic converter.
- DO NOT continue to use the car if the engine burns oil to the extent of leaving a visible trail of blue smoke.
- Remember that the catalytic converter operates at very high temperatures. DO NOT, therefore, park the car in dry undergrowth, over long grass or piles of dead leaves after a long run.
- Remember that the catalytic converter is FRAGILE – do not strike it with tools.
- In some cases a sulphurous smell (like that of rotten eggs) may be noticed from the exhaust. This is common to many catalytic converter-equipped cars and once the car has covered a few thousand miles the problem should disappear.
- If the converter is no longer effective it must be renewed.

Diesel models

2 Refer to parts f, g, h and i of the petrol models information given above.

Chapter 5 Part A
Starting and charging systems

Contents

Section number

Alternator – removal and refitting 7
Alternator – testing and overhaul 8
Alternator drivebelt – removal, refitting and tensioning 6
Battery – disconnection, removal and refitting 4
Battery – testing and charging 3
Charging system – testing 5
Electrical fault finding – general information 2

Section number

General information and precautions 1
Ignition switch – removal and refitting 12
Oil level sensor – removal and refitting 14
Oil pressure warning light switch – removal and refitting 13
Starter motor – removal and refitting 10
Starter motor – testing and overhaul 11
Starting system – testing 9

Degrees of difficulty

| Easy, suitable for novice with little experience | Fairly easy, suitable for beginner with some experience 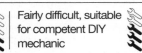 | Fairly difficult, suitable for competent DIY mechanic 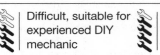 | Difficult, suitable for experienced DIY mechanic | Very difficult, suitable for expert DIY or professional |

Specifications

System type . . . . 12 volt, negative earth

Battery
Type . . . . Low maintenance or 'maintenance-free' sealed for life
Charge condition:
  Poor . . . . 12.5 volts
  Normal . . . . 12.6 volts
  Good . . . . 12.7 volts

Alternator
Type . . . . Denso, Bosch, Magneti Marelli, Valeo or Mitsubishi (depending on model)
Rating:
  Petrol models . . . . 70, 80, 90 or 120 amp
  Diesel models . . . . 150 amp

Starter motor
Type . . . . Mitsubishi, Valeo, Ducellier, Iskra, or Bosch (depending on model)

Torque wrench settings	Nm	lbf ft
Alternator mounting bolts	40	30
Oil pressure switch	30	22
Starter motor:		
Diesel models	20	15
Petrol models	35	26

1 General information and precautions

General information

1 The engine electrical system consists mainly of the charging and starting systems. Because of their engine-related functions, these components are covered separately from the body electrical devices such as the lights, instruments, etc (which are covered in Chapter 12). On petrol engine models refer to Part B for information on the ignition system, and on diesel models refer to Part C for information on the preheating system.

2 The electrical system is of the 12 volt negative earth type.

3 The battery is of the low maintenance or 'maintenance-free' (sealed for life) type and is charged by the alternator, which is belt-driven from the crankshaft pulley.

4 The starter motor is of the pre-engaged type incorporating an integral solenoid. On starting, the solenoid moves the drive pinion into engagement with the flywheel ring gear before the starter motor is energised. Once the engine has started, a one-way clutch prevents the motor armature being driven by the engine.

Precautions

5 Further details of the various systems are given in the relevant Sections of this Chapter. While some repair procedures are given, the usual course of action is to renew the component concerned.

6 It is necessary to take extra care when working on the electrical system to avoid damage to semi-conductor devices (diodes and transistors), and to avoid the risk of personal injury. In addition to the precautions given in Safety first0,2 ! at the beginning of this manual, observe the following when working on the system:

● Always remove rings, watches, etc, before working on the electrical system. Even with the battery disconnected, capacitive discharge could occur if a component's live terminal is earthed through a metal object. This could cause a shock or nasty burn.

● Do not reverse the battery connections. Components such as the alternator, electronic control units, or any other components having semi-conductor circuitry could be irreparably damaged.

● If the engine is being started using jump leads and a slave battery, connect the batteries positive-to-positive and negative-to-negative (see Jump starting). This also applies when connecting a battery charger.

● Never disconnect the battery terminals, the alternator, any electrical wiring or any test instruments when the engine is running.

● Do not allow the engine to turn the alternator when the alternator is not connected.

● Never 'test' for alternator output by 'flashing' the output lead to earth.

● Never use an ohmmeter of the type incorporating a hand-cranked generator for circuit or continuity testing.

● Always ensure that the battery is disconnected when working on the electrical system.

● Before using electric-arc welding equipment on the car, disconnect the battery, alternator and components such as the fuel injection/ignition electronic control unit to protect them from the risk of damage.

2 Electrical fault finding – general information

1 Refer to Chapter 12.

3 Battery – testing and charging

Testing

Standard and low maintenance battery

1 If the vehicle covers a small annual mileage, it is worthwhile checking the specific gravity of the electrolyte every three months to determine the state of charge of the battery. Use a hydrometer to make the check and compare the results with the following table. Note that the specific gravity readings assume an electrolyte temperature of 15°C; for every 10°C below 15°C subtract 0.007. For every 10°C above 15°C add 0.007.

	Above 25°C	Below 25°C
Fully-charged	1.210 to 1.230	1.270 to 1.290
70% charged	1.170 to 1.190	1.230 to 1.250
Discharged	1.050 to 1.070	1.110 to 1.130

2 If the battery condition is suspect, first check the specific gravity of electrolyte in each cell. A variation of 0.040 or more between any cells indicates loss of electrolyte or deterioration of the internal plates.

3 If the specific gravity variation is 0.040 or more, the battery should be renewed. If the cell variation is satisfactory but the battery is discharged, it should be charged as described later in this Section.

Maintenance-free battery

4 In cases where a 'sealed for life' maintenance-free battery is fitted, topping-up and testing of the electrolyte in each cell is not possible. The condition of the battery can therefore only be tested using a battery condition indicator or a voltmeter.

3.5 Battery charge condition indicator (arrowed)

5 Certain models may be fitted with a 'Delco' type maintenance-free battery, with a built-in charge condition indicator. The indicator is located in the top of the battery casing, and indicates the condition of the battery from its colour **(see illustration)**. If the indicator shows green, then the battery is in a good state of charge. If the indicator shows black, then the battery requires charging, as described later in this Section. If the indicator shows blue, then the electrolyte level in the battery is too low to allow further use, and the battery should be renewed.

Caution: Do not attempt to charge, load or jump-start a battery when the indicator shows clear/yellow.

All battery types

6 If testing the battery using a voltmeter, connect the voltmeter across the battery and compare the result with those given in the Specifications under 'charge condition'. The test is only accurate if the battery has not been subjected to any kind of charge for the previous six hours. If this is not the case, switch on the headlights for 30 seconds, then wait four to five minutes before testing the battery after switching off the headlights. All other electrical circuits must be switched off, so check that the doors and tailgate are fully shut when making the test.

7 If the voltage reading is less than 12.2 volts, then the battery is discharged, whilst a reading of 12.2 to 12.4 volts indicates a partially-discharged condition.

8 If the battery is to be charged, remove it from the vehicle (Section 4) and charge it as described later in this Section.

Charging

Note: *The following is intended as a guide only. Always refer to the manufacturer's recommendations (often printed on a label attached to the battery) before charging a battery.*

Standard and low maintenance battery

9 Charge the battery at a rate of 3.5 to 4 amps and continue to charge the battery at this rate until no further rise in specific gravity is noted over a four hour period.

10 Alternatively, a trickle charger charging at the rate of 1.5 amps can safely be used overnight.

11 Specially rapid 'boost' charges that are claimed to restore the power of the battery in 1 to 2 hours are not recommended, as they can cause serious damage to the battery plates through overheating.

12 While charging the battery, note that the temperature of the electrolyte should never exceed 38°C.

Maintenance-free battery

13 This battery type takes considerably longer to fully recharge than the standard type, the time taken being dependent on the extent of discharge, but it can take anything up to three days.

14 A constant voltage type charger is required to be set, when connected, to 13.9 to 14.9 volts with a charger current below 25 amps. Using this method, the battery should be usable within three hours, giving a voltage reading of 12.5 volts, but this is for a partially-discharged battery and, as mentioned, full charging can take considerably longer.

15 If the battery is to be charged from a fully-discharged state (condition reading less than 12.2 volts), have it recharged by your Peugeot dealer or local automotive electrician, as the charge rate is higher and constant supervision during charging is necessary.

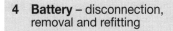

4 Battery – disconnection, removal and refitting

Note: *The audio unit fitted as standard equipment by Peugeot is equipped with an anti-theft system, to deter thieves. If the power source is disconnected, the unit will automatically recode itself as long as it is still fitted to the correct vehicle. If the unit is removed it will not operate in another vehicle.*

Note: *Prior to disconnecting the battery, wait 15 minutes after switching off the ignition to*

4.3a Remove the front cover from the battery…

4.4a Remove the rear cover from the battery…

4.3b… then lift up the quick-release lever and disconnect the positive lead

4.4b… and disconnect the negative lead

allow the vehicle's ECU's to store all learnt values in their memories.

Removal

1 Prior to disconnecting the battery, close all windows and the sunroof, and ensure that the vehicle alarm system is deactivated (see Owner's Handbook or Chapter 12, Section 20).

 Warning: Make sure the keys are not left in the car, in case of the vehicle locking system activating and locking all the doors.

2 The battery is located on the left-hand side of the engine compartment.

Early models

3 First lift off the battery front cover, then lift up the quick-release lever and remove the battery positive lead **(see illustrations)**.

4 Lift off the battery rear cover, then undo the retaining bolt and remove the battery negative lead **(see illustrations)**.

5 Release the securing clip and tilt the battery towards the engine, then lift it out from the battery tray **(see illustrations)**.

Later petrol models

6 On later petrol engines, unclip the battery one-piece cover from over the battery **(see illustration)**.

4.5a Release the securing clamp…

4.5b… and lift out the battery

4.6 Unclip the battery cover

4.7a Release the retaining clips...

4.7b ...to remove the ECU cover, if required

4.8 Disconnect the battery terminals

4.11 Release the electrical panel from the cover

4.12a Lift off the battery cover...

7 Release the retaining clip and withdraw the plastic cover from over the ECU, if required (see illustrations).

8 Undo the retaining bolt and remove the battery negative lead, then lift up the quick-release lever and remove the battery positive lead (see illustration).

9 Release the securing clip (or remove bolt), then tilt the battery towards the engine and lift it out from the battery tray.

Later diesel models

10 First lift up the battery positive terminal front cover, then lift up the quick-release lever and disconnect the battery positive lead.

11 Release the securing clips at the front of the battery, then slide the electrical connector panel towards the rear of the battery to release it from the top of the battery cover (see illustration).

12 Lift off the battery cover, then undo the retaining nut and disconnect the negative lead from the battery (see illustrations).

13 Remove the ECU from the side of the battery, as described in Chapter 4B Section 12.

14 Undo the battery retaining bolt and remove the battery from the engine compartment (see illustration).

Battery tray removal – early models

15 If the battery tray needs to be removed, first remove the ECU (see Chapter 4A or 4B).

16 Remove the air resonator and ducting from around the battery tray by releasing the fasteners and withdrawing them from the engine compartment (see illustration).

4.12b ...and disconnect the negative terminal

4.14 Undo bolt and remove battery

4.16 Remove the air resonator box (depending on model)

4.17a Release the wiring bracket...

4.17b... and unclip the wiring loom

4.18 Disconnect the air vent tube

4.19 Unclip the fusebox from the battery tray

4.20 Release any wiring securing clips

17 Release the retaining clip from around the wiring loom and then unclip it from the bottom of the battery tray **(see illustrations)**.
18 Disconnect the battery tray air vent pipe from the front panel **(see illustration)**.
19 Unclip the fusebox from the rear of the battery tray **(see illustration)**.
20 Unclip the wiring connector from the rear corner of the battery tray **(see illustration)**.
21 Undo the mounting bolts, carefully move aside all cables and hoses, and then lift the battery box out of the engine compartment **(see illustrations)**.

Battery tray removal – later models
22 Undo the mounting bolts, and lift out

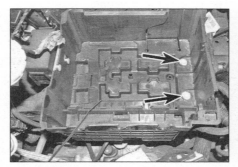

4.21a Undo the bolts (arrowed)...

4.21b... and remove the battery box

the plastic part of the battery tray **(see illustration)**.
23 Release the wiring loom retaining clips

from around the side and rear of the metal part of the battery tray bracket **(see illustrations)**.
24 Undo the mounting bolts and lift the metal

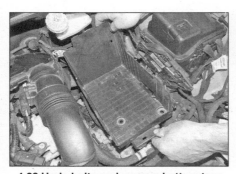

4.22 Undo bolts and remove battery tray

4.23a Unclip the wiring connectors from the side...

4.23b ...and the rear of the mounting bracket

part of the battery tray mounting bracket out of the engine compartment **(see illustration)**.

Refitting

25 Refitting is a reversal of removal, but smear petroleum jelly on the terminals after reconnecting the leads, and reconnect the negative lead first, and positive the lead last.
26 With the battery reconnected, switch on the ignition and wait at least 1 minute before starting the engine. This will allow the vehicle electronic systems and control units to stabilise. Also refer to Chapter 12, Section 20, on models with the anti-theft alarm system.

5 Charging system – testing

Note: *Refer to the warnings given in 'Safety first!' and in Section 1 of this Chapter before starting work.*

1 If the ignition warning light fails to illuminate when the ignition is switched on, first check the alternator wiring connections for security. If satisfactory, check that the warning light bulb has not blown, and that the bulbholder is secure in its location in the instrument panel. If the light still fails to illuminate, check the continuity of the warning light feed wire from the alternator to the bulbholder. If all is satisfactory, the alternator is at fault and should be renewed or taken to an auto-electrician for testing and repair.
2 If the ignition warning light illuminates when the engine is running, stop the engine and check that the drivebelt is correctly fitted and tensioned (see Chapter 1A Section 13 for petrol engines and Chapter 1B Section 16 for diesel engines) and that the alternator connections are secure. If all is so far satisfactory, have the alternator checked by an auto-electrician for testing and repair.
3 If the alternator output is suspect even though the warning light functions correctly, the regulated voltage may be checked as follows.
4 Connect a voltmeter across the battery terminals and start the engine.
5 Increase the engine speed until the voltmeter reading remains steady; the reading

4.24 Undo the bolts and remove the mounting bracket

should be approximately 12 to 13 volts, and no more than 14.2 volts.
6 Switch on as many electrical accessories (eg, the headlights, heated rear window and heater blower) as possible, and check that the alternator maintains the regulated voltage of around 13 to 14.2 volts.
7 If the regulated voltage is not as stated, the fault may be due to worn brushes, weak brush springs, a faulty voltage regulator, a faulty diode, a severed phase winding or worn or damaged slip-rings. The alternator should be renewed or taken to an auto-electrician for testing and repair.

6 Alternator drivebelt – removal, refitting and tensioning

1 Refer to the procedure given for the auxiliary drivebelt in Chapter 1A Section 13 for petrol engines and Chapter 1B Section 16 for diesel engines.

7 Alternator – removal and refitting

Removal

1 Disconnect the battery (see Section 4). Remove the plastic cover from the top of the engine.

7.6 Undo the auxiliary drivebelt tensioner bolts (arrowed)

2 Remove the auxiliary drivebelt as described in Chapter 1A or 1B.
3 On some models, it may be necessary to remove the air-conditioning compressor, as described in Chapter 3 Section 12, to make removal of the alternator easier.
4 So that access to the alternator can be gained both from above and below, apply the handbrake then jack up the front of the vehicle and support it on axle stands (see *Jacking and vehicle support*). Release the screws and remove the engine undershield (where fitted).

Diesel models

5 Remove the air mass meter from above the alternator, as described in Chapter 4B Section 12.
6 Undo the three bolts and remove the auxiliary drivebelt tensioner assembly **(see illustration)**.
7 Remove the rubber cover from the alternator terminal, then unscrew the retaining nut and disconnect the wiring from the rear of the alternator **(see illustration)**. Prise out the retaining clip to release the wiring harness routed around the end of the alternator.
8 Unscrew the alternator mounting bolts **(see illustrations)**. To access the left-hand lower mounting bolt, unbolt the air conditioning compressor (where fitted) and move it to one side. Do not disconnect the refrigerant pipes. Manoeuvre the alternator away from its mounting brackets and out from the engine compartment.

Petrol models

9 Disconnect the wiring connectors from the

7.7 Prise out the rubber cover, then disconnect the alternator wiring and plug

7.8a Alternator right-hand mounting bolts (arrowed)...

7.8b ... and left-hand mounting bolts (arrowed)

7.9a Disconnect the wiring connector...

7.9b... prise out the rubber cover...

7.9c... and undo the retaining nut

7.10a Undo the upper two bolts (arrowed)...

7.10b... and remove the automatic tensioner

7.11 Remove the alternator from its bracket

rear of the alternator, remove the rubber cover (where fitted) from the alternator terminals, and then unscrew the retaining nut **(see illustrations)**. Prise out the retaining clip to release the wiring harness routed around the end of the alternator.

10 On VTi models, undo the alternator two upper retaining bolts and remove the auxiliary belt automatic tensioner **(see illustrations)**.

11 Unscrew the lower nut(s) and/or mounting bolt(s), or undo the nut securing the adjuster bolt bracket to the alternator (as applicable). Note that, where a long through-bolt is used to secure the alternator in position, the bolt does not need to be fully removed, the alternator can be disengaged from the bolt once it has been slackened sufficiently **(see illustration)**. On some models, it may be necessary to remove the drivebelt idler/tensioner pulley to gain access to the alternator mounting nuts and bolts (depending on specification).

12 Manoeuvre the alternator away from its mounting brackets and out from the engine compartment **(see illustration)**.

Refitting

13 Refitting is a reversal of removal, tensioning the auxiliary drivebelt, and ensuring that the alternator mountings are securely tightened. Note that on diesel models, the upper bolt acts as a centraliser and should be tightened first **(see illustration)**.

8 Alternator – testing and overhaul

1 If the alternator is thought to be suspect, it should be removed from the vehicle and taken to an auto-electrician for testing. Most auto-electricians will be able to supply and fit

brushes at a reasonable cost. However, check on the cost of repairs before proceeding, as it may prove more economical to obtain a new or exchange alternator.

9 Starting system – testing

Note: *Refer to the precautions given in 'Safety first!' and in Section 1 of this Chapter before starting work.*

1 If the starter motor fails to operate when the ignition key is turned to the appropriate position, the following possible causes may be to blame.

● The engine immobiliser is faulty.
● The battery is faulty.
● The electrical connections between the switch, solenoid, battery and starter motor are somewhere failing to pass the necessary current from the battery through the starter to earth.
● The solenoid is faulty.
● The starter motor is mechanically or electrically defective.

2 To check the battery, switch on the headlights. If they dim after a few seconds, this indicates that the battery is discharged – recharge (see Section 3) or renew the battery. If the headlights glow brightly, operate the ignition switch and observe the lights. If they dim, then this indicates that current is reaching the starter motor; therefore the fault must lie in the starter motor. If the lights continue to glow

7.12 Manoeuvre the alternator out from under the wheel arch (VTi engine)

7.13 On diesel engines, the upper bolts acts as a centraliser

9.3 Engine/transmission earth strap connection (arrowed)

10.6a Undo the two nuts (arrowed) and disconnect the starter motor wiring

10.6b Undo the bolt (arrowed) securing the wiring loom support plate

brightly (and no clicking sound can be heard from the starter motor solenoid), this indicates that there is a fault in the circuit or solenoid – see following paragraphs. If the starter motor turns slowly when operated, but the battery is in good condition, then this indicates that either the starter motor is faulty, or there is considerable resistance somewhere in the circuit.

3 If a fault in the circuit is suspected, disconnect the battery leads (including the earth connection to the body of the vehicle), the starter/solenoid wiring and the engine/transmission earth strap – located on the top of the transmission housing **(see illustration)**. Thoroughly clean the connections and reconnect the leads and wiring, then use a voltmeter or test lamp to check that full battery voltage is available at the battery positive lead connection to the solenoid, and that the earth is sound. Smear petroleum jelly around the battery terminals to prevent corrosion – corroded connections are amongst the most frequent causes of electrical system faults.

4 If the battery and all connections are in good condition, check the circuit by disconnecting the wire from the solenoid blade terminal. Connect a voltmeter or test lamp between the wire end and a good earth (such as the battery negative terminal), and check that the wire is live when the ignition switch is turned to the 'start' position. If it is, then the circuit is sound – if not the circuit wiring can be checked as described in Chapter 12.

5 The contacts inside the solenoid can be checked, by connecting a voltmeter or test

lamp between the battery positive feed connection on the starter side of the solenoid and earth. When the ignition switch is turned to the 'start' position, there should be a reading or lighted bulb, as applicable. If there is no reading or lighted bulb, the solenoid is faulty and should be renewed.

6 If the circuit and solenoid are proved sound, the fault must lie in the starter motor. In this event, it may be possible to have the starter motor overhauled by a specialist, but check on the cost of spares before proceeding, as it may prove more economical to obtain a new or exchange motor.

10 Starter motor – removal and refitting

Removal

1 Disconnect the battery (see Section 4).
2 So that access to the motor can be gained both from above and below, apply the handbrake then jack up the front of the vehicle and support it on axle stands (see *Jacking and vehicle support*). Release the screws and remove the engine undershield (where fitted).
3 Remove the air cleaner housing and air ducting, as described in Chapter 4A Section 2 for petrol engines and Chapter 4B Section 4 for diesel engines.
4 On all models except non-VTi SOHC petrol engines, remove the battery and battery tray as described in Section 4.

Petrol engines

5 On non-VTi DOHC petrol engines, remove the inlet manifold as described in Chapter 4A Section 13.
6 Slacken and remove the retaining nut(s) and disconnect the wiring from the starter motor solenoid. Recover the washers under the nuts. Where applicable, release the wiring loom from the retaining clips, then undo the bolt securing the wiring loom support plate above the starter motor **(see illustrations)**.
7 Undo the three mounting bolts (two at the rear of the motor, and one which comes through from the top of the transmission housing), supporting the motor as the bolts are withdrawn. Recover the washers from under the bolt heads and note the locations of any wiring or hose brackets secured by the bolts **(see illustration)**.
8 Manoeuvre the starter motor out from underneath the engine and recover the locating dowel(s) from the motor/transmission (as applicable) **(see illustration)**.

Diesel engines

9 To make access easier, disconnect the exhaust front pipe from the intermediate pipe and move the exhaust to one side, taking care not to damage the flexible joint. On some 1.6 litre diesel engines, undo the retaining bolts and move the vacuum reservoir from the rear of the cylinder block to access the starter motor bolts.
10 The starter motor is located on the rear of the cylinder block **(see illustration)**.
11 Undo the starter motor lower mounting

10.7 Starter motor mounting bolts (arrowed)

10.8 Remove the starter motor

10.10 Location of starter motor

10.11 Note location of wiring loom bracket

10.12 Undo the two wiring securing nuts

13.3 Disconnect the wiring connector from the oil pressure switch (VTi engine)

bolt from underneath, noting the wiring loom mounting bracket located on the bolt (see illustration).

12 Note their fitted positions, then undo the two securing nuts and disconnect the wiring connections from the starter motor (see illustration).

13 Unclip the wiring loom retaining clip from one of the upper mounting bolts, then undo the upper mounting bolts, and remove the starter motor. The starter motor will need to be lowered down and out from under the vehicle. As the upper bolts are removed, an assistant will be required to support the starter from underneath. To make removal easier, disconnect the wiring connector from the oxygen sensor to make more room for the starter to be lowered and removed.

Refitting

14 Refitting is a reversal of removal, ensuring that the locating dowel(s) are correctly positioned. Also make sure that any wiring or hose brackets are in place under the bolt heads as noted prior to removal.

11 Starter motor – testing and overhaul

1 If the starter motor is thought to be suspect, it should be removed from the vehicle and taken to an auto-electrician for testing. Most auto-electricians will be able to supply and fit brushes at a reasonable cost.

However, check on the cost of repairs before proceeding, as it may prove more economical to obtain a new or exchange motor.

12 Ignition switch – removal and refitting

1 The ignition switch is integral with the steering column lock, and can be removed as described in Chapter 10 Section 19.

13 Oil pressure warning light switch – removal and refitting

1 On some models access to the switch may be improved if the vehicle is jacked up and supported on axle stands, and the engine undershield removed (where fitted), so that the switch can be reached from underneath (see Jacking and vehicle support).

Removal

2 The switch is fitted to the engine, in the following locations:
● Non-VTi petrol engines: Screwed into the base of the oil filter housing on the front of the cylinder block.
● VTi petrol engines: Screwed into the left-hand end of the cylinder head.
● Diesel engines: Adjacent to the oil dipstick guide tube on the front of the cylinder block.

3 Remove the protective sleeve from the wiring

plug (where applicable), and then disconnect the wiring from the switch(see illustration).

4 Unscrew the switch from the cylinder block, and recover the sealing washer (see illustrations). Be prepared for oil spillage, and if the switch is to be left removed from the engine for any length of time, plug the hole in the cylinder block.

Refitting

5 Examine the sealing washer for signs of damage or deterioration and if necessary renew.

6 Refit the switch, complete with washer, and tighten it securely. Reconnect the wiring connector.

7 Lower the vehicle to the ground, and then check the engine oil level. If necessary, top-up the engine oil as described in Weekly checks.

14 Oil level sensor – removal and refitting

1 The sensor is fitted in the following locations:
● Non-VTi petrol engines: Front side of the cylinder block adjacent to the oil filter housing.
● VTi petrol engines: Rear side of the cylinder block, at the lower centre.
● Diesel engines: Rear side of the cylinder block, between cylinders 2 and 3.

2 The removal and refitting procedure is as described for the oil pressure switch in Section 13. Access is most easily obtained from underneath the vehicle (see illustration).

13.4a The oil pressure switch is located at the front of the cylinder block (diesel engine)...

13.4b... or by the oil filter housing (petrol engine)

14.2 Disconnect the wiring connector from the oil level sensor

Chapter 5 Part B
Ignition system – petrol models

Contents

Degrees of difficulty

| Easy, suitable for novice with little experience | | Fairly easy, suitable for beginner with some experience | | Fairly difficult, suitable for competent DIY mechanic | | Difficult, suitable for experienced DIY mechanic | | Very difficult, suitable for expert DIY or professional | |

Specifications

General

System type	Static (distributorless) ignition system controlled by engine management ECU
Firing order.	1-3-4-2 (No 1 cylinder at transmission end)
Spark plugs	See Chapter 1A Specifications
Ignition timing.	Controlled by engine management ECU

Torque wrench setting

	Nm	lbf ft
Knock sensor securing bolt	20	15

1 Ignition system –
general information

1 The ignition system is integrated with the fuel injection system to form a combined engine management system under the control of one ECU (see Chapter 4A for further information). The ignition side of the system is of the static (distributorless) type, consisting of the ignition coils and spark plugs. The ignition coils are housed in a single unit mounted directly above the spark plugs. The coils are integral with the spark plug caps and are pushed directly onto the spark plugs, one for each plug. This removes the need for any HT leads connecting the coils to the plugs.

2 Under the control of the ECU, the ignition coils operate on the 'wasted spark' principle, ie, each plug sparks twice for every cycle of the engine, once during the compression stroke and once during the exhaust stroke. The spark voltage is greatest in the cylinder which is under compression; in the cylinder on its exhaust stroke the compression is low and this produces a very weak spark which has no effect on the exhaust gases.

3 The ECU uses its inputs from the various sensors to calculate the required ignition advance setting and coil charging time, depending on engine temperature, load and speed. At idle speeds, the ECU varies the ignition timing to alter the torque characteristic of the engine, enabling the idle speed to be controlled. This system operates in conjunction with the idle speed control motor – see Chapter 4A for additional details.

4 A knock sensor is also incorporated into the ignition system. Mounted onto the cylinder block, the sensor detects the high-frequency vibrations caused when the engine starts to pre-ignite, or 'pink'. Under these conditions, the knock sensor sends an electrical signal to the ECU, which in turn retards the ignition advance setting in small steps until the 'pinking' ceases.

2 Ignition system – testing

⚠️ *Warning: Voltages produced by an electronic ignition system are considerably higher than those produced by conventional ignition systems. Extreme care must be taken when working on the system with the ignition switched on. Persons with surgically implanted cardiac pacemaker devices should keep well clear of the ignition circuits, components and test equipment.*

1 If a fault appears in the engine management (fuel injection/ignition) system, first ensure that the fault is not due to a poor electrical connection or poor maintenance; ie, check that the air cleaner filter element is clean, the spark plugs are in good condition and correctly gapped, that the engine breather hoses are clear and undamaged, referring to Chapter 1A Section 7 for further information. If the engine is running very roughly, check the compression pressures and the valve clearances as described in Chapter 2A Section 9, where applicable.

2 If these checks fail to reveal the cause of the problem the vehicle should be taken to a suitably-equipped Peugeot dealer or specialist for testing. A wiring block diagnostic connector is incorporated in the engine management circuit into which a special electronic diagnostic tester can be plugged **(see illustration)**. The tester will locate the fault quickly and simply alleviating the need to test all the system components individually, which is a time-consuming operation that carries a high risk of damaging the ECU.

3 The only ignition system checks which can be carried out by the home mechanic are those described in Chapter 1A Section 19 relating to the spark plugs.

3 Ignition coil unit – removal, testing and refitting

Removal

SOHC engine

1 Disconnect the engine breather hose at the quick-release connections on the air cleaner air inlet duct, cylinder head cover and inlet manifold **(see illustration)**. Move the hose to one side.

2 Unplug the wiring connector from the top of the ignition coil unit **(see illustration)**.

3 Undo the nut securing each end of the ignition coil unit to the mounting studs **(see illustration)**. Note that it is quite likely that the stud will be released with the nut.

2.2 Diagnostic plug connector (arrowed)

4 Lift the ignition coil unit upwards off the mounting studs and at the same time carefully ease the HT extension pillars away from the tops of the spark plugs. Lift the unit off the plugs and withdraw it from the engine **(see illustration)**.

Non-VTi DOHC engines

5 Undo the six screws and remove the plastic coil pack cover from the top of the engine between the two camshaft covers.

6 Disconnect the wiring plug from the left-hand end of the ignition coil unit **(see illustration)**.

7 Depress the clips and remove the two breather pipes from between the camshaft covers **(see illustration)**.

3.1 Disconnect the breather hose from the cylinder head cover

3.2 Disconnect the wiring plug from the ignition HT coil

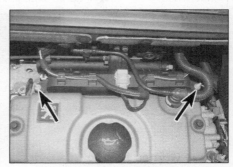

3.3 Undo the coil retaining bolts (arrowed)…

3.4… then ease the ignition HT coil assembly off the spark plugs and remove it from the engine

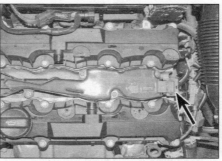

3.6 Disconnect the wiring plug from the HT coils (arrowed)

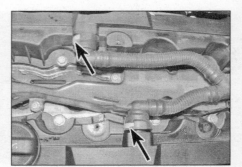

3.7 Depress the clips (arrowed) and disconnect the breather pipes

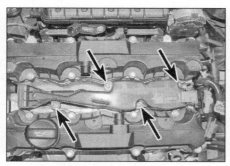

3.8 Undo the four coil pack retaining screws (arrowed)

3.10 Remove the upper cover

3.11a Release the locking clip...

3.11b... disconnect the wiring connector...

3.12... and withdraw the ignition coil

5.3 Disconnect the knock sensor wiring plug

8 Undo the four mounting screws securing the coil pack **(see illustration)**.
9 Lift the ignition coil unit upwards and at the same time carefully ease the HT extension pillars away from the tops of the spark plugs. Lift the unit off the plugs and withdraw it from the engine.

VTi engines

10 Undo the two retaining screws and unclip the front of the plastic cover from the cylinder head cover **(see illustration)**.
11 Release the locking lever and disconnect the wiring connectors from the top of the ignition coil units **(see illustrations)**.
12 Lift the coil unit upwards, off the spark plugs and from its location in the cylinder head cover **(see illustration)**.

Testing

13 The circuitry arrangement of the ignition coil unit on these engines is such that testing of an individual coil in isolation from the remainder of the engine management system is unlikely to prove effective in diagnosing a particular fault. Should there be any reason to suspect a faulty individual coil, the engine

management system should be tested by a Peugeot dealer or specialist using diagnostic test equipment (see Section 2).

Refitting

14 Refitting is a reversal of the relevant removal procedure ensuring the wiring connectors are securely reconnected.

4 Ignition timing – checking and adjustment

1 There are no timing marks on the flywheel or crankshaft pulley. The timing is constantly being monitored and adjusted by the engine management ECU, and nominal values cannot be given. Therefore, it is not possible for the home mechanic to check the ignition timing.
2 The only way in which the ignition timing can be checked is using special electronic test equipment, connected to the engine management system diagnostic connector; see Section 2 or refer to Chapter 4A for further information.

5 Knock sensor – removal and refitting

Removal

1 The knock sensor is screwed into the rear face of the cylinder block.
2 Firmly apply the handbrake, and then jack up the front of the vehicle and support it securely on axle stands (see *Jacking and vehicle support*). Undo the screws and remove the engine undershield (where fitted).
3 Depending on type of knock sensor fitted, either trace the wiring back from the sensor to its wiring connector, and disconnect it from the main loom or disconnect the wiring connector directly from the sensor **(see illustration)**.
4 Undo the sensor securing bolt and remove the sensor from the cylinder block.

Refitting

5 Refitting is a reversal of the removal procedure, ensuring that the securing bolt for the knock sensor is tightened to the specified torque.

Chapter 5 Part C
Pre/post-heating system – diesel models

Contents

Degrees of difficulty

Easy, suitable for novice with little experience		Fairly easy, suitable for beginner with some experience		Fairly difficult, suitable for competent DIY mechanic		Difficult, suitable for experienced DIY mechanic		Very difficult, suitable for expert DIY or professional	

Specifications

Preheating system

Note: *At the time of writing no information concerning the 1.4 litre engine was available.*
Pre-heating period at coolant temperatures of (approximate values):
    1.6 litre engine:

-30°C	15 seconds
-10°C	5 seconds
0°C	0.5 seconds
20°C	0 seconds

Post-heating system

Note: *At the time of writing no information concerning the 1.4 litre engine was available.*
Post-heating period at coolant temperatures of (approximate values):
    1.6 litre engine:

-30°C	3 minutes
-10°C	3 minutes
0°C	3 minutes
20°	0.5 seconds
80°	0 seconds

Torque wrench settings

	Nm	lbf ft
Glow plugs:		
1.4 litre engine	8	6
1.6 litre engine	10	7

1 Pre/post-heating system – description and testing

Description

1 To assist cold starting, diesel engines are fitted with a preheating system, which consists of four of glow plugs (one per cylinder), a glow plug relay unit, a facia-mounted warning lamp, the engine management ECU, and the associated electrical wiring.

2 The glow plugs are miniature electric heating elements, encapsulated in a metal case with a probe at one end and electrical connection at the other. Each combustion chamber has one glow plug threaded into it, with the tip of the glow plug probe positioned directly in line with incoming spray of fuel from the injectors. When the glow plug is energised, it heats up rapidly, causing the fuel passing over the glow plug probe to be heated to its optimum temperature, ready for combustion. In addition, some of the fuel passing over the glow plugs is ignited and this helps to trigger the combustion process.

3 The preheating system begins to operate as soon as the ignition key is switched to the second position, but only if the engine coolant temperature is below 20°C and the engine is turned at more than 70 rpm for 0.2 seconds. A facia-mounted warning lamp informs the driver that preheating is taking place. The lamp extinguishes when sufficient preheating has taken place to allow the engine to be started, but power will still be supplied to the glow plugs for a further period until the engine is started. If no attempt is made to start the engine, the power supply to the glow plugs is switched off after 10 seconds to prevent battery drain and glow plug burnout.

4 With the electronically-controlled diesel injection systems fitted to models in this manual, the glow plug relay unit is controlled by the engine management system ECU, which determines the necessary preheating time based on inputs from the various system sensors. The system monitors the temperature of the inlet air, and then alters the preheating time (the length for which the glow plugs are supplied with current) to suit the conditions.

5 Post-heating takes place after the ignition key has been released from the 'start' position, but only if the engine coolant temperature is below 20°C, the injected fuel flow is less than a certain rate, and the engine speed is less than 2000 rpm. The glow plugs continue to operate for a maximum of 60 seconds, helping to improve fuel combustion whilst the engine is warming-up, resulting in quieter, smoother running and reduced exhaust emissions.

Testing

6 If the system malfunctions, testing is ultimately by substitution of known good units, but some preliminary checks may be made as follows.

7 Connect a voltmeter or 12 volt test lamp between the glow plug supply cable and earth (engine or vehicle metal). Make sure that the live connection is kept clear of the engine and bodywork.

8 Have an assistant switch on the ignition, and check that voltage is applied to the glow plugs. Note the time for which the warning light is lit, and the total time for which voltage is applied before the system cuts out. Switch off the ignition.

9 Compare the results with the information given in the Specifications. Warning light time will increase with lower temperatures and decrease with higher temperatures.

10 If there is no supply at all, the control unit or associated wiring is at fault.

11 On 1.4 and 1.6 litre DOHC engines, to gain access to the glow plugs for further testing, remove the cylinder head cover/manifold assembly.

12 On 1.6 litre SOHC engines, to gain access to the glow plugs for further testing, remove the engine plastic cover and sound insulation from the rear of the cylinder head.

13 Disconnect the main supply cable and the interconnecting wire or strap from the top of the glow plugs. Where applicable, take care not to drop the nuts and washers.

14 Use a continuity tester, or a 12 volt test lamp connected to the battery positive terminal, to check for continuity between each glow plug terminal and earth. The resistance of a glow plug in good condition is very low (less than 1 ohm), so if the test lamp does not light or the continuity tester shows a high resistance, the glow plug is certainly defective.

15 If an ammeter is available, the current draw of each glow plug can be checked. After an initial surge of 15 to 20 amps, each plug should draw 12 amps. Any plug which draws much more or less than this is probably defective.

16 As a final check, the glow plugs can be removed and inspected as described in the following Section. On completion, refit any components removed for access.

2 Glow plugs – removal, inspection and refitting

Caution: If the preheating system has just been energised, or if the engine has been running, the glow plugs will be very hot.

Removal

1 Ensure the ignition is turned off. To gain access to the glow plugs, remove the components described in Section 1, according to engine.

2 Unscrew the nuts from the glow plug terminals, and recover the washers. Note that on some models, an interconnecting wire/shunt is fitted between the four plugs (see illustration).

3 Where applicable, carefully move any obstructing pipes or wires to one side to enable access to the relevant glow plug(s).

4 Unscrew the glow plug(s) and remove from the cylinder head (see illustration).

2.2 Undo the nuts securing the glow plug connections (arrowed)

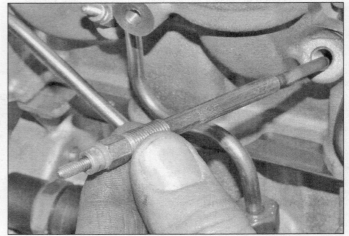

2.4 Unscrew the glow plugs from the cylinder head

Inspection

5 Inspect each glow plug for physical damage. Burnt or eroded glow plug tips can be caused by a bad injector spray pattern. Have the injectors checked if this sort of damage is found.

6 If the glow plugs are in good physical condition, check them electrically using a 12 volt test lamp or continuity tester as described in the previous Section.

7 The glow plugs can be energised by applying 12 volts to them to verify that they heat up evenly and in the required time. Observe the following precautions.

● Support the glow plug by clamping it carefully in a vice or self-locking pliers. Remember it will become red-hot.

● Make sure that the power supply or test lead incorporates a fuse or overload trip to protect against damage from a short-circuit.

● After testing, allow the glow plug to cool for several minutes before attempting to handle it.

8 A glow plug in good condition will start to glow red at the tip after drawing current for 5 seconds or so. Any plug, which takes much longer to start glowing, or which starts glowing in the middle instead of at the tip, is defective.

Refitting

9 Thoroughly clean the glow plugs and the glow plug seating areas in the cylinder head.

3.3a Undo the glow plug control unit mounting nut – early models

3.3b Control unit on later models

10 Apply a smear of copper-based anti-seize compound to the plug threads and tighten the glow plugs to the specified torque.

11 Reconnect the wiring to the glow plug taking care not to damage the glow plug element.

12 The remainder of refitting is a reversal of removal, refit any components that have been removed for access.

---

3 Pre/post-heating system relay unit – removal and refitting

Removal

1 The unit is located on the left-hand front side of the engine compartment where it is mounted on a bracket just in front of the fuse/relay box or bolted to the inner wing/chassis panel.

2 Disconnect the battery (see Chapter 5A Section 4).

3 Unscrew the retaining nut securing the unit to the mounting bracket **(see illustrations)**.

4 Unscrew the two retaining nuts and free the main feed and supply wires from the base of the unit, then disconnect the wiring connector. Remove the unit from the engine compartment.

Refitting

5 Refitting is a reversal of removal, ensuring that the wiring connectors are correctly connected.

Notes

Chapter 6
Clutch

Contents

Degrees of difficulty

Easy, suitable for novice with little experience	Fairly easy, suitable for beginner with some experience	Fairly difficult, suitable for competent DIY mechanic	Difficult, suitable for experienced DIY mechanic	Very difficult, suitable for expert DIY or professional

Specifications

General

Type	Single dry disc with diaphragm spring, hydraulic operation

Friction disc diameter

Petrol engine models:

SOHC	180 mm
DOHC	200 mm

Diesel engine models:

1.4 litre	200 mm
1.6 litre	225 mm or 235 mm

Torque wrench setting	Nm	lbf ft
Pressure plate retaining bolts.	20	15

1 General Information

1 The clutch consists of a friction disc, a pressure plate assembly, a release bearing and release fork; all of these components are contained in the large cast-aluminium alloy bellhousing, sandwiched between the engine and the transmission. The release mechanism is hydraulic on all models.

2 The friction disc is fitted between the engine flywheel and the clutch pressure plate, and is allowed to slide on the transmission input shaft splines.

3 The pressure plate assembly is bolted to the engine flywheel. When the engine is running, drive is transmitted from the crankshaft, via the flywheel, to the friction disc (these components being clamped securely together by the pressure plate assembly) and from the friction disc to the transmission input shaft.

4 To interrupt the drive, the spring pressure must be relaxed. This is done by means of the clutch release bearing, fitted concentrically around the transmission input shaft. The bearing is pushed onto the pressure plate assembly by means of the release fork actuated by clutch slave cylinder pushrod.

5 The clutch pedal is connected to the clutch master cylinder by a short pushrod. The master cylinder is mounted on the engine side of the bulkhead in front of the driver and receives its hydraulic fluid supply from the brake master cylinder reservoir. Depressing the clutch pedal moves the piston in the master cylinder forwards, so forcing hydraulic fluid through the clutch hydraulic pipe to the slave cylinder. The piston in the slave cylinder moves forward on the entry of the fluid and actuates the clutch release fork by means of a short pushrod. The release fork pivots on its mounting stud, and the other end of the fork then presses the release bearing against the pressure plate spring fingers. This causes the springs to deform and releases the clamping force on the pressure plate.

6 On all models the clutch operating mechanism is self-adjusting, and no manual adjustment is required.

2 Clutch hydraulic system – bleeding

⚠️ **Warning: Hydraulic fluid is poisonous; wash off immediately and thoroughly in the case of skin contact, and seek immediate medical advice if any fluid is swallowed or gets into the eyes. Certain types of hydraulic fluid are inflammable, and may ignite when allowed into contact with hot components; when servicing any hydraulic system, it is safest to assume that the fluid IS inflammable, and to take precautions against the risk of fire as though it is petrol that is being handled. Hydraulic fluid is also an effective paint stripper, and will attack plastics; if any is spilt, it should be washed off immediately, using copious quantities of clean water. When topping-up or renewing the fluid, always use the recommended type, and ensure that it comes from a freshly-opened sealed container.**

1 Obtain a clean jar, a suitable length of rubber or clear plastic tubing, which is a tight fit over the bleed screw on the clutch slave cylinder, and a tin of the specified hydraulic fluid. The help of an assistant will also be required. (If a one-man do-it-yourself bleeding kit for bleeding the brake hydraulic system is available, this can be used quite satisfactorily for the clutch also).

2 Remove the air cleaner housing as described in Chapter 4A Section 2 for petrol engines or Chapter 4B Section 4 for diesel engines.

3 Remove the filler cap from the brake master cylinder reservoir, and if necessary top-up the fluid. Keep the reservoir topped-up during subsequent operations.

4 Remove the dust cap from the slave cylinder bleed screw, located on the lower front facing side of the transmission (see illustration).

5 Connect one end of the bleed tube to the bleed screw, and insert the other end of the tube in the jar containing sufficient clean hydraulic fluid to keep the end of the tube submerged.

6 Open the bleed screw half a turn and have your assistant depress the clutch pedal and then slowly release it. Continue this procedure until clean hydraulic fluid, free from air bubbles, emerges from the tube. Now tighten the bleed screw at the end of a downstroke. Make sure that the brake master cylinder reservoir is checked frequently to ensure that the level does not drop too far, allowing air into the system.

7 Check the operation of the clutch pedal. After a few strokes it should feel normal. Any sponginess would indicate air still present in the system.

8 On completion remove the bleed tube and refit the dust cover. Top-up the master cylinder reservoir if necessary and refit the cap. Fluid expelled from the hydraulic system should now be discarded, as it will be contaminated with moisture, air and dirt, making it unsuitable for further use.

3 Clutch master cylinder – removal and refitting

Note: *Before starting work, refer to the note at the beginning of Section 2 concerning the dangers of hydraulic fluid.*

Removal

1 Working inside the driver's footwell, unclip the cover from the lower part of the facia below the steering column. Then release the securing clips and remove the trim panel from above the pedals (see illustrations).

2 Carefully release the securing clips and disconnect the master cylinder pushrod from the clutch pedal (see illustration).

3 Working inside the engine compartment, remove the brake master cylinder reservoir filler cap, and then tighten it down onto a piece of polythene to obtain an airtight seal. This will minimise hydraulic fluid loss.

4 To gain better access, remove the air filter/cleaner housing and air inlet ducting as described in Chapter 4A Section 2 for petrol engines or Chapter 4B Section 4 for diesel engines.

5 Place absorbent rags under the clutch master cylinder pipe connections in the engine compartment and be prepared for hydraulic fluid loss.

2.4 Remove the dust cap from the bleed screw

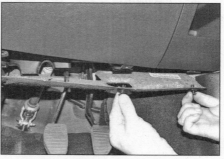

3.1a Unclip the lower trim panel...

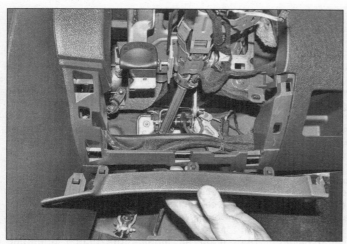

3.1b ... and the facia trim panel

3.2 Release the pushrod from the pedal (arrowed)

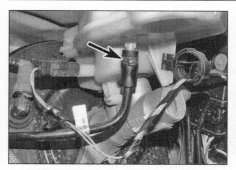

3.6 Hydraulic pipe connection from the master cylinder (arrowed)

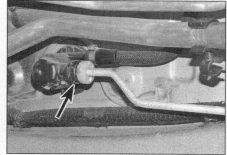

3.7 Release the securing clip (arrowed)

3.8 Turn the master cylinder 90° clockwise, and remove it from the bulkhead

6 Release the securing clip and disconnect the hydraulic fluid supply pipe, either from the clutch master cylinder or from the brake fluid reservoir **(see illustration)**. Plug or cap the pipe end to prevent further fluid loss and dirt entry.

7 Prise out the retaining wire clip and disconnect the hydraulic pressure pipe from the clutch master cylinder on the bulkhead **(see illustration)**. Plug or cap the pipe end to prevent further fluid loss and dirt entry.

8 Rotate the master cylinder 45 degrees clockwise, and remove it from the bulkhead **(see illustration)**.

Refitting

9 Refitting the master cylinder is the reverse sequence to removal, bearing in mind the following points.
● Ensure all retaining clips are correctly refitted and the master cylinder is located securely in the bulkhead.
● On completion, bleed the clutch hydraulic system as described in Section 2.

---

4 Clutch slave cylinder –
removal and refitting

Note: *Before starting work, refer to the note at the beginning of Section 2 concerning the dangers of hydraulic fluid.*

Removal

Early models

1 To minimise hydraulic fluid loss, remove the brake master cylinder reservoir filler cap then tighten it down onto a piece of polythene to obtain an airtight seal.

2 To gain better access, remove the air inlet ducting/resonator, as described in Chapter 4A Section 2 for petrol engines or Chapter 4B Section 4 for diesel engines.

3 Place absorbent rags under the clutch slave cylinder located on the lower front facing side of the transmission. Be prepared for hydraulic fluid loss.

4 Where necessary for access, release the wiring harness from the retaining clips and move the harness clear of the slave cylinder.

5 Lever out the retaining clip a little, and then disconnect the hydraulic pipe from the slave cylinder **(see illustration)**. Suitably plug or cap the pipe end to prevent further fluid loss and dirt entry. **Note:** *Some models may have two retaining clips securing the hydraulic pipe.*

6 Undo the two retaining bolts and remove the cylinder from the transmission housing **(see illustrations)**.

Later models

7 The clutch slave cylinder is part of the release bearing assembly. Refer to Section 7 for the removal and refitting procedure.

Refitting

8 Refitting the slave cylinder is the reverse sequence to removal, bearing in mind the following points.

4.5 Lever out the hydraulic pipe retaining clip

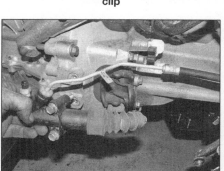

4.6b... and remove the clutch slave cylinder – MA5 transmission

● Apply a little Molykote BR2 Plus grease to the end of the slave cylinder pushrod.
● On completion, bleed the clutch hydraulic system as described in Section 2.

---

5 Clutch pedal –
removal and refitting

Removal

1 Working inside the driver's footwell, unclip the cover from the lower part of the facia below the steering column. Then release the securing clips and remove the trim panel from above the pedals **(see illustrations 3.1a and 3.1b)**.

2 Carefully release the securing clip and

4.6a Undo the two bolts (arrowed)...

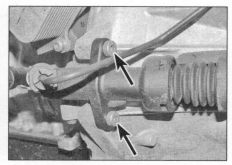

4.6c Undo the two bolts (arrowed) – BE4/5 transmission

5.3 The clutch pedal bolt (arrowed) is also the pivot for the brake pedal

disconnect the master cylinder pushrod from the clutch pedal **(see illustration 3.2)**.

3 Undo the nut from the clutch pedal pivot bolt and withdraw the bolt **(see illustration)**. Note that the bolt also provides a pivot for the brake pedal.

4 Remove the clutch pedal from the pedal bracket and recover the bush from the pedal pivot.

5 Check the condition of the pedal and pivot bush assembly and renew any components as necessary.

Refitting

6 Lubricate the pedal pivot bolt with multipurpose grease, then locate the pedal in the bracket and insert the pivot bolt. Refit the pivot bolt nut and tighten it securely.

7 Reconnect the master cylinder pushrod to the pedal.

8 Depress the pedal two or three times and check the operation of the clutch release mechanism.

9 Refit the facia lower trim panels on completion.

---

6 Clutch assembly – removal, inspection and refitting

Caution: Dust created by clutch wear and deposited on the clutch components may contain asbestos, which is a health hazard. DON'T blow it out with compressed air, nor inhale any of it. DO NOT use petrol or

petroleum-based solvents to clean off the dust. Brake system cleaner or methylated spirit should be used to flush the dust into a suitable receptacle. After the clutch components are wiped clean with rags, dispose of the contaminated rags and cleaner in a sealed, marked container.

Note: *Although most friction materials no longer contain asbestos, it is safest to assume that some still do, and to take precautions accordingly.*

Removal

1 Unless the complete engine/transmission unit is to be removed from the car and separated for major overhaul, the clutch can be reached by removing the transmission as described in Chapter 7A Section 7.

2 Before disturbing the clutch, use chalk or a marker pen to mark the relationship of the pressure plate assembly to the flywheel.

3 Working in a diagonal sequence, slacken the pressure plate bolts by half a turn at a time, until spring pressure is released and the bolts can be unscrewed by hand **(see illustration)**.

4 Prise the pressure plate assembly off its locating dowels **(see illustration)**, and collect the friction disc, noting which way round the disc is fitted.

Inspection

Note: *Due to the amount of work necessary to remove and refit clutch components, it is considered good practice to renew the clutch friction disc, pressure plate assembly and release bearing as a matched set, even if only one of these is worn enough to require renewal. It is worth considering the renewal of the clutch components on a preventative basis if the engine and/or transmission have been removed for some other reason.*

5 When cleaning clutch components, read first the warning at the beginning of this Section; remove dust using a clean, dry cloth, and working in a well-ventilated atmosphere.

6 Check the friction disc facings for signs of wear, damage or oil contamination. If the friction material is cracked, burnt, scored or damaged, or if it is contaminated with oil or grease (shown by shiny black patches), the friction disc must be renewed.

7 If the friction material is still serviceable, check that the centre boss splines are unworn, that the torsion springs are in good condition and securely fastened, and that all the rivets are tight. If any wear or damage is found, the friction disc must be renewed.

8 If the friction material is fouled with oil, this must be due to an oil leak from the crankshaft left-hand oil seal, from the sump-to-cylinder block joint, or from the transmission input shaft. Renew the seal or repair the joint, as appropriate, before installing the new friction disc.

9 Check the pressure plate assembly for obvious signs of wear or damage; shake it to check for loose rivets or worn or damaged fulcrum rings, and check that the drive straps securing the pressure plate to the cover do not show signs (such as a deep yellow or blue discoloration) of overheating. If the diaphragm spring is worn or damaged, or if its pressure is in any way suspect, the pressure plate assembly should be renewed.

10 Examine the machined bearing surfaces of the pressure plate and of the flywheel; they should be clean, completely flat, and free from scratches or scoring. If either is discoloured from excessive heat, or shows signs of cracks, it should be renewed – although minor damage of this nature can sometimes be polished away using emery paper.

11 Check that the release bearing contact surface rotates smoothly and easily, with no sign of noise or roughness. Also check that the surface itself is smooth and unworn, with no signs of cracks, pitting or scoring. If there is any doubt about its condition, the bearing must be renewed.

Refitting

12 On reassembly, ensure that the bearing surfaces of the flywheel and pressure plate are completely clean, smooth, and free from oil or grease. Use solvent to remove any protective grease from new components.

13 Fit the friction disc so that its spring hub assembly faces away from the flywheel; there may be a marking showing which way round the disc is to be refitted **(see illustration)**.

14 Refit the pressure plate assembly, aligning the marks made on dismantling (if the original pressure plate is re-used), and locating the

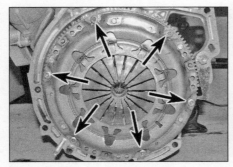

6.3 Undo the pressure plate bolts (arrowed)

6.4 Locating dowel (arrowed) – marked for refitting

6.13 Fit the disc so the spring hub assembly faces away from the flywheel

6.16 Using a clutch aligning tool to centralise the friction disc

6.17 Using a different type of alignment tool

pressure plate on its three locating dowels. Fit the pressure plate bolts, but tighten them only finger-tight, so that the friction disc can still be moved.

15 The friction disc must now be centralised, so that when the transmission is refitted, its input shaft will pass through the splines at the centre of the friction disc.

16 Centralisation can be achieved by passing a screwdriver or other long bar through the friction disc and into the hole in the crankshaft; the friction disc can then be moved around until it is centred on the crankshaft hole. Alternatively, a clutch-aligning tool can be used to eliminate the guesswork; these can be obtained from most accessory shops **(see illustration)**.

17 Another type of alignment tool locks the clutch plate to the pressure plate in the central position, and then they are fitted as a complete assembly **(see illustration)**.

18 When the friction disc is centralised, tighten the pressure plate bolts evenly and in a diagonal sequence to the specified torque setting.

19 Apply a thin smear of molybdenum disulphide grease (Peugeot recommend the use of Molykote BR2 Plus – available from your dealer) to the splines of the friction disc and the transmission input shaft, and also to the release bearing bore and release fork shaft.

20 Refit the transmission as described in Chapter 7A Section 7.

7 Clutch release mechanism – removal, inspection and refitting

Note: *Refer to the warning concerning the dangers of asbestos dust at the beginning of Section 7.*

Removal

1 Unless the complete engine/transmission unit is to be removed from the car and separated for major overhaul, the clutch release mechanism can be reached by removing the transmission only, as described in Chapter 7A Section 7.

Early models

2 With the transmission removed, squeeze together the tabs of the retaining clip and pull

7.2 Squeeze the tabs of the retaining clip together and remove the release fork...

7.4a Recover the shim...

the release fork off the pivot ball-stud **(see illustration)**.

3 Slide the release bearing off the guide tube and disengage the arms of the release fork **(see illustration)**.

4 If required, recover the shim where fitted and unscrew the mounting stud from the transmission housing **(see illustrations)**.

Later models

5 With the transmission removed, undo

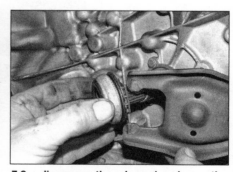

7.3... disengage the release bearing as the release fork is removed

7.4b... and then unscrew the pivot ball-stud (arrowed)

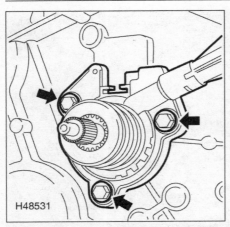

7.5 Undo the slave cylinder/release bearing retaining bolts

the three mounting bolts from inside the bellhousing **(see illustration)**.

6 Withdraw the slave cylinder/release bearing by sliding it over the transmission input shaft.

Inspection

7 Check that the release bearing contact surface rotates smoothly and easily, with no sign of noise or roughness, and that the surface itself is smooth and unworn, with no signs of cracks, pitting or scoring. If there is any doubt about its condition, the bearing must be renewed.

8 On 5-speed transmissions, check the bearing surfaces and points of contact on the release fork and pivot ball-stud, renewing any component, which is worn or damaged.

Refitting

9 On early models, where removed, refit the pivot bolt stud and shim, apply a smear of molybdenum disulphide grease to the pivot ball-stud. Insert the outer end of the release fork through the rubber boot in the side of the transmission bellhousing. Engage the arms of the release fork with the release bearing collar, then slide the release bearing onto the guide tube. Position the shim over the tabs of the pivot ball-stud clip, then push the fork over the stud, ensuring the tabs of the retaining clip engage correctly with the fork **(see illustrations)**.

10 On later models, slide the slave cylinder/release bearing over the transmission input shaft and tighten the retaining bolts to the specified torque setting.

11 Refit the transmission as described in Chapter 7A Section 7.

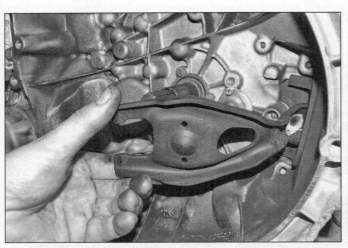

7.9a Refit the release fork into the rubber gaiter and release bearing

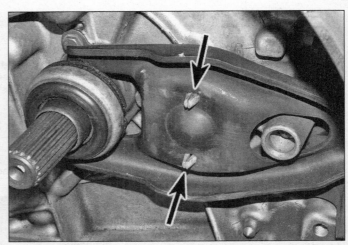

7.9b Ensure the retaining tabs (arrowed) engage correctly with the release fork

Chapter 7 Part A
Manual transmission

Contents

Degrees of difficulty

Easy, suitable for novice with little experience	Fairly easy, suitable for beginner with some experience	Fairly difficult, suitable for competent DIY mechanic	Difficult, suitable for experienced DIY mechanic	Very difficult, suitable for expert DIY or professional

Specifications

General

Type	Manual, five speeds and reverse. Synchromesh on all forward speeds

Designation:

Petrol engine models	MA5

Diesel engine models:

1.4 litre	MA5
1.6 litre	BE4/5

Lubrication

Capacity (after draining):

MA5	2.0 litres
BE4/5	1.9 litres
Recommended oil type	See *Lubricants and fluids*

Torque wrench settings

	Nm	lbf ft
Clutch release bearing guide sleeve bolts	12	9
Engine-to-transmission fixing bolts:		
MA5 transmission	40	30
BE4/5 transmission	45	33
Gearchange lever mounting nuts	8	6
Left-hand engine/transmission mounting	Refer to Chapter 2	
Oil drain plug:		
MA5 transmission	33	24
BE4/5 transmission	35	26
Rear mounting link	Refer to Chapter 2	
Reversing light switch	25	18
Roadwheel bolts	90	66
Speedometer drive housing bolts	15	11
Speedometer drive pinion bracket	10	7

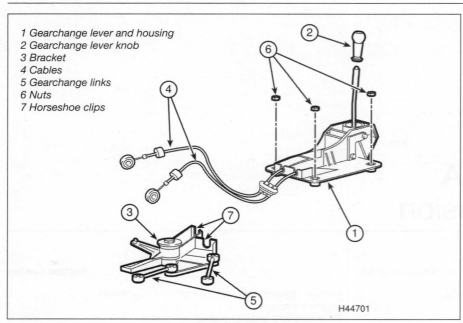

1 Gearchange lever and housing
2 Gearchange lever knob
3 Bracket
4 Cables
5 Gearchange links
6 Nuts
7 Horseshoe clips

H44701

1.4 Gearchange lever and cables

1 General Information

1 The transmission is contained in a cast-aluminium alloy casing bolted to the engine's left-hand end, and consists of the gearbox and final drive differential – often called a transaxle.
2 Drive is transmitted from the crankshaft via the clutch to the input shaft, which has a splined extension to accept the clutch friction disc, and rotates in sealed ball-bearings. From the input shaft, drive is transmitted to the output shaft, which rotates in a roller bearing at its right-hand end, and a sealed ball-bearing at its left-hand end. From the output shaft, the drive is transmitted to the differential crownwheel, which rotates with the differential case and planetary gears, thus driving the sun gears and driveshafts. The rotation of the planetary gears on their shaft allows the inner roadwheel to rotate at a slower speed than the outer roadwheel when the car is cornering.

3 The input and output shafts are arranged side-by-side, parallel to the crankshaft and driveshafts, so that their gear pinion teeth are in constant mesh. In the neutral position, the output shaft gear pinions rotate freely, so that drive cannot be transmitted to the crownwheel.
4 Gear selection is via a floor-mounted lever and cable mechanism **(see illustration)**. The selector/gearchange cables cause the appropriate selector fork to move its respective synchro-sleeve along the shaft, to lock the gear pinion to the synchro-hub. Since the synchro-hubs are splined to the output shaft, this locks the pinion to the shaft, so that drive can be transmitted. To ensure that gearchanging can be made quickly and quietly, a synchromesh system is fitted to all forward gears, consisting of baulk rings and spring-loaded fingers, as well as the gear pinions and synchro-hubs. The synchromesh cones are formed on the mating faces of the baulk rings and gear pinions.
5 Two different manual transmissions are used on the models covered in this manual, see

specifications at the beginning of this Chapter.
6 Both of the transmissions used are 'filled for life' with fluid – there's no recommended interval for changing the fluid, although it may be prudent to do so at some stage in the vehicle's life. During each service, it is advised to check around the transmission for signs of any leaks.

2 Manual transmission – draining and refilling

Note: *On later models, the oil level cannot be checked, as there is no filler/level plug fitted. These transmissions do not require regular maintenance and are filled for life. If the transmission develops a leak or is removed for other work, the oil needs to be completely drained and refilled with the correct amount of oil. The transmission will then be refilled through the vent on the top of the transmission. For checking the level on earlier models, see Chapter 1A Section 22.*
Note: *A suitable square section wrench may be required to undo the transmission drain plug on some models. These wrenches can be obtained from most motor factors or your Peugeot dealer.*
1 This operation is much quicker and more efficient if the car is first taken on a journey of sufficient length to warm the engine/ transmission up to normal operating temperature.
2 Park the car on level ground, switch off the ignition and apply the handbrake firmly. For improved access, jack up the front of the car and support it securely on axle stands (see *Jacking and vehicle support*). Undo the screws and remove the engine undershield (where fitted).
3 To improve access to the filler/breather plug, remove the air cleaner housing/ducting and resonator (depending on model), to access the top of the transmission housing.
4 Pull the breather valve cover upwards to remove **(see illustration)**. **Note:** *The transmission fluid is added through the breather valve on the top face of the transmission.*
5 Position a suitable container under the drain plug (situated on the final drive casing at the rear of the transmission) and unscrew the plug **(see illustrations)**

2.4 Unclip the vent cap from the top of the transmission

2.5a Oil drain plug (arrowed) – MA5 transmission

2.5b Oil drain plug – BE4/5 transmission

2.8a Connect a length of pipe…

2.8b… with a funnel to the vent pipe

2.9 Refilling the transmission

6 Allow the oil to drain completely into the container. If the oil is hot, take precautions against scalding. Clean the drain plug, being especially careful to wipe any metallic particles off the magnetic inserts (where applicable). Discard the original sealing washer; as it should be renewed whenever it is disturbed.
7 When the oil has finished draining, clean the drain plug threads and those of the transmission casing, fit a new sealing washer and refit the drain plug, tightening it to the specified torque wrench setting. Refit the undercover (where fitted) then lower the vehicle to the ground.
8 Refilling the transmission is an extremely awkward operation, to make it easier, connect a piece of hose and a funnel to the breather valve on the top of the transmission **(see illustrations)**.

9 Add the exact amount of transmission oil as specified at the beginning of the Chapter **(see illustration)**. Allow plenty of time for the correct amount of oil to flow down into the transmission.
10 Refit the breather cap.
11 Refit the air cleaner assembly, and the engine/transmission undershield, and lower the vehicle to the ground.

3 Gearchange lever and cables – removal and refitting

Removal

1 Firmly apply the handbrake, and then jack up the front of the vehicle and support it on axle stands (see *Jacking and vehicle support*).
2 Remove the centre console as described in Chapter 11 Section 26.
3 Carefully pull the rear passenger compartment air ducts from above the gear lever housing **(see illustration)**.
4 Undo the four nuts securing the gearchange lever housing to the floor **(see illustration)**.
5 Remove the air cleaner housing and air ducting, as described in Chapter 4A Section 2 for petrol engines and Chapter 4B Section 4 for diesel engines.
6 Remove the battery and battery box, as described in Chapter 5A Section 4.
7 Working in the engine compartment, note their fitted locations, and then carefully prise the two gearchange cable balljoints from the selector levers on the transmission **(see illustration)**.
8 Depending on model, it may be necessary to remove the exhaust heat shield from under the cables. Working underneath the vehicle, remove the front exhaust pipe heat shield fasteners, and allow the heat shield to rest on the exhaust pipe.
9 Release the outer cables from the support bracket on the transmission **(see illustration)**.
10 Working inside the vehicle, release the cable sealing grommet from the floor, and manoeuvre the lever, housing and cables assembly from the vehicle **(see illustration)**.
11 To release the outer cables from the lever

3.3 Remove the air ducts from above the gear lever housing

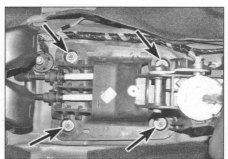

3.4 Undo the four nuts (arrowed) securing the gear lever housing to the floor

3.7 Release the inner cables (arrowed) from the transmission

3.9 Unclip the outer cables from the brackets

3.10 Release the cable sealing grommet from the floor

3.11a Depress the clip tabs (arrowed)...

3.11b... and lever the cable outer upwards

3.12 Lever the cable balljoint from the lever

housing, depress the clips and pull the cable up from the housing (see illustrations)

12 Using a pair of long-nose pliers, lever the cable balljoint from the lever on the gear lever (see illustration)

13 The gearchange lever is integral with the housing, and is not available separately.

Refitting

14 Refitting is a reversal of the removal procedure, noting the following points:
● Tie the two cables together to make it easier to pass them through the floor to their correct locations.
● Apply grease to the balljoints before refitting.
● No adjustment of the gearchange cables is possible.

4 Oil seals – renewal

Driveshaft oil seals

1 Remove the appropriate driveshaft as described in Chapter 8 Section 2.

2 Carefully prise the oil seal out of the transmission, using a large flat-bladed screwdriver (see illustration).

3 Remove all traces of dirt from the area around the oil seal aperture, then apply a smear of grease to the outer lip of the new oil seal. Fit the new seal into its aperture, and drive it squarely into position using a suitable tubular drift (such as a socket) which bears only on the hard outer edge of the seal, until

it abuts its locating shoulder. If the seal was supplied with a plastic protector sleeve, leave this in position until the driveshaft has been refitted (see illustrations).

4 Apply a thin film of grease to the oil seal lip, and then refit the driveshaft as described in Chapter 8 Section 2.

Input shaft oil seal

5 Remove the transmission as described in Section 7, and the clutch release mechanism as described in Chapter 6 Section 7.

6 Undo the three bolts securing the clutch release bearing guide sleeve in position, and slide the guide off the input shaft, along with its sealing ring or gasket (as applicable)(see illustration). Recover any shims or thrustwashers, which have stuck to the rear of the guide sleeve, and refit them to the input shaft. Note that on some transmissions, the oil seal appears to be integral with the guide sleeve. Check with your Peugeot parts specialist.

7 Carefully lever the oil seal out of the guide using a suitable flat-bladed screwdriver(see illustration).

8 Before fitting a new seal, check the input shaft's seal rubbing surface for signs of burrs, scratches or other damage, which may have caused the seal to fail in the first place. It may be possible to polish away minor faults of this sort using fine abrasive paper; however, more serious defects will require the renewal of the input shaft. Ensure that the input shaft

4.2 Use a large flat-bladed screwdriver to prise out the driveshaft oil seals

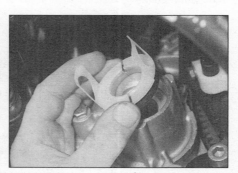

4.3a Fit the new seal to the transmission, noting the plastic seal protector...

4.3b... and tap it into position using a tubular drift

4.6 Undo the three bolts (arrowed) securing the guide sleeve

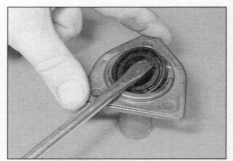

4.7 Remove the input shaft seal from the guide sleeve

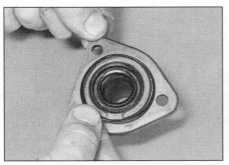

4.10 Fit a new O-ring/gasket (as applicable) to the guide sleeve

5.4a Reversing light switch in top of transmission...

5.4b ...or at the front of the transmission

is clean and greased, to protect the seal lips on refitting.

9 Dip the new seal in clean oil, and fit it to the guide sleeve.

10 Fit a new sealing ring or gasket (as applicable) to the rear of the guide sleeve, then carefully slide the sleeve into position over the input shaft. Refit the retaining bolts and tighten them to the specified torque setting **(see illustration)**.

11 Take the opportunity to inspect the clutch components if not already done. Finally, refit the transmission as described in Section 7.

Selector shaft oil seal

MA5 transmissions

12 On these models, to renew the selector shaft seal, the transmission must be dismantled. This task should therefore be entrusted to a Peugeot dealer or transmission specialist.

BE4/5 transmissions

13 Park the car on level ground, apply the handbrake, slacken the left-hand front roadwheel bolts, then jack up the front of the vehicle and support it on axle stands (see *Jacking and vehicle support*). Remove the left-hand front roadwheel.

14 Using a large flat-bladed screwdriver, lever the link rod balljoint off the transmission selector shaft, and disconnect the link rod.

15 Using a large flat-bladed screwdriver, carefully prise the selector shaft seal out of the housing, and slide it off the end of the shaft.

16 Before fitting a new seal, check the selector shaft's seal rubbing surface for signs of burrs, scratches or other damage, which may have caused the seal to fail in the first place. It may be possible to polish away minor faults of this sort using fine abrasive paper; however, more serious defects will require the renewal of the selector shaft.

17 Apply a smear of grease to the new seal's outer edge and sealing lip, and then carefully slide the seal along the selector rod. Press the seal fully into position in the transmission housing.

18 Refit the link rod to the selector shaft, ensuring that its balljoint is pressed firmly onto the shaft. Lower the car to the ground.

5 Reversing light switch – testing, removal and refitting

Testing

1 The reversing light circuit is controlled by a plunger-type switch, which is screwed into either the top of the transmission casing or in the selector housing on the front of the transmission. If a fault develops, first ensure that the circuit fuse has not blown.

2 To test the switch, disconnect the wiring connector, and use a multimeter (set to the resistance function) or a battery-and-bulb test circuit to check that there is continuity between the switch terminals only when reverse gear is selected. If this is not the case, and there are no obvious breaks or other damage to the wires, the switch is faulty, and must be renewed.

Removal

3 Where necessary, to improve access to the switch, remove the air cleaner housing intake duct assembly/battery and battery box.

4 Disconnect the wiring connector, and then unscrew the switch, along with its sealing washer **(see illustrations)**.

Refitting

5 Fit a new sealing washer to the switch, then screw it back into position in the top of the transmission housing and tighten it to the specified torque setting. Refit the wiring plug, and test the operation of the circuit. Refit any components removed for access.

6 Speedometer drive – removal and refitting

Note: *According to Peugeot, only the transmission fitted to the 1.4 litre SOHC petrol model is equipped with a speedometer drive pinion. On other models, the speedometer receives vehicle speed data from the engine management ECU, supplied by the wheel speed sensors and the ABS ECU.*

Removal

1 Chock the rear wheels, firmly apply the handbrake, and then jack up the front of the car and support it on axle stands (see *Jacking and vehicle support*). The speedometer drive is on the rear of the transmission housing, next to the inner end of the right-hand driveshaft. Undo the screws and remove the engine/transmission undershield (where fitted).

2 Disconnect the wiring connector from the speedometer drive **(see illustration)**.

3 Slacken and remove the retaining bolt and remove the heat shield (where fitted). Withdraw the speedometer drive and driven pinion assembly from the transmission housing, along with its sealing ring.

4 If necessary, the pinion can be slid out of the housing, and the oil seal removed from the top of the housing. Examine the pinion for signs of damage, and renew if necessary. Renew the housing sealing ring as a matter of course.

5 If the driven pinion is worn or damaged, also examine the drive pinion in the transmission housing for similar signs.

6 To renew the drive pinion, the transmission must be dismantled and the differential gear removed. This task should therefore be entrusted to a Peugeot dealer or a transmission specialist.

Refitting

7 Apply a smear of grease to the lips of the seal and to the driven pinion shaft, and slide

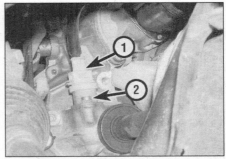

6.2 Disconnect the wiring plug (1) then undo the retaining bolt (2) and withdraw the speedometer drive assembly

the pinion into position in the speedometer drive.

8 Fit a new sealing ring to the speedometer drive and refit it to the transmission, ensuring that the drive and driven pinions are correctly engaged. Refit the drive retaining bolt, complete with heat shield (where fitted), and tighten securely.

9 Reconnect the wiring connector to the speedometer drive then lower the vehicle to the ground.

7.8 Remove the front crossmember...

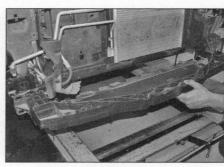

7.9... and lower plastic tray

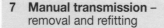

7 Manual transmission – removal and refitting

Removal

1 Chock the rear wheels, then firmly apply the handbrake. Slacken both front roadwheel bolts. Jack up the front of the vehicle, and securely support it on axle stands (see *Jacking and vehicle support*). Remove both front roadwheels.

2 Drain the transmission oil as described in Section 2, then refit the drain plugs, and tighten to their specified torque settings.

3 Remove both driveshafts as described in Chapter 8 Section 2.

4 Remove the battery and battery box (see Chapter 5A Section 4).

5 Remove the air cleaner housing and inlet ducting, as described in Chapter 4A Section 2

for petrol engines or Chapter 4B Section 4 for diesel engines.

6 In order to prevent any damage, remove the exhaust system as described in Chapter 4A Section 15 for petrol engines or Chapter 4B Section 18 for diesel engines.

7 Remove the front bumper, as described in Chapter 11 Section 6.

8 Undo the retaining bolts and remove the front crossmember from the front of the vehicle **(see illustration)**.

9 Undo the retaining bolts and remove the front plastic tray from across the front of the vehicle **(see illustration)**.

10 Undo the retaining bolts and remove the headlamps, with reference to Chapter 12 Section 7.

11 Drain the cooling system and remove the

radiator assembly, as described in Chapter 1A Section 25.

12 Remove the air conditioning condenser, as described in Chapter 3 Section 12. Do not disconnect the condenser from the refrigerant pipes, just move it to one side; making sure it is supported securely.

13 Undo the retaining bolts and remove the radiator housing panel from the front of the engine compartment **(see illustration)**.

14 Undo the retaining bolts and remove the front subframe crossmembers from the left-hand side of the transmission **(see illustrations)**.

15 Remove the starter motor, see relevant Chapter, if required.

16 Detach the clutch slave cylinder from the transmission as described in Chapter 6 Section 4. Note there is no need to disconnect the fluid pipe from the cylinder.

17 Disconnect the gearchange cables from the transmission and support bracket as described in Section 3.

18 Note their fitted positions, and then disconnect all the wiring plugs from the transmission **(see illustrations)**. Release the retaining clips and move the harness to one side, noting its routing.

19 Depending on model, undo the retaining bolt(s), and remove the flywheel lower cover plate (where fitted) from the transmission.

20 Undo the retaining bolts and remove

7.13 Remove the radiator housing front panel

7.14a Undo the retaining bolts (arrowed)...

7.14b... and remove the crossmembers

7.18a Disconnect the reversing light switch...

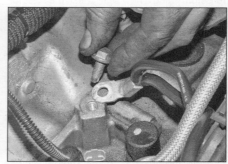

7.18b... and the earth cable from the transmission

7.20 Undo the rear crossbar retaining bolts (arrowed)

7.23 Remove the lower mounting link (arrowed)

the crossbar from under the vehicle (see illustration).

21 Place a jack with a block of wood beneath the engine, to take the weight of the engine. Alternatively, attach a couple of lifting eyes to the engine, and fit a hoist or support bar to take the engine weight.

22 Place a jack and block of wood beneath the transmission, and raise the jack to take the weight of the transmission.

23 Unscrew the nuts and bolts and remove the lower mounting link and bracket from the rear of the engine/transmission (see illustration), with reference to Chapter 2.

24 Slacken and remove the mounting bolts from the upper left-hand transmission mounting (see Illustration).

25 With the jack positioned beneath the transmission taking the weight, slacken and remove the remaining bolts securing the transmission housing to the engine. Note the correct fitted positions of each bolt and the necessary brackets, as they are removed, to use as a reference on refitting (see illustration).

26 Make a final check that all components have been disconnected, and are positioned clear of the transmission so that they will not hinder the removal procedure.

27 With the bolts removed (see Illustration), move the trolley jack and transmission to the left, to free it from its locating dowels. Lower the engine slightly to enable the transmission to be withdrawn.

Caution: Take great care not to damage any components if the engine is moved.

28 Once the transmission is free, lower the jack and manoeuvre the unit out from under the car. Remove the locating dowels from the transmission or engine if they are loose, and keep them in a safe place.

Refitting

29 The transmission is refitted by a reversal of the removal procedure, bearing in mind the following points:
● Prior to refitting, check the clutch assembly and release mechanism components (see Chapter 6 Section 6). Lubricate the release-bearing guide with a little high melting-point grease (Peugeot recommend the use of Molykote BR2 Plus). Do not apply too much grease, otherwise there is a possibility of the grease contaminating the clutch friction disc, and ensure no grease is applied to the input shaft/friction disc splines.

● Ensure that the locating dowels are correctly positioned prior to installation.
● Tighten all nuts and bolts to the specified torque (where given).
● Renew the driveshaft oil seals, then refit the driveshafts.
● Refit the lower rear engine mounting link and bracket (see Chapter 2).
● Refit the slave cylinder (see Chapter 6 Section 4).
● Refill the cooling system with reference to Chapter 1A Section 25.
● On completion, refill the transmission with the specified type and quantity of lubricant, as described in Section 2.

8 Manual transmission overhaul – general information

1 Overhauling a manual transmission is a difficult and involved job for the DIY home mechanic. In addition to dismantling and reassembling many small parts, clearances must be precisely measured and, if necessary, changed by selecting shims and spacers. Internal transmission components are also often difficult to obtain, and in many instances,

7.24 Undo the mounting upper securing bolts (arrowed)

7.25 Note the position of any brackets

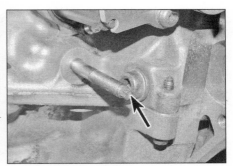

7.27 On diesel engines, remove the mounting stud (arrowed) which obscures the transmission-to-engine bolt

extremely expensive. Because of this, if the transmission develops a fault or becomes noisy, the best course of action is to have the unit overhauled by a specialist repairer, or to obtain an exchange reconditioned unit.

2 Nevertheless, it is not impossible for the more experienced mechanic to overhaul the transmission, provided the special tools are available, and the job is done in a deliberate step-by-step manner, so that nothing is overlooked.

3 The tools necessary for an overhaul include internal and external circlip pliers, bearing pullers, a slide hammer, a set of pin punches, a dial test indicator, and possibly a hydraulic press. In addition, a large, sturdy workbench and a vice will be required.

4 During dismantling of the transmission, make careful notes of how each component is fitted, to make reassembly easier and more accurate.

5 Before dismantling the transmission, it will help if you have some idea what area is malfunctioning. Certain problems can be closely related to specific areas in the transmission, which can make component examination and renewal easier. Refer to the Fault finding Section for more information.

Chapter 7 Part B
Automatic transmission

Contents

Degrees of difficulty

Easy, suitable for novice with little experience	Fairly easy, suitable for beginner with some experience	Fairly difficult, suitable for competent DIY mechanic	Difficult, suitable for experienced DIY mechanic	Very difficult, suitable for expert DIY or professional

Specifications

General

Type	Auto-adaptive four-speed electronically-controlled automatic with three driving modes (normal, sport and snow)
Designation	AL4

Lubrication

Capacity:
Refilling after draining	3.0 litres*
From dry	6.0 litres
Recommended fluid	See *Lubricants and fluids*

* If the torque converter is also removed and drained, add a further 2 litres

Torque wrench settings

	Nm	lbf ft
Engine-to-transmission fixing bolts	35	26
Fluid cooler centre bolt	50	37
Fluid drain plug	33	24
Fluid filler plug	24	18
Fluid level plug:		
To RPO 9855 (hexagonal)	24	18
From RPO 9856 (socket key)	9	7
Fluid pressure sensor bolts	9	7
Input shaft speed sensor bolt	10	7
Left-hand engine/transmission mounting	Refer to Chapter 2	
Multifunction switch retaining bolts	10	7
Output shaft speed sensor bolt	10	7
Rear mounting link	Refer to Chapter 2	
Roadwheel bolts	90	66
Torque converter-to-driveplate nuts:		
Stage 1	10	7
Stage 2	30	22

1 General Information

1 Certain models were offered with the option of a four-speed electronically-controlled automatic transmission, consisting of a torque converter, an epicyclic geartrain, and hydraulically-operated clutches and brakes. The unit is controlled by the electronic control unit (ECU) via the electrically-operated solenoid valves in the hydraulic block within the transmission unit. The transmission has three driving modes: normal, sport and snow; the mode buttons are situated on the right-hand side of the selector lever and the mode indicator lights are incorporated in the instrument panel.

2 The normal mode is the standard mode for driving in which the transmission shifts up at relatively low engine speeds to combine reasonable performance with economy. If the transmission unit is switched into sport mode, the transmission will shift up only at high engine speeds, giving improved acceleration and overtaking performance. In snow mode, the transmission will select 2nd gear when the vehicle pulls away from a standing start; this helps maintain traction on slippery surfaces.

3 The torque converter provides a fluid coupling between the engine and transmission, which acts as an automatic clutch, and also provides a degree of torque multiplication when accelerating.

4 The epicyclic geartrain provides either of the four forward or one reverse gear ratios, according to which of its component parts are held stationary or allowed to turn. The components of the geartrain are held or released by brakes and clutches, which are controlled by the ECU via the electrically-operated solenoid valves in the hydraulic unit. A fluid pump within the transmission provides the necessary hydraulic pressure to operate the brakes and clutches.

5 Driver control of the transmission is by a six-position selector lever. The transmission has a 'drive' position, and a 'hold' facility on the first three gear ratios. The 'drive' position D provides automatic changing throughout the range of all four gear ratios, and is the one to select for normal driving. An automatic kickdown facility shifts the transmission down a gear if the accelerator pedal is fully depressed. The 'hold' facility is very similar, but limits the number of gear ratios available – ie, when the selector lever is in the 3 position, only the first three ratios can be selected; in the 2 position, only the first two can be selected. When the lever is in position 2, the transmission can be locked in first gear using the button on the right-hand side of the selector lever. These lower ratio 'hold' settings are useful for providing engine braking when traveling down steep gradients, or for preventing unwanted selection of top gear on twisty roads. Note, however, that the transmission should never be shifted down at high engine speeds.

6 On some models, the selector lever is equipped with a shift-lock function. This prevents the selector lever being moved from the P position unless the brake pedal is depressed.

7 Due to the complexity of the automatic transmission, any repair or overhaul work must be left to a Peugeot dealer with the necessary special equipment for fault diagnosis and repair. The contents of the following Sections are therefore confined to supplying general information, and any service information and instructions that can be used by the owner.

8 Note: *The automatic transmission unit is of the 'auto-adaptive' type. This means that it takes into account your driving style and modifies the transmission shift points to provide optimum performance and economy to suit. When the battery is disconnected, the transmission will lose its memory and will resort to one of its many base shift programs. The transmission will then relearn the optimum shift points when the vehicle is driven a few miles. During these first few miles of driving, there maybe a noticeable difference in performance whilst the transmission adapts to your individual style.*

2 Automatic transmission fluid – draining and refilling

Note: *A suitable square section wrench may be required to undo the transmission filler plug. These wrenches can be obtained from most motor factors or your Peugeot dealer.*

Note: *The transmission unit is equipped with a fluid wear sensor to inform the driver when the fluid needs renewing (the ECU flashes the Sport and Snow mode indicator lights when fluid renewal is necessary). If the transmission unit is drained and refilled with new fluid, this sensor should be reset. This can only be done using the Peugeot diagnostic test box.*

Draining

1 This operation is much quicker and more efficient if the car is first taken on a journey of sufficient length to warm the engine/transmission up to normal operating temperature.

2 Park the car on level ground, switch off the ignition and apply the handbrake firmly. For improved access, jack up the front of the car and support it securely on axle stands (see *Jacking and vehicle support*). Undo the screws and remove the engine/transmission undershield (where fitted).

3 Position a suitable container under the drain plug, situated on the base of the transmission. Unscrew the drain plug (the smaller plug in the centre of the drain plug is the level plug – see Chapter 1A Section 23) and recover the sealing washer **(see illustration)**. Allow the fluid to drain completely into the container.

> ⚠️ **Warning: If the fluid is hot, take precautions against scalding.**

4 Clean the drain plug, being especially careful to wipe off any metallic particles. Discard the sealing washer; it should be renewed whenever it is disturbed.

5 When the fluid has finished draining, clean the drain plug threads and those of the transmission casing, fit a new sealing washer and refit the drain plug, tightening it to the specified torque wrench setting. If the car was raised for the draining operation, now lower it to the ground.

Refilling

6 To improve access to the filler plug, remove air cleaner housing, and the battery and battery box as described in Chapter 5A Section 4. If necessary, also unclip the selector cable end fitting from its balljoint on the transmission lever.

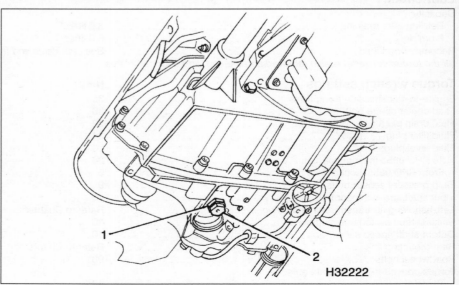

2.3 Transmission fluid drain plug (1) and oil level plug (2), inside the drain plug

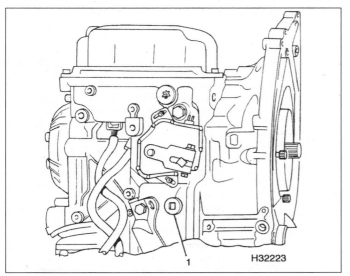

2.7 Transmission fluid filler plug (1) as viewed from above

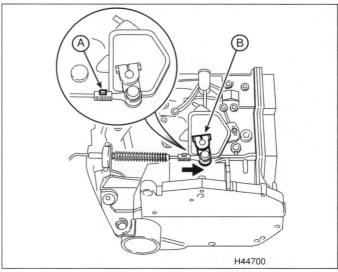

3.3 Press the yellow plastic part (A) to unlock the adjuster, then push the selector lever (B) fully to the front

7 Wipe clean the area around the filler plug, which is situated directly behind the transmission selector lever **(see illustration)**. Unscrew the filler plug from the transmission and recover the sealing washer.
Caution: Do not unscrew the selector shaft bolt (located in front of the selector lever).
8 Carefully refill the transmission with the correct amount of the specified type of fluid. Fit the new sealing washer to the filler plug then refit the plug, tightening it to the specified torque. Reconnect the selector cable to the lever (where disconnected – support the lever when pressing the cable onto its balljoint to prevent the lever being bent) then refit the battery and air cleaner housing.
9 Take the vehicle on a short journey to warm

the transmission up to normal operating temperature.
10 On your return, check the transmission fluid level as described in Chapter 1A Section 23.

3 Selector cable – adjustment

1 To gain access to the transmission end of the selector cable, remove the battery and battery box as described in Chapter 5A Section 4.
2 Position the selector lever firmly against its detent in the P (park) position.
3 Press the yellow plastic part on the cable end fitting to unlock the adjustment system **(see illustration)**.
4 Ensure that the selector lever on top of the transmission is fully forward, then press the yellow part on the selector cable again, to lock it in position.
5 Check the operation of the selector lever before refitting the battery box and battery.

4 Selector lever and cable – removal and refitting

Removal

1 Firmly apply the handbrake, and then jack up the front of the vehicle and support it on axle stands (see *Jacking and vehicle support*). Position the selector lever in the P position.
2 To gain access to the transmission end of the selector cable, remove the battery and battery box/tray.
3 Unclip the selector cable end fitting from the balljoint on the transmission lever. Remove the retaining clip and free the cable from the transmission bracket **(see illustration)**.
4 Remove the centre console as described in Chapter 11 Section 26.
5 Carefully pull the plastic rear air vents from place **(see illustration)**.
6 Note their fitted positions and disconnect all wiring plugs from the lever housing.
7 Undo the four nuts and manoeuvre the lever housing and cables from the vehicle **(see illustration)**. Prise the cable sealing grommet

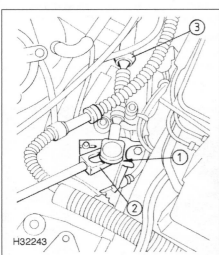

4.3 Prise off the selector cable balljoint (1) using a forked tool (2), then remove the cable from the bracket (3)

4.5 Move the plastic air vents to one side

4.7 Undo the four nuts (arrowed – two each side) and remove the housing

from the floor as the assembly is withdrawn.
8 Lever the selector cable off the selector lever balljoint then pull out the spring-loaded black pin and pull the outer cable from the front of the housing (see illustrations). Note that at the time of writing, the lever and housing were only available as a complete assembly – check with your Peugeot dealer for parts availability.

Refitting

9 Refitting is the reverse of removal, noting the following points.
● Support the transmission selector lever when pressing the cable onto its balljoint to prevent the lever being bent.
● Adjust the cable as described in Section 3 before refitting all components removed for access.

5 Speedometer drive – removal and refitting

1 Refer to Chapter 7A, Section 6.

6 Oil seals – renewal

Driveshaft oil seals

1 Remove the appropriate driveshaft as described in Chapter 8 Section 2.

Right-hand seal

2 Remove the O-ring from the differential sun gear shaft and then carefully remove the oil seal from of the transmission, taking care not to damage the shaft or housing. To remove the seal, carefully punch or drill two small holes opposite each other into the seal. Screw a self-tapping screw into each hole and pull on the screws to extract the seal.
3 Remove all traces of dirt from the area around the oil seal aperture, then apply a smear of grease to the outer edge and sealing lip of the new oil seal. Ease the new seal onto the shaft, taking care not to damage its lip, and into its aperture. Drive the seal squarely

into position using a suitable tubular drift (such as a socket), which bears only on the hard outer edge of the seal.
4 Once the seal is correctly installed, fit a new O-ring to the sun gear shaft and slide along until it abuts the seal.
5 Refit the driveshaft.

Left-hand seal

6 Carefully prise the oil seal out of the transmission, using a large flat-bladed screwdriver.
7 Remove all traces of dirt from the area around the oil seal aperture, then apply a smear of grease to the outer lip of the new oil seal. Fit the new seal into its aperture, and drive it squarely into position using a suitable tubular drift (such as a socket) which bears only on the hard outer edge of the seal, until it abuts its locating shoulder. If the seal was supplied with a plastic protector sleeve, leave this in position until the driveshaft has been refitted.
8 Apply a thin film of grease to the oil seal lip.
9 Refit the driveshaft.

Selector shaft oil seal

10 To gain access to the transmission selector shaft, remove the battery and battery tray as described in Chapter 5A Section 4.
11 Position the selector lever firmly against its detent mechanism in the P position.
12 Slacken and remove the nut and clamp bolt securing the selector lever to the transmission shaft (see illustration). Make alignment marks between the shaft and lever then free the lever from the shaft.
13 Remove the retaining clip and free the selector cable from transmission bracket (see illustration 4.3). Position the cable clear of the selector shaft.
14 Make alignment marks between the multifunction switch and transmission unit then unscrew the retaining bolts and remove the switch.
15 Carefully remove the oil seal from of the transmission, taking care not to damage the shaft or housing. To remove the seal, carefully punch or drill two small holes opposite each other into the seal. Screw a self-tapping screw into each hole and pull on the screws to extract the seal.
16 Remove all traces of dirt from the area around the oil seal aperture, then apply a

smear of grease to the outer edge and sealing lip of the new oil seal. Ease the new seal onto the shaft, taking care not to damage its lip, and press it squarely into its aperture.
17 Locate the multifunction switch back on the selector shaft. Align the marks made prior to removal then refit the switch bolts, tightening them to the specified torque.
18 Seat the selector cable in the transmission bracket and engage the selector lever with the transmission shaft. Ensure the marks made on removal are correctly aligned then refit the lever clamp bolt and nut and tighten securely.
19 Secure the selector cable in position with the retaining clip then adjust the cable as described in Section 3.
20 Refit all components removed for access.

Torque converter seal

21 Remove the transmission unit as described in Section 9.
22 Carefully slide the torque converter off the transmission shaft whilst being prepared for fluid spillage.
23 Note the correct fitted position of the seal in the housing then carefully lever it out of position, taking care not to mark the housing or shaft.
24 Remove all traces of dirt from the area around the oil seal aperture. Ease the new seal into its aperture, ensuring its sealing lip is facing inwards, then press it squarely into position.
25 Engage the torque converter with the transmission shaft splines and slide it into position, taking care not to damage the oil seal.
26 Refit the transmission unit as described in Section 9.

7 Fluid cooler – removal and refitting

Caution: Be careful not to allow dirt into the transmission unit during this procedure.

Removal

1 The fluid cooler is mounted on the rear of the transmission housing. To gain access to the cooler, remove the battery and battery box as described in Chapter 5A Section 4.

4.8a Lever the selector cable end fitting from the balljoint

4.8b Pull out the pin (arrowed) a little, then slide up the outer cable fitting

6.12 Unscrew the nut and clamp bolt (arrowed) and free the selector lever from the transmission shaft

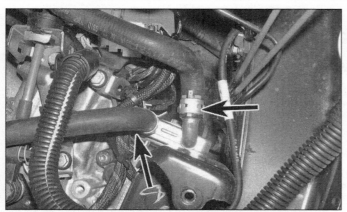

7.4 Release the retaining clips and disconnect the coolant hoses (arrowed) from the fluid cooler (viewed from above)

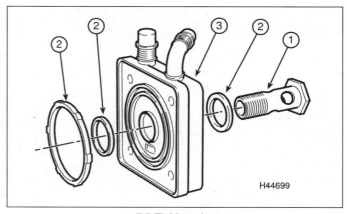

H44699

7.5 Fluid cooler

1 Bolt   2 Seals   3 Fluid cooler

2 Remove all traces of dirt from around the fluid cooler before proceeding.

3 Using a hose clamp or similar, clamp both the fluid cooler coolant hoses to minimise coolant loss during subsequent operations.

4 Release the retaining clips, and disconnect both coolant hoses from the fluid cooler – be prepared for some coolant spillage **(see illustration)**. Wash off any spilt coolant immediately with cold water, and dry the surrounding area before proceeding further.

5 Slacken and remove the fluid cooler centre bolt, and remove the cooler from the transmission. Remove the seal from the centre bolt, and the two seals fitted to the rear of the cooler, and discard them; new ones must be used on refitting **(see illustration)**.

Refitting

6 Lubricate the new seals with clean automatic transmission fluid, then fit the two new seals to the rear of the fluid cooler and a new seal to the centre bolt.

7 Locate the fluid cooler on the rear of transmission housing then refit the centre bolt. Ensure the cooler is correctly positioned then tighten the centre bolt to the specified torque setting.

8 Reconnect the coolant hoses to the fluid cooler, and secure them in position with their retaining clips. Remove the hose clamps.

9 Refit the battery and battery tray.

10 Top-up the cooling system as described in *Weekly checks* and check the transmission unit fluid level as described in Chapter 1A Section 23.

---

8   Transmission control system components – removal and refitting

Electronic control unit (ECU)

Note: *The automatic transmission electronic control system relies on accurate communication between the engine management ECU and the automatic transmission ECU. If the ECU is*
renewed, then both ECUs must be 'initialised'. The initialisation procedure requires access to specialised electronic test equipment and so it is recommended that this operation be entrusted to a suitably-equipped Peugeot dealer or specialist.

Removal

1 Remove the battery and battery box (see Chapter 5A Section 4).

2 Slide out the locking catch and disconnect the wiring connector from the ECU.

3 Undo the two mounting nuts and remove the ECU from the mounting plate.

Refitting

4 Refitting is the reverse of removal, ensuring the wiring connector is securely reconnected.

Output shaft speed sensor

Caution: *Be careful not to allow dirt into the transmission unit during this procedure.*

Removal

5 The output shaft sensor is fitted to the rear of the transmission unit.

6 To gain access to the sensor, jack up the front of the vehicle and support it securely on axle stands (see *Jacking and vehicle support*). Undo the screws and remove the engine/transmission undershield (where fitted).

7 Trace the sensor wiring back to its connector, located next to the transmission main wiring harness connector. Unclip the connector from its bracket then disconnect it.

8 Wipe clean the area around the sensor then slacken and remove the retaining bolt from the sensor. Remove the sensor along with its sealing ring; discard the sealing ring, a new one must be used on refitting.

Refitting

9 Refitting is the reverse of removal, noting the following points.

● Fit a new sealing ring to the sensor and tighten the sensor bolt to the specified torque.

● On completion, check the transmission fluid level as described in Chapter 1A Section 23.

Input shaft speed sensor

Caution: *Be careful not to allow dirt into the transmission unit during this procedure.*

Removal

10 The input shaft speed sensor is located on the left-hand end of the transmission unit.

11 To gain access to the sensor, chock the rear wheels, firmly apply the handbrake, then jack up the front of the vehicle and securely support it on axle stands (see *Jacking and vehicle support*).

12 To gain access to the main wiring connector, remove the battery and battery tray.

13 Lift the retaining clip and disconnect the main wiring connector from the top of the transmission unit.

14 Unscrew the two bolts and free the main wiring connector from the transmission unit. Cut the cable tie securing the wiring to the connector cover then release the clips and slide the cover off the connector.

15 Trace the wiring back from the sensor being removed to the main wiring connector, freeing it from all the relevant retaining clips and ties. Carefully release the retaining clips then slide the sensor connector out from the rear of the main connector, noting which way around it is fitted.

16 Wipe clean the area around the sensor. Slacken and remove the retaining bolt then remove the sensor, along with its sealing ring. Discard the sealing ring; a new one must be used on refitting.

Refitting

17 Refitting is the reverse of removal, noting the following points.

● Fit a new sealing ring to the sensor and tighten the sensor bolt to the specified torque.

● Ensure the sensor wiring is correctly routed and retained by all the necessary clips and ties.

● Clip the sensor wiring back into the main wiring connector, ensuring it is fitted the right way around. Slide the cover back onto the main connector, ensuring it is clipped securely in position, and secure the wiring to the cover with a new cable tie. Secure the connector to the transmission unit with the retaining bolts.

● On completion, check the transmission fluid level as described in Chapter 1A Section 23.

Fluid pressure sensor

Caution: Be careful not to allow dirt into the transmission unit during this procedure.

Removal

18 The fluid pressure sensor is located on the base of the transmission unit.

19 To gain access to the sensor, chock the rear wheels, firmly apply the handbrake then jack up the front of the vehicle and securely support it on axle stands (see *Jacking and vehicle support*).

20 Remove the battery and battery tray.

21 Unscrew the two bolts and free the main wiring connector from the transmission unit. Cut the cable tie securing the wiring to the connector cover then release the clips and slide the cover off the connector.

22 Trace the wiring back from the sensor being removed to the main wiring connector, freeing it from all the relevant retaining clips and ties. Carefully release the retaining clips then slide the green 3-way sensor connector out from the rear of the main connector, noting which way around it is fitted.

23 Wipe clean the area around the sensor. Slacken and remove the retaining bolts then remove the sensor, along with its sealing ring **(see illustration)**. Discard the sealing ring; a new one must be used on refitting. Be prepared for fluid spillage, and plug the opening to minimise fluid loss.

Refitting

24 Refitting is the reverse of removal, noting the following points.

● Fit a new sealing ring to the sensor and tighten the sensor bolts to the specified torque.

● Ensure the sensor wiring is correctly routed and retained by all the necessary clips and ties.

● Clip the sensor wiring back into the main wiring connector, ensuring it is fitted the right way around. Slide the cover back onto the main connector, ensuring it is clipped securely in position, and secure the wiring to the cover with a new cable tie.

● On completion, check the transmission fluid level as described in Chapter 1A Section 23.

Multifunction switch

Note: *The multifunction switch is slotted to allow for adjustment. Accurate adjustment requires the use an accurate multimeter – see the text later in this Section.*

Removal

25 Remove the battery and battery box/tray (see Chapter 5A Section 4).

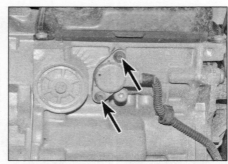

8.23 The fluid pressure sensor is secured to the base of the transmission by two bolts (arrowed)

26 Position the selector lever firmly against its detent mechanism in the P position.

27 Slacken and remove the nut and clamp bolt securing the selector lever to the transmission shaft **(see illustration 6.12)**. Make alignment marks between the shaft and lever then free the lever from the shaft.

28 Remove the retaining clip and free the selector cable from transmission bracket. Position the cable clear of the selector shaft.

29 Unscrew the two bolts and free the main wiring connector from the transmission unit. Cut the cable tie securing the wiring to the connector cover then release the clips and slide the cover off the connector.

30 Trace the wiring back from the switch to the main wiring connector, freeing it from all the relevant retaining clips and ties. Carefully release the retaining clips then slide the green 12-way connector out from the rear of the main connector, noting which way around it is fitted.

31 Make accurate alignment marks between the multifunction switch and transmission unit then unscrew the retaining bolts and remove the switch.

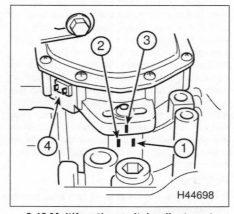

8.42 Multifunction switch adjustment

1 1st alignment mark
2 2nd alignment mark
3 Switch body alignment mark
4 Switch external contacts

Refitting

32 Locate the multi-function switch back on the selector shaft. Align the marks made prior to removal then refit the switch bolts, tightening them to the specified torque.

33 Clip the wiring back into the main wiring connector, ensuring it is fitted the right way around. Slide the cover back onto the main connector, ensuring it is clipped securely in position, and secure the wiring to the cover with a new cable tie. Locate the connector on the transmission unit and securely tighten its retaining bolts.

34 Reconnect the main wiring connector to the transmission unit.

35 Seat the selector cable in the transmission bracket and engage the selector lever with the transmission shaft. Ensure the marks made on removal are correctly aligned then refit the lever clamp bolt and nut, and tighten securely.

36 Secure the selector cable in position with the retaining clip then adjust the cable as described in Section 3, and the multifunction switch as described next.

Adjustment

37 Slacken the switch mounting bolts and rotate the switch fully anti-clockwise as far as it will go.

38 Set the multimeter to measure ohms, and connect meter terminals to the external switch contacts.

39 Slowly rotate the switch clockwise until the switch contacts close (the meter should register zero ohms – no resistance).

40 In this position, make an alignment mark between the switch and the transmission casing.

41 Continue to rotate the switch clockwise until the contacts open (the meter should register infinite ohms or similar)

42 Make another alignment mark between the transmission casing and the mark made previously on the switch **(see illustration)**.

43 Rotate the switch until the alignment mark on the switch body is exactly halfway between the two marks made on the transmission casing. Tighten the switch mounting bolts to the specified torque.

44 Refit the battery and battery box/tray as described in Chapter 5A Section 4.

45 Check that the selector lever position corresponds to the display on the instrument panel.

---

9 Automatic transmission – removal and refitting

1 Chock the rear wheels, then firmly apply the handbrake. Slacken both front roadwheel bolts. Jack up the front of the vehicle, and securely support it on axle stands (see *Jacking and vehicle support*). Remove both front roadwheels.

2 Drain the transmission oil as described in Section 2, then refit the drain plugs, and tighten to their specified torque settings.

3 Remove both driveshafts as described in Chapter 8 Section 2.

4 Remove the battery and battery box/tray, and then remove the automatic transmission ECU as described in Section 8.

5 Remove the air cleaner housing and intake ducting.

6 In order to prevent any damage, remove the exhaust system.

7 Remove the front bumper, as described in Chapter 11 Section 6.

8 Undo the retaining bolts and remove the front crossmember from the front of the vehicle.

9 Undo the retaining bolts and remove the front plastic tray from across the front of the vehicle.

10 Undo the retaining bolts and remove the headlamps, with reference to Chapter 12 Section 7.

11 Drain the cooling system and remove the radiator assembly, as described in Chapter 1A Section 25.

12 Remove the air conditioning condenser, as described in Chapter 3 Section 12. Do not disconnect the condenser from the refrigerant pipes, just move it to one side; making sure it is supported securely.

13 Undo the retaining bolts and remove the radiator housing panel from the front of the engine compartment.

14 Undo the retaining bolts and remove the front subframe crossmember from the left-hand side of the transmission

15 Remove the starter motor, referring to the relevant Chapter, if required.

16 Disconnect the gearchange cables from the transmission and support bracket with reference to Section 4.

17 Release the retaining clips and disconnect both coolant hoses from the fluid cooler – be prepared for some coolant spillage. Wash off any spilt coolant immediately with cold water, and dry the surrounding area before proceeding further.

18 Lift the retaining clip and disconnect the main wiring connector from the transmission wiring block, located at the rear of the unit. Also disconnect the output shaft speed sensor wiring connector (located next to the main connector) then position the wiring harness clear of the transmission unit.

19 Undo the retaining nut/bolt(s), and disconnect the earth straps from the top of the transmission housing. Free the wiring from any relevant retaining clips, and position it clear of the transmission.

20 Undo the retaining bolt(s), and remove the flywheel lower cover plate (where fitted) from the transmission.

21 Undo the retaining bolts and remove the cross bar from under the vehicle.

22 Access to the torque converter retaining nuts is gained via an access hole above the right-hand driveshaft on the back of the cylinder block. Use a socket and extension bar to rotate the crankshaft pulley to align the first nut with the aperture **(see illustration)**. Unscrew the nut then rotate the crankshaft 120°. Remove the second nut then rotate the crankshaft another 120° Unscrew the third and final nut and discard all three nuts; new ones will be required for refitting.

23 To ensure that the torque converter does not fall out as the transmission is removed, secure it in position using a length of metal strip bolted to one of the starter motor bolt holes.

24 Place a jack with a block of wood beneath the engine, to take the weight of the engine. Alternatively, attach a couple of lifting eyes to the engine, and fit a hoist or support bar to take the engine weight.

25 Place a jack and block of wood beneath the transmission, and raise the jack to take the weight of the transmission.

26 Remove the left-hand engine/transmission mounting, undo the retaining bolts and remove it from the top of the transmission.

27 Unscrew the nuts and bolts and remove the mounting link securing the rear engine/transmission mounting to the subframe.

28 With the jack positioned beneath the transmission taking the weight, slacken and remove the remaining bolts securing the transmission housing to the engine. Note the correct fitted positions of each bolt and the necessary brackets, as they are removed, to use as a reference on refitting.

29 Make a final check that all components have been disconnected, and are positioned clear of the transmission so that they will not hinder the removal procedure.

30 With the bolts removed, move the trolley jack and transmission to the left, to free it from its locating dowels. Lower the engine slightly to enable the transmission to be withdrawn.

Caution: Take great care not to damage any components if the engine is moved.

31 Once the transmission is free, lower the jack and manoeuvre the unit out from under the car. Remove the locating dowels from the transmission or engine if they are loose, and keep them in a safe place.

Refitting

32 Ensure that the bush fitted to the centre of the crankshaft is in good condition, and apply a little Molykote BR2 grease to the torque converter centring pin.

Caution: Do not apply too much; otherwise there is a possibility of the grease contaminating the torque converter.

33 Ensure that the engine/transmission locating dowels are correctly positioned then raise the transmission unit into position. Align

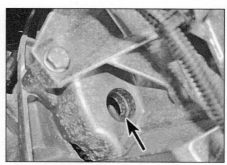

9.22 Access to the torque converter nuts is gained via the access hole (arrowed) above the driveshaft

the torque converter studs with the driveplate holes then engage the transmission unit with the engine.

Caution: Do not allow the weight of the transmission unit to hang on the torque converter as the unit is installed.

34 With the transmission and engine correctly joined, refit the transmission-to-engine unit bolts and tighten them to the specified torque.

35 Screw the new nuts onto the torque converter studs, tightening them lightly only, rotating the crankshaft as necessary. Tighten all three nuts to the specified Stage 1 torque setting. Once all have been tightened to the Stage 1 torque, go around and tighten them to the specified Stage 2 torque setting.

36 The remainder of refitting is the reverse of removal, noting the following points:

● Tighten all nuts and bolts to the specified torque (where given).

● Renew the driveshaft oil seals, then refit the driveshafts.

● Reconnect the selector cable and adjust as described in Section 3.

● Refill the cooling system.

● On completion, check the transmission fluid level as described in Chapter 1A Section 23.

10 Automatic transmission overhaul – general information

1 In the event of a fault occurring with the transmission, it is first necessary to determine whether it is of an electrical, mechanical or hydraulic nature and, to do this, special test equipment is required. It is therefore essential to have the work carried out by a Peugeot dealer or specialist if a transmission fault is suspected.

2 Do not remove the transmission from the car for possible repair before professional fault diagnosis has been carried out, since most tests require the transmission to be in the vehicle.

Chapter 8
Driveshafts

Contents

Degrees of difficulty

Easy, suitable for novice with little experience		Fairly easy, suitable for beginner with some experience		Fairly difficult, suitable for competent DIY mechanic		Difficult, suitable for experienced DIY mechanic		Very difficult, suitable for expert DIY or professional	

Specifications

Lubrication (overhaul only – see text)

Lubricant type/specification . . . . Use only special grease supplied in sachets with gaiter kits – joints are otherwise pre-packed with grease and sealed

Torque wrench settings

	Nm	lbf ft
Driveshaft retaining nut:		
1.4 litre non-VTi petrol engines	245	181
All other engines	325	240
Lower balljoint clamp bolt and nut	40	30
Roadwheel bolts	90	66
Track rod end nut	35	26

1 General Information

1 Drive is transmitted from the differential to the front wheels by means of two solid-steel driveshafts of unequal length.
2 Both driveshafts are splined to accept the wheel hubs, and are threaded at the outer ends so that each hub can be fastened by a large nut. The inner end of each driveshaft is splined, to accept the differential sun gear.
3 Constant velocity (CV) joints are fitted to each end of the driveshafts, to ensure that the smooth and efficient transmission of power at all suspension and steering angles. The outer constant velocity joints are of the ball-and-cage type, and the inner constant velocity joints are of the tripod type.

2 Driveshafts – removal and refitting

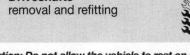

Caution: Do not allow the vehicle to rest on its wheels with one or both driveshafts removed, as damage to the wheel bearing(s) may result. If moving the vehicle is unavoidable, temporarily insert the outer end of the driveshaft(s) in the hub(s) and tighten the hub nut(s): in this case, the inner end(s) of the driveshaft(s) must be supported, for example by suspending with string from the vehicle underbody. Do not allow the driveshaft to hang down under its own weight.
Note: *A new suspension lower balljoint nut, track rod end nut and driveshaft nut will be required on refitting.*

Removal

1 Remove the wheel trim/hub cap (as applicable) and then undo the driveshaft nut with the vehicle resting on its wheels. Also slacken the wheel bolts.
2 On models where the driveshaft nut is staked, using a hammer and a chisel or similar

2.2 Use a chisel to release the securing nut

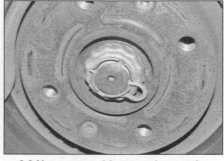

2.3 Use a screwdriver to prise out the R-clip

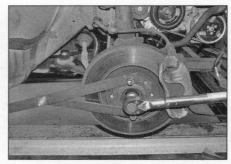

2.6 Using a fabricated tool to hold the front hub stationary

2.7 Disconnect the track rod end

2.8 Remove the lower balljoint retaining bolt

2.10 Pull down on the lower arm to disengage balljoint

tool, tap up the staking securing the driveshaft nut in position **(see illustration)**. Note that a new retaining nut must be used on refitting.

3 On models where the driveshaft nut is secured by an R-clip, withdraw the R-clip and remove the locking cap from the driveshaft nut **(see illustration)**.

4 Chock the rear wheels of the car, firmly apply the handbrake, and then jack up the front of the car and support it on axle stands (see *Jacking and vehicle support*). Remove the appropriate front roadwheel and engine undershield.

5 On manual transmission models drain the transmission oil, on automatic transmission models there is no need to drain the fluid.

6 If the nut was not slackened with the wheels on the ground (see paragraph 1 to 3), refit at least two roadwheel bolts to the front hub, and tighten them securely. Have an assistant firmly depress the brake pedal to prevent the front hub from rotating, then using a socket and a long

extension bar, slacken and remove the driveshaft nut. Alternatively, a tool can be fabricated from two lengths of steel strip (one long, one short) and a nut and bolt, the nut and bolt forming the pivot of a forked tool **(see illustration)**. Bolt the tool to the hub using two wheel bolts, and hold the tool to prevent the hub from rotating as the driveshaft retaining nut is undone. This nut is very tight; make sure that there is no risk of pulling the car off the axle stands (see *Jacking and vehicle support*). **Note:** *If the roadwheel trim allows access to the driveshaft nut, the initial slackening can be done with the vehicle resting on its wheels on the ground.*

7 Undo the retaining nut and disconnect the track rod end from the front stub axle **(see illustration)**.

8 Slacken and remove the suspension lower arm balljoint clamp bolt and nut **(see illustration)**. Discard the nut – a new one must be used on refitting.

Left-hand driveshaft

9 Turn the hub assembly onto a full left-hand lock.

10 Pull down on the lower arm to free its balljoint from the swivel hub **(see illustration)**. Once the balljoint is freed from the swivel hub, pull the hub assembly outwards taking care not to damage the gaiters.

11 If required, recover the protector plate from lower arm balljoint **(see illustration)**.

12 Carefully pull the swivel hub assembly outwards, and withdraw the driveshaft outer constant velocity joint from the hub assembly **(see illustration)**. If necessary, the shaft can be tapped out of the hub using a soft-faced mallet.

13 Support the driveshaft, and then withdraw the inner constant velocity joint from the transmission, taking care not to damage the driveshaft oil seal. Remove the driveshaft from the vehicle **(see illustration)**.

2.11 Check protector plate on balljoint

2.12 Withdraw the driveshaft out from the hub...

2.13... and then from the transmission

2.17 Withdraw the driveshaft out from the hub...

2.18... and then from the transmission

2.24 Align the balljoint with the swivel hub

Right-hand driveshaft

14 Turn the hub assembly onto a full right-hand lock.

15 Pull down on the lower arm to free its ball- joint from the swivel hub **(see illustration 2.10)**. Once the balljoint is freed from the swivel hub, pull the hub assembly outwards taking care not to damage the gaiters.

16 If required, recover the protector plate from lower arm balljoint **(see illustration 2.11)**.

17 Carefully pull the swivel hub assembly outwards, and withdraw the driveshaft outer constant velocity joint from the hub assembly **(see illustration)**. If necessary, the shaft can be tapped out of the hub using a soft-faced mallet.

18 Support the driveshaft, and then withdraw the inner constant velocity joint from the transmission, taking care not to damage the driveshaft oil seal. Remove the driveshaft from the vehicle **(see illustration)**.

Refitting

19 Before installing the driveshaft, examine the driveshaft oil seal in the transmission for signs of damage or deterioration and, if necessary, renew it as described in Chapter 7A or 7B. It is highly recommended that the seal be renewed, regardless of its apparent condition.

20 Thoroughly clean the driveshaft splines, and the apertures in the transmission and hub assembly. Apply a thin film of grease to the oil seal lips, and to the driveshaft splines and shoulders. Check that all gaiter clips are securely fastened.

21 Offer up the driveshaft, and locate the joint splines with those of the differential sun gear, taking great care not to damage the oil seal. Push the joint fully into position.

22 Locate the outer constant velocity joint splines with those of the swivel hub, and slide the joint back into position in the hub.

23 If removed, refit the protector plate to the lower arm balljoint.

24 Align the lower arm balljoint with the swivel hub, and seat the balljoint shank correctly in the swivel hub, aligning the protector plate tang with the hub slot **(see illustration)**. Insert the clamp bolt then fit the new nut and tighten to the specified torque.

25 Lubricate the inner face and threads of the driveshaft nut with clean engine oil (Peugeot recommend the use of Molykote D321R) and fit it to the end of the driveshaft (a new nut must be used on models with a staked nut). Use the method employed on removal to prevent the hub from rotating, and tighten the

2.26 Use a hammer and punch to lock the hub nut

driveshaft nut to the specified torque. Check that the hub rotates freely.

26 On models where the driveshaft nut is staked, stake the new nut into the driveshaft groove using a hammer and punch **(see illustration)**.

27 On models where the driveshaft nut is secured by an R-clip, engage the locking cap with the driveshaft nut so that one of its cut-outs is aligned with the driveshaft hole. Secure the cap in position with the R-clip **(see illustrations)**.

28 Refit the track rod end to the front stub axle and tighten the retaining nut.

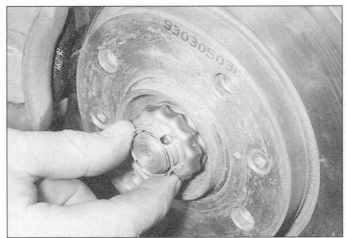

2.27a Tighten the driveshaft nut to the specified torque, then refit the locking cap...

2.27b... and secure it in position with the R-clip

29 Refit the roadwheel and undershield (where fitted), then lower the vehicle to the ground and tighten the roadwheel bolts to the specified torque.

30 Top-up/refill the transmission with the specified type and amount of fluid/oil, and check the level using the information given in Chapter 7A or 7B.

3 Driveshaft rubber gaiters – renewal

Outer joint

1 Remove the driveshaft from the vehicle as described in Section 2.

2 Secure the driveshaft in a vice equipped with soft jaws, and release the two outer gaiter retaining clips. If necessary, the gaiter retaining clips can be cut to release them **(see illustrations)**.

3 Slide the rubber gaiter down the shaft, to expose the outer constant velocity joint **(see illustrations)**. Scoop out the excess grease.

4 If the gaiter is to be renewed, it can be cut off and removed from the driveshaft **(see illustration)**.

5 Using a hammer and suitable soft metal drift, sharply strike the inner member of the outer joint to drive it off the end of the shaft **(see illustration)**. The joint is retained on the driveshaft by a circlip, and striking the joint in this manner forces the circlip into its groove, so allowing the joint to slide off.

Caution: This joint can be very tight, if the outer joint does not appear to be moving, remove the inner joint (as described later in this Section) and slide the gaiter on from the other end of the shaft.

6 Once the joint assembly has been removed, release the circlip from the groove in the driveshaft splines, and discard it. A new circlip must be fitted on reassembly.

7 If not removed already, withdraw the rubber gaiter from the driveshaft.

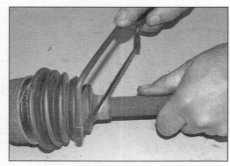
3.2a Cut the retaining clips…

3.2b… and remove from the gaiter

3.3a Pull back the gaiter…

3.3b… and clean out the old grease

8 With the constant velocity joint removed from the driveshaft, thoroughly clean the joint using paraffin, or a suitable solvent, and dry it thoroughly. Carry out a visual inspection of the joint.

9 Move the inner splined driving member from side-to-side to expose each ball in turn at the top of its track. Examine the balls for cracks, flat spots, or signs of surface pitting.

10 Inspect the ball tracks on the inner and outer members. If the tracks have widened, the balls will no longer be a tight fit. At the same time, check the ball cage windows for wear or cracking between the windows.

11 If, on inspection, any of the constant velocity joint components are found to be worn or damaged, it will be necessary to renew the complete joint assembly (where available), or even the complete driveshaft (where no joint components are available separately). Refer to your Peugeot dealer for further information on parts availability. If the joint is in satisfactory condition, obtain a repair kit consisting of a new gaiter, circlip, retaining clips, and the correct type and quantity of grease.

12 Slide the new gaiter and retaining clips onto the shaft and then perform the operations

3.4 Cut the old gaiter and remove

3.5 Using a soft metal drift to release the outer joint

3.12a Fit the new circlip to its groove in the driveshaft splines...

3.12b... then locate the joint outer member on the splines, and slide it into position over the circlip. Ensure that the joint is securely retained by the circlip

3.12c Pack the joint with grease, working it into the ball tracks while twisting the joint, then locate the gaiter outer lip in its groove on the outer member

shown **(see illustrations)**. Be sure to stay in order, and follow the captions carefully.

13 Note that the gaiter retaining clips supplied with the repair kit may be different to those shown in the sequence. To secure this other type of clip in position, lock the ends of the clip together, and then remove any slack in the clip by carefully compressing the raised section of the clip using a pair special pliers **(see illustrations)** or a pair of side-cutters.

14 Check that the constant velocity joint moves freely in all directions, then refit the driveshaft to the vehicle as described in Section 2.

Inner joint

15 Remove the driveshaft from the vehicle as described in Section 2.

16 Secure the driveshaft in a vice equipped with soft jaws, and release the two outer gaiter retaining clips. If necessary, the gaiter retaining clips can be cut to release them **(see illustrations)**.

17 Slide the rubber gaiter down the shaft, to expose the outer constant velocity joint. Scoop out the excess grease.

18 If the gaiter is to be renewed, it can be cut off and removed from the driveshaft **(see illustration 3.4)**.

19 Slide the outer member off the tripod joint and remove the spring (and cup on some models), from inside the outer member of the joint **(see illustrations)**.

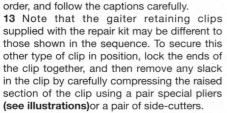

3.12d Fit the outer gaiter retaining clip and, using a hook fabricated out of welding rod and a pair of pliers, pull the clip tight to remove all the slack

3.13b... and, then using a pair of special pliers, tighten the clip onto the gaiter

3.13a Fit the outer gaiter retaining clip...

3.16a Cut the retaining clips...

3.16b... and remove from the gaiter

3.19a Slide the joint apart...

3.19b... and retrieve the spring

3.20a Release the circlip

3.20b Mark the position (arrowed) of the joint on the shaft

3.21 Slide the joint from the end of the shaft

3.25 Slide the inner clip onto the shaft first

3.26 Align the marks on refitting

3.27 Refit the circlip to secure the tripod joint

20 Using circlip pliers, extract the circlip securing the tripod joint to the driveshaft **(see illustrations)**. Mark the position of the tripod in relation to the driveshaft, using a dab of paint or a punch.
21 The tripod joint can now be removed **(see illustration)**. If it is tight, draw the joint off the driveshaft end using a puller. Ensure that the legs of the puller are located behind the joint inner member and do not contact the joint rollers. Alternatively, support the inner member of the tripod joint, and press the shaft out using a hydraulic press, again ensuring that no load is applied to the joint rollers.
22 With the tripod joint removed, if not removed already, slide the gaiter off the end of the driveshaft.

23 Wipe clean the joint components, taking care not to remove the alignment marks made on dismantling. Do not use paraffin or other solvents to clean this type of joint.
24 Examine the tripod joint, rollers and outer member for any signs of scoring or wear. Check that the rollers move smoothly on the tripod stems. If wear is evident, check with your local dealer to see if the tripod joint and roller assembly can be renewed. Obtain a new gaiter, retaining clips and a quantity of the special lubricating grease.
25 Tape over the splines on the end of the driveshaft, then carefully slide the inner retaining clip and gaiter onto the shaft **(see illustration)**.
26 Remove the tape, then, aligning the marks

made on dismantling, engage the tripod joint with the driveshaft splines **(see illustration)**. Use a hammer and soft metal drift to tap the joint onto the shaft, taking great care not to damage the driveshaft splines or joint rollers. Alternatively, support the driveshaft and press the joint into position using a hydraulic press and suitable tubular spacer which bears only on the joint inner member.
27 Secure the tripod joint in position with the circlip, ensuring that it is correctly located in the driveshaft groove **(see illustration)**.
28 Evenly distribute the grease contained in the repair kit inside the outer member, and then refit the spring and cup (where fitted) in the outer member **(see illustrations)**.

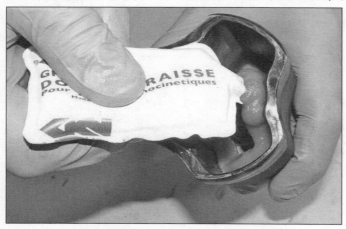

3.28a Pack the outer joint with grease...

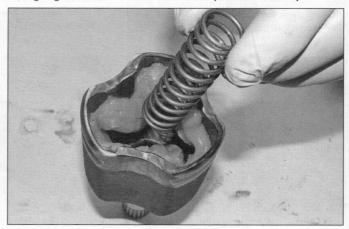

3.28b ... and insert the spring

3.29 Refit the tripod joint into the outer joint

3.33 Secure the gaiter in position with the securing clips

29 Pack the gaiter with the remainder of the grease and slide the two halves of the joint together **(see illustration)**.

30 Slide the gaiter up the driveshaft. Locate the gaiter in the grooves on the driveshaft and outer member.

31 Fit the inner retaining clip into place over the inner end of the gaiter.

32 Using a blunt rod, carefully lift the outer lip of the gaiter to equalise the air pressure.

33 Slip the new retaining clip into place to secure the outer lip of the gaiter to the outer member. Remove any slack in the gaiter retaining clip by carefully compressing the raised section of the clip (depending on type of clip supplied). In the absence of the special tool, a pair of pincers may be used **(see illustration)**. Secure the small retaining clip using the same procedure.

34 Check that the constant velocity joint moves freely in all directions, then refit the driveshaft as described in Section 2.

4 Driveshaft overhaul – general information

1 If any of the checks described in Chapter 1A or 1B reveal wear in any driveshaft joint, first remove the roadwheel trim or centre cap (as appropriate).

2 On models with a staked driveshaft nut, if the staking is still effective, the driveshaft nut should be correctly tightened; if in doubt, relieve the staking, then tighten the nut to the specified torque and restake it into the driveshaft grooves. Refit the roadwheel trim or centre cap (as applicable), and repeat the check on the remaining driveshaft nut.

3 On models where the driveshaft nut is secured by an R-clip, if the R-clip is fitted, the driveshaft nut should be correctly tightened, if in doubt, remove the R-clip and locking cap, and use a torque wrench to check that the nut is securely fastened. Once tightened, refit the locking cap and R-clip, and then refit the centre cap or trim. Repeat this check on the remaining driveshaft nut.

4 Road test the vehicle, and listen for a metallic clicking from the front as the vehicle is driven slowly in a circle on full-lock. If a clicking noise is heard, this indicates wear in the outer constant velocity joint. This means that the joint must be renewed; reconditioning is not possible.

5 If vibration, consistent with roadspeed, is felt through the car when accelerating, there is a possibility of wear in the inner joints.

6 To check the joints for wear, remove the driveshafts, and then dismantle them as described in Section 3 ; if any wear or free play is found, the affected joint must be renewed. In the case of the inner joints (and on some models, the outer joints), this means that the complete driveshaft assembly must be renewed, as the joints are not available separately. Refer to your Peugeot dealer for latest information on the availability of driveshaft components.

Chapter 9
Braking system

Contents

Degrees of difficulty

Easy, suitable for novice with little experience 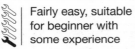	Fairly easy, suitable for beginner with some experience 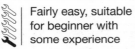	Fairly difficult, suitable for competent DIY mechanic 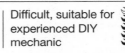	Difficult, suitable for experienced DIY mechanic 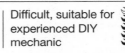	Very difficult, suitable for expert DIY or professional

Specifications

Front brakes

Disc diameter:	
Petrol models:	
1.4 litre engines	266 mm
1.6 litre engines	283 mm
Diesel models:	
1.4 litre engines	266 mm
1.6 litre engines	266 mm or 283 mm
Disc thickness:	
Petrol models:	
1.4 litre engines:	
New	22 mm
Minimum thickness	20 mm
1.6 litre engines:	
New	26 mm
Minimum thickness	24 mm
Diesel models:	
1.4 litre engines:	
New	22 mm
Minimum thickness	20 mm
1.6 litre engines (266 mm diameter discs):	
New	22 mm
Minimum thickness	20 mm
1.6 litre engines (283 mm diameter discs):	
New	26 mm
Minimum thickness	24 mm
Maximum disc run-out	0.05 mm
Caliper piston diameter	54 mm
Brake pad friction material thickness:	
New	13.0 mm
Minimum	2.0 mm

Rear drum brakes

Drum internal diameter:		
New	....	228.6 mm
Maximum	....	229.8 mm
Brake shoe friction material minimum thickness	....	1.5 mm

Rear disc brakes

Disc diameter	....	249 mm
Disc thickness:		
New	....	9.0 mm
Minimum thickness	....	7.0 mm
Maximum disc run-out	....	0.05 mm
Caliper piston diameter	....	38 mm
Brake pad friction material thickness:		
New	....	11.0 mm
Minimum	....	2.0 mm

Torque wrench settings

	Nm	lbf ft
ABS system components:		
Regulator unit mounting bolts	6	4
Wheel sensor retaining bolts*	8	6
Crossover linkage housing nuts and bolts (right-hand drive models) ..	25	18
Disc retaining screws	10	7
Front brake caliper:		
Guide pin bolts*	30	22
Mounting bracket bolts*	105	77
Handbrake lever nuts	15	11
Hydraulic hose/pipe union nuts	15	11
Master cylinder retaining nuts	20	15
Rear brake caliper:		
Guide pin bolts*	30	22
Mounting bracket bolts*	53	39
Rear hub nut: *		
Drum brakes	200	147
Disc brakes	300	221
Rear wheel cylinder retaining bolts*	8	6
Roadwheel bolts	90	66
Vacuum pump mounting bolts:		
1.4 litre diesel	18	13
1.6 litre diesel:		
Stage 1	3	2
Stage 2	5	4
Stage 3	18	13
Stage 4	Slacken by 5°	
Vacuum servo unit mounting nuts	22	16

*Do not re-use

1 General Information

1 The braking system is of the servo-assisted, dual-circuit hydraulic type. The arrangement of the hydraulic system is such that each circuit operates one front and one rear brake from a tandem master cylinder. Under normal circumstances, both circuits operate in unison. However, in the event of hydraulic failure in one circuit, full braking force will still be available at two wheels.

2 All models are equipped with disc front brakes, and disc or drum brakes on the rear depending on model.

3 The disc brakes are actuated by single-piston sliding type calipers, which ensure that equal pressure is applied to each disc pad. ABS is fitted as standard (refer to Section 21 for further information on ABS operation).

4 On models with rear drum brakes, these incorporate leading and trailing shoes, which are actuated by twin-piston wheel cylinders. A self-adjust mechanism is incorporated, to automatically compensate for brake shoe wear. As the brake shoe linings wear, the footbrake operation automatically operates the adjuster mechanism, which effectively lengthens the shoe strut and repositions the brake shoes to maintain the lining-to-drum clearance. The hydraulic pressure applied to the rear brakes is regulated by the pressure control valve(s) to help prevent rear wheel lock-up during emergency braking.

5 The handbrake provides an independent mechanical means of rear brake application. Models with rear brake calipers have an integral handbrake function. The handbrake cable operates a lever on the caliper, which forces the piston to press the pad against the disc surface. A self-adjust mechanism is incorporated, to automatically compensate for brake pad wear.

6 On VTi petrol and diesel engine models, a vacuum pump is fitted to the engine to provide sufficient vacuum to operate the servo unit. The vacuum pump is mounted on the end of the cylinder head, and is driven directly off the end of the camshaft.

Note: *When servicing any of the system, work carefully and methodically; also observe scrupulous cleanliness when overhauling any of the hydraulic system. Always renew components (in axle sets, where applicable) if in doubt about their condition, and use only genuine Peugeot parts, or at least those of known good quality. Note the warnings given in 'Safety first!' and at relevant points in this Chapter concerning the dangers of asbestos dust and hydraulic fluid.*

2 Hydraulic system – bleeding

Warning: Hydraulic fluid is poisonous; wash off immediately and thoroughly in the case of skin contact, and seek immediate medical advice if any fluid is swallowed or gets into the eyes. Certain types of hydraulic fluid are inflammable, and may ignite when allowed into contact with hot components; when servicing any hydraulic system, it is safest to assume that the fluid is inflammable, and to take precautions against the risk of fire as though it is petrol that is being handled. Hydraulic fluid is also an effective paint stripper, and will attack plastics; if any is spilt, it should be washed off immediately, using copious quantities of fresh water. Finally, it is hygroscopic (it absorbs moisture from the air) – old fluid may be contaminated and unfit for further use. When topping-up or renewing the fluid, always use the recommended type, and ensure that it comes from a freshly-opened sealed container.

Caution: Ensure the ignition is switched off before starting the bleeding procedure, to avoid any possibility of voltage being applied to the hydraulic regulator before the bleeding procedure is complete. Ideally, the battery should be disconnected. If voltage is applied to the regulator before the bleeding procedure is complete, this will effectively drain the hydraulic fluid in the regulator, rendering the unit unserviceable. Do not, therefore, attempt to 'run' the regulator in order to bleed the brakes.

Note: *If difficulty is experienced in bleeding the braking circuit, this maybe due to air being trapped in the ABS regulator unit. If this is the case then the vehicle should be taken to a Peugeot dealer or suitably-equipped specialist so that the system can be bled using special electronic test equipment.*

Note: *A hydraulic clutch shares its fluid reservoir with the braking system, and may also need to be bled (see Chapter 6 Section 2).*

General

1 The correct operation of any hydraulic system is only possible after removing all air from the components and circuit; this is achieved by bleeding the system.

2 During the bleeding procedure, add only clean, unused hydraulic fluid of the recommended type; never re-use fluid that has already been bled from the system. Ensure that sufficient fluid is available before starting work.

3 If there is any possibility of incorrect fluid being already in the system, the brake components and circuit must be flushed completely with uncontaminated, correct fluid, and new seals should be fitted to the various components.

4 If hydraulic fluid has been lost from the system, or air has entered because of a leak, ensure that the fault is cured before proceeding further.

5 Park the vehicle on level ground, switch off the engine and select first or reverse gear, then chock the wheels and release the handbrake.

6 Check that all pipes and hoses are secure, unions tight and bleed screws closed. Clean any dirt from around the bleed screws.

7 Unscrew the master cylinder reservoir cap, and top the master cylinder reservoir up to the MAX level line **(see illustration)**; refit the cap loosely, and remember to maintain the fluid level at least above the MIN level line throughout the procedure, or there is a risk of further air entering the system.

8 There is a number of one-man, do-it-yourself brake bleeding kits currently available from motor accessory shops. It is recommended that one of these kits is used whenever possible, as they greatly simplify the bleeding operation, and also reduce the risk of expelled air and fluid being drawn back into the system. If such a kit is not available, the basic (two-man) method must be used, which is described in detail below.

9 If a kit is to be used, prepare the vehicle as described previously, and follow the kit manufacturer's instructions, as the procedure may vary slightly according to the type being used; generally, they are as outlined below in the relevant sub-section.

10 Whichever method is used, the same sequence must be followed (paragraphs 11 and 12) to ensure that the removal of all air from the system.

Bleeding

Sequence

11 If the system has been only partially disconnected, and suitable precautions were taken to minimise fluid loss, it should be necessary only to bleed that of the system (ie, the primary or secondary circuit).

12 If the complete system is to be bled, then it should be done working in the following sequence:

● Left-hand front brake.
● Right-hand front brake.
● Left-hand rear brake.
● Right-hand rear brake.

2.7 Fluid MAX level line (arrowed)

Basic (two-man) method

13 Collect a clean glass jar, a suitable length of plastic or rubber tubing which is a tight fit over the bleed screw, and a ring spanner to fit the screw. The help of an assistant will also be required.

14 Remove the dust cap from the first screw in the sequence. Fit the spanner and tube to the screw, place the other end of the tube in the jar, and pour in sufficient fluid to cover the end of the tube.

15 Ensure that the master cylinder reservoir fluid level is maintained at least above the MIN level line throughout the procedure.

16 Have the assistant fully depress the brake pedal several times to build-up pressure, and then maintain it on the final down stroke.

17 While pedal pressure is maintained, unscrew the bleed screw (approximately one turn) and allow the compressed fluid and air to flow into the jar. The assistant should maintain pedal pressure, following it down to the floor if necessary, and should not release it until instructed to do so. When the flow stops, tighten the bleed screw again, have the assistant release the pedal slowly, and recheck the reservoir fluid level.

18 Repeat the steps given in paragraphs 16 and 17 until the fluid emerging from the bleed screw is free from air bubbles. If the master cylinder has been drained and refilled, and air is being bled from the first screw in the sequence, allow approximately five seconds between cycles for the master cylinder passages to refill.

19 When no more air bubbles appear, tighten the bleed screw securely, remove the tube and spanner, and refit the dust cap. Do not overtighten the bleed screw.

20 Repeat the procedure on the remaining screws in the sequence until all air is removed from the system and the brake pedal feels firm again.

Using a one-way valve kit

21 As their name implies, these kits consist of a length of tubing with a one-way valve fitted, to prevent expelled air and fluid being drawn back into the system; some kits include a translucent container, which can be positioned so that the air bubbles can be more easily seen flowing from the end of the tube.

22 The kit is connected to the bleed screw, which is then opened **(see illustration)**. The

2.22 Connect the kit to the bleed screw

user returns to the driver's seat, depresses the brake pedal with a smooth, steady stroke, and slowly releases it; this is repeated until the expelled fluid is clear of air bubbles.

23 Note that these kits simplify work so much that it is easy to forget the master cylinder reservoir fluid level; ensure that this is maintained at least above the MIN/DANGER level line at all times.

Using a pressure-bleeding kit

24 These kits are usually operated by the reservoir of pressurised air contained in the spare tyre. However, note that it will probably be necessary to reduce the pressure to a lower level than normal; refer to the instructions supplied with the kit.

25 By connecting a pressurised, fluid-filled container to the master cylinder reservoir, bleeding can be carried out simply by opening each screw in turn (in the specified sequence), and allowing the fluid to flow out until no more air bubbles can be seen in the expelled fluid.

26 This method has the advantage that the large reservoir of fluid provides an additional safeguard against air being drawn into the system during bleeding.

27 Pressure-bleeding is particularly effective when bleeding 'difficult' systems, or when bleeding the complete system at the time of routine fluid renewal.

All methods

28 When bleeding is complete, and firm pedal feel is restored, wash off any spilt fluid, tighten the bleed screws securely, and refit their dust caps.

29 Check the hydraulic fluid level in the master cylinder reservoir, and top-up if necessary (see *Weekly checks*).

30 Discard any hydraulic fluid that has been bled from the system; it will not be fit for re-use.

31 Check the feel of the brake pedal. If it feels at all spongy, air must still be present in the system, and further bleeding is required. Failure to bleed satisfactorily after a reasonable repetition of the bleeding procedure may be due to worn master cylinder seals.

3 Hydraulic pipes and hoses – renewal

Caution: Ensure the ignition is switched off before disconnecting any braking system hydraulic union and do not switch it on until after the hydraulic system has been bled. Failure to do this could lead to air entering the regulator unit requiring the unit to be bled using special Peugeot test equipment (see Section 2).

Note: *Before starting work, refer to the note at the beginning of Section 2 concerning the dangers of hydraulic fluid.*

1 If any pipe or hose is to be renewed, minimise fluid loss by first removing the master cylinder reservoir cap, then tightening it down onto a piece of polythene to obtain an airtight seal. Alternatively, flexible hoses can be sealed, if required, using a proprietary brake hose clamp; metal brake pipe unions can be plugged (if care is taken not to allow dirt into the system) or capped immediately they are disconnected. Place a wad of rag under any union that is to be disconnected, to catch any spilt fluid.

2 If a flexible hose is to be disconnected, unscrew the brake pipe union nut before removing the spring clip, which secures the hose to its mounting bracket.

3 To unscrew the union nuts, it is preferable to obtain a brake pipe spanner of the correct size; these are available from most large motor accessory shops. Failing this, a closefitting open-ended spanner will be required, though if the nuts are tight or corroded their flats may be rounded-off if the spanner slips. In such a case, a self-locking wrench is often the only way to unscrew a stubborn union, but it follows that the pipe and the damaged nuts must be renewed on reassembly. Always clean a union and surrounding area before disconnecting it. If disconnecting a component with more than one union, make a careful note of the connections before disturbing any of them.

4 If a brake pipe is to be renewed, it can be obtained, cut to length and with the union nuts and end flares in place, from Peugeot dealers. All that is then necessary is to bend it to shape, following the line of the original, before fitting it to the car. Alternatively, most motor accessory shops can make up brake pipes from kits, but this requires very careful measurement of the original, to ensure that the new one is of the correct length. The safest answer is usually to take the original to the shop as a pattern.

5 On refitting, do not overtighten the union nuts. It is not necessary to exercise brute force to obtain a sound joint.

6 Ensure that the pipes and hoses are correctly routed, with no kinks, and that they are secured in the clips or brackets provided. After fitting, remove the polythene from the reservoir, and bleed the hydraulic system as described in Section 2. Wash off any spilt fluid, and check carefully for any fluid leaks.

4 Front brake pads – renewal

⚠ *Warning: Renew both sets of front brake pads at the same time – never renew the pads on only one wheel, as uneven braking may result. Note that the dust created by wear of the pads may contain asbestos, which is a health hazard. Never blow it out with compressed air, and don't inhale any of it. An approved filtering mask should be worn when working on the brakes. DO NOT use petrol or petroleum-based solvents to clean brake parts; use brake cleaner or methylated spirit only.*

Note: *New guide pin bolts must be used on refitting.*

1 Apply the handbrake, slacken the front roadwheel bolts, then jack up the front of the vehicle and support it on axle stands. Remove the front roadwheels.

2 Push the piston back into its bore slightly, by pulling the caliper outwards.

3 Slacken and remove the caliper lower guide pin bolt **(see illustration)**. Discard the guide pin bolt – a new one must be used on refitting.

4 With the lower guide pin bolt removed, pivot the caliper away from the brake pads and mounting bracket, and tie it to the suspension strut using a suitable piece of wire **(see illustration)**.

5 Withdraw the two brake pads from the caliper mounting bracket; check the shim (where fitted) should be located in the piston of the caliper **(see illustrations)**.

6 First measure the thickness of each brake pad's friction material **(see illustration)**. If either pad is worn at any point to the specified minimum thickness or less, all four pads must be renewed. Also, the pads should be renewed if any are fouled with oil or grease;

4.3 Remove the caliper lower guide pin bolt...

4.4... then pivot the caliper upwards and away from the brake pads, and tie it to the suspension strut

4.5a Withdraw the brake pads from the caliper mounting bracket

4.5b Check the shim in the caliper piston

4.6 Measure the thickness of the pads friction material

there is no satisfactory way of degreasing friction material once contaminated. If any of the brake pads are worn unevenly, or are fouled with oil or grease, trace and rectify the cause before reassembly.

7 If the brake pads are still serviceable, carefully clean them using a clean, fine wire brush or similar, paying particular attention to the sides and back of the metal backing. Clean out the grooves in the friction material, and pick out any large embedded particles of dirt or debris. Carefully clean the pad locations in the caliper mounting bracket.

8 Prior to fitting the pads, check that the guide pins are free to slide easily in the caliper mounting bracket, and check that the rubber guide pin gaiters are undamaged **(see illustrations)**. If required a guide pin kit can be obtained, renew the pins noting their fitted position, using the grease provided.

9 Brush the dust and dirt from the caliper

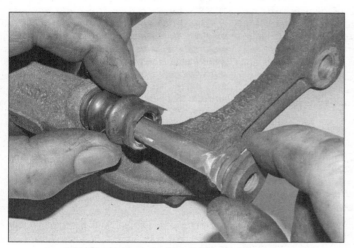

4.8a Check the condition of the guide pins…

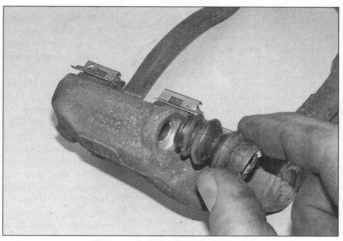

4.8b… and the guide pin rubbers

4.8c Renew guide pins and rubbers, if required

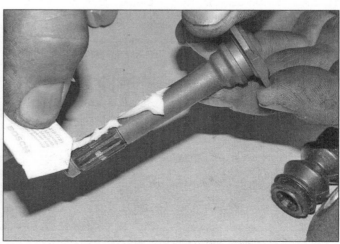

4.8d Use special grease to lubricate pins

4.10 Open the bleed nipple and push the piston back (piston retraction tool shown)

4.11 Ensure the shims at the top and bottom of the caliper mounting bracket are correctly fitted

4.12 Refit the pads, with the arrow (arrowed) in the direction of rotation

and piston, but do not inhale it, as it is a health hazard. Inspect the dust seal around the piston for damage, and the piston for evidence of fluid leaks, corrosion or damage. If attention to any of these components is necessary, refer to Section 10.

10 If new brake pads are to be fitted, the caliper piston must be pushed back into the cylinder to make room for them. Either use a G-clamp or similar tool, or use suitable pieces of wood as levers. Clamp off the flexible brake hose leading to the caliper then connect a brake bleeding kit to the caliper bleed nipple. Open the bleed nipple as the piston is retracted, the surplus brake fluid will then be collected in the bleed kit vessel **(see illustration)**. Close the bleed nipple just before the caliper piston is pushed fully into the caliper. This should ensure no air enters the hydraulic system. **Note:** *The ABS unit contains hydraulic components that are very sensitive to impurities in the brake fluid. Even the smallest particles can cause the system to fail through blockage. The pad retraction method described here prevents any debris in the brake fluid expelled from the caliper from being passed back to the ABS hydraulic unit, as well as preventing any chance of damage to the master cylinder seals.*

11 Check to make sure the shims at the top and bottom of the caliper bracket are correctly fitted **(see illustration)**.

12 Ensuring that the friction material of each pad is against the brake disc, fit the pads

to the caliper mounting bracket. Check the shim is in position in the caliper piston. If the pads have a chamfer at one edge, fit the pads so that the chamfer is at the top or they may have an arrow showing the direction of rotation **(see illustration)**.

13 Pivot the caliper down into position over the pads. If the threads of the new guide pin bolt are not already pre-coated with locking compound, apply a suitable thread-locking compound to them (Peugeot recommend Loctite Frenetanch – available from your Peugeot dealer). Press the caliper into position, and then install the guide pin bolt, tightening it to the specified torque setting **(see illustration)**.

14 Depress the brake pedal repeatedly, until the pads are pressed into firm contact with the brake disc, and normal (non-assisted) pedal pressure is restored.

15 Repeat the above procedure on the remaining front brake caliper.

16 Refit the roadwheels, and then lower the vehicle to the ground and tighten the roadwheel bolts to the specified torque.

17 Check the hydraulic fluid level as described in *Weekly checks*.

Caution: New pads will not give full braking efficiency until they have bedded-in. Be prepared for this, and avoid hard braking as far as possible for the first hundred miles or so after pad renewal.

5 Rear brake pads – renewal

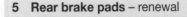

⚠ *Warning: Renew both sets of rear brake pads at the same time – never renew the pads on only one wheel, as uneven braking may result. Note that the dust created by wear of the pads may contain asbestos, which is a health hazard. Never blow it out with compressed air, and don't inhale any of it. An approved filtering mask should be worn when working on the brakes. DO NOT use petrol or petroleum-based solvents to clean brake parts; use brake cleaner or methylated spirit only.*

Note: *New guide pin bolts must be fitted on reassembly.*

1 Chock the front wheels, slacken the rear roadwheel bolts, and then jack up the rear of the vehicle and support it on axle stands (see *Jacking and vehicle support*). Remove the rear roadwheels.

2 Using a pair of pliers, release the handbrake cable from the caliper lever. Compress the clip and pull the cable from the support bracket **(see illustrations)**.

3 Slacken and remove the caliper guide pin bolts, then move the caliper to one side, and tie it in place to prevent any damage to the

4.13 Pivot the caliper down and over the pads, then fit and tighten the new caliper guide pin bolt

5.2a Disengage the handbrake cable from the caliper lever...

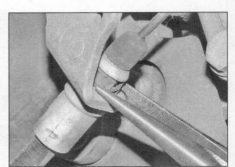

5.2b... then squeeze the clip and pull the outer cable from the support bracket

5.3a On first type of caliper, remove the caliper lower guide pin bolt...

5.3b ... and upper bolt (with fitted damper)

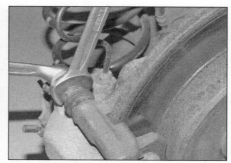

5.3c On second type of caliper, use an open-ended spanner to counter hold the guide pins...

brake hose. Note there are two types of brake calipers fitted to this model, although they have the same procedure for removal, there are some slight differences (see illustrations).

4 Withdraw the outer and inner pads from the caliper bracket, and note the location of the shim fitted to the caliper piston (see illustrations).

5 First measure the thickness of the friction material of each brake pad. If either pad is worn at any point to the specified minimum thickness or less, all four pads must be renewed. Also, the pads should be renewed if any are fouled with oil or grease; there is no satisfactory way of degreasing friction material once contaminated. If any of the brake pads are worn unevenly, or fouled with oil or grease, trace and rectify the cause before reassembly. Examine the retaining pins for signs of wear and renew if necessary. New brake pads and retaining pin kits are available from Peugeot dealers.

6 If the brake pads are still serviceable, carefully clean them using a clean, fine wire brush or similar, paying particular attention to the sides and back of the metal backing. Clean out the grooves in the friction material (where applicable), and pick out any large embedded particles of dirt or debris. Carefully clean the pad locations in the caliper body/ mounting bracket.

7 Prior to fitting the pads, check that the guide sleeves are free to slide easily in the caliper body, and check that the rubber guide sleeve gaiters are undamaged (see illustrations 4.8a, 4.8b, 4.8c and 4.8d).

8 Brush the dust and dirt from the caliper and piston, but do not inhale it, as it is a health hazard. Inspect the dust seal around the piston for damage, and the piston for evidence of fluid leaks, corrosion or damage. If attention to any of these components is necessary, refer to Section 11.

9 If new brake pads are to be fitted, the caliper piston must be pushed back into the cylinder to make room for them. In order to retract the piston, the piston must be rotated as it is pushed into the caliper (see

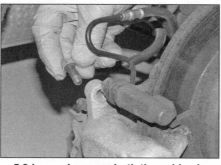

5.3d ... and remove both the guide pin bolts...

5.3e ... then secure the caliper to prevent damage

5.4a On first type of caliper, withdraw the outer...

5.4b ... and inner pads – note the fitted location of shim in piston

5.4c On second type of caliper, withdraw the outer...

5.4d ... and inner brake pads

5.9a Use a retraction tool to rotate the piston whilst pushing at the same time

5.9b Typical piston rotation tool for use with a socket set

5.11 Ensure the pads are fitted with the friction material facing the brake disc

5.12 Fit new guide pin bolts

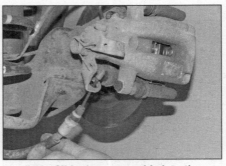

5.13a Slide the outer cable into the bracket...

5.13b ... and refit the inner cable

illustrations). **Note:** *This may be clockwise or anti-clockwise. The ABS unit contains hydraulic components that are very sensitive to impurities in the brake fluid. Even the smallest particles can cause the system to fail through blockage. The pad retraction method described here prevents any debris in the brake fluid expelled from the caliper from being passed back to the ABS hydraulic unit, as well as preventing any chance of damage to the master cylinder seals.*

10 Check to make sure the shims at the top and bottom of the caliper mounting bracket are correctly fitted **(see illustration 4.11)**.

11 Slide the brake pads into position in the caliper; ensuring each pad's friction material is facing the brake disc. If the shim has become detached, ensure that it is correctly positioned in the caliper piston **(see illustration)**.

12 Untie the caliper and fit it into position over the brake pads. Insert the new caliper guide pin bolts **(see illustration)**, which are coated in thread locking compound and tighten them to the specified torque. On the second type of caliper, use an open-ended spanner to secure the guide pin, when tightening the bolt.

13 Slide the outer handbrake cable into the support bracket and then reconnect the inner cable end fitting, back to the arm on the caliper **(see illustrations)**.

14 Depress the brake pedal repeatedly until the pads are pressed into firm contact with the brake disc, and normal (non-assisted) pedal pressure is restored.

15 Repeat the above procedure on the remaining rear brake caliper.

16 Check the operation of the handbrake, and if necessary, carry out the adjustment procedure as described in Section 17.

17 Refit the roadwheels, then lower the vehicle to the ground and tighten the roadwheel bolts to the specified torque setting.

18 Check the hydraulic fluid level as described in *Weekly checks*.

Caution: New pads will not give full braking efficiency until they have bedded-in. Be prepared for this, and avoid hard braking as far as possible for the first hundred miles or so after pad renewal.

6 Rear brake shoes – renewal

Caution: Brake shoes must be renewed on both rear wheels at the same time – never renew the shoes on only one wheel, as uneven braking may result. Also, the dust created by wear of the shoes may contain asbestos, which is a health hazard. Never blow it out with compressed air, and don't inhale any of it. An approved filtering mask should be worn when working on the brakes. DO NOT use petrol or petroleum-based solvents to clean brake parts; use brake cleaner or methylated spirit only.

1 Slacken the handbrake cable adjustment and remove the brake drum (see Section 9).

2 Working carefully, and taking the necessary precautions, remove all traces of brake dust from the brake drum, backplate and shoes.

3 Measure the thickness of the friction material of each brake shoe at several points; if either shoe is worn at any point to the specified minimum thickness or less, all four shoes must be renewed as a set. The shoes should also be renewed if any are fouled with oil or grease; there is no proper way of degreasing friction material, once contaminated.

4 If any of the brake shoes are worn unevenly, or fouled with oil or grease, trace and rectify the cause before reassembly.

5 Prior to removing the shoes, take careful note of the correct fitted positions of the springs and adjuster strut, to use as a guide on reassembly **(see illustration)**.

6.5 Make a note of the position of the brake shoes and springs

6.6a Remove the spring and cup...

6.6b... and recover the retaining pin

6.7 Ease the shoes out from the lower pivot point

6 Using a pair of pliers, remove the shoe retainer spring cups by depressing and turning them through 90º. With the cups removed, lift off the springs and withdraw the retainer pins **(see illustrations)**.

7 Ease the shoes out one at a time from the lower pivot point, to release the tension of the return spring, then disconnect the lower return spring from both shoes **(see illustration)**.

8 Ease the upper end of both shoes out from their wheel cylinder locations, taking care not to damage the wheel cylinder seals, and disconnect the handbrake cable from the trailing shoe. The brake shoe and adjuster strut assembly can then be manoeuvred out of position and away from the backplate. Do not depress the brake pedal until the brakes are reassembled; wrap an elastic band around the wheel cylinder pistons to retain them **(see illustrations)**.

9 With the shoe and adjuster strut assembly on a bench, make a note of the correct fitted positions of the springs and adjuster strut, to use as a guide on reassembly **(see illustrations)**.

10 Carefully unhook the adjuster strut bolt retaining spring from the leading shoe. Pivot the leading shoe out from the adjuster strut bolt then detach the leading shoe and return spring from the trailing shoe. Unhook the adjuster strut from the trailing shoe and recover the spring **(see illustrations)**.

6.8a Release the handbrake cable from the lever

6.8b Put a strong elastic band around the wheel cylinder to prevent the pistons moving out whilst the shoes are removed

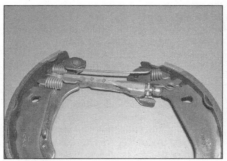

6.9a Note the correct fitted locations of the springs...

6.9b... and the strut components before separating the shoe and strut assembly

6.10a Unhook the adjuster strut bolt spring...

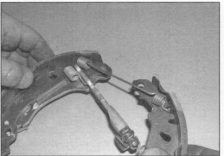

6.10b... then pivot the leading shoe off the bolt and remove the shoe and upper return spring

6.10c Unhook the adjuster strut from the trailing shoe, noting which way around its spring is fitted

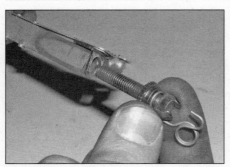

6.11 Check the adjuster strut bolt for signs of wear or damage

11 Withdraw the adjuster bolt from the strut, and carefully examine the assembly for signs of wear or damage **(see illustration)**. Pay particular attention to the threads of the adjuster bolt and the knurled adjuster wheel, and renew if necessary. Note that left-hand and right-hand struts are not interchangeable. Also note that the strut adjuster bolts are not interchangeable: the left-hand strut bolt has a left-handed thread, and the right-hand bolt a right-handed thread.

12 All return springs should be renewed, regardless of their apparent condition; spring kits are available from Peugeot dealers.

13 Ensure that the components on the end of the strut are correctly positioned, and then apply a little high melting-point grease to the threads of the adjuster bolt (Peugeot recommend the use of Lubritherm G200). Screw the adjuster wheel onto the bolt until only a small gap exists between the wheel and the head of the bolt, and then fit the bolt in the strut.

14 Fit the adjuster strut retaining spring to the trailing shoe, ensuring that the shorter hook of the spring is engaged with the shoe. Attach the adjuster strut to the spring end, and then ease the strut into its slot in the trailing shoe**(see illustration)**.

15 Engage the upper return spring with the trailing shoe, then hook the leading shoe onto the other end of the spring. Lever the leading shoe down until the adjuster bolt head is correctly located in its groove. Once the bolt is correctly located, hook its retaining spring into the slot on the leading shoe **(see illustration)**.

16 Peel back the rubber protective caps, and check the wheel cylinder for fluid leaks or other damage; check that both cylinder pistons are free to move easily. Refer to Section 12, if necessary, for information on wheel cylinder renewal.

17 Prior to installation, clean the backplate, and apply a thin smear of high-temperature brake grease or anti-seize compound (Peugeot recommend the use of Lubritherm G200) to all those surfaces of the backplate which bear on the shoes, particularly the wheel cylinder pistons and lower pivot point **(see illustration)**. Do not allow the lubricant to foul the friction material.

18 Remove the elastic band fitted to the wheel cylinder then manoeuvre the shoe and strut assembly into position. Attach the handbrake cable to the trailing shoe then locate the upper end of both shoes correctly with the wheel cylinder pistons. Fit the lower return spring to both shoes then ease the shoes into position on the lower pivot point.

19 Tap the shoes to centralise them with the backplate, then refit the shoe retainer pins and springs, and secure them in position with the spring cups.

20 Using a screwdriver, turn the strut adjuster wheel to expand the shoes until the brake drum just slides over the shoes.

21 Refit the brake drum (see Section 9).

22 Repeat the above procedure on the remaining rear brake.

23 Once both sets of rear shoes have been renewed, adjust the lining-to-drum clearance by repeatedly depressing the brake pedal with the handbrake fully released. Whilst depressing the pedal, have an assistant listen to the rear drums, to check that the adjuster strut is functioning correctly; if so, a clicking sound will be emitted by the strut as the pedal is depressed.

24 Check and, if necessary, adjust the handbrake as described in Section 17.

25 On completion, check the hydraulic fluid level as described in *Weekly checks*.

Caution: New shoes will not give full braking efficiency until they have bedded-in. Be prepared for this, and avoid hard braking as far as possible for the first hundred miles or so after shoe renewal.

---

7 Front brake disc/hub
  – inspection, removal and
  refitting

Note: Before starting work, refer to the note at the beginning of Section 4 concerning the dangers of asbestos dust.

Inspection

Note: If either disc requires renewal, BOTH should be renewed at the same time, to ensure even and consistent braking. New brake pads should also be fitted.

1 Apply the handbrake, slacken the front roadwheel bolts, then jack up the front of the car and support it on axle stands (see *Jacking and vehicle support*). Remove the appropriate front roadwheel.

2 Slowly rotate the brake disc so that the full area of both sides can be checked; remove the brake pads if better access is required to the inboard surface. Light scoring is normal in the area swept by the brake pads, but if heavy scoring or cracks are found, the disc must be renewed.

3 It is normal to find a lip of rust and brake dust around the disc's perimeter; this can be scraped off if required. If, however, a lip has formed due to excessive wear of the brake pad swept area, then the disc's thickness must be measured using a micrometer. Take measurements at several places around the disc, at the inside and outside of the pad swept area; if the disc has worn at any point

---

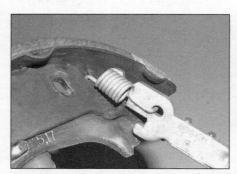

6.14 Hook the shorter end of the spring onto the trailing shoe, then attach the adjuster strut and locate it on the shoe, ensuring it is correctly engaged with the handbrake lever

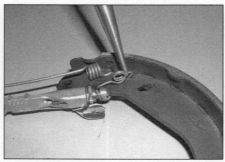

6.15 Fit the upper return spring and leading shoe. Ensure the shoe is correctly located in the bolt slot then hook the bolt spring into position

6.17 Lubricate the shoe contact surfaces of the rear backplate with a smear of high melting-point grease

7.3 Use a micrometer to measure the disc thickness

7.4 Check the disc run-out using a dial gauge

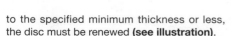

7.7 Undo the two Torx screws, and remove the disc

to the specified minimum thickness or less, the disc must be renewed **(see illustration)**.

4 If the disc is thought to be warped, it can be checked for run-out. Either use a dial gauge mounted on any convenient fixed point while the disc is slowly rotated, or use feeler blades to measure (at several points all around the disc) the clearance between the disc and a fixed point, such as the caliper mounting bracket **(see illustration)**. If the measurements obtained are at the specified maximum or beyond, the disc is excessively warped, and must be renewed; however, it is worth checking first that the hub bearing is in good condition (Chapter 1A or 1B). Also try the effect of removing the disc and turning it through 180°, to reposition it on the hub; if the run-out is still excessive, the disc must be renewed.

5 Check the disc for cracks, especially around the wheel bolt holes, and any other wear or damage, and renew if necessary.

Removal

6 Slacken and remove the two bolts securing the brake caliper mounting bracket to the hub carrier. Slide the assembly off the disc and tie it to the coil spring, using a piece of wire or string, to avoid placing any strain on the hydraulic brake hose.

7 Use chalk or paint to mark the relationship of the disc to the hub, then remove the screws securing the brake disc to the hub, and remove the disc **(see illustration)**. If it is tight, lightly tap its rear face with a hide or plastic mallet.

Refitting

8 Refitting is the reverse of the removal procedure, noting the following points:
- Ensure that the mating surfaces of the disc and hub are clean and flat.
- Align (if applicable) the marks made on removal, and tighten the disc retaining screws to the specified torque setting.
- If a new disc has been fitted, use a suitable solvent to wipe any preservative coating from the disc, before refitting the caliper.
- Refit the roadwheel then lower the vehicle to the ground and tighten the wheel bolts to the specified torque. Apply the

footbrake several times to force the pads back into contact with the disc before driving the vehicle.

<table><tr><td>**8**</td><td>**Rear brake disc/hub** – inspection, removal and refitting</td></tr></table>

Inspection

Note: *The brake disc and hub are an integral part, if either disc requires renewal, BOTH should be renewed at the same time, to ensure even and consistent braking. New brake pads should also be fitted.*

1 Firmly chock the front wheels, slacken the appropriate rear roadwheel bolts, and then

8.4 Slacken the two caliper mounting bracket Torx screws (arrowed)

8.5b ... release the staked part of the nut...

jack up the rear of the car and support it on axle stands (see *Jacking and vehicle support*). Remove the relevant rear roadwheel.

2 Inspect the disc as described in Section 7.

Removal

3 Remove the brake pads as described in Section 5.

4 Slacken the two screws securing the caliper mounting bracket to the stub axle **(see illustration)**.

5 Remove the cap from the centre of the brake disc and release the staked part of the nut, then undo the retaining nut. Use a hammer and chisel or similar tool, to tap up the staking securing the hub nut in position **(see illustrations)**. Note that a new retaining nut must be used on refitting.

8.5a Remove the centre cap...

8.5c ... then slacken the retaining nut

8.6 Withdraw the disc/hub

8.7 Stake the new nut, once it is tightened to specified torque setting

6 If necessary, gently tap the disc/hub from behind and withdraw it from the stub axle **(see illustration)**.

Refitting

7 Refitting is the reverse of the removal procedure, noting the following points:
● Ensure that ABS rotor on the rear of the hub is not damaged.
● Fit a new disc/hub nut to the stub axle and tighten to the specified torque, stake the new nut to lock the nut in position and fit a new centre cap **(see illustration)**.
● If a new disc has been fitted, use a suitable solvent to wipe any preservative coating from the disc, before refitting the caliper.

● Refit the roadwheel, then lower the vehicle to the ground and tighten the roadwheel bolts to the specified torque. Depress the brake pedal several times to force the pads back into contact with the disc.

---

9 Rear brake drum – removal, inspection and refitting

Note: *Before starting work, refer to the note at the beginning of Section 6 concerning the dangers of asbestos dust.*
Note: *A new rear hub nut, cap and seal must be used on refitting.*

Removal

1 Chock the front wheels, then jack up the rear of the vehicle and support it on axle stands (see *Jacking and vehicle support*). Remove the appropriate rear wheel.
2 Using a hammer and a large flat-bladed screwdriver, carefully tap and prise the cap out of the centre of the brake drum **(see illustrations)**. Discard the cap – a new one must be used on refitting.
3 Using a hammer and chisel, tap up the staking securing the hub retaining nut to the groove in the stub axle **(see illustration)**.
4 Using a socket and long bar, slacken and remove the rear hub nut **(see illustration)**. Discard the hub nut – a new nut must be used on refitting.
5 It should now be possible to withdraw the brake drum and hub bearing assembly from the stub axle by hand **(see illustration)**. It may be difficult to remove the drum due to the tightness of the hub bearing on the stub axle, or due to the brake shoes binding on the inner circumference of the drum. If the bearing is tight, tap the periphery of the drum using a hide or plastic mallet, or use a universal puller secured to the drum with the wheel bolts to pull it off. If the brake shoes are binding, first check that the handbrake is fully released. If necessary, fully slacken the handbrake cable

9.2a Using a chisel...

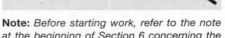

9.2b... to remove the outer cap

9.3 Using a punch to unstake the hub nut

9.4 Washer is combined with the hub nut

9.5 Withdraw the brake drum

9.6a Using a puller to withdraw the seal/ radial target

9.6b Refit the seal/radial target squarely on the centre of the drum

9.6c Carefully tap the seal/target ring into position

adjuster nut, to obtain maximum freeplay in the cable to enable the drum to be removed.

Inspection

Note: *If either drum requires renewal, BOTH should be renewed at the same time, to ensure even and consistent braking. New brake shoes should also be fitted.*

6 Once the drum has been removed, check the condition of the seal on the rear of the drum. If required, discard the seal and fit a new one. Using a puller, withdraw the seal and then carefully fit a new seal making sure it is located squarely **(see illustrations)**.

⚠️ *Warning: The seal is also the radial target for the wheel speed sensor. This needs to be fitted correctly or the sensor may not pick-up a signal for the wheel speed.*

7 Working carefully, remove all traces of brake dust from the drum, but avoid inhaling the dust, as it is injurious to health.

8 Clean the outside of the drum, and check it for obvious signs of wear or damage, such as cracks around the roadwheel bolt holes; renew the drum if necessary.

9 Examine carefully the inside of the drum. Light scoring of the friction surface is normal, but if heavy scoring is found, the drum must be renewed. It is usual to find a lip on the drum's inboard edge, which consists of a mixture of rust and brake dust; this should be scraped away, to leave a smooth surface which can be polished with fine (120- to 150-grade) emery paper. If, however, the lip is due to the friction surface being recessed by excessive wear, then the drum must be renewed.

10 If the drum is thought to be excessively worn, or oval, its internal diameter must be measured at several points using an internal micrometer. Take measurements in pairs, the second at right-angles to the first, and compare the two, to check for signs of ovality. Provided that it does not enlarge the drum to beyond the specified maximum diameter, it may be possible to have the drum refinished by skimming or grinding; if this is not possible, the drums on both sides must be renewed. Note that if the drum is to be skimmed, BOTH drums must be refinished, to maintain a consistent internal diameter on both sides.

Refitting

11 If a new brake drum is to be installed, install the new shoes (see Section 6) and use a suitable solvent to remove any preservative coating that may have been applied to the drum interior.

12 Slide the brake drum assembly into position on the stub axle.

13 Fit the new hub nut and tighten it to the specified torque. Secure the nut in position by staking it firmly into the groove on the stub axle then tap the new hub cap into place in the centre of the brake drum **(see illustrations)**.

14 Depress the footbrake several times to operate the self-adjusting mechanism.

15 Repeat the above procedure on the remaining rear brake assembly (where necessary), then check and, if necessary, adjust the handbrake cable as described in Section 17.

16 On completion, refit the roadwheel(s), then lower the vehicle to the ground and tighten the wheel bolts to the specified torque.

10 Front brake caliper – removal, overhaul and refitting

Caution: Ensure the ignition is switched off before disconnecting any braking system hydraulic union and do not switch it on until after the hydraulic system has been bled. Failure to do this could lead to air entering the regulator unit requiring the unit to be bled using special Peugeot test equipment (see Section 2).

Note: *Before starting work, refer to the note at the beginning of Section 2 concerning the dangers of hydraulic fluid, and to the warning at the beginning of Section 4 concerning the dangers of asbestos dust.*

Note: *New caliper guide pin bolts and caliper mounting bracket bolts will be required on reassembly if removed.*

Removal

1 Apply the handbrake, slacken the relevant front roadwheel bolts, then jack up the front of the vehicle and support it on axle stands (see *Jacking and vehicle support*). Remove the appropriate roadwheel.

2 Minimise fluid loss by first removing the master cylinder reservoir cap, and then tightening it down onto a piece of polythene, to obtain an airtight seal. Alternatively, use a brake hose clamp, a G-clamp or a similar tool to clamp the flexible hose **(see illustration)**.

9.13a Using a punch to lock the hub nut in position...

9.13b... and then fit new cap

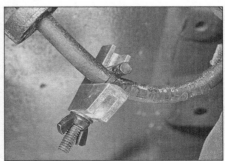

10.2 To minimise fluid loss, fit a brake hose clamp to the flexible hose

10.3 Unscrew the union nut (arrowed)

10.4a Undo the upper…

10.4b… and lower guide pin bolts

3 Clean the area around the caliper hose union, then loosen the union **(see illustration)**.
4 Slacken and remove the upper and lower caliper guide pin bolts **(see illustrations)**. Discard the bolts; new ones must be used on refitting.
5 Lift the caliper away from the brake disc **(see illustration)**, and then unscrew the caliper from the end of the brake hose. Plug the pipe and caliper unions to minimise fluid loss and prevent dirt entry.
6 If required, the caliper mounting bracket can be unbolted from the hub carrier **(see illustration)**; discard the bolts, new ones must be fitted.

Overhaul

Note: *Check the availability of repair kits for the caliper before dismantling.*
7 With the caliper on the bench, wipe away all traces of dust and dirt, but avoid inhaling the dust, as it is a health hazard.
8 Withdraw the partially-ejected piston from the caliper body, and remove the dust seal.
9 Using a small screwdriver, extract the piston hydraulic seal, taking great care not to damage the caliper bore.
10 Thoroughly clean all components, using only methylated spirit, isopropyl alcohol or clean hydraulic fluid as a cleaning medium. Never use mineral-based solvents such as petrol or paraffin, as they will attack the hydraulic system's rubber components. Dry the components immediately, using compressed air or a clean, lint-free cloth.

> **HAYNES HiNT** *If the piston cannot be withdrawn by hand, it can be pushed out by applying compressed air to the brake hose union hole. Only low pressure should be required, such as is generated by a foot pump. As the piston is expelled, take great care not to trap your fingers between the piston and caliper.*

Use compressed air to blow clear the fluid passages.
Caution: Always wear protective clothing, including safety goggles, when using compressed air.
11 Check all components, and renew any that are worn or damaged. Check particularly the cylinder bore and piston; these should be renewed (note that this means the renewal of the complete body assembly) if they are scratched, worn or corroded in any way. Similarly check the condition of the guide pins and their gaiters; both pins should be undamaged and (when cleaned) a reasonably tight sliding fit in the caliper bracket. If there is any doubt about the condition of any component, renew it.
12 If the assembly is fit for further use, obtain the appropriate repair kit; the components should be available from Peugeot dealers in various combinations. All rubber seals should be renewed as a matter of course; these should never be re-used.

13 On reassembly, ensure that all components are clean and dry.
14 Soak the piston and the new piston (fluid) seal in clean brake fluid. Smear clean fluid on the cylinder bore surface.
15 Fit the new piston (fluid) seal, using only your fingers (no tools) to manipulate it into the cylinder bore groove.
16 Fit the new dust seal to the rear of the piston and seat the outer lip of the seal in the caliper body groove. Carefully ease the piston squarely into the cylinder bore using a twisting motion. Press the piston fully into position, and seat the inner lip of the dust seal in the piston groove.
17 If the guide pins are being renewed, lubricate the pin shafts with the special grease supplied in the repair kit, and fit the gaiters to the pin grooves. Insert the pins into the caliper bracket and seat the gaiters correctly in the bracket grooves.

Refitting

18 If previously removed, refit the caliper mounting bracket to the hub carrier, and tighten the new bolts to the specified torque.
19 Screw the caliper body fully onto the flexible hose union.
20 Ensure that the brake pads are correctly fitted in the caliper mounting bracket and refit the caliper (refer to Section 4).
21 If the threads of the new guide pin bolts are not already pre-coated with locking compound, apply a suitable locking compound to them (Peugeot recommend Loctite Frenetanch – available from your Peugeot dealer). Fit the new lower guide pin bolt, then press the caliper into position and fit the new upper guide pin bolt. Tighten both guide pin bolts to the specified torque.
22 Tighten the brake hose union nut to the specified torque, then remove the brake hose clamp or polythene (where fitted).
23 Bleed the hydraulic system as described in Section 2. Note that, providing the precautions described were taken to minimise brake fluid loss, it should only be necessary to bleed the relevant front brake.
24 Refit the roadwheel, then lower the vehicle to the ground and tighten the roadwheel bolts to the specified torque.

10.5 Remove the caliper from over the brake pads

10.6 Caliper mounting bracket retaining bolts (arrowed)

11 Rear brake caliper –
removal, overhaul and refitting

Caution: Ensure the ignition is switched off before disconnecting any braking system hydraulic union and do not switch it back on until after the hydraulic system has been bled. Failure to do this could lead to air entering the regulator unit requiring the unit to be bled using special Peugeot test equipment (see Section 2).

Note: *Before starting work, refer to the note at the beginning of Section 2 concerning the dangers of hydraulic fluid, and to the warning at the beginning of Section 5 concerning the dangers of asbestos dust.*

Note: *New caliper mounting bracket bolts and guide pin bolts when be required on reassembly if removed.*

Removal

1 Chock the front wheels, slacken the relevant rear roadwheel bolts, then jack up the rear of the vehicle and support on axle stands (see *Jacking and vehicle support*). Remove the relevant rear wheel.

2 Remove the brake pads (see Section 5).

3 Minimise fluid loss by first removing the master cylinder reservoir cap, and then tightening it down onto a piece of polythene, to obtain an airtight seal. Alternatively, use a brake hose clamp, a G-clamp or a similar tool to clamp the flexible hose at the nearest convenient point to the brake caliper.

4 Wipe away all traces of dirt around the brake hose union on the caliper. Unscrew the union nut and disconnect the brake pipe from the caliper. Plug the pipe and caliper unions to minimise fluid loss and prevent dirt entry.

5 Remove the caliper from the vehicle. If required, the caliper mounting bracket can be unbolted from the hub carrier. Discard the bolts, new ones must be fitted.

Overhaul

6 At the time of writing, no parts were available to recondition the rear caliper assembly, with the exception of the guide pin bolts, guide pins and guide pin gaiters. Check the condition of the guide pins and their gaiters; both pins should be undamaged and (when cleaned) a reasonably tight sliding fit in the caliper bracket. If there is any doubt about the condition of any component, renew it.

Refitting

7 If previously removed, refit the caliper mounting bracket to the hub carrier, and tighten the new bolts to the specified torque.

8 Refit the brake pads as described in Section 5.

9 Refit the caliper using new guide pin bolts **(see illustration 5.3d)**, tightening them to the specified torque settings.

10 Reconnect the brake pipe to the caliper, and tighten the brake hose union nut to the

12.2 Note the position of the springs before removal

specified torque. Remove the brake hose clamp or polythene (where fitted).

11 Bleed the hydraulic system as described in Section 2. Note that, providing the precautions described were taken to minimise brake fluid loss, it should only be necessary to bleed the relevant rear brake.

12 Refit the roadwheel, then lower the vehicle to the ground and tighten the roadwheel bolts to the specified torque.

12 Rear wheel cylinder –
removal and refitting

Note: *Before starting work, refer to the note at the beginning of Section 2 concerning the dangers of hydraulic fluid, and to the warning at the beginning of Section 6 concerning the dangers of asbestos dust.*

Note: *New wheel cylinder retaining bolts will be needed on refitting.*

Removal

1 Remove the brake drum (see Section 9).

2 Using pliers, carefully unhook the upper brake shoe return spring **(see illustration)**, and remove it from both brake shoes. Pull the upper ends of the shoes away from the wheel cylinder to disengage them from the pistons.

3 Minimise fluid loss by first removing the master cylinder reservoir cap, and then tightening it down onto a piece of polythene, to obtain an airtight seal. Alternatively, use a brake hose clamp, a G-clamp or a similar tool to clamp the flexible hose at the nearest convenient point to the wheel cylinder.

4 Wipe away all traces of dirt around the brake pipe union at the rear of the wheel cylinder, and unscrew the union nut **(see illustration)**. Carefully ease the pipe out of the wheel cylinder, and plug or tape over its end to prevent dirt entry. Wipe off any spilt fluid immediately.

5 Unscrew the wheel cylinder retaining bolt from the rear of the backplate, and remove the cylinder, taking great care not to allow surplus hydraulic fluid to contaminate the brake shoe linings. Discard the bolt – a new one must be used on refitting.

6 Note that it is not possible to overhaul the

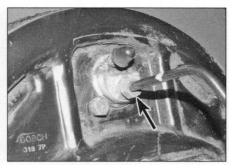

12.4 Unscrew the union nut (arrowed)

cylinder, since no components are available separately. If faulty, the complete wheel cylinder assembly must be renewed.

Refitting

7 Ensure that the backplate and wheel cylinder mating surfaces are clean, then spread the brake shoes and manoeuvre the wheel cylinder into position.

8 Engage the brake pipe, and screw in the union nut two or three turns to ensure that the thread has started.

9 Fit the new retaining bolt to the wheel cylinder and tighten it to the specified torque.

10 Tighten the brake pipe union nut to the specified torque then remove the clamp from the flexible brake hose, or the polythene from the master cylinder reservoir (as applicable).

11 Ensure that the brake shoes are correctly located in the cylinder pistons, and then carefully refit the brake shoe upper return spring. Use a screwdriver to stretch the spring into position.

12 Refit the brake drum (see Section 9).

13 Bleed the brake hydraulic system as described in Section 2. Providing suitable precautions were taken to minimise loss of fluid, it should only be necessary to bleed the relevant rear brake.

13 Master cylinder – removal,
overhaul and refitting

Caution: Ensure the ignition is switched off before disconnecting any braking system hydraulic union and do not switch it back on until after the hydraulic system has been bled. Failure to do this could lead to air entering the regulator unit requiring the unit to be bled using special Peugeot test equipment (see Section 2).

Note: *Before starting work, refer to the warning at the beginning of Section 2 concerning the dangers of hydraulic fluid.*

Removal

1 Remove the battery and battery box as described in Chapter 5A Section 4.

2 Remove the master cylinder reservoir cap and filter, and siphon the hydraulic fluid from

13.3 Disconnect the level sensor wiring plug (arrowed)

13.5 Unscrew the union nuts (arrowed)

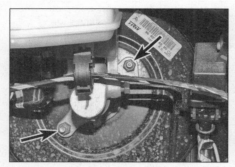

13.6 Brake master cylinder securing nuts (arrowed)

13.7 Undo the bolt (arrowed) securing the reservoir to the master cylinder

the reservoir. **Note:** *Do not siphon the fluid by mouth, as it is poisonous; use a syringe or an old antifreeze tester. Alternatively, open any convenient bleed screw in the system, and gently pump the brake pedal to expel the fluid through a plastic tube connected to the screw until the reservoir is emptied (see Section 2).*

3 Disconnect the wiring connector from the brake fluid level sender unit **(see illustration)**.
4 Disconnect the clutch master cylinder fluid supply pipe from the bottom of the reservoir. Plug the pipe opening to prevent dirt ingress.
5 Wipe clean the area around the brake pipe unions on the side of the master cylinder **(see illustration)** and place absorbent rags beneath the pipe unions to catch any surplus fluid. Make a note of the correct fitted

positions of the unions, then unscrew the union nuts and carefully withdraw the pipes. Plug or tape over the pipe ends and master cylinder orifices, to minimise the loss of brake fluid, and to prevent the entry of dirt into the system. Wash off any spilt fluid immediately with cold water.
6 Slacken and remove the two nuts securing the master cylinder to the vacuum servo unit **(see illustration)**, then withdraw the unit from the engine compartment. If the sealing ring fitted to the rear of the master cylinder shows signs of damage or deterioration, it must be renewed.
7 If required, undo the retaining screw and separate the reservoir from the master cylinder **(see illustration)**.

Overhaul
8 The master cylinder may be overhauled after obtaining the relevant repair kit from a Peugeot dealer. Ensure that the correct repair kit is obtained for the master cylinder being worked on. Note the locations of all components to ensure correct refitting, and lubricate the new seals using clean brake fluid. Follow the assembly instructions supplied with the repair kit.

Refitting
9 Remove all traces of dirt from the master cylinder and servo unit mating surfaces and ensure that the sealing ring is correctly fitted to the rear of the master cylinder.
10 Fit the master cylinder to the servo unit. Refit the master cylinder mounting nuts, and tighten them to the specified torque.
11 Wipe clean the brake pipe unions and refit them to the master cylinder ports, tightening them to the specified torque.
12 If the reservoir has been removed, press the mounting seals fully into the master cylinder ports then carefully ease the fluid reservoir into position. Fit the reservoir retaining screw and secure it in position.
13 Reconnect the clutch master cylinder supply pipe, and level sensor wiring plug.
14 Refit any components removed to improve access then refill the master cylinder reservoir with new fluid. Bleed the complete hydraulic system as described in Section 2. **Note:** *A hydraulic clutch shares its fluid reservoir with the braking system, and will also need to be bled (see Chapter 6 Section 2).*

14 Brake pedal – removal and refitting

Removal
1 Working inside the driver's footwell, unclip the cover from the lower part of the facia below the steering column. Then release the securing clips and remove the trim panel from above the pedals **(see illustrations)**.
2 Slide off the retaining clip and withdraw the clevis pin securing the pedal crossover linkage pushrod to the pedal **(see illustration)**.

14.1a Remove the lower trim panel... / **14.1b ... and facia trim panel**

14.2 Slide off the clevis pin retaining clip (arrowed)

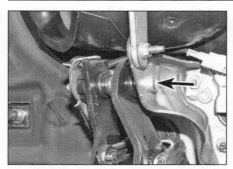

14.3 Slacken and remove the pivot bolt and nut (arrowed)

15.6 Disconnect the vacuum pipe

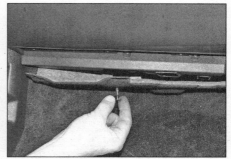

15.7 Unclip the trim panel from below the glovebox

Discard the clevis pin; a new one must be fitted.

3 Slacken and remove the pivot bolt and nut **(see illustration)**, and remove the brake pedal from the vehicle. Slide the spacer and washer (where fitted) out from the pedal pivot. Examine all components for signs of wear or damage, renewing them as necessary.

Refitting

4 Apply a smear of multipurpose grease to the spacer and washer, and insert it into the pedal pivot bore.

5 Manoeuvre the pedal into position, making sure it is correctly engaged with the pushrod, and insert the pivot bolt. Refit the nut to the pivot bolt and tighten it securely.

6 Align the pedal with the pushrod and insert the new clevis pin, securing it in position with the retaining clip(s).

7 Refit the lower panel to the facia.

15 Vacuum servo unit – testing, removal and refitting

Testing

1 To test the operation of the servo unit, depress the footbrake several times to exhaust the vacuum, then start the engine whilst keeping the pedal firmly depressed. As the engine starts, there should be a noticeable 'give' in the brake pedal as the vacuum builds-up. Allow the engine to run for at least

two minutes, and then switch it off. If the brake pedal is now depressed it should feel normal, but further applications should result in the pedal feeling firmer, with the pedal stroke decreasing with each application.

2 If the servo does not operate as described, first inspect the servo unit check valve as described in Section 16. On VTi petrol and diesel engine models, also check the operation of the vacuum pump as described in Section 24.

3 If the servo unit still fails to operate satisfactorily, the fault lies within the unit itself. Repairs to the unit are not possible – if faulty, the servo unit must be renewed.

Removal

4 Remove the master cylinder as described in Section 13.

5 Release the wiring harness adjacent to the servo from its retaining clips, and move it to one side.

6 Slacken or release the retaining clip (depending on type of securing clip), then disconnect the vacuum pipe from the servo unit check valve **(see illustration)**.

7 Working in the passenger's footwell, remove the trim from beneath the passenger's glovebox **(see illustration)**.

8 Rotate the crossover shaft-to-servo pushrod clevis pin and remove it from the linkage **(see illustration)**. Discard the clevis pin; a new one must be fitted.

9 Slacken and remove the four nuts securing the housing to the bulkhead **(see illustration)**.

10 Where fitted, depress the two retaining

clips (one to the left of the servo gaiter, and one to the right), then ease the housing away from the bulkhead **(see illustration)**.

11 Manoeuvre the servo unit out of position, along with its gasket which is fitted between the servo and housing. Renew the gasket if it shows signs of damage.

Refitting

12 Refitting is the reverse of removal, noting the following points.

● Lubricate all crossover linkage pivot points with multipurpose grease.

● Tighten the servo unit and mounting bracket nuts and bolts to their specified torque settings.

● Refit the master cylinder as described in Section 13 and bleed the complete hydraulic system as described in Section 2.

● Always renew the crossover shaft clevis pins.

16 Vacuum servo unit check valve – removal, testing and refitting

Removal

1 Slacken or release the retaining clip (depending on type of securing clip), then disconnect the vacuum hose from the servo unit check valve.

2 Withdraw the valve from its rubber sealing grommet, using a pulling and twisting motion

15.8 Release the clevis pin securing clip (arrowed)

15.9 Undo the four servo mounting nuts (arrowed)

15.10 Release the servo retaining clips (left-hand one arrowed)

16.2 Servo unit check valve

17.2b Unclip the storage tray (later model)

17.2a Unclip the switch trim panel (early model)

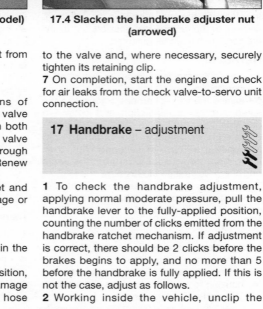

17.4 Slacken the handbrake adjuster nut (arrowed)

(see illustration). Remove the grommet from the servo.

Testing

3 Examine the check valve for signs of damage, and renew if necessary. The valve may be tested by blowing through it in both directions. Air should flow through the valve in one direction only – when blown through from the servo unit end of the valve. Renew the valve if this is not the case.

4 Examine the rubber sealing grommet and flexible vacuum hose for signs of damage or deterioration, and renew as necessary.

Refitting

5 Fit the sealing grommet into position in the servo unit.

6 Carefully ease the check valve into position, taking great care not to displace or damage the grommet. Reconnect the vacuum hose

to the valve and, where necessary, securely tighten its retaining clip.

7 On completion, start the engine and check for air leaks from the check valve-to-servo unit connection.

17 Handbrake – adjustment

1 To check the handbrake adjustment, applying normal moderate pressure, pull the handbrake lever to the fully-applied position, counting the number of clicks emitted from the handbrake ratchet mechanism. If adjustment is correct, there should be 2 clicks before the brakes begins to apply, and no more than 5 before the handbrake is fully applied. If this is not the case, adjust as follows.

2 Working inside the vehicle, unclip the

switch panel/storage tray (depending on model) from the centre console at the side of the handbrake lever (see illustrations).

3 Chock the front wheels, then jack up the rear of the vehicle and support it on axle stands (see *Jacking and vehicle support*).

4 Slacken the adjuster nut through the access hole in the centre console (see illustration).

5 Start the engine and depress the brake pedal approximately 40 times. Stop the engine.

6 Tighten the adjuster nut just enough to eliminate any free play in the cables.

7 Pull the handbrake lever on 10 times. On the last application, pull the lever up and stop after the second click is emitted.

8 Tighten the adjuster nut until the rear brake pads begin to make contact and the wheel begins to drag when it is spun.

9 Release the lever and check by hand that the rear wheels rotate freely, then check that no more than five clicks are emitted before the handbrake is fully applied.

10 Refit the switch panel/storage panel, then lower the vehicle to the floor.

18 Handbrake lever – removal and refitting

Removal

1 Referring to Section 17, release the handbrake lever and back off the adjuster nut to obtain maximum freeplay in the cable.

2 Remove the centre console as described in Chapter 11 Section 26.

3 Disconnect the wiring connector from the handbrake warning light switch at the rear of the lever (see illustration).

4 With the adjuster nut slackened, detach the two handbrake cables from the equaliser plate just behind the lever (see illustration).

5 Slacken and remove the lever retaining nuts, and remove the lever from the vehicle(see illustration).

Refitting

6 Refitting is a reversal of removal. Tighten the lever retaining nuts to the specified torque, and adjust the handbrake as described in Section 17.

18.3 Disconnect the wiring connector (arrowed)

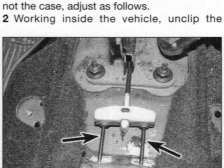

18.4 Disengage the cable end fittings (arrowed) from the equaliser plate

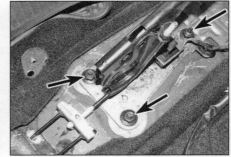

18.5 Undo the handbrake lever securing nuts (arrowed)

19 Handbrake cables – removal and refitting

Removal

1 The handbrake cable consists of a left-hand section and a right-hand section connecting the rear brakes to the adjuster mechanism on the handbrake lever rod. The cables can be removed separately.
2 Firmly chock the front wheels, slacken the relevant rear roadwheel bolts, and then jack up the rear of the vehicle and support it on axle stands (see *Jacking and vehicle support*).
3 Remove the centre console as described in Chapter 11 Section 26.
4 Slacken the handbrake adjuster nut sufficiently to be able to disengage the relevant cable end fitting from the equaliser plate with reference to Section 18 **(see illustration 18.4)**.
5 Release the cable end fitting from the lever on the brake caliper, and remove the cable from the support bracket **(see illustration)**.
6 Working underneath the vehicle, note its fitted location, then free the cable from the various retaining clips/brackets along its route, and pull the front end of the cable from the opening in the floor. Withdraw the cable from underneath the vehicle

Refitting

7 Refitting is a reversal of the removal procedure, adjusting the handbrake as described in Section 17.

20 Stop-light switch – removal, refitting and adjustment

1 The stop-light switch is located on the pedal crossover shaft bracket behind the passenger side of the facia **(see illustration)**. On some models, depending on the specification, there are two switches fitted to the bracket.

Removal

2 Working in the passenger's footwell, remove the trim panel from beneath the passenger's glovebox **(see illustration 15.7)**.
3 Disconnect the wiring, then rotate the switch 90 degrees anti-clockwise and remove it from the bracket **(see illustration)**.

Refitting and adjustment

4 Pull the switch plunger out to its full extent, and then depress the brake pedal by hand.
5 Refit the switch back into position in the mounting bracket, then release the brake pedal, and pull it up as far as it will go. The switch should now be correctly positioned.
6 Reconnect the wiring connector, and check the operation of the stop-lights. Refit the trim panel.

21 Anti-lock braking system (ABS) – general information

1 ABS is fitted to all models as standard; the system comprises a hydraulic regulator unit and the four roadwheel sensors. The regulator unit contains the electronic control unit (ECU), the hydraulic solenoid valves and the electrically-driven return pump. The purpose of the system is to prevent the wheel(s) locking during heavy braking. This is achieved by automatic release of the brake on the relevant wheel, followed by re-application of the brake.
2 The solenoid valves are controlled by the ECU, which itself receives signals from the four wheel sensors (the sensors are fitted to the hubs) which monitor the speed of rotation of each wheel. By comparing these signals, the ECU can determine the speed at which the vehicle is traveling. It can then use this speed to determine when a wheel is decelerating at an abnormal rate, compared to the speed of the vehicle, and therefore predicts when a wheel is about to lock. During normal operation, the system functions in the same way as a non-ABS braking system.
3 If the ECU senses that a wheel is about to lock, it closes the relevant outlet solenoid valves in the hydraulic unit, which then isolates the relevant brake(s) on the wheel(s) which is/are about to lock from the master cylinder, effectively sealing-in the hydraulic pressure.
4 If the speed of rotation of the wheel continues to decrease at an abnormal rate, the ECU opens the inlet solenoid valves on the relevant brake(s), and operates the electrically-driven return pump which pumps the hydraulic fluid back into the master cylinder, releasing the brake. Once the speed of rotation of the wheel returns to an acceptable rate, the pump stops; the solenoid valves switch again, allowing the hydraulic master cylinder pressure to return to the caliper, which then re-applies the brake. This cycle can be carried out many times a second.
5 The action of the solenoid valves and return pump creates pulses in the hydraulic circuit. When the ABS system is functioning, these pulses can be felt through the brake pedal.
6 The operation of the ABS system is entirely dependent on electrical signals. To prevent the system responding to any inaccurate signals, a built-in safety circuit monitors all signals received by the ECU. If an inaccurate signal or low battery voltage is detected, the ABS system is automatically shutdown, and the warning light on the instrument panel is illuminated to inform the driver that the ABS system is not operational. Normal braking should still be available, however.
7 The Peugeot 207 is also equipped with additional safety features built around the ABS system. These systems are EBFD (Electronic Brake Force Distribution), which automatically apportions braking effort between the front and rear wheels, EBA (Emergency Brake Assist) which guarantees full braking effort in the event of an emergency stop by monitoring the rate at which the brake pedal is depressed, and ESP (Electronic Stability Program) which monitors the vehicle's cornering forces and steering wheel angle, then applies the braking force to the appropriate roadwheel to enhance the stability of the vehicle.
8 If a fault does develop in the any of these systems, the vehicle must be taken to a Peugeot dealer or suitably-equipped specialist for fault diagnosis and repair.

19.5 Disengage the handbrake cable from the caliper

20.1 Brake light switch (arrowed)

20.3 Disconnect the wiring connector from the brake light switch

22.4a Unclip the cover...

22.4b... and disconnect the wiring connector

22.5 Mark the location of the various brake pipes before disconnecting them from the regulator

22 Anti-lock braking system (ABS) components – removal and refitting

Regulator assembly

Caution: Disconnect the battery (see Chapter 5A Section 4) before disconnecting the regulator hydraulic unions, and do not reconnect the battery until after the hydraulic system has been bled. Also ensure that the unit is stored upright (in the same position as it is fitted to the vehicle) and is not tipped onto its side or upside down. Failure to do this could lead to air entering the regulator unit, requiring the unit to be bled using special Peugeot test equipment on refitting (see Section 2).

22.6a Remove the two retaining nuts (arrowed)...

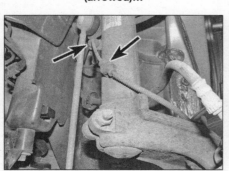

22.15a Unclip the sensor wiring from the retaining clips (arrowed)...

Note: Before starting work, refer to the warning at the beginning of Section 2 concerning the dangers of hydraulic fluid.

Removal

1 Disconnect the battery (see Chapter 5A Section 4).
2 The regulator assembly is located under the front left-hand corner of the front wing. Slacken the left-hand front roadwheel bolts, jack up the front of the vehicle and support it securely on axle stands (see *Jacking and vehicle support*).
3 Remove the front left-hand road wheel and wheel arch liner.
4 Withdraw the plastic cover and release the retaining clip and disconnect the main wiring connector from the regulator assembly **(see illustrations)**. Where applicable, unscrew the

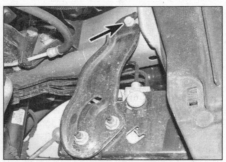

22.6b... and slacken the retaining bolt (arrowed)

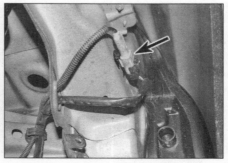

22.15b... and disconnect the wiring connector (arrowed)

retaining nut and disconnect the earth lead from the regulator.
5 Mark the locations of the hydraulic fluid pipes to ensure correct refitting, then unscrew the union nuts, and disconnect the pipes from the regulator assembly **(see illustration)**. Be prepared for fluid spillage, and plug the open ends of the pipes and the regulator to prevent dirt ingress and further fluid loss.
6 Slacken and remove the regulator mounting nuts from the outside of the chassis leg, and then slacken the bolt on the inner side of the chassis leg **(see illustrations)**. The inner bolt does not have to be removed completely, as the bracket has a slot for locating the bolt.
7 The regulator and mounting bracket can then be withdrawn from under the front wheel arch. If necessary, the mounting bracket can then be unbolted and removed from the regulator assembly. Renew the regulator mountings if they show signs of wear or damage.

Refitting

8 Manoeuvre the regulator and mounting bracket into position and tighten the retaining nuts and bolt.
9 Reconnect the hydraulic pipes to the correct unions on the regulator and tighten the union nuts to the specified torque.
10 Reconnect the wiring connector to the regulator and fit the plastic protector cover.
11 Bleed the complete hydraulic system as described in Section 2. Once the system is correctly bled, refit the wheels arch liner, roadwheel and reconnect the battery.

Electronic control unit (ECU)

12 The ECU is integral with the regulator assembly, and is not available separately.

Front wheel sensor

Removal

13 Ensure the ignition is turned off.
14 Apply the handbrake, slacken the appropriate front roadwheel bolts, then jack up the front of the vehicle and support securely on axle stands (see *Jacking and vehicle support*). Remove the wheel arch liner.
15 Trace the wiring back from the sensor, releasing it from all the relevant clips and ties whilst noting its correct routing, and disconnect the wiring connector **(see illustrations)**.

22.16 Front wheel sensor retaining bolt (arrowed)

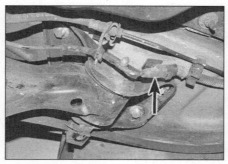

22.24 Disconnect the sensor wiring connector (arrowed)

22.25 Rear wheel sensor retaining bolt (arrowed)

16 Slacken and remove the retaining bolt and withdraw the sensor from the hub carrier **(see illustration)**.

Refitting

17 Ensure that the mating faces of the sensor and the swivel hub are clean, and apply a little anti-seize grease to the swivel hub bore before refitting.

18 Make sure the sensor tip is clean and ease it into position in the swivel hub.

19 Clean the threads of the sensor bolt and apply a few drops of thread-locking compound (Peugeot recommend Loctite Frenetanch – available from your Peugeot dealer). Refit the retaining bolt and tighten it to the specified torque.

20 Work along the sensor wiring, making sure it is correctly routed, securing it in position with all the relevant clips and ties. Reconnect the wiring connector.

21 Lower the vehicle and tighten the wheel bolts to the specified torque.

Rear wheel sensor

Removal

22 Ensure the ignition is turned off.

23 Chock the front wheels, slacken the appropriate rear roadwheel bolts, and then jack up the rear of the vehicle and support it on axle stands (see *Jacking and vehicle support*). Remove the appropriate roadwheel.

24 Trace the wiring back from the sensor, releasing it from all the relevant clips and ties whilst noting its correct routing, and disconnect the wiring connector **(see illustration)**.

25 Slacken and remove the retaining bolt and withdraw the sensor from the stub axle (disc brake models) or brake backplate (drum brake models) **(see illustration)**.

Refitting

26 Ensure that the mating faces of the sensor and the hub are clean, and apply a little anti-seize grease to the hub bore before refitting.

27 Make sure the sensor tip is clean and ease it into position in the stub axle/brake backplate.

28 Clean the threads of the sensor bolt and apply a few drops of thread-locking compound (Peugeot recommend Loctite Frenetanch – available from your Peugeot dealer). Refit the retaining bolt and tighten it to the specified torque.

29 Work along the sensor wiring, making sure it is correctly routed, and secured in position with all the relevant clips and ties. Reconnect the wiring connector, then lower the vehicle and (where necessary) tighten the wheel bolts to the specified torque.

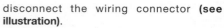

23 Vacuum pump – removal and refitting

Note: *Vacuum pumps are fitted to VTi petrol and all diesel engine models.*

Removal

1 The pump is located at the left-hand end of the cylinder head. To improve access to the vacuum pump, remove the air cleaner duct and air cleaner with reference to Chapter 4A Section 2 for petrol engines and Chapter 4B Section 4 for diesel engines **(see illustration)**.

2 Disconnect the vacuum pipe, then depress the retaining retaining clip and disconnect the brake servo vacuum hose from the pump **(see illustrations)**.

3 Slacken and remove the retaining bolts/nut (as applicable) securing the pump to the left-hand end of the cylinder head, then

23.1 Remove the air ducting

23.2a Disconnect the vacuum pipe – VTi petrol model

23.2b Disconnect the vacuum pipe – diesel model

23.2c Disconnect the brake servo pipe – diesel model

23.3a Vacuum pump mounting bolts (arrowed) – 1.4 litre diesel...

23.3b Vacuum pump mounting nuts – 1.6 litre diesel...

23.3c... and VTi petrol models

remove the pump (see illustrations). Discard the sealing rings – new ones must be used on refitting.

Refitting

4 Fit new sealing ring(s) to the pump recess(es), then align the drive dog with the slot in the end of the camshaft, and refit the pump to the cylinder head, ensuring that the sealing ring(s) remain correctly seated (see illustrations).

5 Refit the pump mounting bolts/nut (as applicable) and tighten them securely.

6 Reconnect the vacuum hose to the pump, ensuring its retaining clip engages correctly, and refit the air cleaner duct.

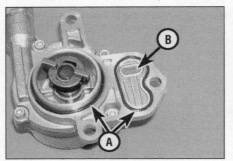

23.4a Renew vacuum pump O-ring seals (A) and gauze filter (B) – depending on model

23.4b Ensure the pump drive dog engages with the slot in the end of the camshaft (arrowed)

24 Vacuum pump – testing

Note: Vacuum pumps are fitted to VTi petrol and all diesel engine models.

1 The operation of the braking system vacuum pump can be checked using a vacuum gauge.

2 Disconnect the vacuum pipe from the pump, and connect the gauge to the pump union using a suitable length of hose.

3 Start the engine and allow it to idle, and then measure the vacuum created by the pump. As a guide, after one minute, a minimum of approximately 500 mm Hg should be recorded. If the vacuum registered is significantly less than this, it is likely that the pump is faulty. However, seek the advice of a Peugeot dealer before condemning the pump.

4 Overhaul of the vacuum pump is not possible, since no components are available separately for it. If faulty, the complete pump assembly must be renewed.

Chapter 10
Suspension and steering

Contents

Degrees of difficulty

Easy, suitable for novice with little experience		Fairly easy, suitable for beginner with some experience		Fairly difficult, suitable for competent DIY mechanic		Difficult, suitable for experienced DIY mechanic		Very difficult, suitable for expert DIY or professional	
Easy, suitable for novice with little experience		Fairly easy, suitable for beginner with some experience		Fairly difficult, suitable for competent DIY mechanic		Difficult, suitable for experienced DIY mechanic		Very difficult, suitable for expert DIY or professional	

Specifications

Wheel alignment and steering angles

Front wheel:
  Toe setting . . . . 0° 8' ± 4'
  Camber:
    1.4 litre models. . . . . -0° 31' ± 30'
    1.6 litre models . . . . -0° 33' ± 30'
  Castor:
    1.4 litre models. . . . . 4° 38' ± 18'
    1.6 litre models . . . . 4° 39' ± 18'
  King pin inclination:
    1.4 litre models. . . . . 11° 26' ± 30'
    1.6 litre models . . . . 11° 28' ± 30'
Rear wheel:
  Toe setting . . . . 0° 21' ± 4'
  Camber. . . . . -1° 42' ± 30'

Roadwheels

Type . . . . Pressed-steel or aluminium alloy (depending on model)
Tyre pressures . . . . *See Lubricants, fluids and tyre pressures*

Torque wrench settings	Nm	lbf ft
Front suspension		
Anti-roll bar:		
Connecting link nuts*	43	32
Mounting clamp bolts.	75	55
Brake caliper mounting bracket bolts	Refer to Chapter 9	
Driveshaft retaining nut:		
1.4 litre non-VTi petrol engines.	245	181
All other models	325	240
Hub carrier-to-lower strut bolt/nut*	54	40
Lower arm-to-subframe bolts	110	81
Lower balljoint-to-hub carrier bolt/nut*	40	30
Lower balljoint-to-suspension arm bolt/nut	55	41
Subframe mounting bolts.	85	63
Subframe front and side crossmember bolts.	95	70
Subframe tie-bar bolts	66	49
Suspension strut:		
Upper mounting plate nut.	75	55
Upper spring seat nut*	75	55
*Do not re-use		
Rear suspension		
Caliper mounting bracket bolts*	53	39
Hub nut: *		
Drum brakes.	200	148
Disc brakes.	300	221
Rear axle mounting bracket-to-body bolts	75	55
Rear axle-to-mounting bracket through-bolt:		
Stage 1	40	30
Stage 2	Angle-tighten 130 °	
Shock absorber:		
Lower mounting bolt.	69	51
Upper mounting bolt	61	45
Stub axle bolts	70	52
*Do not re-use		
Steering		
Column-to-steering rack pinch-bolt*	22	16
Steering column mounting bolts	22	16
Steering rack mounting nuts*	90	66
Steering wheel bolt.	33	24
Track rod:		
Balljoint-to-hub carrier nut*	35	26
Balljoint locknut	75	55
Inner balljoint to steering rack	80	59
*Do not re-use		
Roadwheels		
Wheel bolts.	90	66

1 General Information

1 The independent front suspension is of the MacPherson strut type, incorporating coil springs and integral telescopic shock absorbers. The MacPherson struts are located by transverse lower suspension arms, which utilise rubber inner mounting bushes. The front hub carriers, which carry the wheel bearings, brake calipers, the hub/disc assemblies and lower balljoints, are bolted to the MacPherson struts and connected to the lower arms via the balljoints. A front anti-roll bar is fitted to all models. The anti-roll bar is rubber-mounted onto the subframe, and is connected to the front suspension struts by link rods **(see illustration)**.

2 The rear suspension has separate telescopic shock absorbers and coil springs fitted between the beam axle and the vehicle body. The rear beam axle has an integral torsion bar **(see illustration)**.

3 The steering column has a universal joint fitted to its lower end, which is connected to the steering rack pinion by means of a clamp bolt.

4 The steering rack is mounted onto the front subframe, and is connected to the steering arms projecting rearwards from the hub carriers by two track rods, with balljoints at their outer ends. The track rod ends are threaded, to facilitate adjustment. The steering system is powered by an electrically-operated motor, which is controlled by the engine management ECU.

5 An electric power steering system is fitted to this model. The electric motor only operates when there is torque applied to the steering wheel, so only consumes electrical energy when necessary. The level of steering assistance will depend on the vehicle speed and the force used on the steering wheel. The motor is an integral part of the steering rack assembly and cannot be renewed separately.

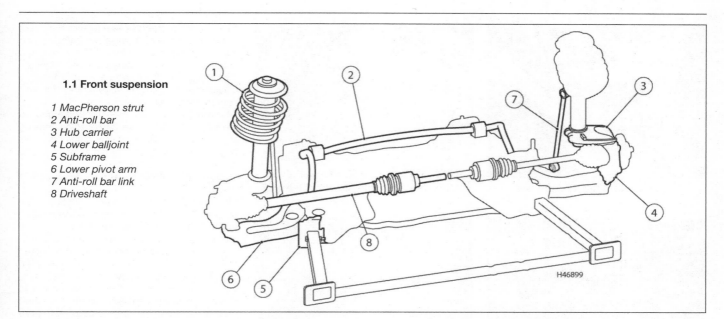

1.1 Front suspension

1 MacPherson strut
2 Anti-roll bar
3 Hub carrier
4 Lower balljoint
5 Subframe
6 Lower pivot arm
7 Anti-roll bar link
8 Driveshaft

2 Front hub carrier assembly – removal and refitting

Note: *A new track rod balljoint nut, lower balljoint nut, brake caliper mounting bracket bolts, and strut-to-hub carrier nut will be required on refitting.*

Removal

1 Remove the wheel trim/hub cap (as applicable) and slacken the driveshaft nut with the vehicle resting on its wheels. On models where the driveshaft nut is staked, using a hammer and a chisel or similar tool, tap up the staking securing the driveshaft nut in position **(see illustration)**. Note that a new retaining nut must be used on refitting. On models where the driveshaft nut is secured by an R-clip, withdraw the R-clip and remove the locking cap from the driveshaft nut **(see illustration)**. Also slacken the wheel bolts.
2 Chock the rear wheels of the car, firmly apply the handbrake, and then jack up the front of the car and support it on axle stands

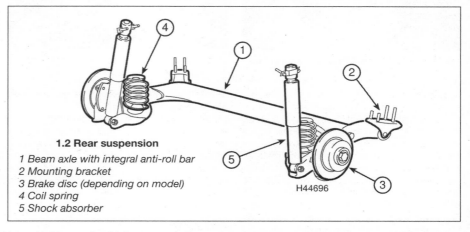

1.2 Rear suspension

1 Beam axle with integral anti-roll bar
2 Mounting bracket
3 Brake disc (depending on model)
4 Coil spring
5 Shock absorber

(see *Jacking and vehicle support*). Remove the appropriate front roadwheel.
3 Unbolt the wheel sensor and position it clear of the hub assembly (refer to Chapter 9 Section 22). Note that there is no need to disconnect the wiring.
4 Slacken and remove the driveshaft retaining nut. If the nut was not slackened with the

wheels on the ground (see paragraph 1). Refit at least two roadwheel bolts to the front hub, tightening them securely, then have an assistant firmly depress the brake pedal to prevent the front hub from rotating whilst you slacken and remove the driveshaft retaining nut. Alternatively, a tool can be fabricated to hold the hub stationary **(see illustration)**.

2.1a Use a chisel to release the securing nut

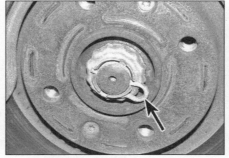

2.1b Prise out the R-clip (arrowed), remove the locking collar and slacken the driveshaft nut

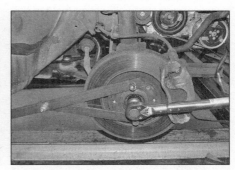

2.4 Using a fabricated tool to hold the front hub stationary

2.5 Disconnect the trackrod end

2.6 Fasten the caliper up out of the way

2.7 Free the balljoint from the swivel hub

2.8 Undo the strut-to-hub carrier bolt (arrowed)

5 Slacken and remove the nut securing the steering rack track rod to the hub carrier then free the balljoint from the hub **(see illustration)**. If the balljoint is tight, use a universal balljoint separator to free it. Discard the nut; a new one should be used on refitting.
6 If the hub bearings are to be disturbed, remove the brake disc as described in Chapter 9 Section 7. If not, unscrew the two bolts securing the brake caliper mounting bracket assembly to the hub carrier, and slide the caliper assembly off the disc. Using a piece of wire or string, tie the caliper out of the way, to avoid placing any strain on the hydraulic brake hose **(see illustration)**.
7 Slacken and remove the lower balljoint nut and bolt, then free the balljoint shank from the lower arm **(see illustration)**. Discard the nut and lift off the protector plate (if loose).
8 Undo the nut and withdraw the hub carrier-to-suspension strut bolt, noting that the bolt

is inserted from the rear of the vehicle **(see illustration)**.
9 Free the hub carrier assembly from the end of the strut, noting its fitted position. Mark the lower part of the strut with the slot in the back of the hub carrier for refitting. Release it from the driveshaft splines, and remove it from the vehicle. Suspend the driveshaft by string from the suspension strut to prevent and damage to the constant velocity joints.

Refitting

10 Ensure that the driveshaft outer constant velocity joint and hub splines are clean, and then slide the hub fully onto the driveshaft splines.
11 Slide the hub assembly fully onto the lower part of the suspension strut. Making sure it is aligned with the marks made on removal. Insert the bolt from the rear using a new nut, and tighten it to the specified torque.

2.17 Use a punch to stake the hub nut

3.2 Press the hub flange from the bearing

12 Refit the protector plate (where removed) to the lower balljoint. Align the balljoint with the lower arm and fit the new retaining nut, tightening it to the specified torque.
13 Engage the track rod balljoint in the hub carrier, then fit the new retaining nut and tighten it to the specified torque.
14 Where necessary, refit the brake disc to the hub. Slide the caliper into position, making sure the pads pass either side of the disc, and tighten the new caliper bracket bolts to the specified torque setting.
15 Refit the wheel sensor as described in Chapter 9 Section 22.
16 Lubricate the inner face and threads of the driveshaft nut with clean engine oil, and refit it to the end of the driveshaft. Use the method employed on removal to prevent the hub from rotating (see paragraph 4), and tighten the driveshaft retaining nut to the specified torque. Check that the hub rotates freely.
17 On models where the driveshaft nut is staked, stake the new nut into the driveshaft groove using a hammer and punch **(see illustration)**.
18 On models where the driveshaft nut is secured by an R-clip, engage the locking cap with the driveshaft nut so that one of its cut-outs is aligned with the driveshaft hole. Secure the cap in position with the R-clip **(see illustration 2.1b)**.
19 Refit the roadwheel, then lower the vehicle to the ground and tighten the roadwheel bolts to the specified torque. If not already having done so, tighten the driveshaft nut to the specified torque. Check the brake operation.

3 Front hub bearings – renewal

Note: *The bearing is a sealed, pre-adjusted and pre-lubricated, double-row roller type, and is intended to last the car's entire service life without maintenance or attention. Never overtighten the driveshaft nut beyond the specified torque wrench setting in an attempt to 'adjust' the bearing.*
Note: *A press will be required to dismantle and rebuild the assembly; if such a tool is not available, a large bench vice and spacers (such as large sockets) will serve as an adequate substitute. The bearing's inner races are an interference fit on the hub; if the inner race remains on the hub when it is pressed out of the hub carrier, a knife-edged bearing puller will be required to remove it. A new bearing retaining circlip must be used on refitting.*
1 Remove the hub carrier assembly as described in Section 2.
2 Support the hub carrier securely on blocks or in a vice. Using a tubular spacer, which bears only on the inner end of the hub flange, press the hub flange out of the bearing **(see illustration)**. If the bearing's outboard inner race remains on the hub, remove it using a bearing puller (see note above).

3.3 Extract the circlip from the inner side of the hub carrier

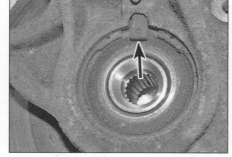

3.7 Take great care not to damage the seal in the bearing – it contains the encoder for the wheel speed sensor (arrowed)

4.2 Use a Torx bit (or Hex bit) to prevent rotation whilst the connecting link nut (arrowed) is undone

3 Extract the bearing retaining circlip from the inner end of the hub carrier assembly **(see illustration)**.

4 Where necessary, refit the inner race back in position over the ball cage, and securely support the inner face of the hub carrier. Using a tubular spacer, which bears only on the inner race, press the complete bearing assembly out of the hub carrier.

5 Thoroughly clean the hub and hub carrier, removing all traces of dirt and grease, and polish away any burrs or raised edges, which might hinder reassembly. Check both for cracks or any other signs of wear or damage, and renew them if necessary. Renew the circlip, regardless of its apparent condition.

6 On reassembly, apply a light film of oil (Peugeot recommend Molykote 321R – available from your Peugeot dealer) to the bearing outer race and hub flange shaft, to aid installation of the bearing.

7 Securely support the hub carrier, and locate the bearing in the hub. Press the bearing fully into position, ensuring that it enters the hub squarely, using a tubular spacer, which bears only on the bearing outer race. Note that the bearing is equipped with a magnetic encoder on its inboard face. When fitting the bearing ensure this face is inboard adjacent to the ABS wheel speed sensor **(see illustration)**. Take care not to damage this encoder, or place it adjacent to a magnetic source. Ensure the encoder face is clean.

8 Once the bearing is correctly seated, secure the bearing in position with the new circlip,

ensuring that it is correctly located in the groove in the hub carrier. **Note:** *Align the gap between the ends of the circlip with the gap for the ABS wheel speed sensor.*

9 Securely support the outer face of the hub flange, and locate the hub carrier bearing inner race over the end of the hub flange. Press the bearing onto the hub, using a tubular spacer that bears only on the inner race of the hub bearing, until it seats against the hub shoulder. Check that the hub flange rotates freely, and wipe off any excess oil or grease.

10 Refit the hub carrier assembly as described in Section 2.

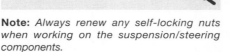

4 Front suspension strut –
   removal and refitting

Note: *Always renew any self-locking nuts when working on the suspension/steering components.*

Removal

1 Chock the rear wheels, apply the handbrake, slacken the appropriate front roadwheel bolts, then jack up the front of the car and support on axle stands (see *Jacking and vehicle support*). Remove the appropriate roadwheel.

2 Unscrew the nut securing the anti-roll bar connecting link to the strut, and position the link clear of the strut; if necessary, retain the balljoint shank with a Torx bit to prevent

rotation whilst the nut is slackened **(see illustration)**. Discard the nut; a new one should be used on refitting. Note on later models, it may be necessary to use a Hex key not a Torx bit to prevent the ball joint shank from rotating.

3 Undo the nut and bolt, and then free the hub carrier assembly from the end of the strut, noting its fitted position. Mark the lower part of the strut with the slot in the back of the hub carrier for refitting **(see illustration)**. To prevent the hub carrier assembly dropping whilst the strut is removed support the lower arm. Take care not to strain the brake hose and the wiring attached to the brake caliper and the hub carrier.

4 Remove both wiper arms as described in Chapter 12 Section 13.

5 Remove the plastic scuttle trim from in front of the windscreen **(see illustration)**. Lift up the ends of the trim to release the trim, then pull it down to release it from the lower edge of the windscreen,

6 Working in the scuttle aperture, slacken and remove the strut upper mounting nut, counterholding the strut rod with an Allen key located in the end of the rod. Withdraw the strut from under the wheel arch **(see illustration)**.
Caution: As soon as the upper mounting nut is removed, the strut will be unsupported.

Refitting

7 Manoeuvre the strut assembly into position, ensuring that the end of the strut rod is

4.3 Slacken the lower strut nut and bolt (arrowed)

4.5 Remove the upper grill panel

4.6 Use an Allen key to counterhold the strut whilst slackening the retaining nut

correctly located in the corresponding hole in the inner wing. Fit the upper mounting nut and tighten it to the specified torque.

8 Engage the lower end of the strut with the hub carrier; making sure it is aligned with the marks made on removal. Insert the bolt from the rear and tighten it to the specified torque.

9 Refit the scuttle plastic trim, and the wiper arms.

10 Reconnect the anti-roll bar connecting link to the strut. Do not omit the wiring support bracket. Tighten the nut to the specified torque.

11 Refit the roadwheel, then lower the vehicle to the ground and tighten the roadwheel bolts to the specified torque.

5 Front suspension strut – overhaul

⚠️ **Warning: Before attempting to dismantle the front suspension strut, a suitable tool to hold the coil spring in compression must be obtained. Adjustable coil spring compressors are readily available, and are recommended for this operation. Any attempt to dismantle the strut without such a tool is likely to result in damage or personal injury.**

Note: *Always renew any self-locking nuts when working on the suspension/steering components.*

5.1 Fit the coil compressors to the springs

5.2 Slacken the top nut whilst retaining the piston with an Allen key

1 With the strut removed from the car (as described in Section 4), clean away all external dirt, and then mount it upright in a vice. Fit the spring compressor and compress the coil spring until tension is relieved from the spring seats **(see illustration)**.

2 Slacken and remove the upper spring seat nut whilst retaining the shock absorber piston with a suitable Allen key **(see illustration)**.

3 Remove the nut then lift off the thrust bearing followed by the spring seat **(see illustrations)**.

4 Lift off the coil spring and remove the cap, dust gaiter and rubber bump stop from the shock absorber piston **(see illustrations)**.

5 Examine the shock absorber for signs of fluid leakage. Check the piston for signs of pitting along its entire length, and check the shock

body for signs of damage. While holding it in an upright position, test the operation of the shock absorber by moving the piston through a full stroke, and then through short strokes of 50 to 100 mm. In both cases, the resistance felt should be smooth and continuous. If the resistance is jerky, or uneven, or if there is any visible sign of wear or damage to the shock absorber, renewal is necessary.

6 Inspect all other components for signs of damage or deterioration, and renew any that are suspect.

7 Slide the rubber bump stop onto the piston. Fit the dust gaiter and cap, making sure the lower end of gaiter is correctly positioned over the shock absorber end.

8 Refit the coil spring; making sure its lower end is correctly seated against the spring seat

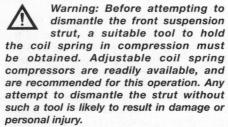
5.3a Remove the nut...

5.3b... the thrust bearing...

5.3c... the spring seat...

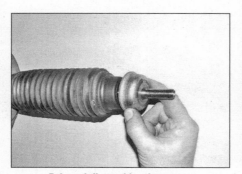
5.4a... followed by the cap...

5.4b... the dust gaiter...

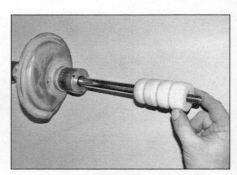
5.4c... and the bump stop

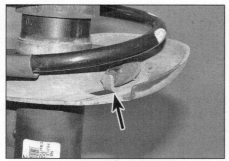

5.8 Ensure the lower end of the spring locates correctly against the spring seat stop (arrowed)

6.1 Pull down on the lower arm to disengage the lower balljoint

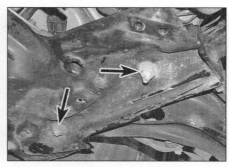

6.2 Undo the lower arm front and rear pivot bolts (arrowed)

stop **(see illustration)**. Fit the upper spring seat, aligning its stop with the spring end, then the thrust bearing.

9 Fit the new nut. Retain the shock absorber piston and tighten the upper spring seat nut to the specified torque.

6 Front suspension lower arm – removal, overhaul and refitting

Note: *Always renew any self-locking nuts when working on the suspension/steering components.*

Removal

1 Slacken and remove the nut and bolt, then free the lower balljoint shank from the lower arm **(see illustration)**. Discard the nut and lift off the protector plate (if loose) from the balljoint.

2 Slacken and remove the lower arm front and rear pivot bolts and nuts **(see illustration)**.

3 Manoeuvre the lower arm assembly out from underneath the vehicle.

Overhaul

4 Thoroughly clean the lower arm and the area around the arm mountings, removing all traces of dirt and underseal if necessary, then check carefully for cracks, distortion or any other signs of wear or damage, paying particular attention to the pivot bushes, and renew components as necessary. The bushes can only be fitted in one position, make a note of the position of the bush in the arm before attempting removal.

5 Renewal of the front and rear pivot bushes will required the use of a hydraulic press, a bearing puller and several spacers and should therefore be entrusted to a Peugeot dealer or specialist with access to the necessary equipment.

Refitting

6 Manoeuvre the lower arm assembly into position, and refit the front pivot bolt and nut, tightening it finger-tight only.

7 Refit the rear pivot bolt and nut, and then tighten them to the specified torque.

8 Refit the protector plate (where removed) to the lower balljoint, and then locate the balljoint shank in the lower arm. Fit the new retaining nut and tighten it to the specified torque.

9 Refit the roadwheel, then lower the vehicle and tighten the roadwheel bolts to the specified torque. Rock the car to settle the disturbed components in position, and then tighten the lower arm front pivot bolt to the specified torque.

10 Check and, if necessary, adjust the front wheel alignment as described in Section 25.

7 Front suspension lower balljoint – removal and refitting

Note: *The balljoint is riveted to the lower arm, so will need to be drilled out and refitted using the bolts supplied in the new balljoint fitting kit.*

Removal

1 Remove the lower suspension arm as described in Section 6.

2 Mount the lower suspension arm securely in a vice, with the balljoint pointing upwards.

3 Using a centre punch, mark the centre of the three rivets that secure the balljoint to the lower arm.

4 Carefully drill the centre of the rivets, using a 10mm drill bit, to a depth of approximately 5 mm.

⚠ **Warning: Make sure the drilling is central in the rivets, so as not to damage the lower suspension arm.**

5 Using a hammer and sharp chisel, cut the drilled part of the rivet head off, and then tap the remainder of the rivet through the suspension arm.

6 The balljoint can then be removed from the suspension arm.

Refitting

7 Fit the new balljoint to the suspension arm, securing it in position with the bolts in the fitting kit. The balljoint fits under the suspension arm and the bolts are inserted

down through the suspension arm and through the balljoint, the retaining nuts are put on the underside of the balljoint.

8 Fit the new protector plate to the balljoint and refit the suspension arm as described in Section 6.

8 Front suspension anti-roll bar – removal and refitting

Note: *Always renew any self-locking nuts when working on the suspension/steering components.*

Removal

1 Chock the rear wheels, firmly apply the handbrake, slacken the front roadwheel bolts, and then jack up the front of the vehicle and support on axle stands (see *Jacking and vehicle support*). Remove both front roadwheels.

2 Slacken and remove the nuts securing the left- and right-hand connecting links to the anti-roll bar, and position the links clear of the bar; if necessary, retain the balljoint shank with a Torx bit to prevent rotation whilst the nut is slackened **(see illustration)**. Discard the nuts; new ones should be used on refitting.

3 Remove the front subframe as described in Section 10.

4 Slacken the two anti-roll bar mounting clamp retaining bolts and nuts, and remove

8.2 Remove the anti-roll bar link nut (arrowed)

8.4 Anti-roll bar clamp (left-hand side arrowed)

8.8 Make sure the clamp is located correctly (arrowed)

Removal

1 Chock the rear wheels, firmly apply the handbrake, slacken the relevant roadwheel bolts, then jack up the front of the vehicle and support on axle stands (see *Jacking and vehicle support*). Remove the relevant roadwheel.

2 Slacken and remove the nuts securing the connecting link to the anti-roll bar and suspension strut and remove the link from the vehicle; if necessary, retain the balljoint shanks with a Torx bit to prevent rotation whilst each nut is slackened **(see illustrations)**.

3 Inspect the link for signs of wear or damage and renew if necessary.

Refitting

4 Refitting is the reverse of removal, using new nuts and tightening them to the specified torque setting.

both clamps from the top of the subframe **(see illustration)**.

5 Manoeuvre the anti-roll bar from subframe, and remove the mounting bushes from the bar.

6 Carefully examine the anti-roll bar components for signs of wear, damage or deterioration, paying particular attention to the mounting bushes renew worn components as necessary.

Refitting

7 Fit the rubber mounting bushes to the anti-roll bar. Position each bush so that its flat surface is at the bottom and its internal flats are correctly engaged with the flats on the anti-roll bar; the slit in the bush should be at the rear of the anti-roll bar.

8 Manoeuvre the anti-roll bar into position on the subframe. Refit the mounting clamps,

ensuring that their ends are correctly located in the hooks on the subframe **(see illustration)**, and refit the retaining bolts and nuts and tighten to the specified torque.

9 Refit the front subframe as described in Section 10.

10 Engage the connecting links with the ends of the anti-roll bar, and then tighten the retaining nuts to the specified torque.

11 Refit the roadwheels then lower the vehicle to the ground and tighten the wheel bolts to the specified torque.

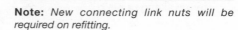

9 Front suspension anti-roll bar connecting link – removal and refitting

Note: *New connecting link nuts will be required on refitting.*

10 Front suspension subframe – removal and refitting

Note: *Always renew any self-locking nuts when working on the suspension/steering components.*

Removal

1 Chock the rear wheels, firmly apply the handbrake, slacken the front roadwheel bolts, and then jack up the front of the vehicle and support it on axle stands (see *Jacking and vehicle support*). Remove both front roadwheels.

2 Disconnect each end of the anti-roll bar from the connecting links, as described in Section 9.

3 Slacken and remove the engine/transmission rear lower mounting bolt and nut, then undo the nut and bolt securing the link rod to the subframe and remove the link **(see illustration)**.

4 Slacken and remove both lower balljoint nut and bolts, then free the balljoint shank from the hub carrier on each side of the vehicle.

5 Slacken and remove both track rod end balljoints from the hub carrier on each side of the vehicle. Discard the nuts; new ones must be fitted.

6 Slacken and remove the steering rack-to-steering column joint bolt and nut and disconnect the steering column from the steering rack noting its fitted position.

7 Disconnect the wiring block connectors from the power steering motor **(see illustration)**.

8 Make a final check that all control cables that are attached to the subframe have been released and positioned clear so that they will not hinder the removal procedure.

9 Place a jack and a suitable block of wood under the subframe to support the subframe as it is lowered.

10 Slacken and remove the subframe mounting bolts then carefully lower the

9.2a Remove the connecting link upper retaining nut (arrowed)…

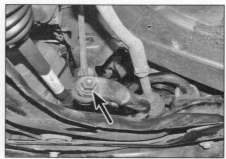

9.2b… and lower retaining nut (arrowed)

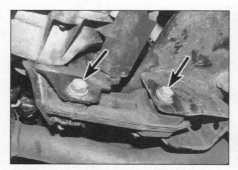

10.3 Undo the bolts (arrowed) securing the rear engine/transmission link rod

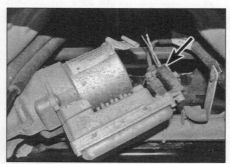

10.7 Disconnect the wiring connector (arrowed) from the power steering motor

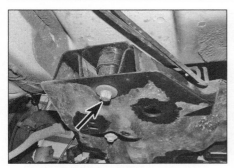

10.10a Undo the rear subframe mounting bolts (left one arrowed)...

10.10b... and the front mounting bolts (left one arrowed)

12.4 Remove the circlip

12.5a Using a threaded bar...

12.5b... to press the bearing out from the hub

subframe assembly out of position and remove it from underneath the vehicle, taking great care to ensure that the subframe assembly does not catch the power steering cables as it is lowered out of position. Recover the washers between the steering rack and the subframe **(see illustrations)**.

Refitting

11 Refitting is a reversal of the removal procedure, noting the following points:
● Use new connecting link and lower balljoint nuts, and steering rack nuts.
● Tighten all nuts and bolts to the specified torque settings (where given).
● On completion check and, if necessary, adjust the front wheel alignment as described in Section 25.

11 Rear hub assembly – removal and refitting

1 The rear hub is an integral part of the brake drum/disc and is not available separately (see Chapter 9 Section 7). If the bearing is worn, renew it as described in Section 12.

12 Rear hub bearings – renewal

Note: *The bearing is a sealed, pre-adjusted and pre-lubricated, double-row roller type, and is intended to last the car's entire service life without maintenance or attention. Never overtighten the hub nut beyond the specified torque wrench setting in an attempt to 'adjust' the bearing.*
Note: *A press will be required to dismantle and rebuild the assembly; if such a tool is not available, a threaded bar and spacers (such as large sockets) will serve as an adequate substitute.*
1 Chock the front wheels, slacken the relevant rear roadwheel bolts, and then jack up the rear of the vehicle and support it on axle stands (see *Jacking and vehicle support*). Remove the relevant roadwheel.

2 Remove the rear brake disc/drum hub assembly as described in Chapter 9 Section 8.
3 Once the disc/drum hub has been removed, use a puller to withdraw the seal from the rear of the hub (see Chapter 9, Section 9). Discard the seal, as a new one will be required for refitting.
4 Extract the bearing retaining circlip from the inner end of the hub assembly **(see illustration)**.
5 Using threaded bar and some large spacers on the inside of the hub, and a socket against the bearing in the outer side of the hub, push the bearing out from the centre of the hub **(see illustrations)**.
6 Thoroughly clean the hub, removing all traces of dirt and grease, and polish away any burrs or raised edges which might

hinder reassembly. Check both for cracks or any other signs of wear or damage, and renew them if necessary. Renew the circlip, regardless of its apparent condition.
7 On reassembly, apply a light film of oil (Peugeot recommend Molykote 321R – available from your Peugeot dealer) to the bearing outer race and hub, to aid installation of the bearing.
8 Securely support the disc/drum hub, and locate the bearing in the hub. Press the bearing fully into position, ensuring that it enters the hub squarely, using a tubular spacer (or old bearing), which bears only on the bearing outer race. Use the same method as removal, with the threaded bar **(see illustrations)**.
9 Once the bearing is correctly seated, secure the bearing in position with the new

12.8a Use the old bearing...

12.8b... and threaded bar to press the new bearing into the hub

12.9 Fit new circlip to bearing recess

12.10a Carefully tap seal/target ring back onto the hub...

12.10b... making sure it sits squarely

circlip, ensuring that it is correctly located in the groove in the hub carrier **(see illustration)**.

10 Carefully fit a new seal making sure it is located squarely on the hub **(see illustrations)**.

 Warning: The seal is also the radial target for the wheel speed sensor, so take care not to damage it. This needs to be fitted correctly or the sensor may not pick-up a signal for the wheel speed.

11 Refit the rear brake disc/drum hub assembly as described in Chapter 9 Section 8.

12 Refit the roadwheels, and then lower the vehicle to the ground and tighten the wheel bolts to the specified torque.

13 Rear suspension shock absorber – removal, testing and refitting

Note: Always renew shock absorbers in pairs, and renew any self-locking nuts when working on the suspension/steering components.

Removal

1 Chock the front wheels, slacken the relevant rear roadwheel bolts, and then jack up the rear of the vehicle and support it on axle stands (see *Jacking and vehicle support*). Remove the relevant rear roadwheel and wheel arch liner **(see illustration)**.

2 Unclip the plastic guard from under the rear axle trailing arm **(see illustration)**.

3 Using a trolley jack positioned under the spring cup, raise the lower arm until the rear suspension coil spring is slightly compressed.

4 Working inside the wheel arch, undo the shock absorber upper mounting bolt **(see illustrations)**. Note the retaining nut is fitted into a plastic holder, which locates into the vehicle body.

5 Slacken and remove the lower mounting bolt, and then manoeuvre the shock absorber out of position **(see illustration)**.

Testing

6 Examine the shock absorber for signs of fluid leakage or damage. Test the operation of the shock absorber, while holding it in an upright position, by moving the piston through a full stroke and then through short strokes of 50 to 100 mm. In both cases, the resistance felt should be smooth and continuous. If the resistance is jerky, or uneven, or if there is any visible sign of wear or damage, renewal is necessary. Also check the rubber mountings for damage and deterioration. Renew worn components as necessary. Inspect the shank of the mounting bolt for signs of wear or damage, and renew as necessary. Any self-locking nuts should be renewed as a matter of course.

Refitting

7 Prior to refitting the shock absorber, mount it upright in the vice, and operate it fully through several strokes in order to prime it. Apply a smear of multipurpose grease to the lower

13.1 Remove the inner wheel arch liner

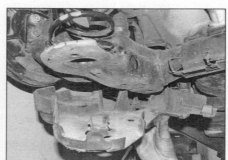

13.2 Unclip the plastic cover from the rear trailing arm

13.4a Remove the upper mounting bolt...

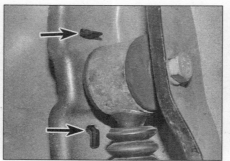

13.4b... noting the nut securing bracket location (arrowed)

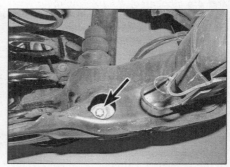

13.5 Shock absorber lower mounting bolt

mounting bolt and contact face of the new nut (Peugeot recommend Molykote G Rapide Plus – available from your Peugeot dealer).

8 Fully extend the piston and manoeuvre the assembly into position. Refit the upper mounting bolt and tighten to the specified torque.

9 Align the shock absorber lower mounting with the lower arm and refit the mounting bolt, tightening it lightly only at this stage.

10 Refit the wheel arch liner and rear roadwheel, then lower the vehicle to the ground and tighten the wheel bolts to the specified torque.

11 Rock the vehicle to settle the shock absorber in position, and then tighten the shock absorber lower mounting bolt to the specified torque setting. Refit the plastic guard under the rear trailing arm.

14 Rear suspension coil spring – removal and refitting

1 Always renew coil springs in pairs, and renew any self-locking nuts when working on the suspension/steering components.

Removal

2 Chock the front wheels, slacken the rear roadwheel bolts, and then jack up the rear of the vehicle and support it on axle stands (see *Jacking and vehicle support*). Remove the rear roadwheels.

3 Unclip the plastic guard from under the rear axle trailing arm **(see illustration 13.2)**.

4 Position a trolley jack underneath one of the lower arm's spring cup and raise the arm until the rear suspension coil spring on that side is slightly compressed.

5 Unscrew the shock absorber lower mounting bolt and withdraw the bolt **(see illustration 13.5)**.

6 Using a spring compressor tool, compress the coil spring until there is no pressure on the rear axle, and then lower the jack slightly to remove the spring complete with tool. Note the fitted position of the spring in the upper and lower seats **(see illustrations)**.

7 Inspect the coil spring and its seats for signs of wear or damage and renew if necessary.

14.6a Spring compressor tool (arrowed) fitted to spring

Refitting

8 Manoeuvre the spring into position and carefully raise the lower arm with the jack, ensuring that the coil spring ends are correctly aligned with both seats.

9 Align the shock absorber with the lower arm and refit its mounting bolt, tightening it lightly only at this stage.

10 With the spring in position, release the pressure and remove the spring compressor from the coil spring.

11 Remove the jack from underneath the lower arm.

12 Refit the rear roadwheel, and then lower the vehicle to the ground; tighten the wheel bolts to the specified torque.

13 Rock the vehicle to settle the shock absorber in position, and then tighten the shock absorber lower mounting bolt to the specified torque setting. Refit the plastic guard under the rear trailing arm.

15 Rear suspension stub axle – removal, overhaul and refitting

Note: *Always renew any self-locking nuts when working on the suspension/steering components.*

Removal

1 Chock the front wheels, slacken the relevant rear roadwheel bolts, and then jack up the rear of the vehicle and support it on axle stands (see *Jacking and vehicle support*). Remove the relevant roadwheel.

14.6b Note the fitted position of the spring in the seat

2 Unbolt the wheel sensor and position it clear of the stub axle (see Chapter 9 Section 22). Note that there is no need to disconnect the wiring.

3 Remove the rear brake disc/drum hub assembly as described in Chapter 9 Section 8.

4 Undo the four retaining bolts from the rear of the stub axle and pull it away from the rear arm slightly **(see illustrations)**.

5 Remove the upper and lower retaining bolts from the backplate and withdraw the stub axle from the backplate **(see illustration)**. **Note:** *On drum brake models, secure the backplate in position to prevent any damage to the brake lines.*

6 Inspect the stub axle for signs of wear or damage. If the stub axle shaft is worn or damaged then the assembly must be renewed.

Refitting

7 Obtain all the new nuts required and lubricate the shanks of the bolts and contact faces of the new nuts with multipurpose grease (Peugeot recommend Molykote G Rapide Plus – available from your Peugeot dealer).

8 Offer up the stub axle and backplate, insert the bolts and tighten them to the specified torque.

9 Fit the brake disc/drum hub assembly.

10 On disc brake models, slide the brake caliper and bracket assembly over the edge of the disc (refer to Chapter 9 Section 11), and tighten the mounting bracket bolts to the specified torque.

15.4a Rear stub axle (arrowed) – drum brakes

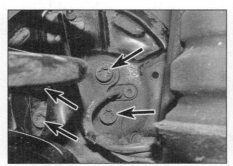

15.4b Rear stub axle retaining bolts (arrowed)

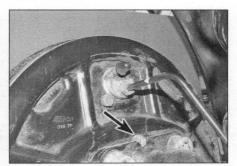

15.5 Brake backplate retaining bolt (upper one arrowed) – drum brakes

16.3a Undo the two retaining bolts (arrowed)...

16.3b... and remove the mounting bracket plastic cover

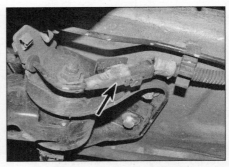

16.5 Disconnect the sensor wiring connector (arrowed)

11 Refit the wheel speed sensor to the stub axle.

12 Refit the rear roadwheel, and then lower the vehicle to the ground and tighten the wheel bolts to the specified torque.

16 Rear beam axle – removal, overhaul and refitting

Note: *Always renew any self-locking nuts when working on the suspension/steering components.*

Removal

1 Chock the front wheels, slacken the rear roadwheel bolts, and then jack up the rear of the vehicle and support it on axle stands (see *Jacking and vehicle support*). Remove the rear roadwheels.

2 Unclip the plastic guards from under the rear axle trailing arms **(see illustration 13.2)**.

3 Undo the retaining bolts and unclip the plastic guards from under the rear axle front mounting bracket **(see illustrations)**.

4 Remove the coil springs as described in Section 14.

5 Trace the ABS wheel speed sensor wiring back to its connector, and unplug it. Free the sensor harness from any retaining clips on the axle **(see illustration)**.

6 Clamp the flexible brake hose, and undo the hose union where the flexible hose connects to the rigid hose **(see illustration)**. Plug the end of the hose/pipe to prevent dirt ingress. Repeat this procedure on the remaining side.

7 Release the handbrake cables from the retaining clips along the axle, then release the ends of the cables from the rear brakes and support brackets (see Chapter 9 Section 19). Repeat the procedure on the remaining side.

8 Make alignment marks between the axle mounting brackets and the vehicle body to aid refitment. Undo the 4 bolts each side securing the mounting brackets to the vehicle body, and lower the axle to the floor **(see illustration)**. If the axle is to be renewed, remove the brake caliper and disc (Chapter 9 Section 8), and the stub axle (Section 15).

Overhaul

9 Thoroughly clean the axle and the area around the axle mountings, removing all traces of dirt and underseal if necessary, then check carefully for cracks, distortion or any signs of wear or damage, paying particular attention to the pivot bushes.

10 Renewal of the pivot bushes will require the use of a hydraulic press and several spacers, and should therefore be entrusted to a Peugeot dealer or specialist with access to the necessary equipment.

Refitting

11 Lubricate the shanks of the axle mounting bracket bolts with multipurpose grease (Peugeot recommend Molykote G Rapide Plus – available from your Peugeot dealer).

12 Offer up the axle and mounting brackets, aligning the previously-made marks, and insert the retaining bolts, tightening them lightly only at this stage.

13 Jack up each side of the rear axle trailing arms until there is a measurement of 160.5 mm, between the upper and lower spring seats (the raised part in the middle of the spring).

14 The rear axle mounting bolts can now be fully tightened to their specified torque. Note the bolts are shouldered, so will align themselves.

15 Refit the handbrake cables to their retaining clips on the axle, and reconnect the cable ends to the rear brakes.

16 Reconnect the rear brake flexible hoses, tightening the hose/pipe unions securely. Remove the hose clamps.

17 Reconnect the wheel speed sensor wiring connectors, and secure the wiring harness in the retaining clips on the axle.

18 Refit the coil spring with reference to Section 14.

19 On completion bleed the brakes as described in Chapter 9 Section 2.

17 Steering wheel – removal and refitting

Warning: Refer to the precautions given in Chapter 12 Section 21 about airbags before proceeding.

Removal

1 Release the securing clip and remove the airbag unit as described in Chapter 12 Section 22 **(see illustration)**.

16.6 Undo the nut where the metal brake pipe joins the flexible pipe

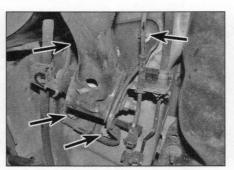

16.8 Undo the four bolts each side (arrowed) securing the axle brackets to the vehicle body

17.1 Insert screwdriver to release airbag retaining spring

2 Unclip the connector from inside the steering wheel and disconnect the wiring **(see illustration)**.

3 Position the front wheels in the straight-ahead position and engage the steering lock.

4 Slacken and remove the steering wheel retaining bolt, noting the alignment marks on the steering wheel and the steering column shaft in relation to each other for refitting **(see illustration)**.

5 Lift the steering wheel off the column splines, feeding the airbag wires through the aperture in the steering wheel as it is withdrawn.

Refitting

6 Prior to refitting the steering wheel, ensure that the front wheels are still in the straight-ahead position.

7 Refitting is a reversal of removal, noting the following points:

● On refitting, align the marks made on removal, taking great care not to damage any wiring, then tighten the retaining bolt to the specified torque.

● On completion, refit the airbag unit as described in Chapter 12 Section 22.

---

18 Steering column – removal, inspection and refitting

Note: *As all models are equipped with a driver's airbag, refer to the precautions*

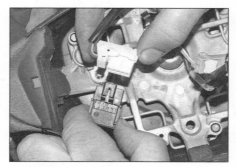
17.2 Disconnect the wiring connectors from inside the steering wheel

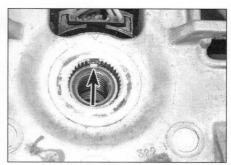
17.4 Note the alignment marks and master spline (arrowed)

given in Chapter 12 Section 21 before proceeding.

Note: *A new pinch-bolt nut will be needed on refitting.*

Removal

1 Remove the steering wheel as described in Section 17.

2 Move the driver's seat as far back as possible.

3 Undo the retaining screws and remove the trim panels from around the steering column **(see illustration)**.

4 Release the retaining clips and remove the lower trim panel from above the driver's pedals and the facia trim panel from the lower

part of the steering column **(see illustrations)**.

5 Working in the driver's footwell, make alignment marks between the universal joint and the steering rack pinion, release the retaining clip, then undo and remove the pinch-bolt/nut from the joint at the base of the column **(see illustration)**.

6 Remove the combination switches from the top of the steering column **(see illustration)**, as described in Chapter 12 Section 10.

7 Disconnect the wiring connector from the ignition switch, and then trace the wiring loom back along the steering column and release it from the retaining clips **(see illustration)**.

8 Slacken and remove the four mounting

18.3 Remove the steering column upper trim panels

18.4a Remove the lower trim panel...

18.4b... and facia trim panel

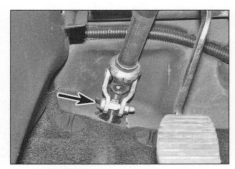
18.5 Release the retaining clip and remove the pinch-bolt/nut (arrowed)

18.6 Remove the combination switches

18.7 Unclip the wiring loom

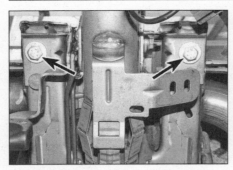

18.8a Undo the upper mounting bolts (arrowed)...

18.8b... and lower mounting bolts (arrowed)

18.9 Withdraw the steering column out from the facia

bolts from the mounting bracket on the upper part of the steering column (**see illustrations**).

9 Slide the column assembly upwards, to free from the steering rack pinion, and remove it from the vehicle (**see illustration**).

Inspection

10 Before refitting the steering column, examine the column and mountings for signs of damage and deformation, and renew as necessary. Check the steering shaft for signs of free play in the column bushes, and check the universal joints for signs of damage or roughness in the joint bearings. If any damage or wear is found on the steering column universal joint or shaft bushes, the column must be renewed as an assembly.

Refitting

11 Align the marks made prior to removal and engage the column universal joint with the steering rack pinion.

12 Slide the column assembly into position making sure its mounting bracket is correctly engaged with the facia bracket. Refit the column mounting bolts and tighten them to the specified torque setting.

13 Refit the universal joint pinch-bolt and nut, tighten them to the specified torque setting, and then refit the retaining clip.

14 The remainder of refitting is a reversal of the removal procedure, noting the following.

● Ensure that all wiring is correctly routed and retained by all the necessary clips and ties.

● Refit the steering wheel as described in Section 17.

19.3 Unclip the ignition switch cover...

19 Ignition switch/lock cylinder/ steering lock – removal and refitting

Ignition switch/steering lock

Removal

1 Disconnect the battery (see Chapter 5A Section 4).

2 Undo the retaining screws securing the steering column lower shroud in position, then lift the rear edge of the upper shroud, and release it from the retaining clips.

3 Withdraw the plastic cover from around the ignition switch (**see illustration**).

4 Disconnect the wiring connector from the ignition switch (**see illustration**).

5 Using a hammer and small chisel undo and remove the securing bolt from under the

19.4... and disconnect the wiring connector

ignition switch (**see illustration**). Discard the bolt as a new one will be required for refitting. **Note:** *The new shear bolt has a head on it which can be tightened and will snap off at a given torque, leaving the remainder of the bolt in place securing the ignition switch.*

6 With the key in the ignition switch, use a small screwdriver to depress the locating peg on the top of the switch, and then slide the assembly from the steering column housing (**see illustrations**).

Refitting

7 Refitting is a reversal of removal, noting the following points:

● Ensure all wiring is correctly routed, and securely clipped back into its original positions.

● Refit the steering lock housing with a new securing bolt, tightening it until it shears the head.

19.5 Using a hammer and chisel to undo the switch securing shear bolt

19.6a Depress the peg with a small screwdriver...

19.6b... and slide the switch from the steering column

Lock cylinder

8 At the time of writing, the lock cylinder was not available separately from the ignition switch assembly.

20 Steering rack assembly – removal, overhaul and refitting

Note: *Always renew any self-locking nuts when working on the suspension/steering components.*

Removal

1 Chock the rear wheels, firmly apply the handbrake, slacken the front roadwheel bolts, and then jack up the front of the vehicle and support on axle stands (see *Jacking and vehicle support*). Remove both front roadwheels.
2 Remove the front subframe as described in Section 10. **Note:** *The subframe does not need to be removed completely for this procedure, lower the subframe on a jack to allow enough room for the steering rack can be withdrawn.*
3 Undo the steering rack mounting nuts **(see illustration)**. Where applicable, recover any washers/spacers fitted between the rack and the subframe, noting their fitted positions. Discard the rack mounting studs and nuts, as new ones must be fitted.
4 Free the steering rack from the subframe and manoeuvre it out from the anti-roll bar.

Overhaul

5 Examine the steering rack assembly for signs of wear or damage, and check that the rack moves freely throughout the full length of its travel, with no signs of roughness or excessive free play between the steering rack pinion and rack.
6 The electric power steering motor is an integral part of the steering rack and cannot be purchased separately from the steering rack. If required, have the motor checked by your local Peugeot dealer or specialist. The steering torque sensor is fitted around the pinion shaft, inside the top of the steering rack housing **(see illustration)**.
7 It may be possible to overhaul the steering rack assembly housing components, but this task should be entrusted to a Peugeot dealer or specialist.

20.3 Steering rack-to-subframe mounting nuts (arrowed)

8 The only components which can be renewed by the home mechanic are the steering rack gaiters, the track rod end balljoints and the track rods, which are covered elsewhere in this Chapter.

Refitting

9 Manoeuvre the steering rack into position on the subframe and tighten the nuts to the specified torque, where applicable, sliding the washers into position between the subframe and steering rack, as noted on removal.
10 Refit the front subframe as described in Section 10.
11 The remainder of refitting is a reversal of removal, noting the following point:
● On completion check and if necessary adjust the front wheel alignment as described in Section 25.

21 Steering rack rubber gaiters – renewal

1 Remove the track rod end balljoint as described in Section 23.
2 Mark the correct fitted position of the gaiter on the track rod, then release the retaining clips and slide the gaiter off the steering rack housing and track rod end **(see illustrations)**.
3 Thoroughly clean the track rod and the steering rack housing, using fine abrasive paper to polish off any corrosion, burrs or sharp edges which might damage the new gaiter's sealing lips on installation. Scrape off all the grease from

20.6 Steering torque sensor (arrowed)

the old gaiter, and apply it to the track rod inner balljoint. (This assumes that grease has not been lost or contaminated as a result of damage to the old gaiter. Use fresh grease if in doubt.)
4 Carefully slide the new gaiter onto the track rod end, and locate it on the steering rack housing. Align the outer edge of the gaiter with the mark made on the track rod prior to removal, and then secure it in position with new retaining clips (where fitted).
5 Refit the track rod balljoint as described in Section 23.

22 Power steering motor – removal and refitting

1 The power steering motor is an integral part of the steering rack assembly and is not available separately **(see illustration)**. Remove the steering rack as described in Section 20.

23 Track rod end balljoint – removal and refitting

1 A new balljoint retaining nut will be required on refitting.

Removal

2 Apply the handbrake, slacken the appropriate front roadwheel bolts, then jack up the front of the vehicle and support it on axle stands (see *Jacking and vehicle support*). Remove the appropriate front roadwheel.

21.2a Steering rack securing clips (arrowed) – right-hand side...

21.2b... and left-hand side

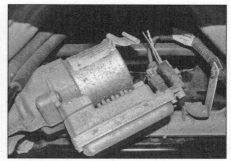

22.1 Power steering motor integral with rack

23.4 Slacken the locknut (arrowed)

3 If the balljoint is to be re-used, mark the threads on the track rod arm in relationship to the track rod end.

4 Hold the track rod end and unscrew the locknut by a quarter of a turn **(see illustration)**. Do not move the locknut from this position, as it will serve as a handy reference mark on refitting.

5 Slacken and remove the nut securing the track rod end balljoint to the hub carrier; discard the nut; a new one will be needed on refitting. Release the balljoint tapered shank using a universal balljoint separator **(see illustrations)**.

6 Counting the exact number of turns necessary to do so, unscrew the track rod end balljoint from the track rod arm.

7 Carefully clean the balljoint and the threads. Renew the balljoint if its movement is sloppy or too stiff, if excessively worn, or if damaged in any way; carefully check the stud taper and threads. If the balljoint gaiter is damaged, the complete track rod end balljoint assembly must be renewed; it is not possible to obtain the gaiter separately.

Refitting

8 Screw the track rod end balljoint onto the track rod arm by the number of turns noted on removal. This should bring the locknut to within a quarter of a turn of the alignment marks that were made on removal (if applicable).

9 Locate the balljoint shank in the hub carrier and fit a new retaining nut; tighten it to the specified torque.

10 Tighten the locknut on the track rod arm,

23.5a Undo the balljoint nut (arrowed)...

refit the roadwheel, and then lower the vehicle to the ground. Tighten the roadwheel bolts to the specified torque.

11 Check and, if necessary, adjust the front wheel alignment as described in Section 25, then securely tighten the track rod end balljoint locknut.

24 Track rod arm –
removal and refitting

Note: *A special wrench (Peugeot number 0721-A and 0721-B) will be required to remove/refit the track rod inner balljoint from the end of the steering rack. Without the clamp, damage to the assembly is likely. The special wrench engages with the balljoint housing allowing the track rod to be easily slackened/tightened without the risk of damage. The other part of the tool clamps around the steering rack shaft to prevent any damage to the steering rack. Note that without access to the special tool, track rod removal will be difficult, especially without causing damage.*

Note: *A new balljoint retaining nut will be required on refitting.*

Removal

1 Remove the front subframe as described in Section 10.

2 Remove the relevant steering rack rubber gaiter as described in Section 21.

3 Using the special wrench (see note at the start of the Section), unscrew the track rod inner balljoint from the steering rack end. Take great care not to place excess strain on the rack, as the joint is unscrewed, if necessary, prevent the steering rack from turning by holding it carefully with a pair of grips. Take great care not to mark the surfaces of the rack and balljoint. To eliminate the possibility of damage, a Peugeot special tool (0721-B) is available to prevent the rack from twisting.

4 Remove the track rod assembly. Examine the track rod inner balljoint for signs of slackness or tight spots, and check that the track rod itself is straight and free from damage. If necessary, renew the track rod; it is also recommended that the steering rack gaiter/dust cover is renewed.

23.5b... then use a balljoint separator to release the tapered shank

Refitting

5 Screw the balljoint into the steering rack, and tighten it to the specified torque. If necessary, retain the steering rack with a pair of grips or the special Peugeot tool, again taking great care not to damage or mark the track rod balljoint or steering rack.

6 Carefully slide on the new gaiter, and locate it on the steering rack housing. Turn the steering fully from lock-to-lock, to check that the gaiter is correctly positioned on the track rod, then secure it in position with new retaining clips (where fitted).

7 Refit the front subframe as described in Section 10.

8 Refit the track rod balljoint as described in Section 23.

25 Wheel alignment and
steering angles – information, checking and adjustment

Definitions

1 A car's steering and suspension geometry is defined in four basic settings – all angles are expressed in degrees; the steering axis is defined as an imaginary line drawn through the axis of the suspension strut, extended where necessary to contact the ground.

2 Camber is the angle between each roadwheel and a vertical line drawn through its centre and tyre contact patch, when viewed from the front or rear of the car. Positive camber is when the roadwheels are tilted outwards from the vertical at the top; negative camber is when they are tilted inwards. The camber angle is not adjustable.

3 Castor is the angle between the steering axis and a vertical line drawn through each roadwheel's centre and tyre contact patch, when viewed from the side of the car. Positive castor is when the steering axis is tilted so that it contacts the ground ahead of the vertical; negative castor is when it contacts the ground behind the vertical. The castor angle is not adjustable.

4 Toe is the difference, viewed from above, between lines drawn through the roadwheel centres and the car's centre-line. 'Toe-in' is when the roadwheels point inwards, towards each other at the front, while 'toe-out' is when they splay outwards from each other at the front.

5 The front wheel toe setting is adjusted by screwing the track rod in or out of its balljoints to alter the effective length of the track rod assembly.

6 Rear wheel toe setting is not adjustable.

Checking and adjustment

7 Due to the special measuring equipment necessary to check the wheel alignment and steering angles, and the skill required to use it properly, the checking and adjustment of these settings is best left to a Peugeot dealer or similar expert. Note that most tyre-fitting shops now possess sophisticated checking equipment.

Chapter 11
Bodywork and fittings

Contents

Degrees of difficulty

Easy, suitable for novice with little experience	Fairly easy, suitable for beginner with some experience	Fairly difficult, suitable for competent DIY mechanic	Difficult, suitable for experienced DIY mechanic	Very difficult, suitable for expert DIY or professional

Specifications

Torque wrench setting	Nm	lbf ft
Seat belt mountings	25	18

1 General Information

1 The bodyshell is made of pressed-steel sections, and is available in a three- or five-door Hatchback version or five-door Estate. Most components are welded together, but some use is made of structural adhesives. The front wings are bolted on.
2 The bonnet, doors and some other vulnerable panels are made of zinc-coated metal, and are further protected by being coated with an anti-chip primer prior to being sprayed.
3 Extensive use is made of plastic materials, mainly in the interior, but also in exterior components. The front and rear bumpers, and the front grille, are injection-moulded from a synthetic material, which is very strong, yet light. Plastic components such as wheel arch liners are fitted to the underside of the vehicle, to improve the body's resistance to corrosion.

2 Maintenance – bodywork and underframe

1 The general condition of a vehicle's bodywork is the one thing that significantly affects its value. Maintenance is easy, but needs to be regular. Neglect, particularly after minor damage, can lead quickly to further deterioration and costly repair bills. It is important also to keep watch on those parts of the vehicle not immediately visible, for instance the underside, inside all the wheel arches, and the lower part of the engine compartment.
2 The basic maintenance routine for the bodywork is washing – preferably with a lot of water, from a hose. This will remove all the loose solids that may have stuck to the vehicle. It is important to flush these off in such a way as to prevent grit from scratching the finish. The wheel arches and underframe need washing in the same way, to remove any accumulated mud, which will retain moisture and tend to encourage rust. Paradoxically enough, the best time to clean the underframe and wheel arches is in wet weather, when the mud is thoroughly wet and soft. In very wet weather, the underframe is usually cleaned of large accumulations automatically, and this is a good time for inspection.
3 Periodically, except on vehicles with a wax based underbody protective coating, it is a good idea to have the whole of the underframe of the vehicle steam-cleaned, engine compartment included, so that a thorough inspection can be carried out to see what

minor repairs and renovations are necessary. Steam cleaning is available at many garages, and is necessary for the removal of the accumulation of oily grime, which sometimes is allowed to become thick in certain areas. If steam-cleaning facilities are not available, there are one or two excellent grease solvents available, which can be brush-applied; the dirt can then be simply hosed off. Note that these methods should not be used on vehicles with wax-based underbody protective coating, or the coating will be removed. Such vehicles should be inspected annually, preferably just prior to winter, when the underbody should be washed down, and any damage to the wax coating repaired using underseal. Ideally, a completely fresh coat should be applied. It would also be worth considering the use of wax-based protection for injection into door panels, sills, box sections, etc, as an additional safeguard against rust damage, where such protection is not provided by the vehicle manufacturer.

4 After washing paintwork, wipe off with a chamois leather to give an unspotted clear finish. A coat of clear protective wax polish will give added protection against chemical pollutants in the air. If the paintwork sheen has dulled or oxidised, use a cleaner/polisher combination to restore the brilliance of the shine. This requires a little effort, but such dulling is usually caused because regular washing has been neglected. Care needs to be taken with metallic paintwork, as a special non-abrasive cleaner/polisher is required to avoid damage to the finish. Always check that the door and ventilator opening drain holes and pipes are completely clear, so that water can be drained out. Brightwork should be treated in the same way as paintwork. Windscreens and windows can be kept clear of the smeary film, which often appears, by the use of proprietary glass cleaner. Never use any form of wax or other body or chromium polish on glass.

3 Maintenance –
upholstery and carpets

1 Mats and carpets should be brushed or vacuum-cleaned regularly, to keep them free of grit. If they are badly stained, remove them from the vehicle for scrubbing or sponging, and make quite sure they are dry before refitting. Seats and interior trim panels can be kept clean by wiping with a damp cloth and a proprietary upholstery cleaner. If they do become stained (which can be more apparent on light-coloured upholstery), use a little liquid detergent and a soft nail brush to scour the grime out of the grain of the material. Do not forget to keep the headlining clean in the same way as the upholstery. When using liquid cleaners inside the vehicle, do not over-wet the surfaces being cleaned. Excessive damp could get into the seams and padded interior, causing stains,

offensive odours or even rot. If the inside of the vehicle gets wet accidentally, it is worthwhile taking some trouble to dry it out properly, particularly where carpets are involved.
Caution: Do not leave oil or electric heaters inside the vehicle for this purpose.

4 Minor body damage – repair

Scratches

1 If the scratch is very superficial, and does not penetrate to the metal of the bodywork, repair is very simple. Lightly rub the area of the scratch with a paintwork renovator, or a very fine cutting paste, to remove loose paint from the scratch, and to clear the surrounding bodywork of wax polish. Rinse the area with clean water.

2 Apply touch-up paint to the scratch using a fine paintbrush; continue to apply fine layers of paint until the surface of the paint in the scratch is level with the surrounding paintwork. Allow the new paint at least two weeks to harden, and then blend it into the surrounding paintwork by rubbing the scratch area with a paintwork renovator or a very fine cutting paste. Finally apply wax polish.

3 Where the scratch has penetrated right through to the metal of the bodywork, causing the metal to rust, a different repair technique is required. Remove any loose rust from the bottom of the scratch with a penknife, and then apply rust-inhibiting paint, to prevent the formation of rust in the future. Using a rubber or nylon applicator, fill the scratch with body stopper paste. If required, this paste can be mixed with cellulose thinners, to provide a very thin paste that is ideal for filling narrow scratches. Before the stopper-paste in the scratch hardens, wrap a piece of smooth cotton rag around the top of a finger. Dip the finger in cellulose thinners, and quickly sweep it across the surface of the stopper-paste in the scratch; this will ensure that the surface of the stopper-paste is slightly hollowed. The scratch can now be painted over as described earlier in this Section.

Dents

4 When deep denting of the vehicle's bodywork has taken place, the first task is to pull the dent out, until the affected bodywork almost attains its original shape. There is little point in trying to restore the original shape completely, as the metal in the damaged area will have stretched on impact, and cannot be reshaped fully to its original contour. It is better to bring the level of the dent up to a point which is about 3 mm below the level of the surrounding bodywork. In cases where the dent is very shallow anyway, it is not worth trying to pull it out at all. If the underside of the dent is accessible, it can be hammered out gently from behind, using a mallet with

a wooden or plastic head. Whilst doing this, hold a suitable block of wood firmly against the outside of the panel, to absorb the impact from the hammer blows and thus prevent a large area of the bodywork from being 'belled-out'.

5 Should the dent be in a section of the bodywork, which has a double skin, or some other factor making it inaccessible from behind, a different technique is called for. Drill several small holes through the metal inside the area – particularly in the deeper section. Then screw long self-tapping screws into the holes, just sufficiently for them to gain a good purchase in the metal. Now the dent can be pulled out by pulling on the protruding heads of the screws with a pair of pliers.

6 The next stage of the repair is the removal of the paint from the damaged area, and from an inch or so of the surrounding 'sound' bodywork. This is accomplished most easily by using a wire brush or abrasive pad on a power drill, although it can be done just as effectively by hand, using sheets of abrasive paper. To complete the preparation for filling, score the surface of the bare metal with a screwdriver or the tang of a file, or alternatively, drill small holes in the affected area. This will provide a really good 'key' for the filler paste.

7 To complete the repair, see the Section on filling and re-spraying.

Rust holes or gashes

8 Remove all paint from the affected area, and from an inch or so of the surrounding 'sound' bodywork, using an abrasive pad or a wire brush on a power drill. If these are not available, a few sheets of abrasive paper will do the job most effectively. With the paint removed, you will be able to judge the severity of the corrosion, and therefore decide whether to renew the whole panel (if this is possible) or to repair the affected area. New body panels are not as expensive as most people think, and it is often quicker and more satisfactory to fit a new panel than to attempt to repair large areas of corrosion.

9 Remove all fittings from the affected area, except those, which will act as a guide to the original shape of the damaged bodywork (eg, headlight shells etc). Then, using tin snips or a hacksaw blade, remove all loose metal and any other metal badly affected by corrosion. Hammer the edges of the hole inwards, in order to create a slight depression for the filler paste.

10 Wire-brush the affected area to remove the powdery rust from the surface of the remaining metal. Paint the affected area with rust-inhibiting paint; if the back of the rusted area is accessible, treat this also.

11 Before filling can take place, it will be necessary to block the hole in some way. This can be achieved by the use of aluminium or plastic mesh, or aluminium tape.

12 Aluminium or plastic mesh, or glass-fibre matting, is probably the best material to use for a large hole. Cut a piece to the approximate size and shape of the hole to be filled, then position it in the hole so that its edges are below the level of the surrounding bodywork. It can be retained in position by several blobs of filler paste around its periphery.

13 Aluminium tape should be used for small or very narrow holes. Pull a piece off the roll, trim it to the approximate size and shape required, then pull off the backing paper (if used) and stick the tape over the hole; it can be overlapped if the thickness of one piece is insufficient. Burnish down the edges of the tape with the handle of a screwdriver or similar, to ensure that the tape is securely attached to the metal underneath.

Filling and respraying

14 Before using this Section, see the Sections on dent, minor scratch, rust holes and gash repairs.

15 Many types of body filler are available, but generally speaking, those proprietary kits, which contain a tin of filler paste and a tube of resin hardener, are best for this type of repair; some can be used directly from the tube. A wide, flexible plastic or nylon applicator will be found invaluable for imparting a smooth and well-contoured finish to the surface of the filler.

16 Mix up a little filler on a clean piece of card or board – measure the hardener carefully (follow the maker's instructions on the pack), otherwise the filler will set too rapidly or too slowly. Using the applicator, apply the filler paste to the prepared area; draw the applicator across the surface of the filler to achieve the correct contour and to level the surface. As soon as a contour that approximates to the correct one is achieved, stop working the paste – if you carry on too long, the paste will become sticky and begin to 'pick-up' on the applicator. Continue to add thin layers of filler paste at 20-minute intervals, until the level of the filler is just proud of the surrounding bodywork.

17 Once the filler has hardened, the excess can be removed using a metal plane or file. From then on, progressively finer grades of abrasive paper should be used, starting with a 40-grade production paper, and finishing with a 400-grade wet-and-dry paper. Always wrap the abrasive paper around a flat rubber, cork, or wooden block – otherwise the surface of the filler will not be completely flat. During the smoothing of the filler surface, the wet-and-dry paper should be periodically rinsed in water. This will ensure that a very smooth finish is imparted to the filler at the final stage.

18 At this stage, the 'dent' should be surrounded by a ring of bare metal, which in turn should be encircled by the finely 'feathered' edge of the good paintwork. Rinse the repair area with clean water, until all of the dust produced by the rubbing-down operation has gone.

19 Spray the whole area with a light coat of primer – this will show up any imperfections in the surface of the filler. Repair these imperfections with fresh filler paste or body stopper, and once more smooth the surface with abrasive paper. If body stopper is used, it can be mixed with cellulose thinners, to form a really thin paste that is ideal for filling small holes. Repeat this spray-and-repair procedure until you are satisfied that the surface of the filler, and the feathered edge of the paintwork, are perfect. Clean the repair area with clean water, and allow to dry fully.

20 The repair area is now ready for final spraying. Paint spraying must be carried out in a warm, dry, windless and dust-free atmosphere. This condition can be created artificially if you have access to a large indoor working area, but if you are forced to work in the open, you will have to pick your day very carefully. If you are working indoors, dousing the floor in the work area with water will help to settle the dust, which would otherwise be in the atmosphere. If the repair area is confined to one body panel, mask off the surrounding panels; this will help to minimise the effects of a slight mismatch in paint colours. Bodywork fittings (e.g. chrome strips, door handles etc) will also need to be masked off. Use genuine masking tape, and several thicknesses of newspaper, for the masking operations.

21 Before commencing to spray, agitate the aerosol can thoroughly, and then spray a test area (an old tin, or similar) until the technique is mastered. Cover the repair area with a thick coat of primer; the thickness should be built up using several thin layers of paint, rather than one thick one. Using 400-grade wet-and-dry paper, rub down the surface of the primer until it is really smooth. While doing this, the work area should be thoroughly doused with water, and the wet-and-dry paper periodically rinsed in water. Allow to dry before spraying on more paint.

22 Spray on the top coat, again building up the thickness by using several thin layers of paint. Start spraying at the top of the repair area, and then, using a side-to-side motion, work downwards until the whole repair area and about 2 inches of the surrounding original paintwork is covered. Remove all masking material 10 to 15 minutes after spraying on the final coat of paint.

23 Allow the new paint at least two weeks to harden, then, using a paintwork renovator or a very fine cutting paste, blend the edges of the paint into the existing paintwork. Finally, apply wax polish.

Plastic components

24 With the use of more and more plastic body components by the vehicle manufacturers (e.g. bumpers. spoilers, and in some cases major body panels), rectification of more serious damage to such items has become a matter of either entrusting repair work to a specialist in this field, or renewing complete components. Repair of such damage by the DIY owner is not really feasible, owing to the cost of the equipment and materials required for effecting such repairs. The basic technique involves making a groove along the line of the crack in the plastic, using a rotary burr in a power drill. The damaged part is then welded back together, using a hot air gun to heat up and fuse a plastic filler rod into the groove. Any excess plastic is then removed, and the area rubbed down to a smooth finish. It is important that a filler rod of the correct plastic is used, as body components can be made of a variety of different types (e.g. polycarbonate, ABS, polypropylene).

25 Damage of a less serious nature (abrasions, minor cracks etc) can be repaired by the DIY owner using a two-part epoxy filler repair material. Once mixed in equal proportions, this is used in similar fashion to the bodywork filler used on metal panels. The filler is usually cured in twenty to thirty minutes, ready for sanding and painting.

26 If the owner is renewing a complete component himself, or if he has repaired it with epoxy filler, he will be left with the problem of finding a suitable paint for finishing which is compatible with the type of plastic used. At one time, the use of a universal paint was not possible, owing to the complex range of plastics encountered in body component applications. Standard paints, generally speaking, will not bond to plastic or rubber satisfactorily. However, it is now possible to obtain a plastic body parts finishing kit that consists of a pre-primer treatment, a primer and coloured top coat. Full instructions are normally supplied with a kit, but basically, the method of use is to first apply the pre-primer to the component concerned, and allow it to dry for up to 30 minutes. Then the primer is applied, and left to dry for about an hour before finally applying the special-coloured top coat. The result is a correctly coloured component, where the paint will flex with the plastic or rubber, a property that standard paint does not normally posses.

5 Major body damage – repair

1 Where serious damage has occurred, or large areas need renewal due to neglect, it means that complete new panels will need welding-in, and this is best left to professionals. If the damage is due to impact, it will also be necessary to check completely the alignment of the bodyshell, and this can only be carried out accurately by a Peugeot dealer, or accident repair specialist, using special jigs. If the body is left misaligned, it is primarily dangerous, as the car will not handle properly, and secondly, uneven stresses will be imposed on the steering, suspension and possibly transmission, causing abnormal wear, or complete failure, particularly to such items as the tyres.

6.3 Release the four securing clips (two arrowed)

6.5 Disconnect the wiring connector

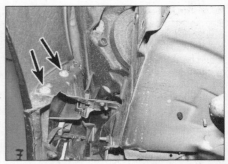

6.7 Undo the bumper-to-wing retaining bolts (arrowed)

6.9a Undo the mounting bolts (one side arrowed)...

6.9b... and remove the front crossmember

9 If required, undo the three bolts each side and remove the bumper front crossmember (see illustrations).

10 Refitting is a reversal of removal, ensuring that the bumper correctly engages with the retaining clips each side as it is located in position.

7 Rear bumper – removal and refitting

1 The help of an assistant is useful to support the bumper during the removal and refitting procedure.

Removal

2 Chock the front wheels, then jack up the rear of the vehicle and support securely on axle stands (see Jacking and vehicle support).

Hatchback models

3 Working under the rear of the vehicle, undo the two retaining bolts from the lower part of the bumper cover (see illustration).

4 Working at the outer edges of the bumper, release the securing clips and remove the side trim panels (see illustrations).

5 Release the ends of the bumper from the retaining clips (where fitted) on the wheel arch liners at each side of the vehicle.

6 Remove the rear light cluster on both sides as described in Chapter 12 Section 7.

6 Front bumper – removal and refitting

Note: The help of an assistant is useful to support the bumper during the removal and refitting procedure.

1 Firmly apply the handbrake, and then jack up the front of the vehicle and support it securely on axle stands (see Jacking and vehicle support). To improve access to the bumper fasteners, remove both front roadwheels.

2 Release the securing clips and fasteners and remove both front wheel arch liners.

3 Open the bonnet and remove the four retaining clips securing the upper edge of

the bumper to the front crossmember (see illustration).

4 Working under the front of the vehicle remove the two retaining bolts from the lower part of the bumper.

5 From under the right-hand front wheel arch, disconnect the foglamp wiring connector (see illustration).

6 Where fitted, also disconnect the headlamp washer pipe. Plug the end of the pipe to prevent spillage.

7 From under the both front wheel arches, undo the two retaining bolts from each side of the front bumper (see illustration).

8 With the help of an assistant, carefully pull the bumper forward and away from the vehicle.

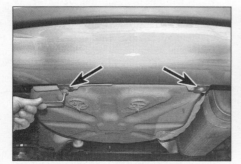

7.3 Undo the two screws from the centre of the bumper underneath

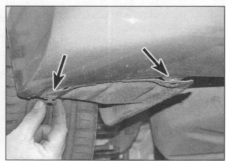

7.4a Unclip the fasteners (arrowed)...

7.4b... and remove the side trim panel – one side shown

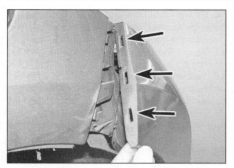

7.7 Carefully release the retaining clips (arrowed) at the side of the bumper...

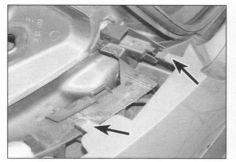

7.8... and the clips (arrowed) at the rear of the bumper

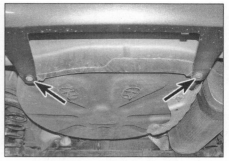

7.9 Undo the two screws (arrowed) from the centre of the bumper underneath

7 Carefully pull the sides of the bumper out from the rear wing panels, releasing it from the retaining clips **(see illustration)**.

8 With the help of an assistant, carefully pull the bumper rearwards and away from the vehicle, releasing it from the retaining clips **(see illustration)**. Depending on model, disconnect any wiring connectors as the bumper cover is removed.

Estate models

9 Working under the rear of the vehicle, undo the two retaining bolts from lower part of the bumper cover **(see illustration)**.

10 Working at the outer edges of the bumper, undo the retaining bolt and release the securing clip from the side trim panels **(see illustration)**.

11 Release the ends of the bumper from the retaining clips (where fitted) on the wheel arch liners at each side of the vehicle.

12 Carefully pull the sides of the bumper out from the rear wing panels, releasing it from the retaining clips **(see illustration)**.

13 With the help of an assistant, carefully pull the bumper rearwards and away from the vehicle. Depending on model, disconnect any wiring connectors as the bumper cover is removed.

Refitting

14 Refitting is a reversal of removal.

---

8 Bonnet – removal, refitting and adjustment

Note: *The help of an assistant is useful to support the bonnet during the removal and refitting procedure.*

Removal

1 Open the bonnet and have an assistant support it then, using a pencil or felt tip pen, mark the outline of each bonnet hinge relative to the bonnet, to use as a guide on refitting.

2 Disconnect the washer jet tubing **(see illustration)**, and jet heater wiring (where fitted). Release the tubing and wiring from any retaining clips.

7.10 Remove the screw and retaining clip from the side trim panel – one side shown

3 Unscrew the bonnet-to-hinge retaining bolts each side **(see illustration)**. With the help of the assistant, carefully lift the bonnet from the vehicle. Store the bonnet out of the way in a safe place.

4 Inspect the bonnet hinges for signs of wear and free play at the pivots, and if necessary renew. Each hinge is secured to the body by two bolts, accessible after removing the scuttle grille panel as described in Section 22. On refitting, apply a smear of multi-purpose grease to the hinges.

Refitting and adjustment

5 With the aid of an assistant, offer up the bonnet, and engage the retaining bolts.

8.2 Disconnect the washer pipe from the bonnet hinge

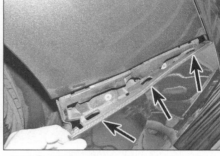

7.12 Carefully release the retaining clips (arrowed) at the side of the bumper

Align the hinges with the marks made on removal, and then tighten the retaining bolts securely.

6 Close the bonnet, and check for alignment with the adjacent panels. If necessary, slacken the hinge bolts and re-align the bonnet to suit. When correctly aligned, tighten the hinge bolts securely.

7 Once the bonnet is correctly aligned, check that the bonnet fastens and releases in a satisfactory manner. If adjustment is necessary, slacken the bonnet lock retaining bolts, and adjust the position of the lock to suit. Once the lock is operating correctly, securely tighten its retaining bolts.

8 Reconnect the washer jet tubing and wiring (where applicable).

8.3 Undo the bonnet hinge nuts (arrowed) – two at each side

9.1a Disconnect the inner cable...

9.1b ... and outer cable from the bonnet catch

9.4a Pull out the securing clip...

9.4b... and remove the trim panel

9 Bonnet release cable – removal and refitting

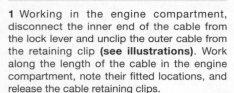

1 Working in the engine compartment, disconnect the inner end of the cable from the lock lever and unclip the outer cable from the retaining clip **(see illustrations)**. Work along the length of the cable in the engine compartment, note their fitted locations, and release the cable retaining clips.
2 Remove the scuttle grille upper panel as described in Section 22.
3 Use a screwdriver to push the cable bulkhead grommet into the passenger cabin.
4 Working in the front passenger footwell, release the locking plug from the sill trim

panel and then unclip it from the sill **(see illustrations)**.
5 Release the lever, and withdraw it from its location under the facia.
6 If required, lower the Built-in Systems Interface/fusebox with reference to Chapter 12 Section 23.
7 Tie a length of string to the end of the cable in the engine compartment, note its routing, then carefully pull the cable through into the passenger compartment. Untie the string from the end of the cable, and leave it in position to aid refitting.
8 Locate the cable in position in the passenger compartment.
9 Tie the end of the new cable to the string, and pull it through into the engine compartment.

10 Check that the bulkhead grommet is securely seated, then remove the string and connect the cable to the bonnet lock lever.
11 Secure the release lever in place, and the sill trim panel.
12 Secure the cable in place with its retaining clips. Check the lock operates satisfactorily.
13 Refit the Built-In Systems interface/fusebox as described in Chapter 12 Section 23.
14 Refit the upper scuttle grille panel as described in Section 22.

10 Bonnet lock – removal and refitting

1 Disconnect the bonnet release cable from the bonnet lock, as described in previous Section.
2 Unscrew the two bolts securing the lock assembly to the body upper crossmember **(see illustration)**.
3 Withdraw the lock and, if required, trace the wiring back from the lock assembly, then disconnect the wiring connector on the offside chassis leg **(see illustration)**.
4 Refitting is a reversal of removal. On completion, check the operation of the lock and, if necessary, adjust the position of the lock within the elongated bolt holes to achieve satisfactory operation prior to closing the bonnet.

11 Door – removal, refitting and adjustment

Note: *The help of an assistant is useful to support the door during the removal and refitting procedure.*

Front door

1 Using a small screwdriver, release the wiring harness guide retaining clips, and pull the harness and guide from the door pillar **(see illustration)**.

10.2 Undo the lock mounting bolts

10.3 Disconnect wiring connector

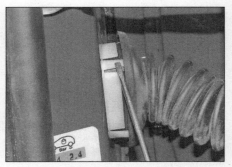

11.1 Prise out the wiring harness guide

11.2 Lever up the locking catch and disconnect the wiring plug

11.3a Undo the upper door hinge retaining bolt (arrowed)...

11.3b... and lower door hinge retaining nut/bolt

2 Prise up the locking catch and disconnect the door wiring connector **(see illustration)**.
3 With the aid of an assistant, ensure that the door is adequately supported. Then remove the upper and lower hinge securing bolts and carefully lift the door from the vehicle **(see illustrations)**.
4 Refitting is a reversal of removal.

Rear door

5 The procedure is as described for the front doors, but the hinge-to-body bolts are accessed for adjustment with the front door open and the rear one closed **(see illustration)**.

11.5 Rear door hinge retaining bolts

12.1a Undo the door handle screw (arrowed)...

12 Door inner trim panel – removal and refitting

Removal

Front door

1 Undo the door handle switch retaining screw, the trim panel rear retaining screw and the front retaining screw **(see illustrations)**.
2 Using a suitable forked tool, work around the edge of the trim panel, and release the securing clips **(see illustration)**.
3 Pull the panel outwards, lift it up and remove it from the door, disconnecting the switch wiring and the door release handle cable from the rear of the door trim panel as it is withdrawn **(see illustrations)**.

12.1b... the door panel rear retaining screw (arrowed)...

12.1c... and front retaining screw (arrowed)

12.2 Using a forked tool, release the retaining clips around the door trim

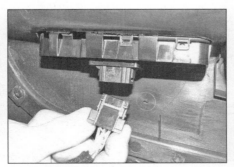

12.3a Disconnect the wiring connector...

12.3b... and the operating cable as the panel is removed

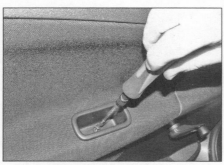

12.4a Undo the door handle screw...

12.4b... the door panel rear retaining screw...

12.4c... and front retaining screw

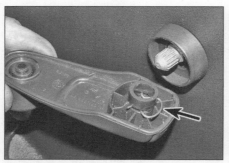

12.5a Release the securing clip (arrowed)...

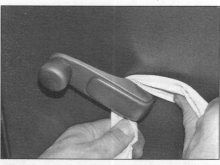

12.5b... using a cloth to unclip the manual window winder handle from the spindle

Rear door

4 Undo the door handle retaining screw, the trim panel rear retaining screw and the front retaining screw **(see illustrations)**.

5 On models with manual windows, release the securing clip and pull the winder handle off the spindle, and then remove the spindle trim spacer **(see illustrations)**. A piece of cloth, working it from side-to-side behind the handle, will release the securing clip.

6 On models with electric windows, unclip the switch from the trim panel and disconnect the wiring connector.

7 Using a suitable forked tool, work around the lower and side edges of the trim panel, and release the securing clips.

8 Pull the panel upwards and outwards, and remove the panel from the door.

Refitting

9 Before refitting, check whether any of the trim panel plastic retaining studs where broken on removal. Renew the panel retaining studs as necessary, and then refit the panel using a reversal of removal.

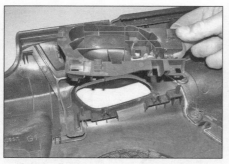

13.2 Unclip the release handle from the door trim panel

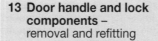

13.4 Remove the rubber grommet...

---

13 Door handle and lock components – removal and refitting

Front interior door release handle

1 Remove the door inner trim panel, as described in Section 12.

2 Remove the handle from its location in the door trim panel by releasing the retaining clips, and then pulling it from the panel **(see illustration)**.

3 Refitting is a reversal of removal, but ensure that the operating cable is correctly reconnected, and then refit the inner trim panel (see Section 12).

Front door lock cylinder

4 Open the front door and unclip the rubber grommet from the edge of the door **(see illustration)**.

5 Slacken the lock retaining screw **(see illustration)**, note this does not have to be removed completely.

6 With the screw slackened, withdraw the lock cylinder from the door handle **(see illustration)**.

13.5... and slacken the securing screw (arrowed)

13.6 Withdraw the lock cylinder from the door handle

13.9 Pull out the rear of the handle and disengage the pin at the front

13.13 Carefully remove the door sealing sheet

13.14a Unclip the rubber gasket...

7 Refitting is a reversal of removal, but ensure that the lock cylinder screw is securely refitted.

Front door exterior handle

8 Remove the door lock cylinder, as described in paragraphs 4 to 6.
9 Pull the rear of the exterior handle outwards, and slide it to the rear of the door to disengage it from the front pivot pin **(see illustration)**. Manoeuvre the handle from the door.
10 Refitting is a reversal of removal, but ensure that the door handle locates on the front pivot pin correctly.

Front door lock assembly

Note: *A new door sealing sheet may be required on refitting.*
11 Remove the front door exterior handle, as described in paragraphs 8 and 9.
12 Remove the door inner trim panel, as described in Section 12.
13 Using a sharp knife, carefully release the door sealing sheet from the adhesive bead and remove the sheet from the door panel **(see illustration)**. If care is taken, it may just be possible to remove the sheet in one piece and re-use it when refitting.
14 Unclip the rubber gasket from the outside of the door, and undo the retaining screw **(see illustrations)**.
15 Working inside the door panel, disengage the door handle mounting bracket and withdraw it from inside the door panel **(see**

13.14b... and undo the retaining screw

13.15b... and disconnect the operating cable

illustrations). Disconnect the operating cable as it is removed.
16 Undo the two screws securing the lock assembly to the edge of the door **(see illustration)**.

13.15a Remove the door handle mounting bracket...

13.16 Undo the two lock retaining screws...

17 Lower the lock assembly and manipulate it out through the door aperture, unclip the plastic cover and disconnect the wiring plug connector from the lock assembly **(see illustrations)**.

13.17a... remove the lock assembly...

13.17b... unclip the plastic cover...

13.17c... and disconnect the wiring connector

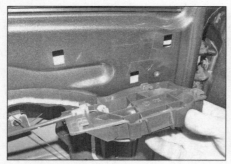

13.20 Unclip the door interior release handle from the door...

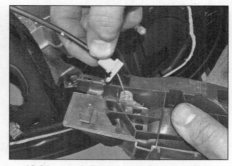

13.21... and disconnect the operating cable

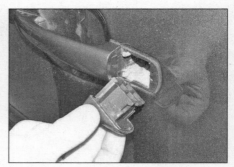

13.25 Withdraw the door handle plastic cap

18 Refitting is a reversal of removal. Fit a new sealing sheet to the door if the original was damaged in any way during removal. On completion, refit the door inner trim panel as described in Section 12.

Rear interior door release handle

19 Remove the door inner trim panel, as described in Section 12.
20 Release the handle from its location by pulling it towards the rear edge of the door and disengaging it from the door panel **(see illustration)**.
21 Unclip the outer cable from the mounting bracket and disconnect the inner cable from the handle **(see illustration)**.
22 Refitting is a reversal of removal, but ensure that the operating cable is reconnected correctly, and then refit the inner trim panel (see Section 12).

13.32 Using a knife to carefully remove the door sealing sheet

13.33b... and slacken the retaining screw

Rear door exterior handle

23 Open the rear door and unclip the rubber grommet from the edge of the door.
24 Slacken the lock/cap retaining screw, note this does not have to be removed completely.
25 With the screw slackened, withdraw the plastic cap from the door handle **(see illustration)**.
26 Pull the rear of the exterior handle outwards, and slide it to the rear of the door to disengage it from the front pivot pin **(see illustration 13.9)**. Manoeuvre the handle from the door.
27 Refitting is a reversal of removal, but ensure that the door handle locates on the front pivot pin correctly.

Rear door lock assembly

28 Note: *A new door sealing sheet may be required on refitting.*

13.33a Unclip the rubber gasket...

13.35 Undo the two lock retaining screws (arrowed)...

29 Remove the front door exterior handle, as described in paragraphs 23 to 26.
30 Remove the door inner trim panel, as described in Section 12.
31 Remove the rear door speaker, as described in Chapter 12, Section 18.
32 Using a sharp knife, carefully release the door sealing sheet from the adhesive bead and remove the sheet from the door panel **(see illustration)**. If care is taken, it may just be possible to remove the sheet in one piece and re-use it when refitting.
33 Unclip the rubber gasket from the outside of the door, and undo the retaining screw **(see illustrations)**.
34 Working inside the door panel, disengage the door handle mounting bracket and withdraw it from inside the door panel. Disconnect the operating cable as it is removed.
35 Undo the two screws securing the lock assembly to the edge of the door **(see illustration)**.
36 Lower the lock assembly and manipulate it out through the door aperture, unclip the plastic cover and disconnect the wiring plug connector from the lock assembly.
37 Refitting is a reversal of removal. Fit a new sealing sheet to the door if the original was damaged in any way during removal. On completion, refit the door inner trim panel as described in Section 12.

14 Door window sliding glass, regulator and fixed glass – removal and refitting

Front door sliding window glass

Note: *A new door sealing sheet may be required on refitting.*
Note: *The help of an assistant is useful to support the door during the removal and refitting procedure.*
1 Remove the door inner trim panel as described in Section 12.
2 Using a sharp knife, carefully release the door sealing sheet from the adhesive bead and remove the sheet from the door panel **(see illustration 13.13)**. If care is taken, it may just be possible to remove the sheet in one piece and re-use it when refitting.

14.3 Glass-to-regulator retaining screws (arrowed)

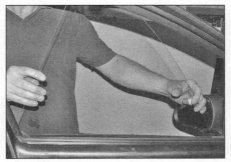

14.4 Lift up the rear end and manoeuvre the window from the door

14.7a Drill out the door channel lower rivet (arrowed)...

14.7b... centre rivet (arrowed)...

14.7c... and upper rivet

14.11 Disconnect the wiring connector

3 Reconnect the electric window switch and lower the window until the window glass to regulator retaining screws can be accessed **(see illustration)**.
4 With the window glass being supported, undo the retaining screws, and then withdraw the window glass upwards, while tilting it up through the aperture, and out of the door **(see illustration)**.
5 Refitting is a reversal of removal, but fit a new sealing sheet to the door if the original was damaged in any way during removal. On completion, refit the inner trim panel as described in Section 12.

Front door fixed window glass

6 Remove the door sliding window glass as described in paragraphs 1 to 4.
7 Drill out the three rivets and remove the front sliding window glass channel **(see illustrations)**.
8 The fixed window glass can now be withdrawn from the front of the window frame.
9 Refitting is a reversal of removal, fitting new rivets to secure the window glass channel. Refit the sliding glass window.

Front door window regulator

10 Remove the door sliding window glass as described in paragraphs 1 to 4. If required, the window glass does not have to be completely removed from the doorframe, slide the glass to the top of the window frame and secure it in place.
11 Disconnect the wiring connector from the window regulator **(see illustration)**.

12 Drill out the two rivets securing the regulator assembly to the door frame **(see illustrations)**.
13 Undo the Torx screw from the regulator assembly to the door panel **(see illustration)**.

14.12a Drill out the upper (arrowed)...

14 Lift the regulator assembly, to release the locating hooks from inside the door panel, and manoeuvre it from the door **(see illustration)**.

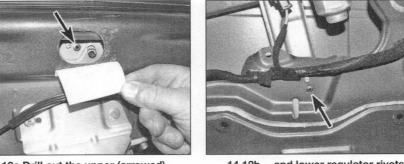

14.12b... and lower regulator rivets (arrowed)

14.13 Undo the window regulator securing screw...

14.14... and manoeuvre the window regulator from the door

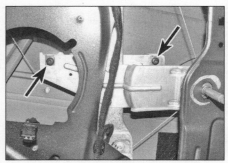

14.20 Glass-to-regulator retaining screws (arrowed)

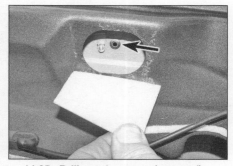

14.25a Drill out the upper (arrowed)...

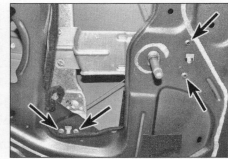

14.25b... and lower regulator rivets (arrowed)

15 Refitting is a reversal of removal, fitting new rivets to secure the window regulator. Refit the sliding glass window.

Rear door sliding window glass

Note: *A new door sealing sheet may be required on refitting.*

16 Remove the door inner trim panel, as described in Section 12.

17 Remove the door interior release handle, as described in Section 13.

18 Remove the rear door speaker, as described in Chapter 12, Section 18.

19 Using a sharp knife, carefully release the door sealing sheet from the adhesive bead and remove the sheet from the door panel **(see illustration 13.31)**. If care is taken, it may just be possible to remove the sheet in one piece and re-use it when refitting.

20 Lower the window until the window glass-

to-regulator retaining screws can be accessed **(see illustration)**.

21 With the window glass being supported, undo the retaining screws, and then withdraw the window glass upwards, while tilting it up through the aperture, and out of the door.

22 Refitting is a reversal of removal, but fit a new sealing sheet to the door if the original was damaged in any way during removal. On completion, refit the inner trim panel as described in Section 12.

Rear door window regulator

23 Remove the door sliding window glass as described in paragraphs 16 to 21. If required, the window glass does not have to be completely removed from the doorframe, slide the glass to the top of the window frame and secure it in place.

24 On electric window model, disconnect the wiring connector from the window regulator.

25 Drill out the five rivets securing the regulator assembly to the door frame **(see illustrations)**.

26 Lift the regulator assembly, to release the locating hooks from inside the door panel and manoeuvre it from the door.

27 Refitting is a reversal of removal, fitting new rivets to secure the window regulator. Refit the sliding glass window.

15 Tailgate and support struts – removal and refitting

Tailgate

1 Remove the tailgate trim panels as described in Section 25.

2 Disconnect the wiring harness connectors at the tailgate internal components **(see illustration)**, referring to the relevant procedures contained in Chapter 12.

3 Release the rubber grommet sleeves from each side of the tailgate and withdraw the wiring harness **(see illustrations)**.

4 Remove the high-level brake light as described in Chapter 12 Section 7.

5 With the aid of an assistant, support the tailgate, and then prise out the support strut spring clips **(see illustration)**, and pull the struts from the balljoints on the tailgate.

6 Unscrew the bolt each side securing the hinges to the tailgate **(see illustration)**, and

15.2 Note the wiring harness routing before removal

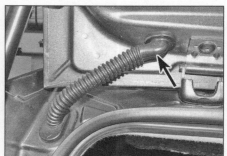

15.3a Unclip the left-hand wiring harness rubber sleeve (arrowed)...

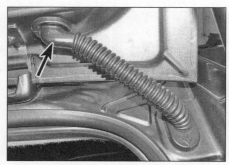

15.3b... and also the right-hand side (arrowed)

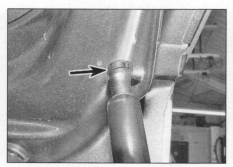

15.5 Release the spring clip (arrowed)

15.6 Tailgate retaining bolt (arrowed) – one side shown

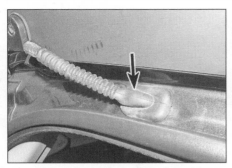

15.10 Unclip the wiring harness rubber sleeve (arrowed)

15.11a Release the spring clip from the top of the strut...

15.11b... and the bottom of the strut balljoint

15.12 Tailgate glass retaining bolt (arrowed) – one side shown

15.15 Prise out the upper clip...

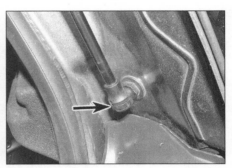

15.16... and the lower clip (arrowed) from the strut balljoint

carefully lift the tailgate from the vehicle. On Hatchback models, it may be necessary to lower the rear of the headlining to access the securing bolts.

7 If a new tailgate is to be fitted, transfer all serviceable components (lock mechanism, wiper motor, etc) to it, with reference to the relevant procedures in this Chapter and in Chapter 12.

8 Refitting is a reversal of removal, bearing in mind the following points:

● If necessary, adjust the rubber buffers to obtain a good fit when the tailgate is shut.

● If necessary, adjust the position of the tailgate lock and/or hinge bolts within their elongated holes to achieve satisfactory lock operation.

Estate tailgate glass

9 Remove the high-evel brake light and dis-connect the wiring connectors, as described in Chapter 12 Section 7.

10 Release the rubber grommet sleeve from the tailgate and withdraw the wiring harness (see illustration).

11 With the aid of an assistant, support the tailgate glass, and then prise out the support strut spring clips (see illustrations), and pull the struts from the balljoints on the tailgate.

12 Unscrew the bolt each side securing the hinges to the tailgate (see illustration), and carefully lift the tailgate glass from the vehicle.

13 Refitting is a reversal of removal.

Support struts

14 Support the tailgate in the open position

with the help of an assistant, or using a stout piece of wood.

15 Using a small screwdriver, release the spring clip, and pull the support strut from its balljoint on the tailgate (see illustration).

16 Similarly, release the strut from the balljoint on the body (see illustration), and withdraw the strut from the vehicle.

17 Refitting is a reversal of removal, but ensure the spring clips are correctly engaged.

16 Tailgate lock components – removal and refitting

Tailgate lock

1 Remove the tailgate lower trim panel as described in Section 25.

16.2 Undo the two bolts (arrowed) and remove the lock

2 Undo the two lock retaining screws and withdraw the lock (see illustration).

3 Disconnect the wiring connector as the lock is removed.

4 Refitting is a reversal of removal, but adjust the tailgate lock striker as necessary to obtain satisfactory closure.

Tailgate lock striker

5 Undo the screws and remove the tailgate aperture lower panel (see Section 25) for access to the striker plate retaining bolts.

6 Mark the position of the striker on the body, for use when refitting. Unscrew the two securing bolts, and remove the striker from the body (see illustration).

7 Refitting is a reversal of removal. Before tightening the securing bolts, the position of the striker should be altered (the securing bolt holes are elongated) until satisfactory lock

16.6 Undo the two bolts (arrowed) and remove the lock striker

16.9 Disconnect the wiring connector

16.10 Undo the trim retaining nuts (arrowed)

16.11 Unclip the handle from the trim panel

operation is obtained. Use the marks made prior to removal, if appropriate.

Tailgate exterior handle

8 Removal the tailgate lower trim panel as described in Section 25.
9 Disconnect the wiring plug connector from the rear of the handle **(see illustration)**.
10 Undo the securing nuts, release the retaining clips and remove the handle housing/number plate light cowling from the exterior of the tailgate **(see illustrations)**.
11 Release the retaining clips, and slide the handle out from the housing **(see illustration)**.
12 Refitting is a reversal of removal.

---

17 Central locking components – removal and refitting

Control unit

1 The central locking system is controlled by the Built-in Systems Interface (BSI) which is the vehicle central computer controlling the main body electrical system functions. The unit is located at the left-hand end of the facia panel, behind the glovebox. Refer to Chapter 12 Section 23 for further information.
2 Should any problems be experienced with the operation of the central locking system or any of the other functions controlled by the BSI, the vehicle should be taken to a Peugeot dealer for diagnostic investigation.

Door lock motor

3 The motor is integral with the door lock assembly. Removal and refitting of the lock assembly is described in Section 13.

Tailgate lock motor

4 Removal of the tailgate lock motor is described as part of the tailgate lock removal and refitting procedure described in Section 16.

Remote control transmitter

Battery renewal

5 When the remote control transmitter battery

is nearing the end of its life, an audible signal will be emitted from within the vehicle, accompanied by a message on the instrument panel multifunction screen. The battery should then be renewed with a type CR 1620 (3 volt) battery.
6 Using a small screwdriver, undo the screw, and carefully prise the two halves of the transmitter apart. Remove the battery, noting which way around it is fitted.
7 Fit the new battery and reassemble the transmitter.

Initialisation

8 To initialise the unit after renewing the battery, switch off the ignition, then switch on the ignition and immediately press the locking button. Switch off the ignition and remove the key from the ignition.

18.2 Electric mirror wiring connectors (arrowed)

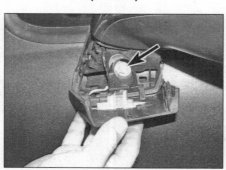

18.4b... and undo the retaining bolt (arrowed)

---

18 Mirrors and mirror glass – removal and refitting

Exterior mirror assembly

1 Remove the door inner trim panel, as described in Section 12.
2 Disconnect the wiring block connectors for the mirror assembly **(see illustration)**. The amount of connectors will vary depending on model specifications.
3 On manually-operated mirrors, disconnect the operating cable from the switch panel.
4 Carefully unclip the cover from the base of the mirror, and undo the mirror mounting bolt **(see illustrations)**.
5 Remove the mirror from the door frame and withdraw the wiring loom through the aperture **(see illustration)**.

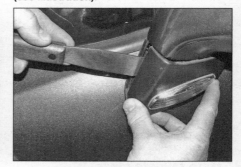

18.4a Unclip the outer cover...

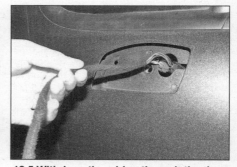

18.5 Withdraw the wiring through the door

6 Refitting is a reversal of removal.

Exterior mirror glass

7 Working through the gap at the lower edge of the mirror glass, using a flat scraper (or similar), unclip the glass from the mirror adjuster **(see illustrations)**.

8 Withdraw the glass, and disconnect the wiring connector (where fitted) **(see illustration)**.

9 If required, release the retaining clips and withdraw the colour-coded trim panel from the rear of the mirror housing **(see illustration)**

10 Push the mirror glass into position in the mirror housing until the clips lock into position around the mirror adjuster.

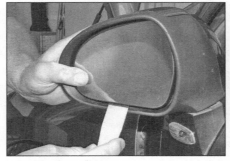

18.7a Insert a flat scraper at the lower edge…

18.7b… to release the mirror glass from its retaining clips

19 Windscreen, tailgate and fixed/hinged side window glass – general information

1 These areas of glass are secured by the tight fit of the weatherstrip in the body aperture, and are bonded in position with a special adhesive. Renewal of such fixed glass is a difficult, messy and time-consuming task, which is considered beyond the scope of the home mechanic. It is difficult, unless one has plenty of practice, to obtain a secure, waterproof fit. Furthermore, the task carries a high risk of breakage; this applies especially to the laminated glass windscreen. In view of this, owners are strongly advised to have this sort of work carried out by one of the many specialist windscreen fitters.

2 Note that the rear side hinged windows on the 3-door models are also bonded in at the front edge, and therefore renewal should be entrusted to a specialist.

Rear side window hinge

3-door Hatchback models

3 Remove the C-pillar trim as described in Section 25.

4 Carefully prise the cap from place, and then undo the retaining nut at the window end of the hinge **(see illustration)**.

18.8 Disconnect the wiring connectors

18.9 Unclip the trim panel from the mirror

5 Drill out the rivets securing the hinge to the C-pillar **(see illustration)**.

6 Refitting is a reversal of removal.

20 Sunroof – general information

1 The factory-fitted sunroof is of the electric tilt/slide type.

2 Due to the complexity of the sunroof mechanism, considerable expertise is required to repair, renew or adjust the sunroof components successfully. Removal of the roof first requires the headlining to be removed, which is a tedious operation, and not a task to be undertaken lightly. Any problems with

the sunroof should be referred to a Peugeot dealer.

21 Body exterior fittings – removal and refitting

Wheel arch liners/mud shields

1 The wheel arch liners are secured mainly by expanding plastic rivets. To remove the liners, push in the centre pins a little, and then prise the complete rivet from place. With all the rivets removed, manoeuvre the liner from the wheel arch. Depending on model, there may be other fasteners, such as screws and nuts securing the liners **(see illustration)**.

19.4 Prise off the cap and undo the hinge nut (arrowed)

19.5 Drill out the three rivets (arrowed)

21.1 Remove the inner wheel arch liner

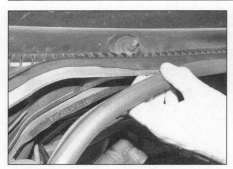

22.3 Pull the rubber seal from the scuttle panel

22.4a Unclip the upper grille panel from the right-hand side...

22.4b... and the left-hand side of the scuttle panel

Body trim strips and badges

2 The various body trim strips and badges are held in position with a special adhesive membrane. Removal requires the trim/badge to be heated to soften the adhesive, and then cut away from the surface. Due to the high risk of damage to the vehicle paintwork during this operation, it is recommended that this task should be entrusted to a Peugeot dealer.

3 The door side trims are held on by retaining clips, remove the inner door trim panels (as described in Section 12) to access the securing clips.

22 Scuttle grille panel – removal and refitting

Removal

Upper scuttle grille panel

1 Open the bonnet and support it in the highest position.

2 Remove the windscreen wiper arms as described in Chapter 12 Section 13.

3 Working along the front edge of the scuttle panel, remove the rubber seal (see illustration).

4 Pull the scuttle panel up at each end to

release it from the windscreen clips, then downwards and forwards to release it from the lower part of the windscreen (see illustrations).

Lower scuttle panel

5 Remove the upper scuttle grille panel as described in paragraphs 1 to 4.

6 Unclip the plastic covers from each end of the scuttle panel (see illustration).

7 Undo the securing bolts at each end of the lower scuttle panel, and the two securing nuts at the centre of the panel (see illustrations).

8 Disconnect the wiper motor wiring connector and the earth cable, and then withdraw the wiring loom through the scuttle panel (see illustrations).

22.6 Unclip the plastic covers from each side of the scuttle panel

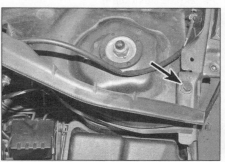

22.7a Undo the bolts from each side of the scuttle panel (one side shown)...

22.7b... and undo the two centre retaining nuts (arrowed)

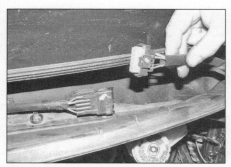

22.8a Disconnect the wiring connector...

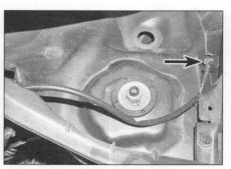

22.8b... earth cable retaining bolt (arrowed)...

22.8c... and withdraw the wiring through the panel

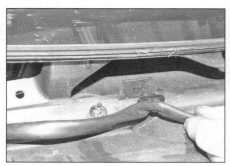

22.9a Release the wiring loom retaining clips...

22.9b... and remove the scuttle panel from the bulkhead

23.2 Undo the two bolts at the rear of the seat rails (arrowed)

9 Unclip the wiper motor wiring loom from the lower scuttle panel and then panel from the rear of the engine compartment **(see illustrations)**.

Refitting

10 Refitting is a reversal of removal.

23 Seats – removal and refitting

Front seats

⚠️ *Warning: The front seats are equipped with side airbags built into the outer sides of the seats. Refer to Chapter 12 Section 21 for the precautions, which should be observed when dealing with an airbag system. Do not tamper with the airbag unit in any way, and do not attempt to test any airbag system components. Note that the airbag is triggered if the mechanism is supplied with an electrical current (including via an ohmmeter), or if the assembly is subjected to a temperature of greater than 100°C.*

1 De-activate the airbag system (see Chapter 12 Section 22) before attempting to remove the seat.

2 Move the seat fully forwards, and then remove the bolts (one on each side) securing the rear of the seat rails to the vehicle floor **(see illustration)**.

3 Move the seat fully rearwards, and then remove the bolts (one bolt on each side) securing the front of the seat frame to the floor **(see illustration)**.

4 Release the two retaining clips and remove the plastic cover from the floor panel, then unclip the wiring from the plastic trim **(see illustrations)**.

5 Release the locking catch and disconnect the wiring plug connector **(see illustration)**. The seat can now be carefully removed from the passenger compartment.

6 Refitting is a reversal of removal, but observe the following precautions before reconnecting the battery.

● Ensure that there are no occupants in the vehicle, and that there are no loose objects around the vicinity of the seats.

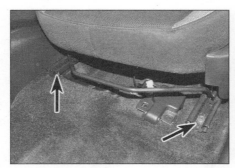

23.3 Undo the two bolts at the front of the seat rails (arrowed)

● Ensure that the ignition is switched off then reconnect the airbag ECU and the battery.
● Open the driver's door and switch on the ignition. Check that the airbag warning light illuminates briefly then extinguishes.
● Switch off the ignition.
● If the airbag warning light does not operate as described in paragraph c), consult a Peugeot dealer before driving the vehicle.

Rear seats

Estate models

7 Move the front seats fully forwards, and then remove the bolts securing the front of the rear seat to the vehicle floor **(see illustration)**.

8 Open the tailgate and remove the boot floor mat.

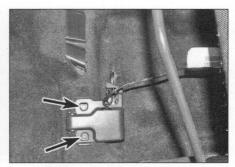

23.4a Release the retaining clips (arrowed)...

23.4b... unclip the plastic cover...

23.5... and disconnect the wiring connector

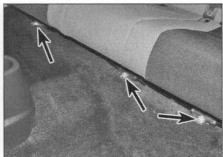

23.7 Undo the three bolts at the front of the seat cushions (arrowed)

23.9 Undo the hinge nuts and bolt in the centre

23.10a Undo the seat belt stalk retaining bolt (arrowed)...

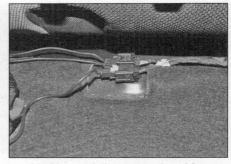

23.10b... and disconnect the wiring connectors

9 Undo the rear seat mounting bolt/nuts from where the rear seats join together (see illustration).
10 Undo the securing bolts and remove the seat belt stalks; disconnect the wiring connectors as they are removed (see illustrations).
11 Fold the seat back forward and pull the seat forward, releasing it from the side pivot mounting; carefully lift the seat from the passenger cabin (see illustration).
12 Refitting is a reversal of removal, tightening the hinge bolts securely.

Hatchback models

13 Lift the front edge first, followed by the rear edge, then push the stays to the side and remove the seat from the vehicle.
14 Open the tailgate and remove the boot floor mat, undo the bolt and nut securing

the centre hinge to the vehicle floor (see illustration).
15 Lift the seat back up at the hinge, disengage the outer hinge (see illustration 23.11), and remove it from the vehicle.
16 If required, undo the securing bolts and remove the seat belt stalks; disconnect the wiring connectors as they are removed.
17 Refitting is a reversal of removal, tightening the hinge bolts securely.

Rear seat catch

18 To remove the rear seat back catch, unclip the inner lower and side edges of the seat cover (see illustration).
19 Unclip the trim from around the top of the seat catch (see illustration).
20 Pull the seat cover back and undo the seat catch retaining screws; manoeuvre the catch from the seat back (see illustration).

21 Refitting is a reversal of removal, tightening the hinge bolts securely.

24 Seat belt components – removal and refitting

Note: *Record the positions of any washers and spacers on the seat belt anchors, and ensure they are refitted in their original positions.*

Front seat belt

⚠️ **Warning: The front seat belt inertia reels are equipped with a pyrotechnic pretensioner mechanism. Refer to the airbag system precautions contained in Chapter 12 Section 21, which apply equally to the seat belt pretensioners. Do not tamper with the inertia reel pretensioner unit in any way, and do not attempt to test the unit. Note that the unit is triggered if the mechanism is supplied with an electrical current (including via an ohmmeter), or if the assembly is subjected to a temperature of greater than 100°C.**
1 De-activate the airbag system (which will also de-activate the pyrotechnic pretensioner mechanism) as described in Chapter 12 Section 22 before attempting to remove the seat belt.
2 If desired, to improve access, remove the relevant front seat as described in Section 23.

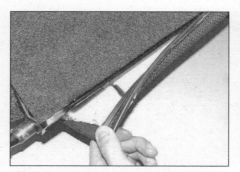

23.11 Rear seat pivot mounting (arrowed)

23.14 Undo the hinge nut and bolt in the centre

23.18 Unclip the seat cover from the seat frame

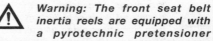

23.19 Unclip the seat catch trim

23.20 Seat catch retaining bolts (arrowed)

24.3 Unclip the cover and undo the retaining bolt

24.5 Release the locking clip (arrowed)

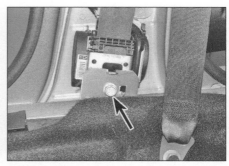

24.6 Inertia reel mounting bolt (arrowed)

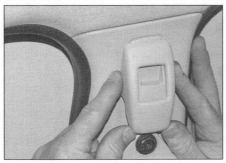

24.7a Carefully push the trim upwards...

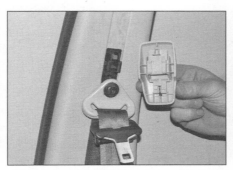

24.7b... to release it from the seat height mechanism

24.8 Undo the seat belt upper anchor bolt

3 Unclip the plastic cover and undo the seat belt lower anchor bolt and recover the washers **(see illustration)**.
4 Remove the B-pillar trim panels as described in Section 25.
5 Disconnect the wiring connector from the inertia reel pretensioner unit **(see illustration)**.
6 Slacken and remove the inertia reel anchor bolt **(see illustration)**.
7 Push the plastic adjuster trim upwards, to release it from the upper seat belt anchorage point **(see illustrations)**.
8 Undo the seat belt upper anchor bolt and withdraw the inertia reel from the door pillar **(see illustration)**.
9 Release the seat belt from the guide on the

pillar and remove the seat belt assembly from the vehicle **(see illustration)**.
10 To remove the seat belt stalk, remove the front seat as described in Section 23, and then undo the bolt securing the seat belt stalk to the seat frame **(see illustration)**. Trace the wiring from the stalk and disconnect the wiring connector.
11 Refitting is a reversal of removal, but observe the following precautions before reconnecting the battery.
● Ensure that there are no occupants in the vehicle, and that there are no loose objects around the vicinity of the seats.
● Ensure that the ignition is switched off then reconnect the battery.

● Open the driver's door and switch on the ignition. Check that the airbag warning light illuminates briefly then extinguishes.
● Switch off the ignition.
● If the airbag warning light does not operate (as described in paragraph c), consult a Peugeot dealer before driving the vehicle.
● Tighten the seat belt mountings securely.

Rear seat outer belts

12 On Estate models, unclip the plastic cover and undo the seat belt upper anchor bolt from the pillar **(see illustration)**.
13 Remove the C-pillar trim panels as described in Section 25.
14 On Hatchback models, undo the seat

24.9 Unclip the seat belt guide from the pillar

24.10 Seat belt stalk securing bolt (arrowed)

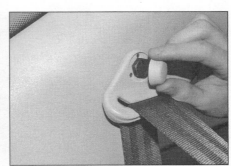

24.12 Unclip the cover and undo the retaining bolt

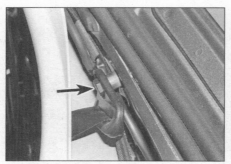

24.14 Seat belt upper anchor bolt (arrowed)

24.15a Inertia reel mounting bolt (arrowed) – Estate model

24.15b Inertia reel mounting bolt (arrowed) – Hatchback model

24.16a Unclip the cover…

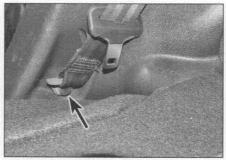

24.16b… and undo the lower anchor bolt (arrowed)

24.17 Centre seat belt lower anchor bolt (arrowed)

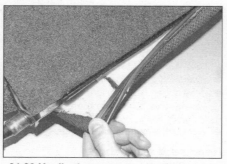

24.20 Unclip the seat cover from the seat frame

belt upper anchor bolt from the pillar **(see illustration)**.

15 Undo the bolt securing the seat belt inertia reel to the vehicle body **(see illustrations)**.

16 Unclip the plastic cover and undo the seat belt lower anchor bolt from the pillar **(see illustrations)**.

17 To remove the seat belt stalk, fold forward the rear seat cushions, and undo the bolt securing the seat belt stalk to the vehicle body **(see illustration)**. Trace the wiring from the stalk and disconnect the wiring connector.

18 Refitting is a reversal of removal. Tighten the mounting bolts securely.

Rear seat centre belt

19 Remove the rear seat as described in Section 23.

20 Unclip the seat cover from the lower part of the seat **(see illustration)**.

21 Reach up inside the seat back and release the headrest retaining clips **(see illustration)**.

22 Unclip the plastic trim cover(s) from the top of the rear seat back **(see illustration)**.

23 Remove the seat cover, then undo the nut

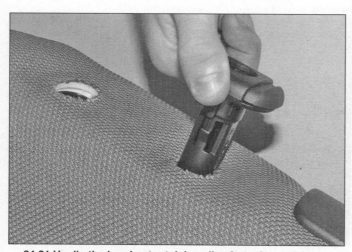

24.21 Unclip the headrest retaining clips from the seat frame

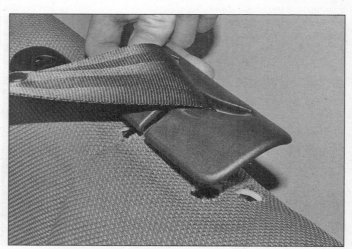

24.22 Unclip the seat belt trim from the seat frame

24.23a Pull back the seat cover and foam...

24.23b... undo the inertia reel mounting nut (arrowed)...

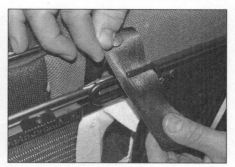

24.23c... and disengage the seat belt from the guide

and remove the inertia reel and belt assembly **(see illustrations)**.
24 Refitting is a reversal of removal. Tighten the mounting bolts securely.

25 Interior trim – removal and refitting

Door inner trim

1 Refer to Section 12.

A-pillar trim

2 Prise the weatherstrip from the front door aperture in the vicinity of the pillar trim.
3 Carefully prise the trim away from the pillar, and then pull upwards to disengage it from the facia panel **(see illustration)**.
4 Refitting is a reversal of removal, but ensure that all retaining clips are fully engaged and that the weatherstrip is fully-seated.

Lower B-pillar trim

5-door Hatchback and Estate models

5 Carefully pull the front sill trim upwards to release its retaining clips **(see illustration)**.
6 On the passenger side, withdraw the clip from the bonnet release lever to release the front edge of the sill trim **(see illustrations)**. Pull the rear end of the sill trim upwards to release it from lower B-pillar trim.
7 Prise the weatherstrip from the front door aperture in the vicinity of the pillar trim **(see illustration)**.

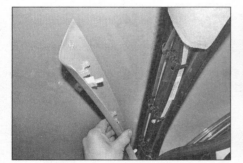

25.3 Unclip the trim from the A-pillar

25.5 Pull the door sill trim up from its clips

25.6a Pull out the securing clip...

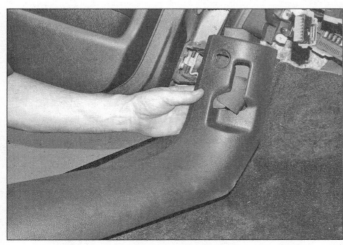

25.6b... and pull the door sill trim up from its clips

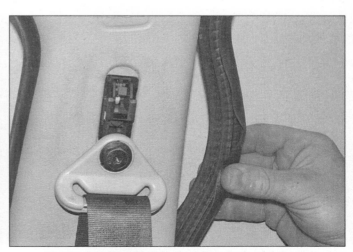

25.7 Carefully pull the door seal from the door frame

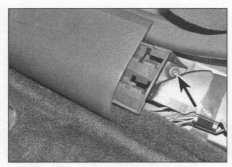

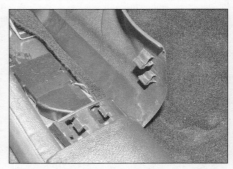

25.8 Undo the trim securing screw (arrowed)

25.9a Remove the lower trim panel...

25.9b... unclipping it from the rear sill trim panel

8 Undo the retaining screw from the lower front edge of the B-pillar trim **(see illustration)**.

9 Unclip the trim panel from the pillar, disengaging it from the rear sill trim panel **(see illustrations)**.

Upper B-pillar trim

3-door Hatchback models

10 Remove the rear side trim panel as described in this Section.

11 Undo the bolt securing the lower seat belt anchor rail to the vehicle.

12 Release the clip at is base, then pull the trim towards the centre of the vehicle, and release it from the retaining clips **(see illustration)**. Feed the seat belt through as the trim is removed.

13 Refitting is a reversal of removal, but ensure that all retaining clips are fully engaged.

5-door Hatchback and Estate models

14 Remove the lower B-pillar trim as described in paragraphs 5 to 9.

15 Undo the bolt securing the upper seat belt anchor to the door pillar **(see illustrations 24.7a and 24.7b)**.

16 Release the retaining clips securing the lower edge of the trim to the pillar **(see illustration)**.

17 Pull the trim away from the pillar, releasing it from the retaining clips **(see illustration)**.

18 Refitting is a reversal of removal, but ensure that all retaining clips are fully engaged.

C-pillar trim

5-door Hatchback models

19 Remove the parcel shelf support as described below.

20 Undo the screw securing the lower edge of the C-pillar/rear door sill trim panel, then carefully pull the pillar trim from the vehicle body to release its retaining clips **(see illustration)**.

21 Refitting is a reversal of removal.

3-door Hatchback models

22 Remove the parcel shelf support and side trim panel as described below.

23 Carefully pull the trim from the pillar, releasing the push-on retaining clips.

25.12 Release the securing clip (arrowed)

25.16 Release the two securing clips...

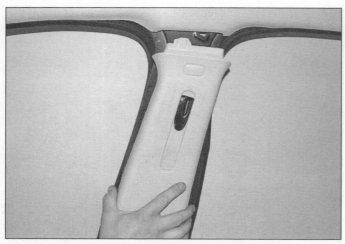

25.17... and remove the upper trim panel

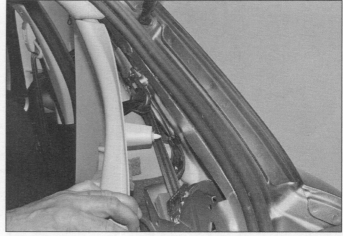

25.20 Removing the rear upper trim panel – Hatchback model

25.26 Removing the rear upper trim panel –
Estate model

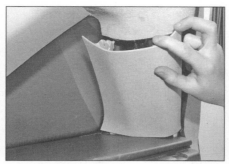

25.29 Unclip the trim panel from the rear
pillar – Estate model

25.36a Removing the rear pillar lower trim
panel...

Estate models

24 Remove the parcel shelf support panel and
lower trim panels as described below.
25 Prise off the plastic cap, then undo the bolt
securing the seat belt upper bracket.
26 Release the retaining clips and carefully
pull the trim from the pillar and withdrawing it
down from the headlining **(see illustration)**.

All models

27 Refitting is a reversal of removal.

D-pillar trim

Estate models

28 Pull away the rubber weatherstrip from the
tailgate aperture adjacent to the D-pillar trim.
29 Carefully pull the D-pillar trim away,
releasing the retaining clips as it is removed
(see illustration).
30 Refitting is a reversal of removal.

Parcel shelf support panel

Hatchback models

31 Fold the relevant rear seat back forward.
32 Undo the screw and nut securing the
parcel shelf support to the body sidemember.
33 Disconnect the wiring connectors from
the accessories socket and interior light (as
applicable) as the support is removed.

25.36b... disengaging it from the sill trim –
Estate model

Estate models

34 Remove the D-pillar trim as described
in this Section. Lift the luggage
compartment cover/crossmember from the
vehicle.
35 Tilt the rear seat forward and undo the
lower seat belt anchorage bolt.
36 Unclip the C-pillar lower trim panel,
disengaging it from the sill trim panel **(see
illustrations)**.
37 Where applicable, unclip the luggage
compartment light and disconnect the wiring
connector.

25.38 Unclip the rear seat belt trim

38 Prise out the seat belt flap at the top of
the panel **(see illustration)**.
39 Undo the two screws, release the
retaining clips and remove the support panel
(see illustrations). Pass the seat belt through
the panel as required.

All models

40 Refitting is a reversal of removal, but ensure
that all retaining clips are fully engaged, that
the seat belt is correctly located, and the
luggage compartment light wiring is correctly
routed (where applicable).

25.39a Undo the two retaining screws...

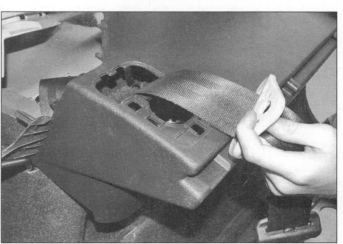

25.39b... and remove the rear support panel

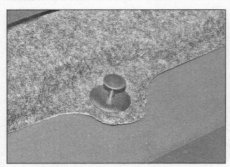

25.45 One type of trim securing clips

25.49a Using a forked trim tool...

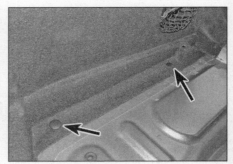

25.49b... remove the trim securing clips (arrowed)

Luggage area lower side trim

41 Remove the parcel shelf support bracket as described previously.

Hatchback models

42 Prise the weatherstrip from the bottom of the tailgate aperture.

43 Lift the luggage compartment floor panel carpet.

44 Pull the sill trim panel straight upwards to release the retaining clips, and remove the panel.

45 Prise up the centre pin, then lever up the complete expanding plastic rivet(s) at the lower edge of the trim **(see illustration)**.

46 Undo the screw securing the upper edge of the lower C-pillar/rear door sill trim panel. Pull the top edge of the panel out and manoeuvre the luggage area lower side trim from the vehicle.

Estate models

47 Lift the luggage compartment floor panel carpet.

48 Remove the parcel shelf support panel as described in paragraphs 34 to 39.

49 Use a forked tool to release the securing clips from the lower edge of the trim **(see illustrations)**.

50 Lift the luggage compartment carpet side trim from the luggage compartment **(see illustration)**.

All models

51 Refitting is a reversal of removal, but ensure that all retaining clips are fully engaged.

Tailgate trim

52 Open the tailgate and, where applicable, unclip the upper side trims panels from the tailgate **(see illustration)**.

53 Undo the two screws (where fitted), in the handle recesses.

54 On Estate models, open the upper glass hatch and unclip the plastic trim from around the wiper control **(see illustration)**.

55 Carefully pull the panel away from the tailgate, releasing the retaining clips.

56 Refitting is a reversal of removal, but ensure that all retaining clips are fully engaged.

Headlining

Note: *Headlining removal requires considerable skill and experience if it is to be carried out without damage, and is therefore best entrusted to a Peugeot dealer or bodywork specialist. A general overview of the procedure is given below for those with the expertise to attempt the operation on a DIY basis.*

57 The headlining is clipped and glued to the roof, and can be withdrawn only once all fittings such as the grab handles, courtesy lights, sunvisors, sunroof (if fitted), pillar trim panels, and associated additional panels have been removed. The door, tailgate and sunroof aperture weatherstrips will also have to be prised clear and any additional screws and clips removed. Once the headlining attachments are released, the adhesive bonding in the centre panels must be broken using a hot air gun and spatula, starting at the front and working rearwards.

58 When refitting, a coat of neoprene adhesive (available from Peugeot dealers) must be applied to the centre panels in the locations noted during removal. Position the headlining carefully and refit all components disturbed during removal. Clean the headlining with soap and water, or white spirit, on completion.

Overhead console

59 Using a small screwdriver carefully prise the lens from the interior light unit **(see illustrations)**.

60 Lever back the two retaining clips and remove the light unit from its console.

25.50 Removing the luggage compartment side trim – Estate model

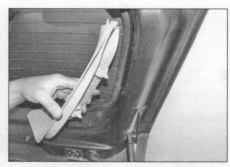

25.52 Unclip the two tailgate side trims

25.54 Unclip the trim panel from the wiper motor

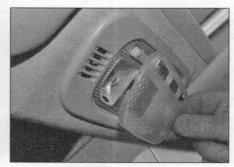

25.59 Unclip the light lens

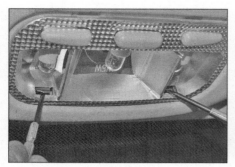

25.60a Lever back the two clips...

25.60b... remove the light unit...

25.60c... and disconnect the wiring connector

25.61 Undo the retaining screw (arrowed)

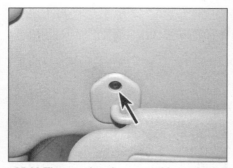

25.63 The sunvisor is secured by a single screw (arrowed)

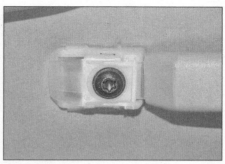

25.68 Undo the screw at each end of the grab handle

Disconnect the wiring connector as the unit is withdrawn **(see illustrations)**.

61 Undo the securing screw and pull the front of the plastic console from the headlining **(see illustration)**. Where applicable, disconnect any wiring plugs as the console is removed.

62 Refitting is a reversal of removal.

Sunvisor

63 The sunvisor is retained by a single screw **(see illustration)**. Prior to removing the sunvisor, remove the interior light unit as described in Paragraph 60, and disconnect the wiring plugs.

64 Remove the sunvisor retaining screw and unclip the mounting from the headlining.

Identify the sunvisor vanity light wiring plug at the overhead console, and tie a length of string to it. Withdrawn the sunvisor, pulling the string through the interior light aperture. When the string emerges at the sunvisor mount aperture, untie it from the wiring plug.

65 Tie the length of string to the visor wiring, and pull it through to the interior light aperture. Reconnect the wiring plug.

66 Refit the sunvisor mount to the headlining, and tighten the retaining screw securely.

Grab handle

67 Levering at the top and bottom edges, prise the plastic covers from the front and rear ends of the grab handle.

68 Undo the retaining screws and remove the handle **(see illustration)**.

69 Refitting is a reversal of removal.

26 Centre console – removal and refitting

1 Slide the front seats back as far as possible.

2 Carefully unclip the centre facia trim panels from each side of the heater control panel **(see illustration)**.

3 Undo the two retaining screws from the front of the centre console **(see illustration)**.

26.2 Unclip the side trims

26.3 Undo the two retaining screws (arrowed)

26.4a Unclip the gear lever gaiter – manual transmission

26.4b Unclip the gear lever trim – automatic transmission

26.5 Prise out the cover and undo the retaining nut

26.6 Remove the rubber cover

26.7a Release the securing clip…

4 Unclip the gear lever gaiter (manual models) or plastic surround (automatic models) from the centre console (**see illustrations**).

5 Prise out the plastic cover at the base of the cup holder and undo the retaining nut at the rear of the centre console (**see illustration**).

6 Withdraw the rubber cover from the front of the centre console (**see illustration**).

7 Unclip the console upper cover and with- draw it over the gear lever, disconnect the wiring connector as it is removed (**see illustrations**).

8 Unclip the switch panel/small compartment from the side of the handbrake lever and disconnect the wiring connector (**see illustrations**).

26.7b… and remove the upper trim panel – automatic transmission

26.7c Remove the upper trim panel – manual transmission

26.7d Disconnect the wiring connector

26.8a Unclip the switch trim panel…

26.8b … and disconnect the wiring connector…

26.8c …or unclip small compartment

26.9 Lift the centre console up to remove

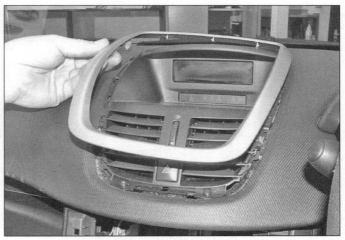

27.1 Carefully unclip the trim from the facia

27.2a Undo the two retaining screws (arrowed)...

27.2b... and withdraw the panel from the facia

27.3 Disconnect the wiring connectors as it is removed

9 Raise the rear of the console, and lift the console over the handbrake lever, and rearwards out of the vehicle (see illustration).
10 Refitting is a reversal of removal.

27 Facia panel components – removal and refitting

Upper centre panel

1 Carefully unclip the plastic surround from the upper centre panel (see illustration).
2 Undo the two screws and withdraw the panel from the top of the facia (see illustrations).
3 Disconnect the wiring connectors as the panel is removed (see illustration).
4 Refitting is a reversal of removal.

Lower centre side panels

5 Release the retaining clip at the front of the trim panel (see illustration).

6 Withdraw the panel from the front of the centre console (see illustration).
7 Refitting is a reversal of removal.

Instrument panel cover

8 Carefully pull the instrument cover out from the facia panel, releasing it from the retaining clips (see illustration).
9 Refitting is a reversal of removal.

Driver's side compartment panel

10 Carefully pull the instrument cover out

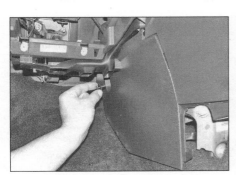

27.5 Release the securing clip...

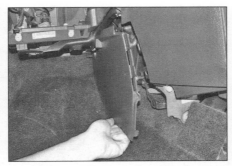

27.6... and remove the side trim

27.8 Unclip the cover from the facia

27.10 Unclip the storage compartment panel from the facia

27.12a Undo the retaining screws (arrowed)...

27.12b... and remove the lower trim

from the facia panel, releasing it from the retaining clips **(see illustration)**.
11 Refitting is a reversal of removal.

27.13a Release the elastic strap...

Steering column shrouds

12 Unscrew the two lower steering column shroud securing screws and unclip it from the upper shroud **(see illustrations)**.
13 Unclip the elastic strap from around the ignition switch and lift the upper cover from the steering column **(see illustrations)**.
14 Refitting is a reversal of removal.

Steering column lower panel

15 Carefully pull the panel out from the facia, releasing it from the retaining clips **(see illustration)**.
16 Refitting is a reversal of removal.

Lower panel above pedals

17 Release the retaining clips along the rear

edge of the trim panel and withdraw it from under the facia **(see illustration)**.
18 Refitting is a reversal of removal.

Facia end covers

19 Carefully unclip the plastic surround from the air vents **(see illustration)**.
20 Unclip the end cover from the facia panel **(see illustration)**.
21 Refitting is a reversal of removal.

Side air vents

22 Carefully unclip the plastic surround from the air vents **(see illustration 27.19)**.
23 Undo the retaining screw at the front of the air vent **(see illustration)**.
24 Release the retaining clip, through the

27.13b... and remove the upper trim

27.15 Unclip the lower trim panel from the facia

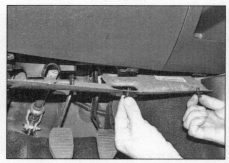

27.17 Release the clips and remove lower trim panel from the driver's footwell

27.19 Carefully unclip the trim from the air vents

27.20 Unclip the side trims from each end of the facia

27.23 Undo the retaining screw (arrowed)...

27.24a... release the retaining clip...

27.24b... and withdraw the vent from the facia

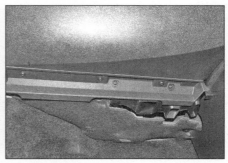

27.26 Glovebox lower retaining screws

grille of the air vent and withdraw the vent from the facia (see illustrations).

25 Refitting is a reversal of removal.

Passenger side glovebox

26 Working inside the passenger front footwell, undo the retaining screws from the lower edge of the glovebox assembly (see illustration).

27 Release the securing clips, and remove the trim beneath the facia (see illustration).

28 Open the glovebox, and unclip the cover from the left-hand side of the compartment (see illustration).

29 Undo the screws securing the inside of the glovebox to the facia (see illustrations).

30 Release the wiring block connectors and diagnostic plug, from the glovebox housing (see illustration).

31 Withdraw the glovebox housing from the facia panel; disconnect the wiring plug connectors as it is withdrawn (see illustrations). On models with air-conditioning, it may be necessary to disconnect the air ducting hose from the rear of the glovebox housing.

32 Refitting is a reversal of removal.

Complete facia assembly

Note: *This is an involved operation entailing the removal of numerous components and assemblies, and the disconnection of a multitude of wiring connectors. Make notes of the location of all disconnected wiring, or attach labels to the connectors, to avoid confusion when refitting.*

33 Disconnect the battery (see Chapter 5A Section 4).

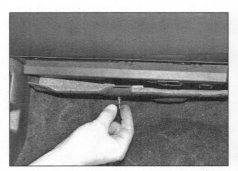

27.27 Release the clips and remove lower trim panel from the passenger footwell

27.28 Unclip the cover from inside the glovebox

27.29a Undo the upper retaining screws...

27.29b... and the side retaining screws

34 Move the front seats as far back as possible. Set the steering wheel in the straight-ahead position, and engage the steering lock.

35 Remove the centre console as described in Section 26.

36 Remove the steering wheel and steering column, as described in Chapter 10 Section 17 & 18.

37 Remove the heater control panel, as described in Chapter 3 Section 10.

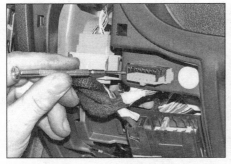

27.30 Unclip the wiring plug connectors from the facia

27.31a Withdraw the glovebox from the facia...

27.31b... and disconnect the wiring connectors

27.39 Undo the screws behind each side air vent

27.40 Undo the screw behind instrument panel

27.41 Undo the screws at each side of the facia

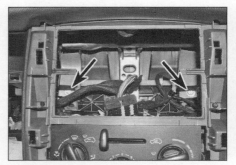

27.42 Undo the two bolts inside the centre of the facia

27.43 Unclip the cover and undo the screws (arrowed)

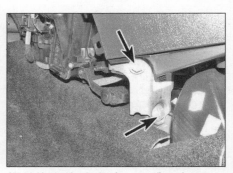

27.44 Undo the bolts (arrowed) and remove the centre bracket

27.45a Unclip the wiring from the crossmember...

38 Remove all the following facia panels as described previously in this Section:
● Facia upper centre panel.
● Facia lower centre side panels.
● Instrument panel cover.
● Driver's side compartment panel.
● Steering column shrouds.
● Steering column lower panel.
● Lower panel above pedal assembly.
● Facia end covers and air vents.
● Passenger side glovebox.
39 Undo the two retaining screws (one each side) from inside the side air vent apertures **(see illustration)**.
40 Undo the retaining screw from inside the instrument panel apertures **(see illustration)**.

41 Undo the two retaining screws (one each side) from the lower corners of the facia panel **(see illustration)**.
42 Undo the two retaining bolts from inside the centre of the facia panel **(see illustration)**.
43 Unclip the plastic cover and undo the two retaining screws from the lower centre of the facia panel **(see illustration)**.
44 Undo the retaining bolt from the mounting bracket on the lower centre of the facia panel **(see illustration)**.
45 Working along the facia panel, release the retaining clips and unclip the wiring loom. Disconnect any connections, making sure the position of the wiring is noted for refitting **(see illustrations)**.

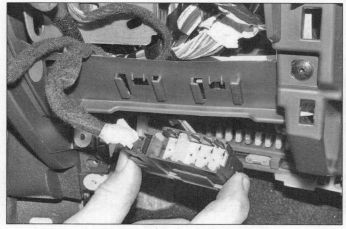

27.45b... and the facia panel...

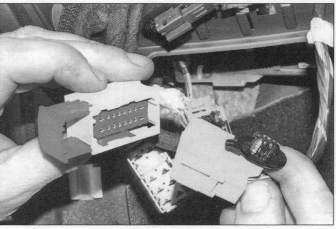

27.45c... noting their fitted positions

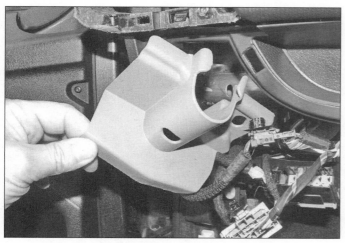

27.46a Unclip the crossmember end covers...

27.46b... and undo the left-hand mounting bolts (arrowed)...

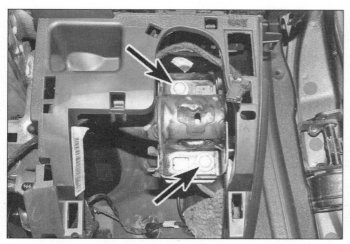

27.46c... and the right-hand mounting bolts (arrowed)

27.48 Undo the mounting bolt from inside the instrument panel aperture (arrowed)

46 Unclip the plastic covers from the ends of the facia crossmember, and then undo the retaining bolts **(see illustrations)**.

47 Check along the length of the facia panel, noting the fitted positions and harness routing, and then disconnect the facia wiring plugs. Take note of the location of the various wiring harness retaining clips to aid refitment.

48 Working through the apertures behind the instrument panel, unscrew the bolt securing the facia crossmember **(see illustration)**.

49 With the help of an assistant, lift the facia from place, and remove it from the vehicle.

50 Refitting is a reversal of removal, ensuring that all wiring is correctly reconnected and all mountings securely tightened.

Notes

Chapter 12
Body electrical systems

Contents

Degrees of difficulty

Easy, suitable for novice with little experience	Fairly easy, suitable for beginner with some experience 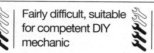	Fairly difficult, suitable for competent DIY mechanic	Difficult, suitable for experienced DIY mechanic 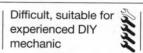	Very difficult, suitable for expert DIY or professional

Specifications

General
System type . . . . 12 volt negative earth

Bulbs

	Type	Wattage
Ashtray light	Push-fit	1.2
Direction indicator light	Bayonet	21
Direction indicator side repeater	Push-fit	5
Front foglight:		
Early models	H1	55
Later models	H11	
Glovebox light	Push-fit	5
Headlights:		
Main beam bulbs	H1	55
Dip beam bulbs	H7	55
Elliptical/Directional bulb (later models)	H7	55
High-level stop light	Push-fit	5
Interior/courtesy light	Push-fit	5
Luggage compartment light	Push-fit	5
Number plate light	Push-fit	5
Rear foglight	Bayonet	21
Reversing light	Bayonet	21
Sidelights	Push-fit	5
Stop-light	Bayonet	21
Tail light	Bayonet	5
Vanity lights	Festoon	3

Torque wrench settings

	Nm	lbf ft
Airbag control unit retaining nuts	8	6
Side airbag acceleration sensor retaining nuts	8	6

1 General Information

⚠️ *Warning: Before carrying out any work on the electrical system, read through the precautions given in 'Safety first!' at the beginning of this manual, and in Chapter 5A Section 1.*

1 The electrical system is of 12 volt negative earth type. Power for the lights and all electrical accessories is supplied by a lead-acid type battery, which is charged by the alternator.

2 Many of the body electrical systems are controlled by individual electronic control units (ECUs) and these are in turn controlled by a main ECU known as a Built-in Systems Interface (BSI). The various ECUs and the BSI exchange data with each other via a multiplex network. The multiplex network is a two-wire system linking the BSI with the system ECUs and is termed by Peugeot as CAN (controlled area network) and VAN (vehicle area network). Essentially this means that the BSI and the ECUs controlling the 'comfort' systems, safety systems, security systems, and entertainment systems in the vehicle, are all interconnected via Vehicle Area Networks **(see illustration)**.

3 An ECU connected to the multiplex network only receives some of the data needed for it to operate directly, with the remaining data being supplied by the other ECUs on the network. Because the ECUs share information via the network, several ECUs can control the operation of the same system. Also, one ECU can control several systems in an autonomous manner. The BSI is the manager of this information interchange as well as also being responsible for the control of certain vehicle systems itself. The BSI has a full diagnostic capability whereby any fault in any of the ECUs on the multiplex network can be traced using diagnostic equipment connected to the vehicle diagnostic connector. Should any fault develop with a system on the network, have the self-diagnosis facility interrogated by a Peugeot dealer or suitably-equipped specialist.

4 This Chapter covers repair and service procedures for the various electrical components not associated with the engine. Information on the battery, alternator and starter motor can be found in Chapter 5A Section 7 & 10.

5 It should be noted that, prior to working on any component in the electrical system, the battery should first be disconnected to prevent the possibility of electrical short-circuits (see Chapter 5A Section 4).

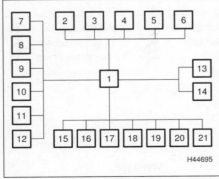

1.1 Multiplexing – Vehicle Area Network (VAN)

1 Built-in Systems Interface (BSI)
2 Electric windows
3 Fuel additive ECU (diesel model with particulate filter)
4 Anti-theft alarm
5 Central locking transmitter
6 Sunroof motor
7 Power steering pump
8 Engine management ECU
9 Steering column combination switches
10 ABS control unit
11 ESP control unit
12 Automatic transmission ECU
13 Airbag ECU
14 Fusebox
15 Air conditioning ECU
16 Instrument cluster
17 CD player
18 Multifunction display
19 Parking aid ECU
20 Radio
21 Radio/telephone ECU

2 Electrical fault finding – general information

Note: *Refer to the precautions given in 'Safety first!' and in Chapter 5A Section 1 before starting work. The following tests relate to testing of the main electrical circuits, and should not be used to test delicate electronic circuits (such as anti-lock braking systems), particularly where an electronic control unit (ECU) or multiplexing is used (see Section 1).*

General

1 A typical electrical circuit consists of an electrical component, any switches, relays,

1.2 Diagnostic plug connector (arrowed)

motors, fuses, fusible links or circuit breakers related to that component, and the wiring and connectors which link the component to both the battery and the chassis. To help to pinpoint a problem in an electrical circuit, wiring diagrams are included at the end of this Chapter.

2 Before attempting to diagnose an electrical fault, first study the appropriate wiring diagram, to obtain a more complete understanding of the components included in the particular circuit concerned. The possible sources of a fault can be narrowed down by noting whether other components related to the circuit are operating properly. If several components or circuits fail at one time, the problem is likely to be related to a shared fuse or earth connection.

3 Electrical problems usually stem from simple causes, such as loose or corroded connections, a faulty earth connection, a blown fuse, a melted fusible link, or a faulty relay (refer to Section 3 for details of testing relays). Visually inspect the condition of all fuses, wires and connections in a problem circuit before testing the components. Use the wiring diagrams to determine which terminal connections will need to be checked, in order to pinpoint the trouble spot.

4 The basic tools required for electrical fault finding include a circuit tester or voltmeter; an ohmmeter (to measure resistance); a battery and set of test leads; and a jumper wire, preferably with a circuit breaker or fuse incorporated, which can be used to bypass suspect wires or electrical components. Before attempting to locate a problem with test instruments, use the wiring diagram to determine where to make the connections.

5 To find the source of an intermittent wiring fault (usually due to a poor or dirty connection, or damaged wiring insulation), a 'wiggle' test can be performed on the wiring. This involves wiggling the wiring by hand, to see if the fault occurs as the wiring is moved. It should be possible to narrow down the source of the fault to a particular section of wiring. This method of testing can be used in conjunction with any of the tests described in the following sub-Sections.

6 Apart from problems due to poor connections, two basic types of fault can occur in an electrical circuit – open-circuit, or short-circuit.

7 Open-circuit faults are caused by a break somewhere in the circuit, which prevents current from flowing. An open-circuit fault will prevent a component from working, but will not cause the relevant circuit fuse to blow.

8 Short-circuit faults are caused by a 'short' somewhere in the circuit, which allows the current flowing in the circuit to 'escape' along an alternative route, usually to earth. Short circuit faults are normally caused by a breakdown in wiring insulation, which allows a feed wire to touch either another wire, or an earthed component such as the bodyshell. A short-circuit fault will normally cause the

2.21a Earth connection under centre console...

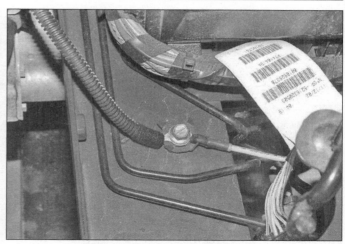

2.21b... in front of the battery box...

relevant circuit fuse to blow. **Note:** *As an aid to economy and to prevent battery discharge, certain functions of the electrical system can only be used for 30 minutes after the engine has been stopped. Bear this in mind when tracing power supply faults on these systems.*

Functions affected
● Windscreen wipers.
● Electric windows.
● Sunroof.
● Courtesy lights.
● Audio equipment.

9 After this period the BSI (Built-in Systems Interface) cuts the power to these circuits. To restore power, start the engine. It is also possible for the BSI to turn off certain functions (heater blower, heated rear window) depending on the state of charge of the battery. When tracing a fault, ensure the battery is in a good state of charge.

Finding an open-circuit

10 To check for an open-circuit, connect one lead of a voltmeter to either the negative battery terminal or a known good earth.
11 Connect the other lead to a connector in the circuit being tested, preferably nearest to the battery or fuse.
12 Switch on the circuit, bearing in mind that some circuits are live only when the ignition switch is moved to a particular position.
13 If voltage is present (indicated either by the tester bulb lighting or a voltmeter reading, as applicable), this means that the section of the circuit between the relevant connector and the battery is problem-free.
14 Continue to check the remainder of the circuit in the same fashion.
15 When a point is reached at which no voltage is present, the problem must lie between that point and the previous test point with voltage. Most problems can be traced to a broken, corroded or loose connection.

Finding a short-circuit

16 To check for a short-circuit; first disconnect

the load(s) from the circuit (loads are the components which draw current from a circuit, such as bulbs, motors, heating elements, etc).
17 Remove the relevant fuse from the circuit, and connect a circuit tester or voltmeter to the fuse connections.
18 Switch on the circuit, bearing in mind that some circuits are live only when the ignition switch is moved to a particular position.
19 If voltage is present (indicated either by the tester bulb lighting or a voltmeter reading, as applicable), this means that there is a short-circuit.
20 If no voltage is present, but the fuse still blows with the load(s) connected, this indicates an internal fault in the load(s).

Finding an earth fault

21 The battery negative terminal is connected to 'earth' – the metal of the engine/ transmission and the car body – and most systems are wired so that they only receive a positive feed, the current returning via the metal of the car body. This means that the component mounting and the body form part of that circuit. Loose or corroded mountings can therefore cause a range of electrical faults, ranging from total failure of a circuit, to a puzzling partial fault. In particular, lights may shine dimly (especially when another circuit sharing the same earth point is in operation), motors (eg, wiper motors or the radiator cooling fan motor) may run slowly, and the operation of one circuit may have an apparently unrelated effect on another. Note that on many vehicles, earth straps are used between certain components, such as the engine/transmission and the body, usually where there is no metal-to-metal contact between components, due to flexible rubber mountings, etc. **(see illustrations)**.
22 To check whether a component is properly earthed, disconnect the battery, and connect one lead of an ohmmeter to a known good earth point. Connect the other lead to the wire or earth connection being tested. The

2.21c... on the top of the transmission (arrowed)

resistance reading should be zero; if not, check the connection as follows.
23 If an earth connection is thought to be faulty, dismantle the connection, and clean back to bare metal both the bodyshell and the wire terminal or the component earth connection-mating surface. Be careful to remove all traces of dirt and corrosion, and then use a knife to trim away any paint, so that a clean metal-to-metal joint is made. On reassembly, tighten the joint fasteners securely; if a wire terminal is being refitted, use serrated washers between the terminal and the bodyshell, to ensure a clean and secure connection. When the connection is remade, prevent the onset of corrosion in the future by applying a coat of petroleum jelly or silicone-based grease, or by spraying on (at regular intervals) a proprietary ignition sealer or water-dispersant lubricant.

3 Fuses and relays – general information

Fuses

1 Fuses are designed to break a circuit when a predetermined current is reached, in order

3.3a Unclip the cover…

3.3b… to access the fuses (arrowed)

3.3c Engine compartment fuse/relay box

3.3d Heavy duty fuses at the rear of the battery box

to protect the components and wiring which could be damaged by excessive current flow. Any excessive current flow will be due to a fault in the circuit, usually a short-circuit (see Section 2).

2 The majority of fuses are located behind the glovebox lid on the passenger's side of the facia. Additional fuses (including the larger, higher-rated fuses) are located in the fuse/relay box on the left-hand side of the engine compartment. Some models have a fusebox attached to the rear of the battery tray.

3 To gain access to the facia fuses, open the glovebox and unclip the cover from the facia **(see illustrations)**. To gain access to the fuses in the engine compartment, simply unclip the cover from the fuse/relay box.

4 A list of circuits each fuse protects is given on the fusebox cover.

5 To remove a fuse, first switch off the circuit

concerned (or the ignition), and then pull the fuse out of its terminals. The wire within the fuse should be visible; if the fuse has blown it will be broken or melted.

6 Always renew a fuse with one of the correct rating; never use a fuse with a different rating from that specified. The fuse rating is stamped on the top of the fuse; the fuses are also colour-coded as follows. Refer to the wiring diagrams for details of the fuse ratings and the circuits protected.

Colour	Rating
Orange	5A
Red	10A
Blue	15A
Yellow	20A
Clear or white	25A
Green	30A

7 Never renew a fuse more than once without tracing the source of the trouble. If the new fuse blows immediately, find the cause before renewing it again; a short to earth as a result of faulty insulation is most likely. Where a fuse protects more than one circuit, try to isolate the fault by switching on each circuit in turn (where possible) until the fuse blows again. Always carry a supply of spare fuses of each relevant rating on the vehicle; a spare of each rating should be clipped into the fusebox.

Relays

8 The majority of relay functions are incorporated into the Built-in System Interface (BSI) unit (see Section 23). Other relays are located in the fuse/relay box in the engine compartment and the cooling fan relay(s) is/are located in front panel **(see illustration)**.

9 If a circuit or system controlled by a relay develops a fault and the relay is suspect, operate the system. If the relay is functioning, it should be possible to hear it 'click' as it is energised. If this is the case, the fault lies with the components or wiring of the system. If the relay is not being energised, then either the relay is not receiving a main supply or a switching voltage, or the relay itself is faulty. Testing is by the substitution of a known good unit, but be careful – while some relays are identical in appearance and in operation, others look similar but perform different functions.

10 To remove a relay, first ensure that the relevant circuit is switched off. The relay can then simply be pulled out from the socket, and pushed back into position.

3.8 Cooling fan relay (arrowed)

4.3 Disconnect the wiring connectors at the rear of the switch assembly

---

4   Switches –
removal and refitting

Note: *Disconnect the battery before removing any switch, and reconnect the lead after refitting the switch (see Chapter 5A Section 4).*

Ignition switch

1 Refer to Chapter 10 Section 19.

Steering column switches (lights, wipers, audio)

2 Remove the steering column lower and upper shrouds as described in Chapter 11 Section 27.

3 Disconnect the wiring plug connectors from the rear of the switch unit **(see illustration)**.

4 Turn the steering wheel to access the switch retaining screws and then undo the relevant screws, depending on which

4.4a Undo the retaining screws (arrowed)...

4.4b... to remove an individual switch

4.5 Release the clip to slide audio switch from the housing

switch requires removing **(see illustrations)**.

5 Using a small screwdriver, release the retaining clip and slide the switch out from the housing **(see illustration)**.

6 Refitting is the reversal of removal.

Facia-mounted switches

7 The facia-mounted switches for the central locking, alarm and ESP (depending on model) are located below the heater controls. Using a plastic or wooden spatula, carefully prise the trim panels from the each side of the centre panel. Undo the two retaining screws and remove the switch panel from the facia, disconnecting the wiring plug as it is withdrawn **(see illustrations)**. Take care not to mark the surrounding trim.

8 To remove the headlight height control switch, remove the driver's side compartment panel as described in Chapter 11 Section 27. Release the retaining clip and remove the switch from the facia **(see illustrations)**. Disconnect the wiring connector as it is removed.

9 To remove the hazard warning switch, remove the facia upper centre air vent panel as described in Chapter 11 Section 27. Release the retaining clip and remove the switch from the panel **(see illustrations)**.

10 Refitting is the reverse of removal.

Heating/ventilation control

11 The switches are an integral part of the heater/ventilation control panel, and cannot

4.7a Unclip the side trims...

4.7b... undo the retaining screw (arrowed)...

4.7c... and remove the switch panel

4.8a Withdraw the switch from the facia...

4.8b... and disconnect the wiring connector

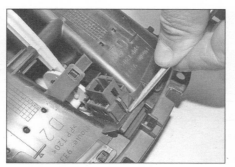

4.9a Release the securing clip...

4.9b... and withdraw the switch

4.14 Handbrake switch (arrowed)

4.18 Unclip the light from inside the glovebox

be renewed separately. If any switch is faulty, the complete control panel must be renewed – refer to Chapter 3 Section 10 for details.

Stop-light switch

12 Refer to Chapter 9 Section 20.

Handbrake warning light switch

13 Remove the centre console as described in Chapter 11 Section 26.
14 Disconnect the switch wiring connector, then push the switch out of the mounting bracket to remove it **(see illustration)**.
15 Refitting is the reverse of removal.

5.2 Unclip the headlight bulb protective cover

Courtesy light switch

16 The courtesy light switches are an integral part of the door lock assemblies. Refer to Chapter 11 Section 13 for door lock removal and refitting details.

Luggage area light switch

17 The luggage compartment light switch function is integral with the tailgate lock assembly. For tailgate lock removal, refer to Chapter 11 Section 16.

Glovebox illumination switch

18 The switch is integral with the light. Unclip the light unit from inside the glove compartment **(see illustration)**. Disconnect the wiring connector as it is removed.

5 Bulbs (exterior lights) – renewal

General

1 Whenever a bulb is renewed, note the following points:
● Remember that, if the light has just been in use, the bulb may be extremely hot.
● Always check the bulb contacts and holder, ensuring that there is clean metal-to-metal contact between the bulb and its

live(s) and earth. Clean off any corrosion or dirt before fitting a new bulb.
● Wherever bayonet-type bulbs are fitted (see Specifications), ensure that the live contact(s) bear firmly against the bulb contact.
● Always ensure that the new bulb is of the correct rating, and that it is completely clean before fitting it; this applies particularly to headlight/foglight bulbs (see below).
● On later models, there may be LED's fitted to the light units and not standard bulbs, on this type the light unit may be a complete unit.

Headlight

Note: *On early models (conventional lights), there are two headlight bulbs fitted, the outer one being the dipped beam and the inner one being the main beam. On later models (elliptical/directional lights), there are three headlight bulbs fitted, one of the outer bulbs being the main beam and the other outer being the directional bulb, the inner bulb on this type is the dipped beam.*

2 The headlight bulbs are all separate. Reach behind the headlamp, and unclip relevant beam's protective cover and remove it **(see illustration)**.
3 Disconnect the wiring plug from the dipped beam bulb (early models), then release the bulb retaining clip and withdraw the bulb **(see illustrations)**.

5.3a Disconnect the headlight bulb wiring plug

5.3b Release the retaining clip...

5.3c ... and remove the bulb

5.4a Disconnect the headlight bulb wiring plug

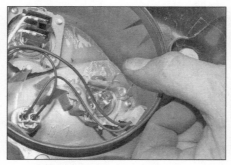

5.4b Release the retaining clip...

5.4c ... and remove the bulb

5.5a Disconnect the headlight bulb wiring plug

5.5b Release the retaining clip...

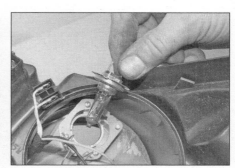

5.5c ... and remove the bulb

4 Disconnect the wiring plug from the main beam bulb (later models), then release the bulb retaining clip and withdraw the bulb **(see illustrations)**.

5 Disconnect the wiring plug from the elliptical/directional bulb (later models), then release the bulb retaining clip and withdraw the bulb **(see illustrations)**.

Caution: When handling the new bulb, use a tissue or clean cloth to avoid touching the glass with the fingers; moisture and grease from the skin can cause blackening and rapid failure of this type of bulb. If the glass is accidentally touched, wipe it clean using methylated spirit.

6 Install the new bulb, ensuring that its locating tabs are correctly seated in the light cut-outs, and secure it in position with the retaining clip.

7 Reconnect the wiring plug, and refit the protective cover.

Sidelight

8 Reach behind the headlight and unclip the protective cover **(see illustration 5.2)**, Squeeze together the retaining clips and pull the bulbholder from the headlight. The bulb is of the capless (push-fit) type, and can be removed by simply pulling it out of the holder **(see illustrations)**.

9 Refitting is the reverse of the removal procedure, ensuring that the bulbholder seal is in good condition.

Foglight

10 The front foglights are located in the front bumper. Chock the rear wheels then jack up the front of the vehicle and support it on axle stands (see *Jacking and vehicle support*). For easier access to the foglights, it is necessary to release the front of the wheel arch liner by removing the fasteners.

5.8a Remove the bulbholder from the light unit...

11 Reach up under the front bumper and disconnect the wiring from the foglight bulb holder (early model). Turn the bulb holder 90° anti-clockwise and withdraw it from the rear of the foglight **(see illustrations)**.

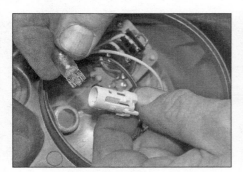

5.8b... and pull the bulb from the holder

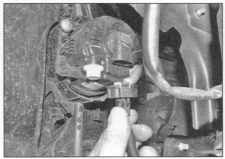

5.11a Disconnect the foglight wiring plug...

5.11b ... rotate the bulbholder to remove

5.12a Disconnect the foglight wiring plug...

5.12b ... squeeze locking clips and remove

5.15a Twist the bulbholder to remove...

5.15b... then press in the bulb and rotate it anti-clockwise to remove it

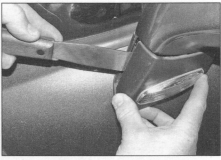

5.17a Unclip the trim from the mirror...

5.17b... and disconnect the wiring connector

12 Reach up under the front bumper and disconnect the wiring from the foglight bulb holder (later model). Squeeze the locking clips and release the bulb holder from the rear of the foglight **(see illustrations)**. To change the bulb on the offside front foglight, it may be necessary to remove the complete light unit, as described in Section 7.

Caution: When handling the new bulb, use a tissue or clean cloth to avoid touching the glass with the fingers; moisture and grease from the skin can cause blackening and rapid failure of this type of bulb. If the glass is accidentally touched, wipe it clean using methylated spirit.

13 Purchase the new bulb before attempting to remove the bulb from the bulb holder, as the bulb may be part of the bulb holder.

14 Fit the new bulb using a reversal of the removal procedure.

Direction indicator

15 Reach up to the top corner of the headlight unit and rotate the bulbholder anti-clockwise, and free it from the rear of the headlight unit. The bulb is a bayonet-fit in the holder, and can be removed by pressing it in and rotating it anti-clockwise**(see illustrations)**.

16 Refitting is the reverse of the removal procedure, ensuring that the bulbholder seal is in good condition.

Direction indicator side repeater

17 The side repeaters are located in the base of the door mirrors. Using a plastic or wooden spatula, carefully prise the trim panel from the base of the door mirror **(see illustrations)**. Disconnect the wiring connector as it is removed. Each bulb is of the capless (push-fit) type, and can be removed by simply pulling it out of the bulbholder. On some models the bulb is part of the light assembly and cannot be renewed separately.

18 Refitting is a reversal of the removal procedure.

Rear light cluster

19 Remove the relevant rear light unit as described in Section 7.

20 Release the retaining tabs and remove the bulbholder from the light unit **(see illustrations)**.

21 All the bulbs have bayonet fittings, press the relevant bulb in and rotate it anti-clockwise to remove **(see illustration)**.

22 Refitting is the reverse of removal, ensuring

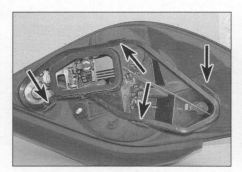

5.20a Squeeze together the tabs (arrowed)...

5.20b... and remove the bulbholder assembly

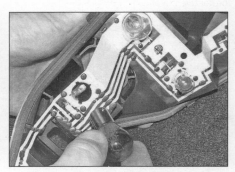

5.21 Press in and rotate the bulb anti-clockwise to remove

5.24a Release the securing clips (arrowed)…

5.24b… and remove the bulbholder…

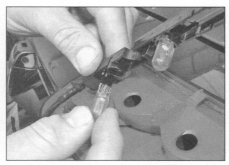

5.24c… then pull the capless bulb out

the light unit and bulbholder seals are in good condition.

High-level stop-light

23 Remove the light unit as described in Section 7.

24 On Estate models, release the retaining clips and detach the bulbholder from the light unit. Each bulb is of the capless (push-fit) type, and can be removed by simply pulling it out of the bulbholder **(see illustrations)**.

25 On Hatchback models, rotate the bulbholders 90 degrees anti-clockwise and detach the bulbholder from the light unit. Each bulb is of the capless (push-fit) type, and can be removed by simply pulling it out of the bulbholder **(see illustrations)**.

26 Refitting is the reverse of removal. Do not overtighten the light unit retaining nuts, as the plastic is easily broken.

Number plate light

27 Using a small flat-bladed screwdriver, carefully prise the end of the lens downwards, and remove it. The bulb is of the capless (push-fit) type, and can be removed by simply pulling it out of the light unit **(see illustrations)**.

28 Refitting is the reverse of the removal procedure, ensuring that the lens is securely clipped in position.

5.25a Rotate the bulbholder anti-clockwise and pull it from the light…

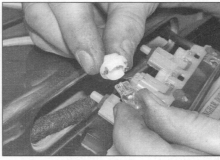

5.25b… then pull the capless bulb out

5.27a Unclip the lens…

5.27b… and then pull the capless bulb out

---

6 Bulbs (interior lights) – renewal

General

1 Refer to Section 5, paragraph 1.

Passenger compartment light

2 Using a flat bladed-screwdriver, carefully prise the lens from the light unit **(see illustration)**.

3 The bulb is of the capless (push-fit) type, and can be removed by simply pulling it out of the bulbholder **(see illustration)**.

4 Refitting is the reverse of the removal procedure

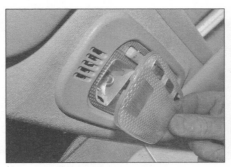

6.2 Unclip the lens…

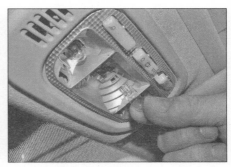

6.3… and then pull the capless bulb out

6.5a Unclip the light unit…

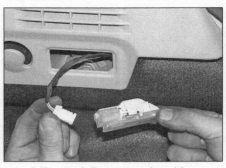

6.5b… and disconnect the wiring connector

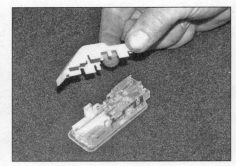

6.6a Unclip the rear cover…

Luggage compartment light

5 Using a flat-bladed screwdriver, carefully ease the light unit out of position and disconnect it from the wiring connector (see illustrations).

6 Unclip the cover from the rear of the light unit. The bulb is of the capless (push-fit) type, and can be removed by simply pulling it out of the bulbholder (see illustrations).

7 Refitting is the reverse of the removal procedure.

Instrument panel lights

8 The instrument panel and warning lights are illuminated by integral LEDs. It is not possible to renew them independently of the panel.

Instrument panel renewal is described in Section 9.

Heating/ventilation control illumination

9 Remove the heater control panel as described in Chapter 3.

10 Rotate the bulb holder anti-clockwise and remove it. The capless bulb simply pulls from the bulb holder (see illustration).

Multifunction display illumination

11 The multifunction display warning lights are illuminated by integral LEDs. It is not possible to renew them independently of the panel. Multifunction display panel renewal is described in Section 10.

Accessory socket/ cigarette lighter illumination

12 Remove the accessory socket/cigarette lighter as described in Section 11.

13 Free the bulb from its holder. The capless bulb simply pulls from the bulbholder

14 Securely fit the new bulb then clip the holder back into position on the console. Refit the accessory socket/cigarette lighter as described in Section 11.

Switch illumination

15 All of the switches that are illuminated are done so by LEDs. These LEDs are an integral part of the switch and cannot be renewed separately. Renewal will therefore require renewal of the complete switch assembly (see Section 4).

Glovebox illumination

16 Open the glovebox, and carefully prise the rear of the light from the facia. Remove the light unit, and disconnect the wiring plug as it is withdrawn (see illustrations). Note that the switch is integral with the light.

17 Unclip the cover from the rear of the light unit. The capless bulb simply pulls from the bulb holder (see illustrations 6.6a and 6.6b).

Vanity mirror illumination

18 Carefully prise the lens and mirror from the sunvisor (see illustration).

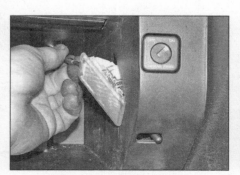

6.6b… and then pull the capless bulb out

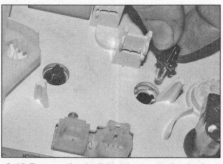

6.10 Rotate the bulbholder anti-clockwise and remove it from the rear of the control panel

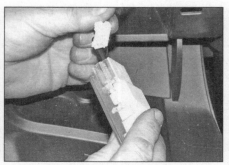

6.16a Unclip the light unit…

6.16b… and disconnect the wiring connector

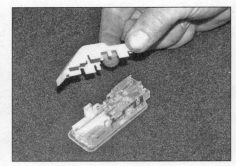

6.18 Carefully prise the lens and mirror from place…

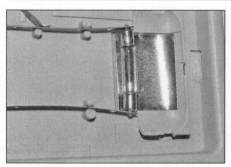

6.19... then lever out the festoon bulb

7.4a Undo the outer headlamp mounting bolt (arrowed)...

7.4b... inner mounting bolt (arrowed)...

19 Prise the festoon bulb(s) from place **(see illustration)**.

7 Exterior light units – removal and refitting

Headlight

1 Remove the front bumper as described in Chapter 11 Section 6.
2 If removing the left-hand headlight, it may be necessary to remove the air intake ducting adjacent to the headlight.
3 Unclip the washer jet from the headlight lens (where fitted).
4 Slacken and remove the three mounting bolts and free the headlight unit from its mounting **(see illustrations)**.
5 Slide out the locking clip and disconnect the wiring connector(s) from the headlight unit, then manoeuvre the unit out of position **(see illustration)**.
6 Refitting is the reverse of the removal procedure. Refit the bumper as described in Chapter 11 Section 6.
7 Check the headlight beam alignment using the information given in Section 8.

Direction indicator side repeater

8 The side repeaters are located in the base of the door mirrors.
9 Remove the side repeaters as described in Section 5 **(see illustrations 5.17a and 5.17b)**.

Rear light unit

Hatchback models

10 Working inside the luggage compartment, undo the retaining nut (one on each side) from the rear of the light unit **(see illustration)**.
11 Pull the light unit, to detach it from the rear of the vehicle disconnecting it from the locating peg **(see illustration)**.
12 Disconnect the wiring connector from the light unit then remove the light unit from the vehicle **(see illustration)**.
13 Refitting is the reverse of removal, ensuring the light unit seal is in good condition and the locating peg is aligned correctly.

Estate models

14 Open the tailgate, and unclip the trim panel behind the light unit **(see illustration)**.

7.4c... and lower mounting bolt

7.5 Slide out the locking latch and disconnect the wiring plug

7.10 Undo the rear light unit securing nut

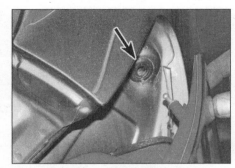

7.11 Withdraw the rear light from the locating peg (arrowed)

7.12 Disconnect the wiring connector

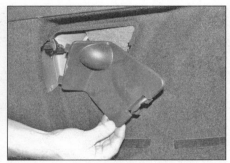

7.14 Unclip the access cover

7.15a Disconnect the wiring connector and undo the retaining nut (arrowed)

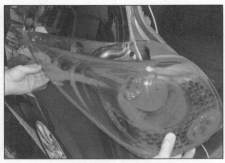

7.15b Remove the light unit...

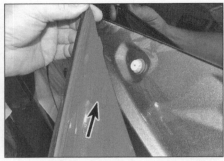

7.16a ... disengaging it from the securing clip (arrowed)...

7.16b ... and locating peg (arrowed)

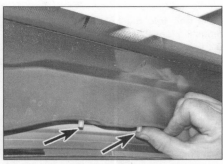

7.18 Press out the locating pegs (arrowed) – Hatchback models

High-level stop-light

Hatchback

18 Open the tailgate, and then carefully push on the light unit studs to ease the unit out from the tailgate **(see illustration)**.
19 Disconnect the washer tube from the end of the light unit **(see illustration)**.
20 Disconnect the wiring connector, and then remove the light unit from the tailgate **(see illustration)**.
21 Refitting is the reverse of removal. Make sure the light unit is located correctly.

Estate models

22 Open the tailgate, and then unscrew the nuts securing the light unit to the tailgate **(see illustrations)**. Carefully push on the light unit studs to ease the unit out.
23 Disconnect the wiring connector and washer tube, and then remove the light unit from the tailgate **(see illustrations)**.
24 Refitting is the reverse of removal. Do not

15 Disconnect the wiring connector from the rear of the light unit, and then undo the plastic wing nut (one on each side), and remove the light unit from the vehicle **(see illustrations)**.
16 Pull the light unit to detach it from the rear of the vehicle, disconnecting it from the two retaining clips and the locating peg **(see illustrations)**.
17 Refitting is the reverse of removal, ensuring the light unit seal is in good condition and the locating peg/clips are aligned correctly.

7.19 Disconnect the washer pipe...

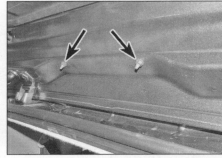

7.20 ... and wiring plug connector

7.22a Undo the retaining nuts – Estate models...

7.22b ... and remove the high-level stop-light

7.23a Disconnect the wiring connector...

7.23b ... and the washer pipe...

7.26 Disconnect the wiring connector…

7.27… and the remove the light unit

7.30a Disconnect the wiring connector

overtighten the light unit retaining nuts as the plastic is easily broken.

Number plate light

25 Remove the tailgate trim panel as described in Chapter 11.
26 Disconnect the wiring plug connector from the rear of the light unit (see illustration).
27 Carefully release the relevant light unit clips, and ease the light unit out from the outside of the tailgate (see illustration).
28 Refitting is a reversal of removal.

Foglights

29 Chock the rear wheels then jack up the front of the vehicle and support it on axle stands (see *Jacking and vehicle support*). Release the front of the wheel arch liners from the front bumper by removing the fasteners.
30 On early models, reach up under the front bumper and disconnect the wiring from the foglight bulb holder, then undo the mounting screws and remove the foglight from the rear of the front bumper (see illustrations).
31 On later models, carefully unclip the plastic trim from around the foglight, then undo the mounting screws. Withdraw the foglight from the front bumper and disconnect the wiring connector (see illustrations).
32 Refitting is a reversal of removal. Alignment of the foglights can be adjusted by rotating the adjuster, which is accessible from the bottom of the foglight casing (see illustration).

7.30b Foglight retaining screws (arrowed)

7.31a Carefully unclip the trim panel…

8 Headlight beam alignment
– general information

1 Accurate adjustment of the headlight beam is only possible using optical beam-setting equipment, and this work should therefore be carried out by a Peugeot dealer or suitably-equipped workshop.
2 For reference, the vertical alignment of the headlights can be adjusted using a suitable-sized Allen key to rotate the adjuster assemblies accessible from the top of the headlight casing, whilst the horizontal alignment is adjusted by rotating the adjuster with a spanner/socket (see illustration).
3 On models equipped with headlight leveling, ensure the adjuster switch is set to position 0 before the headlights are adjusted.

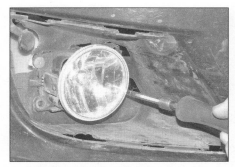

7.31b … undo the retaining screws…

7.31c … and disconnect the wiring connector

7.32 Foglight adjusting screw (arrowed)

8.2 Headlight adjusting screws (arrowed)

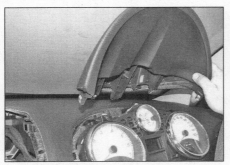

9.2 Unclip the instrument panel cover

9.3 Undo the two screws (arrowed)

9.4a Disconnect the wiring connector...

9.4b... and remove the instrument panel

10.2a Undo the two retaining screws...

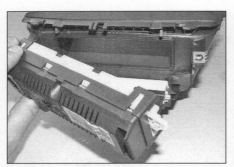

10.2b... and remove the display unit

11.2a Release the securing clip...

11.2b... and slide the centre socket out

11.3 Unclip the outer plastic from the trim

9 Instrument panel – removal and refitting

1 Disconnect the battery as described in Chapter 5A Section 4.
2 Carefully pull the instrument cover out from the facia panel, releasing it from the retaining clips **(see illustration)**.
3 Undo the two retaining screws from the top of the instrument panel **(see illustration)**.
4 Disconnect the panel wiring plug(s) as the unit is withdrawn from the facia. Should the instrument panel develop a fault, have the vehicle's self-diagnosis facility interrogated by a Peugeot dealer or suitably-equipped specialist **(see illustrations)**.
5 Refitting is a reversal of removal, ensuring that the locating lugs of the panel engage correctly.

10 Clock/multifunction unit – removal and refitting

1 Remove the upper centre panel as described in Chapter 11, Section 27.
2 Undo the two screws from the rear of the panel and unclip the display from the cowling **(see illustrations)**.
3 Refitting is a reversal of removal.

11 Accessory socket/cigarette lighter – removal and refitting

1 Unclip the centre console upper trim panel as described on Chapter 11, Section 26.
2 Release the retaining clips from inside the socket, and then slide the metal part of the socket out from the plastic outer part **(see illustrations)**.
3 Free the outer plastic part of the accessory socket from the console **(see illustration)**.
4 Refitting is a reversal of removal, ensuring the accessory socket is correctly assembled, and then refit the centre console upper trim panel.

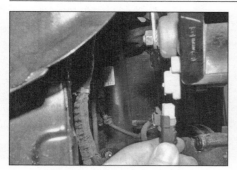

12.3 Disconnect the wiring connector

12.4 Undo the horn mounting bracket retaining nut

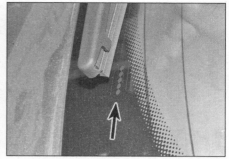

13.1 Wiper blade alignment mark (arrowed)

12 Horn – removal and refitting

1 The horn is located behind the front bumper, on the left-hand side.
2 Chock the rear wheels then jack up the front of the vehicle and support it on axle stands (see *Jacking and vehicle support*). Release the front of the wheel arch liner from the front bumper by removing the fasteners on the left-hand side.
3 Reach up under the front bumper and disconnect the wiring from the horn **(see illustration)**.
4 Undo the mounting nut and remove the horn from the inner wing panel **(see illustration)**.
5 Refitting is a reversal of removal.

13 Wiper arm – removal and refitting

Note: *The wiper arms are a very tight fit on their spindles and it is likely that a puller will be needed to remove them safely and without damage.*

1 Operate the wiper motor, and then switch it off so that the wiper arm returns to the at-rest position. Stick tape to the screen alongside the wiper blade to ensure correct refitment. There may also be an alignment mark provided on the windscreen **(see illustration)**.
2 On the front wiper arms, open the bonnet and remove the wiper arm spindle nut cover, then slacken and remove the spindle nut **(see illustrations)**.
3 On rear Hatchback wiper arms, lift up the wiper arm spindle nut cover, and then slacken and remove the spindle nut **(see illustration)**.
4 On rear Estate wiper arms, release the securing clip and withdraw the plastic wiper arm spindle nut cover, and then slacken and remove the spindle nut **(see illustration)**.
5 Lift the blade off the glass, and then pull the wiper arm off its spindle **(see illustration)**.
6 If the arm is very tight, free it from the spindle using a suitable puller **(see illustration)**.

13.2a Remove the cover...

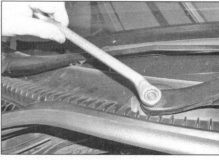

13.2b... and undo the wiper spindle nut

13.3 Lift up the cover and undo the wiper spindle nut

13.4 Release the locating peg to remove cover

13.5 Remove the wiper arm from the spindle

13.6 If the wiper arm is tight on the spindle, use a puller

14.4a Undo the mounting bolts (arrowed)...

14.4b... and remove the wiper linkage assembly

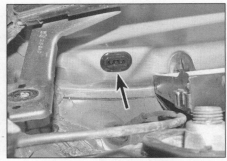

14.6 Locating grommet in bulkhead (arrowed)

7 Ensure that the wiper arm and spindle splines are clean and dry, then refit the arm to the spindle, aligning the wiper blade with the tape fitted on removal, or the alignment marks provided.

8 Refit the spindle nut, tightening it securely, and clip the nut cover back into position.

14 Windscreen wiper motor and linkage – removal and refitting

1 Remove the wiper arms (see Section 13).
2 Remove the scuttle grille panels as described in Chapter 11, Section 22.
3 If not already done, disconnect the wiper motor wiring plug connector.
4 Undo the bolts at each end of the wiper linkage assembly, and then withdraw the

assembly from the locating peg at the rear of the bulkhead (see illustrations).
5 At the time of writing, it would appear that the motor is not available separately from the linkage assembly. Check availability with your Peugeot dealer.
6 Refitting is a reversal of removal, ensuring all fasteners are securely tightened. Note that before tightening the linkage mounting bolts, ensure the assembly is correctly located in the bulkhead grommet (see illustration).

15 Tailgate window wiper motor – removal and refitting

Note: A pop rivet gun and suitable rivets will be required on refitting.

Removal

1 Ensure the ignition is turned off.
2 Remove the wiper arm (see Section 13).
3 Remove the tailgate lower trim panel as described in Chapter 11, Section 25.

Estate models

4 Disconnect the wiring connector from the wiper motor (see illustration).
5 Using a 7.5 mm drill, carefully drill the heads off the pop rivets securing the wiper motor bracket to the tailgate (see illustration). To prevent the rivets falling into the tailgate, position a cloth on either side of the motor.
Caution: Take care not to damage the motor and tailgate when drilling out the rivets.
6 With the three rivets removed, remove the wiper motor from the tailgate. Take care not to lose the collars from the motor mounting rubbers.
7 If required, remove the wiper motor sealing grommet from the tailgate glass.
8 Remove the cloths and recover the remnants of each rivet from the motor bracket/tailgate. Ensure all traces of rivet are removed.

Hatchback models

9 Disconnect the wiring connector from the wiper motor (see illustration).
10 Release the three securing clips and rotate the motor assembly anti-clockwise to release it from the tailgate (see illustrations).

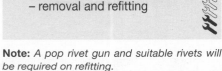

15.4 Disconnect the wiring connector

15.5 Drill out the three rivets (arrowed)

15.9 Disconnect the wiring connector

15.10a Release the securing clips...

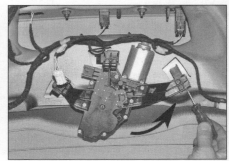

15.10b... and rotate the motor anti-clockwise (arrowed)...

15.11... and remove the wiper motor from the tailgate

16.4 Note the fitted position of the washer pipes

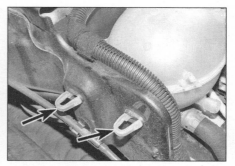

16.6 Coolant reservoir securing clips (arrowed)

11 Carefully withdraw the wiper assembly from the grommet in the tailgate glass **(see illustration)**.

12 If required, remove the wiper motor sealing grommet from the tailgate glass.

Refitting

13 Prior to refitting check the sealing grommet and rubber mountings for signs of damage or deterioration and renew as necessary.

14 Ensure the rubber grommet is correctly fitted to the tailgate glass and, where applicable, the rubber mountings and collars are correctly fitted to the motor mounting bracket.

15 Manoeuvre the wiper motor into position and secure it in position with new pop rivets (estate models) and securing clips (Hatchback models).

16 Reconnect the wiring connector to the motor then refit the trim panel to the tailgate. Turn on the ignition, then operate the wiper and allow it to stop in the park position.

17 Refit the wiper arm as described in Section 13.

16 Washer system components – removal and refitting

1 The washer reservoir is located behind the right-hand front wing and supplies both the windscreen and tailgate washers via

the same pump. On models equipped with headlight washers, the reservoir also supplies the headlight washer jets via an additional pump.

Washer fluid reservoir

2 Slacken the right-hand front roadwheel bolts. Jack up the front of the vehicle, and support it securely on axle stands (see *Jacking and vehicle support*). Remove the right-hand roadwheel.

3 Remove the front bumper as described in Chapter 11 Section 6.

4 Note the correct fitted location of the washer hoses (if necessary, mark them for identification purposes) then disconnect the hoses from the washer pump(s) **(see illustration)**.

5 Disconnect the wiring connector(s) from the washer pump(s).

6 Working in the engine compartment, unclip the coolant bottle from the inner wing panel and move it to one side **(see illustration)**.

7 Undo the two upper retaining nuts from the reservoir filler neck and withdraw the neck up from the lower part of the reservoir.

8 Slacken and remove the retaining bolt then move the reservoir downwards, and free it from the body panel. Manoeuvre it out from underneath the wing **(see illustration)**.

9 Refitting is the reverse of removal, ensuring that the hoses are securely reconnected. Refill the reservoir and check for leaks.

Washer pump

10 Proceed as described in paragraphs 2 to 5 and disconnect the hose(s) and wiring connector from the pump.

11 Position a container beneath the reservoir to catch the washer fluid as the pump is removed.

12 Carefully ease the pump out from the reservoir, and recover its sealing grommet **(see illustration)**. Wash off any spilt fluid with cold water.

13 Refitting is the reverse of removal, using a new sealing grommet if the original shows signs of damage or deterioration. Refill the reservoir and check the pump grommet for leaks on completion.

Windscreen washer jet

14 Open the bonnet. Prise up the centre pins a little, lever out the complete plastic expanding rivets, and remove the bonnet insulation panel to gain access to the base of the windscreen washer jets. Disconnect the washer hose(s) from the relevant jet, then depress the retaining clips and ease the jet out of position **(see illustration)**.

15 On refitting, clip the jet into the bonnet and reconnect the hose. The aim of the washer jets is not adjustable.

Tailgate washer jet

16 Remove the high-level stop-light unit as described in Section 7.

17 Disconnect the washer hose from the jet

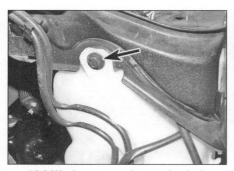

16.8 Washer reservoir securing bolt (arrowed)

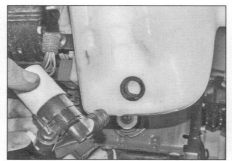

16.12 Ease the washer pump from the reservoir

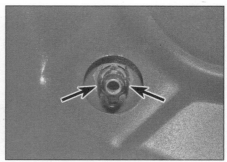

16.14 Squeeze together the clips (arrowed) and ease the jet from the bonnet

16.17 Carefully release the clips and remove the washer jet

17.3 Insert two pins into each side of the audio unit to release the clips, then pull the unit from place

17.4 Disconnect the wiring connectors

then free the jet from the light unit by releasing the two retaining clips **(see illustration)**. Recover the jet O-ring.

18 Refitting is the reverse of removal. Do not overtighten the light unit retaining nuts (where applicable), as the plastic is easily broken. The washer jet is not adjustable.

Headlight washer jet

19 Carefully prise the jet cover from the bumper, and pull the assembly out to its full extent.

20 Have an assistant grip the washer jet tube with a pair or grips, then depress the two retaining clips and pull the jet from the tube.

21 To remove the washer cylinders, remove the front bumper as described in Chapter 11 Section 6, then disconnect the washer tubing and unclip the cylinders.

22 Refitting is the reverse of removal.

17 Audio unit – removal and refitting

1 The following procedure is for the range of equipment fitted by Peugeot.

2 Ensure the audio unit and ignition is switched off.

3 Insert the removal clips into the holes at the sides of the unit until they release the retaining clips. Push the clips outwards to release the unit from the facia **(see illustration)**. If the removal clips are not available, insert a small

screwdriver/punch into the holes on each side of the unit to release the clips.

4 Once both retaining clips have been released, slide the audio unit out of position. Disconnect the wiring connections and aerial lead (where applicable) and remove the unit from the vehicle **(see illustration)**.

5 Prior to refitting, reset the unit retaining clips.

6 Securely reconnect the aerial lead (where applicable) and wiring connectors then slide the unit back into position, taking care not to trap the wiring.

18 Loudspeakers – removal and refitting

Removal

Front door speaker

1 Remove the door inner trim panel as described in Chapter 11 Section 12.

2 Slacken and remove the retaining screws then remove the speaker from the door, disconnecting the wiring connector as it becomes accessible **(see illustrations)**.

Front tweeter

3 Carefully prise the tweeter cover from the top of the facia and remove it along with the tweeter **(see illustration)**. Disconnect the wiring plug as it is withdrawn.

4 Rotate the tweeter speaker clockwise to free

it from the cover.

Rear speaker – 5-door models

5 Remove the door inner trim panel as described in Chapter 11 Section 12.

6 Undo the screws and remove the speaker from the door, disconnecting the wiring plug as it becomes accessible.

Rear speaker – 3-door models

7 Remove the rear side trim panel as described in Chapter 11, Section 25.

8 Pull the foam surround from place then slacken and remove the retaining screws, then remove the speaker from the body, disconnecting the wiring connector as it becomes accessible.

Refitting

9 Refitting is a reversal of removal. Ensure the trim panels are clipped securely in position and are correctly located behind the edges of the sealing strips.

19 Radio aerial – removal and refitting

1 The aerial mast is a screw-fit in its base and is easily removed.

2 To remove the complete aerial on models where the aerial is mounted on the rear of the roof, open the tailgate then free the tailgate sealing strip from the top of its aperture. Undo the two screw fixings and carefully lower the

18.2a Undo the screws (arrowed)…

18.2b… and remove the speaker

18.3 Unclip the speaker from the facia

rear of the headlining to gain access to the aerial nut.

3 Disconnect the wiring plug, undo the nut and remove the aerial.

4 Refitting is the reverse of removal.

20 Engine immobiliser and anti-theft alarm system – general information

Note: *This information is applicable only to the systems fitted by Peugeot as standard equipment.*

Engine immobiliser

1 An engine immobiliser system is fitted as standard to all models and the system is operated automatically every time the ignition key is inserted/removed.

2 The immobiliser system ensures the vehicle can only be started using the original Peugeot ignition key. The key contains an electronic chip (transponder), which is programmed with a code. When the key is inserted into the ignition switch it uses the current present in the sensor ring (which is fitted to the ignition switch housing) to send a signal to the immobiliser electronic control unit (ECU). The ECU is incorporated into the Built-in Systems Interface (BSI) unit (see Section 23). The ECU checks this code every time the ignition is switched on. If the key code does not match the ECU code, the ECU will disable the starter, fuel and ignition (as applicable) to prevent the engine being started.

3 When the vehicle is new, a confidential security card is supplied along with the other vehicle documentation. This card contains the security code, which your Peugeot dealer requires when carrying out any work on the immobiliser system. Keep this card in a safe place at home; never store it in the vehicle. If the ignition key is lost, a new one can be obtained from a Peugeot dealer. Take the confidential security card and all the existing keys along to your Peugeot dealer who will supply a new key and reprogramme all the keys with a new security code; this will render the lost key useless.

Caution: Without the confidential security card, it will not be possible to have the keys and immobiliser system reprogrammed.

4 Any problems with the engine immobiliser system should be referred to a Peugeot dealer.

Anti-theft alarm system

5 Most models covered in this manual were also equipped with an anti-theft alarm system as standard equipment. The system was available as a option on all other models. The alarm is automatically armed when the deadlocking is set using the remote central locking transmitter and is disarmed when the doors are unlocked using the remote transmitter. The alarm system has switches on the bonnet, tailgate and each of the doors and also has ultrasonic sensing, which detects

movement inside the vehicle via sensors mounted on either side of the vehicle interior.

6 When the system is activated, the direction indicators will flash continuously for two seconds and the indicator light on the alarm switch, fitted to the rear section of the centre console, will flash continuously. **Note:** *If the bonnet, tailgate or one of the doors are not properly closed when the alarm is set, the siren will sound briefly. If the bonnet/tailgate/ door (as applicable) is properly closed within 45 seconds the alarm will be armed. If not the alarm will remain disarmed.*

7 If for some reason the remote central locking transmitter fails whilst the alarm is armed, the alarm can be disarmed using the key. To do this, open the door with the key, and then enter the vehicle, noting that the alarm will sound as the door is opened. Insert the key and switch on the ignition, the immobiliser will recognise the key and will switch off the alarm.

8 If required, the ultrasonic sensing facility of the alarm can be switched off whilst retaining the switched side of the system. To switch off the ultrasonic sensing, with the ignition switched off, depress the alarm switch (mounted on the facia above the centre air vents) until the alarm indicator light on the switch is continuously lit. Get out of the vehicle and operate the deadlocking function using the remote transmitter to arm the alarm. The direction indicators will flash as normal but only the switched (door, tailgate and bonnet) side of the alarm system will be operational. This facility is useful, as it allows you to leave the windows/sunroof open, and still arm the alarm. If the windows/sunroof are left open with the ultrasonic sensing not switched off, the alarm may be falsely triggered by a gust of wind.

9 Prior to Disconnecting the battery13,6, the alarm system should be disabled; this will prevent the alarm sounding when the battery is disconnected/reconnected. To do this, switch on the ignition then immediately depress and hold the alarm switch for two seconds; the indicator light on the switch should then flash rapidly for approximately three seconds indicating the alarm has been disabled. Switch off the ignition and disconnect the battery.

10 Once the battery has been reconnected, operate the deadlocking with the remote transmitter then unlock the vehicle. The alarm will be set as normal; the next time the deadlocking is set.

11 Should the alarm system become faulty, the vehicle should be taken to a Peugeot dealer for examination.

21 Airbag system – general information and precautions

1 All models in the range are fitted with a driver's airbag, passenger's airbag, side front airbags, and side curtain airbags.

2 The airbag system is triggered in the event of

a heavy frontal impact above a predetermined force, depending on the point of impact. The airbag is then inflated within milliseconds, and forms a safety cushion between the cabin occupants and the vehicle interior. This prevents contact between the upper body and vehicle interior, and therefore greatly reduces the risk of injury. The airbag then deflates almost immediately. The control unit also operates the front seat belt tensioner mechanisms at the same time (see Chapter 11).

3 The side airbags are fitted to the seat back of each front seat. Each airbag unit has its own lateral acceleration sensor, which is mounted onto the vehicle body on the outside of each front seat. The side airbags are not linked in anyway and operate individually.

4 The curtain airbags are fitted behind the windscreen pillars and headlining on each side of the passenger cabin.

5 Every time the ignition is switched on, the airbag control unit performs a self-test. The self-test takes approximately six seconds and during this time the warning light in the instrument panel will be illuminated. After the self-test is complete, the warning light will go out (unless the passenger airbag unit has been deactivated – see paragraph 6). If the warning light fails to come on, remains illuminated after the self-test period, or comes on at any time when the vehicle is being driven, there is a fault in the airbag system. The vehicle should be taken to a Peugeot dealer for examination at the earliest possible opportunity.

6 Most vehicles with a passenger airbag are equipped with a disabling switch fitted to the centre console. The switch is operated using the ignition key and switches off the passenger airbag (it is not possible to disable the driver's or side/curtain airbags) to enable a rear-facing child seat to be installed in the passenger seat. Whilst the passenger airbag is disabled, the airbag warning light on the instrument panel will remain illuminated all the time.

 Warning: Before carrying out any operations on the airbag system, disconnect the battery (see Chapter 5A Section 4) and wait at least two minutes. Remove the centre console (see Chapter 11 Section 26) and then release the retaining clip and disconnect the wiring connector(s) from the airbag control unit. When the operations are complete, securely reconnect the control unit then refit the centre console. Make sure no one is inside the vehicle when the battery is reconnected then, with the driver's door open, switch the ignition on from outside vehicle and check the operation of the airbag warning light.

● Do not subject the area of the body around the control unit to any form of shock, which could trigger the system.

● Note that the airbags must not be subjected to temperatures in excess of 100°C. When the airbag is removed, ensure that it is stored the correct way up to prevent possible inflation.

22.3 Airbag control unit (arrowed)

22.4a Using a long screwdriver...

22.4b... release the securing clip (arrowed)

● Do not allow any solvents or cleaning agents to contact the airbag assemblies. They must be cleaned using only a damp cloth.
● The airbags and control unit are both sensitive to impact. If either is dropped or damaged they should be renewed.
● Disconnect the airbag control unit wiring connector prior to using arc welding equipment on the vehicle.
● Never fit a rear-facing child seat to the front passenger seat unless the passenger airbag has been disabled (paragraph 6).
● Peugeot recommend that the airbag units be renewed every ten years.

22 Airbag system components – removal and refitting

1 Refer to the precautions given in Section 21 before carrying out the following operations.
2 Before carrying out work on any of the components in the airbag system, disconnect the battery and wait at least 5 minutes.
3 Remove the centre console as described in Chapter 11 Section 26, and disconnect the wiring connectors from the airbag control unit, which is situated just behind the gear lever housing (see illustration).

Driver's airbag

4 With the wheel in the straight-ahead position and the steering lock engaged, insert a thin flat-bladed screwdriver into the hole in the bottom of the steering wheel boss,

and push to release the retaining clip (see illustrations).
5 Carefully lift the airbag unit away from the wheel, disconnecting the wiring connectors as they become accessible, noting their fitted positions (see illustrations).

⚠ **Warning: Do not knock or drop the airbag unit and store it the correct way up with its padded surface uppermost.**

6 Securely reconnect the wiring connectors then seat the airbag unit in the steering wheel, ensuring the wiring does not become trapped. Note that the main connectors are colour-coded to correspond with their respective sockets.
7 Fit the airbag unit; press it into place until the retaining clip engages.
8 Make sure no one is inside the vehicle then reconnect the battery. With the driver's door

open, switch the ignition on from outside vehicle and check the operation of the warning light.

Passenger airbag

9 Remove the glovebox assembly, as described in Chapter 11 Section 27.
10 Working up under the facia panel, release the air vent ducting at each end and remove it from below the passenger airbag.
11 Disconnect the two wiring plug connectors for the airbag, located at the right-hand side of the airbag unit (see illustration). Release the wiring harness from any retaining clips, noting their fitted position and harness routing.
12 Undo the retaining screw from the mounting bracket on the facia crossmember (see illustration).
13 Undo the four securing screws, and remove the airbag from under the facia(see illustration).

22.5a Release the securing clip (arrowed)...

22.5b... and disconnect the wiring connectors

22.11 Passenger airbag wiring connectors (arrowed)

22.12 Undo the retaining bolt (arrowed)

22.13 Passenger airbag retaining screws (arrowed)

22.17 Airbag control unit retaining nuts (arrowed)

22.25 Side airbag acceleration sensor (arrowed)

22.32 Figure 0 should be viewed through the white circle (arrowed)

14 Fit the airbag unit under the facia panel, ensuring the wiring is correctly routed, and the screws are securely tightened.

15 The remainder of refitting is the reverse of removal. On completion, securely reconnect the airbag control unit wiring connector(s). Refit the centre console. Make sure no one is inside the vehicle then reconnect the battery. With the driver's door open, switch the ignition on from outside vehicle and check the operation of the warning light.

Airbag control unit

16 Disconnect the battery (see Chapter 5A Section 4) and wait at least five minutes. Remove the centre console (see Chapter 11 Section 26), then release the retaining clip and disconnect the wiring connectors from the airbag control unit.

17 Unscrew the retaining nuts then remove the control unit from the vehicle (see illustration).

18 Refit the control unit, making sure the arrow on the top of the unit is pointing towards the front of the vehicle (see illustration 22.16). Refit the control unit retaining nuts and tighten them to the specified torque.

19 Securely reconnect the airbag control unit wiring connectors.

20 Refit the centre console. Make sure no one is inside the vehicle, and then reconnect the battery. With the driver's door open, switch the ignition on from outside vehicle and check the operation of the warning light.

Side airbag

21 Removal and refitting of the side airbag

units should be entrusted to a Peugeot dealer. The seat must be dismantled to enable the airbag unit to removed/refitted. Remove the front seat as described in Chapter 11 Section 23.

Side airbag acceleration sensor

22 There are two sensors fitted, one at each side of the vehicle. Remove the relevant front seat as described in Chapter 11 Section 23.

23 Referring to Section of Chapter 11, on three-door models remove the rear side trim panel, and on five-door models remove the B-pillar upper and lower trim panels.

24 On all models, remove the sill trim.

25 Peel back the carpet to gain access to the side airbag acceleration sensor (see illustration).

26 Disconnect the wiring connector then undo the retaining nut and remove the sensor from the vehicle.

27 Refitting is the reverse of removal, tightening the acceleration sensor nut to the specified torque.

Curtain airbag

28 Removal and refitting of the curtain airbag units should be entrusted to a Peugeot dealer. The headlining must be partially removed to enable the airbag unit to removed/refitted.

Steering column airbag rotary contact switch

29 Remove the driver's airbag as described at the beginning of this Section.

30 Remove the steering wheel as described in Chapter 10 Section 17.

31 Remove the steering column lower and upper shrouds as described in Chapter 11, Section 27.

32 With the steering in the straight-ahead position, there should be the figure 0 viewed through the white circle on the bottom right of the switch unit (see illustration).

33 Slacken the switch assembly retaining clamp, then using a small screwdriver, carefully prise the retaining catches away from the column and lift the switch assembly from place (see illustrations).
Caution: Take great care to not damage the switch assembly retaining catches.

34 Disconnect the wiring connectors from the rear of the contact switch assembly as the switch is removed (see illustration).

35 If required, remove the retaining screws and slide the switches out from the centre rotary switch unit, with reference to Section 4.

36 Although refitting is a reversal of removal, the airbag contact unit built into the switch assembly must be set in the correct position as noted on removal, with the figure 0 viewed through the white circle on the bottom right of the switch unit (see illustration 22.31). If it is not aligned, press the centre of the switch in, and turn it clockwise (without forcing) until the figure 0 appears.

37 Units supplied by other manufacturers may be supplied with the contact ring immobilised in the correct position with a self-adhesive label which should be removed just prior to steering wheel refitment.

22.33a Undo the retaining clamp bolt (arrowed)...

22.33b... and remove the switch assembly

22.34 Disconnect the wiring connectors

23.5 Unclip the wiring connectors from the facia

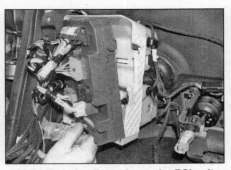

23.6 Lift and pull to release the BSI unit

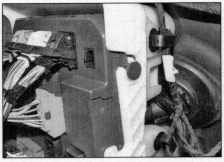

23.8 Make sure the unit is located securely on refitting

23 Built-in systems interface (BSI) unit/fusebox – general, removal and refitting

General information

1 The Built-in Systems Interface (BSI) unit is an electronic control unit, which controls a variety of functions normally controlled by individual control units and relays. The BSI unit is located behind the glovebox assembly on the passenger's side of the facia where it is situated directly above the fusebox. The BSI unit controls the following functions (not all functions are fitted to all models).

● Direction indicator/hazard warning lights.
● Windscreen/tailgate wiper motors.
● Rear screen heating element.
● Immobiliser system.
● Anti-theft alarm system.
● Lights on/ignition key warning buzzer.
● Central locking/deadlocking, including the remote central locking receiver.
● Door open indicator.
● Courtesy light delay timer.
● Automatic transmission audible warning system.

2 Should any of the above functions become faulty, first check the condition of the fuses. If this fails to locate the problem, take the vehicle to a Peugeot dealer for testing. The only satisfactory way to test the BSI unit is by substitution with another unit which is known to be functioning correctly.

Removal

3 Disconnect the battery (see Chapter 5A Section 4).

4 Remove the passenger side glovebox assembly, as described in Section of Chapter 11.

5 Unclip the wiring connectors and loom from the facia panel, noting their fitted positions **(see illustration)**.

6 Lift the BSI unit/fusebox and pull it forwards to unclip it from the plastic housing **(see illustration)**.

7 Note their fitted positions, then release the retaining clips then disconnect all the wiring connectors and remove the BSI unit from the vehicle. Note that there are several different designs of locking catches for the various connectors. Take your time to study the wiring connectors, and release them without using excessive force as they are easily damaged.

Refitting

8 Refitting is the reverse of removal, ensuring the BSI unit/fusebox is located securely in the housing **(see illustration)**. Check the wiring connectors are all securely reconnected. Note that the connector colours are listed adjacent to their respective sockets on the BSI.

Peugeot 207 wiring diagrams

Diagram 1

 WARNING: This vehicle is fitted with a supplemental restraint system (SRS) consisting of a combination of driver (and passenger) airbag(s), side impact protection airbags and seatbelt pre-tensioners. The use of electrical test equipment on any SRS wiring systems may cause the seatbelt pre-tensioners to abruptly retract and airbags to explosively deploy, resulting in potentially severe personal injury. Extreme care should be taken to correctly identify any circuits to be tested to avoid choosing any of the SRS wiring in error.
For further information see airbag system precautions in body electrical systems chapter.
Note: The SRS wiring harness can normally be identified by yellow and/or orange harness or harness connectors.

The prime method of wire identification is by the number code printed on each wire. Additionally, the wires can be identified by using the terminal pin numbers (moulded into each component or connector and shown in the diagrams).
To relate each diagram to the vehicle wiring, locate the relevant component or connector illustrated and find the wire(s) connected to the terminal pin(s) as shown in the diagram.
Caution: Whilst a number (indicating the function of that wire) may be printed on each wire, this is not always the case, and in such instances, this is reflected by the absence of such wire numbering on our diagrams. Similarly, numbering of the connector/component terminal pins is not always available from the manufacturers' source information and may also be missing from our diagrams.

Key to symbols

Solenoid actuator	Bulb	Wire splice, soldered joint, or unspecified connector
Earth point	Switch	Connecting wires
Multiplexed network — 90186	Fuse F26	Diode
Wire identification and colour — MC50A —	Maxifuse fusible link MF1	Light-emitting diode
Dashed outline denotes part of a larger item, containing in this case an electronic or solid state device.	Resistor	Item number 12
	Variable resistor	Motor/pump M
16GR - 16 pin grey connector, pins 5 & 9	Variable resistor	Heating element

Engine fusebox 4

Fuse	Rating	Circuit protected
F1	20A	Engine management
F2	15A	Horn
F3	10A	Front/rear screen washer pump
F4	20A	Headlight washer pump
F5	15A	Fuel gauge, fuel pump
F6	10A	Vehicle speed sensor
F7	20A	Electric power steering, headlight levelling, dip beam relay
F8	15A	Starter
F9	10A	ABS/ESP, stop light switch
F10	30A	Engine management
F11	40A	Air conditioning
F12	30A	Front wiper
F13	40A	Built-in systems interface
F14	-	Spare
F15	10A	RH headlight main beam
F16	10A	LH headlight main beam
F17	15A	LH headlight dip beam
F18	15A	RH headlight dip beam

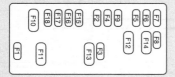

Built-in systems interface 6

Fuse	Rating	Circuit protected
F1	5A	Rear wiper motor
F2	-	Spare
F3	5A	SRS
F4	10A	Diagnostic connector, fuel additive pump, clutch switch, steering column control unit, air conditioning, photochromic rear view mirror
F5	30A	Sunroof, rear electric windows, electric window switches
F6	30A	Front electric windows
F7	5A	Clock, glovebox light
F8	20A	Tyre pressure monitor, clock, steering column control unit, audio system, telephone, multifunction screen
F9	30A	Front accessory socket
F10	15A	Dip beam relay
F11	15A	Diagnostic connector, ignition switch
F12	15A	Fuel injection, audio amplifier, rain & light sensor
F13	5A	Stop light switch, ABS
F14	15A	Instrument panel, parking assistance, SRS, hands-free kit, air conditioning, seatbelt warning light, headlight levelling
F15	30A	Central locking
F16	-	Spare
F17	40A	Electric mirrors, heated rear window

H47007

Colour codes

BA	White	OR	Orange
BE	Blue	RG	Red
BG	Beige	RS	Pink
GR	Grey	VE	Green
JN	Yellow	VI	Mauve
MR	Brown	VJ	Green/
NR	Black		Yellow

Key to items

1 Battery
2 Starter motor
3 Alternator
4 Engine fusebox
5 Ignition switch
6 Built-in systems interface
7 Instrument cluster
8 Engine management control unit
9 Horn
10 Steering column control unit
11 Cooling fan control unit
12 Engine coolant temperature sensor
13 Air conditioning pressostat
14 Engine cooling fan

Diagram 2

H47008

Typical starting & charging

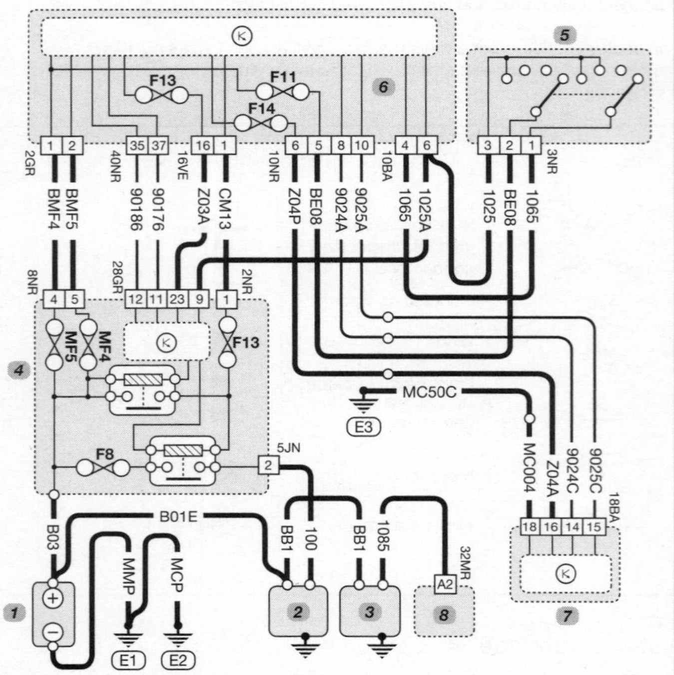

Typical horn

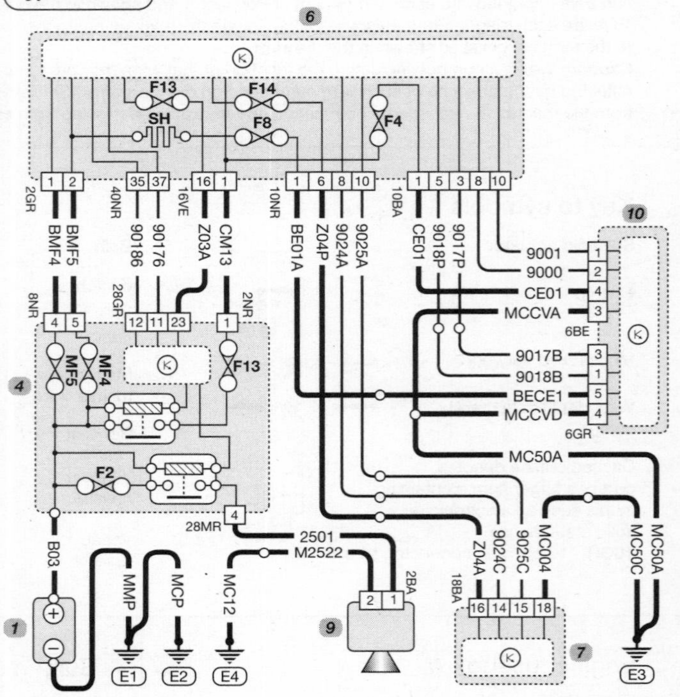

Typical engine cooling fan

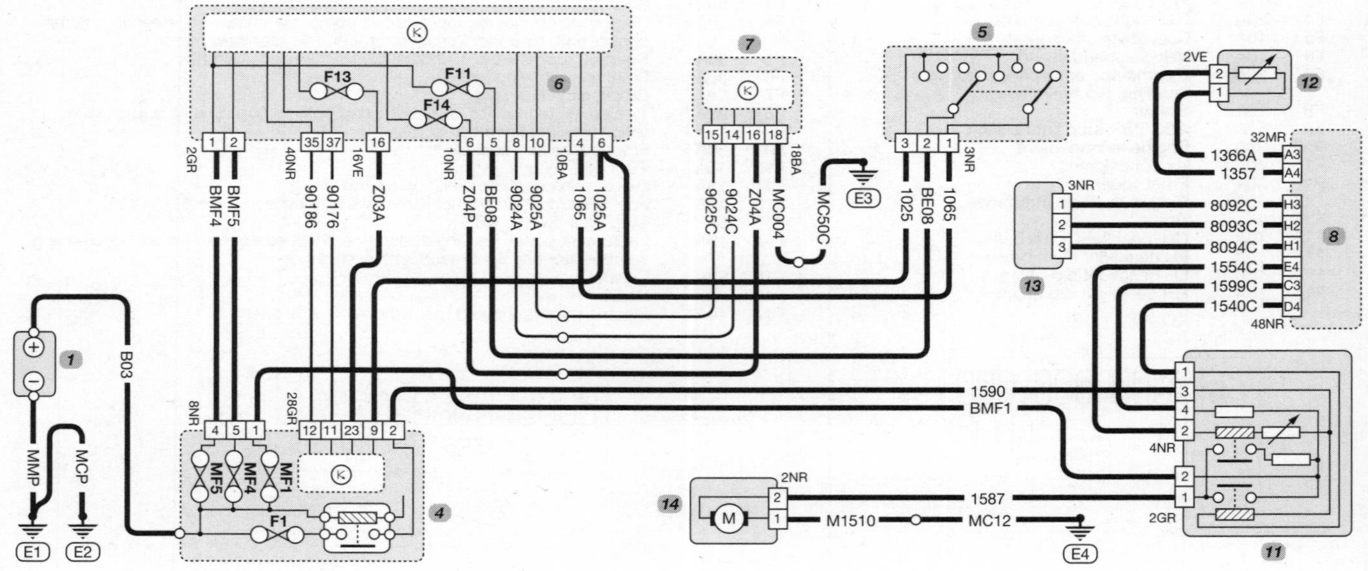

Colour codes

BA	White	**OR**	Orange
BE	Blue	**RG**	Red
BG	Beige	**RS**	Pink
GR	Grey	**VE**	Green
JN	Yellow	**VI**	Mauve
MR	Brown	**VJ**	Green/
NR	Black		Yellow

Key to items

1 Battery
4 Engine fusebox
6 Built-in systems interface
7 Instrument cluster
8 Engine management control unit
10 Steering column control unit
17 High level brake light
18 Stop light switch
19 Reversing light switch
20 LH rear light unit
  a = reversing light
  b = stop light
  c = tail light
21 RH rear light unit
  (as above)
22 LH number plate light
23 RH number plate light
24 LH front light unit
  a = main beam
  b = side light
  c = dip beam
25 RH front light unit
  (as above)
26 Rain/light sensor

Diagram 3

H47009

Typical stop & reversing lights

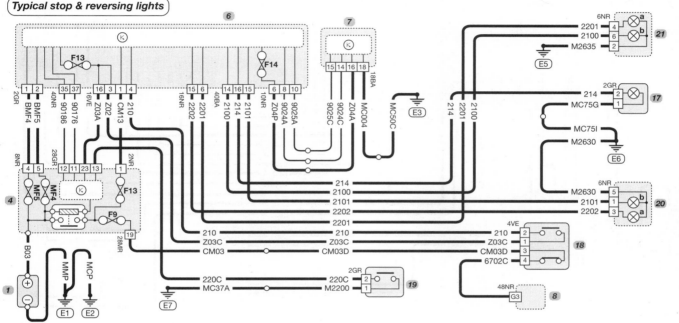

Typical side, tail, number plate & headlights

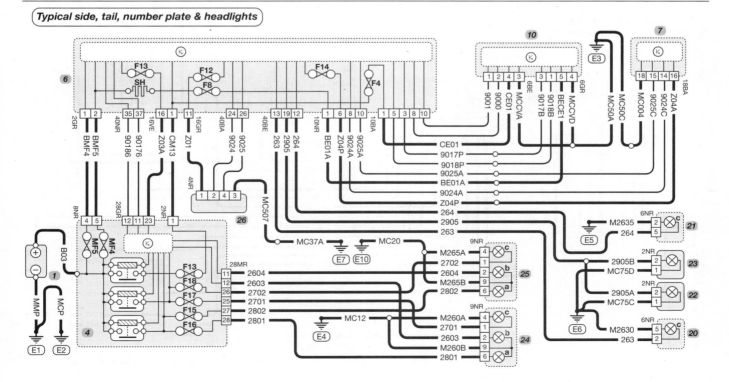

Colour codes

BA	White	OR	Orange
BE	Blue	RG	Red
BG	Beige	RS	Pink
GR	Grey	VE	Green
JN	Yellow	VI	Mauve
MR	Brown	VJ	Green/
NR	Black		Yellow

Key to items

1 Battery
4 Engine fusebox
6 Built-in systems interface
7 Instrument cluster
10 Steering column control unit
20 LH rear light unit
  d = fog light
  e = direction indicator
21 RH rear light unit
  (as above)
24 LH front light unit
  d = direction indicator
25 RH front light unit
  (as above)
28 LH front fog light
29 RH front fog light
30 LH mirror assembly
  a = direction indicator side repeater
31 RH mirror assembly
  a = direction indicator side repeater
32 Hazard warning switch

Diagram 4

H47010

Typical front & rear fog lights

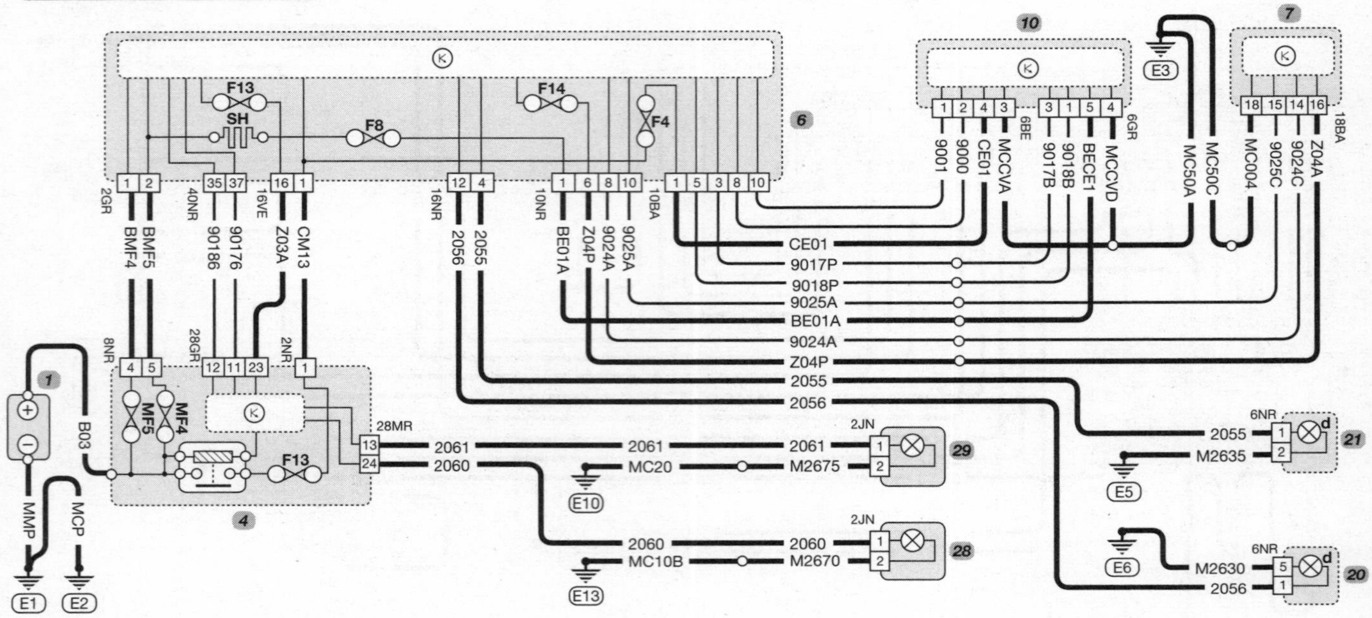

Typical direction indicator & hazard warning lights

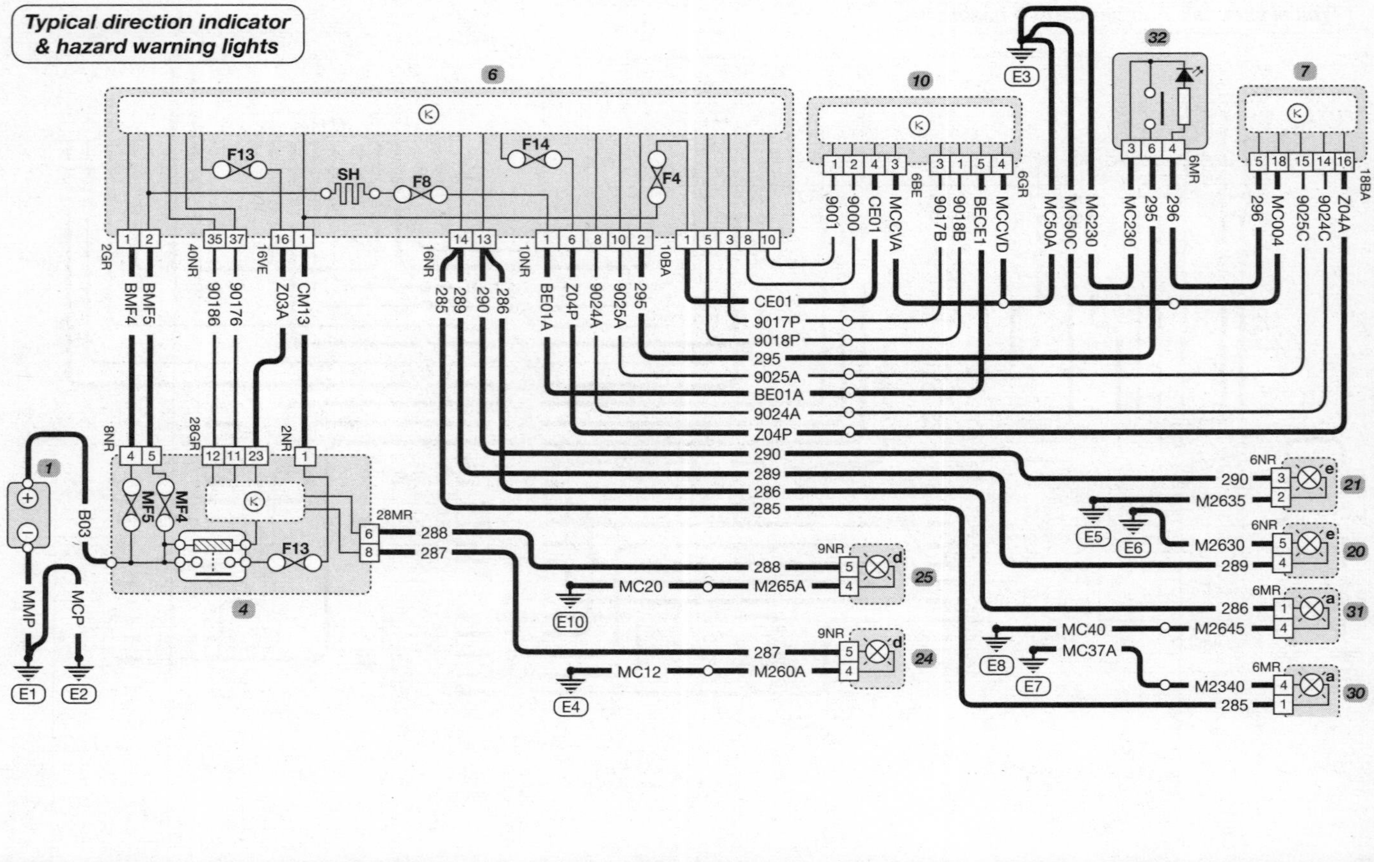

Colour codes

BA	White	OR	Orange
BE	Blue	RG	Red
BG	Beige	RS	Pink
GR	Grey	VE	Green
JN	Yellow	VI	Mauve
MR	Brown	VJ	Green/
NR	Black		Yellow

Key to items

1 Battery
4 Engine fusebox
5 Ignition switch
6 Built-in systems interface
7 Instrument cluster
10 Steering column control unit
26 Rain/light sensor

35 Front courtesy light
36 Rear courtesy light
37 LH vanity mirror light
38 RH vanity mirror light
39 Glovebox light/switch
40 Luggage compartment light
41 Front wiper motor

42 Rear wiper motor
43 Front/rear washer pump
44 Washer level sensor
45 Headlight washer pump

Diagram 5

H47011

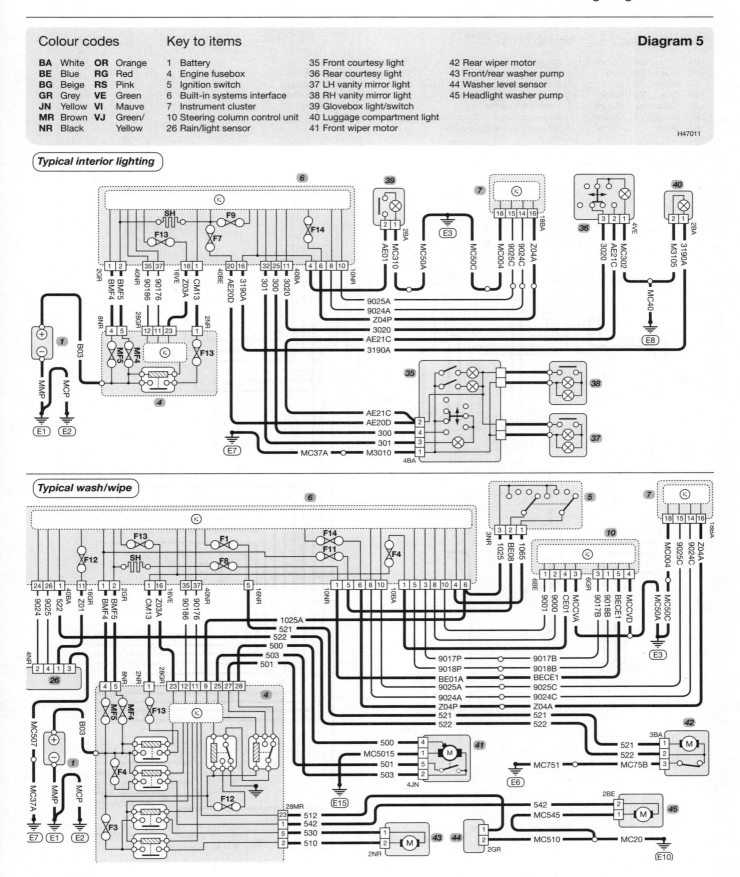

Typical interior lighting

Typical wash/wipe

Colour codes

BA	White	OR	Orange
BE	Blue	RG	Red
BG	Beige	RS	Pink
GR	Grey	VE	Green
JN	Yellow	VI	Mauve
MR	Brown	VJ	Green/
NR	Black		Yellow

Key to items

1 Battery
4 Engine fusebox
5 Ignition switch
6 Built-in systems interface
7 Instrument cluster
8 Engine management control unit
13 Air conditioning pressostat

48 ESP control unit
49 Evaporator thermistor
50 Air conditioning compressor
51 Air conditioning control panel
52 Heater blower resistors
53 Blower motor

Diagram 6

H47012

Typical air conditioning

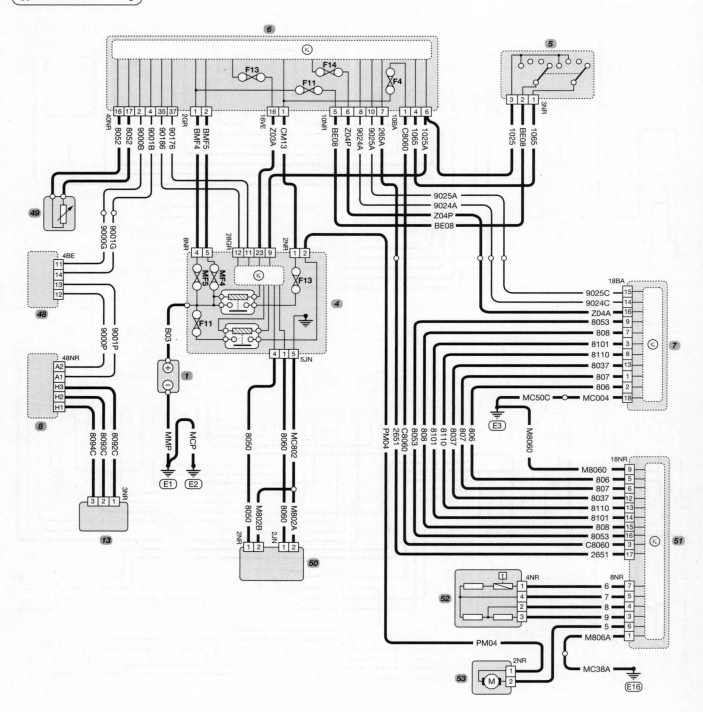

Colour codes

BA	White	OR	Orange
BE	Blue	RG	Red
BG	Beige	RS	Pink
GR	Grey	VE	Green
JN	Yellow	VI	Mauve
MR	Brown	VJ	Green/
NR	Black		Yellow

Key to items

1 Battery
4 Engine fusebox
5 Ignition switch
6 Built-in systems interface
7 Instrument cluster
8 Engine management control unit
12 Engine coolant temperature sensor

48 ESP control unit
51 Air conditioning control panel
55 Low brake fluid switch
56 Handrake switch
57 Oil pressure switch
58 Oil level sensor
59 Fuel gauge sender/fuel pump

60 Cigar lighter
61 Clock
62 Electric window/mirror control switch
63 LH door window control switch
64 LH window motor
65 RH window motor

Diagram 7

H47013

Typical instrument cluster, clock & cigar lighter

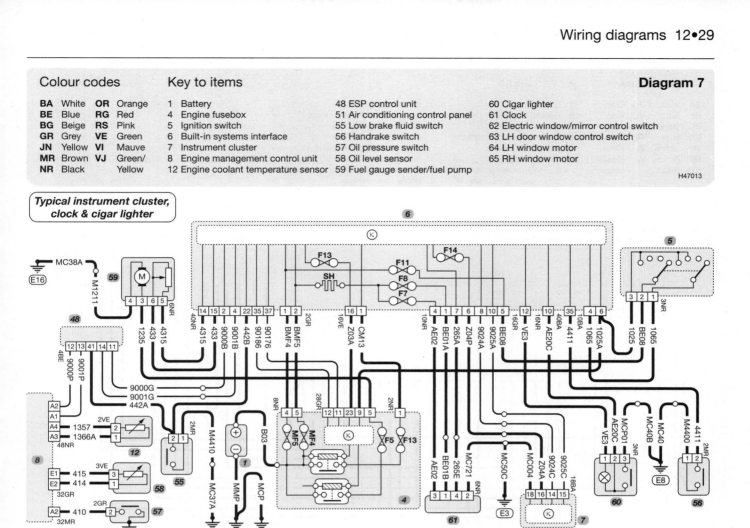

Typical electric windows

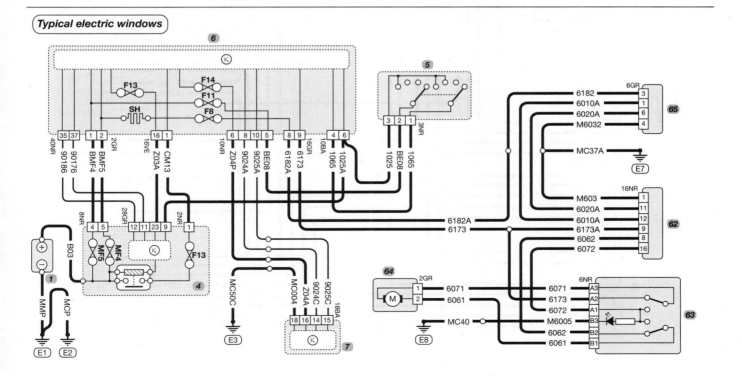

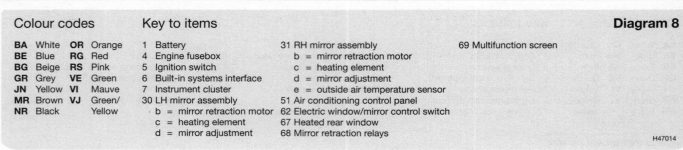

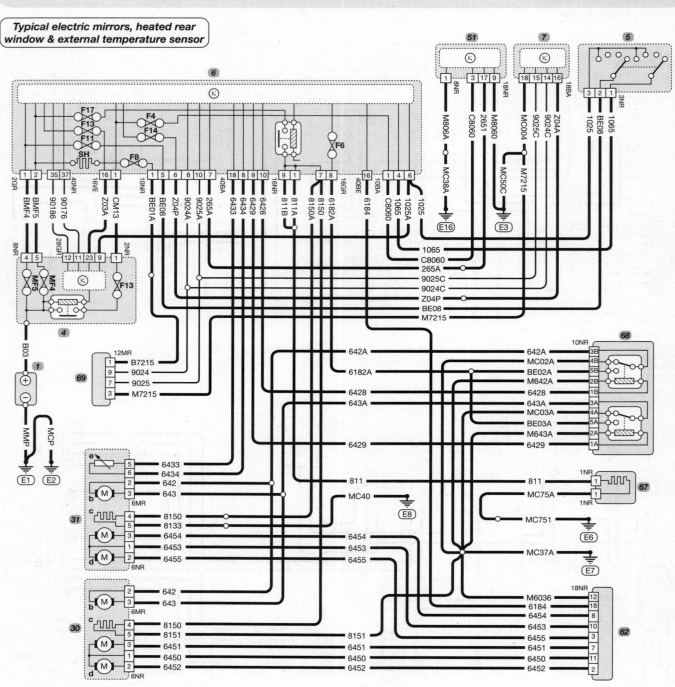

Colour codes

BA	White	OR	Orange
BE	Blue	RG	Red
BG	Beige	RS	Pink
GR	Grey	VE	Green
JN	Yellow	VI	Mauve
MR	Brown	VJ	Green/
NR	Black		Yellow

Key to items

1 Battery
4 Engine fusebox
5 Ignition switch
6 Built-in systems interface
7 Instrument cluster
73 Door lock master switch
74 Child lock switch

75 Front LH door lock
76 Rear LH door lock
77 Front RH door lock
78 Rear RH door lock
79 Tailgate lock
80 Tailgate release switch

Diagram 9

H47015

Typical central locking

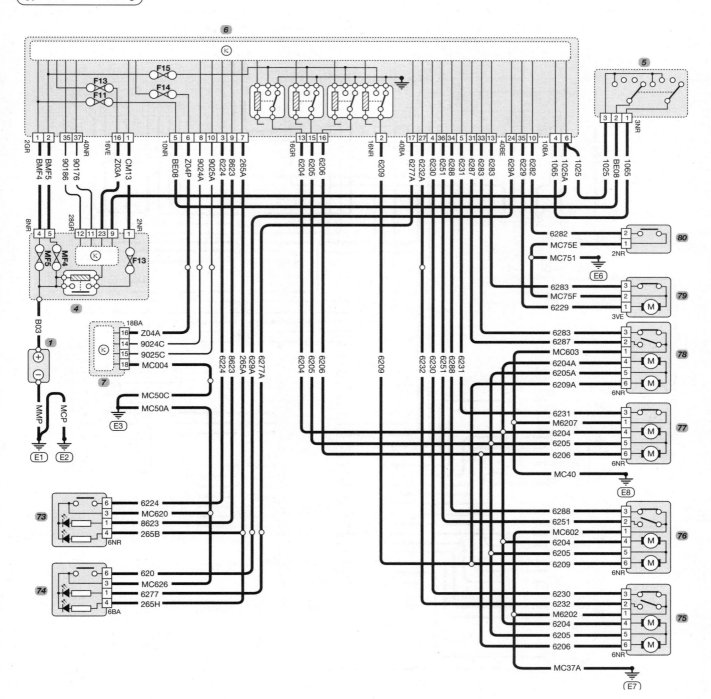

Colour codes

BA	White	OR	Orange
BE	Blue	RG	Red
BG	Beige	RS	Pink
GR	Grey	VE	Green
JN	Yellow	VI	Mauve
MR	Brown	VJ	Green/
NR	Black		Yellow

Key to items

1 Battery
4 Engine fusebox
5 Ignition switch
6 Built-in systems interface
10 Steering column control unit
69 Multifunction screen
83 Audio unit
84 CD player
85 Hands free kit
86 Microphone
87 Aerial
88 Radio aerial amplifier
89 Rear window aerial
90 LH rear speaker
91 LH door speaker
92 LH tweeter
93 RH tweeter
94 RH front door speaker
95 RH rear speaker
96 Aerial switching control unit

Diagram 10

H47016

Typical audio system

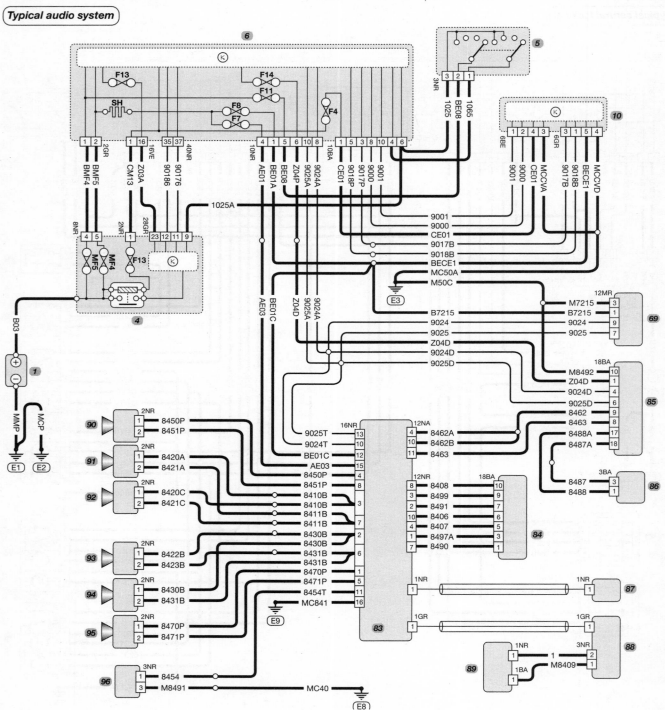

Dimensions and weights

Note: *All figures are approximate, and may vary according to model. Refer to manufacturer's data for exact figures.*

Dimensions

	Hatchback	Estate
Overall length	4212 mm	4428 mm
Overall width (excluding mirrors)	1762 mm	1762 mm
Overall height (unladen)	1530 mm	1580 mm
Wheelbase	2608 mm	2708 mm

Weights

Kerb weight:	
Petrol engine models:	
1.4 litre engine	1234 kg
1.6 litre engine	1268 kg
Diesel engine models:	
1.4 litre engine	1271 kg
1.6 litre engine	1325 kg
Maximum gross vehicle weight: *	
Petrol engine models:	
1.4 litre engine	1659 kg
1.6 litre engine	1693 kg
Diesel engine models:	
1.4 litre engine	1696 kg
1.6 litre engine	1770 kg
Maximum gross train (vehicle and trailer) weight: *	
Petrol engine models:	
1.4 litre engine	2659 kg
1.6 litre engine	2893 kg
Diesel engine models:	
1.4 litre engine	2836 kg
1.6 litre engine	3130 kg
Maximum towing weight: †	
Unbraked trailer:	
Petrol engine models:	
1.4 litre engine	590 kg
1.6 litre engine	610 kg
Diesel engine models:	
1.4 litre engine	635 kg
1.6 litre engine	655 kg
Braked trailer:	
Petrol engine models	1200 kg
Diesel engine models:	
1.4 litre engine	1140 kg
1.6 litre engine	1360 kg

* Refer to the Vehicle Identification Plate for the exact figures for your vehicle – see *Vehicle identification numbers*
† Ensure the combined weight of the trailer and vehicle never exceeds the gross train weight when towing.

Fuel economy

Although depreciation is still the biggest part of the cost of motoring for most car owners, the cost of fuel is more immediately noticeable. These pages give some tips on how to get the best fuel economy.

Working it out

Manufacturer's figures

Car manufacturers are required by law to provide fuel consumption information on all new vehicles sold. These 'official' figures are obtained by simulating various driving conditions on a rolling road or a test track. Real life conditions are different, so the fuel consumption actually achieved may not bear much resemblance to the quoted figures.

How to calculate it

Many cars now have trip computers which will

display fuel consumption, both instantaneous and average. Refer to the owner's handbook for details of how to use these.

To calculate consumption yourself (and maybe to check that the trip computer is accurate), proceed as follows.

1. Fill up with fuel and note the mileage, or zero the trip recorder.
2. Drive as usual until you need to fill up again.
3. Note the amount of fuel required to refill the tank, and the mileage covered since the previous fill-up.
4. Divide the mileage by the amount of fuel used to obtain the consumption figure.

For example:

Mileage at first fill-up (a) = 27,903
Mileage at second fill-up (b) = 28,346
Mileage covered (b - a) = 443
Fuel required at second fill-up = 48.6 litres

The half-completed changeover to metric units in the UK means that we buy our fuel

in litres, measure distances in miles and talk about fuel consumption in miles per gallon. There are two ways round this: the first is to convert the litres to gallons before doing the calculation (by dividing by 4.546, or see Table 1). So in the example:

48.6 litres ÷ 4.546 = 10.69 gallons
443 miles ÷ 10.69 gallons = 41.4 mpg

The second way is to calculate the consumption in miles per litre, then multiply that figure by 4.546 (or see Table 2).

So in the example, fuel consumption is:

443 miles ÷ 48.6 litres = 9.1 mpl
9.1 mpl x 4.546 = 41.4 mpg

The rest of Europe expresses fuel consumption in litres of fuel required to travel 100 km (l/100 km). For interest, the conversions are given in Table 3. In practice it doesn't matter what units you use, provided you know what your normal consumption is and can spot if it's getting better or worse.

Table 1: conversion of litres to Imperial gallons

litres	1	2	3	4	5	10	20	30	40	50	60	70
gallons	0.22	0.44	0.66	0.88	1.10	2.24	4.49	6.73	8.98	11.22	13.47	15.71

Table 2: conversion of miles per litre to miles per gallon

miles per litre	5	6	7	8	9	10	11	12	13	14
miles per gallon	23	27	32	36	41	46	50	55	59	64

Table 3: conversion of litres per 100 km to miles per gallon

litres per 100 km	4	4.5	5	5.5	6	6.5	7	8	9	10
miles per gallon	71	63	56	51	47	43	40	35	31	28

Maintenance

A well-maintained car uses less fuel and creates less pollution. In particular:

Filters

Change air and fuel filters at the specified intervals.

Oil

Use a good quality oil of the lowest viscosity specified by the vehicle manufacturer (see *Lubricants and fluids*). Check the level often and be careful not to overfill.

Spark plugs

When applicable, renew at the specified intervals.

Tyres

Check tyre pressures regularly. Under-inflated tyres have an increased rolling resistance. It is generally safe to use the higher pressures specified for full load conditions even when not fully laden, but keep an eye on the centre band of tread for signs of wear due to over-inflation.

When buying new tyres, consider the 'fuel saving' models which most manufacturers include in their ranges.

Driving style

Acceleration

Acceleration uses more fuel than driving at a steady speed. The best technique with modern cars is to accelerate reasonably briskly to the desired speed, changing up through the gears as soon as possible without making the engine labour.

Air conditioning

Air conditioning absorbs quite a bit of energy from the engine – typically 3 kW (4 hp) or so. The effect on fuel consumption is at its worst in slow traffic. Switch it off when not required.

Anticipation

Drive smoothly and try to read the traffic flow so as to avoid unnecessary acceleration and braking.

Automatic transmission

When accelerating in an automatic, avoid depressing the throttle so far as to make the transmission hold onto lower gears at higher speeds. Don't use the 'Sport' setting, if applicable.

When stationary with the engine running, select 'N' or 'P'. When moving, keep your left foot away from the brake.

Braking

Braking converts the car's energy of motion into heat – essentially, it is wasted. Obviously some braking is always going to be necessary, but with good anticipation it is surprising how much can be avoided, especially on routes that you know well.

Carshare

Consider sharing lifts to work or to the shops. Even once a week will make a difference.

Electrical loads

Electricity is 'fuel' too; the alternator which charges the battery does so by converting some of the engine's energy of motion into electrical energy. The more electrical accessories are in use, the greater the load on the alternator. Switch off big consumers like the heated rear window when not required.

Freewheeling

Freewheeling (coasting) in neutral with the engine switched off is dangerous. The effort required to operate power-assisted brakes and steering increases when the engine is not running, with a potential lack of control in emergency situations.

In any case, modern fuel injection systems automatically cut off the engine's fuel supply on the overrun (moving and in gear, but with the accelerator pedal released).

Gadgets

Bolt-on devices claiming to save fuel have been around for nearly as long as the motor car itself. Those which worked were rapidly adopted as standard equipment by the vehicle manufacturers. Others worked only in certain situations, or saved fuel only at the expense of unacceptable effects on performance, driveability or the life of engine components.

The most effective fuel saving gadget is the driver's right foot.

Journey planning

Combine (eg) a trip to the supermarket with a visit to the recycling centre and the DIY store, rather than making separate journeys.

When possible choose a travelling time outside rush hours.

Load

The more heavily a car is laden, the greater the energy required to accelerate it to a given speed. Remove heavy items which you don't need to carry.

One load which is often overlooked is the contents of the fuel tank. A tankful of fuel (55 litres / 12 gallons) weighs 45 kg (100 lb) or so. Just half filling it may be worthwhile.

Lost?

At the risk of stating the obvious, if you're going somewhere new, have details of the route to hand. There's not much point in achieving record mpg if you also go miles out of your way.

Parking

If possible, carry out any reversing or turning manoeuvres when you arrive at a parking space so that you can drive straight out when you leave. Manoeuvering when the engine is cold uses a lot more fuel.

Driving around looking for free on-street parking may cost more in fuel than buying a car park ticket.

Premium fuel

Most major oil companies (and some supermarkets) have premium grades of fuel which are several pence a litre dearer than the standard grades. Reports vary, but the consensus seems to be that if these fuels improve economy at all, they do not do so by enough to justify their extra cost.

Roof rack

When loading a roof rack, try to produce a wedge shape with the narrow end at the front. Any cover should be securely fastened – if it flaps it's creating turbulence and absorbing energy.

Remove roof racks and boxes when not in use – they increase air resistance and can create a surprising amount of noise.

Short journeys

The engine is at its least efficient, and wear is highest, during the first few miles after a cold start. Consider walking, cycling or using public transport.

Speed

The engine is at its most efficient when running at a steady speed and load at the rpm where it develops maximum torque. (You can find this figure in the car's handbook.) For most cars this corresponds to between 55 and 65 mph in top gear.

Above the optimum cruising speed, fuel consumption starts to rise quite sharply. A car travelling at 80 mph will typically be using 30% more fuel than at 60 mph.

Supermarket fuel

It may be cheap but is it any good? In the UK all supermarket fuel must meet the relevant British Standard. The major oil companies will say that their branded fuels have better additive packages which may stop carbon and other deposits building up. A reasonable compromise might be to use one tank of branded fuel to three or four from the supermarket.

Switch off when stationary

Switch off the engine if you look like being stationary for more than 30 seconds or so. This is good for the environment as well as for your pocket. Be aware though that frequent restarts are hard on the battery and the starter motor.

Windows

Driving with the windows open increases air turbulence around the vehicle. Closing the windows promotes smooth airflow and

reduced resistance. The faster you go, the more significant this is.

And finally . . .

Driving techniques associated with good fuel economy tend to involve moderate acceleration and low top speeds. Be considerate to the needs of other road users who may need to make brisker progress; even if you do not agree with them this is not an excuse to be obstructive.

Safety must always take precedence over economy, whether it is a question of accelerating hard to complete an overtaking manoeuvre, killing your speed when confronted with a potential hazard or switching the lights on when it starts to get dark.

Conversion factors

Length (distance)

Inches (in)	x 25.4	= Millimetres (mm)	x 0.0394	= Inches (in)
Feet (ft)	x 0.305	= Metres (m)	x 3.281	= Feet (ft)
Miles	x 1.609	= Kilometres (km)	x 0.621	= Miles

Volume (capacity)

Cubic inches (cu in; in³)	x 16.387	= Cubic centimetres (cc; cm³)	x 0.061	= Cubic inches (cu in; in³)
Imperial pints (Imp pt)	x 0.568	= Litres (l)	x 1.76	= Imperial pints (Imp pt)
Imperial quarts (Imp qt)	x 1.137	= Litres (l)	x 0.88	= Imperial quarts (Imp qt)
Imperial quarts (Imp qt)	x 1.201	= US quarts (US qt)	x 0.833	= Imperial quarts (Imp qt)
US quarts (US qt)	x 0.946	= Litres (l)	x 1.057	= US quarts (US qt)
Imperial gallons (Imp gal)	x 4.546	= Litres (l)	x 0.22	= Imperial gallons (Imp gal)
Imperial gallons (Imp gal)	x 1.201	= US gallons (US gal)	x 0.833	= Imperial gallons (Imp gal)
US gallons (US gal)	x 3.785	= Litres (l)	x 0.264	= US gallons (US gal)

Mass (weight)

Ounces (oz)	x 28.35	= Grams (g)	x 0.035	= Ounces (oz)
Pounds (lb)	x 0.454	= Kilograms (kg)	x 2.205	= Pounds (lb)

Force

Ounces-force (ozf; oz)	x 0.278	= Newtons (N)	x 3.6	= Ounces-force (ozf; oz)
Pounds-force (lbf; lb)	x 4.448	= Newtons (N)	x 0.225	= Pounds-force (lbf; lb)
Newtons (N)	x 0.1	= Kilograms-force (kgf; kg)	x 9.81	= Newtons (N)

Pressure

Pounds-force per square inch (psi; lbf/in²; lb/in²)	x 0.070	= Kilograms-force per square centimetre (kgf/cm²; kg/cm²)	x 14.223	= Pounds-force per square inch (psi; lbf/in²; lb/in²)
Pounds-force per square inch (psi; lbf/in²; lb/in²)	x 0.068	= Atmospheres (atm)	x 14.696	= Pounds-force per square inch (psi; lbf/in²; lb/in²)
Pounds-force per square inch (psi; lbf/in²; lb/in²)	x 0.069	= Bars	x 14.5	= Pounds-force per square inch (psi; lbf/in²; lb/in²)
Pounds-force per square inch (psi; lbf/in²; lb/in²)	x 6.895	= Kilopascals (kPa)	x 0.145	= Pounds-force per square inch (psi; lbf/in²; lb/in²)
Kilopascals (kPa)	x 0.01	= Kilograms-force per square centimetre (kgf/cm²; kg/cm²)	x 98.1	= Kilopascals (kPa)
Millibar (mbar)	x 100	= Pascals (Pa)	x 0.01	= Millibar (mbar)
Millibar (mbar)	x 0.0145	= Pounds-force per square inch (psi; lbf/in²; lb/in²)	x 68.947	= Millibar (mbar)
Millibar (mbar)	x 0.75	= Millimetres of mercury (mmHg)	x 1.333	= Millibar (mbar)
Millibar (mbar)	x 0.401	= Inches of water (inH₂O)	x 2.491	= Millibar (mbar)
Millimetres of mercury (mmHg)	x 0.535	= Inches of water (inH₂O)	x 1.868	= Millimetres of mercury (mmHg)
Inches of water (inH₂O)	x 0.036	= Pounds-force per square inch (psi; lbf/in²; lb/in²)	x 27.68	= Inches of water (inH₂O)

Torque (moment of force)

Pounds-force inches (lbf in; lb in)	x 1.152	= Kilograms-force centimetre (kgf cm; kg cm)	x 0.868	= Pounds-force inches (lbf in; lb in)
Pounds-force inches (lbf in; lb in)	x 0.113	= Newton metres (Nm)	x 8.85	= Pounds-force inches (lbf in; lb in)
Pounds-force inches (lbf in; lb in)	x 0.083	= Pounds-force feet (lbf ft; lb ft)	x 12	= Pounds-force inches (lbf in; lb in)
Pounds-force feet (lbf ft; lb ft)	x 0.138	= Kilograms-force metres (kgf m; kg m)	x 7.233	= Pounds-force feet (lbf ft; lb ft)
Pounds-force feet (lbf ft; lb ft)	x 1.356	= Newton metres (Nm)	x 0.738	= Pounds-force feet (lbf ft; lb ft)
Newton metres (Nm)	x 0.102	= Kilograms-force metres (kgf m; kg m)	x 9.804	= Newton metres (Nm)

Power

Horsepower (hp)	x 745.7	= Watts (W)	x 0.0013	= Horsepower (hp)

Velocity (speed)

Miles per hour (miles/hr; mph)	x 1.609	= Kilometres per hour (km/hr; kph)	x 0.621	= Miles per hour (miles/hr; mph)

Fuel consumption*

Miles per gallon, Imperial (mpg)	x 0.354	= Kilometres per litre (km/l)	x 2.825	= Miles per gallon, Imperial (mpg)
Miles per gallon, US (mpg)	x 0.425	= Kilometres per litre (km/l)	x 2.352	= Miles per gallon, US (mpg)

Temperature

Degrees Fahrenheit = (°C x 1.8) + 32   Degrees Celsius (Degrees Centigrade; °C) = (°F - 32) x 0.56

It is common practice to convert from miles per gallon (mpg) to litres/100 kilometres (l/100km), where mpg x l/100 km = 282

Spare parts are available from many sources, including maker's appointed garages, accessory shops, and motor factors. To be sure of obtaining the correct parts, it may sometimes be necessary to quote the vehicle identification number. If possible, it can also be useful to take the old parts along for positive identification. Items such as starter motors and alternators maybe available under a service exchange scheme – any parts returned should be clean.

Our advice regarding spare part sources is:

Officially appointed garages

This is the best source of parts, which are peculiar to your car, and are not otherwise generally available (eg, badges, interior trim, certain body panels, etc). It is also the only place at which you should buy parts if the vehicle is still under warranty.

Accessory shops

These are very good places to buy materials and components needed for the maintenance of your car (oil, air and fuel filters, spark plugs, light bulbs, drivebelts, oils and greases, brake pads, touch-up paint, etc). Components of this nature sold by a reputable shop are of the same standard as those used by the car manufacturer.

Besides components, these shops will also sell tools and general accessories, usually have convenient opening hours, charge lower prices, and can often be found close to home. Some accessory shops also have parts counters where components needed for almost any repair job can be purchased or ordered.

Motor factors

Good factors will stock all the more important components, which wear out comparatively quickly and can sometimes supply individual components needed for the overhaul of a larger assembly. They may also handle work such as cylinder block reboring, crankshaft regrinding and balancing, etc.

Tyre and exhaust specialists

These outlets may be independent or members of a local or national chain. They frequently offer competitive prices when compared with a main dealer or local garage, but it will pay to obtain several quotes before making a decision. Also ask what 'extras' may be added to the quote – for instance, fitting a new valve and balancing the wheel are both often charged on top of the price of a new tyre.

Other sources

Beware of parts or materials obtained from market stalls, car boot sales or similar outlets. Such items are not invariably sub-standard, but there is little chance of compensation if they do prove unsatisfactory. In the case of safety-critical components such as brake pads there is the risk not only of financial loss but also of an accident causing injury or death.

Whenever servicing, repair or overhaul work is carried out on the car or its components, observe the following procedures and instructions. This will assist in carrying out the operation efficiently and to a professional standard of workmanship.

Joint mating faces and gaskets

When separating components at their mating faces, never insert screwdrivers or similar implements into the joint between the faces in order to prise them apart. This can cause severe damage which results in oil leaks, coolant leaks, etc upon reassembly. Separation is usually achieved by tapping along the joint with a soft-faced hammer in order to break the seal. However, note that this method may not be suitable where dowels are used for component location.

Where a gasket is used between the mating faces of two components, a new one must be fitted on reassembly; fit it dry unless otherwise stated in the repair procedure. Make sure that the mating faces are clean and dry, with all traces of old gasket removed. When cleaning a joint face, use a tool which is unlikely to score or damage the face, and remove any burrs or nicks with an oilstone or fine file.

Make sure that tapped holes are cleaned with a pipe cleaner, and keep them free of jointing compound, if this is being used, unless specifically instructed otherwise.

Ensure that all orifices, channels or pipes are clear, and blow through them, preferably using compressed air.

Oil seals

Oil seals can be removed by levering them out with a wide flat-bladed screwdriver or similar implement. Alternatively, a number of self-tapping screws may be screwed into the seal, and these used as a purchase for pliers or some similar device in order to pull the seal free.

Whenever an oil seal is removed from its working location, either individually or as part of an assembly, it should be renewed.

The very fine sealing lip of the seal is easily damaged, and will not seal if the surface it contacts is not completely clean and free from scratches, nicks or grooves. If the original sealing surface of the component cannot be restored, and the manufacturer has not made provision for slight relocation of the seal relative to the sealing surface, the component should be renewed.

Protect the lips of the seal from any surface which may damage them in the course of fitting. Use tape or a conical sleeve where possible. Where indicated, lubricate the seal lips with oil before fitting and, on dual-lipped seals, fill the space between the lips with grease.

Unless otherwise stated, oil seals must be fitted with their sealing lips toward the lubricant to be sealed.

Use a tubular drift or block of wood of the appropriate size to install the seal and, if the seal housing is shouldered, drive the seal down to the shoulder. If the seal housing is unshouldered, the seal should be fitted with its face flush with the housing top face (unless otherwise instructed).

Screw threads and fastenings

Seized nuts, bolts and screws are quite a common occurrence where corrosion has set in, and the use of penetrating oil or releasing fluid will often overcome this problem if the offending item is soaked for a while before attempting to release it. The use of an impact driver may also provide a means of releasing such stubborn fastening devices, when used in conjunction with the appropriate screwdriver bit or socket. If none of these methods works, it may be necessary to resort to the careful application of heat, or the use of a hacksaw or nut splitter device. Before resorting to extreme methods, check that you are not dealing with a left-hand thread!

Studs are usually removed by locking two nuts together on the threaded part, and then using a spanner on the lower nut to unscrew the stud. Studs or bolts which have broken off below the surface of the component in which they are mounted can sometimes be removed using a stud extractor.

Always ensure that a blind tapped hole is completely free from oil, grease, water or other fluid before installing the bolt or stud. Failure to do this could cause the housing to crack due to the hydraulic action of the bolt or stud as it is screwed in.

For some screw fastenings, notably cylinder head bolts or nuts, torque wrench settings are no longer specified for the latter stages of tightening, "angle-tightening" being called up instead. Typically, a fairly low torque wrench setting will be applied to the bolts/nuts in the correct sequence, followed by one or more stages of tightening through specified angles.

When checking or retightening a nut or bolt to a specified torque setting, slacken the nut or bolt by a quarter of a turn, and then retighten to the specified setting. However, this should not be attempted where angular tightening has been used.

Locknuts, locktabs and washers

Any fastening which will rotate against a component or housing during tightening should always have a washer between it and the relevant component or housing.

Spring or split washers should always be renewed when they are used to lock a critical component such as a big-end bearing retaining bolt or nut. Locktabs which are folded over to retain a nut or bolt should always be renewed.

Self-locking nuts can be re-used in non-critical areas, providing resistance can be felt when the locking portion passes over the bolt or stud thread. However, it should be noted that self-locking stiffnuts tend to lose their effectiveness after long periods of use, and should then be renewed as a matter of course.

Split pins must always be replaced with new ones of the correct size for the hole.

When thread-locking compound is found on the threads of a fastener which is to be re-used, it should be cleaned off with a wire brush and solvent, and fresh compound applied on reassembly.

Special tools

Some repair procedures in this manual entail the use of special tools such as a press, two or three-legged pullers, spring compressors, etc. Wherever possible, suitable readily-available alternatives to the manufacturer's special tools are described, and are shown in use. In some instances, where no alternative is possible, it has been necessary to resort to the use of a manufacturer's tool, and this has been done for reasons of safety as well as the efficient completion of the repair operation. Unless you are highly-skilled and have a thorough understanding of the procedures described, never attempt to bypass the use of any special tool when the procedure described specifies its use. Not only is there a very great risk of personal injury, but expensive damage could be caused to the components involved.

Environmental considerations

When disposing of used engine oil, brake fluid, antifreeze, etc, give due consideration to any detrimental environmental effects. Do not, for instance, pour any of the above liquids down drains into the general sewage system, or onto the ground to soak away, as this is likely to pollute your local environment. Many local council refuse tips provide a facility for waste oil disposal, as do some garages. You can find your nearest disposal point by calling the Environment Agency on 03708 506 506 or by visiting www.oilbankline.org.uk.

Note: It is illegal and anti-social to dump oil down the drain. To find the location of your local oil recycling bank, call 03708 506 506 or visit www.oilbankline.org.uk.

Modifications are a continuing and unpublicised process in vehicle manufacture, quite apart from major model changes. Spare parts manuals and lists are compiled upon a numerical basis, the individual vehicle identification numbers being essential for correct identification of the part concerned.

When ordering spare parts, always give as much information as possible. Quote the car model, year of manufacture, body and engine numbers, but most importantly, the 4-digit production code (sometimes referred to as the 'spares number').

The vehicle Identification number is on a label, which is stuck onto the left-hand B-pillar, adjacent to the rear door hinges. The label carries the vehicle identification number (VIN) and vehicle weight information **(see illustration)**.

The vehicle identification number (VIN) is also stamped onto rear bulkhead panel at the right-hand side of the engine compartment **(see illustration)**.

The vehicle identification number (VIN) is stamped onto a plate visible through the base of the windscreen **(see illustration)**.

The engine number is situated on the front face of the cylinder block, and can be found in the following locations:

a) *On petrol engines the engine number is located on the left-hand side of the cylinder block (transmission end). The number is either stamped directly onto the block or is stamped onto a plate, which is riveted to the block.*

b) *On diesel engines the engine number is stamped on the base of the cylinder block on the flat surface located on the right-hand side of the oil filter/cooler.*

Note: *The first part of the engine number gives the engine code, eg, 8FR (1.4 litre petrol model).*

The vehicle identification label is located on the left-hand B-pillar

The vehicle identification number is stamped on the right-hand rear of the engine compartment

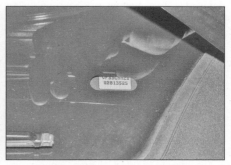

The VIN is also visible through the windscreen

Jacking and vehicle support

The jack supplied with the vehicle should **only** be used for changing the roadwheels – see *Wheel changing* at the front of this manual. When carrying out any other kind of work, raise the vehicle using a hydraulic (or 'trolley') jack, and always supplement the jack with axle stands at the vehicle jacking points.

When using a hydraulic jack or axle stands, always position the jack head or axle stand head under one of the relevant jacking points; the jacking point is the strengthened part of the sill **(see illustration)**. Use a block of wood between the jack or axle stand and the sill –

the block of wood should have a groove cut into it, into which the welded flange of the sill will locate.

Do not attempt to jack the vehicle under the front crossmember, the sump, or any of the suspension components.

The jack supplied with the vehicle locates in the jacking points on the underside of the sills – see *Wheel changing*. Ensure that the jack head is correctly engaged before attempting to raise the vehicle.

Never work under, around, or near a raised vehicle, unless it is adequately supported in at least two places.

Jacking point

Introduction

A selection of good tools is a fundamental requirement for anyone contemplating the maintenance and repair of a motor vehicle. For the owner who does not possess any, their purchase will prove a considerable expense, offsetting some of the savings made by doing-it-yourself. However, provided that the tools purchased meet the relevant national safety standards and are of good quality, they will last for many years and prove an extremely worthwhile investment.

To help the average owner to decide which tools are needed to carry out the various tasks detailed in this manual, we have compiled three lists of tools under the following headings: *Maintenance and minor repair*, *Repair and overhaul*, and *Special*. Newcomers to practical mechanics should start off with the *Maintenance and minor repair* tool kit, and confine themselves to the simpler jobs around the vehicle. Then, as confidence and experience grow, more difficult tasks can be undertaken, with extra tools being purchased as, and when, they are needed. In this way, a *Maintenance and minor repair* tool kit can be built up into a *Repair and overhaul* tool kit over a considerable period of time, without any major cash outlays. The experienced do-it-yourselfer will have a tool kit good enough for most repair and overhaul procedures, and will add tools from the *Special* category when it is felt that the expense is justified by the amount of use to which these tools will be put.

Maintenance and minor repair tool kit

The tools given in this list should be considered as a minimum requirement if routine maintenance, servicing and minor repair operations are to be undertaken. We recommend the purchase of combination spanners (ring one end, open-ended the other); although more expensive than open-ended ones, they do give the advantages of both types of spanner.

☐ *Combination spanners:*
  Metric - 8 to 19 mm inclusive
☐ *Adjustable spanner - 35 mm jaw (approx.)*
☐ *Spark plug spanner (with rubber insert) - petrol models*
☐ *Spark plug gap adjustment tool - petrol models*
☐ *Set of feeler gauges*
☐ *Brake bleed nipple spanner*
☐ *Screwdrivers:*
  Flat blade - 100 mm long x 6 mm dia
  Cross blade - 100 mm long x 6 mm dia
  Torx - various sizes (not all vehicles)
☐ *Combination pliers*
☐ *Hacksaw (junior)*
☐ *Tyre pump*
☐ *Tyre pressure gauge*
☐ *Oil can*
☐ *Oil filter removal tool (if applicable)*
☐ *Fine emery cloth*
☐ *Wire brush (small)*
☐ *Funnel (medium size)*
☐ *Sump drain plug key (not all vehicles)*

Repair and overhaul tool kit

These tools are virtually essential for anyone undertaking any major repairs to a motor vehicle, and are additional to those given in the *Maintenance and minor repair* list. Included in this list is a comprehensive set of sockets. Although these are expensive, they will be found invaluable as they are so versatile - particularly if various drives are included in the set. We recommend the half-inch square-drive type, as this can be used with most proprietary torque wrenches.

The tools in this list will sometimes need to be supplemented by tools from the *Special* list:

☐ *Sockets to cover range in previous list (including Torx sockets)*
☐ *Reversible ratchet drive (for use with sockets)*
☐ *Extension piece, 250 mm (for use with sockets)*
☐ *Universal joint (for use with sockets)*
☐ *Flexible handle or sliding T "breaker bar" (for use with sockets)*
☐ *Torque wrench (for use with sockets)*
☐ *Self-locking grips*
☐ *Ball pein hammer*
☐ *Soft-faced mallet (plastic or rubber)*
☐ *Screwdrivers:*
  Flat blade - long & sturdy, short (chubby), and narrow (electrician's) types
  Cross blade – long & sturdy, and short (chubby) types
☐ *Pliers:*
  Long-nosed
  Side cutters (electrician's)
  Circlip (internal and external)
☐ *Cold chisel - 25 mm*
☐ *Scriber*
☐ *Scraper*
☐ *Centre-punch*
☐ *Pin punch*
☐ *Hacksaw*
☐ *Brake hose clamp*
☐ *Brake/clutch bleeding kit*
☐ *Selection of twist drills*
☐ *Steel rule/straight-edge*
☐ *Allen keys (inc. splined/Torx type)*
☐ *Selection of files*
☐ *Wire brush*
☐ *Axle stands*
☐ *Jack (strong trolley or hydraulic type)*
☐ *Light with extension lead*
☐ *Universal electrical multi-meter*

Sockets and reversible ratchet drive

Brake bleeding kit

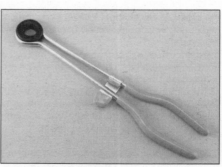

Torx key, socket and bit

Hose clamp

Angular-tightening gauge

Special tools

The tools in this list are those which are not used regularly, are expensive to buy, or which need to be used in accordance with their manufacturers' instructions. Unless relatively difficult mechanical jobs are undertaken frequently, it will not be economic to buy many of these tools. Where this is the case, you could consider clubbing together with friends (or joining a motorists' club) to make a joint purchase, or borrowing the tools against a deposit from a local garage or tool hire specialist.

The following list contains only those tools and instruments freely available to the public, and not those special tools produced by the vehicle manufacturer specifically for its dealer network. You will find occasional references to these manufacturers' special tools in the text of this manual. Generally, an alternative method of doing the job without the vehicle manufacturers' special tool is given. However, sometimes there is no alternative to using them. Where this is the case and the relevant tool cannot be bought or borrowed, you will have to entrust the work to a dealer.

- [ ] Angular-tightening gauge
- [ ] Valve spring compressor
- [ ] Valve grinding tool
- [ ] Piston ring compressor
- [ ] Piston ring removal/installation tool
- [ ] Cylinder bore hone
- [ ] Balljoint separator
- [ ] Coil spring compressors (where applicable)
- [ ] Two/three-legged hub and bearing puller
- [ ] Impact screwdriver
- [ ] Micrometer and/or vernier calipers
- [ ] Dial gauge
- [ ] Tachometer
- [ ] Fault code reader
- [ ] Cylinder compression gauge
- [ ] Hand-operated vacuum pump and gauge
- [ ] Clutch plate alignment set
- [ ] Brake shoe steady spring cup removal tool
- [ ] Bush and bearing removal/installation set
- [ ] Stud extractors
- [ ] Tap and die set
- [ ] Lifting tackle

Buying tools

Reputable motor accessory shops and superstores often offer excellent quality tools at discount prices, so it pays to shop around.

Remember, you don't have to buy the most expensive items on the shelf, but it is always advisable to steer clear of the very cheap tools. Beware of 'bargains' offered on market stalls, on-line or at car boot sales. There are plenty of good tools around at reasonable prices, but always aim to purchase items which meet the relevant national safety standards. If in doubt, ask the proprietor or manager of the shop for advice before making a purchase.

Care and maintenance of tools

Having purchased a reasonable tool kit, it is necessary to keep the tools in a clean and serviceable condition. After use, always wipe off any dirt, grease and metal particles using a clean, dry cloth, before putting the tools away. Never leave them lying around after they have been used. A simple tool rack on the garage or workshop wall for items such as screwdrivers and pliers is a good idea. Store all normal spanners and sockets in a metal box. Any measuring instruments, gauges, meters, etc, must be carefully stored where they cannot be damaged or become rusty.

Take a little care when tools are used. Hammer heads inevitably become marked, and screwdrivers lose the keen edge on their blades from time to time. A little timely attention with emery cloth or a file will soon restore items like this to a good finish.

Working facilities

Not to be forgotten when discussing tools is the workshop itself. If anything more than routine maintenance is to be carried out, a suitable working area becomes essential.

It is appreciated that many an owner-mechanic is forced by circumstances to remove an engine or similar item without the benefit of a garage or workshop. Having done this, any repairs should always be done under the cover of a roof.

Wherever possible, any dismantling should be done on a clean, flat workbench or table at a suitable working height.

Any workbench needs a vice; one with a jaw opening of 100 mm is suitable for most jobs. As mentioned previously, some clean dry storage space is also required for tools, as well as for any lubricants, cleaning fluids, touch-up paints etc, which become necessary.

Another item which may be required, and which has a much more general usage, is an electric drill with a chuck capacity of at least 8 mm. This, together with a good range of twist drills, is virtually essential for fitting accessories.

Last, but not least, always keep a supply of old newspapers and clean, lint-free rags available, and try to keep any working area as clean as possible.

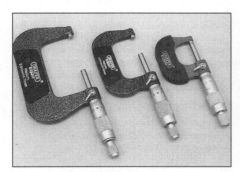
Micrometers

Dial test indicator ("dial gauge")

Oil filter removal tool (strap wrench type)

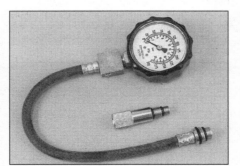
Compression tester

Bearing puller

This is a guide to getting your vehicle through the MOT test. Obviously it will not be possible to examine the vehicle to the same standard as the professional MOT tester. However, working through the following checks will enable you to identify any problem areas before submitting the vehicle for the test.

It has only been possible to summarise the test requirements here, based on the regulations in force at the time of printing. Test standards are becoming increasingly stringent, although there are some exemptions for older vehicles.

An assistant will be needed to help carry out some of these checks.

The checks have been sub-divided into four categories, as follows:

1 Checks carried out **FROM THE VEHICLE INTERIOR**

2 Checks carried out **WITH THE VEHICLE ON THE GROUND**

3 Checks carried out **WITH THE VEHICLE RAISED AND THE WHEELS FREE TO TURN**

4 Checks carried out on **YOUR VEHICLE'S EXHAUST EMISSION SYSTEM**

1 Checks carried out **FROM THE VEHICLE INTERIOR**

Handbrake (parking brake)

☐ Test the operation of the handbrake. Excessive travel (too many clicks) indicates incorrect brake or cable adjustment.

☐ Check that the handbrake cannot be released by tapping the lever sideways. Check the security of the lever mountings.

☐ If the parking brake is foot-operated, check that the pedal is secure and without excessive travel, and that the release mechanism operates correctly.

☐ Where applicable, test the operation of the electronic handbrake. The brake should engage and disengage without excessive delay. If the warning light does not extinguish, or a warning message is displayed when the brake is disengaged, this could indicate a fault which will need further investigation.

Footbrake

☐ Depress the brake pedal and check that it does not creep down to the floor, indicating a master cylinder fault. Release the pedal, wait a few seconds, then depress it again. If the pedal travels nearly to the floor before firm resistance is felt, brake adjustment or repair is necessary. If the pedal feels spongy, there is air in the hydraulic system which must be removed by bleeding.

☐ Check that the brake pedal is secure and in good condition. Check also for signs of fluid leaks on the pedal, floor or carpets, which would indicate failed seals in the brake master cylinder.

☐ Check the servo unit (when applicable) by operating the brake pedal several times, then keeping the pedal depressed and starting the engine. As the engine starts, the pedal will move down. If not, the vacuum hose or the servo itself may be faulty.

Steering wheel and column

☐ Examine the steering wheel for fractures or looseness of the hub, spokes or rim.

☐ Move the steering wheel from side to side and then up and down. Check that the steering wheel is not loose on the column, indicating wear or a loose retaining nut. Continue moving the steering wheel as before, but also turn it slightly from left to right.

☐ Check that the steering wheel is not loose on the column, and that there is no abnormal movement of the steering wheel, indicating wear in the column support bearings or couplings.

☐ Check that the ignition lock (where fitted) engages and disengages correctly.

☐ Steering column adjustment mechanisms (where fitted) must be able to lock the column securely in place with no play evident.

Windscreen, mirrors and sunvisor

☐ The windscreen must be free of cracks or other significant damage within the 'swept area' of the windscreen. This is the area swept by the windscreen wipers. A second test area, known as 'Zone A', is the part of the swept area 290 mm wide, centred on the steering wheel centre line. Any damage in Zone A that cannot be contained in a 10 mm diameter circle, or any damage in the remainder of the swept area that cannot be contained in a 40 mm diameter circle, may cause the vehicle to fail the test.

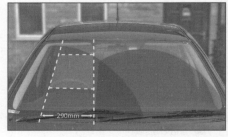

☐ Any items that may obscure the drivers view, such as stickers, sat-navs, anything hanging from the interior mirror, should be removed prior to the test.

☐ Vehicles registered after 1st August 1978 must have a drivers side mirror, and either an interior mirror, or a passenger's side mirror. Cameras (or indirect vision devices) may replace the mirrors, but they must function correctly.

☐ The driver's sunvisor must be capable of being stored in the "up" position.

Seat belts, seats and supplementary restraint systems (SRS)

Note: *The following checks are applicable to all seat belts, front and rear.*

□ Examine the webbing of all the belts (including rear belts if fitted) for cuts, serious fraying or deterioration. Fasten and unfasten each belt to check the buckles. If applicable, check the retracting mechanism. Check the security of all seat belt mountings accessible from inside the vehicle, ensuring any height adjustable mountings lock securely in place.

□ Where the seat belt is attached to a seat, the frame and mountings of the seat form part of the belt mountings, and are to be inspected as such.

□ Any airbag, or SRS warning light must extinguish a few seconds after the ignition is switched on. Failure to do so indicates a fault which must be investigated.

□ Seat belts with pre-tensioners, once activated, have a "flag" or similar showing on the seat belt stalk. This, in itself, is a reason for test failure.

□ Check that the original airbag(s) is/are present, and not obviously defective.

□ The seats themselves must be securely attached and the backrests must lock in the upright position. The driver's seat must also be able to slide forwards/rearwards, and lock in several positions.

Doors

□ Both front doors must be able to be opened and closed from outside and inside, and must latch securely when closed.

□ The rear doors must open from the outside.

□ Examine all door hinges, catches and striker plates for missing, deteriorated, or insecure parts that could effect the opening and closing of the doors.

Speedometer

□ The vehicle speedometer must be present, and appear operative. The figures on the speedometer must be legible, and illuminated when the lights are switched on.

2 Checks carried out WITH THE VEHICLE ON THE GROUND

Vehicle identification

□ Number plates must be in good condition, secure and legible, with letters and numbers correctly spaced – spacing at (A) should be 33 mm and at (B) 11 mm. At the front, digits must be black on a white background and at the rear

black on a yellow background. Other background designs (such as honeycomb) are not permitted.

□ The VIN plate and/or homologation plate must be permanently displayed and legible.

Electrical equipment

□ Switch on the ignition and check the operation of the horn.

□ Check the windscreen washers and wipers, examining the wiper blades; renew damaged or perished blades. The wiper blades must clear a large enough area of the windscreen to provide an 'adequate' view of the road, and be able to be parked in a position where they will not affect the drivers' view.

□ On vehicles first used from 1st September 2009, the headlight washers (where fitted) must operate correctly.

□ Check the operation of the stop-lights. This includes any lights that appear to be connected – Eg. high-level lights.

□ Check the operation of the sidelights and number plate lights. The lenses and reflectors must be secure, clean and undamaged.

□ Check the operation and alignment of the headlights. The headlight reflectors must not be tarnished and the lenses must be undamaged. Where plastic lenses are fitted, check they haven't deteriorated to the extent where they affect the light ouput or beam image. It's often possible to restore the plastic lens using a suitable polish or aftermarket treatment.

□ Where HID or LED headlights are fitted, check the operation of the cleaning and self-levelling functions.

□ The headlight main beam warning lamp must be functional.

□ On vehicles first used from 1st March 2018, the daytime running lights (where fitted) must operate correctly.

□ Switch on the ignition and check the operation of the direction indicators (including the instrument panel tell-tale) and the hazard warning lights. Operation of the sidelights and stop-lights must not affect the indicators – if it does, the cause is usually a bad earth at the rear light cluster. Indicators should flash at a rate of between 60 and 120 times per minute – faster or slower than this could indicate a fault with the flasher unit or a bad earth at one of the light units.

□ The hazard warning lights must operate with the ignition on and off.

□ Check the operation of the rear foglight(s), including the warning light on the instrument panel or in the switch. Note that the foglight

must be positioned in the centre or driver's side of the vehicle. If only the passenger's side illuminates, the test will fail.

□ The warning lights must illuminate in accordance with the manufacturers' design (this includes any warning messages). For most vehicles, the ABS and other warning lights should illuminate when the ignition is switched on, and (if the system is operating properly) extinguish after a few seconds. Refer to the owner's handbook.

□ On vehicles first used from 1st September 2009, the reversing lights must operate correctly when reverse gear is selected.

□ Check the vehicle battery for security and leakage.

□ Check the visible/accessible vehicle wiring is adequately supported, with no evidence of damage or deterioration that could result in a short-circuit.

Footbrake

□ Examine the master cylinder, brake pipes and servo unit for leaks, loose mountings, corrosion or other damage. If ABS is fitted, this unit should also be examined for signs of leaks or corrosion.

□ The fluid reservoir must be secure and the fluid level must be between the upper (A) and lower (B) markings.

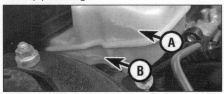

□ Check the fluid in the reservoir for signs of contamination.

□ Inspect both front brake flexible hoses for cracks or deterioration of the rubber. Turn the steering from lock to lock, and ensure that the hoses do not contact the wheel, tyre, or any part of the steering or suspension mechanism. With the brake pedal firmly depressed, check the hoses for bulges or leaks under pressure.

Steering and suspension

□ Have your assistant turn the steering wheel from side to side slightly, up to the point where the steering gear just begins to transmit this movement to the roadwheels. Check for excessive free play between the steering wheel and the steering gear, indicating wear or insecurity of the steering column joints, the column-to-steering gear coupling, or the steering gear itself. With a standard (380 mm diameter) steering wheel, there should be no more than 13 mm of free play for rack-and-pinion systems, and no more than 75 mm for non-rack-and-pinion designs.

□ Have your assistant turn the steering

wheel more vigorously in each direction, so that the roadwheels just begin to turn. As this is done, examine all the steering joints, linkages, fittings and attachments. Renew any component that shows signs of wear or damage. On vehicles with hydraulic power steering, check the security and condition of the steering pump, drivebelt and hoses.

☐ Note that all movement checks on power steering systems are carried out with the engine running.

☐ Check that the vehicle is standing level, and at approximately the correct ride height.

Exhaust system

☐ Start the engine. With your assistant holding a rag over the tailpipe, check the entire system for leaks. Repair or renew leaking sections.

3 Checks carried out **WITH THE VEHICLE RAISED AND THE WHEELS FREE TO TURN**

Jack up the front and rear of the vehicle, and securely support it on axle stands. Position the stands clear of the suspension assemblies. Ensure that the wheels are clear of the ground and that the steering can be turned from lock to lock.

Steering mechanism

☐ Have your assistant turn the steering from lock to lock. Check that the steering turns smoothly, and that no part of the steering mechanism, including a wheel or tyre, fouls any brake hose or pipe or any part of the body structure.

☐ Examine the steering rack rubber gaiters for damage or insecurity of the retaining clips. If power steering is fitted, check for signs of damage or leakage of the fluid hoses, pipes or connections. Also check for excessive stiffness or binding of the steering, a missing split pin or locking device, or severe corrosion of the body structure within 30 cm of any steering component attachment point.

☐ Check the track rod end ball joint dust covers. Any covers that are missing, seriously damaged, deteriorated or insecure, may fail inspection.

Front and rear suspension and wheel bearings

☐ Starting at the front right-hand side, grasp the roadwheel at the 3 o'clock and 9 o'clock positions and rock gently but firmly. Check for free play or insecurity at the wheel bearings, suspension balljoints, or suspension mountings, pivots and attachments.

☐ Now grasp the wheel at the 12 o'clock and 6 o'clock positions and repeat the previous inspection. Spin the wheel, and check for roughness or tightness of the front wheel bearing.

☐ If excess free play is suspected at a component pivot point, this can be confirmed by using a large screwdriver or similar tool and levering between the mounting and the component attachment. This will confirm whether the wear is in the pivot bush, its retaining bolt, or in the mounting itself (the bolt holes can often become elongated).

☐ Carry out all the above checks at the other front wheel, and then at both rear wheels.

Springs and shock absorbers

☐ Examine the suspension struts (when applicable) for serious fluid leakage, corrosion, or damage to the casing. Also check the security of the mounting points.

☐ If coil springs are fitted, check that the spring ends locate in their seats, and that the spring is not corroded, cracked or broken.

☐ If leaf springs are fitted, check that all leaves are intact, that the axle is securely attached to each spring, and that there is no deterioration of the spring eye mountings, bushes, and shackles.

☐ The same general checks apply to vehicles fitted with other suspension types, such as torsion bars, hydraulic displacer units, etc. Ensure that all mountings and attachments are secure, that there are no signs of excessive wear, corrosion or damage, and (on hydraulic types) that there are no fluid leaks or damaged pipes.

☐ Check any suspension and anti-roll bar link ball joint dust covers. Any covers that are missing, seriously damaged, deteriorated or insecure, may fail inspection.

☐ Examine each shock absorber for signs of leakage, corrosion of the casing, missing, detached or worn pivots and/or rubber bushes.

Driveshafts (fwd vehicles only)

☐ Rotate each front wheel in turn and inspect the inner and outer joint gaiters for splits or damage. Also check that each driveshaft is straight and undamaged.

Braking system

☐ If possible without dismantling, check brake pad wear and disc condition. Ensure that the friction lining material has not worn excessively, (A) and that the discs are not fractured, pitted, scored or badly worn (B). As a general rule, if the friction material is less than 1.5 mm thick, the inspection will fail.

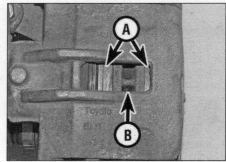

☐ Examine all the rigid brake pipes underneath the vehicle, and the flexible hose(s) at the rear. Look for corrosion, chafing or insecurity of the pipes, and for signs of bulging under pressure, chafing, splits or deterioration of the flexible hoses.

☐ Look for signs of fluid leaks at the brake calipers or on the brake backplates. Repair or renew leaking components.

☐ Slowly spin each wheel, while your assistant depresses and releases the footbrake. Ensure that each brake is operating and does not bind when the pedal is released.

☐ Examine the handbrake mechanism, checking for frayed or broken cables, excessive corrosion, or wear or insecurity of the linkage. Check that the mechanism works on each relevant wheel, and releases fully, without binding.

☐ Check the ABS sensors' wiring for signs of damage, deterioration or insecurity.

☐ It is not possible to test brake efficiency without special equipment, but a road test can be carried out later to check that the vehicle pulls up in a straight line.

Fuel and exhaust systems

☐ Inspect the fuel tank (including the filler cap), fuel pipes, hoses and unions. All components must be secure and free from leaks. Locking fuel caps must lock securely and the key must be provided for the MOT test.

☐ Examine the exhaust system over its entire length, checking for any damaged, broken or missing mountings, security of the retaining clamps and rust or corrosion.

☐ If the vehicle was originally equipped with a catalytic converter or particulate filter, one must be fitted.

Wheels and tyres

☐ Examine the sidewalls and tread area of each tyre in turn. Check for cuts, tears, lumps, bulges, separation of the tread, and exposure of the ply or cord due to wear or damage. Check that the tyre bead is correctly seated on the wheel rim, that the valve is sound and properly seated, and that the wheel is not distorted or damaged.

☐ Check that the tyres are of the correct size for the vehicle, that they are of the same size and type on each axle, and that the pressures are correct. The vehicle will fail the test if the tyres are obviously under-inflated.

☐ Check the tyre tread depth. The legal minimum at the time of writing is 1.6 mm over the central three-quarters of the tread width. Abnormal tread wear may indicate incorrect front wheel alignment or wear in steering or suspension components.

☐ Check that all wheel bolts/nuts are present.

☐ If the spare wheel is fitted externally or in a separate carrier beneath the vehicle, check that mountings are secure and free of excessive corrosion.

Body corrosion

☐ Check the condition of the entire vehicle structure for signs of corrosion in load-bearing areas. (These include chassis box sections, side sills, cross-members, pillars, and all suspension, steering, braking system and seat belt mountings and anchorages.) Any corrosion which has seriously reduced the thickness of a load-bearing area (or is within 30 cm of safety-related components such as steering or suspension) is likely to cause the vehicle to fail. In this case professional repairs are likely to be needed.

☐ Damage or corrosion which causes sharp or otherwise dangerous edges to be exposed will also cause the vehicle to fail.

Towbars

☐ Check the condition of mounting points (both beneath the vehicle and within boot/hatchback areas) for signs of corrosion, ensuring that all fixings are secure and not worn or damaged. There must be no excessive play in detachable tow ball arms or quick-release mechanisms.

☐ Examine the security and condition of the towbar electrics socket. If the later 13-pin socket is fitted, the MOT tester will check its' wiring functions/connections are correct.

General leaks

☐ The vehicle will fail the test if there is a fluid leak of any kind that poses an environmental risk.

4 Checks carried out on YOUR VEHICLE'S EXHAUST EMISSION SYSTEM

Petrol models

☐ The engine should be warmed up, and running well (ignition system in good order, air filter element clean, etc).

☐ Before testing, run the engine at around 2500 rpm for 20 seconds. Let the engine drop to idle, and watch for smoke from the exhaust. If the idle speed is too high, or if dense blue or black smoke emerges for more than 5 seconds, the vehicle will fail. Typically, blue smoke signifies oil burning (engine wear); black smoke means unburnt fuel (dirty air cleaner element, or other fuel system fault).

☐ An exhaust gas analyser for measuring carbon monoxide (CO) and hydrocarbons (HC) is now needed. If one cannot be hired or borrowed, have a local garage perform the check.

CO emissions (mixture)

☐ The MOT tester has access to the CO limits for all vehicles from 1st August 1992. The CO level is measured at idle speed, and at 'fast idle' (2500 to 3000 rpm). The following limits are given as a general guide:

At idle speed – Less than 0.3% CO
At 'fast idle' – Less than 0.2% CO
Lambda reading – 0.97 to 1.03

☐ If the CO level is too high, this may point to poor maintenance, a fuel injection system problem, faulty lambda (oxygen) sensor or catalytic converter. Try an injector cleaning treatment, and check the vehicle's ECU for fault codes.

HC emissions

☐ The MOT tester has access to HC limits for all vehicles. The HC level is measured at 'fast idle' (2500 to 3000 rpm). The following limits are given as a general guide:

At 'fast idle' – Less than 200 ppm

☐ Excessive HC emissions are typically caused by oil being burnt (worn engine), or by a blocked crankcase ventilation system ('breather'). If the engine oil is old and thin, an oil change may help. If the engine is running badly, check the vehicle's ECU for fault codes.

Diesel models

☐ If the vehicle was fitted with a DPF (Diesel Particulate Filter) when it left the factory, it will fail the test if the MOT tester can see smoke of any colour emitting from the exhaust, or finds evidence that the filter has been tampered with.

☐ The only emission test for diesel engines is measuring exhaust smoke density, using a calibrated smoke meter.

☐ This test involves accelerating the engine to its maximum unloaded speed a minimum of once, and a maximum of 6 times. With the smoke meter connected, the engine is accelerated quickly to its maximum speed. If the smoke level is at or below the limit specified, the vehicle will pass. If the level is more than the specified limit then two further accelerations are carried out, and an average of the readings calculated. If the vehicle is still over the limit, a further three accelerations are carried out, with the average of the last three calculated after each check. **Note:** *On engines with a timing belt, it is VITAL that the belt is in good condition before the test is carried out.*

Vehicles registered after 1st July 2008
Smoke level must not exceed 1.5m-1 – Turbo-charged and non-Turbocharged engines

Vehicles registered before 1st July 2008
Smoke level must not exceed 2.5m-1 – Non-turbo vehicles
Smoke level must not exceed 3.0m-1 – Turbocharged vehicles:

☐ If excess smoke is produced, try fitting a new air cleaner element, or using an injector cleaning treatment. If the engine is running badly, where applicable, check the vehicle's ECU for fault codes. Also check the vehicle's EGR system, where applicable. At high mileages, the injectors may require professional attention.

Engine

- [ ] Engine fails to rotate when attempting to start
- [ ] Engine rotates, but will not start
- [ ] Engine difficult to start when cold
- [ ] Engine difficult to start when hot
- [ ] Starter motor noisy or excessively rough in engagement
- [ ] Engine starts, but stops immediately
- [ ] Engine idles erratically
- [ ] Engine misfires at idle speed
- [ ] Engine misfires throughout the driving speed range
- [ ] Engine hesitates on acceleration
- [ ] Engine stalls
- [ ] Engine lacks power
- [ ] Engine backfires
- [ ] Oil pressure warning light on with engine running
- [ ] Engine runs-on after switching off
- [ ] Engine noises

Cooling system

- [ ] Overheating
- [ ] Overcooling
- [ ] External coolant leakage
- [ ] Internal coolant leakage
- [ ] Corrosion

Fuel and exhaust systems

- [ ] Excessive fuel consumption
- [ ] Fuel leakage and/or fuel odour
- [ ] Excessive noise or fumes from exhaust system

Clutch

- [ ] Pedal travels to floor – no pressure or very little resistance
- [ ] Clutch fails to disengage (unable to select gears)
- [ ] Clutch slips (engine speed rises, with no increase in vehicle speed)
- [ ] Judder as clutch is engaged
- [ ] Noise when depressing or releasing clutch pedal

Manual transmission

- [ ] Noisy in neutral with engine running
- [ ] Noisy in one particular gear
- [ ] Difficulty engaging gears
- [ ] Jumps out of gear
- [ ] Vibration
- [ ] Lubricant leaks

Automatic transmission

- [ ] Fluid leakage
- [ ] Transmission fluid brown, or has burned smell
- [ ] General gear selection problems
- [ ] Transmission will not downshift (kickdown) at full throttle
- [ ] Engine won't start in any gear, or starts in gears other than Park or Neutral
- [ ] Transmission slips, shifts roughly, is noisy, or has no drive in forward or reverse gears

Driveshafts

- [ ] Clicking or knocking noise on turns (at slow speed on full-lock)
- [ ] Vibration when accelerating or decelerating

Braking system

- [ ] Vehicle pulls to one side under braking
- [ ] Noise (grinding or high-pitched squeal) when brakes applied
- [ ] Excessive brake pedal travel
- [ ] Brake pedal feels spongy when depressed
- [ ] Excessive brake pedal effort required stopping vehicle
- [ ] Judder felt through brake pedal or steering wheel when braking
- [ ] Brakes binding
- [ ] Rear wheels locking under normal braking

Suspension and steering

- [ ] Vehicle pulls to one side
- [ ] Wheel wobble and vibration
- [ ] Excessive pitching and/or rolling around corners, or during braking
- [ ] Wandering or general instability
- [ ] Excessively-stiff steering
- [ ] Excessive play in steering
- [ ] Lack of power assistance
- [ ] Tyre wear excessive

Electrical system

- [ ] Battery won't hold a charge for more than a few days
- [ ] Ignition/no-charge warning light stays on with engine running
- [ ] Ignition/no-charge warning light fails to come on
- [ ] Lights inoperative
- [ ] Instrument readings inaccurate or erratic
- [ ] Horn inoperative, or unsatisfactory in operation
- [ ] Windscreen/tailgate wipers failed, or unsatisfactory in operation
- [ ] Windscreen/tailgate washers failed, or unsatisfactory in operation
- [ ] Electric windows inoperative, or unsatisfactory in operation
- [ ] Central locking system inoperative, or unsatisfactory in operation

Introduction

The vehicle owner who does his or her own maintenance according to the recommended service schedules should not have to use this section of the manual very often. Modern component reliability is such that provided those items subject to wear or deterioration are inspected or renewed at the specified intervals, sudden failure is comparatively rare. Faults do not usually just happen as a result of sudden failure, but develop over a period of time. Major mechanical failures in particular are usually preceded by characteristic symptoms over hundreds or even thousands of miles. Those components, which do occasionally fail without warning, are often small and easily carried in the vehicle.

With any fault-finding, the first step is to decide where to begin investigations. Sometimes this is obvious, but on other occasions, a little detective work will be necessary. The owner who makes half a dozen haphazard adjustments or replacements may be successful in curing a fault (or its symptoms), but will be none the wiser if the fault recurs, and ultimately may have spent more time and money than was necessary. A calm and logical approach will be found to be more satisfactory in the long run. Always take into account any warning signs or abnormalities that may have been noticed in the period preceding the fault – power loss, high or low gauge readings, unusual smells, etc – and remember that failure of components such as fuses or spark plugs may only be pointers to some underlying fault.

The pages, which follow, provide an easy-reference guide to the more common problems, which may occur during the operation of the vehicle. These problems and their possible causes are grouped under headings denoting various components or systems, such as Engine, Cooling system, etc. The general Chapter that deals with the problem is also shown in brackets; refer to the relevant part of that Chapter for system-specific information. Whatever the fault, certain basic principles apply. These are as follows:

Verify the fault. This is simply a matter of being sure that you know what the symptoms are before starting work. This is particularly important if you are investigating a fault for someone else, who may not have described it very accurately.

Don't overlook the obvious. For example, if the vehicle won't start, is there fuel in the tank? (Don't take anyone else's word on this particular point, and don't trust the fuel gauge either!) If an electrical fault is indicated, look for loose or broken wires before digging out the test gear.

Cure the disease, not the symptom. Substituting a flat battery with a fully charged one will get you off the hard shoulder, but if the underlying cause is not attended to, the new battery will go the same way. Similarly, changing oil-fouled spark plugs (petrol models) for a new set will get you moving again, but remember that the reason for the fouling (if it wasn't simply an incorrect grade of plug) will have to be found and corrected.

Don't take anything for granted. Particularly, don't forget that a 'new' component may itself be defective (especially if it's been rattling around in the boot for months), and don't leave components out of a fault diagnosis sequence just because they are new or recently fitted. When you do finally diagnose a difficult fault, you'll probably realise that all the evidence was there from the start.

Diesel fault diagnosis

The majority of starting problems on small diesel engines are electrical in origin. The mechanic who is familiar with petrol engines but less so with diesel may be inclined to view the diesel's injectors and pump in the same light as the spark plugs and distributor, but this is generally a mistake.

When investigating complaints of difficult starting for someone else, make sure that the correct starting procedure is understood and is being followed. Some drivers are unaware of the significance of the preheating warning light – many modern engines are sufficiently forgiving for this not to matter in mild weather, but with the onset of winter, problems begin. Glow plugs in particular are often neglected – just one faulty plug will make cold-weather starting very difficult.

As a rule of thumb, if the engine is difficult to start but runs well when it has finally got going, the problem is electrical (battery, starter motor or preheating system). If poor performance is combined with difficult starting, the problem is likely to be in the fuel system. The low-pressure (supply) side of the fuel system should be checked before suspecting the injectors and high-pressure pump. The most common fuel supply problem is air getting into the system, and any pipe from the fuel tank forwards must be scrutinised if air leakage is suspected.

Engine

Engine fails to rotate when attempting to start

☐ Battery terminal connections loose or corroded (*Weekly checks*).
☐ Battery discharged or faulty (Chapter 5A Section 3 & 4).
☐ Broken, loose or disconnected wiring in the starting circuit (Chapter 5A Section 4).
☐ Defective starter motor (Chapter 5A Section 9).
☐ Starter pinion or flywheel/driveplate ring gear teeth loose or broken (Chapter, 2B, 2C or 2D and 5A).
☐ Engine earth strap broken or disconnected (Chapter 5A Section 2).

Engine rotates, but will not start

☐ Fuel tank empty.
☐ Battery discharged (engine rotates slowly) (Chapter 5A Section 3).
☐ Battery terminal connections loose or corroded (*Weekly checks*).
☐ Worn, faulty or incorrectly-gapped spark plugs – petrol models (Chapter 1A Section 19).
☐ Preheating system faulty – diesel models (Chapter 5C Section 3).
☐ Engine management system fault – petrol models (Chapter 4A Section 5).
☐ Air in fuel system – diesel models (Chapter 4B Section 3).
☐ Fuel injector/injection pump fault – diesel models (Chapter 4B Section 9).
☐ Low cylinder compressions (Chapter, 2B, 2C or 2D).
☐ Major mechanical failure (eg, camshaft drive) (Chapter, 2B, 2C or 2D).

Engine difficult to start when cold

☐ Battery discharged (Chapter 5A Section 3).
☐ Battery terminal connections loose or corroded (*Weekly checks*).
☐ Worn, faulty or incorrectly-gapped spark plugs – petrol models (Chapter 1A Section 19).
☐ Preheating system faulty – diesel models (Chapter 5C Section 3).
☐ Engine management system fault – petrol models (Chapter 4A Section 5).
☐ Fuel injector/injection pump fault – diesel models (Chapter 4B Section 2).

Engine difficult to start when hot

☐ Engine management system fault – petrol models (Chapter 4A Section 10).
☐ Fuel injector/injection pump fault – diesel models (Chapter 4B Section 2).
☐ Low cylinder compressions (Chapter, 2B, 2C or 2D).

Starter motor noisy or excessively rough in engagement

☐ Starter pinion or flywheel/driveplate ring gear teeth loose or broken (Chapters, 2B, 2C or 2D and 5A).
☐ Starter motor mounting bolts loose or missing (Chapter 5A Section 10).
☐ Defective starter motor (Chapter 5A Section 10 & 11).

Engine starts, but stops immediately

☐ Vacuum leak at the throttle housing/inlet manifold – petrol models (Chapter 4A Section 10).
☐ Engine management system fault – petrol models (Chapter 4A Section 10).
☐ Air in fuel system – diesel models (Chapter 4B Section 3).
☐ Fuel injector/injection pump fault – diesel models (Chapter 4B Section 2).

Engine idles erratically

☐ Vacuum leak at the throttle housing/inlet manifold – petrol models (Chapter 4A).
☐ Worn, faulty or incorrectly-gapped spark plugs – petrol models (Chapter 1A).
☐ Engine management system fault – petrol models (Chapter 4A).
☐ Air in fuel system – diesel models (Chapter 4B).
☐ Fuel injector/injection pump fault – diesel models (Chapter 4B).
☐ Uneven or low cylinder compressions (Chapter, 2B, 2C or 2D).
☐ Camshaft lobes worn (Chapter, 2B, 2C or 2D).
☐ Timing belt/chain incorrectly fitted (Chapter, 2B, 2C or 2D).

Engine (continued)

Engine misfires at idle speed

- ☐ Worn, faulty or incorrectly-gapped spark plugs – petrol models (Chapter 1A).
- ☐ Vacuum leak at the throttle housing/inlet manifold – petrol models (Chapter 4A).
- ☐ Engine management system fault – petrol models (Chapter 4A).
- ☐ Faulty injector(s) – diesel models (Chapter 4B).
- ☐ Uneven or low cylinder compressions (Chapter, 2B, 2C or 2D).
- ☐ Disconnected, leaking, or perished crankcase ventilation hoses (Chapter 4C).

Engine misfires throughout the driving speed range

- ☐ Fuel filter blocked (Chapter 1A or 1B).
- ☐ Fuel pump faulty (Chapter 4A or 4B).
- ☐ Fuel tank vent blocked, or fuel pipes restricted (Chapter 4A or 4B).
- ☐ Worn, faulty or incorrectly-gapped spark plugs – petrol models (Chapter 1A).
- ☐ Vacuum leak at the throttle housing/inlet manifold – petrol models (Chapter 4A).
- ☐ Engine management system fault – petrol models (Chapter 4A).
- ☐ Fuel injector/injection pump fault – diesel models (Chapter 4B).
- ☐ Faulty ignition HT coil – petrol models (Chapter 5B).
- ☐ Uneven or low cylinder compressions (Chapter, 2B, 2C or 2D).

Engine hesitates on acceleration

- ☐ Worn, faulty or incorrectly-gapped spark plugs – petrol models (Chapter 1A).
- ☐ Vacuum leak at the throttle housing/inlet manifold – petrol models (Chapter 4A).
- ☐ Engine management system fault – petrol models (Chapter 4A).
- ☐ Fuel injector/injection pump fault – diesel models (Chapter 4B).

Engine stalls

- ☐ Fuel filter blocked (Chapter 1A or 1B).
- ☐ Fuel pump faulty (Chapter 4A or 4B).
- ☐ Fuel tank vent blocked, or fuel pipes restricted (Chapter 4A or 4B).
- ☐ Worn, faulty or incorrectly-gapped spark plugs – petrol models (Chapter 1A).
- ☐ Vacuum leak at the throttle housing/inlet manifold – petrol models (Chapter 4A).
- ☐ Engine management system fault – petrol models (Chapter 4A).
- ☐ Fuel injector/injection pump fault – diesel models (Chapter 4B).

Engine lacks power

- ☐ Timing belt/chain incorrectly fitted (Chapter, 2B, 2C or 2D).
- ☐ Fuel filter blocked (Chapter 1A or 1B).
- ☐ Fuel pump faulty (Chapter 4A or 4B).
- ☐ Uneven or low cylinder compressions (Chapter, 2B, 2C or 2D).
- ☐ Worn, faulty or incorrectly-gapped spark plugs – petrol models (Chapter 1A).
- ☐ Vacuum leak at the throttle housing/inlet manifold – petrol models (Chapter 4A).
- ☐ Engine management system fault – petrol models (Chapter 4A).
- ☐ Fuel injector/injection pump fault – diesel models (Chapter 4B).
- ☐ Brakes binding (Chapters 1A or 1B and 9).
- ☐ Clutch slipping (Chapter 6).

Engine backfires

- ☐ Timing belt/chain incorrectly fitted (Chapter, 2B, 2C or 2D).
- ☐ Vacuum leak at the throttle housing/inlet manifold – petrol models (Chapter 4A).
- ☐ Engine management system fault – petrol models (Chapter 4A).

Oil pressure warning light on with engine running

- ☐ Low oil level, or incorrect oil grade (*Weekly checks*).
- ☐ Faulty oil pressure warning light switch (Chapter 5A).
- ☐ Worn engine bearings and/or oil pump (Chapter 2F).
- ☐ High engine operating temperature (Chapter 3).
- ☐ Oil pressure relief valve defective (Chapter, 2B, 2C or 2D).
- ☐ Oil pick-up strainer clogged (Chapter, 2B, 2C or 2D).

Engine runs-on after switching off

- ☐ Excessive carbon build-up in engine (Chapter 2F).
- ☐ High engine operating temperature (Chapter 3).
- ☐ Engine management system fault – petrol models (Chapter 4A).
- ☐ Fuel injection pump fault – diesel models (Chapter 4B).

Engine noises

Pre-ignition (pinking) or knocking during acceleration or under load

- ☐ Engine management system fault – petrol models (Chapter 4A).
- ☐ Incorrect grade of spark plug – petrol models (Chapter 1A).
- ☐ Incorrect grade of fuel – petrol models (Chapter 4A).
- ☐ Vacuum leak at the throttle housing/inlet manifold – petrol models (Chapter 4A).
- ☐ Excessive carbon build-up in engine (Chapter 2F).

Whistling or wheezing noises

- ☐ Leaking inlet manifold or throttle housing gasket – petrol models (Chapter 4A).
- ☐ Leaking vacuum hose (Chapters 4A or 4B and 9).
- ☐ Blowing cylinder head gasket (Chapter, 2B, 2C or 2D).

Tapping or rattling noises

- ☐ Worn valve gear or camshaft (Chapter, 2B, 2C or 2D).
- ☐ Ancillary component fault (coolant pump, alternator, etc) (Chapters 3, 5A, etc).

Knocking or thumping noises

- ☐ Worn big-end bearings (regular heavy knocking, perhaps less under load) (Chapter 2F).
- ☐ Worn main bearings (rumbling and knocking, perhaps worsening under load) (Chapter 2F).
- ☐ Piston slap (most noticeable when cold) (Chapter 2F).
- ☐ Ancillary component fault (coolant pump, alternator, etc) (Chapters 3, 5A, etc).

Cooling system

Overheating

☐ Insufficient coolant in system (*Weekly checks*).
☐ Thermostat faulty (stuck closed) (Chapter 3).
☐ Radiator core blocked, or grille restricted (Chapter 3).
☐ Electric cooling fan or sensor faulty (Chapter 3).
☐ Pressure cap faulty (Chapter 3).
☐ Inaccurate temperature gauge/sensor (Chapter 3).
☐ Airlock in cooling system (Chapter 1A or 1B).
☐ Engine management system fault (Chapter 4A).

Overcooling

☐ Thermostat faulty (stuck open) (Chapter 3).
☐ Inaccurate temperature gauge/sensor (Chapter 3).

External coolant leakage

☐ Deteriorated or damaged hoses or hose clips (Chapter 1A or 1B).
☐ Radiator core or heater matrix leaking (Chapter 3).
☐ Pressure cap faulty (Chapter 3).
☐ Coolant pump leaking (Chapter 3).
☐ Boiling due to overheating (Chapter 3).
☐ Core plug leaking (Chapter 2F).

Internal coolant leakage

☐ Leaking cylinder head gasket (Chapter, 2B, 2C or 2D).
☐ Cracked cylinder head or cylinder bore (Chapter, 2B, 2C, 2D or 2F).

Corrosion

☐ Infrequent draining and flushing (Chapter 1A or 1B).
☐ Incorrect coolant mixture or inappropriate coolant type (Chapter 1A or 1B).

Fuel and exhaust systems

Excessive fuel consumption

☐ Air filter element dirty or clogged (Chapter 1A or 1B).
☐ Engine management system fault (Chapter 4A).
☐ Faulty injector(s) (Chapter 4A).
☐ Tyres under-inflated (*Weekly checks*).
☐ Brakes binding (Chapters 1A or 1B and 9).

Fuel leakage and/or fuel odour

☐ Damaged or corroded fuel tank, pipes or connections (Chapter 4A or 4B).

Excessive noise or fumes from exhaust system

☐ Leaking exhaust system or manifold joints (Chapters 1A or 1B and 4A or 4B).
☐ Leaking, corroded or damaged silencers or pipe (Chapters 1A or 1B and 4A or 4B).
☐ Broken mountings causing body or suspension contact (Chapters 1A or 1B and 4A or 4B).

Clutch

Pedal travels to floor – no pressure or very little resistance

- ☐ Air in hydraulic system/faulty master or slave cylinder (Chapter 6).
- ☐ Broken clutch release bearing or fork (Chapter 6).
- ☐ Broken diaphragm spring in clutch pressure plate (Chapter 6).

Clutch fails to disengage (unable to select gears)

- ☐ Air in hydraulic system/faulty master or slave cylinder (Chapter 6).
- ☐ Clutch disc sticking on gearbox input shaft splines (Chapter 6).
- ☐ Clutch disc sticking to flywheel or pressure plate (Chapter 6).
- ☐ Faulty pressure plate assembly (Chapter 6).
- ☐ Clutch release mechanism worn or incorrectly assembled (Chapter 6).

Clutch slips (engine speed rises, with no increase in vehicle speed)

- ☐ Faulty hydraulic release system (Chapter 6).
- ☐ Clutch disc linings excessively worn (Chapter 6).
- ☐ Clutch disc linings contaminated with oil or grease (Chapter 6).
- ☐ Faulty pressure plate or weak diaphragm spring (Chapter 6).

Judder as clutch is engaged

- ☐ Clutch disc linings contaminated with oil or grease (Chapter 6).
- ☐ Clutch disc linings excessively worn (Chapter 6).
- ☐ Faulty or distorted pressure plate or diaphragm spring (Chapter 6).
- ☐ Worn or loose engine or gearbox mountings (Chapter).
- ☐ Clutch disc hub or gearbox input shaft splines worn (Chapter 6).

Noise when depressing or releasing clutch pedal

- ☐ Worn clutch release bearing (Chapter 6).
- ☐ Worn or dry clutch pedal bushes (Chapter 6).
- ☐ Faulty pressure plate assembly (Chapter 6).
- ☐ Pressure plate diaphragm spring broken (Chapter 6).
- ☐ Broken clutch disc cushioning springs (Chapter 6).

Manual transmission

Noisy in neutral with engine running

- ☐ Input shaft bearings worn (noise apparent with clutch pedal released, but not when depressed) (Chapter 7A).*
- ☐ Clutch release bearing worn (noise apparent with clutch pedal depressed, possibly less when released) (Chapter 6).

Noisy in one particular gear

- ☐ Worn, damaged or chipped gear teeth (Chapter 7A).*

Difficulty engaging gears

- ☐ Clutch fault (Chapter 6).
- ☐ Worn or damaged gear selection cables (Chapter 7A).
- ☐ Worn synchroniser units (Chapter 7A).*

Jumps out of gear

- ☐ Worn or damaged gear selection cables (Chapter 7A).
- ☐ Worn synchroniser units (Chapter 7A).*
- ☐ Worn selector forks (Chapter 7A).*

Vibration

- ☐ Lack of oil (Chapters 1A and 7A).
- ☐ Worn bearings (Chapter 7A).*

Lubricant leaks

- ☐ Leaking differential output oil seal (Chapter 7A).
- ☐ Leaking housing joint (Chapter 7A).*
- ☐ Leaking input shaft oil seal (Chapter 7A).

Although the corrective action necessary to remedy the symptoms described is beyond the scope of the home mechanic, the above information should be helpful in isolating the cause of the condition, so that the owner can communicate clearly with a professional mechanic.

Automatic transmission

Fluid leakage

Note: *Due to the complexity of the automatic transmission, it is difficult for the home mechanic to properly diagnose and service this unit. For problems other than the following, the vehicle should be taken to a Peugeot dealer service department or suitably equipped specialist.*

☐ Automatic transmission fluid is usually dark in colour. Fluid leaks should not be confused with engine oil, which can easily be blown onto the transmission by airflow.

☐ To determine the source of a leak, first remove all built-up dirt and grime from the transmission housing and surrounding areas using a degreasing agent, or by steam-cleaning. Drive the vehicle at low speed, so airflow will not blow the leak far from its source. Raise and support the vehicle, and determine where the leak is coming from.

Transmission fluid brown, or has burned smell

☐ Transmission fluid level low, or fluid in need of renewal (Chapter 1A and 7B).

General gear selection problems

Chapter 7B deals with checking and adjusting the selector cable on automatic transmissions. The following are common problems which may be caused by a poorly-adjusted cable:

☐ Engine starting in gears other than Park or Neutral.
☐ Indicator panel showing a gear other than that being used.
☐ Vehicle moves when in Park or Neutral.
☐ Poor gear shift quality or erratic gear changes.
Refer to Chapter 7B for the selector cable adjustment procedure.

Transmission will not downshift (kickdown) at full throttle

☐ Low transmission fluid level (Chapter 1A).
☐ Incorrect selector cable adjustment (Chapter 7B).

Engine won't start in any gear, or starts in gears other than Park or Neutral

☐ Incorrect multi-function switch adjustment (Chapter 7B).
☐ Incorrect selector cable adjustment (Chapter 7B).

Transmission slips, shifts roughly, is noisy, or has no drive in forward or reverse gears

There are many probable causes for the above problems, but the home mechanic should be concerned with only one possibility – fluid level. Before taking the vehicle to a dealer or transmission specialist, check the fluid level as described in Chapter 1A. Correct the fluid level as necessary, or change the fluid. If the problem persists, professional help will be necessary.

Driveshafts

Clicking or knocking noise on turns (at slow speed on full-lock)

☐ Lack of constant velocity joint lubricant, possibly due to damaged gaiter (Chapter 8).
☐ Worn outer constant velocity joint (Chapter 8).

Vibration when accelerating or decelerating

☐ Worn inner constant velocity joint (Chapter 8).
☐ Bent or distorted driveshaft (Chapter 8).
☐ Worn intermediate bearing (Chapter 8).

Braking system

Vehicle pulls to one side under braking

Note: *Before assuming that a brake problem exists, make sure that the tyres are in good condition and correctly inflated, that the front wheel alignment is correct, and that the vehicle is not loaded with weight in an unequal manner. Apart from checking the condition of all pipe and hose connections, any faults occurring on the anti-lock braking system should be referred to a Peugeot dealer for diagnosis.*

☐ Worn, defective, damaged or contaminated brake pads on one side (Chapter 9).
☐ Seized or partially-seized front brake caliper (Chapter 9).
☐ A mixture of brake pad materials fitted between sides (Chapter 9).
☐ Brake caliper mounting bolts loose (Chapter 9).
☐ Worn or damaged steering or suspension components (Chapters 1A or 1B and 10).

Noise (grinding or high-pitched squeal) when brakes applied

☐ Brake pad material worn down to metal backing (Chapters 1A or 1B and 9).
☐ Excessive corrosion of brake disc. May be apparent after the vehicle has been standing for some time (Chapter 9).
☐ Foreign object (stone chipping, etc) trapped between brake disc and shield (Chapter 9).

Excessive brake pedal travel

☐ Faulty master cylinder (Chapter 9).
☐ Air in hydraulic system (Chapter 9).
☐ Faulty vacuum servo unit (Chapter 9).

Brake pedal feels spongy when depressed

☐ Air in hydraulic system (Chapter 9).
☐ Deteriorated flexible rubber brake hoses (Chapters 1A or 1B and 9).
☐ Master cylinder mounting nuts loose (Chapter 9).
☐ Faulty master cylinder (Chapter 9).

Excessive brake pedal effort required stopping vehicle

☐ Faulty vacuum servo unit (Chapter 9).
☐ Disconnected, damaged or insecure brake servo vacuum hose (Chapter 9).
☐ Primary or secondary hydraulic circuit failure (Chapter 9).
☐ Seized brake caliper (Chapter 9).
☐ Brake pads incorrectly fitted (Chapter 9).
☐ Incorrect grade of brake pads fitted (Chapter 9).
☐ Brake pads contaminated (Chapter 9).

Judder felt through brake pedal or steering wheel when braking

☐ Excessive run-out or distortion of discs (Chapters 9).
☐ Brake pads worn (Chapters 1A or 1B and 9).
☐ Brake caliper mounting bolts loose (Chapter 9).
☐ Wear in suspension or steering components or mountings (Chapters 1A or 1B and 10).

Brakes binding

☐ Seized brake caliper (Chapter 9).
☐ Incorrectly-adjusted handbrake mechanism (Chapter 9).
☐ Faulty master cylinder (Chapter 9).

Rear wheels locking under normal braking

☐ Rear brake pads contaminated (Chapters 1A or 1B and 9).
☐ ABS system fault (Chapter 9).

Suspension and steering

Vehicle pulls to one side

Note: *Before diagnosing suspension or steering faults, be sure that the trouble is not due to incorrect tyre pressures, mixtures of tyre types, or binding brakes.*

- ☐ Defective tyre (*Weekly checks*).
- ☐ Excessive wear in suspension or steering components (Chapters 1A or 1B and 10).
- ☐ Incorrect front wheel alignment (Chapter 10).
- ☐ Damage to steering or suspension components (Chapter 1A or 1B).

Wheel wobble and vibration

- ☐ Front roadwheels out of balance (vibration felt mainly through the steering wheel) (Chapters 1A or 1B and 10).
- ☐ Rear roadwheels out of balance (vibration felt throughout the vehicle) (Chapters 1A or 1B and 10).
- ☐ Roadwheels damaged or distorted (Chapters 1A or 1B and 10).
- ☐ Faulty or damaged tyre (*Weekly checks*).
- ☐ Worn steering or suspension joints, bushes or components (Chapters 1A or 1B and 10).
- ☐ Wheel bolts loose (Chapters 1A or 1B and 10).

Excessive pitching and/or rolling around corners, or during braking

- ☐ Defective shock absorbers (Chapters 1A or 1B and 10).
- ☐ Broken or weak spring and/or suspension part (Chapters 1A or 1B and 10).
- ☐ Worn or damaged anti-roll bar or mountings (Chapter 10).

Wandering or general instability

- ☐ Incorrect front wheel alignment (Chapter 10).
- ☐ Worn steering or suspension joints, bushes or components (Chapters 1A or 1B and 10).
- ☐ Roadwheels out of balance (Chapters 1A or 1B and 10).
- ☐ Faulty or damaged tyre (*Weekly checks*).
- ☐ Wheel bolts loose (Chapters 1A or 1B and 10).
- ☐ Defective shock absorbers (Chapters 1A or 1B and 10).

Excessively-stiff steering

- ☐ Seized track rod end balljoint or suspension balljoint (Chapters 1A or 1B and 10).
- ☐ Incorrect front wheel alignment (Chapter 10).
- ☐ Steering rack or column bent or damaged (Chapter 10).
- ☐ Power steering fault (Chapter 10).

Excessive play in steering

- ☐ Worn steering column universal joint (Chapter 10).
- ☐ Worn steering track rod end balljoints (Chapters 1A or 1B and 10).
- ☐ Worn steering rack (Chapter 10).
- ☐ Worn steering or suspension joints, bushes or components (Chapters 1A or 1B and 10).

Lack of power assistance

- ☐ Faulty power steering (Chapter 10).
- ☐ Faulty steering rack (Chapter 10).

Tyre wear excessive

Tyre treads exhibit feathered edges

- ☐ Incorrect toe setting (Chapter 10).

Tyres worn in centre of tread

- ☐ Tyres over-inflated (*Weekly checks*).

Tyres worn on inside and outside edges

- ☐ Tyres under-inflated (*Weekly checks*).

Tyres worn on inside or outside edges

- ☐ Incorrect camber/castor angles (wear on one edge only) (Chapter 10).
- ☐ Worn steering or suspension joints, bushes or components (Chapters 1A or 1B and 10).
- ☐ Excessively-hard cornering.
- ☐ Accident damage.

Tyres worn unevenly

- ☐ Tyres/wheels out of balance (*Weekly checks*).
- ☐ Excessive wheel or tyre run-out (Chapter 1A or 1B).
- ☐ Worn shock absorbers (Chapters 1A or 1B and 10).
- ☐ Faulty tyre (*Weekly checks*).

Electrical system

Battery won't hold a charge for more than a few days

Note: *For problems associated with the starting system, refer to the faults listed under 'Engine' earlier in this Section.*

- ☐ Battery defective internally (Chapter 5A).
- ☐ Battery terminal connections loose or corroded (*Weekly checks*).
- ☐ Auxiliary drivebelt broken, worn or incorrectly adjusted (Chapter 1A or 1B).
- ☐ Alternator not charging at correct output (Chapter 5A).
- ☐ Alternator or voltage regulator faulty (Chapter 5A).
- ☐ Short-circuit causing continual battery drain (Chapters 5A and 12).

Ignition/no-charge warning light stays on with engine running

- ☐ Auxiliary drivebelt broken, worn, or incorrectly adjusted (Chapter 1A or 1B).
- ☐ Internal fault in alternator or voltage regulator (Chapter 5A).
- ☐ Broken, disconnected, or loose wiring in charging circuit (Chapter 5A).

Ignition/no-charge warning light fails to come on

- ☐ Warning light bulb blown (Chapter 12).
- ☐ Broken, disconnected, or loose wiring in warning light circuit (Chapter 12).
- ☐ Alternator faulty (Chapter 5A).

Lights inoperative

- ☐ Bulb blown (Chapter 12).
- ☐ Corrosion of bulb or bulbholder contacts (Chapter 12).
- ☐ Blown fuse (Chapter 12).
- ☐ Faulty relay (Chapter 12).
- ☐ Broken, loose, or disconnected wiring (Chapter 12).
- ☐ Faulty switch (Chapter 12).

Instrument readings inaccurate or erratic

Fuel or temperature gauges give no reading

- ☐ Faulty gauge sensor unit (Chapter 3 or 4A).
- ☐ Wiring open-circuit (Chapter 12).
- ☐ Faulty gauge (Chapter 12).

Fuel or temperature gauges give continuous maximum reading

- ☐ Faulty gauge sensor unit (Chapter 3 or 4A).
- ☐ Wiring short-circuit (Chapter 12).
- ☐ Faulty gauge (Chapter 12).

Horn inoperative, or unsatisfactory in operation

Horn operates all the time

- ☐ Horn push either earthed or stuck down (Chapter 12).
- ☐ Horn cable-to-horn push earthed (Chapter 12).

Horn fails to operate

- ☐ Blown fuse (Chapter 12).
- ☐ Cable or cable connections loose, broken or disconnected (Chapter 12).
- ☐ Faulty horn (Chapter 12).

Horn emits intermittent or unsatisfactory sound

- ☐ Cable connections loose (Chapter 12).
- ☐ Horn mountings loose (Chapter 12).
- ☐ Faulty horn (Chapter 12).

Windscreen/tailgate wipers failed, or unsatisfactory in operation

Wipers fail to operate, or operate very slowly

- ☐ Wiper blades stuck to screen, or linkage seized or binding

(Chapters 1A or 1B and 12).
- ☐ Blown fuse (Chapter 12).
- ☐ Cable or cable connections loose, broken or disconnected (Chapter 12).
- ☐ Faulty Built-in System Interface (BSI) unit (Chapter 12).
- ☐ Faulty wiper motor (Chapter 12).

Wiper blades sweep over too large or too small an area of the glass

- ☐ Wiper arms incorrectly positioned on spindles (Chapter 12).
- ☐ Excessive wear of wiper linkage (Chapter 12).
- ☐ Wiper motor or linkage mountings loose or insecure (Chapter 12).

Wiper blades fail to clean the glass effectively

- ☐ Wiper blade rubbers worn or perished (*Weekly checks*).
- ☐ Wiper arm tension springs broken, or arm pivots seized (Chapter 12).
- ☐ Insufficient windscreen washer additive to adequately remove road film (*Weekly checks*).

Windscreen/tailgate washers failed, or unsatisfactory in operation

One or more washer jets inoperative

- ☐ Blocked washer jet (*Weekly checks*).
- ☐ Disconnected, kinked or restricted fluid hose (Chapter 12).
- ☐ Insufficient fluid in washer reservoir (*Weekly checks*).

Washer pump fails to operate

- ☐ Broken or disconnected wiring or connections (Chapter 12).
- ☐ Blown fuse (Chapter 12).
- ☐ Faulty washer switch (Chapter 12).
- ☐ Faulty washer pump (Chapter 12).

Electric windows inoperative, or unsatisfactory in operation

Window glass will only move in one direction

- ☐ Faulty switch (Chapter 12).

Window glass slow to move

- ☐ Regulator seized or damaged, or in need of lubricant (Chapter 11).
- ☐ Door internal components or trim fouling regulator (Chapter 11).
- ☐ Faulty motor (Chapter 11).

Window glass fails to move

- ☐ Blown fuse (Chapter 12).
- ☐ Broken or disconnected wiring or connections (Chapter 12).
- ☐ Faulty motor (Chapter 11).
- ☐ Faulty Built-in Systems Interface (BSI) unit (Chapter 12).

Central locking system inoperative, or unsatisfactory in operation

Complete system failure

- ☐ Blown fuse (Chapter 12).
- ☐ Broken or disconnected wiring or connections (Chapter 12).
- ☐ Faulty Built-in System Interface (BSI) unit (Chapter 12).

Door/tailgate locks but will not unlock, or unlocks but will not lock

- ☐ Broken or disconnected link rod(s) (Chapter 11).
- ☐ Faulty lock motor (Chapter 11).

One lock fails to operate

- ☐ Broken or disconnected wiring or connections (Chapter 12).
- ☐ Faulty lock motor (Chapter 11).
- ☐ Broken, binding or disconnected link rod(s) (Chapter 11).

A

ABS (Anti-lock brake system) A system, usually electronically controlled, that senses incipient wheel lockup during braking and relieves hydraulic pressure at wheels that are about to skid.

Air bag An inflatable bag hidden in the steering wheel (driver's side) or the dash or glovebox (passenger side). In a head-on collision, the bags inflate, preventing the driver and front passenger from being thrown forward into the steering wheel or windscreen.

Air cleaner A metal or plastic housing, containing a filter element, which removes dust and dirt from the air being drawn into the engine.

Air filter element The actual filter in an air cleaner system, usually manufactured from pleated paper and requiring renewal at regular intervals.

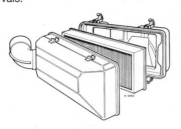

Air filter

Allen key A hexagonal wrench which fits into a recessed hexagonal hole.

Alligator clip A long-nosed spring-loaded metal clip with meshing teeth. Used to make temporary electrical connections.

Alternator A component in the electrical system which converts mechanical energy from a drivebelt into electrical energy to charge the battery and to operate the starting system, ignition system and electrical accessories.

Alternator (exploded view)

Ampere (amp) A unit of measurement for the flow of electric current. One amp is the amount of current produced by one volt acting through a resistance of one ohm.

Anaerobic sealer A substance used to prevent bolts and screws from loosening. Anaerobic means that it does not require oxygen for activation. The Loctite brand is widely used.

Antifreeze A substance (usually ethylene glycol) mixed with water, and added to a vehicle's cooling system, to prevent freezing of the coolant in winter. Antifreeze also contains chemicals to inhibit corrosion and the formation of rust and other deposits that

would tend to clog the radiator and coolant passages and reduce cooling efficiency.

Anti-seize compound A coating that reduces the risk of seizing on fasteners that are subjected to high temperatures, such as exhaust manifold bolts and nuts.

Anti-seize compound

Asbestos A natural fibrous mineral with great heat resistance, commonly used in the composition of brake friction materials. Asbestos is a health hazard and the dust created by brake systems should never be inhaled or ingested.

Axle A shaft on which a wheel revolves, or which revolves with a wheel. Also, a solid beam that connects the two wheels at one end of the vehicle. An axle which also transmits power to the wheels is known as a live axle.

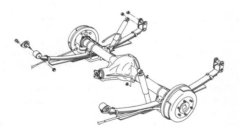

Axle assembly

Axleshaft A single rotating shaft, on either side of the differential, which delivers power from the final drive assembly to the drive wheels. Also called a driveshaft or a halfshaft.

B

Ball bearing An anti-friction bearing consisting of a hardened inner and outer race with hardened steel balls between two races.

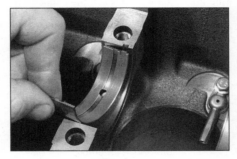

Bearing

Bearing The curved surface on a shaft or in a bore, or the part assembled into either, that permits relative motion between them with minimum wear and friction.

Big-end bearing The bearing in the end of the connecting rod that's attached to the crankshaft.

Bleed nipple A valve on a brake wheel cylinder, caliper or other hydraulic component that is opened to purge the hydraulic system of air. Also called a bleed screw.

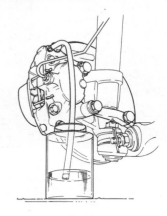

Brake bleeding

Brake bleeding Procedure for removing air from lines of a hydraulic brake system.

Brake disc The component of a disc brake that rotates with the wheels.

Brake drum The component of a drum brake that rotates with the wheels.

Brake linings The friction material which contacts the brake disc or drum to retard the vehicle's speed. The linings are bonded or riveted to the brake pads or shoes.

Brake pads The replaceable friction pads that pinch the brake disc when the brakes are applied. Brake pads consist of a friction material bonded or riveted to a rigid backing plate.

Brake shoe The crescent-shaped carrier to which the brake linings are mounted and which forces the lining against the rotating drum during braking.

Braking systems For more information on braking systems, consult the *Haynes Automotive Brake Manual*.

Breaker bar A long socket wrench handle providing greater leverage.

Bulkhead The insulated partition between the engine and the passenger compartment.

C

Caliper The non-rotating part of a disc-brake assembly that straddles the disc and carries the brake pads. The caliper also contains the hydraulic components that cause the pads to pinch the disc when the brakes are applied. A caliper is also a measuring tool that can be set to measure inside or outside dimensions of an object.

Camshaft A rotating shaft on which a series of cam lobes operate the valve mechanisms. The camshaft may be driven by gears, by sprockets and chain or by sprockets and a belt.

Canister A container in an evaporative emission control system; contains activated charcoal granules to trap vapours from the fuel system.

Canister

Carburettor A device which mixes fuel with air in the proper proportions to provide a desired power output from a spark ignition internal combustion engine.

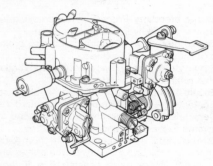

Carburettor

Castellated Resembling the parapets along the top of a castle wall. For example, a castellated balljoint stud nut.

Castellated nut

Castor In wheel alignment, the backward or forward tilt of the steering axis. Castor is positive when the steering axis is inclined rearward at the top.

Catalytic converter A silencer-like device in the exhaust system which converts certain pollutants in the exhaust gases into less harmful substances.

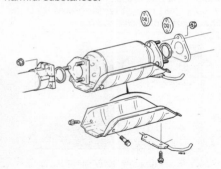

Catalytic converter

Circlip A ring-shaped clip used to prevent endwise movement of cylindrical parts and shafts. An internal circlip is installed in a groove in a housing; an external circlip fits into a groove on the outside of a cylindrical piece such as a shaft.

Clearance The amount of space between two parts. For example, between a piston and a cylinder, between a bearing and a journal, etc.

Coil spring A spiral of elastic steel found in various sizes throughout a vehicle, for example as a springing medium in the suspension and in the valve train.

Compression Reduction in volume, and increase in pressure and temperature, of a gas, caused by squeezing it into a smaller space.

Compression ratio The relationship between cylinder volume when the piston is at top dead centre and cylinder volume when the piston is at bottom dead centre.

Constant velocity (CV) joint A type of universal joint that cancels out vibrations caused by driving power being transmitted through an angle.

Core plug A disc or cup-shaped metal device inserted in a hole in a casting through which core was removed when the casting was formed. Also known as a freeze plug or expansion plug.

Crankcase The lower part of the engine block in which the crankshaft rotates.

Crankshaft The main rotating member, or shaft, running the length of the crankcase, with offset "throws" to which the connecting rods are attached.

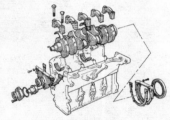

Crankshaft assembly

Crocodile clip See Alligator clip

D

Diagnostic code Code numbers obtained by accessing the diagnostic mode of an engine management computer. This code can be used to determine the area in the system where a malfunction may be located.

Disc brake A brake design incorporating a rotating disc onto which brake pads are squeezed. The resulting friction converts the energy of a moving vehicle into heat.

Double-overhead cam (DOHC) An engine that uses two overhead camshafts, usually one for the intake valves and one for the exhaust valves.

Drivebelt(s) The belt(s) used to drive accessories such as the alternator, water pump, power steering pump, air conditioning compressor, etc. off the crankshaft pulley.

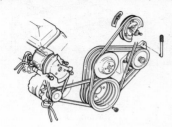

Accessory drivebelts

Driveshaft Any shaft used to transmit motion. Commonly used when referring to the axleshafts on a front wheel drive vehicle.

Driveshaft

Drum brake A type of brake using a drum-shaped metal cylinder attached to the inner surface of the wheel. When the brake pedal is pressed, curved brake shoes with friction linings press against the inside of the drum to slow or stop the vehicle.

Drum brake assembly

E

EGR valve A valve used to introduce exhaust gases into the intake air stream.

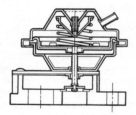

EGR valve

Electronic control unit (ECU) A computer which controls (for instance) ignition and fuel injection systems, or an anti-lock braking system. For more information refer to the *Haynes Automotive Electrical and Electronic Systems Manual*.

Electronic Fuel Injection (EFI) A computer controlled fuel system that distributes fuel through an injector located in each intake port of the engine.

Emergency brake A braking system, independent of the main hydraulic system, that can be used to slow or stop the vehicle if the primary brakes fail, or to hold the vehicle stationary even though the brake pedal isn't depressed. It usually consists of a hand lever that actuates either front or rear brakes mechanically through a series of cables and linkages. Also known as a handbrake or parking brake.

Endfloat The amount of lengthwise movement between two parts. As applied to a crankshaft, the distance that the crankshaft can move forward and back in the cylinder block.

Engine management system (EMS) A computer controlled system which manages the fuel injection and the ignition systems in an integrated fashion.

Exhaust manifold A part with several passages through which exhaust gases leave the engine combustion chambers and enter the exhaust pipe.

Exhaust manifold

F

Fan clutch A viscous (fluid) drive coupling device which permits variable engine fan speeds in relation to engine speeds.

Feeler blade A thin strip or blade of hardened steel, ground to an exact thickness, used to check or measure clearances between parts.

Feeler blade

Firing order The order in which the engine cylinders fire, or deliver their power strokes, beginning with the number one cylinder.

Flywheel A heavy spinning wheel in which energy is absorbed and stored by means of momentum. On cars, the flywheel is attached to the crankshaft to smooth out firing impulses.

Free play The amount of travel before any action takes place. The "looseness" in a linkage, or an assembly of parts, between the initial application of force and actual movement. For example, the distance the brake pedal moves before the pistons in the master cylinder are actuated.

Fuse An electrical device which protects a circuit against accidental overload. The typical fuse contains a soft piece of metal which is calibrated to melt at a predetermined current flow (expressed as amps) and break the circuit.

Fusible link A circuit protection device consisting of a conductor surrounded by heat-resistant insulation. The conductor is smaller than the wire it protects, so it acts as the weakest link in the circuit. Unlike a blown fuse, a failed fusible link must frequently be cut from the wire for replacement.

G

Gap The distance the spark must travel in jumping from the centre electrode to the side

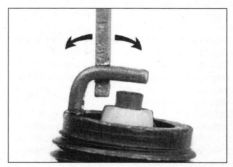

Adjusting spark plug gap

electrode in a spark plug. Also refers to the spacing between the points in a contact breaker assembly in a conventional points-type ignition, or to the distance between the reluctor or rotor and the pickup coil in an electronic ignition.

Gasket Any thin, soft material - usually cork, cardboard, asbestos or soft metal - installed between two metal surfaces to ensure a good seal. For instance, the cylinder head gasket seals the joint between the block and the cylinder head.

Gasket

Gauge An instrument panel display used to monitor engine conditions. A gauge with a movable pointer on a dial or a fixed scale is an analogue gauge. A gauge with a numerical readout is called a digital gauge.

H

Halfshaft A rotating shaft that transmits power from the final drive unit to a drive wheel, usually when referring to a live rear axle.

Harmonic balancer A device designed to reduce torsion or twisting vibration in the crankshaft. May be incorporated in the crankshaft pulley. Also known as a vibration damper.

Hone An abrasive tool for correcting small irregularities or differences in diameter in an engine cylinder, brake cylinder, etc.

Hydraulic tappet A tappet that utilises hydraulic pressure from the engine's lubrication system to maintain zero clearance (constant contact with both camshaft and valve stem). Automatically adjusts to variation in valve stem length. Hydraulic tappets also reduce valve noise.

I

Ignition timing The moment at which the spark plug fires, usually expressed in the number of crankshaft degrees before the piston reaches the top of its stroke.

Inlet manifold A tube or housing with passages through which flows the air-fuel mixture (carburettor vehicles and vehicles with throttle body injection) or air only (port fuel-injected vehicles) to the port openings in the cylinder head.

J

Jump start Starting the engine of a vehicle with a discharged or weak battery by attaching jump leads from the weak battery to a charged or helper battery.

L

Load Sensing Proportioning Valve (LSPV) A brake hydraulic system control valve that works like a proportioning valve, but also takes into consideration the amount of weight carried by the rear axle.

Locknut A nut used to lock an adjustment nut, or other threaded component, in place. For example, a locknut is employed to keep the adjusting nut on the rocker arm in position.

Lockwasher A form of washer designed to prevent an attaching nut from working loose.

M

MacPherson strut A type of front suspension system devised by Earle MacPherson at Ford of England. In its original form, a simple lateral link with the anti-roll bar creates the lower control arm. A long strut - an integral coil spring and shock absorber - is mounted between the body and the steering knuckle. Many modern so-called MacPherson strut systems use a conventional lower A-arm and don't rely on the anti-roll bar for location.

Multimeter An electrical test instrument with the capability to measure voltage, current and resistance.

N

NOx Oxides of Nitrogen. A common toxic pollutant emitted by petrol and diesel engines at higher temperatures.

O

Ohm The unit of electrical resistance. One volt applied to a resistance of one ohm will produce a current of one amp.

Ohmmeter An instrument for measuring electrical resistance.

O-ring A type of sealing ring made of a special rubber-like material; in use, the O-ring is compressed into a groove to provide the sealing action.

O-ring

Overhead cam (ohc) engine An engine with the camshaft(s) located on top of the cylinder head(s).

Overhead valve (ohv) engine An engine with the valves located in the cylinder head, but with the camshaft located in the engine block.

Oxygen sensor A device installed in the engine exhaust manifold, which senses the oxygen content in the exhaust and converts this information into an electric current. Also called a Lambda sensor.

P

Phillips screw A type of screw head having a cross instead of a slot for a corresponding type of screwdriver.

Plastigage A thin strip of plastic thread, available in different sizes, used for measuring clearances. For example, a strip of Plastigage is laid across a bearing journal. The parts are assembled and dismantled; the width of the crushed strip indicates the clearance between journal and bearing.

Plastigage

Propeller shaft The long hollow tube with universal joints at both ends that carries power from the transmission to the differential on front-engined rear wheel drive vehicles.

Proportioning valve A hydraulic control valve which limits the amount of pressure to the rear brakes during panic stops to prevent wheel lock-up.

R

Rack-and-pinion steering A steering system with a pinion gear on the end of the steering shaft that mates with a rack (think of a geared wheel opened up and laid flat). When the steering wheel is turned, the pinion turns, moving the rack to the left or right. This movement is transmitted through the track rods to the steering arms at the wheels.

Radiator A liquid-to-air heat transfer device designed to reduce the temperature of the coolant in an internal combustion engine cooling system.

Refrigerant Any substance used as a heat transfer agent in an air-conditioning system. R-12 has been the principle refrigerant for many years; recently, however, manufacturers have begun using R-134a, a non-CFC substance that is considered less harmful to the ozone in the upper atmosphere.

Rocker arm A lever arm that rocks on a shaft or pivots on a stud. In an overhead valve engine, the rocker arm converts the upward movement of the pushrod into a downward movement to open a valve.

Rotor In a distributor, the rotating device inside the cap that connects the centre electrode and the outer terminals as it turns, distributing the high voltage from the coil secondary winding to the proper spark plug. Also, that part of an alternator which rotates inside the stator. Also, the rotating assembly of a turbocharger, including the compressor wheel, shaft and turbine wheel.

Runout The amount of wobble (in-and-out movement) of a gear or wheel as it's rotated. The amount a shaft rotates "out-of-true." The out-of-round condition of a rotating part.

S

Sealant A liquid or paste used to prevent leakage at a joint. Sometimes used in conjunction with a gasket.

Sealed beam lamp An older headlight design which integrates the reflector, lens and filaments into a hermetically-sealed one-piece unit. When a filament burns out or the lens cracks, the entire unit is simply replaced.

Serpentine drivebelt A single, long, wide accessory drivebelt that's used on some newer vehicles to drive all the accessories, instead of a series of smaller, shorter belts. Serpentine drivebelts are usually tensioned by an automatic tensioner.

Serpentine drivebelt

Shim Thin spacer, commonly used to adjust the clearance or relative positions between two parts. For example, shims inserted into or under bucket tappets control valve clearances. Clearance is adjusted by changing the thickness of the shim.

Slide hammer A special puller that screws into or hooks onto a component such as a shaft or bearing; a heavy sliding handle on the shaft bottoms against the end of the shaft to knock the component free.

Sprocket A tooth or projection on the periphery of a wheel, shaped to engage with a chain or drivebelt. Commonly used to refer to the sprocket wheel itself.

Starter inhibitor switch On vehicles with an automatic transmission, a switch that prevents starting if the vehicle is not in Neutral or Park.

Strut See MacPherson strut.

T

Tappet A cylindrical component which transmits motion from the cam to the valve stem, either directly or via a pushrod and rocker arm. Also called a cam follower.

Thermostat A heat-controlled valve that regulates the flow of coolant between the cylinder block and the radiator, so maintaining optimum engine operating temperature. A thermostat is also used in some air cleaners in which the temperature is regulated.

Thrust bearing The bearing in the clutch assembly that is moved in to the release levers by clutch pedal action to disengage the clutch. Also referred to as a release bearing.

Timing belt A toothed belt which drives the camshaft. Serious engine damage may result if it breaks in service.

Timing chain A chain which drives the camshaft.

Toe-in The amount the front wheels are closer together at the front than at the rear. On rear wheel drive vehicles, a slight amount of toe-in is usually specified to keep the front wheels running parallel on the road by offsetting other forces that tend to spread the wheels apart.

Toe-out The amount the front wheels are closer together at the rear than at the front. On front wheel drive vehicles, a slight amount of toe-out is usually specified.

Tools For full information on choosing and using tools, refer to the *Haynes Automotive Tools Manual*.

Tracer A stripe of a second colour applied to a wire insulator to distinguish that wire from another one with the same colour insulator.

Tune-up A process of accurate and careful adjustments and parts replacement to obtain the best possible engine performance.

Turbocharger A centrifugal device, driven by exhaust gases, that pressurises the intake air. Normally used to increase the power output from a given engine displacement, but can also be used primarily to reduce exhaust emissions (as on VW's "Umwelt" Diesel engine).

U

Universal joint or U-joint A double-pivoted connection for transmitting power from a driving to a driven shaft through an angle. A U-joint consists of two Y-shaped yokes and a cross-shaped member called the spider.

V

Valve A device through which the flow of liquid, gas, vacuum, or loose material in bulk may be started, stopped, or regulated by a movable part that opens, shuts, or partially obstructs one or more ports or passageways. A valve is also the movable part of such a device.

Valve clearance The clearance between the valve tip (the end of the valve stem) and the rocker arm or tappet. The valve clearance is measured when the valve is closed.

Vernier caliper A precision measuring instrument that measures inside and outside dimensions. Not quite as accurate as a micrometer, but more convenient.

Viscosity The thickness of a liquid or its resistance to flow.

Volt A unit for expressing electrical "pressure" in a circuit. One volt that will produce a current of one ampere through a resistance of one ohm.

W

Welding Various processes used to join metal items by heating the areas to be joined to a molten state and fusing them together. For more information refer to the *Haynes Automotive Welding Manual*.

Wiring diagram A drawing portraying the components and wires in a vehicle's electrical system, using standardised symbols. For more information refer to the *Haynes Automotive Electrical and Electronic Systems Manual*.

Note: *References throughout this index are in the form "**Chapter number**" • "**Page number**". So, for example, 2C•15 refers to page 15 of Chapter 2C.*

Note: *References throughout this index are in the form* "**Chapter number**" • "**Page number**". *So, for example, 2C•15 refers to page 15 of Chapter 2C.*

Note: *References throughout this index are in the form* **"Chapter number"** • **"Page number".** *So, for example, 2C•15 refers to page 15 of Chapter 2C.*

Note: *References throughout this index are in the form* "**Chapter number**" • "**Page number**". *So, for example, 2C•15 refers to page 15 of Chapter 2C.*

Preserving Our Motoring Heritage

< *The Model J Duesenberg Derham Tourster. Only eight of these magnificent cars were ever built – this is the only example to be found outside the United States of America*

Almost every car you've ever loved, loathed or desired is gathered under one roof at the Haynes Motor Museum. Over 300 immaculately presented cars and motorbikes represent every aspect of our motoring heritage, from elegant reminders of bygone days, such as the superb Model J Duesenberg to curiosities like the bug-eyed BMW Isetta. There are also many old friends and flames. Perhaps you remember the 1959 Ford Popular that you did your courting in? The magnificent 'Red Collection' is a spectacle of classic sports cars including AC, Alfa Romeo, Austin Healey, Ferrari, Lamborghini, Maserati, MG, Riley, Porsche and Triumph.

A Perfect Day Out

Each and every vehicle at the Haynes Motor Museum has played its part in the history and culture of Motoring. Today, they make a wonderful spectacle and a great day out for all the family. Bring the kids, bring Mum and Dad, but above all bring your camera to capture those golden memories for ever. You will also find an impressive array of motoring memorabilia, a comfortable 70 seat video cinema and one of the most extensive transport book shops in Britain. The Pit Stop Cafe serves everything from a cup of tea to wholesome, home-made meals or, if you prefer, you can enjoy the large picnic area nestled in the beautiful rural surroundings of Somerset.

John Haynes O.B.E., Founder and Chairman of the museum at the wheel of a Haynes Light 12. >

< *Graham Hill's Lola Cosworth Formula 1 car next to a 1934 Riley Sports.*

The Museum is situated on the A359 Yeovil to Frome road at Sparkford, just off the A303 in Somerset. It is about 40 miles south of Bristol, and 25 minutes drive from the M5 intersection at Taunton.
Open 9.30am - 5.30pm (10.00am - 4.00pm Winter) 7 days a week, *except Christmas Day, Boxing Day and New Years Day*
Special rates available for schools, coach parties and outings Charitable Trust No. 292048